GENETIC RESOURCES IN PLANTS– THEIR EXPLORATION AND CONSERVATION

IBP HANDBOOK No. 11

GENETIC RESOURCES IN PLANTS— THEIR EXPLORATION AND CONSERVATION

EDITED BY

O. H. FRANKEL and E. BENNETT

IN ASSOCIATION WITH

R. D. BROCK   A. H. BUNTING

J. R. HARLAN   E. SCHREINER

INTERNATIONAL BIOLOGICAL PROGRAMME

7 MARYLEBONE ROAD, LONDON NW1

BLACKWELL SCIENTIFIC PUBLICATIONS

OXFORD AND EDINBURGH

SBN 632 05730 0

FIRST PUBLISHED 1970

Printed in Great Britain by
BELL AND BAIN LTD., GLASGOW

and bound by
THE KEMP HALL BINDERY, OXFORD

To N.I.VAVILOV

FOREWORD

The decades through which we are living are critical and disturbing ones. An increasing world population means increasing demands on its environment. This has resulted in an intensified exploitation of the biosphere, very often without long-term planning or the necessary research background, and without coordination between nations. As a consequence, there is an alarming deterioration of natural resources, which not only adversely affects the present human habitat but constitutes a threat to the well-being of future generations. Man's technological development, so essential to the attainment of a full life for all as defined in the Charter of the United Nations, has often proceeded in such a way as to enlarge rather than reduce the grounds for concern.

The preamble of the Constitution of the Food and Agriculture Organization of the United Nations defines the objectives of the Organization as raising the levels of nutrition and standards of living of peoples, improving the efficiency of production and distribution of all food and agricultural products, bettering the condition of rural populations and thus contributing to an expanding world economy and ensuring humanity's freedom from hunger.

Recently, in reconsidering the whole problem of human living conditions from the nutritional, economic and social points of view, FAO has laid stress on a number of areas in which national and international efforts should be concentrated in order to move faster towards the objectives set forth in its Constitution. These fields of concentration are concerned with the use of high-yielding varieties of cereal crops, the expansion of world protein production, the reduction and prevention of waste, the mobilization of human resources to promote rural development and the saving and earning of foreign exchange.

In the thousands of years since cultivation first began, men in many parts of the earth have unwittingly created a great wealth of crop forms. At the present time, the genetic resources which these forms represent are more necessary than ever before because of the growing need for the creation of new varieties. They are the raw material with which the plant-breeder works. On the all-too-infrequent occasions on which native varieties have been screened systematically for desirable characteristics, they have been shown to be a rich and as yet scarcely-exploited resource.

vii

The full use of the genetic resources present in primitive crop races is just beginning. Occurring as they do more often than not in the developing countries, their use provides a valuable stimulus to local efforts that can do much to create confidence, self-reliance and experience, and prepare the ground for a further development of human and scientific resources. Conversely, the loss or destruction of the world's genetic resources by short-sighted or ill-directed planning is something so wasteful that its consequences can be disastrous both for world food production and for man himself.

I am therefore happy to commend this book, which attempts to outline the way in which genetic resources may best be turned to man's profitable use. I am also very glad that it should have been through the collaborative efforts of FAO and the International Biological Programme of the International Council of Scientific Unions that this book—which is the combined product of the talents of scientists from many nations—has come into being. I hope that this work—and the cooperation on which it is based—will provide a model for much future cooperation and that it will help towards the successful mobilization of a global effort to preserve what is an invaluable and irreplaceable world heritage.

A. H. BOERMA
Director-General
Food and Agriculture Organization
of the United Nations

ACKNOWLEDGMENT

The editorial committee wishes to express its appreciation for the support given to its work by F A O, and especially wishes to thank Dr José Vallega for his encouragement and cooperation. Acknowledgment is also due to A.V.Hill who compiled the index. One of the editors (O.H.F.) wishes to thank Mrs Dorothy McShane for checking references and preparing most of the final typescripts of the contributions. The other (E.B.) wishes to express her appreciation to Miss Frances Searle who prepared many of the initial typescripts for final revision. Both editors wish also to convey their thanks to all those secretaries who at one time or another have willingly assisted in stages of this work.

A*

CONTENTS

SECTION 2

TACTICS OF EXPLORATION AND COLLECTION

SECTION 3
EXAMPLES OF EXPLORATION

A.   Exploration in Agriculture and Horticulture

B.   Exploration in Forestry

SECTION 4
EVALUATION AND UTILIZATION

SECTION 5
DOCUMENTATION, RECORDS AND
RETRIEVAL

SECTION 6
CONSERVATION

APPENDIX

PREFACE

It is about forty years since N.I.Vavilov and his collaborators at the U.S.S.R. Institute of Plant Industry located and described what we have come to call the geographical centres of genetic diversity of our cultivated plants and of their wild relatives. A vast wealth of variation was discovered, including many characteristics which had not been seen before. It became clear that in these regions of ancient cultivation, where modern methods of selection had as yet made no impact, veritable genetic treasuries had accumulated. These greatly extended the known range of variation in domesticated and related species, yielded invaluable material for genetic, cytogenetic and evolutionary studies, and provided a seemingly inexhaustible reservoir for plant breeders.

In recent years interest in, and concern about 'natural gene pools' has been heightened, on the one hand by a growing awareness of the immense value of representative germ plasm collections for plant breeders, geneticists, pathologists, evolutionists and others, and on the other by the growing threat to the continued existence of the gene pools in their areas of diversity. The subject of this book is the exploration, evaluation, utilization and conservation of the genetic resources represented by primitive cultivated plants and related wild and weed species.

The book is the result of the close consultation and collaboration which has been established between the Food and Agriculture Organization of the United Nations (FAO) and the International Biological Programme (IBP) of the International Council of Scientific Unions (ICSU). For many years FAO has taken an active part in stimulating and assisting plant exploration, introduction and seed exchange, in disseminating information in these fields, and in publishing descriptive catalogues of plant genetic stocks. IBP, at its inception in 1964, set up a sub-committee to study ways and means for collecting and conserving plant genetic resources which were threatened by agricultural development in many of the centres of genetic diversity.

In 1961, the FAO Division of Plant Production and Protection held a Technical Meeting on plant exploration and introduction which reviewed the situation and made valuable recommendations. In the course of preparations for a further conference to be held in 1967, FAO decided to examine its own role and responsibilities, and the possibilities for an intensification of national and international participation. During a brief consultancy at F A O in 1966 it was my task to initiate this examination and to lay plans for the Conference. The aim of the enquiry was to examine the current availability of genetic resources, and the status and organization of their evaluation, utilization and conservation.

There are five more or less distinct kinds of germ plasm material which are involved : (1) cultivars in current use, (2) obsolete cultivars, (3) special genetic stocks such as resistance stocks, genetic and cyto-genetic material, induced mutations, etc., (4) primitive varieties or land races, and (5) wild and weed species related to cultivated species.

F A O's recent World Survey of Plant Collections indicates that *currently or recently used cultivars* are included in various collections and are as a rule available from the country of origin or through the F A O seed exchange. *Special genetic stocks* also are available as long as they are used in current research. *Obsolete* cultivars and genetic stocks which are deemed worthy of perpetuation may require special arrangements for their preservation. This, however, poses few if any scientific or technical problems.

By comparison, *primitive and wild material* presents a host of practical and scientific problems. To start with, unlike breeders' varieties and stocks, it is not readily available. With a few and notable exceptions, representation of primitive and wild material in existing collections is scant, rarely representative of regions or taxa, sometimes inadequately classified and documented, and all too often subject to 'genetic erosion' in maintenance. The reason for this is not lack of interest, but the widespread feeling that the ancient centres of diversity would stay undisturbed in the future as they had remained for hundreds or thou-sands of years, so that one had no need to concern oneself with collecting or preserving material that was not of immediate interest or use ; one could always go out for more.

It became clear during the enquiry that this is no longer the case, since, as is now generally recognized, many of the ancient genetic reservoirs are rapidly disappearing. But what became equally clear was the lack of agreement on, or even of awareness of the many basic, practical and organizational problems which beset every step in the complex process from survey and collection to conservation and docu-mentation. This situation would have to be remedied if the world's genetic resources were to be salvaged, utilized and preserved for the good of present and of future generations. Clearly, also, the urgency of this operation, as well as its importance and magnitude, was such as to make necessary a high degree of rationalization and co-ordination along sound scientific principles. It was concluded that there was an urgent need for a comprehensive review of the field as a whole which would develop approaches and methods, clarify contentious issues, point to areas in need of further research, and, above all, stimulate widepsread interest and involvement. It was felt at the same time that the forth-coming conference would offer an opportunity to bring together reviews and discussions of the problems in preparation for a book.

Accordingly, the Conference was planned to include a section on scientific and technical issues relating to primitive and wild genetic resources. In the detailed planning of this section the I B P committee for plant gene pools played a major role, and I B P assumed responsibility for the resulting publication within its series of Biological Handbooks.

The Conference was held on 18-26 September, 1967, at F A O Head-quarters in Rome.* It was held under the joint authority of Dr J. Vallega, Director of the Division of Plant Production and Protection, and Dr N.A.Osara, Director of the Division of Forestry and Forest Products. With certain changes of subject and author this book corres-ponds to the papers presented during the Conference, although most chapters have been re-written or substantially amended.

The book attempts to define and develop the principles underlying the various stages of exploration, conservation and utilization. Its use-fulness will depend on the degree to which it succeeds in illuminating practical problems, rather than in offering prescriptions or instructions. It presents in its first section an outline of the biological background to the subject as a whole, followed by a section which is intended as a guide to the thoughts, plans and activities of the plant explorer before and during collecting expeditions. The examples of exploration, intro-ducing the realism of actual experience, were selected for diversity of subject and treatment. Evaluation and utilization could, by the nature of the subject, receive no more than a token presentation. The two final sections, Documentation and Conservation, break new and impor-tant ground. Both are eminently practical; yet so little has been thought and written about the *principles* of conservation that the subject still appears somewhat controversial. One may hope that this section is the forerunner to a more comprehensive treatment and study in the near future.

---

* BENNETT, E. ed. (1968) *FAO/IBP Technical Conference on the Exploration, Utilization and Conservation of Plant Genetic Resources*, F A O, Rome.

It was not intended to include reports on the work of individual contributors or their institutions; yet a statement by Dr Brezhnev on the current organization and research programme of Vavilov's institute —now carrying his name—was welcome, especially since it perpetuates Vavilov's collections and traditions.

In a collective work by many authors from many countries, some overlap or repetition of treatment or subject matter is unavoidable. This, however, does have the virtue of giving emphasis to the main points this book intends to make; and, in some instances, of presenting differing, or even contradictory views on contentious issues.

Canberra   O. H. FRANKEL

SECTION 1
BIOLOGICAL BACKGROUND

1

GENETIC RESOURCES

O. H. FRANKEL[1] and E. BENNETT[2]

[1] Division of Plant Industry, CSIRO, Canberra, Australia
[2] Crop Ecology and Genetic Resources Branch, F A O, Rome, Italy

INTRODUCTION

Plant breeding—or in Vavilov's phrase 'evolution at the will of man'—is, like all evolution, dependent on *variation*. This is true whatever the selective agent, whether it be nature, or the effect of the superimposition on natural selection of the efforts of primitive man, the observant cultivator, or the modern plant breeder with an array of scientific, technological and statistical discriminants at his disposal. What has changed in the transition from neolithic to scientific plant breeding is not only the nature of selection—with which we are not here concerned—but the nature and range of variation.

Until the advent of scientific agriculture about the middle of the nineteenth century, variability was an ever present feature of every sexually reproduced crop. Generated by mutation and natural hybridization and maintained by natural selection, variation was as yet virtually unchecked by deliberate selection. Cultivation alone played a great part in the creation of local 'land races' or primitive varietal populations each of which evolved in response to a common physical and socioeconomic environment. But observant cultivators, perhaps from the early beginnings of crop evolution, also played a part in identifying and maintaining local land races.

Land races are crop populations in balance with their environment and remain relatively stable over long periods of time. Yet their population structure has the effect of retaining a potential for adaptive change, especially where there are opportunities for gene exchange and introgression. Though relatively isolated by physical, cultural or political barriers, they are rarely completely insulated from all intrusions from outside. Human migration and trade (quite apart from birds and bees) led to a not insignificant exchange of genetic material; they also led, in the particularly varied habitats of primitive agriculture, to introgression from extraneous gene pools.

7

This kind of population structure was almost universal until disrupted by individual selection in the nineteenth century. Today it is found only where primitive varieties are still in use in areas as yet not deeply affected by modern scientific agriculture, among them—until recently—those areas which Vavilov identified as 'centres of diversity'.*

Indubitably, a great part has been played by introgression from related weed and wild progenitor species to create the diversity which, in the 'gene centres' of Vavilov, is greater than in other areas. This has been stressed by many authors from Vavilov onward (see, for example, Harlan, 1951); but other biological, as well as physical, cultural, economic and political factors have played their part in the evolution of the crop races which are found in the present day gene centres. Exposed to environmental stresses and the opportunities afforded by cultivation over long periods of time, competing and introgressing with associated crop, weed and wild species, these populations have evolved those gene blocks which, in the course of the last hundred years, have been used to build our modern high-yielding cultivars.

The transition from primitive to 'advanced' cultivars has had the effect of narrowing the genetic base. This has happened in two distinct ways. Selection for relative uniformity, resulting in 'pure' lines, multilines, single or double hybrids, etc., and, further, selection for closely defined objectives has led to a marked reduction in genetic variation, even beyond the reduction normally associated with any kind of selection. There has been, at the same time, a tendency to restrict the gene pool from which parental material has been drawn. This has been largely a consequence of the high levels of productivity achieved when breeding within a restricted but well-adapted gene pool, and of the back-crossing technique which made it possible to introduce specifically desired improvements, such as disease resistance and quality characteristics into breeding stocks with a minimum of disturbance to genotypic structure.

The tendency towards a narrowing genetic base has intensified in recent years as a result of the widespread introduction of cultural measures which have done much to minimize or even remove environmental differences over wide areas (see Frankel, 1959). This is, of course, a familiar pattern in intensive horticulture, where control of the environment by the application of fertilizers and the use of standard soils, controlled irrigation, temperature and light control and plant protective

* For a discussion of Vavilov's 'centres of origin' and the present day concept of 'centres of genetic diversity' see Kuckuck (1962) and chapters 2 and 3 of this book.

measures have created conditions in which certain varieties may be grown over large parts of the earth. Similarly, crop varieties selected in France, the Netherlands or Sweden have spread successfully through the high-intensity farming areas of northwestern Europe. This process will undoubtedly continue. Indeed, as Krull and Borlaug point out in chapter 37 of this book, plant breeding manpower and resources may be more efficiently concentrated in what might become major regional research institutions. It may be noted that even an appreciable limitation of the numbers of varieties grown over wide areas, which might be a consequence, need not materially affect evolutionary trends in crops *provided* evolutionary potential in the form of genetic resources is safeguarded. In the more developed regions of the world the active sites of crop evolution have already moved from the crop in the field to the plant collections and breeding populations at the experiment stations—from the cultivator to the plant breeder.

By contrast, in the belt of low latitudes where more than one half of mankind lives under conditions of serious under-nutrition and where the gene centres are to be found, a complex situation of grave consequence exists. Here again we witness the same chain of events: factors limiting production, such as nutrient or moisture deficiencies, are mitigated or removed; and varieties are introduced which possess a relatively high degree of adaptability.

In this instance, the effects are a good deal more drastic than in developed regions since the area involved includes some of the richest primary and secondary gene centres (see chapter 3) of the two most important food crops. The highly successful wheats produced by the Rockefeller team in Mexico are transforming the agricultural picture over much of Asia and Latin America, as are the new rice varieties produced at the International Rice Research Institute in the Philippines. Yet their success represents a very real and immediate threat that the treasuries of variation in the centres of genetic diversity will disappear without a trace.

This threat is neither new, nor restricted to wheat and rice, although in these crops the dynamics of the process are greatly accelerated by the dramatic developments which are taking place. The displacement of natural gene pools by selections and introductions began years ago (see p. 12) and has come to affect or threaten all crops and all areas where primitive varieties still exist, and, as foresters in particular stress in several chapters of this book, it has come to affect some wild gene pools as well. There is therefore an *a priori* case for urgent measures to protect and preserve valuable primitive and wild gene pools which are threatened with extinction.

But here we must pause to consider the significance of the genetic resources which are of immediate or long-term value, bearing in mind not only present, but also possible future needs.

For *research* in a broad range of studies—from evolution and genetics to physiology and biochemistry—a full representation of the genetic variation of domesticated and related species is a continuing and increasing need. As Harlan points out in chapter 2, the evolutionary history of not one of our crops is fully known. Yet what glimpses we have had already have not only thrown light on the origins of our civilization but have enriched our knowledge of the processes of domestication and extended our capacity for crop improvement.

We are now beginning to understand the physiology and biochemistry of crop productivity, and before long may be able to apply the growing knowledge of production processes to the manipulation of their genetic controls. The same may be said of current studies of host-pathogen relationships at the physiological, biochemical and genetic levels. In many, if not most, of these studies a diversity of gene pools—differing in their levels of evolutionary progress, in their ecological adaptation and adaptability, and in their population structures—is an essential requirement.

Research into the population structure of primitive varieties, gen-ecological studies of primitive populations and their wild and weed relatives, host-pathogen relationships, and studies on the nature, causes and distribution of variability—these and other studies can only be conducted in the centres of diversity themselves. The preservation of populations is therefore as highly desirable for purposes of research as it is for storing variation for plant breeding. Whether and to what extent primitive varietal populations, as distinct from wild communities, can be maintained *in situ* in the face of wide-spread agricultural development is far from clear; prospects are discussed in chapters 20 and 40.

Plant breeders take the need for extensive gene pools for granted. Yet for reasons which have already been touched upon, many breeders in the advanced countries until recently have tended to restrict parental gene pools to well-adapted types. However, most breeders now resort to the use of primitive and of wild material in the search for resistance to diseases and pests, and this is likely to increase with the need for new and more effective sources of resistance; indeed, wild material is increasingly being screened for resistance characters, and elegant methods for the transfer of segments from 'wild' to 'cultivated' chromosomes have been devised. Apart from resistance, new needs for specific characteristics arise from advances in science and technology. These may be difficult to predict but are nevertheless likely to multiply in years to come. Who would have predicted a decade ago that extensive gene pools would be screened for high-lysine stocks, or for restorer genes for pollen fertility? There is general agreement among plant breeders that large and diverse gene pools are increasingly required to meet the ever-changing demands, opportunities and challenges of the future.

However, as may be seen in chapter 33 and in the appendix by Brezhnev, there are good reasons for believing that primitive varieties can play a broader and more significant role than in correcting specific shortcomings of otherwise adapted varieties. Primitive varieties have a common background of evolution under cultivation, but differ in the range of environments in which they have evolved. Physical, biological and social factors which constitute or modify the environment, have had the effect of moulding both the cultivator and the crops which had become the basis of human life and civilization.

Thus man and plant, in interaction with each other and with a range of environments—good, bad and indifferent—produced the range of populations from which our gene centres are derived. One may assume—and evidence comes from present-day cultivars—that a range of environments resulted in a corresponding range of adaptations, enabling the plant or the population not only to withstand physical and biological stresses, but productively to exploit the opportunities each environment presents. Primitive varieties may then be seen as differing in their *genetic organization for productivity*, and thus to offer opportunities for recombinations which have not been systematically exploited or explored, except by Vavilov and his colleagues and successors at the Institute of Plant Industry which now bears his name. Vavilov was among the first to advocate combining genotypes from widely differing environments, and many of the varieties produced by his Institute are the result of such combinations, as are, notably, the successful Mexican and Philippine wheat and rice varieties to which we have referred above.

As repositories of gene assemblies of adaptive value, primitive varieties are unlikely to be superseded by induced mutations. As Brock (1969) points out, mutation breeding is promising and economical—by comparison with gene transfer—if a desirable or undesirable character is determined by a single recessive gene, if undesirable linkages or

B

pleiotropic effects are associated with gene transfer, or if the transfer involves inter-specific or inter-generic combinations. Mutation has produced morphological and physiological changes which drastically improve productivity and this field of 'macro-mutation' breeding for productivity is perhaps only in its infancy. Mutagens have also led to increased variance in quantitative characters which are then responsive to selection. But it is too early to predict the potential any more than the limitations of mutation breeding. It is most improbable, however, that the balanced gene complexes which are the consequences of long-term selection for adaptation can be assembled by mutation breeding techniques.

It may well be that it is the enormous diversity of gene complexes determining adaptation and productivity, assembled and incorporated over centuries of cultivation in widely differing environments, which must be recognised as the outstanding and unrivalled characteristic of primitive varietal populations. The more familiar specific adaptations are characteristics which are inherited in a relatively straightforward manner have been, and no doubt will continue to be, extensively exploited. Although induction of mutations may at least in part replace the introduction of specific genes from natural sources, one would be foolhardy to jettison the latter in reliance on induced mutability.

The extinction of the natural sources of adaptation and productivity represented by primitive varieties may turn out to be an irreparable loss to future generations. The destruction of wild populations such as forest tree species and range plants, which are valuable genetic resources for plant improvement also, would be an equal disaster.

In the regions of the earth in which the centres of genetic diversity occur, the question of the continued existence of primitive crop races must evoke contradictory reactions. The productivity of primitive races is frequently less than that of introduced advanced cultivars under conditions of moderately improved fertility, although selections from indigenous races may surpass advanced introductions in yield and quality, especially under conditions of low fertility. Forest and pasture species, which are represented by what are in reality wild populations, may also perform substantially better than introduced material. As fertility rises, however, the balance usually shifts in favour of the modern cultivar, and at this point the dilemma must be faced that the cultivation of variable indigenous populations, whatever their value, and the introduction of modern techniques and high-fertility farming, are mutually exclusive objectives. But this does not mean that such populations can be allowed to perish. We cannot pretend that at present we know the full technical answer; this book endeavours to show what immediate steps should be taken to make genetic resources available and safe, and how some at least of the many problems can be solved.

One thing can be said with certainty. Those regions in which the centres of genetic diversity occur, and where primitive crops are still cultivated, have a direct and pressing interest in the use of indigenous populations which is at least as strong as the interest of other regions in the same material, since in many instances it has been found that some selections from indigenous crop populations have proved superior to introduced varieties, or to be valuable breeding material in combination with introduced varieties. Thus the interest of these regions coincides with that of the rest of the world as a whole : *that the genetic diversity they still possess should be preserved*; it must be added that *this does not infringe upon the development of the regions themselves.*

At the organizational level, the steps which need to be taken to promote the availability and conservation of genetic resources are outlined in the Recommendations of the FAO/IBP Conference of 1967 (see p. 3). Here we discuss only the background and implications of the principal recommendations.

1. In the first place it is necessary to determine the location and nature of *genetic resources in the field*, i.e. in centres of genetic diversity. This survey should be as comprehensive as possible; but, considering the magnitude of the task and, in many cases, the need for urgent salvage, an order of priorities is required in conducting the survey, taking into consideration the importance of the crop, the degree of urgency, availability of information, etc. For reasons already given, as a rule a higher priority would go to primitive than to wild material, though there would be exceptions. Of necessity this survey would be somewhat superficial and incomplete, in view of the need for rapid action; but further information can be added as it comes to hand, and incorporated in a data handling system.

In principle, the aim of the survey would be analogous to the world survey of natural communities by the Section CT (Conservation Terrestrial) of the International Biological Programme (IBP), which has for its objective 'the establishment of the necessary scientific basis for a comprehensive world programme of preservation . . .' IBP is concerned with the preservation of ecosystems, whereas we are concerned with material for research and utilization; further, IBP is concerned with communities, whereas we are concerned with populations mainly of one species or of closely related species. Yet the approach to data collecting (Peterken, 1967) could be similar.

One may envisage a survey conducted by a combination of local and international experts pooling their information to compile a 'check list' of important species, regions and sites. An enormous amount of information is available in publications and unpublished reports, in notebooks and in people's minds. There are plant explorers, ecologists, taxonomists, and evolutionists with a broad knowledge of regions and habitats of importance for particular species. If information already in existence were to be marshalled and coordinated, the resulting check lists are likely to provide a great deal of the data we require. Undoubtedly there would arise needs for *ad hoc* surveys of some areas which are as yet little explored, and such leads would also be listed, and become widely known, as a result of the survey.

The organization of the survey would not be possible without international collaboration and without the co-ordinating services of an international agency (see 6 below). Responsibility for its execution, however, could and should be widely spread—on a regional basis, as in IBP, on a crop or species basis, or both. If well organized, the collection of the data and their collation through a records and retrieval system should be relatively simple, rapid and inexpensive—as it proved to be in IBP. Compilation of such data has already begun in the Genetic Resources Information Centre of the Crop Ecology and Genetic Resources Branch of FAO.

This survey should result in an annotated list of genetic resources of value to present and future scientists. It should assist international and national organizations, foundations and institutions to establish an *order of priorities and a plan of campaign for future exploration* in which due weight can be given to material which is regarded as particularly important or promising, which is threatened with extinction, or both.

Let it clearly be understood that such a survey will serve a purpose only if it proves an aid to concerted action. Comprehensive collections must be made, and it is emphasised in various parts of this book that time is already short for this to be done. The practical problems of collection are great, and not the least of these is the great cost in time and money of expeditions to the field. It is therefore essential that expeditions be planned to secure the greatest benefit for all concerned. Crop-specific and region-specific check lists can provide the informational basis upon which cooperation in the field may be attained by establishing links which materialise in joint action and joint support.

2. There is need for a corresponding survey of *material in existing collections*. With some outstanding exceptions, the holdings of primitive material in collections are small and representative neither of species nor of areas. Yet some collections contain material which is of great value because it is no longer available in the field, as, for example, the collections of Iranian wheats made by Professor H. Kuckuck, or because it is difficult or costly to collect, such as the collections, mainly of wild species, made in Central Asia by Professor Kihara and his colleagues, and the 1968 FAO collection of primitive wheats made in Afghanistan. It is of the greatest importance that such valuable stocks be made widely known and adequately preserved, and a survey of material held in collections would provide the information required for both.

3. There is little purpose in assembling material unless it is effectively used and preserved. The efficient *utilization of genetic resources* requires that they are adequately classified and evaluated. This, as is shown in several chapters, is a task which needs the participation of diverse specialists, and therefore, except in large and diversified institutions, collaboration on a national or even international scale. This phase would greatly gain from advice, assistance and coordination from an international agency.

4. *Conservation of genetic resources*, as we have seen, deserves the strongest emphasis, especially because its importance and urgency are as yet not fully appreciated. The section on conservation endeavours to clarify the scientific issues involved, in the hope of promoting agreement on approaches and techniques which is essential if concerted international action is to ensue.

The task of preserving genetic resources is one which concerns the whole of mankind, and the responsibility is not confined towards those now living; nor can it be adequately discharged by any one nation. This is readily appreciated with regard to wild species which are most effectively preserved in their natural state. Several chapters of this book refer to specific conservation projects which call for international collaboration. There is, however, one need of general and overriding importance, and that is the need for international seed storage facilities. An international gene bank, at least in the form of a 'clearing house' available to all nations and complemented by agreements on the reconstitution, or 'rejuvenation' (see chapter 40), would give strong encouragement to long-term conservation. It should be recalled that first-rate seed storage laboratories are few in number, and that they are

devoted to national or specialist tasks. In consequence, some of the
world's most valuable collections are maintained without the use of
adequate storage facilities, hence have to be grown every few years;
they are thus exposed to the process of 'genetic erosion' described in
chapters 40 and 41; losses due to inadequate storage can also be
alarming.

A world gene bank may be envisaged as an association of national
or regional institutions operating under international agreements relating to techniques and the availability of material, supported by a central
international clearing house under the control of an international
agency of the United Nations. Regional gene banks which have been
proposed could make a contribution provided two conditions are met—
a high degree of technical efficiency, and unrestricted international
access. It is of the greatest importance that both these provisos are
secured; an international gene bank ceases to fulfil its proper function
if it is subject to national or political discrimination.

The emphasis placed on facilities for the long-term preservation of
seed—which we believe to be the most urgent single measure at the
present time to ensure genetic conservation—is not exclusive of other
steps which are discussed in the section on conservation.

5. There is now wide-spread recognition of the need for *documentation*
at all stages; from site description and classification, to morphological
and physiological characterization, evaluation, utilization in research
and breeding, and conservation. The value of collections to contemporary and future workers anywhere, is enormously enhanced by documentation in a standard and internationally recognised form (see
chapter 39). Needless to say, documentation of collections should,
wherever possible, include reference to voucher herbarium specimens
from the collection site.

6. The geographic dispersion, complexity, magnitude and importance of this programme demand *international co-ordination, guidance and
administrative backing* at the highest level, which can only come from an
United Nations agency. FAO is indicated by reason of its long-standing
interest and participation in plant exploration and introduction, and its
general responsibility for international activities of importance to agricultural progress. The recent creation of a new unit dealing with Crop
Ecology and Genetic Resources, and of a Genetic Resources Information Centre using computer-based methods of data storage, retrieval
and analysis, strengthen the involvement of this agency, whose links
with active science have now been reinforced through a permanent

panel of internationally recognised authorities in the relevant fields. UNESCO has interests and responsibilities in conservation also, though in a more general sense. The importance of the conservation of genetic resources was stressed at the Conference on the Scientific Basis for the Rational Use and Conservation of the Resources of the Biosphere held in Paris in September 1968. This amply supported the conclusions of the Rome Conference of FAO and IBP in September 1967. The exploration, collection and utilization of resources stressed by FAO, and the long-term conservation of biological resources stressed by UNESCO, are indissolubly associated. It is now essential and urgent that unequivocal and unhesitating leadership be assumed if the survival of some of man's most vital resources is to be ensured.

REFERENCES

BROCK R.D. (1969) When to use mutations in plant breeding. *Manual of Mutation Breeding*, IAEA, Vienna (in press).
FRANKEL O.H. (1959) Variation under domestication. *Austral. J. Sci.* **22,** 27–32.
HARLAN J.R. (1951) Anatomy of gene centres. *Am. Nat.* **85,** 97–103.
KUCKUCK H. (1962) Vavilov's Genzentrentheorie in heutiger Sicht. *III Congress Eucarpia, Paris,* 177–196.
PETERKEN G.F. (1967) *Guide to the check sheet of IBP areas,* IBP Handbook No. 4. Blackwell Scientific Publications, Oxford.

EVOLUTION OF CULTIVATED PLANTS

J. R. HARLAN

University of Illinois, Urbana,
Illinois, U.S.A.

Darwin opened his book 'On the Origin of Species' with a discussion of the evolution of plants and animals under domestication. He was struck by the magnitude of morphological diversity among races which were obviously closely related and fully compatible when crossed, as well as by the enormous divergence of some domesticated forms from their wild relatives and presumptive progenitors. He concluded that domesticated plants and animals have evolved rapidly, indeed are still evolving rapidly, and are consequently good subjects for the study of evolution. Darwin was right, of course, but the understanding of heredity was too rudimentary and the techniques of biosystematic analysis too crude for useful studies to emerge for some decades. In recent years, students of evolution have been turning their attention more and more to cultivated plants and to weeds as suitable subjects for experimental investigations of evolutionary processes.

As a result, our understanding of the origin and evolution of culti-vated plants is improving, but it is surprising how little we still know of the wild and weedy relatives of our important crop species. With all the genetic and cytogenic work that has been done on wheat, we still have only the sketchiest knowledge of the geographic distribution and ecological behaviour of the wild species that have contributed their heredities to the evolution of wheat. There has been a great deal of discussion and a little research about the importance of *Tripsacum* germ plasm in the evolution of maize, but we know virtually nothing about the genus *Tripsacum*. Although the exploitation of alien germ plasm for the improvement of sugarcane is a classic case in the annals of plant breeding, we really know very little about the wild and weedy relatives of sugarcane. The same applies to rice, sorghum, soybean, etc., in fact to essentially all cultivated plants.

It seems extraordinary that there should be so little curiosity about the relatives of the plants that feed and clothe the world's billions. The neglect could well be dangerous. As the world population continues

B*

to increase, the pressure for more yield per acre must inevitably result in discarding a number of the crops with low yield potentials which helped to provide security in the old subsistence agriculture. It may be, for example, that we shall find it appropriate to grow only those cereals which can yield 10 tons per hectare or more. Cereals with a lower yield potential may have to be discarded except for marginal environments. Already a remarkable proportion of the human diet is supplied by four cereals : wheat, rice, maize and sorghum. Imagine, if you can, the scope of the disaster if one of these should fail, if some new and virulent disease should appear with which we are unable to cope in time. Surely it is imperative that we know all that we possibly can about ALL of the germ plasm within genetic reach in our major food plants.

Time and time again we have reached out into wild relatives of our crops to exploit a gene or a few genes for resistance to disease. Some crops have virtually been saved from discard by the process. But, by and large, we have made these transfers of genes piecemeal, as the need arose, and at our leisure. In almost no crop do we have a large collection of wild relatives available in anticipation of need. In no crop at all have we thoroughly explored the germ plasm that is within genetic reach and that could be used if necessary. This may or may not be important in minor crops, but it would be most irresponsible if we failed to do a thorough job of genetic exploration of our major food plants.

For these reasons the study of the origin and evolution of cultivated plants is not only a work of intellectual and academic interest to the evolutionist, but a matter of enormous practical urgency in those crops that carry the burden of supporting the human population. We must not only assemble the gene pools and maintain them, but we must explore them so thoroughly that we will know how to exploit them more efficiently than we have in the past. In a very real sense, the fate of the human species depends upon our ability to understand and exploit the germ plasm of cultivated plants.

ORIGINS

Evidence on the origins of cultivated plants can be obtained from a variety of disciplines, but the most direct evidence, and presumably the most definitive, comes from the field of archaeology. Archaeobotany as a discipline is relatively new and very little work was done before World War II. In recent years, considerable progress has been made, but the techniques are still too crude and the number of studies far too small for an adequate picture of the origin of any crop to emerge on archaeobotanical evidence alone. Two series are complete enough, however, to provide skeleton frameworks into which evidence from other sources can be fitted. I refer to the emergence of wheat–barley agriculture in the Near East, and the evolution of maize–cucurbit–bean agriculture in the New World. There are, of course, many other agricultural complexes, but so far they are very poorly documented in the archaeological record.

An excellent recent review of the general pattern has been provided by Harris (1967) and it would be inappropriate to go into detail here. It now appears that domestication started more or less at the same time in both the Old and New Worlds. At least the earliest evidence of genuinely domesticated forms so far discovered dates to about 7,000 B.C. in both hemispheres. The development in the Near East may have had a longer prelude than we can yet demonstrate archaeobotanically and seems to have moved faster once an effective agriculture was achieved. The general locale for wheat and barley domestication seems to be in or near the oak woodland belts in an arc through the hilly country surrounding the Syrian–Mesopotamian plains. The arc stretches from Kuzestan in Iran through the Western Zagros, the Tauros of Turkey and down the Antilebanon to the Southern Jordan highlands near the Dead Sea rift.

As Harlan and Zohary (1966) point out, it is likely that einkorn, emmer, and barley were each initially taken into cultivation in different subregions of the nuclear zone. The cluster of peculiar and endemic wheats in Soviet Georgia and Armenia appear to be products of local attempts to domesticate other wild races as well as introgression derivatives between cultivated and the local wild races. Archaeological evidence for the diffusion out of the nuclear area is summarized by Clark (1965) and the archaeobotanical evidence by Helbaek (1965). Some basic botanical considerations are further brought together by Harlan (1967 and n.d.). All of the evidence taken together makes a fairly consistent picture although sketchy and far from complete.

Similar evidence in the New World is summarized by MacNeish (1965) and Harris (1967). The longest and most complete record is that of the Tehuacan Valley in Mexico in which a domesticated *Cucurbita mixta* appears by 7,000 B.C. as well as *Persea*, *Capsicum*, cotton and amaranth, but none of these was especially important in the diet at the time. By slow stages, maize, beans, bottle gourd, and other cucurbits were added. Present estimates suggest that cultivated plants did not contribute over 50% of the diet until the approach of the classical period only some two centuries or so B.C. A somewhat similar series is demonstrable in Tamaulipas in North-eastern Mexico, and involving a somewhat different sequence of crops as well as additional ones such as *Helianthus*. The achievement of an effective agriculture was a very slow and gradual process. A sequence from coastal Peru shows the use of several cucurbits, cotton, and lima beans by 2,500 B.C. but most of the diet was supplied by sea food. An effective agriculture based on maize, beans, manioc, peanut, potato and sweet potato made its appearance a few centuries before the Christian era.

Such is the state of our information at the present time. It is so sketchy and the studies conducted to date so widely separated and so few that future discoveries could change our thinking rather radically. Other potential nuclear areas such as parts of Africa and South-east Asia are too little studied to date for archaeobotanical sequences to emerge. Meanwhile, we must depend more than is desirable on the indirect evidences that come to us through geography, botany, and genetics.

One pattern that emerges rather consistently from geobotanical and genetic studies is one I have called *diffuse origins* (Harlan, 1956, 1961, 1966). Cultivated plants did not enter into domestication as the full-blown crops we know today. They started as something much less impressive and more or less equivalent to their wild progenitors. Since, in some cases, we do not know the wild progenitors, we have only a general idea of what the earliest domesticates were like. We do have good evidence, in a number of instances, that the crops picked up additional germ plasm as they spread out of their nuclear areas of origination and came into contact with wild relatives. In maize, we have evidence of periodic infusions of *Tripsacum* germ plasm. In wheat, we know that the heredity of *Aegilops squarrosa* was added to tetraploid wheat some time after domestication. In sugarcane, we have evidence of the incorporation of germ plasm from several relatives as the crop moved out of local areas in New Guinea (Grassl, 1963; Price, 1957, 1963). A similar pattern can be demonstrated in *Manihot* (Rogers, 1965), potato (Dodds, 1966), sorghum (Doggett, 1965) and many others.

Thus, a crop as we know it today did not originate in one nuclear area. What originated was a primitive domesticate that may not even exist today. Modern strains and races have mostly evolved recently and in places far removed from the locale of original domestication. Origins are diffuse in both time and space, and consequently the problem of a 'center of origin' can never quite be solved. As a matter of fact our understanding would be much improved if we threw out the concept of 'center of origin' altogether and referred to nuclear areas of initial domestication and centers of diversity as two different things.

The concept of diffuse origins in which a species enlarges its geographic range, changing and evolving and picking up additional germ plasm from its relatives on the way, leads in its ultimate extension to the concept of the *compilospecies* put forth a few years ago by Harlan and de Wet (1963). Certain species have a remarkable faculty for absorbing heredities of their relatives. Such genetic agression may, in fact, swamp some races or species and cause their extinction. It is suggested that this may well have been the fate of some missing crop progenitors. It may be that we do not know a wild progenitor of maize simply because the successful domesticate completely absorbed its ancestor genetically. A progenitor potato could easily have disappeared into the remarkable wild, weed, and cultivated complex found today through the highlands of western South America, etc.

In addition, crops may have multiple centers of attempted domestication and multiple centers of introgression with wild or weedy relatives. In rice, we clearly have at least two centers of domestication, one in West Africa producing *Oryza glaberrima*, and one in Asia producing *O.sativa*. The second domesticate has been far more successful than the first. In wheat, there is some indication that einkorn was domesticated independently of emmer (Harlan and Zohary, 1966) and that the forms of Soviet Georgia such as *Triticum timopheevi* (4x) and *T.zhukowskyi* (6x) were derived from a different race of wild emmer than that which produced the bulk of the tetraploid wheats. (Menabde, 1960; Wagenaar, 1961, 1966). The variation pattern in Africa suggests that at least three major races of *Sorghum bicolor* with different ecological amplitudes and different but overlapping geographical distributions were incorporated in the development of cultivated sorghum (Doggett, 1965; de Wet and Huckabay, 1968). Many crops exhibit local areas of extraordinary morphological diversity which we have called *microcenters* and which appear to be based on introgression among domestic races or wild or weedy relatives or all three in combination (Harlan, 1951, 1963, 1965). Thus, the geographic concentration of diversity may not illustrate centers of origin so much as centers of origination of current introgression products.

We may conclude from all this that a study of the origin of cultivated plants requires the unravelling of very complex and intricate patterns and is not nearly so simple as formerly supposed. We are still in a rather primitive stage in our understanding and it will take the investigations of many people from many disciplines over many years to arrive at a reasonably comprehensive interpretation of the phenomenon.

EVOLUTION UNDER DOMESTICATION

Cultivated plants have the capacity to evolve rapidly. Rapid bursts of evolution are possible only through some variation on the theme of the differentiation–hybridization cycle in which variability already accumulated can be exploited. The ultimate source of variability may be mutation but it must operate in many populations over a long period of time in order to accumulate sufficient diversity for great change in a short period of time.

I have described elsewhere (Harlan, 1966) some variations of the differentiation–hybridization cycles in cultivated plants. It may be desirable to reproduce here the schematic diagram used to illustrate the effect of genetic buffering on the length of the cycles (Fig. 2.1). By genetic buffering we mean essentially the effects of redundancy of

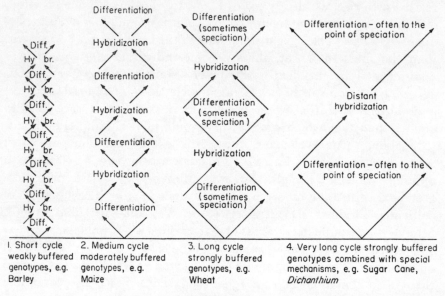

FIGURE 2.1. Schematic diagram of differentiation—hybridization cycles depending upon the degree of buffering of genotypes in cultivated plants.

genetic information. A self-fertilizing diploid would be presumed to be weakly buffered. Crossing between varieties should result in a rather major release of potential variability ; the variability should be largely oligogenic in which a relatively few genes have conspicuous effects, and truly wide hybridizations should be disastrous if possible at all. This system is rather well illustrated by barley.

A cross-fertilizing diploid such as maize should be somewhat better buffered through carrying many genes in a heterozygous condition. Narrow crosses should have less obvious effects, and wider crosses should be tolerated. Variation should still tend toward the oligogenic, at least when compared to a polyploid like wheat. Hexaploid wheat is better buffered than tetraploid wheat since the redundancy in genetic information is greater. Narrow crosses have relatively little effect and decidedly wide crosses, e.g., with *Aegilops*, *Secale*, and *Agropyron*, are tolerated. Finally, the most highly buffered system in the scheme is the case of a high polyploid propagated vegetatively so as to escape the penalties of sterility. Such systems can withstand the shock of distinctly alien germ plasm and the widest crosses are thereby tolerated. There are, of course, many gradations between the illustrations given and a sufficient number of examples would give a continuous series.

It is to be noted that all of the systems work. Barley with its short cycle was probably the foremost cereal crop on earth at one time. It is still important, conspicuously variable, and has a rather high yield potential. The variability may be somewhat deceiving because of its oligogenic nature, but there seems to be no great advantage or disadvantage in either a long or short differentiation–hybridization cycle. The variability accumulated during the differentiation phase is exploited by hybridization at the appropriate stage of differentiation in each case. Natural selection appears to have operated to adjust the length of the cycle to the degree of buffering. If the cycle is too short, there is little effect ; if it is too long the cycle cannot be completed.

In order for differentiation to take place, populations must be fragmented in some fashion and kept apart genetically. A variety of isolating mechanisms is well known. Geographic separation, ecological separation, differences in time of blooming, self-fertilization, apomixis, translocation races, polyploid races, cryptic structural differences in chromosome homologues, physiological imbalances resulting in weak, poorly adapted, or sterile hybrids, are some of the mechanisms studied to date, and all of them can be illustrated by cases in cultivated plants. Again, no one scheme is necessarily better than another. Any barrier to gene flow will permit populations to fragment and accumulate genetic differences among the subpopulations. Sometimes a combination of several mechanisms can be demonstrated. The only qualification is that if the differentiation–hybridization cycle is to function, the isolation can not be absolute nor permanent. Sooner or later the separated populations must be brought together again to permit some hybridization.

One differentiation–hybridization cycle of a short-range type is more or less automatically built into the traditional agricultural system. Farmers are basically sedentary. They settle down in an area and occupy it for long periods of time. This results in an array of varieties adapted to that particular area. But, occasionally, farmers move, taking their seed stocks or other planting materials with them. In the new location there is an opportunity for the transported varieties to cross with the local sorts. Populations separated geographically and differentiated ecologically are thus brought together and a cycle completed. The past movement of certain races of maize can be traced today from Mexico to South America, where the races were modified by introgression with South American races ; then this material returned at a later date to Mexico where it introgressed anew with Mexican races (Wellhausen *et al.*, 1952 ; Roberts *et al.*, 1957). An analysis of the great diversity in Turkish popcorns by Anderson and Brown (1953) indicated that the irruption of variability could be traced to the introduction of two different races into Turkey by different routes. The migration of identifiable races of American cottons and their periodic introgression has been documented by Hutchinson (1959).

Patterns of this nature can be traced in a number of crops. Populations of cultivated plants are far more mobile than populations of wild species, because they are transported by man and go with him on his wanderings over the face of the earth. This can readily result in the separation of plant populations by geographic isolation and the breakdown of isolation by bringing populations together again. There can be little doubt that these movements and migrations have profoundly affected the evolution of cultivated plants, by exposing populations to infusions of germ plasm from other domesticated races as well as from various wild relatives of the crop.

The operation of such differentiation–hybridization cycles is inherent in the nature of agriculture and human behavior and is expected and predictable. What is not so predictable and *a priori* unexpected is the operation of differentiation–hybridization cycles based on companion weeds. As I have pointed out on a number of occasions (Harlan, 1961, 1965) most crop plants have companion weed races. There are weed races of wheat, barley, rice, sorghum, maize, rye, oats, carrot, radish, lettuce, potato, tomato, pepper, watermelon, sugarcane, and so on and so on. Even an obscure crop like *Guizotia abyssinica* has its weed and cultivated races. It is such a general phenomenon that some explanation is demanded. At one time, it was rather generally thought that the weed races were the progenitors of the crops. More detailed studies soon showed that this explanation would not hold in many cases (and possibly in no case), and that the cultivated and weed forms must be considered companion derivatives from the same wild progenitor.

Thus, we frequently have wild, weed, and cultivated races, all in the same biological species, whatever the taxonomic treatment might say to the contrary. To make my own terminology clear, I mean by *cultivated*, forms that are habitually established by man with the purpose and expectation of a later harvest. By a *weed*, I mean a race or species adapted to habitats disturbed by man or his activities*, and by *wild* I mean a race or species neither cultivated nor markedly encouraged by human disturbance. A wild plant can survive without man, most weeds would not, nor would cultivated plants in their present form.

At any rate, there is good evidence that the companion weeds of cultivated plants have played important roles in the evolution of the crops (Harlan, 1965). Wherever the crop and the weed occur together on a massive scale, hybrid swarms and evidence of introgression can be found by diligent search. The barriers to gene flow are always rather strong, and hybridization does not occur on a massive scale. One population is not going to be swallowed up by the other. Instead, we have two separate populations growing side by side and maintaining their own heredities, but occasionally and locally they do cross and germ plasm is exchanged. The differentiation–hybridization cycle is completed and potential variability is released.

The system is a remarkably elegant evolutionary adaptation. Too much crossing would degrade the crop and the weed and cultivated races would merge into one population, possibly resulting in abandonment of the crop. Too little crossing would be ineffective. The barriers to gene flow must be strong but incomplete for the system to work, and the fact that crop–weed pairs have evolved in so many crops is an indication that natural selection has operated to adjust the amount

*For a more extended discussion of our understanding of weeds see Harlan and de Wet, 1965.

and frequency of hybridization to a range somewhere near the optimum evolutionary efficiency.

The barriers themselves are often of a rather ordinary kind, but perhaps the more easily adjusted because of it. The wild progenitor of rice, for example, is largely cross-fertilized. The cultivated and weed derivatives are rather highly self-fertilized, yet not so much so that occasional hybrids and local introgression are prevented. The rather simple shift from outbreeding to inbreeding with an adjusted low frequency of outcrossing has been quite effective. Not only does rice feed a large proportion of the world population, but weed rice is one of the most serious and exasperating problems in its culture. Both crop and weed are smashing evolutionary successes under current circumstances.

A shift from a perennial to annual habit is also to be noted in rice. The same is true in rye and cotton. In the case of rye, the cultivated and companion weed form maintained the cross-fertilizing habit of the wild progenitor. The barrier to gene flow that developed between the wild form on the one hand and the crop-weed pair on the other is based on chromosome translocations. When wild rye is crossed with crop-weed rye, a ring of six chromosomes is usually obtained.

Another rather common barrier to gene flow is polyploidy, but as in self-fertilization, the barrier leaks. In the Near East when tetraploid wheat is often grown surrounded by massive stands of weedy diploid wheats, such as *Triticum boeoticum* and *Aegilops speltoides*, triploids can be found if one searches for them. They are not common and one might have to search diligently over a period of years, but they do occur. Furthermore, under field conditions, surrounded by tetraploid plants they are not completely sterile (Zohary, 1965). They produce some seed and the plants derived from them are likely to be tetraploids or aneuploids very close to the tetraploid number. By the next generation, tetraploidy is recovered, but exchange of germ plasm has taken place ; potential variability is released. Introgression of diploid heredities into tetraploid and tetraploid into hexaploid has been documented in a number of cases. Because of the buffering effect, infusions of strange germ plasm are more common at tetraploid and higher levels than at the diploid level.

Apomixis can accomplish exactly the same results provided some sexual potential is maintained, which is usually the case.

Rice and potatoes appear to be examples in which populations are fragmented by some sort of cryptic structural differences in homologous chromosomes. Crosses between japonica and indica races of rice are not difficult to make; the chromosomes pair well, but the F_1 is rather sterile. Fertility may be recovered in some lines in later generations, but fragmentation into races is one of the characteristics of the species.

Variations on the theme are not endless, of course, but a fairly extensive array of devices have functioned in the evolution of cultivated plants to fragment populations, permit the accumulation of differences and to bring the populations together again through hybridization which in turn releases some of the potential variability. Natural and artificial selection operating on this variability has resulted in the enormous diversity so characteristic of cultivated plants and which impressed Darwin over a century ago.

The conspicuous and exuberant variation in cultivated plants and their relatives has raised taxonomic problems that have never been solved nor adequately treated. The methods of classical taxonomy seem to fail altogether and inevitably result in the establishment of dozens of epithets for races that are fully compatible when crossed. One example among many is Snowdon's treatment of *Sorghum* in which he named 52 species among the cultivated sorghums alone. All of these 'species' are fully compatible when hybridized with one another. The wild or weed barley, usually called *Hordeum spontaneum*, can be easily crossed with cultivated barley; the chromosomes pair in the F_1, and the hybrid is fully fertile. There is no biological reason for maintaining a separate epithet for this plant; it is only a race of *H. vulgare*. Similarly, teosinte which has even been assigned its own generic name (*Euchlaena mexicana*) is biologically only a race of *Zea mays*.

Our understanding of the germ plasm of cultivated plants and even the use and exploitation of it has been seriously handicapped by this kind of taxonomy. Since we have put some of the wheat group into *Aegilops* and some into *Triticum* we have developed mental blocks in our thinking and more reluctance than desirable in utilizing available germ plasm. Plant breeders are generally cautious about going into programs involving interspecific hybridization and practically refuse to attempt 'intergeneric' approaches. If we lumped 'genera' and 'species' according to the cytogenetical evidence of relationship, i.e., used the concept of the biological species, we could remove many misconceptions that have crept into our thinking because of the taxonomy that has been used.

This procedure, if followed consistently, would leave us with the unsolved problem of what to do with all that variability. It could, for example, result in lumping all of the one hundred or more tuber-bearing forms of *Solanum* into one giant biological species. This might be useful in demonstrating biological relationship, but would not solve the problem of semantics. The utility of taxonomy is primarily in giving names to groups or populations so that we can talk about them as a unit. The purpose of all classification is to establish groups of like things so that we can deal with the group rather than the individual. The variability of cultivated plants is not necessarily of a different order of magnitude from that of some wild species, but in dealing with cultivated plants we have special demands for the purpose of communication. To meet these demands, useful and appropriate classifications are required, and these have not been systematically developed to date. These difficult problems will be considered more fully by others in this book.

However we may solve the problem of dealing with it, the variation in cultivated plants is enormous. We have inherited an immensely rich resource which is currently in mortal danger. The varietal wealth of the plants that feed and clothe the world is slipping away before our eyes, and the human race simply cannot afford to lose it.

It is to be hoped that the assembly and conservation of gene pools will be taken seriously on an international scale and that early enthusiasm does not give way in the routine maintenance of stocks. We must expect a great deal of dull donkey-work in this project, but the genetic exploration of germ plasm can be as exciting and rewarding as the collection of exotic materials from far-off places.

I shall close with only one more point, but I wish to make it as strong as I possibly can. For the sake of future generations, we MUST collect and study the wild and weedy relatives of our cultivated plants as well as the domesticated races. These sources of germ plasm have been dangerously neglected in the past, but the future may not be so tolerant. In the plant breeding programs of tomorrow we cannot afford to ignore *any* source of useable genes.

REFERENCES

ANDERSON E. & BROWN W.L. (1953) The popcorns of Turkey. *Ann. Mo. bot. Gdn.*
   40, 33–49.
CLARK J.G.D. (1965) Radiocarbon dating and the spread of farming economy.
   Antiquity **39,** 45–48.
DE WET J.M.J. & HUCKABAY J.P. (1968) The origin of *Sorghum bicolor.* II. Distribution and domestication. *Evolution* **21,** 787–802.
DODDS K.S. (1966) The evolution of the cultivated potato. *Endeavour.* **25,** 83–88.

Doggett H. (1965) The development of the cultivated sorghums. In *Essays on Crop Plant Evolution* (Ed. Hutchinson J.) Cambridge University Press, Cambridge.

Grassl C.O. (1963) Problems and potentialities of intergeneric hybridization in a sugar cane breeding programme. *Proc. 11th Congr. int. Soc. Sug. Cane Technol.* 447–456.

Harlan J.R. (1951) Anatomy of gene centers. *Am. Nat.* **85,** 97–103.

Harlan J.R. (1956) Distribution and utilization of natural variability in cultivated plants. In *Genetics in Plant Breeding. Brookhaven Symp. Biol.* **9,** 191–206.

Harlan J.R. (1961) Geographic origin of plants useful to agriculture. In *Germ Plasm Resources. Publs. Am. Ass. Advmt. Sci.* **66,** 3–19.

Harlan J.R. (1963) Two kinds of gene centers in Bothriochloininae. *Am. Nat.* **97,** 91–98.

Harlan J.R. (1965) The possible role of weed races in the evolution of cultivated plants. *Euphytica* **14,** 173–176.

Harlan J.R. (1966) Plant introduction and biosystematics. In *Plant Breeding.* Iowa State University Press, Ames.

Harlan J.R. (1967) A wild wheat harvest in Turkey. *Archaeology* **20,** 197–201.

Harlan J.R. (1969) Botanical considerations in the domestication of wheat and barley. *Univ. Köln Pub.* (in press).

Harlan J.R. & de Wet J.M.J. (1963) The compilospecies concept. *Evolution* **17,** 497–501.

Harlan J.R. & de Wet J.M.J. (1965) Some thoughts about weeds. *Econ. Bot.* **19,** 16–24.

Harlan J.R. & Zohary D. (1966) Distribution of wild wheats and barley. *Science* **153,** 1074–1080.

Harris D.R. (1967) New light on plant domestication and the origins of agriculture. A Review. *Geogrl. Rev.* **57,** 90–107

Helbaek H. (1965) Archaelogical evidence for genetic changes in wheat and barley. *CSIRO Pl. Introd. Rev.* Canberra **2**(1), 10–16.

Hutchinson J. (1959) *The application of Genetics to Cotton Improvement.* Cambridge University Press, Cambridge.

MacNeish R.S. (1965) The origins of American agriculture. *Antiquity* **39,** 87–94.

Menabde V.L. (1960) Wheats of Georgia and their part in general evolution of the Genus *Triticum L. Trudy tbilis. bot. Inst.* **21,** 229–259.

Price S. (1957) Cytological studies in *Saccharum* and allied genera. III. Chromosome numbers in interspecific hybrids. *Bot. Gaz.* **118,** 146–159.

Price S. (1963) Cytogenetics of modern sugarcane. *Econ. Bot.* **17,** 97–106.

Roberts L.M., Grant U.J., Ricardo R.E., Hatheway W.H., & Smith D.L. (1957) Races of maize in Columbia. National Academy of Sciences. *Publs. natn. Res. Coun., Wash.* Publ. 510.

Rogers D.J. (1965) Some botanical and ethnological considerations of *Manihot esculenta. Econ. Bot.* **19,** 369–377.

Wagenaar E.B. (1961) Studies on the genome constitution of *Triticum timopheevi* Zhuk. I. Evidence for genetic control of meiotic irregularities in tetraploid hybrids. *Can. J. Genet. Cytol.* **3,** 47–60.

WAGENAAR E.B. (1966) Studies on the genome constitution of *Triticum timopheevi* Zhuk. II. The *T. timopheevi* complex and its origin. *Evolution* **20,** 150–164.

WELLHAUSEN E.J., ROBERTS L.M. & HERNANDEZ X.E., in collaboration with MANGELSDORF P.C. (1952) *Races of Maize in Mexico*. Bussey Institute, Harvard University.

ZOHARY D. (1965) Colonizer species in the wheat group. In *The Genetics of Colonizing Species*. (Eds. Baker H.G. and Stebbins G.L.) Academic Press, New York, 404–420.

3

CENTERS OF DIVERSITY AND CENTERS OF ORIGIN

DANIEL ZOHARY

Department of Botany, The Hebrew University,
Jerusalem, Israel

INTRODUCTION

Nikolai Ivanovich Vavilov is to be credited for first setting the phyto-geographic basis for plant exploration. It is mainly due to him that plant breeders have become aware of the fact that variation in cultivated plants is geographically unevenly spread and that the bulk of genetic diversity in our important agricultural crops is geographically confined to relatively few restricted areas or centers. Since this exposition of centers of diversity by Vavilov in the 1920's, much more information has been gathered, but the general picture remains the same. Centers of diversity are a fact, and intelligent exploration and breeding programs in a given crop should be aimed at collection and full utilization of the genetic variation stored in them.

We frequently confuse the concept of *centers of diversity* with another Vavilovian concept, namely *centers of origin*. When distribution patterns of variation in crop plants became obvious to Vavilov, he also proposed that areas of maximum diversity are places of origin. In fact, in his publications Vavilov uses the term 'centers of origin' instead of 'centers of diversity' and we too frequently follow this tradition. But while centers of diversity are a biological fact, the term 'centers of origin' is only an interpretation. Since its exposition in the 1920's, geneticists and students of cultivated plants have sometimes had heated discussions about the validity of this interpretation. This Chapter aims at a brief survey of the world centers of diversity, and discussion of their origin and nature.

CENTERS OF DIVERSITY

Centers of diversity were recognized and mapped by Vavilov and his group on the basis of the tremendous amount of material which they had collected and brought back to Russia in the 1920's and the early 1930's. Vavilov's collections consisted mainly of cultivated varieties. He had a relatively poor representation of wild species. Historically, perhaps the most significant feature in Vavilov's approach was his ambitious, and successful, effort to 'cover the whole globe'. In crop after crop Vavilov found that over very extensive territories cultivated plants showed relatively few varieties, while in some restricted areas, multitudes of varieties and aggregates of species occurred. Wheat is a classical example to illustrate this pattern.

Over most of Europe, as well as Siberia, wheat cultivation is based on a rather restricted number of varieties, mostly hexaploid bread wheats. But when Vavilov and his colleagues explored the Middle East and particularly Anatolia, Syria, Palestine and Transcaucasia, they were amazed at the multitude of forms and types of wheat grown in these territories. The wide range of variation encountered here is apparent from the taxonomic treatments by Soviet botanists. They recognized here a wealth of 'species', 'subspecies', and 'varieties'— diploid, tetraploid and hexaploid.

In addition to this Near Asiatic center of diversity, Vavilov found that, in wheat, several other variation centers exist as well. In a relatively small and geographically isolated area of the Ethiopian plateau, Vavilov found hundreds of endemic 'varieties' and 'subspecies' of tetraploid wheats. Ethiopia is indeed an excellent illustration of a variation center. The area here is so restricted and the wealth of forms is so conspicuously large!

Other concentrations of wheat variability were found by Vavilov's expeditions in Afghanistan (mainly hexaploid varieties) and in the Mediterranean basin (mainly tetraploid varieties).

Wheat (which was the classical example of Vavilov) serves as an illustration for the patterns of variation and distribution found in scores of cultivated crops. Each agricultural crop shows concentration of genetic variation in one (or relatively few) geographic areas.

Another feature which was immediately apparent to Vavilov is that centers of diversity of different crops often overlap. In other words there is a strong correlation in the distribution patterns of different cultivated plants. Western Asia, for instance, where wheat diversity is so conspicuous is not a wheat center alone! The same area harbours a vast wealth of cultivars of barley, rye, lentil, pea, flax, vines, figs and pistachios. Similar situations are found in other centres. The Andes of South America, for instance, are famous for their richness in potato species and varieties (Dodds, 1956). But this area is also a center of variation in tomato, tobacco, lima bean and several other crops. Based on the really 'colossal' amount of material assembled by numerous collecting expeditions, Vavilov first set up (1926) six main geographic centers for cultivated plants, and later (1935) increased their number to about ten. Since then we have gathered further information which perhaps makes it necessary to somewhat revise boundaries or to lump together some of these centers. Turkey, Syria, Palestine, Transcaucasia, Iran and Afghanistan, for example, should be regarded as a single center of diversity rather than two or three independent ones. But the general notion of centers of diversity remains basically unchanged. The main world centers as proposed by Vavilov (1935, 1951) are enumerated in Table 1 (p. 40) each with a representative list of crops.

CENTERS OF ORIGIN

Vavilov proposed that the centers of diversity are places of origin or *centers of origin* of cultivated plants. In fact, in most of his publications, centers of diversity are referred to as centers of origin. Vavilov's concept in a nutshell is : *The place of origin of a species of a cultivated plant is to be found in the area which contains the largest number of genetic varieties of this plant.* As already pointed out by Stebbins (1950), Vavilov's interpretation of diversity patterns are an elaboration on Willis' age-and-area hypothesis. It is based on the assumption that selective forces of the environment are operating in about the same manner throughout the evolutionary history of a given species or biological group. And thus the longer a given biological entity occupies a given area, the bigger would be the number of variables it would produce.

Since its exposition in the early 1930's, we are more and more aware of the fact that such an explanation is an oversimplification of the case and that the build-up of variation in the majority of biological entities proceeds at different paces in different places. It is now obvious that the Vavilovian concept of centers of origin should be discarded or at least greatly revised. In the following sections, several aspects pertinent to 'place of origin' and to factors involved in the build-up of variation are presented and discussed.

'PRIMARY CENTERS' VS. 'SECONDARY CENTERS'

Schiemann has to be given credit for pointing out a major difficulty in Vavilov's assumption that a variation center is a place of origin (see review in Schiemann, 1943). In many cases Vavilov found centers of diversity for given crops very far away from the areas in which their wild relatives occur. A conspicuous case is the Ethiopian center. Here wheats, barleys, peas, flax and lentils occur in an extraordinarily rich collection of varieties. Tetraploid wheats, for instance, manifested here according to Vavilov their widest variation. But significantly for all of these crops, they have not a single wild relative in Ethiopia. They therefore could not have possibly been domesticated there. Already Schiemann argued that the wild relatives of these crops, and particularly wheat, are found only in the Middle East, many thousands of kilometers away from Ethiopia. Today, we have sound information to conclude that most, if not all, of these cereals have been domesticated in the Middle East during the neolithic agricultural revolution. They were brought to Ethiopia already as agricultural crops long afterwards, most probably by Hamitic agricultural migrators.

In view of this obvious criticism, Vavilov had to reconsider his concept of centers of origin and to distinguish between *primary centers* (i.e., places where domestication originated) and *secondary centers* which are only explicable in terms of what happened after domestication was achieved.

TOPOGRAPHY AND ITS ROLE

Vavilov was aware of the fact that the centers of variation he encountered occurred mainly in mountainous regions or hilly areas. Such reliefs provide us with much more heterogeneous environment than a flat country does. Furthermore, when you have a dissected country, valleys, plateaux and mountainsides are somewhat isolated from one another spatially and contacts between agricultural communities are less frequent as compared with flat country.

Evolutionists have come to appreciate the role of population structure in relation to divergence. There is a considerable difference in what could happen in cases of continuous large populations as compared with a pattern of clusters of small, partially isolated populations. Already in the 1930's Sewall Wright pointed out that an ideal situation for rapid divergence would be given by a collection of small populations partially isolated from one another, and each occupying its specific niche. Mountain areas with their spatially semi-isolated farming communities and 'cultivation in patches' on the one hand, and with their wide amplitude of climates and soils on the other hand, conform very much with the requirements set up by Sewall Wright's model for rapid evolution. Here apparently lies, at least in part, the explanation for Vavilov's secondary centers of origin. But, this is only part of the story, because one usually finds in these areas enormous diversity in a single cultivated field. There is much more to a center of diversity than a variety of ecological situations.

PLACES OF ORIGIN

A logical and most sound approach to the problem of place of origin would be to find out (on the basis of genetic affinities) which are the wild progenitors of cultivated plants and where they are distributed. If one can plot the distribution of a given progenitor (or more specifically the area where this progenitor occupies primary habitats and is genuinely wild!) one can delimit the area in which domestication could have taken place. Vavilov necessarily based his judgement on variation patterns in cultivated plants. Information on wild plants in his day was much more fragmentary than it is today. Even now genetic and ecological information on wild relatives of most of our cultivated plants is indeed incomplete and in such cases assessment of a place of origin is hard to make. But at least in several crops we have today the necessary information on genetic affinities between wild and tame, on distribution areas and on ecological affinities of the wild progenitors. We thus have the necessary elements for determining the initial place of origin. Furthermore, at least in one or two areas of the world, the newly risen archeological interest in the early development of agriculture makes it possible for us to corroborate our biological finds with archeological evidence. Perhaps the best example for such an approach is the place of origin of the cultivated plants associated with the Old World neolithic agricultural revolution. On combined evidence of genetic affinities between wild and tame, accumulated knowledge on the ecology and distribution of the wild forms and recent analysis of plant remains in archeological digs, we can locate the initial place of origin of at least one dozen of the Old World cultivated plants. Harlan and Zohary (1966) attempted such delimitation of places of origin for wheat and barley. Most of the elements for such an assessment are also already available for rye, oats, peas, lentils, chickpeas, broad beans, vines, olives, figs and pistachios.

INTROGRESSION AND THE BUILD UP OF VARIATION

In the last twenty years introgressive hybridization in plants has received more and more attention from evolutionists (see reviews by Anderson, 1953 ; Anderson and Stebbins, 1954). A considerable amount of information is already available to indicate that introgression operates as a major evolutionary factor in plants, particularly when areas are drastically disturbed by man or when new habitats are being opened up. In fact, some of the best illustrations of introgression and its consequences are provided by cultivated plants and their closely related weeds.

The annual sunflowers of North America can serve as a demonstration for what actually happens when introgression operates in full force. Here, as Hieser so beautifully demonstrated, one species, i.e., *Helianthus annuus*, considerably expanded its geographical distribution and ecological amplitude by 'absorbing' genetic variation (through interspecific hybridization) from at least half a dozen other *Helianthus* species. As a result of this process, *H.annuus* presents us today with a vast polytypic complex and an extraordinarily large gene pool. All indications point out that the build-up of genetic variation by introgression here is recent. It apparently all happened in the last 100–200 years when man drastically churned up the landscape across the North American continent. 'Donations' of genes from *different* species situated in *different* locations and adapted to *different* environments enabled *H.annuus* to rapidly expand over the *entire* area and successfully and *continuously* occupy the vast climatic and edaphic range on which it is now found.

H.annuus thus serves as a model for what apparently happened in many of our crop plants. There is a great deal of accumulated evidence to indicate that introgression is responsible for rapid build-up of variation in many of our crops. A well cited case is introgression from *Tripsacum* to maize. But today we have sufficient information to assume that introgressive hybridization played a major role in the build-up of variation in *Triticum-Aegilops* (Zohary, 1965), rye (Zohary, unpublished), oats (Ladizinsky, unpublished), tomato (Rick, 1958), sorghum (Doggett, 1965), and various other crops.

I am willing to risk my neck and emphasize the role of introgression even more strongly. It seems that introgression in cultivated plants should be regarded as a rule, not as an exception. Everywhere when I have had a chance to examine places of contact between cultivated plants and their wild relatives, I have found indications for hybridization, and introgressive hybridization patterns could be detected. We should strongly suspect a full scale operation of this process in all cases where initial domesticates expanded their distribution with the help of men and came into contact with new wild races or additional wild species of their genera.

Introgression, of course, complicates the whole concept of a definite 'place of origin'. Instead of an exactly delimited area of a single progenitor, we are faced with blurred boundaries. Harlan (1956, 1961) already suggested the term *diffuse origin* for such situations.

POLYPLOIDY AND PLACE OF ORIGIN

A large proportion of our cultivated plants are polyploids, and polyploidy has its own complications for the concept of place of origin. In a few cases polyploidy actually provides us with a real advantage for determining places of origin. When faced with simple allopolyploidy, we can pinpoint the origin of the polyploid entity by finding the area of contact between the two involved diploid donors. Such examples are often cited in literature, but they present us with rather simple and rare text book models. In many plant groups, and in cultivated crops in particular, the nature of polyploidy is much more complex. Instead of simple cases, we are faced with *polyploid complexes*. At the base of such a complex we have ecologically and morphologically easily definable 'diploid pillars'. Superimposed on them is a 'polyploid superstructure' with a wide range of continuous or almost continuous variation which combines and fuses the separate gene pools found in the diploid level. Only a few polyploid complexes have been satisfactorily analyzed. These include, for example, *Dactylis* (Stebbins and Zohary, 1959), *Triticum–Aegilops* (Zohary, 1965), and blue stem grasses (Harlan, 1963). In many other cultivated crops, such as potatoes, alfalfa, oats, sugar cane, rice, apparently similar compound situations exist.

The crux of the matter in polyploid complexes is that the formation of polyploids is not an end by itself. It is an effective means to fuse gene pools of numerous independent sources and to rapidly build up variation. The polyploid level serves as a buffer; it facilitates hybridization and introgression. It makes possible the fusion of gene pools which are fully isolated between diploids. In polyploid complexes, the polyploid superstructure can be compared to a sponge that sucks variation from numerous sources. Thus the problem of place of origin in polyploid complexes is again vastly complicated, even more than in cases of simple introgression in diploid plants. Diffuse (or may we say 'confused') origin is the proper term here.

TABLE 1. *World Centers of Diversity* (Centers of Origin *Sensu* Vavilov) *of Cultivated Plants* (after Vavilov, 1951.)

1. THE CHINESE CENTER

Avena nuda, Naked oat (Secondary center of origin).
Glycine hispida, Soybean.
Phaseolus angularis, Adzuki bean.
Phaseolus vulgaris, Bean (Recessive form; secondary center).
Phyllostachys spp., Small bamboos.
Brassica juncea, Leaf mustard (Secondary center of origin).
Prunus armeniaca, Apricot.
Prunus persica, Peach.
Citrus sinensis, Orange.
Sesamum indicum, Sesame (Endemic group of dwarf varieties. Secondary center).
Camellia (Thea) sinensis, China tea.

2. THE INDIAN CENTER

Oryza sativa, Rice.
Eleusine coracana, African millet.
Cicer arietinum, Chick pea.
Phaseolus aconitifolius, Math Bean.
Phaseolus calcaratus, Rice bean.
Dolichos biflorus, Horse gram.
Vigna sinensis, Asparagus bean.
Solanum melongena, Egg plant.
Raphanus caudatus, Rat's tail radish.
Colocasia antiquorum, Taro yam.
Cucumis sativus, Cucumber.
Gossypium arboreum, Tree cotton, 2x.
Corchorus olitorius, Jute.
Piper nigrum, Pepper.
Indigofera tinctoria, Indigo.

2a. THE INDO-MALAYAN CENTER

Dioscorea spp., Yam.
Citrus maxima, Pomelo.
Musa spp., Banana.
Cocos nucifera, Coconut.

3. THE CENTRAL ASIATIC CENTER

Triticum aestivum, Bread wheat.
Triticum compactum, Club wheat.
Triticum sphaerococcum, Shot wheat.
Secale cereale, Rye (Secondary center).
Pisum sativum, Pea.
Lens esculenta, Lentil.
Cicer arietinum, Chick pea.
Sesamum indicum, Sesame (One of the centers of origin).
Linum usitatissimum, Flax (One of the centers of origin).
Carthamus tinctorius, Safflower (One of the centers of origin).
Daucus carota, Carrot (Basic center of Asiatic varieties).
Raphanus sativus, Radish (One of the centers of origin).
Pyrus communis, Pear.
Pyrus malus, Apple.
Juglans regia, Walnut.

4. THE NEAR EASTERN CENTER

Triticum monococcum, Einkorn wheat.
Triticum durum, Durum wheat.
Triticum turgidum, Poulard wheat.
Triticum aestivum, Bread wheat (Endemic awnless group. One of the centers of origin).
Hordeum vulgare, Endemic group of cultivated two-rowed barleys.
Secale cereale, Rye.
Avena byzantina, Red oat.
Cicer arietinum, Chick pea (Secondary center).
Lens esculenta, Lentil (A large endemic group of varieties).
Pisum sativum, Pea (A large endemic group. Secondary center).
Medicago sativa, Blue alfalfa.
Sesamum indicum, Sesame (A separate geographic group).

Linum usitatissimum, Flax (Many endemic varieties).

Cucumis melo, Melon.

Amygdalus communis, Almond.

Ficus carica, Fig.

Punica granatum, Pomegranate.

Vitis vinifera, Grape.

Prunus armeniaca, Apricot (One of centers of origin).

Pistacia vera, Pistachio (One of the centers).

5. THE MEDITERRANEAN CENTER

Triticum durum, Durum wheat.

Avena strigosa, Hulled oats.

Vicia faba, Broad bean.

Brassica oleracea, Cabbage.

Olea europaea, Olive.

Lactuca sativa, Lettuce.

6. THE ABYSSINIAN CENTER

Triticum durum, Durum wheat (An amazing wealth of forms).

Triticum turgidum, Poulard wheat (An exceptional wealth of forms).

Triticum dicoccum, Emmer.

Hordeum vulgare, Barley (An exceptional diversity of forms).

Cicer arietinum, Chick pea (A center).

Lens esculenta, Lentil (A center).

Eragrostis abyssinica, Teff.

Eleusine coracana, African millet.

Pisum sativum, Pea (One of the centers).

Linum usitatissimum, Flax (A center).

Sesamum indicum, Sesame (Basic center).

Ricinus communis, Castor bean (A center).

Coffea arabica, Coffee.

7. THE SOUTH MEXICAN AND CENTRAL AMERICAN CENTER

Zea mays, Corn.

Phaseolus vulgaris, Common bean.

Capsicum annum, Pepper.

Gossypium hirsutum, Upland cotton.

Agave sisalana, Sisal hemp.

Cucurbita spp., Squash, Pumpkin, Gourd.

8. SOUTH AMERICAN (PERUVIAN-ECUA-DOREAN-BOLIVIAN) CENTER

Ipomoea batatas, Sweet Potato.

Solanum tuberosum, Potato.

Phaseolus lunatus, Lima bean.

Lycopersicum esculentum, Tomato.

Gossypium barbadense, Sea Island Cotton (4x).

Carica papaya, Papaya.

Nicotiana tabacum, Tobacco.

8a. THE CHILOE CENTER

Solanum tuberosum, Potato.

8b. BRAZILIAN-PARAGUAYAN CENTER

Manihot utilissima, Manioc.

Arachis hypogaea, Peanut.

Theobroma cacao, Cacao (Secondary center).

Hevea brasiliensis, Rubber tree.

Ananas comosa, Pineapple.

Passiflora edulis, Purple granadilla.

REFERENCES

ANDERSON E. (1953) Introgressive hybridization. *Biol. Rev.* **28**, 280–307.

ANDERSON E. & STEBBINS G.L. (1954) Hybridization as an evolutionary stimulus. *Evolution* **8**, 378–388.

DODDS K.S. (1966) The evolution of the cultivated potato. *Endeavour* **25**, 83–88.

DOGGETT H. (1965) The development of the cultivated sorghums. In *Essays on Crop Plant Evolution*. (Ed. Hutchinson J.) Cambridge University Press, Cambridge.

HARLAN J.R. (1956) Distribution and utilization of natural variability in cultivated plants. In *Genetics in Plant Breeding. Brookhaven Symp. Biol.* **9,** 191–206.

HARLAN J.R. (1961) Geographic origin of plants useful to agriculture. In *Germ Plasm Resources. Publs. Am. Ass. Advmt Sci.* **66,** 3–19.

HARLAN J. R. (1963) Two kinds of gene centers in Bothriochloininae. *Am. Nat.* **97,** 91–98.

HARLAN J.R. & ZOHARY D. (1966) Distribution of wild wheat and barley. *Science* **153,** 1074–1080.

RICK C.M. (1958) The role of natural hybridization in the derivation of cultivated tomatoes of Western South America. *Econ. Bot.* **12,** 346–367.

SCHIEMANN E. (1943) Entstehung der Kulturpflanzen. *Ergebn. Biol.* **19,** 409–552.

STEBBINS G.L. (1950) *Variation and Evolution in Plants*. Columbia University Press, New York.

STEBBINS G.L. & ZOHARY D. (1959) Cytogenetic and evolutionary studies in the genus *Dactylis*. I. Morphology, distribution and interrelationships of the diploid sub species. *Univ. Calif. Publs. Bot.* **31,** 1–40.

VAVILOV N.I. (1926) Studies on the origin of cultivated plants. *Trudy Byuro prikl. Bot.* **16,** 139–248.

VAVILOV, N.I. (1935) *Theoretical Bases of Plant Breeding*. Moscow (Russian).

VAVILOV N.I. (1951) Phytogeographic basis of plant breeding. The origin, variation, immunity and breeding of cultivated plants. *Chronica Bot.* **13,** 1–366.

ZOHARY D. (1965) Colonizer species in the wheat group. In *The Genetics of Colonizing Species*. (Eds. Baker H.G. and Stebbins G.L.), 403–423. Academic Press, New York.

4

GEOGRAPHIC VARIATION
IN FOREST TREES

R. Z. CALLAHAM

Forest Service, U.S. Department of Agriculture,
Washington D.C.

INTRODUCTION

The purpose of this Chapter is to relate what has been learned about
genetic variation associated with geographic distribution to the
utilization of this variation in the genetic improvement of forest tree
species. For more than a hundred years, foresters have recognized that
trees from different geographic areas within the range of a species
vary in growth rate, form, adaptation to environmental conditions,
and resistance to insect and disease enemies. Their incidental observations have been followed by purposeful research. The result is a good
scientific understanding and practical use of geographic patterns of
inherent variation in some important commercial forest timber species
in the temperate regions of the northern hemisphere.

Foresters, in contrast to agriculturists, are almost exclusively
concerned with wild species. The only exceptions are the few species
that are grown from cuttings. These occur in genera like *Populus*, *Salix*,
Cryptomeria, and *Metasequoia*. But even in these exceptional cases, the
cultivars now being grown correspond to the primitive cultivars of
agriculture. Little or no breeding has gone into the development of
these superior forms. Similarly, selections of plus trees in many advanced
forestry regions also correspond to primitive agricultural varieties.
In general, we can say that foresters are not faced with the imminent
loss of their wild species. Thus, preservation of gene pools is not a
pressing matter.

The laws of evolution and genecological responses in plants apply
equally well to forest trees as to domestic crop plants; forest trees are
not unique in the plant kingdom. They are, however, less well understood than crop plants. Their domestication and cultivation as crop
plants on a broad scale have only started recently. Basically the evolutionary mechanisms of gene mutation, migration and recombination

43

are the same for forest trees as for crop plants. However, the rate of evolutionary change is much slower, reflecting the long life of forest trees and the relatively long period before sexual maturity and repro- duction. Research to date indicates that forest trees, like crop plants, have evolved inherent adaptations to the factors of the environment at the site where they grow. Summaries of available information are presented by Wright (1962) and by F A O (1964).

HISTORIC BACKGROUND

Foresters as early as the 16th century recognized inherent differences among trees of forest species. However, not until the 19th century did they come to realize the great practical importance of the inherent variation associated with geography. At this time large quantities of seed were being moved among nations of Europe. Great economic losses occurred from moving seed north from Germany to reafforest portions of Sweden, to name just one example. These losses in yield resulted from lack of adaptation to climate and from susceptibility to pests, and they led to the sophisticated genecological research on forest tree species which started about 1900.

Studies of variation within species made over the past seven decades have led to these general conclusions and their corollaries :

1. A diverse environment throughout the range of the species leads to a genetically variable species. Widespread species tend to be more variable than restricted species.
2. Patterns of inherent variation parallel patterns of environmental variation. Discontinuities in patterns of inherent variation are related to breaks in the distribution of species or rapid changes in environmental factors.
3. Races of a species growing in different climatic regions may differ in inherent adaptation to environmental factors. In one region a certain factor of the environment may be critical ; in another region this factor may be less important than some other critical factor.
4. Sympatric species will be similar but not identical in inherent adaptations to the same environment. Limiting factors generally are not always the same for cohabiting species.
5. Two or more successive seed sources trials will be needed to determine an optimum source. Most species and environments are too variable to be analyzed completely in one experiment.

6. Seed source studies of native species undisturbed by man generally show the local seed source to be the best adapted but not necessarily the most productive. Exotic populations usually do not equal local populations in adaptation to the unique combination of factors of the local environment.

7. The local seed source is safest if little is known about variation in a native species. If local seed is not available, seed sources from environments comparable to the planting site should be used.

8. Strong genotype-environment interactions can be expected in all seed source studies. Widely separated provenances of a species should be tried in several diverse environments to find the best source for each environment.

9. Performance will be unpredictable for species grown for a long time under cultivation or disturbance by man or for species transferred to radically different environments, as in the case of species of *Eucalyptus* and *Cedrus*.

10. Exploration should not be confined to finding and cataloguing of forest species. Rather it should be concerned with exposing variability that exists between and within species particularly in relation to environmental changes.

11. Exploration routes obviously should follow major environmental gradients which must be understood before exploration starts. Exploration routes should pass from warm to cold regions, from long-day zones at high latitudes to short-day zones at low latitudes, and from moist to dry regions across mountain ranges.

12. Explorations should seek out the margins of distribution of each species. Outlying populations should be found and sampled to detect possible significant evolutionary changes that have occurred in these populations.

Provenances of forest trees usually display major inherent differences in tolerances for critical environmental factors—light, temperature, moisture, and soils. With respect to light, photoperiod during the growing period is the most critical factor. For temperature, both thermoperiod during the growing season and seasonal temperature extremes are important. The moisture supply is critical both in terms of the total amount provided and in terms of seasonal precipitation patterns. Relative atmospheric humidity is probably also important but critical evidence of adaptation to humidity has not been forthcoming as yet. Soil factors undoubtedly are very important in determining local patterns of inherent variation, but few studies have been made of genetic adaptation to soil difference.

We know considerably less about genetic differences between adjacent populations than we do about differences between distant populations of forest tree species. A few studies suggest that important genetic differences exist between adjacent stands. Considerable research is underway now to expose differences between trees growing on adjacent sites. Only when experimentation of this kind has progressed much further will we begin to understand populations of forest tree species.

Unfortunately most of the research basic to our present knowledge has involved species of forest trees growing in temperate regions of the northern hemisphere. We can probably say that nearly every important forest tree species in these regions has had some genetic investigation. By contrast we know practically nothing of the genetic variability of forest trees growing in tropical or south temperate regions. Teak, some acacias and a few tropical pines are the only species from these regions that have been studied to any great extent. Extensive study of species in these regions probably will not lead to any new principles regarding genetic ecology, but they must be investigated before we have adequate information for conclusions about taxonomy, centers of variation, and opportunities for genetic improvement of species and genera.

INTERNATIONAL COOPERATION

International cooperation is essential in the study and use of geographic variation in forest trees. Past international provenance trials have been most productive. They have uncovered patterns of variation in several important forest tree species, and the practical significance of this variation. The International Union of Forestry Research Organizations (I U F R O) helped establish some of the early studies. Working Groups of I U F R O are now developing standardized methods for provenance research and facilitating seed collections on the western coast of North America and in Central Europe.

Individual countries also are contributing greatly to the international effort. For example, the United States Forest Service has distributed more than 3,300 seed lots to 59 nations in the period 1961 to 1967. It is hoped that the Government of Mexico, with the assistance of FAO, will establish a center for the collection of seeds of pines and other forest tree species. The Australian Commonwealth Forestry

Bureau has appointed a seed collection officer who already has made range-wide collections of seed from some of the most important species of the eucalypts.

REFERENCES

FOOD & AGRICULTURE ORGANIZATION (1964) Forest genetics and tree improvement. Report of the 1963 World Consultation. *Unasylva* **18,** (2–3), 1–144.

WRIGHT J.W. (1962) Genetics of forest tree improvement. *FAO Forestry and Forest Products Studies* **16,** 1–399.

5

TAXONOMY AND THE BIOLOGICAL SPECIES CONCEPT IN CULTIVATED PLANTS

H. G. BAKER

University of California, Berkeley,
California, U.S.A.

INTRODUCTION

There are very few 'classical' taxonomists left now. By this I mean that very few present-day workers are content to judge the taxonomic disposition of a plant simply on the basis of its external morphology, let alone its morphology when dead, dried and stuck down on a herbarium sheet. Almost everyone is agreed that whenever possible information about the physiology, the ecology, the geographical distribution, the cytology, the genetics (and particularly the population genetics and the breeding behavior) of the plants should be considered along with their morphology. Even herbarium botanists are supplementing their hand lenses with compound microscopes and paying attention to microscopic features of the plants—most notably pollen grain size and morphology—and they are accepting the evidence from internal structure, sometimes even from fine-structure studies and, to an increasing extent, from biochemistry.

But it is no news to the reader that there is considerable di agreement among taxonomists as to the most desirable methods of dealing with this abundance of information. Which kind of information, if any, is to be considered more important when attempts are made to draw taxonomic conclusions?

On the surface it seems reasonable that the classification which is based upon the greatest number of attributes will be the most natural and will mirror most accurately the evolutionary events which have produced the contemporary flora. No problems would arise if all the data to come from all the attributes of the plants pointed in the same direction. If this should be the case, any kind of attribute would be as suitable as any other and the sum total of the data would leave no doubt as to the taxonomic decisions to be made. But often there are what appear to be conflicting trends and decision-making is required. Nowhere has this been more evident than when cytological and genetical data have had to be integrated with the morphological. Obviously this is a matter to which we must give serious attention in a book whose concern is with the utilization and conservation of gene pools.

There are those—the numerical taxonomists—who insist (like their patron saint Michel Adanson) that all characters used in assessing the similarity and, therefore, the taxonomic relationship of organisms should be given equal weight, whether they be morphological, physiological, ecological or cytological. Their extreme position is almost matched by that of those more conventional taxonomists who agree to accept cytological and genetical information into their basically morphological–chorological classificatory schemes but who insist that chromosome number, chromosome size and chromosome shape are morphological characters just like petal number, petal size and petal shape—and should be given comparable weight in making taxonomic decisions.

We are surely justified in expostulating, like Löve (1960), that 'we must remember that chromosomes are *not* just another character comparable with the superficial morphological characters taxonomists are forced to use for the indentification of herbarium material. The chromosomes determine the characters, whereas the characters do not determine the chromosomes'. Fortunately, possibly with a slight change in wording, most contemporary taxonomists would agree with this statement and they do give special attention to cytological features and those genetical features which reveal most about genomic constitutions.

However, it is true that the numerical taxonomists and, too often, other synthetic taxonomists, have usually not the time to grow their plants and, even more important, to attempt to make crosses between them. This is particularly unfortunate because it has taken an experimental approach to find a key to taxonomy at the species level—i.e., reproductive isolation.

THE 'BIOLOGICAL SPECIES' CONCEPT

When attempts are made to cross distinct species, or when hybrids between them are sought in natural populations, it is usually found that there are reproductive barriers which reduce gene-flow (miscibility) between the populations of the two species without, at the same time, reducing it within each one (cf. Mayr, 1957). This is the feature of the taxonomic species which seems to be of primary importance. Morphological and physiological differences between species become fixed because of reproductive isolation; sometimes they are direct results of the evolutionary processes which bring reproductive isolation into existence.

The barriers to miscibility may show up as barriers to interpollination or as impediments to normal growth and to fertility in the hybrids (Clausen, 1951). It is to be emphasized that they are taxonomically significant only when they separate populations; sporadic occurrences of a mutant of a teratological nature do not qualify the individuals concerned for new latin binomials. The most widely accepted definition of a species on a miscibility basis is that by Mayr (1942) 'Species are groups of actually or potentially interbreeding natural populations, which are reproductively isolated from other such groups'. This has been referred to by its author as a 'biological species' concept (in contrast to 'typological' and other concepts) and a history of the concept has been published by Löve (1962), and discussed by Bennett (1964).

Despite the nearly universal recognition of the evolutionary importance of reproductive isolation and the concession that it is almost always there between species, still the 'biological species' concept with its basic connection with gene pools, their maintenance and restriction, is not universally applied by botanical taxonomists. I think it is worthwhile for us to examine why this is the case because I want to use the arguments which have been made against its application as arguments in *favor* of adopting it for the taxonomic treatment of cultivated plants and their close wild relatives.

Arguments against using a 'biological species' concept fall into two classes; (*a*) those opposed to the concept itself; and (*b*) those opposed to its application on practical grounds.

THEORETICAL ARGUMENTS AGAINST THE 'BIOLOGICAL SPECIES' CONCEPT

Defenders of those classificatory systems which give greater weight to morphological and distributional criteria than they accord to evidences of reproductive isolation sometimes justify their attitude by the argument that morphological differentiation may be expected to provide a good guide to the amount of evolutionary divergence which has taken place in the descent of any two taxa from a common ancestor, whereas a barrier to gene exchange merely indicates that evolutionary

C*

divergence is likely to occur in the future. They maintain that it is the duty of taxonomy to record the former whereas speculation as to the future is outside the scope of the discipline.

It is further argued, often by the same taxonomists, that barriers to gene flow, such as those between taxa which are at different ploidy levels or which, although having the same chromosome number differ by a limited number of chromosomal rearrangements, are real but are no greater than those between spatially separated populations of an undeniable species. Consequently, it is argued that unless morphological differentiation warrants the distinction it should not be made on the basis of an internal barrier to gene flow (cf. Lewis, 1967).

Additionally, there is the Adansonian objection to giving any degree of weighting to any character whatever its nature.

PRACTICAL ARGUMENTS AGAINST THE 'BIOLOGICAL SPECIES' CONCEPT

Only a very tiny fraction of the world's flora can be brought into cultivation even if all the botanical gardens and experiment stations in all countries should be given over to this purpose. Even for those putative taxa which can be brought into experimental gardens where they can be hybridized the problem arises as to how many specimens are needed to represent adequately the natural intraspecific variation. The number of hybridization attempts which must be made, the number of plants which must be raised in the first hybrid generation and the number of subsequent generations which must be grown to see whether fertility is maintained and whether segregation occurs, all place limitations upon the comprehensiveness of the experiments. And, theoretically, attempts should be made to cross each specimen with each other one. The total task, for naturally occurring plants, is beyond human capacity for achievement.

Of course, some of the difficulties can be overcome by allowing nature to make the experiments and observing the results. However, the fact that two adjacent (rather than sympatric) taxa do not show obvious miscibility may be due to environmental influence (e.g., lack of a suitable intermediate habitat for the hybrids or even a habitat for seedling establishment at all) and the populations concerned may be differentiated only at the ecotype level with no inherent barriers to crossing at all (Baker, 1951, 1952). In addition, nature is not always making the experiments now, even though she may have done so in the past; many closely related taxa may no longer come into contact with each other.

A second major difficulty in applying the 'biological species' concept to naturally occurring plants is that it cannot be applied to those cases in which sexual reproduction has been completely (or nearly completely) set aside and replaced by asexual reproduction (either as agamospermy or substitutive vegetative reproduction). As Mayr (1957, p. 379) pointed out, 'The essence of the biological species concept is discontinuity due to reproductive isolation. Without sexuality this concept cannot be applied. In truly asexual organisms there are no "populations" in the sense in which this term exists in sexual species nor can "reproductive isolation" be tested'.

Morphological differences between 'biological species' are sometimes very slight and, in a number of cases, require microscopy, most notably where polyploidy is involved (and differences in pollen grain volume or guard cell size may be the only adequate characters for use in separating plants at different levels of ploidy). In such cases as the populations of *Holocarpha obconica* (Compositae) in the Inner Coast Ranges of California, there is full interfertility within any local population (which may contain millions of individuals) but each such population may be a breeding unit by itself and sharply separated from its neighbors (to the extent of forming only sterile hybrids) (Clausen, 1952). In gross morphology there are only slight differences between the populations and it is only by careful cytological study that the reproductive barriers can be traced to repatterning of the chromosomes.

ARGUMENT IN FAVOR OF A 'BIOLOGICAL SPECIES' CONCEPT FOR CULTIVATED PLANTS

All of the objections to the consistent application of a 'biological species' concept to naturally occurring taxa are more or less valid. I wish to state, however, that I believe their validity is greatly reduced when cultivated plants are the object of attention. Our needs are different; if we have an evolutionary interest (or a conservational interest) in any group, we must consider the possible futures of the taxa contained in it and not merely be concerned with their pasts.

Each of the objections described above can be answered when our concern is with cultivated plants and their close wild relatives. For example, instead of a seemingly infinite array of wild taxa we are dealing with a circumscribed number of cultivated taxa, most of which are already in cultivation and which have proven themselves amenable to it.

Furthermore, much of the ground work for an experimental investigation has been laid already; these plants have been grown under environmentally controlled conditions and differences which have no genetic basis will have been noted and can be avoided. In addition, plant breeders already have recorded much of the data on fertility in the hybrid generations and the potentialities for transfer of genetic material.

An important practical consideration concerns the availability of financial support for the controlled environment experiments and crossing experiments. Often this is hard to obtain where the objects of research are wild species of no known economic value; for taxa whose value to man is demonstrable the situation may be quite different. Not only may the facilities of government agricultural departments be available but also those of international agencies (and international biological programs!).

In this book we are concerned with the conservation of gene pools; for this we must have information about the genetics of the organisms involved, meaning that the crossings have to be made in any case. Also, as I have said, being concerned with gene pools, we must be more concerned than the general taxonomists are with the potentialities of the taxa; the degree of reproductive isolation between taxa becomes a matter of more than merely academic interest.

For each of these reasons, I believe that the time has come when we should insist on the *biosystematic* treatment of cultivated plants and their wild relatives. A biosystematic treatment of a taxonomic problem is one which is based upon experimentation with plants, not merely observation of them (Table 5.1). Cultivation under controlled conditions, investigation of breeding systems, cytological studies, investigation of crossing relationships and the fertility of hybrids, physiological and biochemical studies, all of these have their places in biosystematics. Artificial crossings should be attempted as well as the planting together of the test plants in 'isolation plots' where the possibilities of crossing by natural pollination agencies can be investigated. It is obvious that the latter test will be most meaningful if it is carried out in the geographical area in which the populations normally grow and more than one plant from each population should always be involved. Finally, the judgement as to whether there is reproductive isolation between the populations should be made on the basis of *all* the experimental and observational evidence taken together.

An example of the improvement in understanding which can be brought about when biosystematic methods are used and a 'biological species' concept is invoked is provided by the study of the species-complex which includes *Vicia sativa*. This has been in confusion as various morphological-distributional treatments from those of Seringe (1825) to Fiori and Paoletti (1925) have variously assigned and distributed taxa (with a range of one to fourteen recognized species). Mettin and Hanelt (1964) and Hanelt and Mettin (1966) have studied

TABLE 5.1 Bases of 'biological species' determination in cultivated plants

Observational	Full description of morphological variation.
	Physiological and biochemical information.
	Chromosome number and karyotype analyses.
	Evidences of natural hybridization.
Experimental	Cultivation of population samples in uniform and varied environments (using experimental gardens or controlled environmental chambers)—observing evidences of race-formation, ranges of environmental tolerance, plasticity, etc.
	Attempts at hybridization (artificially) and by setting test plants in 'isolation plots' exposed to appropriate pollinating insects.
	Estimation of vigor of F_1 hybrids, F_2, etc.
	Estimation of fertility of F_1 hybrids, F_2, etc.
	Chromosome constitution of F_1 hybrids, F_2, etc.
	Analysis of meiosis in F_1 and subsequent generations.

the complex intensively using biosystematic methods and recognize as separate species *Vicia cordata* ($2n = 10$), *V.angustifolia*, *V.macrocarpa* and *V.sativa* (all with $2n = 12$), and *V.amphicarpa*, *V.incisa*, and *V.pilosa* (all with $2n = 14$). *V.angustifolia* contains two subspecies; *angustifolia*, a distinct wild form, and *segetalis*, a weedy plant associated with cereal crops. *V.sativa* is divided into a variety *cosentini* (which contains weedy as well as probably primitive cultivated forms) as well as the cultivated variety *sativa*. This degree of appreciation of the history and contemporary relationships of a complex of wild, weedy and cultivated plants would have been quite impossible without biosystematics.

In the case of a large genus which contains only a few species of economic importance, it is likely that for a long time only a part of the genus (containing the economic plants) will receive biosystematic treatment while the remainder does not. Such genera as *Ipomoea*, *Trifolium* and *Cocos* may suffer this fate. This need not be very serious as long as a complete infra-generic group such as the subgenus, section or species-complex containing the cultivated species can be treated at one time.

SPECIAL FEATURES OF 'BIOLOGICAL SPECIES' IN CULTIVATED PLANTS

The monographer of a genus which contains cultivated as well as wild taxa may reasonably carve out species in the former with roughly the same morphological range as for those in the latter. Subsequent biosystematic investigation, however, sometimes shows that the assumption of similar morphological ranges is incorrect and it may be worth our while to examine some of the reasons why this can be the case.

In the first place, the circumstances of cultivation, particularly of the more advanced kinds where crop plants are kept weed-free, and are optimally spaced, fertilized and irrigated, may permit the survival and reproduction of biotypes which would have been strongly selected against in nature. In cultivation there may even be positive artificial selection for some of the very characteristics which would be deleterious in nature. Mangelsdorf (1965) has presented evidence that the major part of the leaf area of a 'wild maize' which he and his colleagues have reconstructed serves to nourish an extensive root system. By contrast, artificial selection through many centuries in cultivated material has increasingly shifted the photosynthetic support to the nourishment of ever larger quantities of grain. The cumulative effects of changes in a number of such characters may make a profound difference in the morphology and physiology of the plants being studied.

In the case of maize, as Mangelsdorf (1965, p. 48) has pointed out, 'Four evolutionary forces: mutation, genetic drift, selection and hybridization interacting to a degree seldom encountered in nature and accelerated and intensified by the activities of man have produced in the maize plant evolutionary changes so profound and in so short a time that a paleontologist seeing the species only at the beginning and the end might well suspect that evolution under domestication is cataclysmic and the product of violent saltation'. And yet is is probable that there has been no speciation.

In nature, those characters of the plant which are directly concerned with its reproduction tend to be conservative. Successful seed dispersal systems, in particular, involve the coordination of a number of characters of the flower and fruit and only certain combinations are so appropriately balanced that they are successful (cf. Zohary, 1965, for *Triticum*). In cultivation where man can take care of such seed-dispersal as is called for (and seed dispersal by other means may even be disadvantageous if it is a seed-crop which is to be harvested), floral and inflorescence features may be selected which would be disastrous in nature. The classic case here is the stout, laterally borne cob of maize carrying firmly affixed grain and sheathed in an envelope of leaves, a combination of characters which renders seed-dispersal impossible.

So different is a modern maize from the probable wild ancestor of the species and from the weedy species which is called teosinte that before the experimentalists demonstrated that they are unquestionably congeneric (and have influenced each other significantly through hybridization) they were usually treated as species of the separate genera *Zea* and *Euchlaena*, respectively. It might even be argued that both of these taxa could be included in the same genus with the species of *Tripsacum* (which genus appears to have been involved in hybridization with *Zea mays* to produce *Zea* (*Euchlaena*) *mexicana*). The maize story is summarized in Mangelsdorf, MacNeish and Galinat (1964), and a modern treatment of *Euchlaena* is provided by Wilkes (1967).

Another example of the selection by man of a mutant form which would be suicidal in nature is to be seen in the kapok tree (*Ceiba pentandra*) of the tropics. I have shown (Baker, 1965) by experimental crossings and cultivation that the kapok tree of commerce is most probably derived from the hybridization of two kinds of native trees growing in West Africa but that an extra character has been added— that of the permanently closed fruit which retains both the seed and the kapok fibers around it so that they may be harvested. Presumably this closed-pod character arose by mutation and was taken advantage of by West African cultivators. Neither of the parents possesses this character (nor could they survive in the wild if they did). Prior to my experimental study the taxonomy of the trees in the *Ceiba pentandra* complex was in a very confused state with some names having been awarded on the mistaken belief that the closed or dehiscent nature of the fruit could be used as a primary division of the species (e.g., Ulbrich, 1913).

In the cases just cited, dramatic differences in floral or inflorescence characters of a magnitude sometimes associated with generic distinction when they occur in nature prove to be inadequate even to indicate specific distinction in the cultivated plants.

Artificial selection with striking morphological consequences may affect other parts of the plant than the inflorescence : the production of tubers in *Ipomoea*, a switch from a perennial to an effectively annual habit in *Gossypium*; these and other changes are apt to mislead the taxonomist whose morphological species concept is derived from experience with wild species. They should be less upsetting to a bio-systematic investigation.

In a number of cases there have been significant changes in breeding systems at the time when potential economic plants have been taken into cultivation or subsequently. The switch from cross-pollination to selfing in *Lycopersicon* (Rick, 1950) is well known. Hutchinson (1965) has pointed out that in all crop plants the flower structure is such that cross pollination must have occurred in some ancestors ; the switch to selfing and its utilization by man to preserve desired characteristics in the crop plants means that in many of them the taxa have either become mixtures of virtually pure lines or at any rate mixtures of lines homozygous for particular marker genes. In such a case the experimental approach is needed to counteract any tendency to be over-impressed by the clarity of the distinctions between these lines and to give them exaggerated taxonomic status.

More extreme examples of the same phenomenon can be seen where the switch has been from outcrossing sexuality to apomixis or to habitual vegetative reproduction. The taxonomic difficulties presented by clones in such genera as *Rubus* and *Musa* are well known. Occasional cross-pollination between different biotypes followed by the perpetuation of the resulting new biotypes by apomixis or vegetative reproduction can produce a network of phenotypes with which it is beyond the capacity of conventional taxonomic methods to deal. The perennial meadowgrasses of the genus *Poa*, so many of which have risen in artificial situations, provide a striking example (cf. Clausen, 1952). If sexual reproduction (amphimixis) never occurs in the plants of a taxon, the status of that taxon vis-a-vis another taxon on a 'biological species' basis is untestable. Among facultative apomicts, on the other hand, even the products of wide crosses may be reproductively successful by producing seed through agamospermy and thereby avoiding the meiotic sieve. This makes the plotting of the boundaries of 'biological species' a very difficult and time-consuming matter (although it has been carried out successfully in such a case as the forage grass genus *Dichanthium* by Harlan and de Wet, 1963, where it has been valuable in indicating the evolutionary history of the complex). One of the chief advantages of establishing 'biological species' boundaries in amphimictic groups is the information about combining power which is provided for plant breeders; if, in an apomictic complex, this reward is not available, the expenditure of effort in establishing the boundaries may not seem worthwhile. In such circumstances, it may be adequate to circumscribe 'species' in the apomictic group in such a fashion that the range of morphological variation included corresponds to the amount found in the closest related amphimictic species. Discussion of this problem can be found in Davis and Heywood (1963, pp. 381–6).

If it does nothing else, the experimental investigation of cases such as these will reveal the nature of the problems and prevent false optimism and subsequent disappointment for the investigator. I am haunted by the memory of the late W.C.R. Watson's lifetime of devotion to the attempted classification on a purely morphological basis of the British blackberries (*Rubus*) without understanding of the implications of their apomixis (Watson, 1958).

HYBRIDIZATION AND THE TAXONOMY OF CULTIVATED PLANTS

A special taxonomic problem posed by cultivated plants is the origin of some of them by hybridization between taxa which would never have come together naturally. Little difficulty is caused by such a hybrid as the London Plane tree (*Platanus × hybrida*) derived from the hybridization of an Old World species (*P.orientalis*) and a New World one (*P.occidentalis*) without change in chromosome number. Slightly more difficult is the case of the pink flowered horse-chestnut (*Aesculus × carnea*) which is the amphidiploid derivative of an artificial hybrid between Old World *A.hippocastanum* and New World *A.pavia* (Skovsted, 1929). The origin of *A.carnea* is biologically equivalent to that of any natural allopolyploid species but, because it is unknown outside cultivation, it has to be considered an 'interspecific hybrid' according to the International Code of Botanical Nomenclature and the corresponding International Code of Nomenclature for Cultivated Plants (and bear the cross in front of its specific name). Only because it is not technically a species are we saved from embarrassment by the fact that it cannot be fitted into either the Section Aesculus or the Section Pavia which house *A.hippocastanum* and *A.pavia*, respectively.

However, without biosystematic study it might have been very difficult to interpret the history and determine the taxonomic status of such a species as *Sorghum almum* which appears to have arisen from the hybridization of a member of the Section Arundinacea of *Sorghum* with a member of the Section Halepensia after *both* had been introduced from the Old World to South America. The Halepensia are tetraploid while the Arundinacea are diploid and the origin of *S.almum* must have involved the union of an unreduced gamete from the diploid with a normal gamete from the tetraploid (Doggett, 1965). Again the problem of sectional affiliation arises. It may be suggested that biosystematics is dealing death blows to most of the formal infra-generic *sections* which so delight the morphologically minded monographers (cf. arguments put forward by Bowden (1959) in dealing with the wheat genus *Triticum*).

Genetic barriers between taxa which are not separated by them in nature may arise under the conditions of cultivation. Pickersgill (1967) advances some evidence for the evolution of such a reproductive barrier through cryptic structural hybridity which has developed in the chromosomes of the South American peppers *Capsicum chinense* and *C.pendulum* since these previously allopatric species have come into contact during cultivation in rather primitive agricultural systems. Hybrids between *C.chinense* and wild forms of *C.pendulum* are less abnormal than hybrids made from cultivated forms of *pendulum*.

An apparently opposite situation occurs in the genus *Raphanus* (Panetsos and Baker, 1968) but it, too, would never have been discovered without experimentation, nor could it have been properly dealt with taxonomically without a biosystematic investigation. *Raphanus sativus*, the cultivated radish, differs chromosomally from *R. raphanistrum* (a weed of cultivated fields) by a single rather large translocation. In some European and Californian populations of *R.sativus* which have escaped from cultivation into a life of weediness, hybridization with *R.raphanistrum* has taken place and progeny have been formed which are homozygous for the *raphanistrum* state of the translocation. When further hybridization occurs between these plants (which, in most cases, could pass as *R.sativus*) and *R.raphanistrum* there is no longer any reduction in fertility in the offspring.

These examples from *Capsicum* and *Raphanus* emphasize the point that an adequate taxonomic treatment of a group of cultivated plants must also take account of their wild relatives, whether these be primitively wild or feral.

Hybridization between taxonomically distinct individuals whether deliberately controlled or accidentally (naturally) occurring creates, of course, enormous opportunities for the evolution of new taxa as well as for the increase of genetical variation within taxa. The effects may be expressed in two ways, in introgression or in allopolyploidy. It may be worth while to spend a little time considering these evolutionary mechanisms and their taxonomical consequences.

INTROGRESSION

Introgression, or introgressive hybridization, the subtle introduction of genetic material from one taxon into another through hybridization followed by backcrossing had to fight for scientific respectability in the early years of Edgar Anderson's development of the theory (cf. Anderson, 1949, etc.). Now, it may be that we are too ready to offer an explanation on this basis for any case where two extreme forms are connected by intermediates. In some of these cases we may be witnessing the differentiation of extreme forms out of a heterogeneous collection of biotypes rather than the fusion of distinct forms through hybridization. Such differentiation (or purification into 'lines') may be especially likely to occur under human selective pressure and especially in those cultivated taxa where self-pollination is the rule.

Even when hybridization is actually occurring the breeding systems of the plants are of extreme importance in determining the probable outcome. Grant (1958) and Baker (1959) have discussed various aspects of this. Among self-compatible annuals hybridization is most likely to lead to allopolyploidy through the functioning of unreduced gametes; in perennials strong vegetative reproduction also facilitates polyploidization through somatic doubling. By contrast, introgressive hybridization is facilitated by self-incompatibility (because of the importance of back-crossing between hybrids and parental species in producing the subtle infiltration of genes).

A few apparent exceptions to this exist, notably in the evolution of cultivated barley (Section Cerealia of the genus *Hordeum*), where Zohary (1959) has produced evidence of considerable hybridization which apparently produced introgressive effects. Very recently, Grant (1967) has suggested an explanation of what looks like introgression in these predominantly self-pollinating (autogamous) plants, depending upon a linkage between genes which control certain morphological characters and others which affect growth and vigor in early developmental stages of the sporophyte or gametophyte. After a rare hybridization, self-pollination would produce an F_2 and subsequent generations; however, because of the linkage only plants more or less resembling the parent types will survive in the progeny. Recombination of the unlinked genes, together with the linkage of the others, will simulate the subtle infiltration of genes that characterizes introgression without any backcrossing actually taking place.

In cases of introgression, substitution of alleles may occur on an individual gene basis or there may be substitution of entire blocks of alleles from one taxon into another. When these blocks contain a number of genes concerned with various aspects of the same character, as, for example, the 'speltoid' character of the inflorescence in hexaploid wheat (Frankel and Munday, 1962) or the stamen and style morphology and physiology of a heterostylous flowering plant (Baker, 1966) the block may be called a 'super-gene' or 'complex gene'. Evidence is accumulating that super-genes are not uncommon.

Even characters affecting functionally unrelated characters of the species may be inherited *en bloc*. Thus, it has been pointed out already that the only obvious chromosomal difference between *Raphanus sativus* and *R.raphanistrum* is in respect of a single translocation (Panetsos and Baker, 1968). In crosses between the species, the interspecific differences in root-structure and flowering time are inherited as a unit, suggesting that the major genes determining them may be located on the translocated portion of one chromosome. As a special example of the inheritance of super-genes, Grant (1966) has reviewed the block inheritance of viability genes in plant species, giving attention to several genera of economic importance, e.g., *Gossypium*, *Phaseolus*, *Zea* and *Triticum*. Ting (1967) has demonstrated cytologically the existence of a chromosome inversion common to maize and to teosinte and produced evidence that it (and the genes which it must carry) has introgressed from teosinte into maize.

As a consequence of these various demonstrations of block inheritance of characters and of linkages between the blocks and viability determiners, we can no longer take seriously the contention of the taxonomists, numerical and otherwise, who believe that characters for their use can be chosen without prior experiment and that all which can be useful are of equal value.

POLYPLOIDY

Introgression involves the replacement of genetic material from one taxon with material from another; in cases of allopolyploidy (or alloploidy) whole genomes are added together. This kind of speciation with its origin in the hybridization of well-differentiated species followed by doubling of the chromosome number is so well known as to need little comment here except, perhaps, the suggestion that it takes experimentation to prove allopolyploidy—either by re-synthesis of a polyploid from its putative parents or by crossing the polyploid with each of its putative parents and observing the pairing of the chromosomes at meiosis in the resulting hybrids. The number of cases which have been completely authenticated in such a manner is still limited.

However, between the unambiguous allopolyploid and the strict autopolyploid (formed by doubling the chromosome complement of a plant which is not any kind of a hybrid) there is a large area of intermediate conditions. Löve (1964) has suggested a classification based on the taxonomic status of the diploids which contribute the genomes to the polyploids. In between typical allopolyploids (called 'panalloploids' by Löve) and strict autopolyploids (called 'panautoploids') are 'hemialloploids' which are formed from not fully sterile species hybrids and 'hemiautoploids' which are derived from intraspecific hybrids or by the differentiation of the chromosome sets of successful panautoploids. According to Löve (*op. cit.* p. 41) the two intermediate groups constitute the majority of known cases.

Panautoploids are likely to be sporadic in occurrence and, because of infertility resulting from multivalent formation at meiosis followed by uneven disjunction, are relatively unlikely to persist. All workers agree that, for wild plants, sporadic autopolyploid plants of this sort do not merit taxonomic recognition. If we accept the criterion that species 'must exist as independent differentiated populations' (Davis and Heywood, 1963, p. 217), these occasional plants clearly do not qualify. Even if autopolyploids occur (or are created, for example, by colchicine treatment) in cultivation and are perpetuated as clones by vegetative propagation, they still constitute individuals rather than populations. However, in the latter circumstances there may be real merit to the acknowledgement of the polyploidy by giving the clones taxonomic recognition at the cultivar level.

With the hemiautopolyploids and hemiallopolyploids (which usually do form independent populations in nature), an appropriate taxonomic treatment is harder to recommend. The contention that allopolyploids are worthy of specific recognition but that autopolyploids, by reason of diminished fertility (as well as inadequate morphological differentiation), should have, at best, some infraspecific designation can no longer be upheld, particularly for cultivated plants. The demonstration by Riley and Chapman (1958) of genic control of pairing between homeologous (rather than completely homologous) chromosomes in wheat (see the general account in Riley, 1965) which also appears to apply to cotton and tobacco (Kimber, 1960) means that full fertility may be found in hemiautopolyploids as well as in allopolyploids.

The paucity of morphological distinctions may prevent full species recognition of the hemiautopolyploids in wild plants and in cultivated plants in primitive agriculture, where pure lines or clones are not maintained (cf. Dodds, 1965, for some potatoes). On the other hand, with the taxa involved in more sophisticated agriculture the case for giving fertile hemiautopolyploids taxonomic recognition may be as strong as for allopolyploids. In such cultivated material it will be known, or should be capable of determination, that a particular population is diploid or at some level of polyploidy, and, being identifiable, the polyploid should be given recognition.

The question of the appropriate taxonomic treatment of polyploids has excited more discussion than almost any other subject in biosystematics. Opinions have ranged from those of Löve (1951, etc.)who maintains that all polyploids which form populations of their own should be recognized as specifically distinct from their diploid relatives to the much greater number of authors who advocate only subspecific or varietal naming for those polyploids which can be distinguished morphologically without microscopy (unless they are clear allopolyploids).

The reproductive isolation between a polyploid population and the populations at lower levels of ploidy from which it is derived is the biological basis of advocating the specific recognition of polyploids. However, the extent of this isolation varies all the way from slight to complete, depending upon the structure and behaviour of the chromosomes. In addition, Marks (1966a, b) has produced some results to show that in tuberous *Solanum* triploids are rarely produced even when crosses are made between diploids (as pistillate parents) and tetraploids. The predominance of tetraploids in the offspring results from the functioning of unreduced female gametes. Marks points out that the avoidance of the production of sterile triploids means that 'polyploidy may not always be such an efficient isolating mechanism as is generally supposed' (Marks, 1966a, p. 556). Despite the difficulty of producing triploids in many taxa by artificial crossing and their rarity in many natural cases, triploid cultivars of bananas, watermelons, sugar-beet, cassava and apples give superior yields (Marks, 1966b) and therefore cannot be ignored. Thus, for practical purposes, with cultivated plants, there seems little doubt that recognition of the existence of polyploidy is important; the decision as to the level at which that recognition is given must be made by well-informed students of the particular genera concerned.

AGMATOPLOIDY

Fortunately, neither the *Juncaceae* nor the *Cyperaceae* contain many economically important plants. Consequently, we are saved from the difficulty of having to discuss the taxonomic treatment of agmatoploidy (Davis and Heywood, 1963, p. 226) that results from the chromosome fragmentation which is facilitated in these families by the diffuse (or multiple) kinetochores (or centromeres) in those chromosomes. Certainly differences in chromosome number in these cases have no intrinsic taxonomic significance.

EFFECTS OF USING A
'BIOLOGICAL SPECIES' CONCEPT

The overall effect of substituting biosystematics and a 'biological species' concept for a taxonomy which does not make basic use of genetical data in the treatment of cultivated plants and their wild relatives is likely to be a narrowing of species limits in some cases due to the revelation of polyploidy and other barriers to miscibility in what had previously been treated as a single species. However, where a cultigen consists of a number of cultivars, each of which is preserved through time in relatively pure populations (possibly with the aid of regular self-fertilization), there has always been a temptation for the 'classical' taxonomist to give these varieties exaggerated status. In this case, as in the classification of the wheats by Bowden (1959), the application of a 'biological species' concept has an opposite effect by discounting the significance of certain morphological characters for species distinction. Most often at the generic level there is likely to be a broadening of the limits rather than narrowing as intercompatibilities are demonstrated

—and *Aegilops* is fused into *Triticum* on this basis by Bowden (op. cit.) (although Chennaveeraiah, 1960, does not agree entirely with this treatment). In all cases, it may be expected that the taxonomic system will be improved by the change.

A classification system which emphasizes genetical relationships and discontinuities has advantages for breeders, pathologists and others who work with cultivated plants and their wild relatives. By enlarging genera on a basis of miscibility (probably keeping the old genera as subgenera) it can be made clear to these workers where gene-exchange is possible (for breeding new forms). When two species are separated by being placed in different genera, they are less likely to be tried as sources of genetic material. Also, of course, if the most important gene pools are to be conserved they must first be recognized.

REFERENCES

ANDERSON E. (1949) *Introgressive Hybridization*. Wiley and Sons, New York.

BAKER H.G. (1951) Hybridization and natural gene-flow between higher plants. *Biol. Rev.* **26**, 302–337.

BAKER H.G. (1952) The ecospecies—prelude to discussion. *Evolution* **6**, 61–68.

BAKER H.G. (1959) Reproductive methods as factors in speciation in flowering plants. *Cold Spring Harb. Symp. quant. Biol.* **24**, 177–191.

BAKER H.G. (1965) Characteristics and modes of origin of weeds. In *The Genetics of Colonizing Species* (Eds. Baker H.G. and Stebbins G.L.), 147–168. Academic Press, New York.

BAKER H.G. (1966) The evolution, functioning and breakdown of heteromorphic incompatibility systems. I. The Plumbaginaceae. *Evolution* **20**, 349–368.

BOWDEN W.M. (1959) The taxonomy and nomenclature of the wheats, barleys and ryes and their wild relatives. *Can. J. Bot.* **37**, 657–684.

CHENNAVEERAIAH M.S. (1960) Karyomorphologic and cytotaxonomic studies in *Aegilops*. *Acta Horti gothoburg.* **23**, 85–178.

CLAUSEN J. (1951) *Stages in the Evolution of Plant Species*. Cornell University Press, Ithaca.

CLAUSEN J. (1952) New bluegrasses by combining and rearranging genomes of contrasting *Poa* species. *Proc. 6th Int. Grassl. Congr.* **1**, 216 seq.

DAVIS P.H. & HEYWOOD V.H. (1963) *Principles of Angiosperm Taxonomy*. D. van Nostrand Co, London and Princeton.

DODDS K.S. (1965) The history and relationship of cultivated potatoes. In *Essays on Crop Plant Evolution* (Ed. Hutchinson J.B.), Cambridge University Press, Cambridge.

DOGGETT H. (1965) The development of the cultivated sorghums. In *Essays on Crop Plant Evolution* (Ed. Hutchinson J.B.), Cambridge University Press, Cambridge.

FIORI A. & PAOLETTI G. (1925) *Nuova Flora Analitica d'Italia*, Firenze.

FRANKEL O.H. & MUNDAY ANNE (1962) The evolution of wheat. In *The Evolution of Living Organisms*, 173–180. Melbourne University Press, Melbourne.

GRANT V.E. (1958) The regulation of recombination in plants. *Cold Spring Harb. Symp. quant. Biol.* **23,** 337–363.

GRANT V.E. (1966) Block inheritance of viability genes in plant species. *Am. Nat.* **100,** 591–601.

GRANT V.E. (1967) Linkage between morphology and viability in plant species. *Am. Nat.* **101,** 125–140.

HANELT P. & METTIN D. (1966) Cytosystematische Untersuchungen in der Artengruppe um *Vicia sativa* L. II. *Kulturpflanze* **14,** 137–161.

HARLAN J.R. & DE WET J.M.J. (1963) Role of apomixis in the evolution of the *Bothriochloa-Dichanthium* complex. *Crop Science* **3,** 314–316.

HUTCHINSON J.B. (1965) Crop plant evolution: a general discussion. In *Essays on Crop Plant Evolution* (Ed. Hutchinson J.B.), Cambridge University Press, Cambridge.

KIMBER G. (1960) The association of chromosomes in haploid cotton. *Heredity* **15,** 453.

LEWIS H. (1967) The taxonomic significance of autopolyploidy. *Taxon* **16,** 267–271.

LÖVE A. (1951) Taxonomical evaluation of polyploids. *Caryologia* **3,** 263–284.

LÖVE A. (1960) Taxonomy and chromosomes—a reiteration. *Feddes Rep.* **62,** 192–202.

LÖVE A. (1962) The biosystematic species concept. *Preslia* **34,** 127–139.

LÖVE A. (1964) The biological species concept and its evolutionary structure. *Taxon* **13,** 33–45.

MANGELSDORF P.C. (1965) The evolution of maize. In *Essays on Crop Plant Evolution* (Ed. Hutchinson J.B.), Cambridge University Press, Cambridge.

MANGELSDORF P.C., MACNEISH R.S. & GALINAT W.C. (1964) Domestication of corn. *Science*, **143,** 538–545.

MARKS G.E. (1966a) The origin and significance of intraspecific polyploidy: experimental evidence from *Solanum chacoense*. *Evolution* **20,** 552–557.

MARKS G.E. (1966b) The enigma of triploid potatoes. *Euphytica* **15,** 285–290.

MAYR E. (1942) *Systematics and the Origin of Species*. Columbia University Press, New York.

MAYR E. (1957) *The Species Problem*. *Publs. Am. Ass. Advmt. Sc.* **50.**

METTIN D. & HANELT P. (1964) Cytosystematische Untersuchungen in der Artengruppe um *Vicia sativa* I. *Kulturpflanze* **12,** 163–225.

PANETOS C. & BAKER H.G. (1968) The origin of variation in 'wild' *Raphanus sativus* (Cruciferae) in California. *Genetica* **38,** 243–274.

PICKERSGILL BARBARA (1967) Interspecific isolating mechanisms in some South American chili peppers. *Am. J. Bot.* **54,** 654.

RICK C.M. (1950) Pollination relations of *Lycopersicon esculentum* in native and foreign regions. *Evolution* **4,** 110–122.

RILEY R. (1965) Cytogenetics and the evolution of wheat. In *Essays on Crop Plant Evolution* (Ed. Hutchinson J.B.), Cambridge University Press, Cambridge.

RILEY R. & CHAPMAN V. (1958) Genetic control of the cytologically diploid behaviour of hexaploid wheat. *Nature, Lond.* **182,** 713–715.

SERINGE N.C. (1825) *Vicia*. In *Prodromus Systematis Naturalis Regni Vegetabilis*, Vol. II. (Ed. A. P. de Candolle), Paris.

SKOVSTED A. (1929) Cytological investigations of the genus *Aesculus* L. *Hereditas* **12**, 64–70.

TING Y.C. (1967) Common inversion in maize and teosinte. *Am. Nat.* **101**, 87–89.

ULBRICH, E. (1913) Die Kapok liefernden Baumwollbäume der deutschen Kolonien im tropischen Afrika. *Notizbl. des Königl. botan. Gartens und Museums zu Dahlem bei Stieglitz* (Berlin), **6**, 1–37.

WATSON W.C.R. (1958) *Handbook of the Rubi of Great Britain and Ireland*. Cambridge University Press, Cambridge.

WILKES H.G. (1967) *Teosinte: the closest relative of maize*. Bussey Inst., Harvard University.

ZOHARY D. (1959) Is *Hordeum agriocrithon* the ancestor of six-rowed cultivated barley? *Evolution* **13**, 279–280.

ZOHARY D. (1965) Colonizer species in the wheat group. In *The Genetics of Colonizing Species* (Eds. Baker H.G. and Stebbins G.L.), Academic Press, New York.

THE TAXONOMY OF CULTIVATED PLANTS

J. G. HAWKES

University of Birmingham,
Birmingham, United Kingdom

INTRODUCTION

Cultivated plants are notoriously difficult to classify. This is largely because of the bewildering series of variants, the lack of any very clear-cut boundaries between taxa when these are proposed, and the unclear relationships of the cultivated to the wild species from which they were presumably derived, to name only a few of the most frustrating aspects of the situation. Some taxonomists, bolder than the rest, have cut the Gordian Knot by classifying everything belonging to a complex group of cultivars under one species, and have included even the wild relatives under the same head. This has the advantage of simplicity, but its very austerity often negates the purpose of systematics, which is in essence to construct a series of groups into which other facts can be integrated as they become available. The other extreme is to divide and subdivide the groupings into a hierarchical system of such complexity that it approaches the point of providing a separate taxon for every cultivar and so again negates the purpose of classification.

We must, therefore, with cultivated as with wild plants, try to steer a middle course between these two extremes; however, the greater difficulties and special problems relating to cultivated plants make it essential first to examine the reasons underlying the variability in these organisms.

The highly complex pattern of variability in cultivated plants is undoubtedly due largely to the complex selective forces that have been acting on them during the long period of their cultivation. Apart from the general effect of natural selection in modifying or eliminating certain variants, it is obvious that artificial selection under cultivation is of extreme importance, adding a complete new dimension to the pattern of variability of a species once it has been taken into cultivation. Man has changed the natural environment by reducing or eliminating competition with other plants and has raised the level of fertility of the soil and supplied water by irrigation in regions where natural rainfall is insufficient. Thus, variants which in nature would be eliminated may now survive and even be at a selective advantage. Man has also selected variants which aid in harvest, so that in cereals, for instance, brittle rhachis is replaced by non-shattering rhachis. In all seed crops in fact, delayed or ineffective dehiscence is a great advantage to man in helping him to gather all the seeds he can. In tuber or rhizome crops, short stolons are also of great advantage for the same reason. These are examples of *unconscious* selection, and we must be clear that until the advent of plant breeders—a very brief span of time in the history of an ancient cultigen—most artificial selection was, in fact, of an unconscious sort. Perhaps a more conscious sort has been the retention of pleasing colours and shapes in fruits, such as the innumerable fruit sizes and shapes in Capsicums, the innumerable potato tuber colour patterns, the wide range of colours in maize grains, etc. It seems probable that such variants were retained by primitive man often for aesthetic or even religious reasons, but little is known about the selective forces under which they were evolved. Ancient cultivated plants have, no doubt, been carried with migrating tribes into regions where their original wild ancestors never grew and into areas where to begin with they were ill-adapted. Under these circumstances new selection pressures of a general climatic nature, such as different day-length, wet and dry season, temperatures, etc., began to modify them. These factors, together with differences in agricultural practices, often led to the evolution of distinct groups of cultivars which might at first sight be mistaken for distinct species. An example of this may be seen in the three distinct subspecies of *Triticum dicoccum* recognised by Vavilov, subsp. *abyssinicum, europaeum* and *asiaticum,* for Ethiopia, western Europe and west to central Asia, respectively. Similar, though not, of course, identical subspeciation may be seen in *T.durum, T.polonicum* and *T.turgidum,* where Ethiopian and European subspecies may be distinguished.

Another result of bringing cultivated species to new areas far away from their centres of origin may be their hybridisation with wild plants and the spread or introgression of genes from these wild plants into the gene pool of the cultivated ones. Furthermore, if hybridisation takes place between cultivated and wild species of distinct genomes then polyploidy is likely to result. Much polyploidy indeed exists in groups of cultivated plants such as wheats, cottons, potatoes and oats. These processes of introgression and polyploidy bring new dimensions of variability into the cultivated plant, which must be accommodated in the taxonomic system.

Because of the immense range of variability in cultivated plants of ancient origin, the Russian botanist N.I. Vavilov devised very detailed methods of classification into subspecies, grex, variety, subvariety, form, etc., based chiefly on morphological features. This complex analysis, linked to geographical distribution, enabled him to assess variation and determine areas of maximum variability. Such areas were considered by Vavilov generally to represent centres of origin, and by this so-called differential geographical method he drew valuable conclusions on the place and mode of origin of our crop plants. This is to some extent outside the scope of our present theme, but no discussion of the taxonomy of cultivated plants can omit a mention of the great contribution of Vavilov to our knowledge of cultivated plants and animals.

Nowadays, it would seem that much of this detailed formulation of varieties, subvarieties, forms, etc. might be considered as somewhat superfluous. Vavilov needed to make morpho-geographical analyses of variation. We can do this now by other methods, in a less cumbersome way, such as by scoring characters and expressing them in histograms and pictorialised scatter diagrams (see Edgar Anderson's work with maize (1946)), or by using a statistical approach.

TYPES OF CLASSIFICATION

How then can reasonably satisfactory classifications for cultivated plants be constructed?

'Special purpose' or artificial classifications of plant cultivars, based on fruit, seed or vegetative characters are not particularly difficult, since a very limited number of characters is considered, perhaps no more than colour, shape and size of the part of the plant which is eaten. One is here often recording no more than single gene differences, as with aleurone colour and grain type in maize or fruit colour in tomatoes. Though such a classification is excellent for the purposes for which it was designed, namely, to recognize cultivars for commercial, agricultural or horticultural purposes, it is of no value outside this. Other quite distinct arrangements can be made by using different characters, such as seed size, biochemical attributes, etc. These may also be valuable, and one can in theory produce an enormous number of special purpose classifications, according to need, limited only by the number of characters available.

However, what we generally have in mind when we speak of the classification of cultivated plants is a 'general purpose' classification, spoken of in the past as a 'natural' classification, one in which as many characters as possible are used in arriving at a scheme in which plants are grouped together because of their general similarities and separated from others because of the sum total of their differences.

There are two ways in which we can construct such general purpose classifications. We can use characters as we see them, of whatever type, without any reference to evolutionary relationships and classify on a maximum correlation of characters. This is spoken of as a phenetic classification (Cain and Harrison, 1960). On the other hand, we can use such similarities to give an indication of what we presume to be evolutionary or genetic relationships and try to construct thereby a phyletic or phylogenetic classification. Gilmour (1940) would group the phyletic classification as a special purpose one but there are so many uses to which a phyletic classification can be put that it seems to me to be better to include it in the general purpose category.

In practice, phenetic and phyletic classifications often give very similar results, since in general we are using the same characters of present-day plants as the criteria, though ideally our phyletic systems ought to be based on a study of complete fossil sequences. This normally cannot be done, since fossil sequences are either fragmentary or non-existent for most plant groups. And according to which plant character in present-day plants is assumed to be more important or constant from an evolutionary point of view, so more weight is accorded to that character in devising the phyletic classification. Since the views of different taxonomists differ widely as to which feature is most important there are several quite distinct phyletic systems in use, and this has clearly brought the practice of phyletic classification into some disrepute. When fossil evidence is lacking and the value of a character for phylogenetic purposes is determined largely by inspired guesswork it is best to put ideas of phylogeny to one side and classify on the basis of what can be actually observed, giving each character equal importance.

This, then, is the reason for the swing of the pendulum away from phyletic and towards phenetic classifications which are based on similarities or differences of the phenotype rather than on some supposed but non-verifiable phylogenetic relationship.

Having made the position clear so far as broad general classifications are concerned we must now turn to the problem of cultivated plant classifications. Here we are concerned in each case with a small group of species or presumed species, represented by a large array of cultivars and a varying number of related wild species, though occasionally such wild species may be absent altogether, as in maize. This group of species or cultivars seems so similar that we are forced to conclude, as good evolutionists, that they might well be closely related to each other in some way or other.

At this level of classification we can and indeed should consider phylogenetic implications, for we possess other tools of investigation denied to the botanist who is trying to construct a classification at the level of families and orders. These tools are those of cytology and genetics, which furnish us with comparative characters rather than absolute ones, as we shall discuss in more detail below. The cytologist, geneticist and plant breeder can point out close evolutionary relationships between species, based on experimental results. For example, by synthesising naturally occurring polyploid species they can show how such polyploids were evolved from their parental diploids, and can point also to the degree of relationship between pairs of diploid species from an analysis of chromosome pairing in the hybrids between them. The geneticist can elucidate the degree of genetic affinity between species if they can be made to form hybrids, and the sero-taxonomist can similarly point to serological affinities which he assumes to be due to a close evolutionary position.

On the basis of data from these sources we can trace the phylogeny of a group of closely related species, whether wholly wild or wholly cultivated or a mixture of the two. Such a classification is of value in that it draws attention to the evolutionary processes at work in a way that the phenetic classification by definition could never do, and it helps the plant breeder to understand his material and to utilize the variation available to him in breeding for a wider range of adaptation or resistance to disease. However, there are some circumstances in which a completely phyletic system, even for cultivated plants and related wild species, is not so useful from a practical point of view. For example, if we wish to construct a formal classification within a single highly variable cultivated species it might well be better not to search for phyletic affinities but to classify the variation phenetically, purely on the basis of observable characters or character combinations.

TECHNIQUES AND CRITERIA

Before discussing problems of species concepts in cultivated plants it will first be necessary to review the techniques and criteria which have been or could be used in classifying them. Basically, of course, the techniques are similar to those for wild plants. We use morphological characters largely, since they are the simplest to see and can be most easily preserved in dried material. And to these we add the old techniques of anatomy and geographical distribution, as well as the newer ones of cytology, genetics and biochemistry.

The criteria or characters used in classifying plants are basically of two types :

(i) *Absolute characters*. These are the features of the plant itself, without reference to any other plant. Such characters are morphological and anatomical features, chromosome numbers, shapes and sizes, ultrastructural characters, etc. Many classifications are based on morphological characters alone, without any reference to other features of the plant. It is quite clear, however, that cultivated plants cannot be classified by using such a narrow range of criteria, even if living rather than dried herbarium specimens are studied. This is true for any 'difficult' group of plants, perhaps. Morphology is useful but is not enough by itself.

In recent years biochemical criteria have been increasingly used in plant classification. An enormous amount of material exists on the biochemistry of secondary metabolites—anthocyanins, terpenes, alkaloids, for instance—both in cultivated and wild plants, and many quick and ingenious ways of obtaining the data, such as two-way paper chromatography (fingerprinting—see Haskell and Garrie, 1966) and gas chromatography (Harborne, 1968) have been utilised by taxonomists with a great deal of success. These techniques should be applied to the study of cultivated plants much more than they have been up to now, however.

The biochemical analysis of larger molecules, amino-acids and proteins, may also provide characters of importance in classification. Again, quick methods of analysis such as acrylamide gel diffusion techniques (Boulter *et al.*, 1966) have been used with success with wild species as well as cultivated ones (Johnson and Hall, 1965, 1966). The method shows considerable promise for the future.

Much information exists for the important cultivated plants on physiological adaptation and disease resistance. The taxonomist who is conversant with the crop concerned and willing to sift through the plant breeding and phytopathological literature may obtain information of value, providing it is linked to taxa and that provenance data are available for the lines tested. Nevertheless, many attributes may occur at random, uncorrelated with other characters. As an example of this one might cite the presence of genes conferring resistance to wart disease of potatoes (*Synchytrium endobioticum*) or field immunity to potato virus X, found sporadically in several different species and in various places, with no apparent pattern of any kind that would render the information of taxonomic value (Hawkes, 1958). The same might be said about much of the information on secondary metabolites, especially of alkaloids, which also seem to occur largely at random.

Other variation is correlated with geographical regions rather than with species specific characters, and is again of little direct taxonomic value. This may be explained by the presence of selection pressures which act on several species impartially in a given area because of the particular climatic or agricultural conditions there or the presence of a particular disease or parasite in that area. Classic examples are the presence of early maturing wheats and barleys in Ethiopia due to the agricultural practices there, or the resistance to potato root eelworm in varieties belonging to several different cultivated and wild potatoes in southern Peru, Bolivia and northern Argentina (Hawkes, 1958). Vavilov (1922) of course, had this sort of situation in mind when he formulated the Law of Homologous Series (see also Kupzov, 1959).

Such biochemical, physiological or genetical characters, which are uncorrelated with other characters or are correlated only with geographical area may well be of great value to the breeder, but from a taxonomic point of view they are of little use, since the value of a character for classification is directly related both to its constancy in any particular group and to the degree with which it is correlated with other characters.

(ii) *Comparative characters.* In contrast to the various types of absolute characters which can be scored for single plants, irrespective of whether we wish to use them for comparison later, other characters exist which are only obtainable by comparing one individual or species with another. This contrast between the two groups of characters has not apparently been pointed out before. It is of especial interest to the biologist who is interested in problems of evolution, since the comparative characters compel us to make comparisons of relationships and move us forcibly towards a phyletic type of classification.

Thus, when we form hybrids between species or make an attempt to do so we are comparing one species with the other in respect of crossability and the viability and fertility of the F_1 and F_2 generations. The character of fertility is only valid as between these two species, since if we cross each with another species a completely different piece

D

of information will result. Again, we compare the relationships between
two species in a hybrid by investigating the degree of chromosome
pairing, the degree of genetic compatibility and the genetical barriers,
if any, to gene exchange between them.

Similarly, when we synthesise polyploids in an attempt to follow
the course of evolution of a group of plants, we are comparing fertility,
chromosome pairing, etc. And the emphasis, quite clearly, is on
phylogeny. The classic example for cultivated plants is, of course,
wheat. Here, a knowledge of chromosome number and the results of
genome analysis have not only helped us to understand the mode of
formation of the species at different levels of ploidy but have also
provided the key to a satisfactory classification. The same can also be
claimed for cotton, since without the genetical and cytological information, most of it of a comparative nature, no reasonable system of
classification can be formulated. One has only to compare the present-
day classifications of these two genera with older ones based on
morphological characters alone to see how clumsy and unilluminating
these older classifications were. These modern classifications are clearly
and unashamedly phyletic, and must be so since they are based
largely on comparative characters.

Serological criteria are also of a comparative nature. We can
compare each species to another in a group by raising antisera to each
in turn and comparing the homologous with the cross reactions in
simple gel-diffusion plates. We can make even more precise comparisons
by separating the antigens by electrophoresis before allowing them to
diffuse through the agar gel towards each other and form the
characteristic spectrum of precipitin bands. Such techniques of
immuno-electrophoresis, as they are called, have been employed to
elucidate species relationships in a number of groups of cultivated
plants, as with my own work on potatoes (Gell *et al.*, 1956, 1960), that
of Hall (1959) with wheat and rye and that of Klozová and Kloz
(1966) and Kloz (1962) with *Phaseolus* beans. These techniques, which
depend only on a readily available protein store in seeds or vegetative
organs, show great promise for the future in cultivated plant studies.

The newly developed DNA hybridisation techniques are also most
promising, for they enable us to look at similarities or differences in
the very molecules in which the genetic code for each species is stored.
Unfortunately, the methods have not been widely applied to cultivated
plants but there is no reason why this should not be done in the near

future, apart from the extreme complexity of the techniques involved (see Kohne, 1968).

It is of interest to note that serological and DNA hybridisation techniques may be used for any level of comparison since they do not require that the taxa under investigation should be hybridised in the conventional sense before results can be obtained, and hence are applicable in the construction of major classifications. Cytogenetical techniques are limited however, in that they can be applied only where viable hybrids can be obtained between pairs of species.

For reasons of space it has only been possible to deal very briefly with the newer chemical and serological techniques. Those interested in further reading on this matter are referred to the proceedings of a recent symposium edited by the present writer, entitled 'Chemotaxonomy and Serotaxonomy', published in 1968.

SPECIES CONCEPTS

We come to the point now of considering how species can be defined and delimited. Can we find a single precise and objective definition of the species that will lighten the task of the taxonomist of cultivated plants? The short answer is that we cannot, just as we cannot find one for wild plants, either. Evolution is progressing in many different ways, the pattern of variability in different groups varies according to different reproductive behaviour and different selection pressures, and it is therefore impossible to find a single system into which this varying material will fit exactly without any problems.

If we examine variation in nature we can clearly discern groups of organisms which are fairly similar to each other but which are dissimilar to other groups of organisms. We have come to accept each such group as a species, but although we can readily distinguish between maize on the one hand and sugar beet on the other, the task is not so easy when we wish to distinguish two species of wheat, for instance. Between maize and sugar beet there are many character differences and no intergrading, but the two species of wheat possess many characters in common and therefore cannot be so easily distinguished. Indeed, most cultivated plants seem at first sight to vary almost more within the species than between them, and the wide range of morphological variation in groups of species makes it extremely difficult to arrive at a clear idea of cultivated species on the basis of morphology alone. Yet one is forced in the end to return to morphological characters, even though they should not be used exclusively, and the 'morphological species concept' which was rebelled against by the biosystematists has returned, although in a slightly modified form.

The older botanists quite clearly defined their species in morphological terms, since they had no other criteria available. The morphological or taxonomic species concept was well formulated at a more sophisticated level by Du Rietz (1930) as 'the smallest natural populations permanently separated from each other by a distinct discontinuity in the series of biotypes'. This definition is excellent, since it lays emphasis on populations rather than single dried herbarium specimens ; it brings in the concept of the biotype, which is one or more individuals of very similar genotype ; and it lays stress on discontinuity between species, whether of a morphological or any other type.

Unfortunately, as we have seen, discontinuities in cultivated plants are not always easily found, if one is looking for large ones, or are embarassingly frequent if one decides to make do with small ones. However, if in a study of cultivated plant variability one uses not only morphological but cytogenetical, biochemical, geographical and any other type of available information, then it is often possible to find boundaries which are real and satisfactory.

Such morphological or taxonomic species, as Heywood (1958) pointed out, 'are only equivalent by designation and not by virtue of the nature or extent of their evolutionary differentiation'. In other words, they are convenient general purpose groupings for sorting out the vast amount of different types of variation existing in nature. Although there may be an element of subjectivity in such a species concept, this is at a minimum in the sexually reproducing outbreeding species where the discontinuities represent the real boundaries to gene exchange between that species and the others most closely related to it.

In opposition, the biological species concept, which has been advanced by biosystematists, genecologists and cytogeneticists, stresses reproductive isolation, either actual or potential, as the method of determining species boundaries. Thus, Grant (1957) defines species as 'a community of cross-fertilizing individuals linked together by bonds of mating and isolated reproductively from other species by barriers to mating'.

When considering cultivated plants, the biological species concept has much to commend it, and is especially attractive to the plant breeder who thinks very much in terms of gene pools and barriers to mating, and of how such barriers may be broken down in order to introduce a valuable character from some related wild species into the crop in which he is interested. A definition which involves the concept of interbreeding between populations within a species and sterility between populations of one species and another is simple and satisfying at first glance, but presents many difficulties in practice. For instance, the fact that two species do not exchange genes at present does not mean that they did not do so in the past or could not do so in the future. Furthermore, even though in nature no gene exchange may take place because the two species in question do not overlap geographically or ecologically, they may well be readily crossable together under experimental conditions. But all degrees of fertility are known, both in nature and under experimental conditions, and it is extremely difficult in practice to decide on the exact point at which to draw the dividing line. As techniques of embryo culture and hormone control of embryo development under experimental conditions develop, so more and more populations may be crossed with the original biological species and need to be accommodated in it. Because it is now possible to cross, say, wheat with *Aegilops*, *Secale* and *Agropyron*, as well as a number of other grass genera, should we then include the whole of these genera as a single species? On the biological species concept we should, but to give one species name to the whole of these genera would surely not only be absurd but impracticable. After all, species names are useful handles as well as indicators of some kind of natural groupings. In this sort of circumstance it is far better to use the terms of genecology and class all these genera under one comparium, since this defines them in terms of crossability, which is basically the definition of the biological species concept.

If, on the other hand, it is argued that we should define the biological species as a series of populations which do not exchange genes between one species and another under natural conditions or at least outside the experimental field or laboratory, then we should be forced to concede that every individual of all inbreeding cereals was a distinct species until proved otherwise by the presence of occasional crossbreeding. This, clearly, is also an absurd conclusion, but one which is reached logically from a rigid application of the biological species concept.

Then again, within what seems to be a perfectly 'respectable' species there are often to be found chromosomal or genetic barriers to gene exchange which separate groups of populations from each other reproductively. On the biological species concept each of these groups which is separated from the others by sterility barriers should be considered as a distinct species, even though it is impossible to distinguish it from its fellows by other than breeding experiments. Since only a very small proportion of the world's plants have been studied experimentally this would mean that we should not yet be able to give species names to any but a small fraction of our vegetation, and the writers of Floras and those who work in the fields of ecology, plant geography, economic botany and all the other aspects of botany unconnected with breeding and genetics would lack names for the plants they worked with.

A further difficulty arises in dealing with vegetative crops such as the potato. Thus in certain species autotriploids are quite frequent, and are formed almost certainly from diploids by the fusion of reduced and unreduced gametes. These autotriploids are reproductively isolated from each other and from their parental diploids, since they do not exchange genes with anything else and in fact reproduce entirely vegetatively. It is impracticable, surely, to class each of these as a distinct species just because it is reproductively isolated, just as it is impracticable to class every clonally reproducing cultivar or every apomict as a distinct species. The parallel series of terms devised especially for the biosystematist and the genecologist, such as the ecotype, ecospecies and coenospecies terminology of Turesson (1922) and the deme terminology of Gilmour and Gregor (1939) are available and are much more appropriate for typifying the kinds of reproductive isolation I have just mentioned.

In many groups of cultivated plants (cottons and potatoes, for instance) there seems to be no lack of fertility between F_1 hybrids though genetic breakdown occurs in the F_2 hybrids due to basic dissimilarity in the 'genetic architecture' of the species concerned. Such an F_2 test is clearly artificial but can nevertheless be used to add greater emphasis to species boundaries that are already defined in morphological terms. In nature, the F_1 families are much more likely to back-cross with the original parents; yet because the adaptive norms of the parents are well-defined and the hybrids fall into some intermediate non-adapted position one finds in nature that although hybridization can be common and the hybrids seem vigorous and fertile, nevertheless they do not seem to survive for long. Having inherited parts of the adaptive complexes of each parent they do not seem able to survive under adverse conditions since the adaptive mechanisms are only fully effective when present in each parent in a more or less pure state (see Hawkes and Hjerting, 1969; Appendix III). Such species remain apart and quite distinct in nature even though they can hybridize and exchange genes. The taxonomic species concept places them as distinct and recognizable units; the biological concept would put them together and so obscure a clear series of natural differences.

The pragmatic or empirical approach to the species problem on the other hand lays emphasis on the need for a practical way of identification and naming on the basis of easily recognizable characters, morphological ones in the main. Other information from the sources we have mentioned in an earlier section can then be added to deepen and help define more clearly the specific units. Gaps or discontinuities between species in the morphological sense are recognized as due to a lack of gene exchange in nature, or a very restricted gene flow, but if the morphological discontinuities are absent, no matter what the breeding or reproductive isolation is, then no taxonomic species boundaries are created. In a sexually reproducing outbreeding species the taxonomic and biological species definitions often coincide, but not always. Taxonomic species may be separated from each other by a variety of barriers, not only cyto-genetical ones, but geographical, ecological, physiological or ethological ones (these latter occur in plants due to the behaviour patterns of the pollinators).

The taxonomist working with cultivated plants and related wild species must therefore retain a fairly broad pragmatic species definition, looking for boundaries and discontinuities in variability patterns, separating species on the basis of a reasonably large number of characters and making sure that no large and continuous areas of gradation from one species to another exist. If they do, then his species are not really to be considered as distinct, though he would be probably justified in thinking of them as two subspecies, with areas of limited gene flow. In a wild species one frequently finds a chain of geographical subspecies, connected by areas of intergradation; in a cultivated species the subspecies concept may conveniently be applied to large groups of cultivars showing physiological adaptation to certain geographical regions, coupled with at least some recognizable morphological differences.

INTEGRATION OF DATA AND PRACTICAL APPLICATIONS

We have reviewed the basic ideas underlying classification, the criteria involved and species concepts in relation to cultivated plants and wild species. How then should we deal with the practical task of species delimitation and classification? This is admittedly not very easy, as has been stressed several times already. The most difficult situation, perhaps, is where two or more species may possess considerable 'overlap' of characters, with parallel series of variations running through them due to the effects of certain natural and artificial selection pressures acting on them in the areas where they are both cultivated.

As an example we might quote the difficulties described by Smith and Heiser (1951, 1957) for the two species of cultivated pepper, *Capsicum annuum* and *C.frutescens*. In these two species a parallel series of variants makes delimitation of the species almost impossible if every character is to be given equal weight. Yet F_1 hybrids between them are extremely difficult to obtain, most seeds are inviable when they *are* obtained and the plants grown from these are very poor and unthrifty. Therefore there are strong genetic barriers between these species, though only one or two morphological characters such as flower colour, constantly distinguish them. Probably, however, biochemical and serological tests would reveal many other character differences between these two species. On the biological species concept there is no doubt at all that these are two distinct species. On the whole, since they can be distinguished, even with difficulty, the taxonomic species concept would follow suit. If we consider for a moment the probable events in the history of pepper cultivation it would seem likely that two wild species of rather similar but nevertheless distinct morphological characteristics were taken into cultivation and grown by the same peoples under a range of very similar conditions. Perhaps fruit size differed in the two original species, but this difference has now become completely obscured. The only way of differentiating these two species now with certainty is by corolla colour and crossability. If the two original species had been evolving under conditions of geographical or ecological isolation and were then taken into cultivation in the same region they would have hybridized together frequently and become one ; the identity of each would have been lost completely and we should not be aware that they had ever been once distinct. Probably this has taken place frequently amongst cultivated plants.

It is clearly of the greatest importance in studying the taxonomy of cultivated plants to try to understand their relationship to and mode of origin from wild species in the same group. Clearly, different selection pressures act on cultivated and wild plants, but it is for this very reason that a study of variation patterns in wild and cultivated plants is so important. We can see to some extent by this comparison the sort of variation that is due to recent intensive artificial selection in the cultivated species and, so to speak, eliminate it mentally or make allowances for it. The types of variation found both in the cultivated species and in its wild relatives are likely to be of greater taxonomic value and should be looked for whenever possible. Thus, in classifying cultivated potato species we pay very little attention to tuber colours and patterns since these have been evolved very recently under artificial selection and have no value in species delimitation.

Finally, every taxonomist in the field of cultivated plants should keep a lively eye open for archaeological evidence that can throw light on the course of evolution of the plant under domestication. Archaeological evidence is slow to come in, and may never be very satisfactory in some crops. However, the work of Mangelsdorf and MacNeish (Mangelsdorf *et al.*, 1964) has shown what can be done for maize, just as Helbaek's studies on Old World cereals have thrown great light on their evolution under domestication. It is clearly necessary to know something, if we can, of the habits, customs, agricultural practices and religious beliefs of the peoples who grew these plants in primitive times, as well as those who cultivate the primitive cultivars at the present day, in order to understand evolutionary development during prehistoric and historic periods.

CONCLUSIONS

The value to the breeder and the conservationist of a basic knowledge of taxonomy and species concepts must be emphasized. Equally important is that the modern taxonomist of cultivated plants should possess a working knowledge of cytogenetics and some concept of what developments are taking place in plant biochemistry and also be conversant with the work and problems of the plant breeder in his group. If the taxonomic work on cultivated plants is to be of the slightest use to the consumer (in this case chiefly the plant breeder) the taxonomist must leave the herbarium and make his sphere of operations the experimental field, the laboratory and, if possible, the centres of variability of the crop concerned. The taxonomist should be in a position to provide a system in which all further information can be accommodated and which has high predictive value. Such a system should act as an efficient data storage and retrieval framework. It should also act as a central core for evolutionary studies and a stimulus for a fuller

D*

understanding and use of the genetic material available to plant breeders now or in the future. Finally, it should integrate studies on living and archaeological material, indicating thereby the possible course of evolution under domestication. In other words, it should hope to promote a better understanding of the material available, thus leading to its more efficient conservation and use.

REFERENCES

ANDERSON E. (1946) Maize in Mexico. A preliminary survey. *Ann. Mo. bot. Gdn.* **33,** 147–247.

BOULTER D., THURMAN D. A. & TURNER B.L. (1966) The use of disc electrophoresis of plant proteins in systematics. *Taxon* **15,** 135–143.

CAIN A.J. & HARRISON G.A. (1960) Phyletic weighting. *Proc. zool. Soc. Lond.,* **135,** 1–31.

DU RIETZ G.E. (1930) The fundamental units of biological taxonomy. *Bot. Tidsskr.* **24,** 333–428.

GELL P.G.H., WRIGHT S.T.C. & HAWKES J.G. (1956) Immunological methods in plant taxonomy. *Nature, Lond.* **177,** 573.

GELL P.G.H., HAWKES J.G. & WRIGHT S.T.C. (1960) The application of immunological methods to the taxonomy of species within the genus *Solanum. Proc. roy. Soc. B.* **151,** 364–383.

GILMOUR J.S.L. (1940) Taxonomy and philosophy. In *The New Systematics* (Ed. Huxley J.), Oxford University Press.

GILMOUR J.S.L. & GREGOR J.W. (1939) Demes: a suggested new terminology. *Nature, Lond.* **144,** 333–334.

GRANT V.E. (1957) The plant species in theory and practice. In *The Species Problem* (Ed. Mayr E.), 39–80. Am. Assoc. Adv. Sci. Washington, D.C.

HARBORNE J.B. (1968) The use of secondary chemical characters in the systematics of higher plants. In *Chemotaxonomy and Serotaxonomy* (Ed. Hawkes J.G.), Academic Press, London.

HALL O. (1959) Immuno-electrophoretic analyses of allopolyploid ryewheat and its parental species. *Hereditas* **45,** 495–504.

HASKELL G. & GARRIE J.B. (1966) Fingerprinting raspberry cultivars by empirical paper chromatography. *J. Sci. Fd. Agric.* **17,** 189–192.

HAWKES J.G. (1958) Significance of wild species and primitive forms for potato breeding. *Euphytica* **7,** 257–270.

HAWKES, J.G. (1968) *Chemotaxonomy and Serotaxonomy.* Academic Press, London.

HAWKES J.G. & HJERTING J.P. (1969) The potatoes of Argentina, Brazil, Paraguay and Uraguay. A biosystematic study. *Ann. Bot. Mem.* **3,** Oxford University Press.

HEYWOOD V.H. (1958) *The Presentation of Taxonomic Information: a short guide for contributors to Flora Europaea.* Leicester University Press, Leicester.

JOHNSON L. & HALL O. (1965) Analysis of phylogenetic affinities in the Triticinae by protein electrophoresis. *Am. J. Bot.* **52,** 506–513.

JOHNSON L. & HALL O. (1966) Electrophoretic studies of species relationships in *Triticum. Acta agr. Scand. suppl.* **16,** 222–224.

KLOZ J. (1962) An investigation of the protein characters of four *Phaseolus* species with special reference to the question of their phylogenesis. *Biol. Plant., Praha* **4,** 85–90.

KLOZOVÁ E. & KLOZ J. (1966) Protein characters in species hybrids of the genus *Phaseolus* studied by means of serological methods. *Acta. agric. Scand. suppl.* **16,** 225–228.

KOHNE D.E. (1968) Taxonomic applications of DNA hybridization techniques. In *Chemotaxonomy and Serotaxonomy* (Ed. Hawkes J.G.), Academic Press, London.

KUPZOV A.J. (1959) Parallelism in the variability of plant species with certain common characters. *Z. Pflanzenz.* **41,** 313–325.

MANGELSDORF P.C., MacNEISH R.S. & GALINAT W.C. (1964) Domestication of corn. *Science* **143,** 538–545.

SMITH P.G. & HEISER C.B. (1951) Taxonomic and genetic studies on the cultivated peppers, *Capsicum annum* L. and C. *frutescens* L. *Am. J. Bot.* **38,** 362–368.

SMITH P.G. & HEISER C.B. (1957) Taxonomy of *Capsicum sinense* Jacq. and the geographic distribution of the cultivated Capsicum peppers. *Bull. Torrey Bot. Club* **84,** 413–420.

TURESSON G. (1922) The species and variety as ecological units. *Hereditas* **3,** 100–113.

VAVILOV N.I. (1922) The law of homologous series in variation. *J. Genet.* **12,** 57–89.

THE SIGNIFICANCE OF POLYPLOIDY IN THE ORIGIN OF SPECIES AND SPECIES GROUPS

M. S. SWAMINATHAN

Indian Agricultural Research Institute,
New Delhi, India.

INTRODUCTION

Polyploidy is common and widespread throughout the Spermatophytes, recurring over and over again in unrelated groups. It must, therefore, have adaptive value and must be considered one of the most important evolutionary trends among the higher plants. Early students of polyploidy were impressed by giganticism, sometimes associated with it, and by the potential for evolution by large quantum jumps. We are reminded of Haldane (1958) who changed Blake's (1792) verse to read: 'To create a little flower is the labour of ages, *except by allopolyploidy*' (portion in italics added by Haldane). Later students have come to realize that the primary evolutionary advantage of increasing the number of genomic chromosome complements in plant cells is in genetic buffering or stabilization. This permits the survival of more radical mutations without destroying viability and permits wider hybridization and greater exploitation of genetic variability. A highly complex, reticulate polyploid superstructure overriding a series of basic diploid species is now recognized as a common pattern of variation in many groups of plants, wild and cultivated. Numerous variations of the polyploid theme are now recognized and Löve (1964) has proposed a classification based on the genetic and taxonomic characteristics of the diploid(s) involved in the origin of the polyploid. His 'panautoploids' and 'panalloploids' correspond to Stebbins' (1950) auto- and allo-polyploids, while his 'hemialloploids' formed from F_1 hybrids which are partially fertile and 'hemiautoploids' formed either through differentiation of the chromosome set of successful panautoploids (as could have happened in *Solanum tuberosum*, Swaminathan, 1954) or through chromosomes doubling in intra-specific hybrids (as might have happened in *Dactylis glomerata*) would cover the segmental-allopolyploid and auto-allopolyploid groups of Stebbins. All these categories provide in varying degrees opportunities for a synthesis of disomic and polysomic genetic constitution and thereby to an efficient exploitation of phenomena such as mutation, recombination and additive and heterotic interaction of genes. Abrupt and gradual speciation are both facilitated. The elaboration of an altogether new developmental and physiological rhythm is rendered possible through changes in the surface-volume relationships of the cell. Thus, polyploidy is a potent mechanism for traversing the evolutionary scale with jumps of larger quanta in terms of time.

NATURE OF CEILING ON THE INCREASE OF CHROMOSOME NUMBER

From observations on the behaviour of experimentally induced polyploids there has often been a tendency to regard the octoploid level as about the ceiling for the multiplication of the basic number. Studies in lower plants, particularly ferns, have, however, revealed that polyploidy may be a recurrent theme in the origin and diversification of species. For example, in the family *Ophioglossaceae* of the order Fillicales, the species *Ophioglossum reticulatum* has a chromosome number $2n = 1260$ but exhibits functional diploidy in cytological behaviour (Abraham and Ninan, 1954). The basic number in the genus is regarded to be $x = 120$ and Stebbins (1966) regards the evolutionary pathway adopted by this genus as an example of the fact that successful polyploids can become adjusted or 'diploidized' over long periods of time, so that further elevation of the chromosome number by recurrent cycles of polyploidy then becomes possible. The situation in *Ophioglossaceae* thus suggests that given a sufficiently long span of time, accompanied by diploidization at successively higher chromosome levels, almost no limit exists to the upward trend of polyploid chromosome numbers. This will be particularly true if the plant has required an apomictic mode of reproduction, as has happened in *O.reticulatum*, which lends itself to propagation through root buds.

The ceiling on levels of chromosome duplication also seems to vary, depending upon whether a species is wild or domesticated. For example, in the genus *Solanum*, triploids are infrequent among the wild species, whereas in the cultivars the opposite is true (Marks, 1966).

MECHANISMS OF DIPLOIDIZATION

(a) *Chromosome mechanisms* : The incidence of structural differences among the chromosomes of the component genomes, either present already prior to the origin of the polyploid or developed during the subsequent evolution, has long been considered as the causal factor for the diploid-like cytological behaviour of most naturally occurring polyploids (Giles and Randolph, 1951 ; Stebbins, 1950, and Gerstel, 1963). Darlington (1937) proposed that preferential pairing arising from differential affinity is responsible for the fairly regular bivalent formation occurring in polyploids like *Primula kewensis*, where the F_1 hybrids between *P.floribunda* and *P.verticillata* also exhibit bivalent formation. The orientation of quadrivalents so as to promote regular segregation, as found in *Dactylis glomerata* (Myers, 1943) and the occurrence of sub-terminal centromeres limiting chiasma formation to one arm as in *Medicago sativa* (Clement and Stanford, 1963) have been other mechanisms for reducing the chances of disjunctional abnormalities and multivalent formation respectively. Gerstel (1963) has suggested that in *Nicotiana tabacum* and *Gossypium hirsutum* the accumulation of structural differences during evolution may have taken place to a greater degree in one genome than in the other. He thus supported the view of Zohary and Feldman (1962) who observed that the members of at least one closely interrelated group of allopolyploid species in the genus *Aegilops* have one genome in common whereas the other genome or genomes vary from species to species or even within the species.

(b) *Genetic Mechanisms* : Sears and Okamoto (1958) and Riley and Chapman (1958) discovered that regularity in bivalent pairing is achieved in *Triticum aestivum* by one or more factors located in the long arm of chromosome 5B, which in some still unknown way prevents homoeologous pairing. Riley (1960) referred to this phenomenon as the 'genetic enhancement of differential affinity'. Many years prior to this discovery Müntzing and Prakken (1940) had already invoked genetic suppression of multivalent formation to explain regular bivalent pairing in polyploid *Phleum pratense*. Since the publication of the wheat findings, interest in understanding the genetic regulation of the formation of chiasmata and multivalents has grown and control over the time and rate of chromosome condensation has been found to be an important pathway in this phenomenon (Endrizzi, 1962 ; Upadhya and Swaminathan, 1967).

Seed fertility of autoploids can be subjected to improvement and even brought to the level of the diploid through selection, thus indicating that when raw polyploids undergo a period of evolution, their characteristics might undergo considerable alteration. This has been clearly demonstrated in the induced autotetraploids of *Brassica campestris* var. *toria* ($2n = 4x = 40$) where the seed fertility was raised from 2 to 3 seeds per siliqua in the C_2 generation to over 15 per siliqua in the C_{18} generation through the adoption of the mass pedigree system of selection (Rajan, 1955; Swaminathan and Sulbha, 1959).

POLYPLOIDY AS A MEANS OF EVOLUTION THROUGH MACRO- OR SYSTEMIC MUTATIONS

It is now recognized that evolution has largely progressed through selection operating upon 'blind' mutations and their recombination products, a process termed by Muller as 'muddling through'. It is also known that the frequency of mutations increases with a decrease in the magnitude of the change involved. The rigour of the somatic and gametic sieves, which determines the extent to which mutations survive and find phenotypic expression, is largely determined by the genetic architecture of the plant. The rigour is acute in a highly evolved diploid, while it is much less severe in a polyploid with either homoeologous relationships among the constituent genomes or a predominantly polysomic genotype. Zohary (1965), while discussing the characters of polyploid colonizer species in *Aegilops*, has postulated that a successful polyploid cluster may evolve from the operation of a dual system differentiation. First, there should be a conservative gene complex in control of the evolutionary 'theme' (designated the pivotal genome) and second, there should be genomes which have undergone modification through the accumulation of mutations and the operation of recombination. If the pivotal-cum-differentiated genome concept is generally operative, polyploidy would be an ideal mechanism for striking a balance between stability (immediate adaptation) and mutability (adaptability). In addition, it would offer scope for the exploitation of judicious combinations of disomic and polysomic genetic constitution and of additive as well as dominant, epistatic and other forms of gene action and interaction.

The hemialloploids and hemiautoploids of Löve (1964) have proved in many cases to be extremely valuable for domestication not so much because of the excellence of the original genotype but because of polyploidy having provided the wherewithal for the expression and realisation of various types of mutations without any coincident lowering of the reproductive potential. Thus, new systematic categories have arisen through mutations (termed macro- or systematic-mutations by Goldschmidt, 1955) in genera like *Triticum* and *Avena*. The subspecies *spelta*, *compactum* and *sphaerococcum* of *T.aestivum* differ from subspecies *vulgare* only in the genes Q, C and S respectively. These loci seem to have arisen through tandem repeats (Swaminathan, 1963) and are good examples of the abrupt origin of taxa through mutations. Thus, polyploidy is not only by itself a potent mechanism for quantum jumps in evolution but is also an excellent substrate for the incidence and survival of systemic mutations of the type envisaged by Goldschmidt (1955).

A shift from one adaptive norm to another is usually needed for a major evolutionary advance (Simpson, 1953). Some of the systematic mutants in *Triticum* enable such a shift. For example, *T.sphaerococcum* which has been recorded only in north west Pakistan and Baluchistan is extremely drought-resistant, a characteristic which seems to account for its selective survival in the area. A population with a high potential for the creation, conservation and release of genetic variability has obviously a great future in rapidly changing and exacting environments. Since polyploidy confers these advantages, its frequent incidence among angiosperms becomes explicable.

The studies of Frankel (Frankel and Munday, 1962) on flower morphogenesis in *T.aestivum* have revealed that in polyploids loci which exhibit a detrimental effect in the absence of a regulatory gene, may survive due to 'genetic inertia'. Swaminathan (1963) suggested that such loci may have a positive function under normal conditions. Thanks to the development of a complete set of aneuploids in *T. aestivum* by Sears (1954), the various forms of gene expression and interaction are better understood in this hexaploid plant than in any other polyploid. These studies reveal that some loci like the free-threshing gene Q may have several regulatory functions. Thus, Q not only suppresses speltoidy but also the expression of various forms of flower abnormalities, vavilovoid expression and rachis brittleness. Linkage relationships are also highly complex in polyploids, particularly in autoploids and the consequences of inbreeding are different. Thus, polyploids have several unique genetic features (Fisher, 1947).

GENOME AND GENETIC COHERENCE IN RELATION TO
SURVIVAL OF POLYPLOIDS

The poor vigour and survival value of most trisomics and tetrasomics of diploids suggest that the presence of one set of genes alone in a multiple condition has usually no advantage. What is important is the relative balance in gene products. Autoploids and hemiautoploids can, however, develop a balanced genotype, once the sterility problem has been overcome. In alloploids, not all genome combinations are successful, as, for example, in *Triticum* where out of the numerous combinations possible at the hexaploid level, only that involving *Aegilops squarrosa* has had success. The importance of genome combinations capable of functioning in an integrated manner or possessing what Clausen and Hiesey (1960) have called 'genetic coherence' for the stability and survival of polyploids is apparent from numerous studies on induced amphidiploids. In the genus *Oryza*, for example, Shastry (1966) has shown that desynapsis and failure of pairing occur in several F_1 hybrids and amphidiploids due to the non-synchronous time sequence of meiotic division phases and condensation. Besides difficulties in division, developmental imbalance could also arise due to the lack of coherence in gene action. A comparative analysis of the entire spectrum of growth and development in polyploids with successful and unsuccessful genome combinations would help to identify the operational components of coherence.

THE ADAPTIVE SIGNIFICANCE OF POLYPLOIDY

For understanding the circumstances under which polyploidy confers an adaptive advantage on a species group, it may be worthwhile examining why polyploidy is rare in some groups of plants. A conspicuous instance of a general absence of polyploidy is in the gymnosperms (especially *Gingko* and coniferales). These occupy relatively stable mesophytic habitats where they form great forest belts. Polyploidy is also rare among the woody angiosperms of the temperate zone. These plants have long life, frequent vegetative vigour and small chromosomes, factors which have been regarded as favourable for the incidence of polyploidy. The basic chromosome number of many of these genera is often high, thus suggesting that they may actually be ancient polyploids. In any case, it is clear that polyploids in this group ought to have been at a selective disadvantage during their recent evolutionary history. Thus, where the habitat requirements are rather stringent and specific, as in the case of gymnosperms and woody angiosperms, changes in the physiological and developmental rhythm often arising from polyploidy seem to be of negative selective value. Conversely, in changing and altogether new habitats, polyploids have been successful colonizers, as demonstrated by Hagerup (1932). Even reduced vegetative vigour resulting in early flowering could be an advantage when temperature conditions during seed development are likely to become either too high or too low.

Under conditions of intensive seedling competition a large seed size, as may occur in polyploids, will be an advantage. Many chromosome races or cytotypes occur in species of grasses and in most cases the polyploids have been very successful. For example, *Heteropogon contortus* consists of a polyploid complex native to the tropical and sub-tropical regions of both the Old World and the New, the North American forms consisting entirely of apomictic hexaploids (Emery and Brown, 1958).

Stebbins (1956) suggested that diploid plants which do not respond favourably to artificial chromosome doubling might have already acquired an optimum cell volume, with the result that any disturbance in this character has an adverse consequence. The importance of an optimum balance in the surface-volume relationship of the cell (Schwanitz, 1949) is also clear from the parallelism observed in many primary diploids between response to gibberellic acid application and colchicine-induced polyploidy (Swaminathan, Rana and Gupta, 1968).

POLYPLOIDY, APOMIXIS AND TAXONOMY

Gustafsson (1946–47) explained many years ago how polyploidy promotes the survival of mutations for agamospermy. Besides promoting the occurrence of apomixis itself, polyploidy helps to generate variability in such plants through the less rigorous elimination of somatic mutations.

The problem of nomenclature is particularly difficult in the case of intra-specific chromosome races. The view that such chromosome races should all be given specific status was expressed by Löve (1951), while several others have felt that this will not be correct, particularly if a specific systematic key is difficult to evolve. In my view it would be better to apply the same genetic and systematic criteria as far as the fixation of status is concerned, for all plants, whether diploids or polyploids. Delimitation of the boundaries of recombination would help to define the confines of the species. When this criterion is employed, obligate apomicts alone will present a major problem in classification. Systematic and spatial isolation characteristics may have to be used to a greater extent in them than genetic criteria. Morphological differ-

entiation usually accompanies chromosome number differences except
in recently evolved polyploids.

ORIGIN OF POLYPLOIDS

The origin of polyploidy from basic diploid species is not very well
understood. Under conditions of cultivation, polyploids have been
obtained by somatic mutation, especially in fruits and ornamentals.
They have been produced experimentally from callus tissue following
mutilation and by application of drugs such as colchicine that interfere with normal cell division. In nature, the most frequent mechanism
reported is the function of unreduced gametes. Once polyploids have
been produced, germ plasm can be transferred from diploids to tetraploids through the operation of unreduced gametes at moderately
high frequency levels. The initial production of a tetraploid from one
or more diploids, however, is a much less common event.

PLANT COLLECTIONS IN RELATION TO POLYPLOIDY
AND PLANT BREEDING

From the foregoing, it would be clear that polyploidy confers a means
of achieving both abrupt and gradual speciation, a balance between
adaptation and adaptability and new developmental rhythms which
enable the colonisation of diverse ecological niches. An analysis of the
needs of a specific habitat in terms of the dynamics of plant adaptation
would help to identify broadly the regions where polyploids may
thrive. In plant collections, the isolation and accumulation of wild
polyploid relatives by themselves will constitute only one aspect of the
requirements of the plant breeder. Now that the diploid donors of many
of the genomes of polyploid crop plants are fairly well understood,
greater emphasis should be paid to the collection of the genotypes
of the putative parents. This would help to resynthesise the polyploid
crop plants using parents of a different genetic background. Hagberg
and Akerberg (1961) have summarized the value of this approach in
the breeding of oilseed crops. While monosomic analysis of the location
of genes for rust resistance in varieties of *T.aestivum* has shown that the
D genome derived from *A.squarrosa* seldom contains genes for resistance,
the Japanese collections of *A.squarrosa* have revealed some strains with a
high degree of resistance (Yamashita, 1959). With the growing application of fertilizers and intensity of farming all over the world, the

importance of isolating altogether new genes for resistance to the principal diseases and pests hardly needs emphasis. The resynthesis of some of the existing polyploid plants using altogether new parental material may have an important impact in future plant breeding. This is particularly so because of our growing understanding of the methods of manipulating gene recombination.

REFERENCES

ABRAHAM A. & NINAN C.A. (1954) The chromosomes of *Ophioglossum reticulatum*. *Curr. Sci.* **23**, 213–214.

CLAUSEN J. & HIESEY W.M. (1960) The balance between coherence and variation in evolution. *Proc. nat. Acad. Sci. Wash.* **46**, 494–506.

CLEMENT W.M. JR. & STANFORD E.H. (1963) Pachytene studies at the diploid level in *Medicago. Crop. Sci.* **3**, 142–145.

DARLINGTON C.D. (1937) *Recent Advances in Cytology.* Churchill, London.

EMERY W.H.P. & BROWN W.V. (1958) Apomixis in the *Gramineae* tribe *Andropogoneae : Heteropogon contortus. Madrono* **14**, 238–246.

ENDRIZZI J.E. (1962) The diploid like cytological behaviour of tetraploid cotton. *Evolution* **16**, 325–329.

FISHER R.A. (1947) The theory of linkage in polysomic inheritance. *Phil. Trans. R. Soc. Series B.* **233**, 55–87.

FRANKEL O.H. & MUNDAY A. (1962) 'Supergenes' and 'genetic inertia' in hexaploid wheat. (*Australian*) *Plant Breeding & Genetics Newsletter* **20**, 32–34

GERSTEL D.U. (1963) Evolutionary problems in some polyploid crop plants. *Proc. 2nd. Int. Wheat Genet. Symp. Hereditas Suppl.* **2**, 481–504.

GILES A. & RANDOLPH L.F. (1951) Reduction of quadrivalent frequency in autotetraploid maize during a period of ten years. *Am. J. Bot.* **38**, 12–17.

GOLDSCHMIDT R.B. (1955) *Theoretical Genetics.* Univ. California Press, Berkeley.

GUSTAFSSON Å. (1946–47) Apomixis in higher plants. I–III. *Acta Univ. lund., N.F. Avd.* 2, **42**, 1–6, 69–180 and 181–370.

HAGBERG A. & ÅKERBERG E. (1961) *Mutations and Polyploidy in Plant Breeding.* Svenska Bokforlaget, Stockholm.

HAGERUP O. (1932) Über Polyploidie in Beziehung zu Klima, Ökologie, und Phylogenie. *Hereditas* **16**, 19–40.

LÖVE A. (1951) Taxonomical evaluation of polyploids. *Caryologia* **3**, 263–284.

LÖVE A. (1964) The biological species concept and its evolutionary structure. *Taxon* **13**, 33–45.

MARKS G.E. (1966) The enigma of triploid potatoes. *Euphytica* **15**, 285–290.

MÜNTZING A. & PRAKKEN R. (1940) The mode of chromosome pairing in Phleum twins with 63 chromosomes and its cytogenetic consequences. *Hereditas* **26**, 463–501.

MYERS W.M. (1943) Analysis of variance and covariance of chromosomal association and behaviour during meiosis in clones of *Dactylis glomerata. Bot. Gaz.* **104**, 541–552.

RAJAN S.S. (1955) The effectiveness of the mass pedigree system of selection in the improvement of seed setting in autotetraploids of *Toria*. *Indian J. Genet.* **15,** 47–49.

RILEY R. (1960) The diploidization of polyploid wheat. *Heredity* **15,** 407–429.

RILEY R. & CHAPMAN V. (1958) Genetic control of the cytologically diploid behaviour of hexaploid wheat. *Nature, Lond.* **182,** 713–715.

SEARS E.R. (1954) The aneuploids of common wheat. *Mo Agri. Exp. Sta. Res. Bull.* **572,** pp. 58.

SEARS E.R. & Okamoto, M. (1958) Intergenomic chromosome relationships in hexaploid wheat. *Proc. Xth Int. Congr. Genet. Montreal* **2,** 258–259.

SCHWANITZ F. (1949) Untersuchungen an polyploiden Pflanzen. II. Zur Keimungs-physiologie diploider und autotetraploider Nutzpflanzen. *Planta* **36,** 389–401.

SHASTRY S.V.S. (1966) Cytogenetic mechanisms in the speciation of *Oryza*. *J. P.G. School* **4,** 91–98.

SIMPSON G.G. (1953) *The Major Features of Evolution.* Columbia University Press, New York.

STEBBINS G.L. (1950) *Variation and evolution in plants.* Oxford University Press.

STEBBINS G.L. (1956) Artificial polyploidy as a tool in plant breeding. *Brookhaven Symp. Biol.* **9,** 37–52.

STEBBINS G.L. (1966) Chromosomal variation and evolution. *Science, N.Y.* **152,** 1463–1469.

SWAMINATHAN M.S. (1954) Nature of polyploidy in some 48-chromosome species of the genus *Solanum*, section *Tuberarium*. *Genetics* **396,** 59–76.

SWAMINATHAN M.S. (1963) Mutational analysis in the hexaploid wheat complex. *Proc. 2nd Int. Wheat Genet. Symp. Hereditas Suppl.* **2,** 418–438.

SWAMINATHAN M.S., RANA R.S. & GUPTA A.K. (1968) Similarities in the response to chromosome doubling and gibberellin application in some plants. *Curr. Sci.* **37,** 305–306.

SWAMINATHAN M.S. & SULBHA K. (1959) Multivalent frequency and seed fertility in raw and evolved tetraploids of *Brassica campestris* var. *toria*. *Z. Vererb. Lehre* **90,** 385–392.

UPADHYA M.D. & SWAMINATHAN M.S. (1967) Mechanisms regulating chromosome pairing in *Triticum*. *Biol. Zbl.* **86** (suppl.), 239–255.

YAMASHITA K. (1959) Discussion following L.H. Shebeski's paper. *Proc. 1st Int. Wheat Genet. Symp.*, Winnipeg, p. 239.

ZOHARY D. (1965) Colonizer species in the wheat group. In *The Genetics of Colonising Species* (Eds. Baker H.G. and Stebbins G.L.) New York, Academic Press.

ZOHARY D. & FELDMAN M. (1962) Hybridization between amphidiploids and the evolution of polyploids in wheat (*Aegilops–Triticum*) group. *Evolution* **16,** 44–61.

8

POPULATION STRUCTURE
AND SAMPLING METHODS

R. W. ALLARD

University of California,
Davis, California

INTRODUCTION

The basic source of the genetic variability on which the improvement of domestic plants depends is that which exists at the present time in advanced and primitive cultivars, and in the wild or weed relatives of cultivated species. If there is any single conclusion to which recent quantitative studies in population and ecological genetics point, it is that both natural and domestic species of plants and animals contain remarkable stores of genetic variability. All species which have been studied in detail show extensive geographical variability, and they also show extensive variability within populations. Each species contains millions or even hundreds of millions of variants; hence when the practicalities of plant exploration are taken into account it is clear that any collection can be only a small sample of the total variability of the species. The problem is how to sample to include the maximum amount of genetically useful variability and still keep the number of items in the sample within practical limits. More specifically, we wish to know the pattern of collecting that will provide the most useful sample of the genetic variability which occurs between different geographical areas and that which occurs within geographical areas. The development of adequate sampling procedures therefore depends on: (1) information concerning the patterns in which genetic variability is distributed over the geographical range of a species; (2) information about the extent of genetic variability within the local population; and (3) information about the ways by which genetic variability can be maintained once the collection has been made.

PATTERNS OF GENETIC VARIABILITY

GEOGRAPHICAL VARIABILITY

It is, of course, well known that collections of a species taken from widely separated geographical areas usually differ from one another in morphological characteristics and that experienced observers can frequently identify the area of origin of a strain from its morphological characteristics. It is also well known that certain characters occur much more frequently in collections made in some areas than in others. For example, in the United States Department of Agriculture barley collections, about 75 per cent of the genotypes which are resistant to net-blotch disease come from Manchuria, an area that contributed only about 12 per cent of the total collection. Similarly, Hessian-fly-resistant collections abound in North Africa, Greenbug-resistant barleys are likely to originate in China or Korea, and genes for resistance to the bunt disease of wheat are most common in Crimean wheats. However, one should not conclude from these examples that genetic variability is always so unevenly distributed over the range of a species. At least an equal number of examples can be cited in which strains carrying resistance to diseases occur with more or less equal frequency through-out the range of distribution of the species.

In addition to geographical variability for disease resistance, morphological characteristics, and other conspicuous differences, there is also geographical variability of a less obvious but perhaps ultimately more important kind, variability in quantitative characters. The late H. V. Harlan, in discussing this type of variability in barley (Harlan, 1957) stated that in each local area 'there has evolved a type peculiarly fitted for conditions as they exist there. Slight changes in altitude are accompanied by corresponding changes in the barleys. The barleys from each tiny area are made up of large numbers of strains that look much alike, but that may differ greatly in ways useful to the plant breeder. Even out on the plains where the superficial appearance of the crop may be the same over a large area, these constituents are present in endless variety and shift as one goes to drier or colder sections'.

It is only recently that precise quantitative studies have been made of variation in measurement characters and that adequate estimates have been made of the components of this type of variability. The basic procedure followed in these studies has been to collect seeds from large numbers of random plants in a number of populations from various geographical regions. These seeds were then sown to establish families in replicated experiments and measurements were made for various morphological and physiological attributes on each individual in each family. Each family was also scored for various conspicuous polymorphisms. The general pattern of geographical variability that is revealed by such studies can be established by considering a few examples.

In one of the earliest studies of natural populations in which adequate quantitative data were taken, Knowles (1943) made collections of soft brome (*Bromus mollis*), a highly self-pollinated annual grass, along a transect from the cold, humid coastal regions of northern California to the warmer semi-arid Sacramento Valley to the interior. Data (Table 8.1) from progenies grown in a common environment showed that size of plant (as measured by height) and time to maturity (as measured by days to flowering) decreased steadily but tillering capacity increased steadily with increasing aridity. In other words,

TABLE 8.1. Genetic variability between and within populations of *Bromus mollis**

Location of population†	Number of progenies	Days to heading		Plant height		Tiller number	
		Mean	Range	Mean	Range	Mean	Range
Del Norte	16	186	174–201	88	58–102	31	22–45
Humboldt	23	174	163–183	77	49–103	27	17–43
Contra Costa	18	164	155–169	80	72– 89	20	20–43
Solano	44	153	151–164	67	55– 92	23	23–62
Yolo	9	154	151–160	71	57– 86	32	32–49
Sutter	6	151	151	60	58– 63	30	30–40

*After Knowles (1943)
†Listed in increasing order of aridity.

genetic variability for these characters followed a clear and distinct *clinal* pattern. There are now large numbers of additional studies of geographical variability and similar clines have been found in all species for which adequate measurement data are available. Thus, for example, seed size in burr clover (*Medicago hispida*) decreases progressively with increasing altitude, petal length in common crowfoot (*Erodium cicutarium*) increases with increasing rainfall, leaf length in foxtail barley (*Hordeum nodosum*) decreases as mean temperature increases and rainfall decreases and wild oats (*Avena fatua*) from deep fertile soils are more robust and tiller more profusely than wild oats from shallow infertile soils.

These quantitative studies reveal that there is another, and at least equally striking, pattern of genetic variation superimposed on this clinal variability. This is a *patchwork* or *mosaic* pattern which is reflected in very sharp differentiations among local populations within a geographical region. The magnitude of such variation can be illustrated by a sample of data (Table 8.2) on wild oats (*Avena fatua*) from the studies of Imam and Allard (1965) and Jain and Marshall (1966). Comparisons of the means of measurements made on the progeny of individuals from a number of sites separated by only a few kilometers show that genetic differences among the sites are often very large. For example, the two week difference in flowering time between site 4 and site 6 is approximately the same as the clinal variation which occurs over a distance of 800 kilometers in the north–south direction.

Striking genetic differentiations often occur in very short distances, in fact, they frequently occur within distances of a few metres. For

TABLE 8.2. Estimated means for different natural populations of wild
oats within a geographical region

Population*	Flowering time (date in April)	Height (cm)	Population†	Spikelet number per panicle	Panicle length (cm)
4	11·5	112	E_1	7·7	9·9
5	16·8	103	E_2	6·3	8·2
6	25·4	107	F_1	14·0	15·2

*After Imam and Allard (1965)
†After Jain and Marshall (in press)

example, within one collection site heading time changed more than 15 days in a distance of 5 meters, apparently in association with local topography. In this particular case the progeny of plants collected in a flat area immediately above a steep slope flowered on April 18 on the average, progeny of plants collected on the steep area flowered on April 11, and progeny of individuals collected on the well-watered flat area at the base of the slope flowered on April 26. This difference is again equivalent to that which occurs over an 800 kilometer distance in the north–south direction.

All of the examples cited above have involved predominantly self-pollinated species and it can be argued that marked local differentiations are more likely to develop in such species because of the limitations imposed on gene interchange by the mating system. However, experimental evidence from studies of several outcrossing species (Gregor, 1930, in *Plantago*; Epling and Dobzhansky, 1942 in

Linanthus parryae; Ehrendorfer, 1953 in *Galium*; Bradshaw, 1959 in *Agrostis*; Cook, 1962 in *Eschscholtzia*) suggest that under panmixia and within a continuous range of distribution, the distance separating sharply contrasting populations can be less than 50 meters, a distance over which gene flow can occur easily. The sharpness of the transitions are well illustrated by the data of Bradshaw and his associates on *Agrostis tenuis* and *Agrostis stolonifera*, both of which are wind-pollinated and self-incompatible. Bradshaw, McNeilly and Gregory (1965), have shown that *Agrostis tenuis* has evolved populations possessing tolerance to various heavy metals in the neighbourhood of old mine workings and that this tolerance is heritable. Tolerant and non-tolerant populations can be found within a distance of 100 meters; detailed studies of the micro-distribution indicate that sharp transitions between the two types of populations sometimes occur within a distance of 20 metres. Similar sharp transitions were found in length of stolons of populations of *Agrostis stolonifera* along a transect which went from an exposed cliff into protected pastures. Recently, Jain and Bradshaw (1966) have reviewed many such cases and have analyzed their theoretical basis.

VARIABILITY WITHIN POPULATIONS

One of the major efforts in genetics in the past 3 or 4 decades has been to determine the extent of genetic variability within populations and to analyze the forces by which it is maintained. It is now clear that all populations of outbreeding species contain large amounts of genetic variability and the work of Wright and Dobzhansky, in particular, has established that the maintenance of this variability depends on complex interactions among a number of genetic and environmental factors. However, there have been many reviews of the extensive literature on this topic and the main features of the results now appear even in elementary textbooks and are well known to most biologists. Consequently, a further review here appears superfluous and it seems appropriate to direct the present discussion toward one aspect of the topic that is not as well known but is particularly relevant in the presnet context. This is the situation in predominantly self-pollinated plant species.

Populations in inbreeding species are commonly supposed to have a very simple genetic structure along the following pattern: the population is supposed to consist of a number of inbred lines each of which maintains itself as a constant, genetically homozygous entity for a large number of generations; each line is represented in the population by hundreds or thousands of individuals ; there may be some variability between lines but there is presumably little heterozygosity, and this is found mostly among the immediate descendants of the occasional hybrids which occur between the different homozygous lines of which the population is composed.

This is the conventional view. But there is now a body of evidence which shows that it is an over-simplification and that there is a great deal of genetic variability, and heterozygosity, within populations of both agricultural and natural populations (Allard, 1965 ; Allard, Jain and Workman, 1966). Whenever adequate quantitative studies have been made of inbreeding species they have shown that the individual population contains individuals of many different genotypes. Polymorphisms are commonplace in natural populations and also in the 'old land races' of agricultural species. Thus, for example, populations of wild oats are frequently polymorphic for characters such as lemma color, rachilla pubescence, and resistance to rust. Similarly, land races of barley are usually polymorphic for a number of morphological characteristics, for reaction to diseases and for various physiological characteristics. Individuals within populations differ from one another, not only with respect to such conspicuous polymorphisms, but also for continuously varying characters. The extent of variation for continuously varying characters is usually striking ; for example, the range in height from the *genetically* shortest to the *genetically* tallest individual within a population of wild oats is often two-fold and between-family variation for other measurement characters is frequently as large or even larger.

One of the most interesting features of this variability within inbreeding populations is that it is in considerable part based on heterozygosity. When the progeny of single individuals are examined for conspicuous polymorphisms it is found that a high proportion of progenies segregate for such characters. Similarly, when plus and minus selection is performed within single progenies for continuously varying characters such as seed size, time of flowering, and height there is almost always a response to the selection. This establishes that much of the variability for measurement characters that is observed in populations has its basis in heterozygosity. It is beyond the scope of the present discussion to consider the basis for the persistence of such extensive genetic variability under heavy inbreeding since it is now clear that it can be understood only in terms of complex models which take into account not only the primary factors of mutation, selection, migration and mating system but also the integrative properties of the gene pool, population size, local and yearly fluctuations in selective pressures, density-dependent selection, seed load in the soil and the like.

SAMPLING METHODS

In any survey of the distribution of genetic variability within an economic species, or its wild relatives, the most obvious pattern which emerges is that of variability associated with broad geographical regions. Collections which are made in one region differ in morphological appearance from those of other regions and they also differ in a host of other ways, such as frequency of genes for resistance to diseases and tolerance to cold or drought. Few investigators would dispute that in planning a sampling program to preserve the maximum amount of genetic variability, it is essential to sample geographical variability on the broadest scale. Thus it is just as important, if not more important, to sample at the extremes of the range of a species, even though genotypic differences in these areas may be small, as it is to sample in the central parts of the range where genotypic differences may be more prominent.

Once it has been decided to collect in some given geographical area it is necessary to determine the most appropriate distribution of collections between and within specific populations. In the F A O study of 'Plant exploration, collection and introduction' (Whyte, 1958), no specific recommendation was made concerning the number of populations which should be collected within a geographical area. However, it was recommended that 'with cross-fertile herbage plants the recipient should, in general, be supplied with 100 seeds from 50 individual plants within a population'. It was also stated that the seeds required from a population were 'few' for apomicts, 'more' for cross-fertile and 'many' for self-fertile plants; this implies that more extensive collections should be made within populations of self-pollinating than of cross-pollinating species. What modifications of the above recommendation, if any, are called for in the light of present information about the distribution of genetic variability within and between populations?

There can be no general answer to this question because each species and each area will represent a unique problem in sampling. A precise answer for each case requires knowledge of the variates of each individual system, such as the breeding system, observable 'marker' characteristics associated with and indicating significant variation, and the ways in which such individual variates interact with climatic or ecological features of the area to produce the overall pattern of variation. In general this information is not available and, even if the extensive studies required to obtain it could be made before the plans for collection were prepared, populations might have disappeared by the end of the study. Therefore, in formulating sampling procedures for unstudied or incompletely studied cases, there is no practical alternative to developing plans from well-studied cases and extrapolating from them to the cases where basic information is not available. Guidelines obtained in this way, while far from what we should prefer, are better than entirely arbitrary guidelines, particularly if they are applied with biological common sense. Consequently, it seems worthwhile to attempt to develop appropriate sampling schemes for those cases where sufficient genetic information is available to make this possible. Unfortunately, the number of cases which have been studied in enough detail to provide the required information is distressingly small.

The case I shall explore is that of wild oats (*Avena fatua*) in Central California (Imam and Allard, 1964). Quantitative studies, of the type reviewed above, show that variability in this case takes the following forms: (1) extensive variability within the local population, (2) a mosaic pattern in which highly localized differentiations are superimposed on (3) clinal variability which extends in both east–west and north–south directions. These three categories of variability are approximately equal in magnitude in the sense that the range of types found within a local population is often as great as the mean change from one local population to another, or from one extreme of the range to the other.

Variability associated with the north–south cline is the easiest to dispose of in sampling, because changes along this cline are very regular ones associated with increasing aridity and temperature towards the south. Analyses of data from collections made along this cline indicate that one must travel about 200 km before a *statistically significant* change occurs in characteristics such as time of flowering, plant height and number of tillers. Presumably change in more subtle physiological characteristics occurs at an equivalent rate. It therefore seems most unlikely that any *significant* genetic variability would be missed if a collecting team were to sample at intervals of 150 or perhaps even 250 km in the north–south direction, *provided* that a sufficient number of collections were made along the east–west transect at each latitude to give an adequate sample.

The east–west transect, although rarely more than 250 km wide, presents a considerably more complicated pattern of variability. This transect, starting with the cold-foggy coastal area on the west, progresses successively through several other main geomorphic regions—the rough topography of the coastal mountains, the low-flat arid central valley, the foothills of the Sierra Nevada mountains, and then into the mountains themselves, ending at approximately 1500 m elevation. Analyses of data from collections made along this transect indicate that in the coastal areas, or in the interior valley, it may be necessary to travel up to 50 km to observe a *significant* change in characteristics such as time of flowering or tiller number. However, in the coast range or foothills of the Sierra Nevada, where there are sharp changes in altitude, significant differences often occur over much shorter distances. Much of the clinal variability along the east–west transect is associated with altitude. Although it is risky to be specific, it seems unlikely that significant genetic variability would be missed if collections were taken at intervals of about 200 m change in *elevation*, *provided* that collections were made at enough sites at each elevation to assure an adequate sample of the various local habitats associated with differences in slope, exposure to the sun, soil types and other features of the local environment.

The final question concerns the number of individuals to be collected within each local population of wild oats. No sample can include all of the variability since it is clear that few, if any, individuals in a local population have the same genotype. However, variability for measurement characters tends to be normally distributed and experience indicates that a sample of a few seeds (one panicle) from each of 200 to 300 plants would capture most of this variability. A sample of this size would also be likely to include alleles of major genes which are present with gene frequencies greater than two or three per cent, and hence to preserve most of the polymorphisms present in the local population.

It therefore appears likely that most of the significant genetic variability in the wild oat species (*Avena fatua*) in an area in California extending approximately 600 km in a north–south and 200 km in an east–west direction would be included in a sample of 1 m seeds, provided the sample were structured as follows :

10 seeds (one panicle) per plant

200 plants per local population (defined as occupying a site approximately 50 × 50 m)

5 local populations per region (defined as an area of approximately
  5 × 5 km)

20 regions per east–west transect, and

5 transects distributed at more or less 200 km intervals from
  northern California to the Mexican border. The distance
  between transects might be less than 200 km in areas of rough
  topography and greater in the flatter terrain.

It should be noted that information on the distribution of genetic
variability in *Lolium multiflorum* and *Collinsia heterophylla* in Central
California suggests exactly the same pattern of sampling, even though
both of these species are highly cross-pollinated.

This imaginary collection of wild oats would, therefore, consist of
500 populations. This would probably be a manageable number from
the standpoint of handling and maintenance, particularly if the 200
plants within each population were to be combined. If, however, each
plant were kept separate, it might be difficult to handle such large
numbers of individuals and the cost of maintenance would become
prohibitive. Considering the probability that there would be similar
collections from several other parts of the world, the frequency of
sampling appears to be rather high. The wild oat example therefore
suggests that it may not be practical as a routine matter to attempt to
preserve 'all significant genetic variation' within wild species nor,
probably, in widely distributed cultivars.

A number of compromises are possible. If the collection does not have
a specific objective, for example, disease resistance or early maturing
types, it might be appropriate to think in terms of a coarser overall grid,
to be followed later by more intense collecting in specific areas. This
pattern was followed in an expedition to assemble and preserve the
genetic variability which exists in the lima bean species. Studies of the
materials collected on a coarse grid revealed that in certain areas there
were very interesting types, whereupon a second expedition went to
these localities to collect on a very fine grid.

An alternative is to collect on a very tight net at the start, followed
by later reduction of the sample to manageable size on the basis of
information gained from progeny tests or other procedures. In experiments with several annual species in California we have found that it is
more efficient to collect on a tight net and eliminate materials later than
it is to apply restrictions at the collection site.

REFERENCES

ALLARD R.W. (1965) Genetic systems associated with colonizing ability in predominately self-pollinated species. In *The Genetics of Colonizing Species*. (Eds. Baker H.G. and Stebbins G.L.), Academic Press, New York, 49–75.

ALLARD R.W., JAIN S.K. & WORKMAN P.L. (1966) The genetics of inbreeding species. *Adv. Genet.* **14,** 55–131.

BRADSHAW A.D. (1959) Population differentiation in *Agrostis tenuis* Sibth I. Morphological differences. *New Phytol.* **59,** 92–103.

BRADSHAW A.D., McNEILLY T.S. & GREGORY R.P.G. (1965) Industrialization, evolution and the development of heavy metal tolerance in plants. *Brit. Ecol. Soc. Symp.* **6,** 327–343.

COOK S.A. (1962) Genetic system, variation and adaptation in *Eschscholtzia californica*. *Evolution* **16,** 278–299.

EHRENDORFER F. (1953) Ökologisch-geographische mikro-differenzierung einer population von *Galium pumilum* Murr. s. str. (Zur Phylogenie der Gattung Galium. III). *Österr. Bot. Z.* **100,** 616–638.

EPLING C. & DOBZHANSKY TH. (1942) Genetics of natural populations. VI. Microgeographical races in *Linanthus parryae*. *Genetics* **27,** 317–332.

GREGOR J.W. (1930) Experiments on the genetics of wild populations. I. *Plantago maritima*. *J. Genet.* **22,** 15–25.

HARLAN H.V. (1957) *One Man's Life with Barley*. Exposition Press, New York.

IMAM A.G. & ALLARD R.W. (1965) Population studies in predominantly self-pollinated species. VI. Genetic variability between and within natural populations of wild oats from differing habitats in California. *Genetics* **51,** 49–62.

JAIN S.K. & BRADSHAW A.D. (1966) Evolutionary divergence among adjacent plant populations. I. The evidence and its theoretical analysis. *Heredity* **21,** 407–441.

JAIN S.K. & MARSHALL D.R. (1966) Population studies in predominantly self-pollinated species. X. Variation in natural populations of *Avena fatua* and *A. barbata*. *Am. Nat.* **101,** 19–33.

KNOWLES P.F. (1943) Improving an annual brome grass, *Bromus mollis* L. for range purposes. *J. Am. Soc. Agron.* **35,** 548–594.

WHYTE R.O. (1958) Plant exploration, collection and introduction. *F.A.O. Agric. Stud.* **41,** Rome.

E

POPULATION STRUCTURE OF FOREST TREE SPECIES

K. STERN

Forstliche Fakultät der Georg-August Universität
Göttingen, Germany

Some of the earliest work in genecology has been done with forest trees. This is most remarkable since forest trees are difficult to handle in field experiments, and it shows that foresters have long been interested in 'tree race studies', 'provenance studies' or whatever name this kind of research has been given (Langlet, 1964). Their interest in the genetic aspects of timber production is easy to understand because foresters are not able to manipulate the environment of forests to the same degree as agriculturists do when growing crops or fruits. The reason is, of course, that much lower returns of forest land set a lower limit on investment.

Provenance studies have been carried out systematically and on a large scale in many countries since early in this century (Langlet, 1938). The International Union of Forestry Research Organizations has done much to coordinate experiments and to standardize methods. Its working group on provenance research is one of the oldest working groups in I U F R O and one of the most successful. The result of this 60-year activity is that we know today much about genetic variation patterns and modes of adaptation of many forest tree species in spite of the long rotation periods of field experiments and the interruption of both experimental activities and personal relations by two world wars.

The genetic structure of natural populations of forest trees in temperate and subarctic climates is mainly determined by systems of large-scale and local clines (Langlet, 1936; Galoux, 1966). As all of the coniferous species and most of the more important hardwoods are wind pollinated and allogamous, gene flow seems to be more effective than in annual plants and, in some cases, even seems to restrict major modifications in adaptation to extreme environments of local niches and at the edge of species ranges (Sarvas, 1966; Anderson, 1965). Discontinuous 'races' are of minor importance (Stern, 1964).

The following example may illustrate this. It has been taken from an earlier publication (Stern, 1964) and might stand as only one example of the vast literature on genetic variation patterns in forest tree species that cannot be discussed here in detail. The data are from a nursery experiment with young plants of two sympatric birch species from Japan, *Betula japonica* and *B.maximowicziana*. The first is a weed species, the second a species of climax forests.

In both species most of the variation between subpopulations is clinal ('between regions'), as shown by the data in Table 9.1 for cessation of growth in 1960. But the genetic variation within subpopulations is also relatively high ('between families' here relates to families of half-sibs, and this component, therefore, should be multiplied by four). Genetic variation between subpopulations of the same region is higher for the weed-species having a more irregular regeneration and giving, therefore, better chances for drift and other accidents of sampling.

TABLE 9.1. Partition of the genetic variance (%) of the character, cessation of annual growth, in a provenance experiment with two sympatric birch species

Source of variation	% of genetic variance	
	Betula japonica	*B.maximowicziana*
Between regions	78·5	59·8
Subpopulations within regions	11·3	12·0
Families within subpopulations	10·2	28·4

Inbreeding coefficients of subpopulations have been determined as approximately 0.10 for the weed species and 0.03 for the other, using 15 characters measured on the same plants of the same experiment. Mean intensity of natural selection along the latitudinal cline which is responsible for most of the geographic variation in both species, has also been estimated. In order to change a subpopulation mean into that of another subpopulation one degree of latitude apart, one has to select on the average 85% of the individuals in the direction selected for, if heritability is unity. This indicates quite high selection intensities, in spite of relatively small differences of subpopulation means in single characters, when selection acts simultaneously on several characters.

One of the main characteristics of the genetic systems of forest tree species is thought to be a high recombination index and, consequently, broad genetic variation within local populations (Stebbins, 1950). Most evidence from cytogenetic research on forest trees is in favour of this hypothesis as are the estimates of genetic variances for many characters.

The genetic system of some species seems to be extremely conservative leading to the formation of cosmopolitan species adapted to very different niches in various parts of their respective ranges. Examples of this type of adaptation are to be seen in such species as *Picea abies*, *Pseudotsuga menziesii*, *Betula pendula* and others. But other species tend to split into different species if a variety of niches becomes available as, for instance, eucalypts, oaks and pines.

Polyploidy is common in a few genera and it then can be an effective tool for adaptation and specialization as in other plants. Willows offer the most impressive example. The ranges of some species are more or less contiguous whereas other species occupy small and isolated niches. Some trees behave as weeds, reproducing abundantly and thriving under disturbance, while other species are amongst the most typical examples of species of climax vegetation. Vegetative reproduction is frequent in some genera (Barnes, 1966) to such an extent that local populations can be uniclonal, but it is completely lacking in other species of the same genus or in other genera.

Even more complexity is encountered if account is taken also of those species of temperate regions occurring less frequently (species adapted to semi-arid climates), and of those of tropical rain forests, but, unfortunately, very little is known about the genetics of these groups. As species of tropical rain forests are becoming increasingly important, ecologists and geneticists should intensify research into their particular modes of adaptation and the main characteristics of their genetic systems which, probably, are different from those of other tree species (Grant, 1963). Extreme specialization to biotic microniches, as in the case of species of tropical rain forests, must have consequences for their genetic systems.

A complete picture of the genetic systems of forest tree species and their genetic variation patterns and evolution, would not be very different from that of higher plants in general, as outlined above. Hence, the question of how to preserve gene pools of forest tree species, how to design sampling of both species and local populations, etc. has to be answered differently if different species are concerned. The same applies for populations of the same species adapted to different niches.

Populations of forest trees are thought to be wild populations. This is right with a few exceptions (poplars, willows, *Cryptomeria*), if a population which has not yet been affected by artificial selection or breeding is called a wild population. But this does not mean that population structure or selective forces acting upon populations could not have been influenced directly or indirectly by other actions of man. The genetic structure, and the composition of forest tree populations in Europe for instance, have been affected for many generations by artificial regeneration which must have resulted in a new population structure and composition compared with the original state of those populations.

Moreover, the range of such species as *Picea abies* and *Pinus silvestris* has been widely extended by foresters. Nursery and planting techniques, control of competition both within and between species by means of thinning have completely changed the different ecological niches, and hence the way natural or uncontrolled selection acts upon populations. But even in species still regenerated naturally, the direction and intensity of natural selection must have been changed by man's use of the best sites for farmland, the removal of fuelwood and timber from the remaining forests, and by keeping domesticated animals in the forests. If we take account of the changes in population structure brought about by man's activities we can find all kinds of intermediate populations ranging from fully wild populations the structure of which is solely determined by natural forces of evolution, to uniclonal or oligoclonal artificial stands where the clones have been selected by man primarily for high rootability and good growth. This certainly further complicates population structure but is, of course, by no means restricted to forest trees.

Provenance mixtures and their descendants, grown in countries where forestry is long-established, have considerably complicated tree breeding. Population parameters such as heritabilities and genetic correlations cannot be connected with models as random mating populations or sets of subpopulations in a known genetic variation pattern. Moreover, the use of provenance mixtures has widely destroyed the adaptive population structures: directly, by replacing well-adapted local populations or, indirectly, by hybridization. Forest tree breeders in Europe have made many attempts to identify and to save the relics of indigenous populations. Tree breeders in countries where the original population structures have not yet been destroyed try to preserve as many samples of representative local populations as possible. The general rules for sampling are the same as in annual plants since the principles and population structures involved are identical in both forest trees and annual plants.

REFERENCES

ANDERSON E. (1965) Cone and seed studies in Norway spruce (*Picea abies* (L.) Karst.). *Stud. For. Suecica* **23,** 214.

BARNES B.V. (1966) The clonal growth habit of American aspens. *Ecology* **47,** 439–447.

GALOUX A. (1966) La variabilité génécologique du Hetre commun (*Fagus silvatica*) en Belgique. Station de Recherches des Eaux et Forêts, Ser. A., 11.

GRANT V. (1963) *The Origin of Adaptations*. Columbia University Press, New York.

LANGLET O. (1936) Studier över tallens physiologiska variabilitet och dess samband med klimatet. *Medd. St. SkogsförsAnst.* **29,** (4), 219–470.

LANGLET O. (1938) Proveniens försök med olika trädslag. *Svenska SkogsFör. Tidskr.* **1–2,** 55–378.

LANGLET O. (1964) Tvåhundra år genecologi. *Svenskbot. Tidskr.* **58,** 273–308.

SARVAS R. (1966) Temperature sum as a restricting factor in the development of forest in the Sub-Arctic. *Unesco Nat. Res. Org. Symp. on Ecol. of Sub-Arctic Regions, Helsinki.*

STEBBINS G.L. (1950) *Variation and Evolution in Plants*. Columbia University Press, New York.

STERN K. (1964) Herkunftsversuche für Zwecke der Forstpflanzenzüchtung. *Der Züchter* **34,** 181–219.

10

ADAPTATION IN WILD AND CULTIVATED PLANT POPULATIONS

ERNA BENNETT

Crop Ecology and Genetic Resources Branch, F A O, Rome

INTRODUCTION

Stability and mutability are uniquely combined in living organisms; genetic constancy and genetic variability are equally characteristic of them. The frequent occurrence of deviations from 'type' impresses the observer hardly less than the capacity of like to beget like. Acting in unison, these contrary properties contribute a tremendous evolutionary potential to living processes.

Close correspondence under natural conditions between morphological and physiological traits and the characteristics of the habitats in which the traits are expressed has now been established by a great deal of experimental work and may be regarded as general. The genotypic constitution of populations is a consequence of the innate capacity of organisms to vary, and of populations to respond to environmental pressures by differentiation into a range of distinctive gene pools of considerable diversity.

The purpose of the present chapter is to consider the forces operating on and within plant populations under the action of selection in the wild and in cultivation, and to relate these to practical problems of plant exploration and genetic conservation and to the most effective utilisation of the genetic potential which the interaction between genetic variability and selective forces creates.

ADAPTATION AND GENETIC VARIABILITY

Whether in the wild or under conditions of cultivation, genetic variation is essential to the adaptive process. Adaptation cannot take place without genetic variability, and the greater part of the variation involved is quantitative. Adaptation is a complex response, affected by many interacting individual and population functions, including morphology, physiology, biochemistry, mating systems and chromosome behaviour, in such a way that these, taken as a whole, render a popula-ion more fit than other populations differently endowed. This is not to imply that the same population is necessarily more fit in its existing habitat than in any other to which it might be transferred or which may result from changes in any one or a number of the various factors which constitute the environment, nor does it imply superior fitness of the members of the population at all stages of development. Genotypes of superior physiological fitness during a period of vegetative growth, for example, may be at a net selective disadvantage because of a lower reproductive rate sufficient to reduce the contribution of that particular genotype to the gene pool of the population.

Adaptation conferred by simple character differences has not been established by experiment. It is unlikely that adaptive traits can be attributed to single or even small numbers of genes. Adaptation to soil nutrient levels (reviewed by Vose, 1963), or tolerance to toxic ions, which has been regarded previously as relatively simply inherited and under the control of one or a few genes of major effect, is now believed to be quite complex. Climatic adaptation, an important con-sideration in plant introduction, probably involves even more complex relationships. Not only are photoperiodic, temperature and vernalis-ation responses involved, but also physiological and morphological responses to changes in soil-moisture regime, and respiratory and photo-synthetic responses to light and temperature levels and cycles. Internal co-adaptive adjustments of the genotype are also involved. The accumu-lation of polygenic modifier complexes may superimpose a quantitative character upon basically oligogenic effects, as in the case of the 'quasi-continuous' variation described by Cooper (1963).

The interaction between phenotype and environment at each successive stage of the individual life-cycle must also be considered as an important aspect of the population-environment interactions which are involved in adaptation and the resultant evolution of ecotypes and races in both natural and cultivated plant populations. In short, experi-ence indicates that not single characters but whole groups of characters affecting the phenotype at many levels and in many ways are responsible for adaptive fitness.

ADAPTIVE LINKAGE AND ECOTYPE FORMATION

A long series of investigations by Sinskaya (1931, 1942 *inter alia*) on ecotype formation in *Medicago sativa* and in species of the family *Cruci-ferae* has examined the ecological and geographical distribution of adaptive character complexes and the manner in which they may become incorporated into the genetic structure of the species. She has described how under certain conditions populations may present a mixture of a very large number of forms, sometimes without any marked or fixed difference in the frequency of separate characters. Adaptive differences are absent, characters may combine randomly, and Sinskaya refers to such forms as 'iso-reagents' in the sense proposed by Raunkiaer (1918) to describe biotypes reacting alike to the same environment. Gregor (1945) has suggested that iso-reagents may be a result of the action of selective pressures upon previous generations under different environmental conditions or of genetic drift in small and more or less reproductively isolated breeding groups. They may also originate as segregation products of crosses which, because they are inter-ecotypic for example, have resulted in the breakdown of adaptive complexes or of close linkages. Whatever their origin, in conditions in which iso-reagents are freely present in the population genetic variance will be high for many traits, correlations will be low and, according to Sinskaya, ecotype formation will not yet have begun.

The crucifer *Eruca sativa*, which is cultivated in Afghanistan as an oil crop, has a wide distribution as a weed from central and southern Europe and north Africa to southwest and central Asia. It occurs as a weed in flax fields in central Asia, the Hindu Kush of northern Afghanistan and in western China. It is an extremely polymorphic species, and in populations in the mountainous areas of Bokhara and northern Afghanistan many forms exist side by side without the marked prevalence of any one of them. In Bokhara, however, the majority of populations exhibit certain distinct character combinations more frequently than others, certain other characters are absent altogether, and character-complexes of adaptive value have become more or less fixed by selection and by genetic linkage, and have been described as 'eco-elements' by Sinskaya. Eco-elements, or groups of biotypes possessing a number of adaptive features which are *genetically linked*, may be regarded as a first stage in the stabilisation of ecotypic populations. Ecotype formation follows by the merging of different eco-elements and their integration into a system of co-adapted traits conferring adaptive advantage to the system of populations involved. In *Eruca sativa* populations from Kashgar in western China certain characteristic character-complexes are present without exception, other forms have been eliminated, and in these fully ecotypic populations genetic variance is low and character correlations are high.

Ecotype formation as outlined by Sinskaya may be slow or rapid depending on the intensity of selection pressures, on the extent to which isolation is a factor, and upon the nature of the breeding system of a species. Evidence has accumulated from other studies, however, to indicate that the rate of ecotype formation may be unexpectedly rapid (see Bennett, 1965). Harland (1948) has suggested that genetic diversity in *Pisum* on the South American continent, far removed from the primary centre of genetic diversity of the genus, is nevertheless sufficiently great to warrant the exploration of the area and the utilisation of the resources which this diversity represents, although *Pisum* was introduced to South America only after the Spanish conquest. Swaminathan (1968) has referred to a similar situation in the case of the cultivated potato in India, and the great diversity of maize in areas far from its primary centre of diversity is well-known. But the evolution of distinct races in crop species in much shorter periods, ranging from some hundred generations to as few as two or three, has also been reported. Baur (1932) and Gregor (1938, 1939) have both demonstrated the maintenance of ecotypic distinctness and the presence of adaptive clines over very short distances in outbreeding species in spite of extensive annual gene-exchange. Thus ecotype differentiation may take place not only rapidly but also in the absence of reproductive isolation.

ADAPTATION AND POPULATION VARIANCE

Anderson (1949) has described in his classical work on introgressive hybridisation how coordinated character-complexes may be transmitted genetically as units and how characters exhibit 'coherence', so that the amount of genetic recombination which follows hybridisation can be markedly less than expected from *a priori* considerations. It has been shown by other studies that adaptive gene-complexes may be built up under the action of selection pressure and conserved by linkage and chromosome inversions and possibly also by direct genetic control of crossing-over, and may function as 'super-genes'. The work of Harland (1936) on cotton which showed that *Gossypium hirsutum* and *G.barbadense* have very many genes in common but differ in the presence of distinct modifier complexes—Harland attributed the lack of success in interspecific crosses to the breakdown of the internal genetic balance in these complexes—was extended by Stephens (1949) to show that the modifier genes are linked and transmitted as coherent groups in minute chromosome inversions.

Population variance has been related by a number of investigators to the intensity of selection experienced by a population and also to population size, the latter itself undoubtedly associated with selection pressure (Fisher, 1937 ; Mather, 1953). It is clear that in addition to the gene-pool as a population parameter defined either in terms of allelic or genotypic frequencies, or by the frequency of adaptive gene-complexes associated with particular ecotypes and of the genetic mechanisms serving to stabilise them, also the genetic variance of populations is of distinct value in the study of adaptation. Not only may it reflect the stages of the adaptive process and of ecotype formation, as we have seen, but it may serve to trace the disruption of adaptive complexes which results from gene-exchange between populations at different stages of ecotypic differentiation and may interrupt ecotype formation at any stage. There is evidence that variance differs between populations of the same species, and that its level is related to adaptive adjustments to selection pressures or to the breakdown of such adjustments, but in either case there is much need for further studies. Anderson (1931) asks, 'for what species can the following simple questions be answered : What is its actual distribution? Does it grow in different situations in different parts of its range? What are the largest and smallest values (of a given character) for the species as a whole? Do values for different localities depart significantly from the mean of the species? Over what part of its range is it the most variable, over what part the least? Are there distinctive forms, and if so what is their comparative frequency in different localities?' The answers to these questions are of great practical importance in exploring the genetic potential of species. For the vast majority of species of economic importance they remain unanswered. Work such as that of Sinskaya may be regarded as providing a pattern for studies in this neglected field.

ADAPTATION A POPULATION CHARACTERISTIC

A further point of some importance emerges from the ecological studies of Sinskaya, and is confirmed by the work of Gregor (1938) on populations of the out-breeding species *Plantago maritima*, which revealed that 'local population differences were not necessarily associated with the presence of peculiar or distinctive growth forms, but were due to changes in the numerical relations between types' of plant growth habit. This is an observation of considerable interest when considering adaptation, and has been recorded for many species. Jones (1967) describes many examples, to which might be added the case of *Medicago sativa* in Anatolia (Christiansen-Weniger and Tarman, 1939), and the striking manner in which primitive wheat populations in Iran and Afghanistan may be distinguished by characteristic frequencies of varieties and forms, which are often quite rapidly re-established if altered by temporary external interference. The analysis of *Eruca sativa* populations in central Asia by Sinskaya offers a mechanism to explain this effect. Huxley, to whom the author is indebted for having brought to her attention the relevance of his discussion on genetic morphism and evolution (1955), shows how morph ratios and ratio clines may be maintained in populations under the action of selection. He cites evidence that selection favours the close linkage of genes associated with related morphic effects, so that gene-complexes or super-genes may become stabilised.

Adaptation is thus seen, more and more, to be a population rather than an individual effect, and is a characteristic of populations rather than of individuals as such.* Although adaptation takes place as a consequence of the effects of environmental selection pressures on the phenotypes of the individuals which make up a population in such a way as to cause the differential survival of the most fit, the quantitative evaluation of adaptive processes must necessarily be by reference to population rather than individual parameters. Reference to the most important of these parameters—the gene-pool and the genetic variance of populations—has been made already. This view of adaptation, however, has practical consequences also. These have a bearing on plant exploration techniques, and upon the enormous, urgent but as yet unsolved problems of genetic conservation.

In the same way that plant breeding and taxonomy have developed vigorously under the impact of population concepts in genetics and genecology, so also must the evaluation of adaptive processes and the utilisation of the gene-pools which are their consequences remain relatively ineffective as long as they are based on observations on merely average, or 'type', material. Populations must be sampled in accordance with statistically valid techniques, procedures of collection and experiment must be designed to reveal population characteristics, utilisation must draw upon the full resources of population variability, and for every individual or sample it is necessary to know to what extent it is representative of the population from which it is drawn. There is a relationship between breeding system and the genetic structure of a

*The physiological and morphological adjustment of individuals to habitat changes, often referred to as adaptation, is better described as acclimatisation.

population, and it is therefore important to know to what extent the breeding system is affected or altered by environmental or other conditions existing in the population under consideration, and to know how this affects the degree of heterozygosity in the population and the nature and stability of its adaptive complexes.

In plant collecting, the size of seed samples which may be considered genetically representative of a population is at present barely known. There exist only the figures suggested by Whyte (1958) and those derived from the work of Allard and his associates, referred to in chapter 8. Apart from these figures, no data exist to guide population sampling. At present, therefore, and until sufficient further studies have been conducted, only by taking large samples can we be reasonably sure that the gene-pool of a population has been adequately sampled and that the conservation of the samples will not be affected subsequently by genetic drift or the effects of differential survival.

VARIABILITY OF WILD AND PRIMITIVE POPULATIONS

One may contrast the variability of natural and primitive cultivated populations with the uniformity of modern cultivars; at the same time their capacities for adaptive response may be contrasted. It is possible to relate the adaptive capacities of wild, primitive and cultivated plant populations to the different adaptive demands of wild, primitive and cultivated environments. To the extent that genetic variability confers adaptability one may speak of it as a desirable feature of populations. There is some evidence to support this view, and it has been the subject of some recent discussions (Hutchinson, 1958; Simmonds, 1962; Bennett, 1965).

Natural plant populations and populations of primitive cultivars are genetically variable, often strikingly so. The greater part of this variability is quantitative despite the importance of some genes of major effect. Quantitative variation, conferred by the synergistic action of large numbers of genes of individually small effect permits sensitive responses to even minor environmental influences. In primitive cultivars this has permitted the evolution of numerous locally adapted races. Primitive cultivars peculiarly also possess adaptive complexes associated with the special conditions of cultivation, pure-stand associations, harvesting and other factors of special interest to plant breeders. Co-existence of host and pathogen populations over long periods of time has led frequently to the evolution of disease resistance, often in the form of 'field' or 'horizontal' resistance ; resistance to *Phytophthora infestans* in potato in Mexico, and the association of rust resistance in *Aegilops* with conditions of high humidity favouring pathogen increase, may be cited as examples.

The quantitative genetic variability which is to be found in natural and primitive crop populations reflects a genetic structure such that, although high levels of heterozygosity are more or less normal, it is also normal for recombination and segregation to take place without excessive departures from the population average which reflects the adaptive norm. The release of adaptively responsive variation is attained along with the maintenance of a continuing level of hetero-zygosity sufficient to ensure that reserves of variability, which appear to be very considerable, continue to exist. Adaptation thus exists side by side with adaptability, and conservation of the adaptive norm of the population side by side with the capacity to deviate from this norm in response to appropriate environmental pressures. It must be assumed that the characteristically high levels of heterozy-gosity which have been found to occur in natural populations, even in in-breeding species (Jain and Allard, 1960 ; Imam and Allard, 1965), constitute evidence either for the selective advantage of heterozygosity *per se* since homozygote advantage can only lead to the final and rapid elimination of unfavourable alleles, or for unusually high rates of heterozygote replacement from inter-population recombination, or mutation, or both. The situation, however, is a sensitive and complex one, as is shown by the studies of the Dobzhansky school and of the Davis group under Allard (see, for example, Allard and Hansche, 1964).

Cryptic genetic variability
Phenotypic uniformity may be an indication of a closely adapted population. Such uniformity does not necessarily reflect genotypic uniformity, however. It may, and very frequently does, conceal con-siderable genetic heterogeneity. In the course of adaptation many different linked associations of genes must accumulate and, as envi-ronments fluctuate, become fixed with different frequencies. Departures from and returns to phenotypic 'adaptive peaks', occasioned by envi-ronmental fluctuations, may frequently be attained by quite new allelic and genotypic frequencies contributing through different complexes to similar phenotypic expression. Only changes in environ-mental selection pressures can reveal such cryptic genetic heterogeneity,

since different genotypes, though phenotypically alike in one environment are not necessarily so in another. The term 'environmental segregation' is proposed for this effect, and it has been described particularly by Sinskaya (1958) and by Cooper (1965). Later papers by Sinskaya (e.g., 1963) draw attention to the need to distinguish between 'disintegration under the influence of habitat changes into separate eco-elements' (environmental segregation) and the effect when populations are exposed to such environmental changes that there is a collapse of homeostatic mechanisms; populations may then show a 'very striking picture of disintegration into several morphological types' beyond the limits of the known variability range for the species.

Waddington (1957) has described how environmental segregation may force 'into expression genetic factors, which although present in the population, remain imperceptible under normal circumstances and therefore inaccessible to selective pressures'. By applying suitable environmental stress it is possible to carry out 'forced selection' for these cryptic differences. It is extremely probable that the flexibility occasionally observed in natural populations and primitve cultivars to sudden changes of environmental pressure such as drought—and in general the fluctuations associated with dry-farming under semi-arid conditions —and disease attacks is attributable in part to their capacity for environmental segregation.

Reserves of cryptic variability are generally high in wild and primitive populations. Although the effects of linkage and the formation of co-adapted gene-complexes limit in practice the almost innumerable theoretical possibilities of genetic recombination, the capacity of such populations for adaptive response remains high.

Phenotypic plasticity
Primitive and wild populations may owe something of their variability also to selection in favour of phenotypic plasticity over long periods in environments experiencing short-term fluctuations. In some primitive cultivars of species associated with certain nitrogen-rich conditions created by human settlement selection may likewise have favoured genotypes with a plastic response since such a response, characteristic of 'special' adaptation, may be expected to result in higher yields and favour survival. To the extent that plasticity shields individuals possessing it from the most extreme effects of adverse selection and at the population level avoids unnecessary adaptive response, it may be

regarded as conservationist in effect. By avoiding adaptive responses which could lead to loss of variability and adaptive fitness, wild and primitive populations may survive in rapidly fluctuating environments and other adverse conditions. Populations in which the capacity of plastic response to environment is present may be expected to retain more genetic variability than would be the case in its absence.

UNIFORMITY OF MODERN CULTIVARS

In contrast with natural populations and populations of primitive cultivars, most modern cultivars are extremely uniform. This imposes limits upon the sensitivity of adaptive responses, which frequently have been remarked upon, even in the case of some out-breeding crops such as cotton (Manning, 1955) and forage varieties in which long periods of selection for uniformity are reflected in a slowing of selection responses compared with those of less intensely selected varieties (Cooper, 1961). In inbreeding crops, the limited responses to selection resulting from uniformity are even more marked.

There is little doubt that the genetic basis of modern cultivars is limited. Indeed, the longer a crop has been subject to selection the more limited is the genetic base, the more so since one of the selection objectives has tended to be uniformity *per se*. Selection is usually intense; it is usually also directional; both are selection characteristics which accentuate the loss of genetic variability normally associated with any selection process. As variability diminishes in crop populations, they become less able to respond adaptively to environmental selection pressures. This has been pointed out as a serious defect of modern cultivars. When Simmonds (1962), for example, rightly cast doubt upon the ideal of strictly uniform crop populations, an ideal already criticised by Frankel (1950) as inimical to the attainment of highest production, he remarks at the same time that 'success or failure depends upon adaptability in the crop, that is upon the provision of recombinational variability'.

But such a view neglects one striking aspect of the differences between modern cultivars and populations of their wild or primitive precursors, namely that they do not *need* to respond *adaptively* to their environments. With few exceptions, such as when perennial crops are grown for seed, or when annuals are grown as perennials by regular self-seeding, modern cultivars are produced from new seed more or less regularly each season.

It is in the breeding stocks of modern cultivars that evolution takes place, and these fortunately possess a greater range of variability than the uniform cultivars which arise from them. This difference between breeding stocks on the one hand and crops on the other is most important in considerations of adaptation. Nevertheless, it is absurd to imagine that the peculiarly limiting genetic history of most modern cultivars does not affect to some extent the variability available in breeding stocks, and possibly only mass breeding techniques based upon hybridisations on a large scale—such as polycross or composite crossing techniques—may in the end adequately extend available variability. The evaluation of data emerging from such techniques, however, presents some practical problems.

In connection with the adaptation of modern cultivars two further points of practical interest arise. In the first place, close adaptation of modern cultivars to their environment is difficult to attain. The environments which crops occupy are many times more numerous and diverse than the environments of the relatively few centres in which they originate, in spite of the general uniformity of environments under modern conditions. Selection for 'general' rather than 'special' adaptation characteristics (Finlay and Wilkinson, 1963), or in other words, for constancy of phenotypic expression rather than plasticity, may offer a solution to this.

In the second place, there is no doubt that crops must face certain unexpected and sudden environmental changes which, within the course of a season, may partially or even totally destroy a uniform crop. Evidence from synthetic and multiline varieties (Jenkin, 1931 ; Jensen, 1952 ; Borlaug, 1957) which are phenotypically uniform but genetically heterogeneous indicates that these mixtures can exploit environmental variation more effectively than normal cultivars. The genetic differences which are concealed by a phenotypic uniformity—which, to some extent, crops must possess—may be released under the stimulus of environmental change. Such multilines, or synthetics, may well possess the kind of variable responses under the impact of such adverse environmental changes as disease epidemics, drought and frost that may permit crop survival in otherwise impossible conditions.

ENVIRONMENTAL DIVERSITY AND CROP EVOLUTION

Environments in which primitive and modern cultivars occur may be contrasted in a somewhat similar manner as the populations which inhabit them. Environments created by advanced agricultural practices are, unlike those under primitive conditions, uniform and widespread. Frankel (1959) points out that not only is the number of components of the environment reduced, but also that the variation of each is under some degree of more or less effective control. There is a steady trend towards increasing uniformity. Thus, although adaptation in wild populations leads to the genetic fractionation of species into locally variant populations to a very considerable degree indeed, increasing ecological uniformity is itself a significant factor contributing to genetic uniformity in cultivars.

When man first began as a settled cultivator to establish the habitats his crops required, a change of the utmost genetic consequence in the character of the environment emerged. This was the effect of habitat disturbance which is a consequence and, indeed, the aim of cultivation. The sustained disturbance of cultivated land surfaces, and particularly the origin of countless locally varying transitions between cultivated and non-cultivated environments, created new ecological opportunities for successful hybridisation, introgression and mutation on an unparalleled scale. New possibilities of genetic contact and gene exchange between cultivated populations and their wild and weed relatives arose, and made possible the acquisition of vast new sources of commensal germ plasm and the broadening of the genetic basis of practically every cultivated species. As a result, countless locally adapted races of cultivated species emerged—an incalculable wealth which remained unknown until the explorations of Vavilov and his colleagues in the early decades of this century.

GENETIC RESOURCES

Adaptive origin of genetic resources

The Neolithic revolution was the spark to an unprecedented evolutionary explosion, which only the contemporary advances of uniform agricultural varieties and practices have been able to halt. The range of differentiated agro-ecotypes (Gregor, 1933) in primitive cultivars is as extensive as the manner of their countless separate adaptive origins would indicate, and can be attributed to the extraordinarily sensitive nature of the adaptive response. Ecological differentiation of populations of several wheat species in the basin and the islands of the Mediterranean, for example, was shown by Schreiber (1934) to be reflected in the existence of numerous distinctive forms differing in straw length and strength, earliness, tillering capacity, resistance to disease, and many other characteristics. From one valley to the next in Afghanistan,

Triticum aestivum populations display differences in awning, pubescence, straw thickness and other traits which are associated with differences of aspect, altitude, soil moisture regime, cultural practices and social isolation. Collections of *Vicia sativa* races from Greece and Turkey show striking local and ecological differentiation with marked differences even between populations from neighbouring villages. Vavilov and Bukinich (1929), Zhukovsky (1933), Vavilov (1951) and numerous other authors from Vavilov's institute (e.g. Flaksberger, 1935 ; Sinskaya, 1961), and increasingly from other parts of the world, have described the varietal diversity and adaptive variability of most of man's crops sufficiently to show that local adaptive differentiation in primitive cultivars is general to such an extent that to catalogue its full range is probably not possible. Yet this should be attempted, because the range of adaptive capacity which it represents is now most seriously threatened by genetic erosion.

Urgent need for conservation
It is an irony that before our priceless genetic resources have been even adequately explored, let alone conserved or utilised, increasing environmental and genetic uniformity associated with rapidly advancing standards of agriculture should be stifling the evolutionary process which created them, and that their destruction should coincide with a period of virtually unlimited possibilities of genetic recombination on a world scale. Genetic resources stand now in the greatest danger of irretrievable extinction. Of the races described by Vavilov and his co-workers only a fraction remain, and the rate of extinction is increasing. Within the context of the wide horizons which the new possibilities of utilisation open out before us, our urgent aim must be to conserve whatever adaptive genetic variability short-sighted 'advances' have not already dissipated. There is some irony also in the practical thought that it should be necessary to turn to the primitive cultivars of the past, created unconsciously by the labours of our unnamed and uncultured forbears, for the solution of what might well be tomorrow's greatest single problem—the problem of feeding the human species in the midst of the technological wealth it has created.

REFERENCES

ALLARD R.W. & HANSCHE P.E. (1964) Some parameters of population variability and their implications in plant breeding. *Adv. Agron.* **16,** 281–325.
ANDERSON E. (1931) Internal factors affecting discontinuity between species. *Am. Nat.* **65,** 144–148.

ANDERSON E. (1949) *Introgressive Hybridization*. Wiley and Sons, New York.

BAUR E. (1932) Artumgrenzung und Artbildung in der Gattung *Antirrhinum* Sektion *Antirrhinastrum*. *Z. indukt. Abstamm. –u. Vererb. Lehre.* **63,** 256–302.

BENNETT E. (1965) Plant introduction and genetic conservation: genecological aspects of an urgent world problem. *Rec. Scott. Pl. Breed. Stn.*, 27–113.

BORLAUG N.E. (1957) The development and use of composite varieties based upon the mechanical mixing of phenotypically similar lines developed through backcrossing. *Rep. III Int. Wheat Conf.* 12–18.

CHRISTIANSEN–WENIGER F. & TARMAN O. (1939) Anatolian lucerne. *Herb. Rev.* **7,** 59–69.

COOPER J.P. (1961) Selection and population structure in *Lolium*. V. Continued response and associated changes in fertility and vigour. *Heredity* **16,** 435–453.

COOPER J.P. (1963) Species and population differences in climatic response. In *Environmental Control of Plant Growth* (Ed. Evans L.T.), 381–403. Academic Press, New York.

COOPER J.P. (1965) The evolution of forage grass and legumes. In *Essays on Crop Plant Evolution* (Ed. Hutchinson J.B.), 142–165. Univ. Press, Cambridge.

FINLAY K.W. & WILKINSON G.N. (1963) The analysis of adaptation in a plant breeding program. *Aust. J. Agric. Res.* **14,** 742–754.

FISHER R.A. (1937) The relation between variability and abundance shown by the measurements of the eggs of British nesting birds. *Proc. Roy. Soc. B* **122,** 1–26.

FLAKSBERGER C.A. (1935) *Flora of cultivated plants of the U.S.S.R.* **1,** *Cereals: Wheat*. State Agric. Publ. Company, Moscow and Leningrad.

FRANKEL O.H. (1950) The development and maintenance of superior genetic stocks. *Heredity* **4,** 89–102.

FRANKEL O.H. (1959) Variation under domestication. *Aust. J. Sci.*, **22** 27–32.

GREGOR J.W. (1933) The ecotype concept in relation to the registration of crop plants. *Ann. appl. Biol.* **20,** 205–219.

GREGOR J.W. (1938) Experimental taxonomy. II. Initial population differentiation in *Plantago maritima* L. of Britain. *New Phytol.* **37,** 15–49.

GREGOR J.W. (1939) Experimental taxonomy. IV. Population differentiation in north American and European sea plantains allied to *Plantago maritima* L. *New Phytol.* **38,** 293–322.

GREGOR J.W. (1945) Comments on Sinskaja's paper 'The species problem in modern botanical literature'. (Unpublished typescript.)

HARLAND S.C. (1936) The genetical conception of the species. *Biol. Rev.* **11,** 83–112.

HARLAND S.C. (1948) Inheritance of immunity to mildew in Peruvian forms of *Pisum sativum*. *Heredity* **2,** 263–269.

HUTCHINSON J.B. (1958) *Genetics and the Improvement of Tropical Crops*. University Press, Cambridge.

HUXLEY J. (1955) Morphism and evolution. *Heredity* **9,** 1–52.

IMAM A.G. & ALLARD R.W. (1965) Population studies in predominantly self-pollinated species. VI. Genetic variability between and within natural populations of wild oats from differing habitats in California. *Genetics* **51,** 49–62.

JAIN S.J. & ALLARD R.W. (1960) Population studies in predominantly self-pollinated species. I. Evidence for heterozygote advantage in a closed population of barley. *Proc. Natn. Acad. Sci. Washington* **46,** 1371–1377.

JENKIN T.J. (1931) The method and technique of selection, breeding and strain-building in grasses. *Bull. Imp. Bur. Pl. Genet. Herb.* **3,** 5–34.

JENSEN N.F. (1952) Intra-varietal diversification in oat-breeding. *Agron. J.* **44,** 30–34.

JONES D.A. (1967) Polymorphism, plants and natural populations. *Sci. Prog.* **55,** 379–400.

MANNING H.L. (1955) Response to selection for yield in cotton. *Cold Spring Harb. Symp. quant. Biol.* **20,** 103–110.

MATHER K. (1953) The genetical structure of populations. *Symp. Soc. Exp. Biol.* **7,** 66–95.

RAUNKIAER C. (1918) Uber den Begriff der Elementarart im Lichte der modernen Erblichkeitsforschung. *Z. Indukt. Abstamm. -u. Vererb. Lehre* **19,** 225–240.

SCHREIBER D. (1934) Wheats of the islands of the Mediterranean. *Bull. Appl. Bot. Genet. Pl. Breed. Ser. V.* **2,** 41–240.

SIMMONDS N.W. (1962) Variability in crop plants, its use and conservation. *Biol. Rev.* **37,** 422–465.

SINSKAYA E.N. (1931) The study of species in their dynamics and inter-relation with different types of vegetation. *Bull. Appl. Bot. Genet. Pl. Breed.* **25,** 1–91.

SINSKAYA E.N. (1942) The species problem in modern botanical literature. *Usp. sovrem. Biol.* **15,** 326–359 (transl. Fox H., I.A.B. Cambridge).

SINSKAYA E.N. (1958) Investigations on the composition of ecotypical and varietal populations. *Rep. Scott. Pl. Breed. Stn.,* 31–40.

SINSKAYA E.N. (Ed.) (1961) *Flora of Cultivated Plants of the U.S.S.R.* **13,** Part I. I.P.S.T. Jerusalem.

SINSKAYA E.N. (1963) The problem of populations in higher plants. 2. *Trudy vses. Inst. Rast.* (extended summary in English by Comm. Bur. Pl. Breed. Genet. Cambridge).

STEPHENS S.G. (1949) The cytogenetics of speciation in *Gossypium.* I. Selective elimination of the donor parent genotype in interspecific backcrosses. *Genetics* **34,** 627–637.

SWAMINATHAN M.S. (1968) In *Proceedings FAO/IBP Technical Conference on the Exploration, Utilisation and Conservation of Plant Genetic Resources.* (Ed. Bennett E.), p. 38. FAO, Rome.

VAVILOV N.I. (1951) The origin, variation, immunity and breeding of cultivated plants. *Chron. Bot.* **13,** 1–364.

VAVILOV N.I. & BUKINICH D.D. (1929) *Agricultural Afghanistan.* Institute of Applied Botany, Leningrad.

VOSE P.B. (1963) Varietal differences in plant nutrition. *Herb. Abstr.* **33,** 1–13.

WADDINGTON C.H. (1957) *The Strategy of the Genes.* Allen and Unwin, London.

WHYTE R.O. (1958) *Plant Exploration, Collection and Introduction.* Agricultural Study No. 41. FAO, Rome.

ZHUKOVSKY P.M. (Ed.) (1933) *Agricultural Turkey.* Acad. Sci. U.S.S.R., Moscow.

11

ENVIRONMENTAL PHYSIOLOGY

J. P. COOPER
Welsh Plant Breeding Station,
Aberystwyth

INTRODUCTION

Crop production consists basically of the conversion of solar energy and soil nutrients into economic end-products which may be either human or animal foodstuffs or industrial raw materials. The basic limitation to production is, therefore, the seasonal energy input from the sun, but the ability of the crop to make use of this energy is often limited by other climatic factors, such as low temperature or water stress, or by the availability of soil nutrients.

From a knowledge of the environmental limits to production in a particular locality, and the present level of crop production, it should be possible to assess the relative potentialities of either modifying the crop environment, or selecting better adapted varieties, or both. Certain environmental limitations can be avoided by such measures as irrigation or increased fertilizer input, including the application of trace elements. On the other hand, such climatic features as the seasonal light and temperature regime, including photoperiod, and seasonal precipitation cannot be modified by the farmer and the only solution may be selection of adapted genetic material often with appropriate life cycles which synchronise with the seasonal climatic inputs.

In assessing the potential production of a crop in a particular region, we need to know (i) the environmental limitations to production, both climatic and edaphic, and (ii) the extent to which crop varieties can be developed which are adapted to these environmental limitations. This, in its turn, involves an assessment of how far adaptation, and hence potential production, can be increased by the introduction of new genetic material.

ENVIRONMENTAL LIMITS

A. CLIMATIC FACTORS

(i) Energy input

The primary climatic limitation to production is the seasonal input of solar energy. This is influenced primarily by latitude, being comparatively uniform throughout the year near the equator, but varying tenfold or more at latitudes above 50° (Black, 1956). Singapore, for instance, has 400–450 cal/cm²/day of total radiation for most of the year, while the range in Britain is from a December mean of about 50 to 400–450 in June. It is also modified by the degree of cloudiness, which is often related to the rainfall. The highest total energy inputs are found in intermediate latitudes under Mediterranean or semi-arid conditions; seasonal values in Algiers range from 200 in winter to 700 in summer while in Deniliquin, N.S.W. the corresponding values are 250 to 750. At high latitudes, particularly in maritime climates as in the west of Britain, low light energy may be as important as low temperature in limiting production in the winter. The daylength or photoperiod, which varies regularly with latitude, is also important, since as well as influencing daily energy input, it serves as an important developmental switch in controlling such processes as flowering and tuberisation.

(ii) *Temperature*
The seasonal distribution of temperature in general follows that of energy input, though usually with a time-lag of 1–2 months. Under lowland tropical conditions, a steady mean temperature of between 25° and 30°C is often maintained, with a comparatively small daily range, while the highest temperatures occur in desert or semi-arid regions at intermediate latitudes. Khartoum, for instance, has daily maxima over 35°C for most of the year, and a daily range of about 15°C. High latitudes, particularly on large land masses, are also characterised by a wide temperature range, both between day and night, and between winter and summer. In Moscow, for instance, the mean January temperature is −9°C, with a daily range of 6.5°C, and the mean July temperature is 19°C with the daily range of 12°C. Seasonal temperatures are, however, also modified by altitude, by distance from the sea and by the regular movement of air masses, as with the large increase in temperature over the northwest coast of Europe, compared to similar latitudes elsewhere. The temperature distribution not only influences the rate of growth and assimilation of the crop, but extremes of high or low temperature may determine the actual survival of the crop. High temperatures are usually associated with a high energy input, and hence with a high potential evapo-transpiration. Furthermore, in many temperate species, low temperatures (below 5°C) may have important developmental effects on the induction of flowering and breaking of seed dormancy.

(iii) *Water balance*

The water balance is determined primarily by the seasonal precipitation and by the evapo-transpiration of the crop, though in any particular climatic environment it will also be influenced by the water-holding capacity of the soil, particularly particle size and content of organic matter. In general, evapo-transpiration is closely related to the seasonal energy input, and, unfortunately, high energy input and water deficit are often closely associated. In the Sudan, with a high and uniform energy input, a potential evapo-transpiration of about 6 mm/day (about 2200 mm/year) has been reported, while in Britain the values range from below 0.3 mm/day in winter to over 3 mm/day in the summer, with an annual total between 400 and 500 mm. A number of methods have been suggested for estimating the water balance or degree of drought stress from temperature or radiation data and from precipitation records. These range from the comparatively simple Meyer indices based on seasonal records of temperature and saturation deficit, to the more detailed formula of Penman (1963) and Thornthwaite and Mather (1955) based on estimates of the energy balance through the year. The latter can be used for indicating the periods of water deficit through the year, and hence predicting irrigation needs.

B. EDAPHIC FACTORS

Edaphic limitations operate largely through their influence on the availability of water and nutrients, and although many of them can be modified by the farmer, the selection of adapted genetic material is also important. The influence of soil structure, particularly particle size and content of organic matter, on water-holding capacity has already been mentioned, and soil structure and water content also affect the seasonal course of soil temperature.

Of the major plant nutrients, nitrogen is usually limiting except under very intensive cropping systems, and phosphorus and potash may well be so. In temperate climates, the effects of calcium are often confounded with those of soil pH. In most cases, however, major nutrients are not so deficient as to prevent the growth of the crop completely, and the level of fertiliser application is determined by economic, rather than biological requirements. Deficiency of minor elements, such as copper, zinc and molybdenum, however, may often lead to the complete failure of the crop. This is particularly so in old impoverished soils, which have not been previously cropped, as in many parts of Australia (Stephens and Donald, 1958). It may be possible to select crops or varieties which are not susceptible to the deficiency (Vose, 1963), but usually once the deficiency is recognised, the cost of application of the small quantities required is soon recouped. The presence of toxic elements such as aluminium, manganese and selenium, or of increasing degrees of salinity calls for a different approach. The removal of these elements is usually not possible and the selection of resistant genetic material is often the only solution. Adaptation to soil pH is intermediate since although the pH can be modified by liming, the selection of varieties adapted to lower or higher pH is often practicable.

The important environmental limitations will therefore differ with the climatic region. In most tropical environments there are few temperature limitations, and the energy input and photoperiod are fairly uniform throughout the year, but there may be some seasonal shortage of water, particularly in savanna climates. In semi-arid and Mediterranean environments, on the other hand, the energy input and temperatures are higher, with a greater seasonal range, and drought, either seasonal or irregular, is the most important climatic limitation. At more extreme latitudes, above 45°, with a greater seasonal range in energy input, the chief limitations become winter cold and/or light energy; water is often adequate through the year.

CROP ADAPTATION

(i) *Developmental cycles*
Where seasonal climatic limitations exist, an important approach is to select genetic material whose development cycles are synchronised with the seasonal variations in climate. The developmental cycles required will depend not only on the time and extent of such climatic features as drought or winter cold, but also on whether the crop is annual or perennial and on the form of the economic end-product, whether grain, tubers or leaves.

Many important crop species, including the cereals and grain legumes, are annuals grown for seed and it is important to synchronise their period of flowering and grain production with the most favourable growing season. In a Mediterranean environment, for example, wheat and barley are sown in the autumn, and grow actively through the winter, but in the absence of irrigation, must produce grain before drought begins in the early summer. Similar life cycles are required in annual forage species, such as subterranean clover (Donald, 1960). In Northern continental climates, on the other hand, winter cold is usually the main limiting factor, and summer-annual varieties must be used; these are sown in the spring and ripen in late summer, thereby making use of the high energy input of the summer at high latitudes. In maritime climates, such as the British Isles, where there are fewer limitations of winter cold or summer drought, either winter or spring cereals can be used, depending on the particular cropping system in use. These differences between locally-adapted varieties in the timing of inflorescence development are usually based on developmental response to temperature and photoperiod. Most temperate cereals are long-day plants requiring photoperiods longer than a certain critical value before they can develop heads. Northern varieties of wheat and barley have a long critical photoperiod, and many winter-annual forms require exposure to winter conditions of cold and/or short day before they can flower. By contrast, Mediterranean varieties of wheat and barley have a comparatively low photoperiod requirement and need no winter exposure. Similarly, in rice, locally adapted varieties, grown in the summer monsoon season in the tropics, show latitudinal clines of photoperiodic response, controlling the time of maturity of the crop (Oka, 1958). In contrast, more recent varieties, grown under irrigation, tend to be insensitive to photoperiod and regularly early-maturing.

Similarly, up to 600 years ago all the cultivated cottons were frost-susceptible perennial shrubs, and the crop was confined to frost-free tropical areas. Each of the four cultivated species, however, contained sufficient variation for the selection of forms which fruited early enough to give a useful yield in the first season. Such forms could then be grown as annuals, not only in regions such as China, North India and Iran where the growing season is limited by winter frost, but also in regions such as the Sudan, with hot dry summers. Most of the world's cotton crop now consists of such obligate annuals (Hutchinson, 1959).

In other annual field crops, such as potatoes and sugar beet, the economic end-product consists of vegetative roots or tubers; flowering and seed production may be disadvantageous. Sugar beet for root production is usually sown in the spring, to avoid the flowering and seed development which follows natural vernalisation during the winter; varietal differences in the tendency to bolt following an early spring sowing, are based on variation in the cold requirement for vernalisation. In the potato, the length of the growing season is limited by frost in most environments; tuberisation is under photoperiodic control, early, medium and late varieties differing in their daylength response, but the highest yields are obtained if tuber formation in short days has been

preceded by a period of active assimilation during the long days of
summer.

In an annual field crop, the climatically unfavourable season can
often be avoided without great loss in potential yield by appropriate
dates of planting and harvesting, particularly at high latitudes, where
winter cold is usually associated with low energy input. In a perennial
crop, on the other hand, the plant itself must survive periods of climatic
stress, often through winter or summer dormancy. In perennial forage
grasses, such as perennial ryegrass and cocksfoot, Mediterranean
ecotypes often show a degree of summer dormancy while remaining
active in the winter. If transferred to more northerly climates, they may
be killed by severe winter cold. In contrast, Northern varieties of the
same species usually become winter dormant with considerable cold
resistance, but grow actively in the long days and high temperature of
summer. They usually cannot survive the drought of the Mediterranean
summer (Cooper, 1963).

Similarly, in many deciduous forest trees, growing in temperate
regions, the timing of bud break in the spring and leaf fall in the autumn
is based on response to photoperiod and temperature, and is usually
related to the climatic limitations of the place of origin (Wareing,
1956).

Where there are few or no climatic limits, as in the wet tropics,
either continually bearing perennials, such as oil palm or rubber, or a
succession of short duration crops, such as rice, may provide the greatest
annual production.

(ii) *Photosynthetic activity*

In spite of the large seasonal variation in energy input in many
regions, comparatively little is known of the variation in photosynthetic
activity *within* crop species, although considerable differences exist
between species in light saturation level and maximum photosynthetic
rate (Hesketh and Moss, 1963). Many temperate crops including cocksfoot, red clover, white clover and perennial ryegrass reach light saturation
of the individual leaf at 2–3000 ft candles, well below summer light
intensity at midday. Many sub-tropical species, however, such as
maize, sugar cane and sunflower can continue to increase their photosynthetic rates up to light inputs of 6000 ft candles or more, with a
correspondingly greater maximum photosynthesis. Other crops such
as alfalfa, are intermediate between the temperate and sub-tropical
group. Similar variation in maximum photosynthesis of the individual

leaf has been reported *within* crop species; in perennial ryegrass, for instance, differences of over 50% have been reported; high altitude ecotypes appear to have particularly high light saturation levels (Wilson and Cooper, 1967). Similarly, in sugar cane, individual genotypes differ in their maximum photosynthesis and also in the length of time it can be maintained. Such differences may well be important in determining potential production when other environmental factors are not limiting.

(iii) *Temperature responses*

The temperatures required for assimilation and vegetative growth, and for plant survival, differ between species and varieties. In many temperate crops such as wheat, barley and perennial ryegrass the optimum temperature for both dry matter accumulation and extension growth is around 20–25°C, and there is some activity at 5°C; but for many tropical and sub-tropical species, such as maize, sugar cane and *Paspalum*, the optima are considerably higher, 30–35°C, and little growth or assimilation occurs below 10–15°C. Variation within species, particularly at low and high temperatures, is often related to the climatic origin of the material. In many temperate forage grasses and legumes, leaf expansion at moderately low temperatures (5–10°C) is more active in Mediterranean ecotypes than in Northern varieties, but with correspondingly less frost resistance in the Mediterranean material (Cooper, 1963). Similarly, the degree of cold hardiness in temperate cereals varies considerably, being greatest in continental winter varieties, while, in maize, the ability to germinate satisfactorily at low temperatures is an important component of adaptation to northerly latitudes.

(iv) *Water stress*

Although many crops possess life cycles which allow them to avoid drought limitations, species and varieties also differ in their ability to survive or continue growing under conditions of water deficit (May and Milthorpe, 1962). There are two main ways in which a plant can cope with water stress. Firstly, it can continue to grow at a fairly high plant turgidity either by increasing the root range, thereby tapping a greater supply of available water, as in sorghum compared to maize, or it can reduce transpiration by closing the stomata at moderate water stress, as in alfalfa compared to cotton (Van Bavel, 1967). Alternatively, it can allow plant turgor to decrease, and become dormant except for well

protected buds, as in Mediterranean ecotypes of cocksfoot and other
perennial grasses during the summer drought.

(v) *Nutrient response*

Although the nutrient input is more closely under the control of the
farmer, crop species and varieties differ in the uptake and utilisation of
many of the major and minor nutrients (Vose, 1963). It is important to
distinguish between differences in response to fertiliser application in
terms of dry matter production, and differences in uptake, leading to
higher concentrations of the nutrient in the plant. It is often possible
either to select material which can produce a high dry matter yield
with a low input of the particular nutrient, or to find plants which can
concentrate that nutrient in the economic end-product, often with a
lower total dry matter production. The balance between these two
alternatives will depend on the chemical composition required in the
final product. For a malting barley, for instance, the ability to take up
and concentrate nitrogen is undesirable, but for a forage grass, which is
to be used for production as well as maintenance, this character may be
an important breeding objective. In the same way, certain forage grass
varieties can take up and concentrate large amounts of sodium or
iodine, which may be important in animal nutrition. The physiological
bases of such differences are not clear, but in some cases, differences in
cation exchange capacity are involved.

Similarly crop species and varieties differ in their resistance to or
toleration of toxic elements such as aluminium and manganese and/or
in their response to salinity. Resistant varieties may take up less of the
toxic element, or be able to tolerate a greater internal concentration
(Vose, 1963).

A special case of variation in nutrient response lies in the degree of
nodulation and *Rhizobium* activity in legumes, where the environmental
response of both the bacteria and of the host are important. Legume
genotypes differ in their ability to nodulate, but the *Rhizobia* also vary
in their infectivity and ability to fix nitrogen, and both show differential
response to pH and soil temperature (Norris, 1956).

Enough has been said to indicate the range of variation available to
the plant breeder in those physiological characteristics which make for
adaptation to local environmental limitations, and hence for high
energy and nutrient conversion. Unfortunately, little is known of the
ecological pattern of variation for many of these characters, and more
information is urgently required, particularly in tropical crops.

OPERATIONAL SEQUENCE

From a knowledge of the environmental limitations to production, and the adaptation of crop species and varieties to these limitations, an operational sequence can be drawn up for the collection and introduction of new genetic material, as outlined by Cooper (1966) for forage grass breeding in Britain.

The first step is to specify the environmental limitations, both climatic and edaphic, of the locality where the crop is to be grown. This involves records of the seasonal distribution of solar radiation, temperature, precipitation and evapo-transpiration. Such information is usually available in temperate regions which have a long established agricultural history and adequate meteorological records. It is often difficult to obtain in less developed areas, particularly in the tropics and sub-tropics. Most classifications of climate, such as that of Köppen, are based on the seasonal distribution of temperature and precipitation. For many agronomic purposes, these need to be supplemented by records of seasonal energy input, which make it possible to calculate the seasonal water balance, and to predict the potential production. The next stage is to assess how far these limitations can be overcome by modification of the crop environment, such as irrigation or increased fertiliser input, or how far they must be met by selection of better material. These are not necessarily alternatives; an improved environment will usually require improved varieties. In rice, Oka and Chang (1964) have pointed out that intensive cultivation, with irrigation and high fertilizer input, has been associated with the selection of photoperiodically insensitive forms, with regular early maturity, and high nitrogen response.

Those characteristics of the crop which are needed for more effective adaptation can now be specified; they may include such features as cold resistance, resistance to water stress, a shorter or longer life cycle or more effective fertiliser response. The collection of potentially adapted material from appropriate locations can then be effectively planned.

In many crops, primitive cultivated forms and their wild relatives have a wider ecological range, and are often adapted to more extreme climatic and edaphic conditions and, although themselves of low productivity, often prove a valuable source of variation for the plant breeder (Zohary, 1965). In the potato, for instance, certain primitive cultivated species, such as *Solanum juzepczukii* and *S.curtilobum*, grown

F

at 3500 m and above in the high Andes, are highly frost resistant, while others, such as *S.phureja* from the lower east facing valleys, have no tuber dormancy and can be grown throughout the year. The wild species show an even greater range of adaptation, from drought and heat-resistant species growing at or near sea level, to frost resistant types, such as *S.acaule* from over 4000 m in the high Andes and *S.demissum* in Central Mexico (Hawkes, chapter 23).

Similarly, in wheat and barley, locally adapted Indian or Mediter-ranean varieties, though of low yield, have proved valuable sources of genes for early maturity and short life cycle, providing adaptation to a short growing season, whether limited by summer drought, as in southern Australia (Frankel, 1954) or by winter cold as in Canada.

In the forage grass *Phalaris tuberosa*, which is now grown extensively in Australia, collections of wild populations from the Mediterranean have revealed a wide range of variation in flowering and dormancy responses, related to the length of the potential growing season as limited by summer drought. This wild material is now being used to develop varieties with improved seasonal production and range of maturity for Australian conditions (C S I R O, 1967).

Such wild or primitive forms can also provide valuable sources of genes for disease resistance as in the field resistance to *Phytophthora infestans* from the wild potato, *Solanum demissum*, or resistance to crown and stem rust and to mosaic and barley yellow dwarf virus in collections of *Avena sterilis* from Israel (Murphy *et al.*, 1967); or for important biochemical characters, such as higher protein content from local Indian varieties of ground nut, or higher protein and vitamin C content in some of the primitive cultivated potatoes from South America.

For new environments and/or new crops, as in Australia and New Zealand over the past century (Frankel, 1954), introduction from homologous climates elsewhere may be valuable, but is not necessarily the only or the most useful source of improved material. The success of *Pinus radiata* in New Zealand and parts of Australia, and the use of Mediterranean ecotypes of forage grasses to provide increased winter production in Britain are examples of the value of plants from rather different climatic environments. In the case of climatic limitations such as cold or water stress, it is already possible to predict useful sources of genetic material, and this should be feasible in the future for variation in other physiological attributes such as photosynthetic activity or nutrient response. This prediction on an ecological basis of the most useful sources of variation is not, however, possible for such features as disease resistance or chemical composition, and for these characters wide collection followed by intensive screening is likely to be most useful.

Although some introductions, such as subterranean clover in Australia, may be of immediate use to the farmer, most introduced material requires incorporation into a breeding program before its full value can be realised. Most of the characteristics responsible for local climatic and edaphic adaptation show polygenic control and can be selected and combined by the usual methods of the breeder and geneticist. Even so, difficulties may arise through the association of desirable and unfavourable features in the introduced material, as in the marked correlation between winter growth and frost susceptibility in Mediterranean ecotypes of forage grasses (Cooper, 1963), and that between short straw and shrunken grain in the Japanese Norin dwarf wheats (Krull and Borlaug, chapter 37).

REFERENCES

Black J.N. (1956) The distribution of solar radiation over the earth's surface. *Arch. Met. Geophys. Bioklim.* **B7,** 165–189.

Cooper J.P. (1963) Species and population differences in climatic response. In *Environmental Control of Plant Growth* (Ed. Evans L.T.), 381–403. Academic Press, New York.

Cooper J.P. (1966) The use of physiological variation in forage-grass breeding. *Proc. 12th Easter Sch. agric. Sci. Univ. Nott.* 293–330.

Commonwealth Scientific and Industrial Research Organization. (1967) New horizons for phalaris. *Rur. Res. C.S.I.R.O.* **59,** 2–10.

Donald C.M. (1960) The influence of climatic factors on the distribution of subterranean clover in Australia. *Herb. Abstr.* **30,** 81–90.

Frankel O.H. (1954) Invasion and evolution of plants in Australia and New Zealand. *Caryologia,* Suppl. to Vol. **6,** 600–619.

Hesketh J.D. & Moss D.N. (1963) Variation in the response of photosynthesis to light. *Crop Sci.* **3,** 107–110.

Hutchinson J.B. (1959) *The application of Genetics to Cotton Improvement.* Cambridge University Press, London.

May L.H. & Milthorpe F.L. (1962) Drought resistance of crop plants. *Fld. Crop. Abstr.* **15,** 171–179.

Murphy H.C., Wahl I., Dinoor A., Miller J.D., Morey D.D., Luke H.H., Sechler D. & Reyes L. (1967) Resistance to crown rust and soil borne mosaic virus in *Avena sterilis. Pl. Dis. Reptr.* **51,** 120–124.

Norris D.O. (1956) Legumes and the Rhizobium symbiosis. *Emp. J. exp. agric.* **24,** 247–270.

Oka H. (1958) Photoperiodic adaptation to latitude in rice varieties. *Phyton. B. Aires.* **11,** 153–160.

Oka H. & Chang W.T. (1964) Evolution of responses to growing conditions in wild and cultivated rice forms. *Bot. Bull. Acad. sin., Taipei.* **5,** 120–138.

PENMAN H.L. (1963) Vegetation and hydrology. *Tech. Commun. Commonw. Bur. Soil Sci.* **53**, 1–124.

STEPHENS C.G. & DONALD C.M. (1958) Australian soils and their responses to fertilizers. *Adv. Agron.* **10**, 167–256.

THORNTHWAITE C.W. & MATHER J.R. (1955) The water balance. *Publs. Clim. Drexel Inst. Technol.* **8**, 1–104.

VAN BAVEL C.H.M. (1967) Changes in canopy resistance to water loss from alfalfa, induced by soil water depletion. *Agric. Met.* **4**, 165–176.

VOSE P.B. (1963) Varietal differences in plant nutrition. *Herb. Abstr.* **33**, 1–13.

WAREING P.F. (1956) Photoperiodism in woody plants. *Ann. Rev. Pl. Physiol.* **7**, 191–214.

WILSON D. & COOPER J.P. (1967) Assimilation of *Lolium* in relation to leaf mesophyll. *Nature, Lond.* **214**, 989–992.

ZOHARY D. (1965) Colonizer species in the wheat group. In *The Genetics of Colonizing Species* (Eds. Baker H.G. and Stebbins G.L.), 403–419. Academic Press, New York.

GENERAL REFERENCES

WHYTE R.O. (1960) *Crop Production and Environment.* 2nd Ed. Faber & Faber, London.

WILSIE C.P. (1962) *Crop Adaptation and Distribution.* W.H. Freeman & Co., San Francisco and London.

CLIMATE AND CROP DISTRIBUTION

WILLIAM HARTLEY

Commonwealth Scientific and Industrial Research Organization,
Australia.

Any student of the evolution of the crop plants must be struck by the contrast between the very extensive areas of cultivation of the major crops and the very restricted regions in which they are believed to have originated and in which their wild relatives are found as native species. Notwithstanding many intensive studies—archaeological, taxonomic, genetical and cytological—the precise origin of many of our major crops remains obscure, but in other instances it has been found possible to trace their evolution with some precision, and we have a fair knowledge of both the past and present distribution of the more important parental species from which they were derived. Several examples are discussed in the present volume, and notably in the 'Essays of Crop Plant Evolution' edited by Hutchinson (1965). While the evolutionary pathways appear to be characterized by diversity rather than by uniformity, it appears that most of our major crops have come into cultivation in one or a few restricted regions, and have been derived mainly from one or a few wild species each with a restricted range and rather narrow climatic limits.

As pointed out by Hutchinson : 'One of the major consequences of domestication is an enormous increase in the area of distribution of the species'. The early distribution of the crop plants was associated with the migration of peoples and the spread of cultures, and, especially in the 18th and 19th centuries, with the discovery and settlement of new regions. Some of the stages of this distribution, as reflected in the present cultivation pattern of different crops, have been discussed by Kupzow (1965). During the last century the spread of crop plants has owed much to planned programs of introduction and exploration, and to the work of plant breeders in the development of new cultivars. These new cultivars frequently include in their parentage cultivars from other parts of the world, differing greatly in climate from the regions for which they have been developed. Thus the major wheat cultivars of the prairie regions of Canada have been produced by breeding from cultivars originating in regions as widely separate and as climatically diverse as Poland, India, Russia, Australia, England, Egypt and Portugal (Knott, 1967).

Although, as noted above, most of the crop plants appear to have been derived *mainly* from a few wild species, their spread has been paralleled by the spread of associated weed species, many of which are closely allied taxonomically with the crop species concerned. There is evidence that these weed species 'have served as reservoirs of reserve germ plasm, periodically injecting portions of it into the crop under conditions that would most favor increase in variability, heterozygosity and heterosis' (Harlan, 1965).

Notwithstanding their wide distribution, the cultivated crop plants are by no means ubiquitous. They are absent from many parts of the world, at least as plants of economic significance. This is partly due to social and economic factors, such as food preferences in different regions, distance from suitable markets, etc., but partly also to limited climatic adaptability (Kupzow, *op. cit.*). It is therefore of interest to consider how far this apparent lack of climatic adaptability reflects inherent limitations in the pool of germ plasm from which they have been developed, including not only that of the putative parents but also that of related taxa which have had a common origin in the near or distant past.

Such information on the genetic and evolutionary basis of climatic adaptability could be of direct value to those engaged in plant introduction and plant exploration. A major factor in improving the yield of any crop or in extending its range is the introduction of genes or gene blocks which will improve its adaptation to the environment in which it is to be grown. Such adaptation is invariably polygenic, and the genes contributing to it cannot readily be recognised in natural or artificial populations.

Where, then, are they to be sought? Should one look for genes contributing to cold or drought tolerance in 'homoclimes' or in the major gene centres of the crop plant concerned? Are there, indeed, true 'gene centres' for characters of ecological significance? And what, if any, are the climatic and other environmental limits to crop plant adaptation?

Unfortunately, the data for such a study are at best sketchy and inadequate. While it is possible to obtain reliable statistics and maps showing the commercial production of the major crops, little or no detailed information is available about their domestic production for home consumption. This gap is especially important for many of the tropical and sub-tropical crops in which a high proportion of the production is home-consumed.

It would have been desirable to compare the climatic limits of the crop plants with those of the wild species from which they are believed to have originated, and the weed and other species with which they have hybridised in the course of their development. Here again the information is inadequate and conflicting. As noted by Harlan in the present volume : 'With all the genetic and cytogenetic work that has been done on wheat, we still have only the sketchiest knowledge of the geographic distribution and ecological behaviour of the wild species that have contributed their heredities to the evolution of wheat'.

It is, however, possible to make a useful comparative study of the distribution of some of the crop plants of the family *Gramineae* and that of the larger taxonomic units—the genera and tribes—of which they form part. Not only are these plants of major economic importance, with a long history of cultivation and ample opportunity to spread throughout the world, but studies in recent years have done much to clarify relationships in the family at all taxonomic levels. Further, there is evidence that the distribution and relative specific differentiation of some of the larger tribes is closely related to climatic factors (Hartley, 1964).

A survey has been made of the present distribution and regions of concentration of barley, oats, rice and sugar cane as cultivated crops, and of the distribution and areas of relative specific concentration of the genera and tribes to which they belong. These four crop plants have been selected because they cover a wide range of climatic adaptability, from tropical and subtropical to temperate ; they include three annuals and a perennial, three grain cereals and a plant used vegetatively (sugar cane), and they belong to four different tribes of the family as currently recognised. Wheat is not included because of the apparent complexity of its phylogeny, but one may note the conclusion of Riley (1965) : 'Apparently each step in the polyploid evolution of the genus has permitted adaptation to new environmental situations and has resulted in the extension of its geographical distribution and agricultural utilization'. It should be noted that the areas of specific concentration are those in which species of the genus or tribe concerned form the highest proportion of the total grass flora, and are therefore not necessarily the areas in which most species occur. It has been shown elsewhere (Hartley, 1950) that this concept of relative species concentration provides a useful basis for studies of climatic factors in relation to distribution.

The results of this survey are given in Tables 12.1 to 12.4.

It is evident from the data presented in these Tables, and especially from study of distribution maps, that each of the crop plants discussed has a distribution which is subject to climatic limitations. For three of the crops these limitations are primarily those of temperature. Barley and oats are restricted to the extra-tropical regions except at high altitudes, while sugar cane is primarily tropical and sub-tropical and, outside the tropics, is confined to frost-free areas. Temperature is also of some importance in the distribution of rice, which is absent from cold regions at high latitudes, but the more important factor is the availability of an ample supply of moisture during the growing seasons, either through high rainfall or irrigation.

The distribution of the genera to which these crop plants belong shows broadly similar climatic restrictions. *Hordeum* and *Avena* occur widely in the extra-tropical zones of the northern and southern hemispheres either as native or naturalized genera, but, as with the respective crop plants, are absent from the tropics except in the higher (and cooler) regions. *Saccharum* has a more restricted natural distribution confined to the eastern hemisphere, but does not extend into the higher (and colder) latitudes. *Oryza* has a fairly wide latitudinal range, but is conspicuously absent from arid regions.

However, these broad similarities of pattern in the distribution of the crop plants and their congeners conceal significant differences. In each instance the crop is cultivated beyond the geographical—and apparently also beyond the climatic—limits within which the genus occurs as a constituent of the native or naturalised flora. Thus barley is intensively cultivated in the Ganges Valley, although the genus *Hordeum* does not extend into the Indian Peninsula beyond the north-west corner (Bor, 1960). Oats are grown commercially in the south-eastern United States, although species of *Avena* are naturalised only in the more northern and western parts of the country (Hitchcock, 1950). The areas in which rice is cultivated in northern Italy and Hokkaido are beyond the latitudinal limits of *Oryza* in the native flora.

In contrast to the genera, the distributions of which are limited by historical as well as climatic factors, the tribes occur more widely, with a distribution pattern which more clearly reflects climatic influences. The tribes *Triticeae* and *Aveneae* have distribution limits which do not differ greatly from those of the genera *Hordeum* and

TABLE 12.1 Distribution and centres of concentration of barley and its related taxa.

		Distribution	Centre(s) of Concentration
Crop	Barley	Grown mainly in the middle latitudes of the northern hemisphere (22°–63°N), extending into drier and colder regions than other grains. In the southern hemisphere mainly grown in Argentina and southern Australia. Absent from the tropics except in the highlands of Mexico, north-western South America and east Africa (van Royen, 1954).	Main areas of dense cultivation north and west of the Black Sea, Denmark, Morocco, middle and upper Ganges Valley (India), Korea, north central U.S.A., southern Manitoba, Alberta and California (van Royen, 1954).
Genus	*Hordeum*	Occurs throughout the extra-tropical regions except for parts of northern Mexico, the plains of northern India, parts of eastern South Africa, and western and central Australia. Absent from northern Siberia and throughout the tropics except for the Andean region of western South America.	Main relative specific concentration in the north-eastern Mediterranean region and Asia Minor, from northern Yugoslavia to Israel and Iraq.
Tribe	*Triticeae*	Occurs throughout the temperate and cold regions of both hemispheres. Absent from the tropical and sub-tropical zones (27°N to 39°S) except for the highlands of northern Mexico, western South America, Ethiopia and Yemen.	Highest relative specific concentration south and east of Lake Balkash in Kazakstan, surrounded by a zone of high concentration extending longitudinally from the Black Sea to Mongolia and latitudinally from Afghanistan to northern Kazakstan. A second area of specific concentration occurs in the western prairies and mountains of Canada and northern U.S.A. (Saskatchewan, Alberta, Montana.)

F*

TABLE 12.2. Distribution and centres of concentration of oats and its related taxa.

		Distribution	Centre(s) of Concentration
Crop	Oats	Cultivated mainly in the north temperate zone between latitudes 30°N and 63°N, especially in areas with a cool and damp climate. Also in the southern hemisphere south of 30°S (Argentine, southern Chile, Uruguay, southern Australia). Rare in subtropical regions, and absent from the tropics except occasionally at high altitudes in Central and South America (van Royen, 1954).	Areas of dense cultivation mainly in north-western Europe, the north central and north-eastern U.S.A. and southern Manitoba, Saskatchewan, and Alberta (van Royen, 1954).
Genus	*Avena*	Occurs throughout the extra-tropical zone except at high latitudes (north of 55°N) in Siberia, parts of Kazakstan between the Aral Sea and Lake Balkash, and southeastern U.S.A. Occurs more frequently than *Hordeum* in the tropics, but mainly at higher elevations in South America, east tropical Africa and Malaysia.	Main relative specific concentration in the western Mediterranean countries (Spain, southern France, Morocco). Second area of concentration in the southeastern Mediterranean (Israel, northern Egypt), and outlying high concentration in the Caspian Sea region.
Tribe	*Aveneae*	Throughout the extra-tropical zone at all latitudes. Generally absent from the tropics except at higher elevations in Central and South America, east central Africa, and Malaysia.	Main relative species concentration in the western Mediterranean region (northern Italy, southern France, Spain, Morocco). Second area of species concentration in the eastern Baltic region, from Sweden to southern Finland and adjacent parts of U.S.S.R.

TABLE 12.3. Distribution and centres of concentration of rice and its related taxa.

		Distribution	Centre(s) of Concentration
Crop	Rice	Cultivated in all lowland and hill areas of the tropics where sufficient rain or irrigation water is available. Extends in the northern hemisphere to latitude 46°N in northern Italy, Manchuria and Hokkaido, and in the southern hemisphere to latitude 35°S in Australia. Absent from cold regions at high latitudes and from non-irrigated dry regions (van Royen, 1954, Guidry, 1964).	Main density of cultivation in south-eastern and eastern Asia, especially in southern and eastern India, East Pakistan, southern Burma, Thailand, Vietnam, southern and eastern China, Japan, Philippines, and Indonesia. Local concentration in the Nile Delta, in the Po Valley (Italy), in Louisiana, and in California (van Royen, 1954).
Genus	*Oryza*	Occurs throughout the tropical zone between the tropics of Cancer and Capricorn, except at high elevations (e.g., Andes) and in arid regions (Sahara, Arabia, Southwest Africa, central Australia). Occasionally adventive in the warm temperate regions (e.g., south-eastern U.S.A.). Absent from the cool temperate and cold regions at latitudes above 40°N and 25°S.	Main relative specific concentrations in the Indo-Malayan region from Burma to New-Guinea, with subsidiary concentrations in East Africa (Tanganyika), and in northern Brazil (Tateoka, 1962, 1963).
Tribe	*Oryzeae*	May be present or absent in all latitudinal zones, but occurs consistently in regions with good summer rainfall (eastern U.S.A., West Indies, most of tropical Africa south of the Sahara, eastern and south-eastern Asia). Absent from the cold and arid regions of Siberia, the Sahara region, South West Africa, western and central extra-tropical Australia.	No well-defined centres of high relative specific concentration. Isolated high values in tropical West Africa (Sierra Leone), in the Indo-Malayan region (Ganges Delta, Borneo, Philippines), and in east tropical America (Venezuela, Florida, South Carolina, British Honduras).

TABLE 12.4. Distribution and centres of concentration of sugar cane and its related taxa.

		Distribution	Centre(s) of Concentration
Crop	Sugar cane	Cultivated everywhere in the moist and wet tropics except at high altitudes, but commercial cultivation mainly in the latitudinal belt of 10°–30°, northern and southern hemispheres. Susceptible to frost and absent from higher altitudes (van Royen, 1954).	Cultivated intensively in northeastern India, Java, Philippines, Formosa, Queensland, Natal, West Indies, Louisiana, eastern Mexico, eastern Brazil, and Hawaii (van Royen, 1954).
Genus	*Saccharum*	Occurs in the tropics and sub-tropics of the Old World (40°N to 10°S) from central Africa to Japan and Melanesia. Naturalised in the American tropics (West Indies, Central America, Brazil) and in Natal, Madagascar, Mauritius, Queensland and New Caledonia. Absent from the temperate and cold regions beyond latitudes 45°N and 30°S.	Main specific concentration in northern India and the southern Himalayas between 67°E and 90°E, and 20°N and 33°N (Mukherjee, 1957).
Tribe	*Andro-pogoneae*	Occurs throughout the tropical, sub-tropical and temperate regions below latitude 48°, except in parts of California. Infrequent at higher latitudes and absent from most parts of Siberia, Scandinavia, northwestern Europe and Canada.	Main relative specific concentrations in the monsoonal regions of Bombay (India) and southeastern Indonesia. High concentrations in other parts of India, in southeast Asia from Vietnam to New Guinea, and in parts of central Africa (Hartley, 1958).

Avena at lower latitudes, but which extend to include regions in which barley and oats are cultivated but where the genera do not occur in the wild flora. Both tribes extend to higher latitudes in the northern hemisphere and include areas, notably in north-western Asia, where barley and oats are cultivated, but from which the respective genera are absent as uncultivated plants.

The tribes *Oryzeae* and *Andropogoneae*, which include the genera *Oryza* and *Saccharum*, both have a much wider natural distribution than the genera concerned. They include many areas of cultivation of rice and sugar, especially in the western hemisphere, where the genera are absent from the wild flora.

Most significant is the fact that the areas of cultivation of barley, oats, rice and sugar cane are all in regions in which the respective tribes form part of the wild grass flora, although each of these tribes is limited climatically in its global distribution. The only exceptions to this are a few areas (e.g., the Murrumbidgee Irrigation Area in south-eastern Australia) where rice is grown under irrigation but where species of the tribe *Oryzeae* do not occur in the wild state. In such instances, irrigation may be considered to have created an artificial climate.

If there is a general correspondence between the climatic limits of the crop plants and those of the genera—and more especially the tribes—to which they belong, there is no similar conformity between the areas of dense cultivation of the crops and the areas of maximum relative specific concentration of the respective genera and tribes. Such conformity is not indeed to be expected, largely because the areas of dense cultivation are influenced by many economic and social factors which are quite different from those which determine taxonomic diversity.

The main areas of cultivation of barley and oats lie outside and usually in higher latitudes than the centres of specific concentration of *Hordeum* and *Avena*. Rice and sugar cane are both intensively cultivated in the regions of high specific concentrations of *Oryza* and *Saccharum* respectively, but are also grown intensively in other parts of the world where the genera are absent or represented only by one or two species.

There is only a slightly better conformity between the regions of high specific concentration of the tribes and those in which the derived crop plants are intensively cultivated. While the centres of maximum specific concentration of the *Triticeae* and *Aveneae* in central Asia and the western Mediterranean region respectively are not areas of intensive cultivation of barley and oats, these tribes have secondary centres of specific concentration in the prairie region of north America and in the Baltic States, which correspond more closely to regions of intensive crop cultivation. There is no well-defined centre of specific concentration of the tribe *Oryzeae*, but the regions of high specific concentration of the *Andropogoneae*, in India and south-eastern Asia, include some areas of intensive sugar cane cultivation.

CONCLUSIONS

The crop plants barley, oats, rice and sugar cane are grown commercially in many parts of the world which are geographically distant and climatically different from the regions in which they are believed to have originated. While species of the genera to which they belong occur as wild plants in most of the regions in which they are cultivated, this is not universally the case, and in some instances the crop has extended in cultivation beyond the limits of the congeners either as wild or naturalised plants. On the other hand, the crops do not extend beyond the geographical and climatic limits of the tribes to which they belong, although the tribes themselves show fairly well-defined climatic tolerances.

Thus in so far as the restricted climatic tolerance of these crop plants reflects the limitations of the germ plasm from which they have been developed, it would appear that these limitations are phylogenetically derived from, and are those of, the larger taxa, including especially the tribes from which they have evolved.

This conclusion, if accepted, does not provide firm answers to the queries raised earlier in this chapter. It does perhaps suggest that genes contributing to climatic adaptability should be sought in those regions where the corresponding genus or tribe is richly represented as well as at the gene centre of the species itself or in the homoclimes of the area for which adaptation is required. It may also suggest that it would be wise to have regard to the climatic limits of the tribes and genera in considering the possibilities of extending the range of cultivated crops. Taking into consideration the natural distribution of the *Oryzeae* and *Triticeae*, for instance, it may be concluded that there would be better prospects of developing rice cultivars with cold tolerance than with drought tolerance, and better prospects of extending barley cultivation into cool, dry regions than into tropical ones. The spread of cultivation of these crops in recent years offers some support for these conclusions.

REFERENCES

BOR N.L. (1960) *Grasses of Burma, Ceylon, India and Pakistan.* Pergamon Press, Oxford.

GUIDRY N.P. (1964) *A Graphic Summary of World Agriculture.* U.S.D.A. Misc. Publ. No. 705 (revised).

HARLAN J.R. (1965) The possible role of weed races in the evolution of cultivated plants. *Euphytica* **14,** 173–176.

HARTLEY W. (1950) The global distribution of tribes of the Gramineae in relation to historical and environmental factors. *Aust. J. agric. Res.* **1,** 355–373.

HARTLEY W. (1958) Studies on the origin, evolution, and distribution of the Gramineae. I. The tribe Andropogoneae. *Aust. J. Bot.* **6,** 115–128.

HARTLEY W. (1964) The distribution of the grasses. In *Grasses and Grasslands* (Ed. Barnard C.), Macmillan & Co Ltd, London.

HITCHCOCK A.S. (1950) *Manual of the Grasses of the United States* (2nd edit. revised by A. Chase). U.S.D.A. Misc. Publ. No. 200.

HUTCHINSON J. (1965) Crop plant evolution: A general discussion. In *Essays on Crop Plant Evolution* (Ed. Hutchinson J.), Cambridge University Press, Cambridge.

KNOTT D.R. (1967) The story of prairie wheat varieties, 1812–1966. Univ. of Saskatchewan (mimeo.).

KUPZOW A.J. (1965) The formation of areas of cultivated plants. *Z. Pfl.zücht.* **53,** 53–66.

MUKHERJEE S.K. (1957) Origin and distribution of *Saccharum. Bot. Gaz.* **119,** 55–61.

RILEY R. (1965) Cytogenetics and evolution of wheat. In *Essays on Crop Plant Evolution* (Ed. Hutchinson J.), Cambridge University Press, Cambridge.

VAN ROYEN W. (1954) *The Agricultural Resources of the World.* Prentice-Hall Inc, New York.

TATEOKA T. (1962) Species of the genus *Oryza. Nat. Sci. Mus. Tokyo* **29,** 1–12.

TATEOKA T. (1963) Taxonomic studies of *Oryza.* III. Key to the species and their enumeration. *Bot. Mag., Tokyo* **76,** 165–173.

SECTION 2
TACTICS OF EXPLORATION
AND COLLECTION

13

TACTICS OF PLANT EXPLORATION

ERNA BENNETT

Crop Ecology and Genetic Resources Branch, F A O, Rome

Plant exploration has an essentially practical function. It hardly seems necessary to stress that without the raw materials which it is the function of exploration to provide to the plant breeder mankind would face a very serious situation indeed. But this is not to say that exploration has not a part, and even a major part, to play in the resolution of a number of fundamental problems concerned with the origins and utilisation of genetic variability in plant species, nor that these problems are not themselves of the greatest practical importance.

At the present time the loss of genetic resources is taking place so rapidly that there is cause for grave concern for numerous crop races in the centres of diversity—one might even say with some justification, 'centres of former diversity'. Reference to the collections described by Vavilov and his colleagues, and to more recent collections made in the Mediterranean, the Near East and in central Asia, shows that many local races of wheat and other crops, described by the earlier expeditions, have now disappeared from their native habitats or have become rare, and the same is the case in other parts of the world.

Only extensive cooperation on the widest possible scale between workers in many disciplines and in many countries can prevent the extinction of resources essential to present and future generations. Cooperation and the systematisation of plant exploration, which have been desirable for many years, have now become necessary. Plant exploration based upon the easy-going empiricism of the past has neither the capacity nor the authority to meet the demands of the present situation; it is still something of a personal art with a strong element of the subjective and the 'hunch' about it. The need to formulate basic and standard procedural patterns with the capacity to absorb, integrate, preserve and make available the data of exploration missions is now urgent.

In specific terms, plant exploration may be seen to have the dual role of making available for utilisation the greatest possible amount of genetic variability in cultivated and related non-cultivated species, while at the same time revealing the range of variability of which a species is capable and its ecological and geographic distribution. The basis upon which systematic and objective exploration procedures may be established with these objectives is already provided by the phytogeographic method of Vavilov (1951). Stages in the phytogeographic study of variation in plant species, widely applied with striking success by Vavilov and his school (see Sinskaya, 1961), may be stated briefly as follows : (1) Classification of collections into species and genetic groups making use of all available criteria, including morphology, genetics, physiology, ecology and distribution. (2) Determination of distribution, and identification of the original habitats and areas occupied by these groups. (3) Determination of the total range of genetic variability within species. (4) Determination of those parts of a species' distribution in which the greatest intra-specific variability is to be found, and particularly the geographic centres in which endemic characters are most numerous. (5) Determination of similar patterns in cultivated and non-cultivated species (Vavilov, *loc. cit.*).

To the extent that data resulting from the application of the phytogeographic method can be documented and systematically retrieved, such as in the computer-based system for the storage and retrieval of genetic information on plant resources currently proposed by FAO and the International Atomic Energy Agency, it may provide a base upon which exploration programmes of increasing precision and efficiency may be mounted. At the same time, the corresponding collections will serve to meet the growing need of plant breeding programmes for something more than the haphazard fragments of species that have been available in the past. In the sections which follow, certain basic aspects of the 'mechanics' of exploration and collection procedures are outlined to provide a pattern for action in the immediate future— action which it is hoped will itself create conditions for the formulation of more detailed and developed principles of exploration.

THE TIME FACTOR

Time is a dominant consideration. In spite of the accelerating depletion of genetic resources, there is a calculable limit to the amount of material which can be collected in a given time, and this is determined by purely physical factors. Most expeditions are of relatively short duration, and however undesirable this might be, it is a feature which is unlikely to change greatly in the next few decades during which the greatest demands are likely to be made upon world exploration effort. In any case, even in areas where altitudinal or latitudinal range is wide and the collecting season is relatively prolonged, it is not common for this to last much longer than three or four months of the year. Against this, even under the most favourable conditions it is rarely possible to maintain a sampling intensity of 10 to 20 samples a day of one species for each collecting team. Seasonal averages are generally distinctly lower. At the United Nations Crop Research Centre at Izmir in Turkey, situated within a centre of genetic diversity for many species, with a staff possessing specialised local knowledge of terrain and flora, well-equipped with transport and scientific facilities, it was often possible to have four separate teams in the field at the one time. Nevertheless, it was not possible to maintain a daily average of 50 samples, even though the normal mission from this institute had a multi-species objective. The FAO wheat mission in Afghanistan, though frequently sampling as many as 15 crops in a day, averaged less than 10 a day over the whole season. Such figures refer to an average working day in the field of ten hours or more, and a seven-day week.

An upper limit to the number of samples it is possible to collect in one season, therefore, can be set somewhere close to 1,000 assuming ideal conditions and detailed synchronisation of the mission with crop maturity in every region. The conclusion seems unavoidable that if even a fraction of the crop races which face extinction is to be salvaged, not only must strict regional and species priorities be established but plant exploration must receive wider attention and support than it does at present. Considerations of economy alone, whether in terms of cost or effort—both seriously limited—indicate that *ad hoc* exploration missions should yield to coordinated international activity on a cooperative basis. The same considerations argue the necessity of applying standard plant exploration and collection techniques.

ECOLOGICAL FACTORS AND EXPLORATION

Ecological factors are a major determinant of genetic diversity. Cultivated plants no less than wild species display ecotypic differentiation in response to their habitats (Gregor, 1933); such 'agroecotypes' are, however, most clearly to be distinguished in primitive cultivars which are habitually renewed from local seed, while the ecotypic characteristics of modern cultivars are associated with their habitats of origin. Climatic factors such as maximum and minimum average temperatures, daily and annual temperature range, the annual distribution of temperatures, precipitation and the seasons of dormancy and growth, light intensity, and day-length are all reflected in corresponding developmental characteristics. They also lead to a generally clinal distribution of variation patterns. Topographically and edaphically determined differentiation may show either a clinal (most typically with altitudinal differences) or a mosaic distribution.

Parallel ecotypic differentiation is to be found in diverse and unrelated groups of cultivated plants exposed to similar habitats (Vavilov, 1940). The same parallelism in wild ecotypes led Turesson (1922) to propose experimental taxonomic categories within species to describe the ecotypic forms characteristic of certain types of habitat; the categories 'oecotypus alpinus', 'submontanus' and 'alluvialis' refer taxonomically, for example, to the ecotypic forms characteristic of alpine, sub-montane and lowland habitats respectively. Although these categories have not been adopted generally in taxonomy, they have been applied with success to the taxonomy of cultivated plants by Sinskaya (1961) *inter alia*. Ecotypic parallelism is of great interest in plant exploration, and is a valuable guide in exploration planning. It underlines the importance of studies of the physical habitat as well as of genetic variation and its distribution.

By way of illustration we may refer to the Iranian-Turkestan agroecological region which, according to the classification of Vavilov (1957), comprises the Soviet central Asian republics, northeast Iran, northern Afghanistan and the western Chinese province of Sinkiang. This region is distinguished by an extremely hot and arid climate with summer drought, fierce and persistent drying winds and relatively severe winters. Ecotypes of many different taxa of cultivated plants in this region typically possess a low or semi-prostrate habit with weak shoot development, slow early growth, drought resistance at maturity, and extreme susceptibility, when grown under less arid conditions, to fungal diseases. Wheats are commonly short and coarse strawed, coarsely glumed and awned, difficult to thresh and possess other speltoid characteristics. Here we have found strikingly drought-resistant non-shattering ecotypes of *Triticum aestivum* widely distributed in the dry-farming areas of northeastern Badakhshan, local selections of which equal the best of the introduced high-yielding Mexican wheats in yield, and far surpass them in quality and germinability of the grain. Semi-prostrate or bushy ecotypes of barley, flax and *Medicago sativa* s.l., rapidly maturing and drought-resistant, are also found.

In other agroecological regions similar relationships between climate and the general nature of the indigenous ecotypes may be seen.

In the Mediterranean region, which possesses an exceptionally mild climate with autumn, winter and spring precipitation, cool winters and hot, extremely dry summers, sowing is usually done in the autumn ; cereal ecotypes are winter forms marked by particularly vigorous growth, leguminous crops produce distinctively large seed, and disease-resistant forms occur in many crops. In the Caucasian region, Vavilov reports, increasing rust-resistance in wheat collections made from east to west through the region is associated with a steady decrease in aridity in the same direction. A similar increase in the incidence of rust-resistance is to be seen as the observer moves from the Iranian-Turkestan region through Baluchistan to Pakistan and central India.

Within agroecological regions sub-divisions may be recognised which are determined by local variations of climate, soil, topography or cultivation pattern. Thus within the Iranian-Turkestan region, in the lower reaches of the Amu-Darya river which for a thousand kilometers forms the border between Afghanistan and the U.S.S.R., separated from its source in the snows of the Pamir mountains by expanses of arid steppe and the Karakum desert, the late arrival of spring flood-waters has led to the evolution of particularly late-developing ecotypes. The same effect, though less marked, is to be observed in some of the more isolated oases of northern Afghanistan. In the oases themselves one may find— in contrast with the drought-resistant ecotypes characteristic of the region as a whole—ecotypes of more erect habit, which show striking responses to irrigation and soil fertility. Thus the erect *Medicago* of the Herat oasis in western Afghanistan, *M.asiatica* subsp. *geratica*, with its stouter stems and surface branching may be contrasted with the semi-prostrate, deeper-branching *M.asiatica* subsp. *kandagoro-kabulica* mountain ecotype. Certain cereal ecotypes which have become rather widely diffused as cultivars in Afghanistan perform indifferently when water is scarce, but their cultivation under oasis conditions permits the realisation of latent yield potential and the release of variation. Among such may be mentioned the relatively high-yielding *Triticum turgidum* varieties Zafraní and Mowrí and the *T. aestivum* variety known locally in the Herat oasis as Kalak. In the same way the sweet melon, *Cucumis melo*, which is not widely grown outside the oases, shows the remarkable diversity for which it is noted in this region within the major oases of Herat, Mazar-i-Sharif and particularly Kunduz. Despite the high rust-susceptibility of the wheats and other crops of this generally arid agroecological region it is possible that in the oases and humid river valleys devoted to rice cultivation, where we have frequently recorded relative humidities at midday of more than 95 percent, the search for rust-resistant ecotypes might be most successful.

Altitude differences account for other local departures from the general conditions of an agroecological region. Indeed, quite frequently in the search for the ecological correlates of a genetic distribution pattern altitude intrudes so forcibly as to eclipse other possible factors. In the first place, it is a matter of the ecological tolerance of a species and its ecotypes. The adaptive characteristics of an ecotype may sometimes appear to be solitary if striking deviations from the species' ecological range, or extensions of it, and may require ranking as sub-species. While this may be a secondary effect of isolation and the fixation of recessive characters as in the case of the eligulate wheats and other cereals of the northern Pamirs and Badakhshan, it also reflects the extraordinary persistence of generations of primitive cultivators who, over the centuries have forced cultivated species to their ecological limits and beyond, so much so that in the high northeast of Badakhshan, the Pamirs and in Ladakh dried fruits of the mulberry and apricot, fruits normally confined to very much lower altitudes, form with wheat, barley and rye a large part of the staple diet of the population at an elevation of 4,000 meters and above, where night temperatures lie perpetually below 0°C.

Secondly, some high altitude effects may have a more direct origin than the long process of ecotypic differentiation under such markedly adverse conditions. Schiemann (1951) has drawn attention to the possibility that ultra-violet radiation may account for the occurrence of certain high-mountain endemic forms. Temperature shock and radiation may significantly increase mutation rates. *Inflatum* forms of *T. aestivum* in Afghanistan are only found at high elevations or, as pointed out by Ufer (1956), in the wake of severe frost shock and are not, for this reason, given taxonomic status by him. Clearly, such effects may be important sources of variation, even within those agroecological regions not noted for their diversity of habitat, and data relating to them may greatly enlarge the information base of exploration planning.

Ecotypic differentiation may take place as readily in response to cultivation practices as to climatic and other physical habitat characteristics. The evolution of large-seeded, non-dehiscent forms of *Camelina sativa* described as subsp. *linicola*, mimicking the flax in which it occurs as a weed and with which it is harvested, described by Zinger (1909) and Sinskaya and Beztuzheva (1931), provides a classical example. Many similar cases of such mimic variation in wild or weed species have been described.

Developmental and morphological characteristics which have evolved in cultivated plants in response to harvesting customs are even more striking. In the cereals, resistance to sprouting in the ear can be related to the practice of delayed harvesting or threshing in areas affected by rains or heavy dews at harvest time. In the high plateau of Badakhshan, however, where cereals are commonly sown immediately after threshing, post-harvest ripening of the grain is virtually absent; if these races of cereals are grown in more humid climates serious germination in the ear occurs. Throughout eastern Anatolia and south-central Asia it is common for the semi-nomad farmers to leave ripe cereal crops standing in the field for some time, or to allow the harvested crop to lie before threshing. This is a probable cause for the evolution of the many forms of *Triticum aestivum* and *T.compactum* characteristic of the whole area in which the grain is tightly invested by the glumes and is extremely difficult to thresh. Leguminous and brassica crops are also typically non-shattering, as are *Vicia sativa*, *V.villosa* and other weed species present in these crops. In the extreme north of Afghanistan some forms of *Gossypium herbaceum* in which the ripe boll remains closed may still be found in isolated villages. The high-altitude cereals of the Hindu Kush and the Koh-i-Baba mountains of central Afghanistan afford a contrast. The growing season is short and early frosts annually threaten and frequently destroy the thin, ripening crops. Crops are harvested immediately they mature. Glumes are thin and membranous. The grain is lightly invested, usually partly exposed, and sheds with great ease. High-mountain ecotypes of *Secale cereale*, particularly, resemble the northern European forms of the species and differ markedly from the *rigidum* forms generally characteristic of the region.

PLANT EXPLORATION AND POPULATION SAMPLING

The distribution of genetic variability in crop plants, then, is far from uniform. This is especially so in the case of primitive crop races. Although the agroecological characteristics of a region afford a general guide to plant exploration, it is clear that only detailed local knowledge of habitat variations within regions can provide a reliable basis for exploration planning. The same may be said with regard to sampling and collection.

Not only are habitat variations within agroecological regions often considerable, and ecotypic variation correspondingly great, but population structure is often complex. One must speak of ecotypic populations rather than of ecotypes, typified more by morph ratios than by the exclusive occurrence of distinctive forms. The ecotypes characteristic of a habitat represent rather a dominant facet than the exclusive facies of its populations. This may be illustrated by the *Medicago* populations which are to be found in Ladakh in the Karakorum mountains. Here, under the severe conditions occasioned by the high altitude of more than 4,000 meters, *Medicago* populations are quite uniform with respect to such traits as slow spring growth, early autumn dormancy and quite exceptional drought- and cold-resistance, but in many other respects, including plant habit, pubescence, leaf colour and shape, and disease-resistance, they are extremely heterogeneous. These populations may be regarded as mixtures of ecoelements which retain their heterogeneity as a result of recombination between the separate ecotypic components of a varied environment uniform only in terms of extreme exposure and the adverse selection pressures which go with it. Such situations are probably quite general. The frequency of genes and linked associations of genes varies widely and in a complex manner from population to population in response both to the diverse environments encountered by a species throughout its range and to gene-flow between populations; it is high when ecotypically dominant characteristics are concerned and may be low or zero in other cases.

Field sampling procedures in plant exploration are aimed at the fullest possible recovery of the genetic variation of species, irrespective of the relative frequency or rarity of any genes or linked genetic complexes, and the complexities of genecological distributions raise many difficulties. For any character, population variances are generally unknown and vary greatly from one habitat to another. In addition, ecotypic distribution data are still fragmentary. The size of sampling unit varies with every sample ; and the operational sampling unit, which is the field, does not correspond with the actual unit of ecotype distribution which is more often the village or a river basin, or isolated valley. With so many unknown variables accurate statistical analysis of sampling techniques is not possible.

In practice, however, some form of random sampling is usually employed, which may be modified to meet the demands of specific objectives. Approximate estimates of sampling error are therefore possible, since we know that the standard error of a sample of n individuals is given by

$$s = \frac{\sigma}{\sqrt{n}},$$

where σ is the standard deviation of the population. This expression may be corrected for samples drawn from finite populations by the term $\sqrt{(1-f)}$, where f is the sampling fraction, or the fraction of the total population represented in the sample :

$$s = \frac{\sigma}{\sqrt{n}} \sqrt{(1-f)}.$$

However, if f is small, as is almost invariably the case in crop sampling with the possible exception of tree crops and of wild species with sparse distributions, the correction factor may be ignored. Sampling error is at a minimum when samples are large, though incremental decreases in error are dependent on large increases in sample size. It can also be seen that when population variance is high, sample size should be increased.

In the case of genes and gene-complexes of rare occurrence, for which a Poisson distribution may be assumed, the more serious problem exists that if from a population of, say, 1,000,000 plants of which 50 individuals carry a rare character a sample of 500 plants is drawn, the character will not be represented in the sample in more than 97 percent of cases. For a character which is visible in the field, the problem may be resolved by supplementing the random sample with a second, biased sample, made by deliberately selecting all rare phenotypes, which can usually be detected visually at quite low frequencies of the order of ·01 percent or less in cereals and other field crops. The two samples are bulked unless required for separate study. Zagaja (1968), referring to the special problems encountered in sampling tree fruits where random sampling would lead to impossibly large numbers of trees, describes similar biased sampling techniques. Such techniques, of course, do not lead to the recovery of recessive genetic traits present in the population in the heterozygous state beyond those recovered by the random component of the sample where, as we have seen, the frequency of recovery may be low.

Biased sampling procedures which do not supplement random sampling, and plant collections based on phenotypic selection, have a number of defects. In general, phenotypic performance is little guide to genetic distinctness. Occasionally, many-tillered plants may be seen in thin and poorly-tillered wheat crops growing under conditions of low fertility ; rather than constituting evidence of a rare genotype these may merely indicate the existence of some small, local, nitrogen source and actually reflect the potential behaviour of the whole crop. Needless to say, such plants are sampled when encountered. The point is, however, that phenotypes can be and are much modified by environment and this invalidates any time-consuming procedure *based on* phenotypic selection in the field. Swaminathan (1968) refers to marked environmental differences in the incidence of rust, *Melampsora lini*, in Australian and Indian varieties of flax. In Afghanistan, lucerne, *Medicago asiatica* (*Medicago sativa* L. *sensu lato*) is widely used as fodder which, when dry, is bundled and transported roughly on donkeys for hundreds of kilometers and shows no evidence of leaf loss; the same varieties when grown in Europe suffer severe leaf-shedding. Except when employed for characteristics with a very high heritability (which can only be determined by prior genetic studies), or when conducted in an environment closely resembling that in which the collected material is to be utilised directly without further genetic manipulation, phenotypic selection is an unreliable basis for sampling.

In the field, sampling is carried out by randomly selecting a starting point at the collection site and, in cereals for example, taking a single spike at every second, or third, pace along a number of transects through the crop, holding the sample bag in one hand and collecting with the other until from 200–500 spikes have been taken. Other crops are sampled in an exactly similar manner. A biased sample is added to this random sample when it is considered necessary on the basis of visual evidence of rare types of low frequency in the crop. If spikes or fruit are taxonomically important they are kept intact as far as possible. If the crop has been cut, each stook or sheaf cluster is sampled in such a way that the least possible number of spikes, preferably one, is removed from each sheaf, and all sheaves in the field are sampled; this minimises the risk of sampling the same plant more than once by collecting a number of its tillers from the same sheaf. If the crop is stacked, usually with the ears towards the centre of the stack, single culms are drawn randomly around the face of the stack until a sample of the required size has been collected.

The sparse and diffusely distributed populations (and occasionally scattered individuals) of some weed and wild species often do not yield large samples, nor can one always speak of a gene pool. Two points should be noted. In the first place, the representativeness of a sample is always relative to the situation from which it has been taken; if one individual alone is found and sampled, the sample is clearly representative only of that individual and such genetic contributions, if any, it has been able in its isolation to receive. Samples, in short, cannot be more representative than conditions in the field permit, and these may often be severely limiting. It may be noted also, in passing, that seed samples do not reflect the adaptive genetic equilibrium of the populations from which they have been drawn, but rather represent—to a degree which depends on the amount of out-breeding which has occurred—the results of genetic recombinations which have not yet been fully exposed to natural selection. Variation in the rate of maturation of individuals within a population also imposes an unknown bias on seed samples drawn from it unless it can be sampled at intervals, a procedure which is rarely possible.

In the second place, and more generally, if samples are to be utilised —and there can be no point in collection and conservation if utilisation is not the ultimate aim—sample size is important. In terms of the representativeness of a sample, its size must be such that it is not only representative at the time of collection, within the limits discussed above, but also remain so when reduced viability after storage has reduced effective sample size. But minimum sample size is dictated by the requirement that samples should be distributed as well as conserved, and is often greater than can be collected in the field. The practice adopted by the author has been, therefore, to multiply samples immediately after collection in an environment as close as possible to that in which the bulk of samples in a collection have been taken. If facilities permit, further observations are made on the collections during multiplication, since this is the first cultivation of the material under controlled conditions. The samples are then divided into an approximately 500-gram nucleus for conservation, and a surplus which is available for distribution when required. Small samples may also be bulked before or after multiplication, but this should never be done in the field. In general, small samples are less a disadvantage in out-breeding species than in in-breeders; when small numbers of an in-breeding species are being sampled at least some seed should be collected from every individual.

It can hardly be overstressed that documentation at all stages of sampling is important, and at least as important as the maintenance of records at later stages of study and breeding. The environment occupied by a varietal population defines its adaptive characteristics. As has been shown outstandingly by the work of Vavilov and his colleagues, some of which have already been referred to, the classification of the adaptive characteristics of primitive crop races in particular depends on the classification of the environmental factors which have moulded them, and the starting point of such work is the field observation. Field data are useful in assessing the genetic and breeding potential of cultivated and related species, and they contribute to efficient exploration planning by indicating ecotype-habitat associations, as we have seen. But in taxonomy, also, ecological and geographical distribution data play an increasingly important role. Herbarium voucher material, therefore, should always be collected. Many points of taxonomic distinctness necessary for the reliable taxonomic determination of collections cannot be established in the field, but require comparative herbarium studies. Sufficient material should be collected to illustrate the full range of phenotypic expression and genetic variation present.

During sampling, notes should be taken of the latitude, longitude, elevation, slope, aspect, and other topographical features of the collection site. Soil colour, texture, stoniness, depth, drainage, pH, salinity and irrigation are recorded, and since it is not possible to undertake prolonged quantitative studies in the field most of these characteristics are classified on coded scales (Table 13.1). The nature of the vegetation and notes of associated species are recorded. The height,

TABLE 13.1. Field records

Type of record	How coded	Example
Family	Coded { First five letters	GRAMI
Genus	„ ten „	TRITICUM
Species	„ five „	AESTI
Varietal or common name or names	Names in full or abbreviated	Bahri
Country	Coded: three-letter code according to lists supplied by FAO	AFG
Expedition	Name, year or other identification	FAO 1968
Team, date, site and sample	Coded: generated as follows:— 2 letters—initials of team leader 2 numbers—day of month 2 numbers—month of year 2 numbers—last two figures of year 2 numbers—site number for that date 2 numbers—sample number for that site	EB1109680601
Latitude	Degrees and minutes N or S	N3436
Longitude	Degrees and minutes E or W	E06657
Altitude	Meters + or − above or below sea level	+3300

TABLE 13.1—continued

Type of record	How coded	Example
Aspect	Compass direction in degrees (360 = north, 000 = level)	160
Slope	Degrees from horizontal	05
Topography	Coded: 0 = swamp, 1 = flood plain, 2 = level, 3 = undulating, 4 = rolling, 5 = hilly, 6 = hilly dissected, 7 = steeply dissected, 8 = mountainous, 9 = other (specify)	8
Soil—texture	Coded: 1 = sand, loamy sand, 2 = loam, sandy loam, silt loam, clay loam, 3 = clay, silt clay, 4 = highly organic	2
stoniness	Coded: 0 = no stones, 1 = tillage unaffected, 2 = tillage affected, 3 = tillage difficult, 4 = tillage impossible, 5 = essentially paved	2
depth	Coded: 1 = < plough depth, 2 = approx. plough depth, 3 = > plough depth, 4 = very deep	2
colour	Coded: according to international colour chart (observations made on *moist*, *rubbed*, sample)	3
pH	Coded: 1 = generally too low for cropping, 2 = low, 3 = medium, 4 = high, 5 = generally too high for cropping	3
salinity	Coded: 0 = none, 1 = slight, 2 = moderate, 3 = serious	0
drainage	Coded: 1 = poor, 2 = moderate, 3 = well-drained, 4 = excessively drained	3
Disturbance factors:	All are coded as follows:	
cultivation	0 = none	3
irrigation	1 = margin or marginal	4
fertilisation	2 = low	2
gully erosion	3 = medium	—
sheet erosion	4 = intense	—
wind erosion		1
biotic factors		3
fire		—
others (specify)		—

In addition, the most abundant associated wild and cultivated species at the site of collection and adjacent to it are recorded; the incidence of diseases and pests is noted; and any other relevant ecological or meteorological data, and whether crops are winter-or spring-sown, are similarly noted.

vigour, maturity, lodging, incidence or diseases, and variability of the crop are noted. Meteorological data for the region may or may not exist, but it has been found useful to maintain a daily record of maximum and minimum temperature and relative humidity, as well as notes of wind, and air and soil temperatures at the time of collection. Panoramic and close-up colour photographs are taken at every site in such a way as to illustrate site and crop characteristics and to help in the later identification of the site should this be necessary.

EXPEDITION PLANNING

The complexity of the factors determining the distribution and the eco-genetic characteristics of primitive crop races and their related weed species stresses the need for painstakingly detailed planning in advance of exploration missions. The urgency imposed by advancing genetic erosion, the isolation of most of the centres of genetic diversity, the relative scarcity of ecological or floristic studies of these centres, and the high costs of expeditions all serve to emphasise this need. In terms of time, equipment, personnel and ancillary services, plant exploration missions are costly operations and should not be despatched lightly. Wherever possible they should be undertaken cooperatively and dupli-cation of effort avoided, and early contact should be made with other workers and institutes interested in the same region or the proposed objectives of the mission. In view of the wide organisational contacts of FAO and the extensive involvement of its Crop Ecology and Genetic Resources Branch in exploration and genetic conservation, FAO should be contacted as soon as possible during the preparatory stages.

It is a major disadvantage of plant exploration that it is usually carried out by expeditions of relatively short duration. Ultimately, it is not only desirable but essential for permanently staffed exploration bases to be established within the gene centres of the most important crops; alternatives must be regarded as less satisfactory and temporary compromises. Without such bases and teams of resident specialists, the studies needed reliably to define the ecological and geographical distri-bution of species and varietal populations are not possible, and the efficiency of plant collection is correspondingy reduced.

In the absence of permanent exploration stations such studies as have already been made of the meteorology, climatology, ecology and agriculture of a region in which exploration is to be undertaken assume a particular importance. During planning, therefore, one of the first steps to be taken is to assemble, from whatever sources are available, the fullest possible information relating to :

climate and its local variations,

maximum, minimum and average rainfall and temperatures and their geographical and seasonal distribution,

the characteristics of the natural vegetation cover,

regional soil types and their distribution,

the soil moisture regime and its variations, and the extent of irrigation,

topography and its effects on vegetation, communications and social and ecological isolation,

the distribution of crops,

the names, characteristics and maturation rates of local crop varieties,

agricultural structure and practices,

social structure, customs, and history, and

data from previous expeditions.

Climatic data for the current season, and expected harvesting dates of the crops which are to be collected, should be regularly up-dated through contact with local workers or institutes. Local contacts should be developed as extensively as possible. Their personal knowledge of the country and of locally published studies can contribute much to the success of a mission. Wherever possible, they should be involved in the expedition and in discussions of its objectives. Through them, also, arrangements are made for interpreters and local guides for the whole mission or for sections of it.

Although no expedition should work without an interpreter, the importance of even slight familiarity with local languages is stressed. Relations with local people in isolated areas, with whom it may be necessary to live and work for some time, are vital. These relations are improved beyond belief in terms of trust and mutual confidence when even a rudimentary exchange of words, greetings or ideas is possible. Knowledge of the language may also throw valuable light on otherwise mystifying varietal and crop names and in other ways yield access to information sources which are normally closed.

The accumulation of data resulting from preliminary studies permits the preparation of approximate outline maps of altitudinal zones, crop distributions, vegetational zones, rainfall and temperature distributions, soil types, and the distribution of estimated harvest dates. This work is done on outline maps of 1 : 1,000,000, 1 : 2,000,000 or 1 : 3,000,000

G

scale. Transparent overlays on the same scale are prepared. Existing one-million, quarter-million or even 1 : 100,000 maps are used for reference, bearing in mind that even where such maps exist they are often unreliable.

As information on estimated dates of crop ripening and harvest is received, harvest date distribution maps are up-dated and provide a first guide to the itinerary of the mission. Local reports may vary greatly in reliability. Within a particular region, the dates of crop maturity are also affected by many local factors such as sowing date, local weather variations which will affect soil moisture and temperatures, variations in aspect and exposure and especially altitude. The effect of altitude differences is considerable. In general, for every 1,000 meters gain in elevation average temperatures fall approximately 5°C ; this is sufficient to slow vegetative growth and delay maturity by as much as three or four weeks, other factors being equal. This is allowed for when plotting estimated maturity dates in each proposed collecting area on the maps. In most except high-altitude areas where cereals ripen very late in the season and there is a constant danger from early frosts, allowance may be made for the fact that mature crops frequently stand for some time in the field before harvesting.

When fully up-to-date information is available for all collecting areas the itinerary of the mission is finally prepared and transferred to 1 : 1,000,000 map sheets of the collecting region. Transparent overlays of road, river and valley systems, crop distributions, and the routes of previous expeditions, which have been prepared during earlier stages of the work, are now used in plotting the final itinerary. Alternative routes should be prepared for all sections of the mission as a precaution against unforeseen changes of plan. Time-tables are prepared, and are sent to all local contacts, and arrangements are made for guides, inter-preters, and animal transportation where necessary. Final arrangements are also made for all permits necessary to enter, travel or work in the collecting region, and appointments are made with plant quarantine authorities, with whom the screening, packing and shipment of col-lections must be discussed.

Meanwhile, check-lists of equipment are prepared and equipment is tested. Expedition vehicles should be of cross-country type with four-wheel drive, high and low gear ratios and good reserves of power, and fitted with large heavy-tread low-pressure tyres to which chains may with advantage occasionally be fitted. Equipment or modifications to vehicles should include :

an engine-driven winch and steel cable, so that the vehicle may pull
  itself free from situations where traction has been lost,

a long and powerful nylon cable,

a *complete* range of spares, including nuts and bolts,

a tool kit satisfying all repair and maintenance needs in the field,
  including special manufacturer's tools,

a roof rack and tropical roof,

containers for spare fuel and water, firmly secured in a fixed rack,

lockers and straps for stowing and securing *all* equipment,

dust-proofed compartments for scientific and photographic equipment not in use, padded to prevent damage, and accessible during
  travel,

shelves and strong clips for all equipment which is in use, such as
  field notebooks, pencils, map cases, camera, tape-recorder, binoculars, and so on,

altimeter, hygrometer, and thermometers mounted on vibration-
  proof fittings,

a thermometer and wet-and-dry-bulb hygrometer mounted outside
  in a shaded attachment,

internal lights over driving compartment, dash shelf, rear compartment and engine compartment.

If at all possible, personnel space should be separated from equipment and sample space in order to minimise the risk of injury in the
event of heavy gear being dislodged by severe jolts, and to permit some
degree of comfort. Finally, at least one member of the team should be
thoroughly familiar—and preferably experienced—with mechanical
and electrical maintenance.

In the field, exploration teams must be prepared to work in isolation
from all except local villagers, farmers and nomads for periods of weeks
or months. Although it is usually possible to establish a central base
which may be returned to periodically for the renewal of expendable
supplies and to deposit collections temporarily, all needs in the field
must be satisfied from the stores and equipment carried by the expedition. Bearing in mind the isolation and the extreme severity of the conditions under which it is necessary to operate, equipment must be
reliable. It must also be suitable for the particular objectives of the
mission, and will vary according to these to a greater or lesser extent.
Too much equipment is as much to be avoided as too little ; camping
tables, folding chairs and camp beds, sophisticated cooking equipment,
and even tilley lamps can prove to be trying encumbrances, though air

mattresses are a welcome and justifiable luxury. Where ground insects are serious, the vehicle itself and especially the roof-rack are excellent sleeping places. In Table 13.2, four lists of suggested basic equipment are provided. All equipment should be tested before departure of the expedition. Lists should also be submitted to consular representatives

TABLE 13.2. Field equipment

A   *Scientific equipment*

Small portable altimeters (− 200 to + 5,000 meters)
Fluid-damped pocket marching compasses
Binoculars
Small portable professional quality battery-operated tape-recorder (e.g. Uher 4000L) with low-impedance lip-microphone
Dial-reading hair hygrometers
Soil thermometers
Maximum-minimum thermometers
Handlenses (× 8 and × 12)
Small soil-test kit or indicator papers for rapid pH estimates
At least two cameras equipped with wide-angle (30 mm), normal (50 mm) and telephoto (100 mm) lenses, u/v filters, lens hoods, dust-proof lens or hood caps, through-the-lens light metering, for colour and black-and-white photography
A large supply of lens cloths and tissues
A reliable wristwatch-chronometer

B   *Medical supplies*

Water purifying tablets
Insect repellant cream
DDT or other insect powder
Insecticide spray
Entero-vioform or Mexaform tablets
Antihistamine cream
Antiseptic cream
Methiolate or alcohol for sterilisation of small wounds
Antibiotic cream—acromycin for burns
                        —neomycin for skin infections
Phisohex cream for more extensive skin infections
Antibiotic tablets (terramycin) for dysentries
Eye lotion
Aspirin
Buscopan, for colic pains
Dolviran, for relief of heavy pain
Anti-malarial tablets (e.g. chloroquine) for both prophylaxis and treatment

B *Medical supplies (continued)*

Sera for snakebite (of limited validity and generally more or less specific)

Disposable hypodermic syringes

Cotton wool

Splints

Bandages

Lanolin

Siosteran microtablets for diahhroea in children

Note: The last two, and other items in this list, are useful in treating ailments among local people.

C *Camping Equipment*

Small 2-man tents with flysheets, sealed undersheets, and insect-proof screens

Waterproof sleeping-bags, with hoods

Lightweight folding camp-beds or air mattresses

Battery-operated hand torches and tent lamps

Small hand axes and hammers

Folding butane or solid fuel cooking stove and spare fuel

Supply of wind-proof matches

Cooking utensils

Large supply of spare batteries

A small folding table, if light and stable, may be useful

D *Collecting equipment*

Large supply of cotton bags for seed samples

Polythene bags of various sizes

Seed envelopes for small samples

Field books with consecutively numbered pages and similarly numbered detachable slips

Rubber bands for closing bags

Folding pocket knives

Secateurs

Drying paper for herbarium material

Flimsies for herbarium material

Cord and a supply of bulldog clips for drying herbarium paper

Small solid fuel stoves for drying paper

Insecticide for herbarium material

Small polythene specimen tubes for cytological and other specimens

Alcohol

Acetic acid

Plant presses

Trowels and small pick

Portable refrigerator for vegetative material, if possible

of the countries in the collecting region so that customs clearances may be obtained, if necessary.

FIELD WORK

It has been found that small exploration teams are more efficient and mobile than large. If an expedition is large, it should be divided into two-, three- or four-man teams. Each team should include an experienced field ecologist and a member familiar with the taxonomy of the group or groups of cultivated plants which are the objective of the mission. Both should have a strong genetic background. All should be able to drive and carry international driving documents, so that driving duties may be shared on a shift system. A member should be qualified in first-aid and have some medical knowledge ; this is necessary not only to deal with possible emergencies in the team itself but also with requests for assistance from local people. Good all-round field experience is very desirable.

Work should commence at dawn in order to take the fullest advantage of the daylight hours. In hot areas especially, the relatively cool early hours are so important that they should be fully used, nor should they be jeopardised by wasting sleep in the evenings. It is not advisable therefore, to work late into the night unless travelling over ground already covered or in desert areas. Notes, and the sorting of samples, should be done at the time of sampling and not in the evenings. Usually the changing of herbarium papers is quite enough for the evenings, and it is unwise to work into the night. Insects frequently form such dense swarms after dusk that it is best to sleep before these penetrate lighted tents or mosquito nets. Camp duties should be shared ; if this can be done on the basis of preference rather than on a rota basis it is better. One team member may pitch tents and prepare the encampment while others cook ; another may at the same time begin to change herbarium papers. In the mornings, any early-rising member prepares hot coffee and biscuits which are distributed to the tents of other members while he then strikes his own tent ; the others then carry out the daily check on the vehicle, take the daily temperature and humidity readings, and so on, while the first member continues striking camp. At the beginning of each day, the kilometer reading of the vehicle is carefully noted.

SURVEY PROCEDURES

Plant exploration may be regarded as a screening process which may employ different sampling densities corresponding to several distinct levels of discrimination, according to the needs of different situations and the amount of sampling which has already been done in a region. In previously unexplored regions where little or nothing is known of ecotypic or agricultural variation patterns, sampling density is preferably not high and samples are taken at rather widely separated intervals through relatively large areas. One may therefore speak of coarse-mesh or coarse-grid sampling,* the purpose of which is to determine the synoptic features of distribution patterns. By contrast, when sampling is done in a relatively limited area which has been sampled before and the aim is to search for specific genetic characteristics already known from previous synoptic surveys to exist in the area, or to establish more accurately variation patterns already known to exist, sampling is conducted on a regular grid pattern at sites close to one another and one may speak of close-mesh sampling.

Generally, however, there is no regularity of distance or direction between successive sampling sites. Travel is usually along established routes, such as roads or tracks, of irregular pattern. Whether roads are present or not, one may speak of 'road transects', and samples are taken along these transects in a manner determined by :

crop differences, such as changes in varietal composition, maturity, and the incidence of diseases,

changes of ecological, agricultural or social conditions such as the presence or absence of irrigation, changes of fertiliser practices, of threshing methods, cultivation methods, soil type, and so on,

the occurrence of topographical, ecological or social divides such as mountain passes, northern and southern hill or mountain slopes, upper and lower valley slopes, changes from pastoral to cultural organisation and, generally, from the land of each village to that of the next, and finally

not less frequently than every 10 or 20 kilometers according to the nature of the terrain.

During travel a journey log is kept, in which the names of villages, passes, rivers, and other natural or man-made features are noted and their distances from each other recorded. At intervals, the types of crop present are noted and their relative frequencies recorded. For this a five-point scale is usually employed (Table 13.3). All landmarks, especially those on the maps, are also noted and their positions and relative distances recorded. At each sampling site, its latitudinal and

* Strictly speaking, the term 'grid', when applied to vegetation surveys, should apply only when observations are regularly spaced in distance and direction.

TABLE 13.3. Scale for recording crop frequencies

0	Crop absent: not noted unless information required in specific cases.
1	Crop occurs rarely: only single and isolated fields encountered.
2	Crop not rare: cultivated only in a distinct minority of fields in the locality.
3	Crop frequently cultivated, to the extent that it is characteristic of the locality: other crops may occur at the same frequency.
4	Crop cultivated in a majority of fields encountered, to the extent that no other crop has a frequency higher than 2.
5	Crop exclusively cultivated, except for the rare occurrence (frequency 1) of others.

longitudinal coordinates are plotted on 1 : 1,000,000 map sheets as accurately as possible, and the data are recorded in field notebooks. It is *essential* always to have a clear idea of the team's position on the map. Since roads and tracks are often the least reliable of map features this is sometimes not easy, but position errors are cumulative in effect, and great care—even to the extent of retracing one's tracks as far as a recognisable landmark—is advisable. Not only may they result in prolonged detours or greater inconveniences or even dangers, but errors of position invalidate site location data.

In laying down transects for vegetation surveys, it is a basic principle that these should cross, as far as is possible, whatever ecological gradients exist. Road transects, therefore, have a marked disadvantage in that they tend in large part to travel along rather than across these gradients. Two further disadvantages—their irregularity and their unreliability as map features—have already been referred to. But during coarse-mesh sampling particularly the distances which must be covered leave little choice but to accept these disadvantages. Knowing them, however, it is possible to make short deviations from the main route of travel to take samples and determine distribution patterns. Such short deviations are made by foot or, if longer, by pack animal. Both make heavy (and occasionally unjustified) demands on time, the first on account of the slow rate of travel and the second because of the long discussions that are necessary to obtain transportation at a suitable price. We might close with the thought—already the subject of some more-than-half-serious propositions—that it may be worth-while to consider equipping expedition vehicles with powerful light-weight motor-cycles.

CONCLUSION

In considering the tactics of plant exploration in some detail and the ecological factors which have a bearing on the distribution of agro-ecotypes, this chapter has sought to show that the empirical approach to plant exploration requires to be superseded by one which may better measure up to the needs of the present day as they are seen in the light of increasing genetic erosion. It is considered implicit in the foregoing discussions that plant exploration can, and should, be continually supplemented by a feed-back of ecological genetic information from the field according to the scheme :

survey → collection → data → survey → collection → data

in such a way as to provide increasingly meaningful and useful information which will permit plant exploration to carry out its function of providing plant breeding with the raw materials it needs for continual crop improvement, and to do so with increasing efficiency.

REFERENCES

GREGOR J.W. (1933) The ecotype concept in relation to the registration of crop plants. *Ann. Appl. Biol.* **20,** 205–219.

SCHIEMANN ELISABETH (1951) New results on the history of cultivated cereals. *Heredity* **5,** 305–320.

SINSKAYA E.N. (1961) (ed.) *Flora of Cultivated Plants of the U.S.S.R.* **13,** Part I. I.P.S.T. Jerusalem.

SINSKAYA E.N. and BEZTUZHEVA A.A. (1931) The forms of *Camelina sativa* in connection with climate, flax and man. *Bull. Appl. Bot. Genet. Pl. Breed.* **25,** 98–200.

SWAMINATHAN M.S. (1968) In *Report of the FAO/IBP Technical Conference on the Exploration, Utilization and Conservation of Plant Genetic Resources* (Ed. Bennett E.), p. 87, F.A.O., Rome.

TURESSON, G. (1922) The genotypical response of the plant species to the habitat. *Hereditas* **3,** 211–350.

UFER M. (1956) Studien an afghanischen Weizen. *Zeitschr. Pfl. züchtung* **36,** 133–152.

VAVILOV N.I. (1940) The new systematics of cultivated plants. In *The New Systematics* (Ed. Huxley J.), 549–566. University Press, Oxford.

VAVILOV N.I. (1951) The origin, variation, immunity and breeding of cultivated plants. *Chron. Bot.* **13,** 1–364.

VAVILOV N.I. (1957) *World Resources of Cereals, Leguminous Seed Crops, and Flax, and their Utilization in Breeding,* and *Agroecological Survey of the Main Field Crops.* Acad. Sci. U.S.S.R., Moscow (transl. 1960 I.P.S.T. Jerusalem).

ZAGAJA S.W. (1968) In *Report of the FAO/IBP Technical Conference on the Exploration, Utilization and Conservation of Plant Genetic Resources* (Ed. Bennett E.), p. 35. F.A.O., Rome.

ZINGER H.B. (1909) On the species of *Camelina* and *Spergularia* occurring as weeds in sowings of flax and their origin. *Trudy. Bot. Muz. Akad. Nauk* **6,** 1–303.

14

ECOLOGICAL AND AGRONOMIC STUDIES
RELATED TO PLANT EXPLORATION

A. H. BUNTING[1] and H. KUCKUCK[2]

[1] University of Reading, Reading, United Kingdom
[2] Institut für Angewandte Genetik, Hannover, German Federal Republic

Both the practical and the more purely scientific purposes of plant exploration involve ecological as well as agronomic ideas, and ecological and agronomic studies must therefore be an integral part of the exploration process. Experience with many crops has shown that crop varieties in regions where agriculture and plant breeding are not advanced are frequently quite closely adapted to the local environmental and agricultural conditions, and do not succeed outside them. For example the local sorghum varieties of northern Nigeria flower at dates which are closely linked to the average date of the end of the rainy season, apparently by a delicate photoperiodic reaction (Curtis, 1968 ; Bunting and Curtis, 1968). Frequently exploration is primarily directed to find plants which are specifically adapted to particular features of the environment, such as short seasons or low temperatures. In other cases breeders who have to use the material will be able to work more effectively with it if they know something about the local conditions to which it may be specifically adapted. Even for purely practical reasons, therefore, it is essential that the collector should provide a clear account of the ecological and farming conditions of the place of origin of each accession, and the main purpose of this chapter is to remind him of what is required. This information is equally important for studies of evolution and adaptation.

On a collecting expedition, which is seldom in the same place for very long, and has to do a great deal in a short time, it is impossible, and it is probably often unnecessary, to make detailed quantitative observations. Where the collector is working from a permanent base at a research station or similar institution, he may be able to do a great deal more. Indeed, if he has time and facilities for experiments, he may be able to analyse the physiological and genetical bases of adaptation, and the ecological reasons for genetic diversity, but work at this level of sophistication is not covered by this chapter. Nevertheless, all collections, however practical their primary purposes may be, should be sufficiently well documented with ecological and agronomic information to enable their considerable cost to be recouped in broader studies. This is particularly important in regions where agriculture is changing rapidly and older varieties are likely to disappear as they are replaced by new and improved ones.

ECOLOGICAL FACTORS AND LEVELS OF DESCRIPTION

The ecological factors to be considered may be divided somewhat arbitrarily into two groups: the primarily physical, topographic, edaphic and aerial factors (geography, climate, weather and soils) and the primarily biological (including human) and agricultural factors. Further, the environment must be described at three levels—the region as a whole (for example the clay plains of the Central Sudan), the area (for example the Blue Nile depression in the *Acacia*-tall grass country) and the specific locality of the individual collection. The description at the first two levels is essentially an agro-ecological survey, and should be prepared as far as possible before the exploration begins, from earlier reports. It is then checked as the work of the expedition proceeds. It provides a general account to which the information regarding specific localities can be related. Excellent examples are contained in the monographs by Vavilov and Bukinich (1929) on Afghanistan and Zhukovsky (1933) on Turkey, and the classical account of agriculture in the Sudan (Tothill 1948).

AGRO-ECOLOGICAL DESCRIPTION
OF THE REGION AND AREA

Geography, climate, weather and soils
The main elements to be defined or described here are:

(*a*) geographical position and limits of the region and area, communications, route of the expedition.

(*b*) geology, geomorphology and topography, especially altitude ranges and drainage systems.

(*c*) general character of the climate (a descriptive account including significant numerical data where they are available) including the seasonal course of day length, radiation receipt, temperature, rainfall and other forms of precipitation (amount, distribution in space and time and character), wind, evaporation and water régime. Local variations within the region and area, and the nature of the variation within the season and about the long-term averages, must be described.

Latitude is not enough to indicate the biologically important aspects of day-length. If the greater part of the growing season occurs before the longest day (as in a Mediterranean climate) the photoperiodic relations of crop plants may well be quite different from those of plants growing where the greater part of the season occurs after the longest day, as in the summer rainfall regions of eastern Africa.

(*d*) soils, including physical, chemical and significant biological features, drainage within the profile, run-off, erosion, soil features of water régime, catenas and other distributional patterns.

(*e*) based on the foregoing, the length and character of the agricultural season and the factors (usually temperature or rainfall distribution) which determine its beginning and end. It is not necessary, and may on occasion be misleading, to press information about a particular locality into one of the categories of a standard geographical classification of general or agricultural climate. Such classifications, restricted by the criteria selected by their originators, may obscure important specific features, such as the effect of soil type on the utilization of water and the amount that can be stored in the profile (see Smith, 1949) or omit aspects which, though locally unimportant, may be significant elsewhere. For example, the precise features of the winter season in a Mediterranean region may be important determinants of the growth and survival of pasture plants for particular regions in Britain, in a completely different climatic régime (e.g. Cooper, 1964; Cooper and McWilliam, 1966). 'Homoclime' analogies may be useful in crop introduction, but only very broadly, as every practical breeder knows. I have set out elsewhere in some detail the considerations which are important in these studies in tropical regions of Africa (Bunting, 1961).

The main purpose of this part of the survey is to define the characteristics of the agricultural season and the features which define and limit it. It provides a general background for the biological and agricultural description.

Biological, human and agricultural factors

Features to be defined or described at the level of the region and area are :

(f) wild vegetation : principal types of vegetation and plant successions and their distribution in relation to the physical, climate and soil factors ; effects of disturbance (including fire and overgrazing).

(g) human and historical factors : main anthropological, sociological and linguistic features of the human populations ; history of their origins and entry into the region, earlier populations and their fate, recent migrations into the area (particularly if they have brought with them new crops and methods of production) ; economic organization affecting agriculture, including recent changes (marketing, development of industry) which may affect the relative importance of particular crops or crop varieties in the future.

(h) agricultural systems and practices in the region and area : prehistory and history of agriculture in the region ; principal crops and their pests, diseases and weeds, general methods of production (e.g. cultural practices and rotations, including shifting cultivation, flood cultivation, irrigation, and other devices for extending the length or altering the character of the cropping season, other methods of increasing the supply of plant foods and controlling weeds such as manuring and fire cultivation, methods of tillage) ; agricultural research and teaching institutions, and recent agricultural innovations in the region and area such as introduction of new species and varieties, new cultural methods, mechanization, fertilizers, new crop protection methods.

(i) general biology of particular crops in the region : common and taxonomic names and uses of crops, general methods of production (e.g. winter or spring sown, or grown on water stored in the soil, mixed cropping ; phenology (seasonal time-table of sowing, transplanting, vegetative growth, pruning, initiation of inflorescences, flowering, anthesis and fertilization, filling of fruits and seeds, and other relevant morphological and physiological events, harvest maturity) ; harvesting methods, yields, storage, utilization, factors affecting quality and consumer preferences ; breeding systems in the region or area in general, current and past selection pressures, methods of producing and preserving seed or other propagating material ; specific or adapted weeds ; related wild species and genetic relations with them ; diseases and pests.

The main object of including information of this sort in the general agro-ecological survey is to record as much detailed information as possible about the way in which the individual crop species and varieties are adapted to the local conditions described in the first (geographical and physical) section of the survey. Notes on particular points follow.

Section (f) on vegetation may well serve to bring to light relationships with other regions of similar vegetation and climate, as well as the presence of related wild species, or species which are alternate hosts for pests and diseases, and also to indicate the sorts of selection pressures to which pasture, forage and browse plants have been subjected.

Section (g) on human aspects is particularly important. Crops and farming systems evolve and migrate in the hands of people, and hence information on the human history and prehistory of the region can tell us a great deal about the relations of the crops and varieties of a region to those of other regions. For example, the relations of Ethiopian agriculture with that of the Yemen, the Hadhramaut, ancient Saba, and the great river valleys of Iraq on the one hand, and of Egypt on the other, may lead us back to the primitive cultivars of South-West Asia by different routes. In the Blue Nile region of the Sudan, two systems of farming exist side by side, though in separate villages: a simple and apparently indigenous system, based mainly on sesame and sorghum, using fire cultivation, and including the gathering from the wild of *Hibiscus esculentus*, in the hands of partly nomadic Arab tribes who entered the region from Arabia; and a very much more diverse and more typically African system, brought in by immigrants from West Africa, which includes *Hibiscus cannabinus* and *H. sabdariffa*, and several American crops—maize, groundnuts, beans, cassava, *Capsicum* peppers and pumpkins. A knowledge of historical aspects at this level will help the collector to understand more fully what he finds, and the plant breeder to use it better, and it may be of considerable significance for studies of the evolution of the cultivated forms, which are among the most important of the secondary objects of plant exploration.

The general account of agricultural systems, organization, marketing, and industry, and of recent changes and developments, section (h), will help to explain how farming has been adapted to the region, and it will alert the collector to changes which may be tending to affect or eliminate particular crop species and varieties.

It may not be possible to prepare very much of section (i), on the general biology of particular crops in the region and area, until the collecting has begun, but an attempt to do this will show the collector the possibilities and problems he can help to define and solve.

The greatest possible importance attaches to phenological studies, since they show in detail the seasonal time-table of the species and varieties which is the main basis of their adaptation to the conditions of the region and area. Consequently they help the user of the material to think about the nature and mode of action of the environmental factors which determine that time-table. To take a very crude example, if one does not know when the inflorescence is initiated, it may be impossible to think with any precision about the way in which the development of a variety is controlled by photoperiod.

INFORMATION ABOUT SPECIFIC LOCALITIES OR COLLECTIONS

The information needed for each particular location is an extension of the categories of the general agro-ecological survey. In addition to the date of collection, it is essential to record for each collection :

(*j*) the name of the place and its coordinates or position on a reliable topographic map, or at least its relation to a determined point along a track or road. In less-developed regions air photographs are extremely useful in the field, particularly if 'stereo pairs' can be used.

(*k*) the altitude, aspect, drainage and run-off conditions.

(*l*) local features of climate—shelter or exposure, shading by mountains, peculiarities of rainfall or cloudiness.

(*m*) soil type, using a standard classification if one exists, depth of profile, and levels reached by wetting front, roots or water table.

(*n*) the beginning and end of the crop season in the locality, especially if they are not the same as in other parts of the area, and any specific local circumstances that modify the length of the season.

(*o*) particular local features of the general biological, human and agricultural situation.

(*p*) notes on specific biological features of the collection or of the place in which it grows—special methods of production, unusual features of the phenology or seasonal time-table, or of morphology or growth habit ; local peculiarities concerning, for example, storage ; utilization and consumer preferences ; unusual features of the breeding system or population structure ; important weeds and related wild forms and evidence or indications of hybridization and introgression ; susceptibility to or tolerance of disease and pests.

The foregoing seems to represent the most that a field collector can do unless he is able to make repeated visits—for example if he is based at a research station in the area. It has been suggested that the ecological observations could be so detailed that they could be useful in the analysis of the ecological determination of heritable variation and population structure. This may well be possible as a specific piece of research, but it is unlikely that observations sufficiently numerous and precise to be useful in this way can normally be associated with the day-to-day work of plant exploration.

THE IMPORTANCE OF PREPARATORY STUDIES

The ecological appreciation needed in plant explorations must be based on broad studies of the region as a whole, completed as far as possible before the practical work of exploration is undertaken. The plant explorer should not regard himself as simply a collector of potentially useful novelties or curiosities: he is a research worker consciously seeking to understand and record the bases of the adaptation to their general and specific environment of the plant forms and agricultural systems and methods which he encounters. He can do this best only if he carries out his practical work against the background of knowledge in depth of the ecological, human and agricultural characteristics of the area. To assemble such knowledge must take labour and time spent in mastering the relevant literature and the reports of earlier investigators. Such preparatory work is essential in all research, and plant exploration is no exception.

REFERENCES

BUNTING A.H. (1961) Some problems of agricultural climatology in tropical Africa. *Geography* **46,** 283–294.

BUNTING A.H. & CURTIS D.L. (1968) Local adaptation of sorghum varieties in northern Nigeria. In *Agroclimatological Methods: Proceedings of the Reading Symposium (Natural Resources Research 7).* UNESCO. Paris.

COOPER J.P. (1964) Climatic variation in forage grasses. 1. Leaf development in climatic races of *Lolium* and *Dactylis. J. appl. Ecol.* **1,** 45–62.

COOPER J.P. & McWILLIAM J.R. (1966) Climatic variation in forage grasses. II. Germination, flowering and leaf development in Mediterranean populations of *Phalaris tuberosa. J. appl. Ecol.* **3,** 191–212.

CURTIS D.L. (1968) The relation between the date of heading of Nigerian sorghums and the duration of the growing season. *J. appl. Ecol.* **5,** 215–226.

SMITH J. (1949) *Distribution of Tree Species in the Sudan in Relation to Rainfall and Soil Texture.* Bull. Dep. Agric. Forests. Sudan, No. 4.

TOTHILL J.D. (ed.) (1948) *Agriculture in the Sudan.* Oxford University Press, London.

VAVILOV N.I. & BUKINICH D.D. (1929) *Agricultural Afghanistan*, Republished 1959 in *Collected works of Academician N.I. Vavilov, Vol.* 1, pp. 45–415. Moscow and Leningrad: Academy of Sciences of the U.S.S.R.

ZHUKOVSKY P.M. (ed.) (1933) *Agricultural Turkey*. (Russian; French summary). Academy of Sciences of the U.S.S.R., Moscow.

STANDARDIZATION AND TREATMENT OF ECOLOGICAL OBSERVATIONS

M. GODRON and J. POISSONET

Centre d'Etudes Phytosociologiques et Ecologiques, Montpellier, France

INTRODUCTION

In considering the modern problem of the optimum utilization of the genetic resources offered by the vegetation of the earth it must never be forgotten that the evolution of living organisms could not have produced the immense variety of present taxa save as a result of the diversity of ecological niches. In 1959 Whyte pointed out that empirical methods of plant introduction and utilization should now give way to more systematic exploration. Such exploration should provide accurate knowledge of the ecology of species, and this implies three essential phases : systematic sampling, standardized field observations and rigorous methods of processing and analysing data. The present chapter examines these three phases in turn, and considers the second in some detail.

SAMPLING

Exploration is too often carried out according to the intuition of the explorer. At the other extreme, however, it would be absurd to replace such intuition by a method of sampling which relies solely upon chance to reveal the most valuable ecological niches. *Stratified sampling* offers an intermediate solution between these two extremes since it takes into account certain assumptions which may guide the explorer's intuition. Stratified sampling imposes few restraints and has two main advantages ; it permits those who plan the exploration to consider intuitive judgments and their implications critically (and experience has frequently shown that self-criticism is useful) ; and it permits more rigorous use of the results.

Regional maps of environmental factors, combined with estimates of the variation in plant communities deduced from aerial photographs, may be useful in preparing stratified sampling schemes. We shall not dwell on this point as these methods have already been described at the International Symposium on Methods in Regional Biology held at Bratislava in 1967.

STANDARDIZATION OF FIELD OBSERVATIONS

When a collector decides to take a sample, he necessarily takes into account its special morphological features, but he should also consider the peculiar features of the site in which the population occurs which is of interest to him. A very characteristic case in point concerns the Douglas fir *Pseudotsuga menziesii* (Mirb.)Franco, for which breeders specify the geographic location of the original population, because this determines the production of timber which may be expected in regions into which it is to be introduced. To coordinate the work of plant explorers on the world scale, it is necessary to standardize the observations of the ecological conditions of the sites where the samples are taken.

To collect, code and store such ecological observations is a fairly intricate matter. More than ten years ago, the French National Scientific Research Centre put this problem into the hands of a research team which prepared a detailed text and this was published in 1969, entitled *Code pour Relevé méthodique de la Végétation et du Milieu* (*Principes et Transcription sur Cartes perforées*) (Code for methodical sampling of vegetation and the habitat (principles and transfer to punched cards.)).

In the present paper we limit ourselves to discussing the advantages to be gained from precoded questionnaires, with a few examples.

Use of a precoded questionnaire

Experience has shown that it is a great help in the field to be able to use a printed form or questionnaire which includes, so far as possible, all the essential elements of the standard code. This considerably reduces ambiguities, allows for the use of a common language, and in no way hampers freedom of scientific expression since the code is no more than the indispensable minimum to which each worker can add whatever further details he thinks are necessary.

We began to use precoded questionnaires in the field in 1959. The experience has shown even the most sceptical of our ecological colleagues that precoding is not a handicap, but on the contrary, a help.

The questionnaire contains seven pages, 21 by 27cm. (see Figs. 15.5 & 15.6). Observations are recorded by 'fields' of decreasing size. On page 1, immediately after the headings which are concerned with the *identification of the survey site* (16 variables), *the regional characteristics* (4 variables) and *characteristics* of the *plant formation* (9 variables) are presented. On pages 2, 3 and 4 the characteristics of the *site* as a whole are examined; *biotic features* (15 variables), concerned particularly with land use, cultural practices and damage to plants are distinguished from those relating to *vegetation* (8 variables) and to the *subsoil* so far as this can be observed at the surface without digging a soil pit (18 variables). Characteristics of the *soil profile* (64 variables) are dealt with on pages 5, 6 and 7 of the questionnaire.

In coding, each variable is given one or more columns, according to the range of values it may have in nature. Thus the nature of the parent rock occupies three columns (999 possibilities), while only one column (9 possibilities) is provided for aspect.

At first glance, these questionnaires and the coding which results from them may seem burdensome and complex, but experience has shown that in the field it is quicker to note down analytical observations than to attempt a new synthesis at each site; moreover it should be stressed that the code as a whole is designed to embrace the many individual cases that may be encountered in the course of a survey, and the observer may extract, according to his needs, that part which is useful to him. For certain general studies we use *partial questionnaires* adapted to the case in question. These questionnaires contain only a part of the code headings, but these are treated exactly as in the general code.

For use in the field, a simplified code, not containing the theoretical explanations, is published separately by the National Scientific Research Centre of France in the form of a handbook.

The questionnaire and code are intended for use in the French biogeographical area, but they can be used in certain parts of other regions, particularly in the temperate zone. For broader application, the same type of considerations may be adapted to other major geographic areas*, as we have done for Morocco and the Argentine Chaco.

---

* The principal climatic characteristics must be deduced from observations made at local meteorological stations, and the local stages of plant succession must also be determined. It will not be easy to reach agreement on a world classification of climate, but this difficulty can be avoided by indicating all measurable or assessable variables which define climate, rather than climate type.

EXAMPLES

It is not possible here to examine in detail all the ecological observations which may be recorded when a taxon is collected, but a few examples will serve to demonstrate the procedure.

Angular cover

Some ecotypes are very sensitive to light intensity but many unfounded opinions in this connection have led to serious errors : for example, in central France many foresters were convinced that the chestnut (*Castanea sativa* Mill.) could not be established as an understorey plant among pines. An accurate study was necessary to convince them that young chestnut is actually shade-tolerant for several decades.

It is convenient to estimate the amount of light reaching ground level by the concept of 'angular cover', which expresses the proportion of sky excluded by upperlayer vegetation or by the topography (cliffs, rocks, etc.). Angular cover is coded in eighths or 'octas' ; a value of zero indicates that less than $\frac{1}{8}$ of the sky is visible at ground level, and one of 8 indicates that 8/8 of the sky is visible (Fig. 15.1).

Plant formation

In order to avoid attempting to define the 'physiognomy' of the vegetation, we confine ourselves to recording the cover by herbaceous plants, low woody (<2m) and trees (>2m). This permits plant formation to be described unambiguously according to a simple scheme (Fig. 15.2).

Phenological stages

Figure 15.3 shows how the phenological stages are coded for therophytes, biennials and perennials (the definitions for each are explained clearly in the code).

Topographic location

Figure 15.4 illustrates the coding of topographic features without reproducing the definitions in detail.

Types of questionnaire

It has already been pointed out that the types of questionnaire can be extremely varied providing that the coding under each heading corresponds with that of the general code. This is illustrated by two pages extracted from a complete questionnaire to show how the detailed headings are brought together.

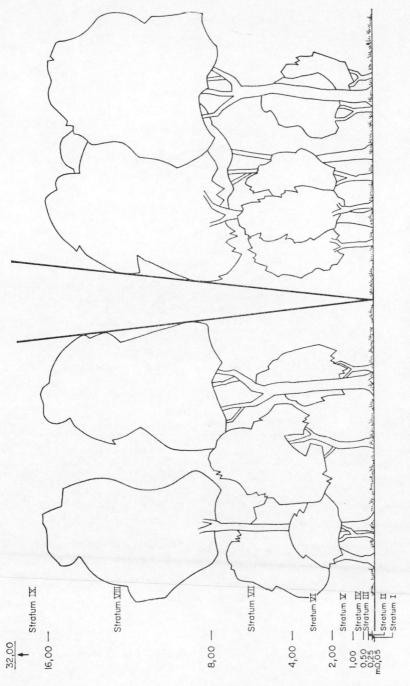

FIGURE 15.1. Angular cover at ground level.

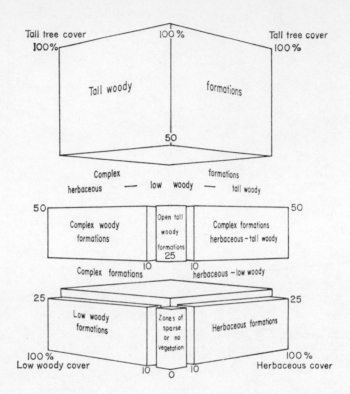

FIGURE 15.2. Scheme illustrating the classification of formations.

Formations	Tall tree cover	Low tree cover	Herbaceous cover
Tall woody	50 to 100%	0 to 100%	0 to 100%
Low woody	0 to 25%	10 to 100%	0 to 10%
Herbaceous	0 to 25%	0 to 10%	10 to 100%
Woody complexes	25 to 50%	10 to 100%	0 to 10%
Herbaceous woody complexes	25 to 50%	0 to 10%	10 to 100%
Herbaceous-low woody complexes	0 to 25%	10 to 100%	10 to 100%
Herbaceous-low woody-tall woody complexes	25 to 50%	10 to 100%	10 to 100%
Open tall woody	25 to 50%	0 to 10%	0 to 10%
Zones of sparse or no vegetation	0 to 25%	0 to 10%	0 to 10%

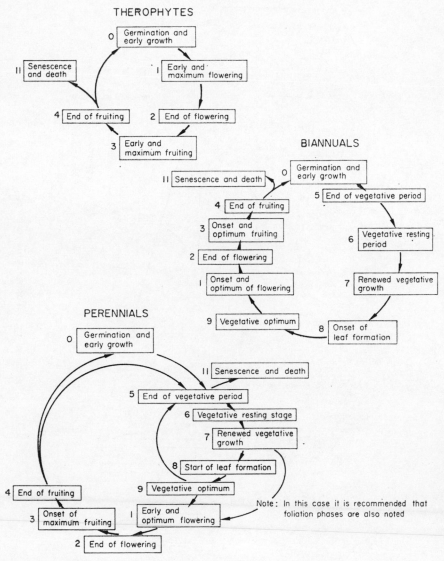

FIGURE 15.3. Scheme indicating the coding of phenological cycles. (After De Floc'h.)

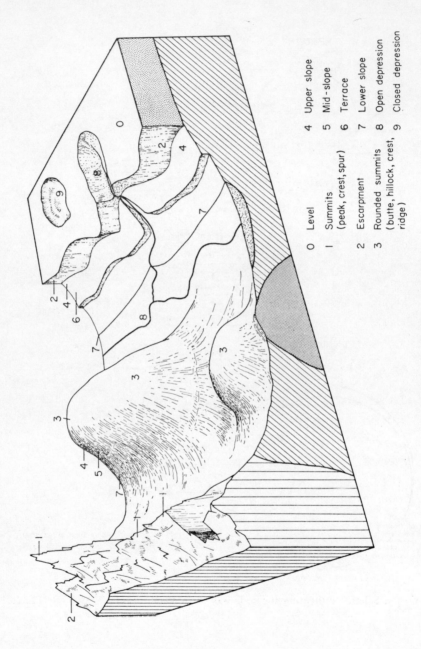

0   Level

1   Summits
    (peak, crest, spur)

2   Escarpment

3   Rounded summits
    (butte, hillock, crest,
    ridge)

4   Upper slope

5   Mid-slope

6   Terrace

7   Lower slope

8   Open depression

9   Closed depression

FIGURE 15.4. Topographic features.

DATA PROCESSING

Transfer to punch cards

The procedure by which observations recorded on the questionnaires are transferred to punch cards involves three phases in which standard cards and regular data-processing equipment (punch machines, sorting and counting machines and tabulators) are used.

In the first stage *Master Data Cards* (CMR) are punched to identify the site and code the ecological observations. Standard cards of 10-line columns, numbered 0 to 9, are used, in which each digit of the code is represented by a punch which is converted into an electric impulse. The observations are too numerous to appear on a single card; they are therefore distributed on a number of cards (CMR_1, CMR_2, CMR_3, etc.).

It is possible to punch the cards directly using a punching machine and reading the questionnaires, but it is more convenient first to prepare a summary statement ('bordereau') form in which each line corresponds to the coded data that are to be punched on one card (Figs. 15.7 and 15.8).

Each plant species at a site is associated with the ecological observations transcribed on the CMR's for that site. In order to build up a complete file that can be processed mechanically, punch cards containing ecological data and phytosociological data must be made. The most convenient solution is to make *Detail cards* (CD). *One CMR-card gives rise to a number of CD-cards equal to the number of species on the site.* If a large-memory computer is available, the procedure can be simplified and more general methods may be proposed. These methods have not yet been completely developed, but when they can be recommended for regular use, it will be advisable to conduct a survey and an analysis and synthesis of them.

Data processing

The ecological observations may be utilized directly to describe the ecological requirements of each taxon sampled; a simple sorting-machine immediately provides the 'ecological profile' of a taxon, that is to say its frequency distribution considered as a function of the various levels of each factor. Thus, Fig. 15.9 shows the distribution of frequency indices of four species at 980 sites in the Mediterranean part of Languedoc in relation to altitude (these include two tree species, one pasture species and one species yielding useful fibres). The ecological

FORMULAIRE D'INVENTAIRE ECOLOGIQUE
DE LA VEGETATION

Nom de la carte .... Date : Jour [12 13] Mois [10 11]

Latitude .... Numéro de la carte [15 16] [17 18]

Longitude .... Auteur (s) ....

Département .... Commune ....

Lieu-dit .... N° de la parcelle cadastrale ....

Nom de l'exploitant ....

Numéro .... [2 3 4]

Auteur .... [5 6]

Année .... [7 8]

Elément .... [9]

Surface de l'élément .... % [14]

Photographies noir ☐

Photographies couleur ☐

Pas de photographie ☐

Surface du relevé .... m² [19] [20]

CROQUIS DE LA STRATIFICATION

CROQUIS DE L'ENVIRONNEMENT ET DES ELEMENTS

Région naturelle : _____ [21 22 23 24]

Séries de végétation : _____ [25 26 27 28]

Influence climatique localement prépondérante [29]

0. Station abritée
1. Station protégée des influences venant du Nord
2. Station protégée des influences venant de l'Est
3. Station protégée des influences venant du Sud
4. Station protégée des influences venant de l'Ouest
5. Vallée ouverte au Nord
6. Vallée ouverte à l'Est
7. Vallée ouverte au Sud
8. Vallée ouverte à l'Ouest
9. Station exposée à tous les vents

Accidents météoriques et climatiques [30 31]

00. Année normale
11. Printemps sec
12. Printemps humide
13. Printemps froid
14. Printemps chaud
21. Eté sec
22. Eté humide
23. Eté froid
24. Eté chaud

31. Automne sec
32. Automne humide
33. Automne froid
34. Automne chaud
41. Hiver sec
42. Hiver humide
43. Hiver froid
44. Hiver chaud

50. Longuement ou massivement enneigé pendant l'hiver précédent
60. Pluies exceptionnelles le mois précédent

Stratification

		Recouvrement (Echelle II en %)	Couvert angulaire au niveau du toit
Strate	I - 0 - 5 cm	32 ..... %	42 ..... / 8
Strate	II - 5 - 25 cm	33 ..... %	43 ..... / 8
Strate	III - 25 - 50 cm	34 ..... %	44 ..... / 8
Strate	IV - 50cm - 1 m	35 ..... %	45 ..... / 8
Strate	V - 1 - 2 m	36 ..... %	46 ..... / 8
Strate	VI - 2 - 4 m	37 ..... %	47 ..... / 8
Strate	VII - 4 - 8 m	38 ..... %	48 ..... / 8
Strate	VIII - 8 - 16 m	39 ..... %	49 ..... / 8
Strate	IX - 16 - 32 m	40 ..... %	50 ..... / 8
Strate	X - 32 m et plus	41 ..... %	51 ..... / 8

Degré d'ouverture des strates basses [52] [53]

ligneux bas .... / herbacées

1. Fermé (> 90 %)
2. Peu ouvert (75 à 90 %)
3. Assez ouvert (50 à 75 %)
4. Ouvert (25 à 50 %)
5. Très ouvert (10 à 25 %)
6. Extrêmement ouvert (0 à 10 %)
7. Totalement ouvert (0 %)

Régularité de la structure [54]

1. Structure verticale et structure horizontale régulières
2. Structure verticale régulière et structure horizontale irrégulière
3. Structure verticale irrégulière et structure horizontale régulière
4. Structure verticale et structure horizontale irrégulières

Formation [55]

0. Zone à végétation très claire ou nulle
1. Formation ligneuse haute dense
2. Formation ligneuse haute assez claire
3. Formation ligneuse haute claire
4. Formation ligneuse basse
5. Formation herbacée
6. Formation complexe ligneuse
7. Formation complexe herbacées-ligneux hauts
8. Formation complexe herbacées-ligneux bas
9. Formation complexe herbacées-ligneux bas-ligneux hauts

Degré d'artificialisation [56]

1. Végétation climacique
2. Artificialisation faible
3. Artificialisation assez faible
4. Artificialisation moyenne
5. Artificialisation assez forte
6. Artificialisation forte
7. Milieux artificiellement dépourvus de végétation

1ère Espèce dominante : _____ [57 58 59 60 61]

2ème Espèce dominante : _____ [62 63 64 65 66]

FIGURE 15-5. Ecological inventory form.

C E P E _ 1967

4

CARACTERES EXTERNES
DU SUBSTRAT DE LA VEGETATION

Numéro............ [2' 3' 4']
Auteur............ [5' 6']
Année............. [7' 8']
Elément........... [9']

CARACTERES TOPOGRAPHIQUES

Altitude .... m   [10' 11']

Exposition   [12']
0. Terrain plat ou sans exposition définie
1. N   5. S
2. NE   6. SW
3. E   7. W
4. SE   8. NW

Position topographique   [13']
0. Terrain plat
1. Sommet vif (pic, arête, éperon)
2. Escarpement (corniche)
3. Sommet arrondi (butte, mamelon, crête, croupe)
4. Haut de versant (talus)
5. Mi-versant
6. Replat
7. Bas de versant
8. Dépression ouverte
9. Dépression fermée

Pente (noter en clair la valeur observée)   [14']
0. 0 à 0,9 %   6. 36 à 48%
1. 1 à 3,9 %   7. 49 à 63%
2. 4 à 8,9 %   8. 64 à 80%
3. 9 à 15 %   9. 81 à 99%
4. 16 à 24 %   11. 100 à 275%

CARACTERES DE LA SURFACE DU SOL

Erosion   [23']
0. Négligeable
1. Hydrique par nappe (faible)
2. Hydrique par nappe (modérée)
3. Hydrique par nappe (forte)
4. Hydrique par rigoles
5. Hydrique par ravins
6. Eolienne
7. Zone de départ d'éboulements
8. Glissements
9. Cas particuliers

Microrelief du sol   [24']
0. Cas particuliers
1. Plan
2. Convexe
3. Concave
4. En planches ou en rigoles
5. Crevassé
6. Alvéolé
7. En billons
8. En polygones
9. Bosselé
11. Ridé-ondulé
12. Mamelonné

Surface couverte par la roche dure et les blocs
dans le relevé .... %   [25' 26']

Surface couverte par les pierrailles .... %   [27' 28']

Surface couverte par la terre fine .... %   [29' 30']

Surface couverte par la végétation .... %   [31' 32']
(recouvrement basal)

Surface couverte par la litière .... %   [33' 34']

Type de litière (voir Code)   [35']
0. Pas de litière
1. Type I (litière foliacée dense)
2. Type II (litière foliacée aérée)
3. Type III (litière ligneuse)
4. Type IV (débris transformés par les animaux)

4

CONDITIONS HYDRIQUES

Humidité apparente de la station
0. Cas particuliers
1. Station très sèche
2. Station sèche
3. Station assez sèche
4. Station moyenne
5. Station assez humide
6. Station humide
7. Station très humide (sol saturé)
8. Station extrêmement humide (sol sursaturé)

$\boxed{36'}$

Submersion
1. Station apparemment jamais inondée
2. Station inondable accidentellement
3. Station submergée périodiquement (moins de 6 mois)
4. Station submergée périodiquement (plus de 6 mois)
5. Station toujours submergée en eau peu profonde
6. Station toujours submergée en eau profonde
11. Eau circulante oxygénée
12. Eau stagnante

$\boxed{37'}$

Aménagements hydriques
0. Aménagements non perceptibles
1. Station non assainie
2. Station assainie mais non drainée
3. Station assainie et drainée
4. Pas d'irrigation
5. Irrigation par déversement ou ruissellement
6. Irrigation par submersion
7. Irrigation par diffusion
8. Irrigation par aspersion

$\boxed{38'}$

CARACTERES GEOLOGIQUES
ET
LITHOLOGIQUES

Age de la roche (voir Code) $\boxed{15' \ 16' \ 17'}$

Pourcentage d'affleurement de la roche dure
et des blocs dans la station   ....% $\boxed{18'}$

Réaction à ClH de la roche affleurante $\boxed{19'}$

0. La roche n'affleure pas
1. La roche affleurante ne fait pas effervescence
2. Effervescence très faible
3. Effervescence faible,
4. Effervescence forte
5. Effervescence très forte
6. Effervescence nettement localisée

Nature de la roche (voir Code) $\boxed{20' \ 21' \ 22'}$

FIGURE 15.6. Form for description of superficial attributes of the substrate.

						Label	Col
2	2	2	2	2	2	Card identification	1
8	9	9	9	9	4	Sample number	2
4	7	6	5	9	4		3
3	6	1	1	7	6		4
3	3	1	3	3	3	Author	5
7	7	7	7	7	7		6
6	6	6	6	6	6	Year	7
3	3	3	3	3	3		8
0	0	0	0	0	0	Element	9
0	0	1	0	0	0	Elevation	10
0	7	0	2	2	0		11
8	4	4	7	6	6	Aspect	12
6	2	2	0	6	0	Topographic code	13
1	0	0	0	0	0	Slope	14
3	2	0	3	5	6	Age of rock	15
5	3	5	3	6	6		16
4	0	4	2	0	8		17
0	0	0	0	0	0	% outcrop of bedrock and boulders	18
0	0	0	0	0	0	HCL reaction of outcrop	19
2	4		4	3	3	Rock type	20
3	0	3	0	3	3		21
4	3	3	7	4	4		22
						Erosion	23
						Micro-relief	24
0	0	0	0	0	0	Surface covered by bedrock and boulders	25
0	0	0	0	0	0		26
0	1	1	0	0	0	Surface covered by gravel	27
5	0	0	5	5	5		28
3	4	2	4	5	4	Surface covered by fine soil	29
5	0	0	5	5	5		30
6	3	1	5	7	5	Surface covered by vegetation	31
0	0	0	0	0	0		32
0	0	0	0	0	0	Surface covered by litter	33
0	0	0	0	0	0		34
0	0	0	0	0	0	Type of litter	35
3	2	2	3	4	6	Apparent humidity of site	36
						Flooding	37
						Water management measures	38

FIGURE 15.7. The first line in this example is the source for the punch card shown in Figure 15.8.

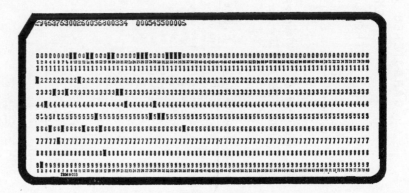

FIGURE 15.8. A standard punch card.

profiles thus established, for example in relation to altitude or pH, are very suggestive, but to interpret them accurately sampling errors must be taken into account. The preliminary interpretation may be com-

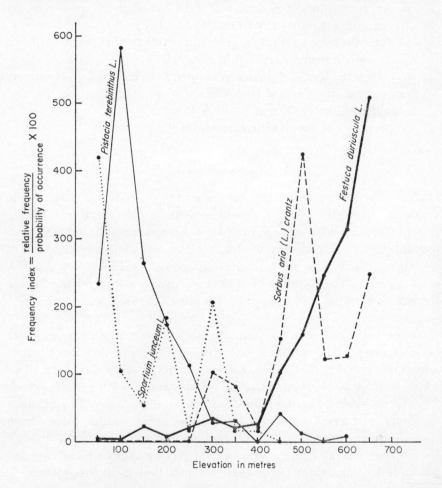

FIGURE 15.9. Ecological profile of four species in Mediterranean Languedoc plotted against elevation.

pleted by a χ^2 test or by an analysis of variance, carried out in respect of each taxon for each ecological factor.

The processing of observations may be carried further if one accepts the idea of a polycriterial classification; the application of multivariate analysis to such data would make it possible:

H

(1) to determine the more important ecological factors, or to define taxon-groups with similar ecological affinities, by principal component analysis;

(2) to determine, by discriminant analysis, whether groups of sites, or of taxa, differ significantly from one another;

(3) to determine, by multiple regression, which factors produce linear effects by complementary action;

(4) to calculate 'distances' between factors, between sites, and between taxa (using the 'generalized distances' of Mahalanobis, or else 'simplified distances'), and

(5) to propose outline classifications from the analysis of these groups.

CONCLUSIONS

If their observations are to be combined into a coherent whole, it is necessary that all observers should use the most objective methods possible, and a *precise language,* in order to compare results and arrive at a synthesis. Standardization of observations and their statistical interpretation call for the use of a uniform code. As Flahault stated, as early as 1901, 'the essential condition for progress in a science is that those who work in it should speak the same language and understand one another'.

Experience has shown repeatedly that the complexity of an exact code is more apparent than real, because the detailed descriptions which it involves serve to dissect observations in order to reduce them to the simplest elements that can be rapidly and unambiguously noted.

The collection, sampling and processing of ecological observations can only be carried out by teams which accept similar rules. Some nations appear to understand this and a solution seems simple enough for international agreement to be initiated, as has been recommended by special commissions of the International Biological Programme.

THE DEVELOPMENT OF AGROBIOCLIMATIC TECHNIQUES

J. M. HENRY

Musée Royal de l'Afrique Centrale, Tervuren, Belgium

For many years farmers, agronomists and others concerned with crops have attempted to classify climates in ways that will identify agrobioclimatic analogues. Such a classification would permit biotypes which are adapted to particular regions to be transferred successfully to ecologically similar environments elsewhere. This paper considers the criteria to be adopted in such studies, surveys some of the approaches, and presents a brief account of some more recently published systems which, although not perfect, appear to have promise in indicating bioclimatic analogies.

CRITERIA

A system of agrobioclimatic analogues requires that:

1. all territorial units to be compared
   (a) are given a matrix number under a universally applied geographic code, and
   (b) are not too large to be ecologically homogeneous;
2. environmental variables (independent variables) such as climate, soil, topography and natural vegetation
   (a) are all considered in making ecological comparisons between territorial units,
   (b) are classified according to parameters arranged in a hierarchic order of decreasing importance, though the system should be able to accept new criteria as required, and
   (c) can be translated into a universal language, the terms of which can be composed of polysyllabic codes representing all the essential criteria for the comparisons;
3. dependent variables—plant species, their growth duration and crop group, races, cultivars, clones or strains—should be given matrix numbers according to their geographic origin;

4. all possible ecological cases can be compared, not only those which cover the whole year, but also those in which the period of plant growth is less than a year, and even as short as three months, whatever their altitude or latitude;

5. every classification
   (a) can be based upon a sufficiently universal system, and
   (b) can continually admit new data and so remain up to date;

6. ecological analogues can be determined rapidly, and lists of biotypes suitable for transfer can be compiled without delay when information is requested.

SURVEY OF AGROBIOCLIMATIC METHODS

Meher-Homji (1963), has reviewed most known methods of agrobioclimatic comparisons, and has classified them as follows:

I PHYSICAL AND METEREOLOGICAL METHODS

A. *Climatic indices, coefficients* and *formulae:* the humidity index (hygrometric coefficient) of Transeau (1905), the Penck formula (1910), the Köppen formula (1918), the rain factor of Lang (1920), the aridity index of de Martonne (1926), the pluviothermal quotient of Emberger (1930), the aridity factor of Gorczynski (1941), the humidity index of Mangenot (1951), the aridity index of Capot Rey (1951), the Thornthwaite formula (1933), Nuttonson's method (1947a), and the precipitation efficacy formula of Bharucha and Shanbhag (1957).

B. *Schematic representation:* the climatic axes and physiographic zones of Azzi (1956), the polygonal representation of Chaptal (1933), the climogram or hythergraph of Taylor (1940), and the ombrothermal diagram of Bagnouls and Gaussen (1957).

C. The method of Meher-Homji (1963), described below.

II BIOLOGICAL METHODS WHICH REFLECT
CLIMATIC ANALOGIES

A. *Floristic methods* of plant classification: *systematic* and *floristic patterns.*

B. *Vegetation:* life-form classifications, structure and physiognomy classifications, and ecological classifications, including the ecologically-based classification of Villar (1929) and single-factor classifications based on water, light, or temperature, classifications based on soil conditions, multi-factor classifications, the static methods based on plant associations and the dynamic methods based on plant successions.

Meher-Homji concludes from his critical review that 'neither the floristic method, the life-form method, nor any ecological method which considers one single factor at a time, nor the static method of plant associations, is satisfactory. These methods do not give a picture of analogues in the vegetable kingdom; the analogues arrived at by these methods do not consider climate.' On the other hand, he showed great interest in certain other classifications including the ecological formulae of Gaussen, and the classifications of the physiognomy of vegetation: in fact, Meher-Homji uses vegetation types to reflect climatic analogies.

METHOD OF MEHER-HOMJI (1963)

Meher-Homji uses a classification of climate, derived from the ombro-thermal diagrams of Bagnouls & Gaussen (1957), within which sub-divisions are based on modifications of the ecological formulae of Gaussen (1955).

CLIMATIC CLASSIFICATION

He distinguishes three major types of climate, divided into twelve climatic regions and further divided into subregions, which are in turn divided into climatic sectors.

I *Hot and warm temperate climates (thermal curve always positive)*
1. Eremic or hot desert
    a True desert
    b Rainfall possible during short days, tending to a Mediterranean type
    c Rainfall possible during long days, tending to a tropical type
    d Rainfall erratic.
2. Hemi eremic or hot sub-desert: 11 to 9 dry months
    a Tending to a Mediterranean type
    b Tending to a tropical type
    c Tendency erratic.
3. Xerotheric: dry long days, tending to Mediterranean, temperature of the coldest month ranging from 0°C to 15°C.
    a Xerothermo mediterranean   7 to 8 dry months
    b Thermo mediterranean   5 to 6 dry months
    c Meso mediterranean   3 to 4 dry months
    d Sub mediterranean   1 to 2 dry months

4. Xerochimenic : Dry short days

| | | | Temperature of the coldest month | | Number of dry months |
			more than 15°C	less than 15°C	
a	Th	Thermoxerochimenic	+	−	7–8
a	Mes	Mesoxerochimenic	−	+	7–8
b	Th	Thermoxerochimenic	+	−	5–6
b	Mes	Mesoxerochimenic	−	+	5–6
c	Th	Thermoxerochimenic	+	−	3–4
c	Mes	Mesoxerochimenic	−	+	3–4
d	Th	Subthermaxeric	+	−	1–2
d	Mes	Submesaxeric	−	+	1–2

5. Bixeric : Two dry seasons (if both dry seasons together exceed 8 months, the climate is bixeric-hemieremic, classed under 2c)

| | | | Temperature of the coldest month | | Number of dry months |
			more than 15°C	less than 15°C	
a	Th	Thermobixeric	+	−	7–8
a	Mes	Mesobixeric	−	+	7–8
b	Th	Thermobixeric	+	−	5–6
b	Mes	Mesobixeric	−	+	5–6
c	Th	Thermobixeric	+	−	3–4
c	Mes	Mesobixeric	−	+	3–4
d	Th	Subthemaxeric	+	−	1–2
d	Mes	Submesaxeric	−	+	1–2

6. Thermaxeric

		Number of dry months
a	Euthermaxeric (equatorial) more than 20°C	0
b	Hypothermaxeric (subequatorial) 15°C to 20°C	0

7. Mesaxeric

			Number of dry months
a	Eumesaxeric	10°C to 15°C	0
b	Hypomesaxeric	0°C to 10°C	0

II *Cold and cold temperate climates* (*thermal curve negative at certain times of the year*)

8. Eremic
    a True desert —Entirely dry nearly every year
    b True desert —No accumulated snow
    c Desert   —A little accumulated snow

9. Hemieremic cold subdesert : 9 to 10 dry months

10. Xerotheric cold	Number of months of frost
a Oroxerotheric : mountainous with dry summer (accentuated)	7–8
b Oroxerotheric : mountainous with dry summer (medium)	5–6
c Oroxerotheric : mountainous with dry summer (mild)	1–2
d Submediterranean : transition to dry xerotheric	1–2

11. Axeric cold	Number of months of frost
a *Very cold*	More than 8
a Oc Oceanic	
a Ct Continental	
b *Cold*	
b Hct Hypercontinental	
b Mt Orohygrotheric (mountainous)	7–8
b Oc Oceanic	
b Ct Continental	
c *Medium Cold*	
c Hct Hypercontinental	4–6
c Mt Orohygrotheric (mountainous)	
d *Temperate cold*	less than 4

III *Glacial climate :* (*thermal curve always negative*)

12. Cryomeric. The cold season lasts all year round	12

ECOLOGICAL FORMULAE

These are based on the combination of values for three factors : temperature (t), humidity (S) and dry season (X).

Temperature (t)

Nine classes are established as a function of the mean for the warmest month (M), the mean for the coldest month (m) or the annual mean (Tn)—see table 16.1.

TABLE 16.1.

Classes and index values	t_1	$t_{1/2}$	t_2	t_3	$t_{3/4}$	t_4	$t_{4/5}$	t_5	t_6
M	less than 10	more than 10	more than 10						
m		less than −15	less than −5	−5–0	0–10	10–15	15–20	more than 20	
Tn								less than 30	less than 30

(Figures = °C)

Humidity (S)

Ten classes are based on total annual precipitation (P) and the number of dry months (n)—see table 16.2.

TABLE 16.2.

Classes and index values	S_1	$S_{1/2}$	S_2	S_3			$S_{3/4}$	S_4	$S_{4/5}$	S_5	$S_{5/6}$	S_6
Rainfall (mm year^{-1})	more than 3000	2999 to 2000	1999 to 1500	1499 to 1000	1499 to 1300	1499 to 750	999 to 750	999 to 750	749 to 500	499 to 250	249 to 100	99 to 0
n				1–2*	3–6	0†	6	7–8				

(*) with 95 days of rainfall
(†) with temperatures below zero at certain times of the year.

Period of drought and xerothermic index (X)

A month is described as dry when $P < 2Tn$. On this basis, the following figures for the xerothermic index are given as a function of the number (n) of dry months—see table 16.3.

TABLE 16.3.

Index figures	X1	X1/2	X2	X2/3	X3	X3/4	X4	X4/5	X5	X5/6	X6
Number of dry months	1	2	3	4	5	6	7	8	9	10	11–12

The aridity—humidity—frost complex $(S + X + g)$

The aridity, or its inverse, the humidity, of a region depends on the length of the dry season and total annual precipitation. By adding the value for index X to that for index S one obtains a sum which is greater the dryer the region. Similar totals can be derived from very different combinations of figures; for example $S_2 + X_4$, $S_4 + X_2$ and $S_3 + X_3$ all give $(S + X) = 6$.

Frost (g) or length of the cold season is the third index considered in this part of the formula. A frosty month is defined as a month in which the mean temperature is $-2°C$ or below. The scale of values in table 16.4 shows frost intensity.

TABLE 16.4.

Value of indices	g1	g1/2	g2	g2/3	g3	g3/4	g4	g4/5	g5	g5/6	g6
Number of months of frost	1	2	3	4	5	6	7	8	9	10	11–12

By combining values of indices composite indices are obtained; for example $(S + X + g)$ may range from 1 for a very humid site to 12 for a very cold or very warm desert. Figures for the sum $(S + X + g)$ should always be linked with the temperature for the coldest month (see above for values of t).

The Meher-Homji indices may also combine as shown in table 16.5.

TABLE 16.5.

Bioclimate	Ecological formula	Value of each ecological factor
1a	$t_4/5(S + X)$ 12	$t_4/5$ S6 X6
1d	t_4 $(S + X)$ 11 1/2	t_4 S5/6 X6
4a Th	t_5 $(S + X)$ 8 1/2	t_5 S4 X4/5
10a	t 1/2 $(S + X + g)$9	t 1/2 S5 $(X + g)$4
10d	t_3 $(S + X + g)$6	t_3 S 4/5 $(X + g)$

H*

The Meher-Homji system is consistent, and deserves further development. It will be necessary to base formulae on a larger number of examples, and to obtain indices for smaller geographical areas. Further, the Meher-Homji system does not involve independent classifications of physiographic and soil units. Nevertheless, this method seems to provide an explanation of the vast range of vegetation-types found in the different bio-climates of the world.

THE METHOD OF PAPADAKIS (1966)

From the point of view of the agronomist, Papadakis has developed the most complete system. He shows that it is necessary to take all factors of the environment into account in determining agricultural potentialities. He rightly rejects synthetic classifications that fail to allow for variations in plant requirements during different life phases. From a practical standpoint, he suggests that fluctuations in synthetic data such as energy balance or water balance are not sufficient to determine the agricultural potential of a habitat. Furthermore, it is necessary to consider the extent of fluctuation, or the extreme values, of certain parameters which constitute critical thresholds for many plants. However, in this system the calculations of indices for classifying a habitat are lengthy and require detailed climatic data, and there is no legitimate means of interpolating for localities between widely-separated observation posts.

Moreover, the bases on which he delimits the major climatic units include the limits of distribution of certain major crops. To draw firm conclusions about the possible distribution of a particular species by reference to the distribution of one or more other cultivated species may be dangerous. From this point of view the method of Papadakis does not take into account the necessity that the variables between which one seeks to establish correlations must be independent. One can observe that a cultivated species may often be encountered within the area of distribution of another species. One need not infer that the optimum areas for cultivation and the limits of the economic cultivation areas of two species need necessarily coincide in all parts of a region or in all parts of the world. What is true of individual species is all the more valid for varieties and lines, and particularly for clones, which are less plastic than ecotypes.

This system of classification, based on areas of cultivation of characteristic species is open to the same objections as systems based on the geographic range of the major plant formations. Like that of Meher-Homji, the method of Papadakis embraces regions which are too large, and the calculation of the characteristics for localities not cited by the author are too time-consuming. However, the symbols used by Papadakis should be established for all the meteorological stations in the world so that their data can be used for interpolation. One may further note that while Papadakis describes major soil and geographic units, he does not provide a detailed, separate classification that allows all elements to be taken into account in characterising regions, or in making valid comparisons of 'climate × soil' and '(climate-soil) × plant formations'. Nevertheless, it should be stressed that this system can be useful and may be combined with others until such time as a better system has been evolved. Therefore, without going into detail, the principles of the Papadakis classification are described briefly by means of a few illustrations.

The classification is based on the following criteria :

A *Thermal regimes*, which are based on different combinations of winter and summer temperatures, each type being defined in relation to the requirements of certain typical plants: oil palm, coconut palm, *Hevea*, *Citrus*, winter wheat, spring wheat, oats and spring-sown crops such as cotton and rice. The following temperature regimes have been defined :

Hot equatorial (EQ) and warm equatorial (Eq) ; Hot tropical (Tr), warm tropical (TR), warm tropical with cold winter (tR) and cold tropical (tr). Polar and alpine climates are classified similarly.

B *Humidity regimes*, determined according to the balance of precipitation and evapotranspiration to establish :

dry periods and wet periods ; leaching rainfall (Ln), rainfall of maximum leaching (Lm) and monthly and annual humidity indices (1a and 1m). Various combinations of these criteria define a number of regimes including very humid (HU), humid (hu), humid Mediterranean (ME), dry Mediterranean (Me), semi-arid Mediterranean (me), dry monsoon (Mo), and absolute desert (da).

Finally, particular combinations of thermal regime and humidity regime distinguish climatic types, which are numbered decimally in ten major classes, each of which is further subdivided into four subclasses. The following subdivisions are thus obtained, see overleaf:

1. Tropical climates

    1.1   Warm, humid Equatorial (Eq combined with HU, Hu or MO)

        1.11 Always humid EqHU (1a > 1)

        1.12 Humid (Hu)

        1.13 Very humid, monsoon (MO) : from 1 to 3 dry months

    1.3   Warm, dry tropical climates

Warm dry, tropical climates, equatorial (Eq)

Warm dry, tropical climates, tropical (Tr)

        1.31 Dry monsoon (Mo) : 4 to 5 dry months

        1.32 Dry monsoon (Mo) : 6 dry or very dry months

        1.35 Wet monsoon (MO) : 0 to 3 dry months

        1.36 Wet monsoon (MO) : 4 to 5 dry months

3. Desert climates (da, de, di, do)

    3.1   Warm tropical deserts, Equatorial (Eq), tropical warm (TR) etc.

    3.7   Continental deserts

        3.71 Hot Co

        3.72 Warm Co

        3.73 Cold Co

6. Mediterranean (ME, Me, me, etc.).

Papadakis has compiled a very small-scale, schematic map of climatic types. The examination of certain defined climatic areas shows that a number of them include regions with different agricultural potentials. For instance, in the Democratic Republic of the Congo, the boundaries between the climate types 1.1, 1.2, 1.4 and 1.7 coincide with neither the boundaries of major plant formations nor the boundaries of the areas suitable for particular crops or animal husbandry.

If the areas compared were smaller and meteorological stations more numerous, the climatic delimitations could be made more accurate. For example Papadakis uses the records of about 20 meteorological stations in the Congo, and about 50 in Indonesia, but rainfall data from more than 1,000 stations are in fact available in the former country and from 5,000 in the latter.

METHOD OF HOLDRIDGE (1947)

Holdridge bases the limits of plant formations on temperature, precipitation, the length of the dry season and the rainfall-evaporation ratio.

He defines plant formation as the major class of plant association and the physiognomic or structural unit which contains specific biological forms, though not necessarily of the same floristic composition in all regions. Within these major formations plant associations are primarily differentiated according to soil and atmospheric factors. On the basis of climatic data, Holdridge has constructed, using appropriate scales, a cellular graph based upon an equilateral triangle.

A geometric scale perpendicular to the base of the triangle represents temperatures covering the range from 0°C to 30°C. From this scale, thermal analogues between effects of latitude and altitude can be shown. The scale at right angles to the left side of the triangle shows rainfall, and a third scale shows the precipitation/evapotranspiration ratio. Since the author calculates evapotranspiration, represented along one side of the triangle, by multiplying the average temperature by a constant, there is a certain parallelism between the temperature and evaporation scales. The surface of the triangle is subdivided into hexagons in bold lines, and into small triangles within them. Over 40 plant formations are characterized by different combinations of the three factors, from evergreen rain forest to dry tundra; combinations falling within triangles are transition zones between adjacent plant formations.

The Holdridge method has been successfully applied in many countries of South and Central America. The correlation between determinations made with the help of the diagram and the major plant formations is generally very good. However, it is still necessary to establish criteria for differences due to soil and atmospheric factors.

Neither Holdridge nor Papadakis consider day-length, their criteria being exclusively thermal or hydrological. Thus, in the Papadakis system, the climate at the Equator in the Congo has the same value (1.1) as the climate on the north-eastern coast of Madagascar (15° latitude South) or at Luzon (17° latitude North). In the Holdridge system, although one latitudinal region, the Boreal, for instance, may show the same overall thermal and hydrological relations as those of the sub-alpine region, it is clear that, according to continental influence, the temperature and day-length distributions in these two regions will be entirely different.

METHOD OF TROLL AND PFAFFEN (1964)

Climatic types defined by these writers depend on the interaction of three factors, namely: duration of daylight, depending on latitude;

annual temperature fluctuations; and seasonal distribution of rainfall.

The climates of oceanic regions are treated merely as variants of the corresponding continental climates, and montane climates are interpreted as altitudinal variations of the general climatic zone around them. On such a basis, these authors distinguish climate types which might serve as the major classes of a classification of climate, the subdivisions of which may be based on altitude classes, or on the degree of continental influence. Troll has been able to indicate more subtle differences in climate by means of isopleth diagrams which present an overall view of daily and seasonal changes in average temperature. The shape and density of the isopleth represent different types of climate in a striking manner. On the same diagram, dotted lines show the length of the day and the positions of the sun at its highest and lowest points. Rainfall and cloud distribution are given on an adjacent graph.

This graphic representation of climate would be much improved if temperature extremes were represented, and if the rainfall curve were replaced by one showing the rainfall/evaporation ratio. Although the compilation of diagrams of this sort for climatic stations throughout the world would entail a tremendous amount of work, pairs of diagrams might be compared as transparencies and larger numbers might be handled by appropriate data-processing methods. Given a complete and detailed atlas of diagrams for all stations throughout the world this method would certainly be used to develop a generalized system of climatic analogues.

METHOD OF PHILLIPS (1959)

Phillips has provided a remarkable synthesis of all the works on climatology, plant geography and agriculture which deal with Africa south of the Sahara. He distinguishes and classifies various plant formations, sub-regions and units, in decreasing order of importance. For each subdivision he gives values or ranges, or else a qualitative appraisal of the climatic factors considered responsible for biogeographic differentiation. For each subregion or unit, the data of characteristic criteria are condensed: annual average precipitation; the division of months into wet, medium humid and ecologically dry months, two classes (very humid and excessively dry) for the distribution of vapour pressure, two classes for saturation deficit; a quantitative and qualitative treatment of temperature to give either a numerical value for fluctuation of the mean temperature or to assign each bioclimate to one of the five following groups—Megathermic (M), intermediate (M/m), mesothermic (m), fairly cold (f cl) and cold (cl).

These data constitute a distinct contribution to the development of bioclimatic analogues, but it is a pity that the climatic data which accompany the descriptions of bioclimatic regions are neither sufficiently detailed nor sufficiently characteristic to provide a basis for detailed comparisons of agricultural methods or estimates of the probable range of adaptation of new varieties or lines. Nor have independent comparisons been established between the phytogeographic classification and the units of climatic classification. Finally, the major soil groups and physiographic effects are not characterised sufficiently to be used for distinct and detailed classification.

METHOD OF NUTTONSON
(1947 a and b, 1948, 1949, 1953, 1955, 1957 a, b, 1962)

Nuttonson has made many studies of agroclimatological analogies between pairs of regions and countries. The comparisons are based on average annual and seasonal precipitation, day-degree sums, mean temperature of the coldest month, mean temperature of the warmest month and mean annual temperature. Latitude is considered in many cases.

These publications are very informative monographs on agriculture, animal husbandry and forestry and varietal adaptation in restricted geographic units. Soils and plant cover are treated generally but not described in detail. Nuttonson's work is of great value in planning the introduction of forms from one country to another.

METHOD OF THE NATICK* LABORATORIES (U.S. ARMY 1959)

These studies, made for military purposes, base comparisons on mean annual and monthly data of precipitation and of average, absolute maximum and minimum, and mean daily maximum and minimum, temperature. Soil and vegetation are not considered, but the Natick studies may be useful in improving agrobioclimatic comparisons.

CONCLUSIONS

Though elements from these methods may help in the construction of a better system, this summary indicates the diversity of criteria used to

* U.S. Army Laboratories, Natick, Massachussetts. U.S.A.

compare and classify climatic types, as well as the difficulty of deriving
analogues on a world scale from systems based on relatively restricted
areas, and of taking topography, soil type and plant cover into account.
None, for example, indicates latitudinal analogues or seasonal analogues between different latitudes, or can be used to produce lists of
new biotypes that may be introduced into a habitat from climatic
analogies. None establishes valid correlations between climatic types,
soil units or composite units and plant formations, and all use only a
relatively restricted number of meteorological stations, so that more or
less elaborate calculations and interpolations are necessary before
analogies can be established.

To be successful, a system should include the registration, using a
numerical code, of all meteorological stations and sites, and a polysyllabic coding, appropriate to all languages, of the factors of climate,
topography, soil and vegetation for each of which separate classifications should be established. For climate, the classification of Walter and
Lieth (1960) is proposed as a basis. It includes several thousand climatic
diagrams constructed according to the principles of Gaussen. Each
climatic type is described by two words. One, the analogue of the genus
in biological classification, is a translation of the subdivisions of Walter
and Lieth. The second (analogous to the species name) is composed of
coded syllables and letters for the physical factors influencing climate,
such as latitude, hemisphere, continentalism, local topography and
altitude. For geography and vegetation the geographical classification
of Monkhouse (1964) could be converted into a polysyllabic code. Soil
types could be classified by combining the 7th Approximation of the
Soil Classification of the U.S. Department of Agriculture (1967 a and b),
the French soil classification (Aubert, 1965), and the classification of
Sijs et al (1961), all of which have been converted into polysyllabic
codes. Separate lists should be built up of the dependent variables—
plant species, biotypes, cultivars, clones—giving not only their names
and standard references but also an appropriate number derived from
the geographical registration of meteorological stations.

In this way it will be possible to determine climatic, phytogeographic
and pedological analogues, to compile lists of plant species and varieties
which may be transferred between analogous environments, to correlate
climate and soil type or plant cover, and to establish comprehensive
bibliographies of analogous regions.

It may be possible to further study agricultural analogies between
environments which differ in several parameters. Factors interact:

altitude counters the effect of latitude, and topographic and soil features (such as natural sub-irrigation) may diminish the effects of extreme climatic conditions. Modern systems for storing and processing data will be essential to handle the very large volume of data needed to construct the multivariate classifications. The system suggested is flexible enough to accept new parameters without radical changes in higher-order categories.

REFERENCES

AUBERT G. (1965) Classification des sols, tableaux des classes, sous-classes, groupes et sous-groupes de sols utilisés par la Section de Pédologie de l'O.R.S.T.O.M. *Cahiers O.R.S.T.O.M., Série Pédologie*, III, **3**.

AZZI G. (1956) *Agricultural Ecology*. London.

BAGNOULS F. & GAUSSEN H. (1957) Les climats biologiques et leur classification. *Annls. Géogr.* **355,** 193–220.

BARUCHA & SHANBHAG (1957) Precipitation effectiveness in relation to the vegetation of India, Pakistan and Burma. *Bot. Memoirs No.* 3, University of Bombay.

CAPOT REY L. (1951) Une carte de l'indice d'aridité au Sahara français. *Bull. Ass. géogr. fr.* 216–7, 73–6.

CHAPTAL L. (1933) Sur un mode de représentation des conditions atmosphèriques en écologie végétale. *Annls. Agron. Nouv. Série*, **3,** 359–365.

DE MARTONNE E. (1926) Aridisme et indice d'aridité. *Compt. Rendo. Acad. Sci., Paris* **182,** 1395–8.

EMBERGER L. (1930) Sur une formule climatique applicable en geographie botanique. *Compt. Rend. Acad. Sci., Paris* **191,** 389–91.

GAUSSEN H. (1955) Determination des climats par la méthode des courbes ombrothermiques. *Compt. Rend. Acad. Sci., Paris* **240,** 642–3.

GORCZYNSKI W. (1941) *Decimal Scheme of World Climate*. Scripps Institute of Oceanography, La Jolla.

HOLDRIDGE L.R. (1947) Determination of world plant formations from simple climatic data. *Science*, **105,** 367–368.

KÖPPEN W. (1918) Klassifikation der Klimate nach Temperatur, Niederschlag und Jahresverlauf. *Petermanns Mitt.* **64,** 193–203, 243–248.

LANG R. (1920) Verwitterung und Bodenbildung als Einführung in die Bodenkunde. *Stuttgart, Schweizer bart'sche Verlag Buchdlg.* 123.

MANGENOT G. (1951) Une formule simple permettant de caracteriser les climats de l'Afrique intertropicale dans leurs rapports avec la végétation. *Rev. Gen. Bot.* **58,** 353–372.

MEHER-HOMJI V.M. (1963) Les bioclimats du sub-continent indien et leurs types analogues dans le monde. *Documn. Cartes Product. Végét., Toulouse, Fasc. Sci. Sér. Génér.* **4.**

MONKHOUSE F. (1964) *Principles of Physical Geography*. New York.

NUTTONSON M.Y. (1947a) International cooperation in crop improvement through the utilisation of the concept of agroclimatic analogues. *Interagra* **1,** 2–8.

NUTTONSON M.Y. (1947b) Ecological crop geography of China and its agroclimatic analogues in North America. *Int. Agro-clim. Ser. Am. Inst. Crop. Ecol.* **7.**

NUTTONSON M.Y. (1948) Some preliminary observations of phenological data as a test in the study of photoperiodic and thermal requirements of various plant materials in vernalisation and photoperiodism. *Chronica Bot.* **12,** 129–143.

NUTTONSON M.Y. (1949) U.S.S.R.: Some physical and agricultural characteristics of the drought area and its climatic analogues in the United States. *Land Econ.* **25,** 347–364.

NUTTONSON M.Y. (1953) *Phenology and thermal environment as a means for a physiological classification of wheat varieties and for predicting maturity dates of wheat.* Am. Inst. Crop. Ecol.

NUTTONSON M.Y. (1955) *Wheat-climate relationships and the use of phenology in ascertaining the thermal and photothermal requirements of wheat.* Am. Inst. Crop Ecol.

NUTTONSON M.Y. (1957a) *Barley-climate relationships and the use of phenology in ascertaining the thermal and photothermal requirements of barley.* Am. Inst. Crop Ecol.

NUTTONSON M.Y. (1957b) The role of bioclimatology in agriculture with special reference to the use of thermal and photothermal requirements of pure-line varieties of plants as a biological indicator in ascertaining climatic analogues (homoclimes). *Int. J. Bioclim. Biomet.* **1,** 1–18.

NUTTONSON M.Y. (1962) Crops and the Weather: the role of bioclimatology in agriculture. *Landscape, Santa Fe* **12,** 1.

PAPADAKIS J. (1966) *Climates of the World and their Agricultural Potentialities.* Buenos Aires.

PENCK A. (1910) Versuch einer Klimaklassifikation auf physiogeographischer Grundlage. *Sber. preuss. Akad. Wiss, phys.-math. Kl.* **1,** 236–46.

PHILLIPS J. (1959) *Agriculture and Ecology in Africa, a study of actual and potential development south of the Sahara.* London.

SIJS C., VAN WAMBEKE A., FRANKART R., GILSON P., JONGEN P., PECROT A., BERCE J.-M. & JAMAGNE M. (1961) La cartographie des sols au Congo: ses principes et ses méthodes. *Publs Inst. natn. Étude agron. Congo Belge, ser. tech.* **66.**

TAYLOR G. (1940) *Australia.* London.

THORNTHWAITE C.W. (1931) The climates of North America according to a new classification. *Geogrl. Rev.* **21,** 633–655.

TRANSEAU E.N. (1905) Forest centres of eastern America. *Am Nat.* **39,** 875–89.

TROLL C. & PFAFFEN K.H. (1964) Die Karte Jahreszeiten-Klimate der Erde, *Erdkunde* **18,** 5–28.

VILLAR E. HUGET DEL (1929) *Geobotanica.* Barcelona.

WALTER H. & LIETH H. (1960–7) *Klimadiagram-Weltatlas.* Jena.

U.S. ARMY (1959) Southwest Asia: environment and its relationship to military activities. *Tech. Rep. U.S. Army Res. Eng. Commd.* EP-118. Natick, Massachusetts.

U.S. DEPARTMENT OF AGRICULTURE (1967a) *Soil Classification, a comprehensive system, 7th approximation.* Soil Conservation Service, U.S.D.A., Washington.

U.S. DEPARTMENT OF AGRICULTURE (1967b) *Supplement to Soil Classification System, 7th approximation.* Soil Conservation Service, U.S.D.A., Washington.

TACTICS OF EXPLORATION
AND COLLECTION

JOHN L. CREECH

New Crops Research Branch, Agricultural Research Service,
U.S. Department of Agriculture, Beltsville, Maryland, U.S.A.

DEFINITION OF PURPOSES:
THE CROP IMPROVEMENT VIEWPOINT

Plant exploration, in its broadest sense, is the survey of remote regions for the purpose of collecting higher plants for biological purposes. This chapter is concerned only with the strictly agricultural aspect of plant exploration—the purposeful collection of wild and cultivated plants and their subsequent introduction into new areas, or their use in plant breeding programmes, for agriculture and industry. Such exploration is a search for both primitive and advanced genetic material that may improve cultivated crops, as well as for unimproved species from which entirely new crops may be developed. It leads to the organized exchange of plant materials, which also helps to shift existing export crops to new regions of culture, and to the establishment of germ plasm collections. The results of such exploration provide material for studies of genetic variability, from which it is possible to define centres of resistance to insects and diseases, of particular types of adaptation to ecological conditions, and of other features which are important to the improvement and diversification of crops. The viewpoint here presented is particularly important in the United States, where (apart from the sunflower) we do not have indigenous sources of variation for our major crops. At the same time we have a large number of plant breeders, whose needs we must attempt to supply. For example, we have over 100 tomato breeders, each of whom has specific needs for his breeding programmes.

COLLECTING FOR THE PLANT BREEDER

The most important purpose of collecting for the plant breeder is to meet the needs of those whose task is to improve particular crops and who therefore seek sources of variability to help solve specific crop problems. Furthermore, in most countries where crop introduction has succeeded, active programs of research and plant breeding are necessary to maintain and improve the commercial stocks and to decrease losses due to insects and disease. Approximately one-third of the plant research in the Crops Research Division of the U.S. Department of Agriculture (USDA) is related to breeding for resistance to insects and diseases. Breeders are looking for specific sources of genetic traits that can readily be incorporated into existing varieties. The source of the desired characteristics is not necessarily important for them. The preferred source is another cultivar, but sometimes a closely related species must be used when resistance cannot be located in cultivated varieties. This is especially true in the case of diseases which are not endemic to the primary centre of origin of the crop.

Where a new crop is to be introduced, plant explorations should seek germ-plasm in countries whose environment is like that of the country to which the crop is to be introduced and where the crop has been grown successfully. Such attempts may be complicated by the effect of individual components of the ecosystem, of which plant pathogens are an important element that is sometimes overlooked. For example, efforts to establish a commercial bean canning industry in East Africa have been thwarted by epidemics of rust, which may destroy the crop at any time during the vegetative growth. The leading varieties in America, where the crop is successful, and where related races of the disease are controlled by variety and cultural methods, do not appear to carry any resistance to the East African races of rust (Howland and Macartney 1966). Our attempts to introduce black pepper (*Piper nigrum*) as a new crop in Puerto Rico (Gentry, 1955), where the climate is entirely suitable, have been completely frustrated because the varieties we have tried have no resistance to *Phytophthora* collar rot, a disease that does not become apparent until the plants begin to flower. Sources of resistance from related species may be essential to success.

In both these instances the major limiting factors to successful production of the crop have been determined. A broad screening programme, using germ-plasm from many sources, is the first step. Plant exploration must provide the germ plasm. Unfortunately, there is no way to predict the occurrence of resistance except through a screening programme that involves a broad range of plant introductions. Thus, the plant breeder turns to existing collections in other countries provided the desired traits have been catalogued.

Hitherto, the accomplishments of plant exploration have been based on the characteristics of particular accessions. However, we are making progress in correlating the useful genetic traits that are found to be in germ-plasm collections of crop species which have primary and secondary centers of origin, particularly where crop traits are phenotypically expressed; or where they exist in related species; or where insects and diseases have been associated with the crop and its progenitors for long periods of time. Resistance to bacterial spot (*Xanthomonas vesicatoria*) in *Capsicum* pepper (Sowell and Langford, 1963) did not develop in South America where *Capsicum frutescens* is native and the disease is seldom found. It resulted from selection pressure exerted on the host by the pathogen after both had been introduced to India, where the disease is prevalent. Additional sources of resistance to bacterial spot must therefore be sought in India.

The excellent Interregional Potato Species Collection (Ross and Rowe, 1963, 1966) at Sturgeon Bay, Madison, Wisconsin, illustrates the results of plant exploration activities. Of the 800 introductions added since 1958, 97 percent were collected during field exploration. This collection of wild relatives of the potato provides breeders with important traits, such as frost resistance and immunity to virus X in *Solanum acaule*, immunity to viruses A and Y in *S.stoloniferum* and *S.chacoense*, field resistance to late blight in *S.demissum*, and resistance to races of nematode in *S.vernei*. Recently, in the screening of 395 of these introductions (Radcliffe and Lauer 1966), involving 65 species, resistance to green peach and potato aphids was identified in 6 species which occur in certain limited areas of Mexico. Within the broad concept of primary centres of origin of economic crops, we are beginning to find subcentres for specific characters.

Among a collection of 630 hexaploid *Avena sterilis* oats introduced to the United States from Israel (Murphy *et al.*, 1967), we have observed new and different genes for resistance to races of crown and stem rust, mosaic and barley yellow dwarf virus, as well as sources of variation in kernel size, vigour, time to maturity, and protein content. This collection may represent a most valuable reservoir of genes for oat improvement. Israel appears to be a geographic centre of diversity where introgressive hybridization has increased the range of genetic diversity.

Over the years, plant explorations have accumulated 150 accessions of wild *Lycopersicon* species and suspected crosses with domesticated species (Muller, 1940; Alexander and Hoover, 1965). These were screened intensively by 58 scientists in the United States and Canada against

19 pathogenic and physiological disorders. Wild species are the major sources of resistance, and they provide objectives for further exploration. *Lycopersicon pimpinellifolium* (which is wild only in Peru, Ecuador, and the Galapagos Islands) has contributed marked resistance, or immunity, to *Fusarium* wilt, *Alternaria* leaf spot, *Cladosporium* leaf mould, and *Phytophthora* late blight. *L.peruvianum* resists several of the same diseases and is also the most resistant form to several species of root-knot nematode.

Plant explorations in China by the USDA since 1900, have led to the introduction of more than 3,000 forms of soybeans. This genetic stockpile is constantly being screened, as new problems arise. Although we have examined introductions for resistance to several diseases, we have found no marked resistance to brown stem rot (*Cephalosporum gregatum*). Trials in Central America of varieties which give large yields in the United States have shown that they are poorly adapted to the tropics and subtropics. In order to meet requirements of these regions and continue the search for disease resistance, we shall have to undertake more plant exploration in the subtropical areas of Asia, and expand the gene pool. The successful adaptation of varieties from the Philippines and southeast Asia to Tanganyika is indicative of the potentials that exist in this direction.

New disorders in peanuts, such as the highly destructive stunt virus, suggest that new collections should be made in the primary centres of South America, and in the secondary centers in India and Africa. There is no immunity in our existing collections which include material obtained as recently as 1966 from those parts of South America where the genus *Arachis* is concentrated. Therefore an expedition to the primary centers was undertaken by the USDA in 1968.

In wheats, where protein content is usually related inversely to yield, selections from the progeny of crosses between high-protein types collected in Brazil and high-yielding North American varieties were very satisfactory both in protein content and in yield.

Recent cooperative exploration for ornamental plants by the USDA and Longwood Foundation (Creech, 1966) have provided new evidence on the distribution of *Rhododendron japonicum* in Japan. Collections of this ornamental species throughout the entire range of its distribution identified geographic centers of biotypes, in which the important ornamental character of the flower colour can be related to specific geographic localities. This knowledge will allow horticulturists to develop stable seed lines to replace the vegetatively-propagated races that are difficult to propagate.

International cooperation may greatly further plant exploration activities. In 1954, arrangements were made between the FAO and CSIRO of Australia for a joint plant exploration in the Mediterranean area (Neal-Smith, 1955). The objective of this project was to collect ecotypes of pasture plants from the natural vegetation with a view to introducing and testing them in member countries and Australia. A total of 686 collections were made and subsequently grown in part in a nursery near Rome, Italy, for distribution purposes. Under this scheme, many countries had the opportunity to share in the benefits of plant exploration.

THE SEARCH FOR NEW CROPS

A new purpose of plant exploration (Creech, 1963) is to procure germ plasm of wild species not previously considered for crop purposes. The search is for species which are promising sources of industrial end-products, such as fibre and pulp from annual species, unique industrial oils, gum-like products, waxes, pharmaceuticals, insecticides, and other products with specific chemical properties. This complex effort requires the cooperation of the chemist, economic botanist, agronomist, and economist. First, the literature about a potentially useful plant group is surveyed jointly by a botanist and a chemist. Collections are then obtained within the genera selected for consideration. For example, *Vernonia anthelmintica*, a weed from India, may be valuable on account of the unique epoxy-acid in its seed oil, which may be useful for protective coatings, synthetic rubber, and other industrial purposes. Unfortunately, the agronomic characteristics of this species need considerable improvement. To obtain a wider range of variation, and to determine the centre of origin of the *Vernonia* species, explorations were conducted by the USDA in 1966 to Africa, where *Vernonia anthelmintica* appears to have originated. This species and its relatives were collected to clarify their taxonomic affinities as well as to obtain species with more useful characters, such as greater seed size and oil content, and improved plant habit. After this agronomic stage of development, there follows a pilot plant stage to study the commercial utilization of the new crop. Thus the pattern of development for this entirely new crop follows that for established crops.

The search for plant precursors of cortisone (Correll, Schubert, Gentry and Hawley, 1955), represents the most successful venture into this field. It did not necessarily establish *Dioscorea* as a successful domes-

ticated crop. However, this programme, in which centres of species in
Africa, Central and North America were explored, and the subsequent
chemical analysis, established *Dioscorea* as the most promising source of
steroids, displacing *Strophanthus*, *Agave*, *Veratrum*, *Trillium*, and *Yucca*.
Further intense exploration for *Dioscorea* species decreased the field to
Dioscorea composita, *D.floribunda*, and *D.spiculiflora*, out of scores of species
sampled. Harvesting in the wilds of Mexico still provides the crude
material for steroid intermediates. However, the effort to develop
productive commercial plantings continues.

THE STUDY AND PRESERVATION OF VARIATION

Plant exploration has also the more basic purpose of preserving genetic
materials that are irreplaceable resources for agriculture. We are well
aware of the various world collections of crop plants which have been
assembled in part by plant exploration. The outstanding example of this
is the collection of more than 12,000 variants of Indian corn (maize)
(Clark, 1956) throughout the western hemisphere. More recently, the
New Crops Research Branch of the USDA has conducted a series of
explorations to Central America and Mexico for variants of common
bean (*Phaseolus vulgaris*). Three expeditions had been completed, and
have yielded more than 1,800 lines. A fourth exploration was undertaken
in October 1967. The purpose of this repeated collecting is to establish
the basis for a germ plasm collection for sources of resistance to diseases
and insects, and for screening in the developing effort to increase our
protein supplies. As the cycles of collection follow one another, the collectors become more and more familiar with the materials they seek,
and the localities where they may be found, and so, though the numbers
of collections may decrease, their usefulness increases. These collections
will be screened for seed-borne pathogens at the Regional Plant Introduction Station in Pullman, Washington, before they are released to
breeders.

A secondary but hardly less valuable purpose of plant exploration is
the investigation of the origin and botanical documentation of those
crop plants which are not necessarily associated with centres of civilization. The New Crops Research Branch of the USDA recently conducted
explorations in Africa for coffee germ plasm. FAO continued the search.
Meyer (1965) collected 650 introductions and sufficient botanical
evidence to place the origin of *Coffea arabica* in the rainforest areas of
southwest Ethiopia. A similar objective was included in the 1957 USDA

sugarcane exploration made in Melanesia by Warner and Grassl (1958). Truly wild members of the genus *Saccharum*, *S.robustum* and *S.spontaneum*, collected from several sources, will probably shed light on the origin of *S.officinarum* and the taxonomic relationships between the species.

As a permanent basis for future improvement of potatoes, the Rockefeller Foundation is sponsoring the Inter-American *Solanum* Germ Plasm Project along lines similar to those used to develop the maize collection. Included in this 2-year project is the establishment of germ-plasm centres in Mexico and Colombia. Through exploration and collection, wild and cultivated tuber-bearing *Solanum* species will be preserved, classified, catalogued, and distributed. The existing collections from the Interregional Potato Project at Madison, Wisconsin, will serve as a base, and they will be augmented by collections derived from future explorations. This project will provide scientists with the material that is needed in order to coordinate and develop the Latin American centres. Eventually, it is hoped that germ plasm centres will be established in Peru and Argentina.

THE COLLECTING TEAM

The collecting team must be technically competent to meet the objectives of the exploration. Air travel has changed the whole concept of exploration. No longer do we rely on the professional explorer who spends years in arduous travel and endures extreme hardships to bring back his collections.

At present, most collecting teams consist of one or two highly specialized scientists, one of whom may have had prior experience in the area of the exploration. If the exploration is a general collecting effort for a commodity group, such as fruits, forages, or ornamentals, in which a range of species is to be sampled, the selection of team members is less important than the choice of an area. If the purpose is to collect germ plasm for a specific crop, where the collection area is already determined, expert knowledge of the crop is of primary importance. In the recent Rockefeller–USDA exploration of Ethiopia for sorghum, the team members were sorghum specialists. Where the objective of the exploration is a broad sampling of the native flora for plants to be utilized in screening programmes for potentially important constituents (for example, activity against tumour systems), only an economic botanist can fulfill the mission. The principal factors in choosing a team of collectors are the objectives of the exploration, and knowledge of the specific crops with which it is concerned.

Present-day explorations are of short duration, usually 3 to 5 months only. They are timed to coincide with the significant phase of development of the species or crop. All this allows a wider choice of members from several institutions. In the United States, we frequently borrow scientists from State Experiment Stations. Up to the present time, we have not included pathologists or entomologists in our plant exploration teams. There is no reason why this should not be done when the funds and purposes of an expedition allow several members to be included.

No exploration mounted from a foreign country can be successfully conducted without the assistance of local scientists. Their intimate knowledge of the distribution of the crops or species and the facilities they can make available for collecting, including local assistance, are essential to success. Their cooperation leads to an exchange of knowledge in methods of plant exploration; it allows for new materials to be added to local germ plasm collections, and, most important, it can ensure that collection can be continued if necessary after the foreign team has departed.

The selection of the collecting team determines, in large measure, the success of the field work and also the subsequent usefulness of the collections. Many valuable plant introductions have been lost because the collectors and sponsoring institutions have failed to understand one of their most important responsibilities—to provide proper documentation for each accession and to ensure continuity of recording and control as the collections move through quarantine and are distributed to the scientists who are to use them.

Field exploration succeeds best when it is sponsored by an authorative and continuing institution whose main objective is the introduction, utilization, and preservation of germ plasm. Without such backing, precious materials may be lost when they have served some immediate purpose, and when a new objective arises they have to be collected again. It goes without saying that such an institution should already have a wealth of experience in planning expeditions, supervising details of itineraries, and providing supplies and equipment. Planners should be familiar with the conditions of entry and work in foreign countries, and know how to maintain and support an expedition in the field. When the exploration has been completed, trained staff and facilities are required to list, quarantine, increase, and distribute the collections. The collectors should be able to return to their own institutions, confident that the results of their efforts are secure.

REFERENCES

ALEXANDER L.J. & HOOVER M.H. (1955) Disease resistance in wild species of tomato. *Res. Bull. Ohio agric. Exp. Sta.* 752.

CLARK J.A. (1956) Collection, preservation, and utilization of indigenous strains of maize. *Econ. Bot.* **10,** 194–200.

CORRELL D.S., SCHUBERT B.G., GENTRY H.S., & HAWLEY W.O. (1955). The search for plant precursors of cortisone. *Econ. Bot.* **9,** 307–375.

CREECH J.L. (1963) New crops prospects. *Chemurg. Dig.* **21,** 7–9.

CREECH J.L. (1966) Ornamental plant explorations—Japan, 1961. USDA–ARS 34–75.

GENTRY H.S. (1955) Introducing black pepper into America. *Econ. Bot.* **9,** 256–268.

HOWLAND A.K. & MACARTNEY J.C. (1966) East African bean rust studies. *E. Afr. Agric. For. J.* **32,** 208–210.

MEYER F.G. (1965) Notes on wild *Coffea arabica* from southwestern Ethiopia, with some historical consideration. *Econ. Bot.* **19,** 136–151.

MULLER C.H. (1940) A revision of the genus *Lycopersicon*. *Misc. Publs. U.S. Dep. Agric.* 382.

MURPHY H.C., WAHL I., DINVOR A., MILLER J.D., MOREY D.D., LUKE H.H., SECHLER D., & REYES L. (1967) Resistance to crown rust and soilborne mosaic virus in *Avena sterilis*. *Pl. Dis. Reptr.* **51,** 120–124.

NEAL-SMITH C.A. (1955) Report on herbage plant exploration in the Mediterranean region. *FAO Rpt.* 415.

RADCLIFFE E.B. & LAUER F.I. (1966) A survey of aphid resistance in the tuber-bearing *Solanum* (Tourn.) L. species. *Bull. Minn. agric. Exp. Stn.* 253.

ROSS R.W. & ROWE P.R. (1965) Inventory of tuber-bearing *Solanum* species. *Bull. Wis. agric. Exp. Stn.* 533.

ROSS, R.W. & ROWE P.R. (1966) Supplement to inventory of tuber-bearing *Solanum* species. *Bull. Wis. agric. Exp. Stn.* 533 (Supplement).

SOWELL G., Jr., & LANGFORD W.R. (1963) Evaluation of introduced peppers for resistance to bacterial spot. *Proc. Am. Soc. hort. Sci.* **83,** 609–612.

WARNER J.N. & GRASSL C.D. (1958) The 1957 sugar cane expedition to Melanesia. *Hawaii Plrs. Rec.* **15,** 209–236.

SECTION 3
EXAMPLES OF EXPLORATION

A. EXPLORATION IN AGRICULTURE AND HORTICULTURE

INTRODUCTION

ERNA BENNETT

Crop Ecology and Genetic Resources Branch, FAO, Rome

It is not possible at the present time to present a detailed and comprehensive assessment of the state of the genetic reserves of cultivated plant species. That is a task which is, as this book goes to press, in its earliest stages and has yet to face quite formidable scientific and organizational problems. In this section of the book, however, an attempt is made to survey briefly the extent of the variability at present available in some crops of major importance, to examine the sources of this variability, and to estimate the degree to which plant exploration and collection of primitive forms and wild related species may usefully extend the genetic bases of crop plants.

In the introduction of the book (p. 13) reasons have been advanced for establishing a system of priorities for the exploration, collection and conservation of crop genetic resources. This will not be discussed further here except to say that priorities will require to be established on the basis of a survey now being initiated through the Food and Agriculture Organization of the United Nations. To be sure, certain priorities are already very obvious, such as the wheats of the Near East whose extinction is now taking place rapidly, and the rices of the African and Asian continents. But in the chapters which follow the selection of crops which has been made is not intended to reflect any special sense of priority apart from the fact that major crops, being generally the most gravely threatened by genetic erosion, may be assumed to occupy a priority position. Beyond that, no implication of priority is intended.

The intention is rather to show, by reference to a range of crop types of diverse distribution and breeding systems, what are the similarities and the differences between the many possible approaches to the same general problem of plant exploration and the extension of the utilizable genetic variability of crop species. One chapter only, that on *Pisum*, departs from this plan to describe organizational matters. Through the Pisum Genetics Association which it describes it is hoped to channel *Pisum* information and to coordinate exploration and other activities relating to the genus. It is included here to offer a model—a model that

J

is, indeed, not new—on the basis of which more effective work on a world scale may be cooperatively achieved. It is to be hoped that similar organizations concerned with single crops or related groups of crops will be formed where they do not already exist, because through such measures the work of directing exploration, conservation and utilization of genetic resources can be significantly improved.

Despite differences in the biology and ecology of the crops considered here, the uniformity of approach which emerges is striking. The same unanimity has continually revealed itself in discussions between workers in the most diverse fields. The situation may be summed up by saying that for every crop only a fraction of the genetic variation of which it is capable is known. Plant collections up to the present have tended to be based on more or less haphazard collections rather than on systematic and wide-ranging exploration over the whole ecological and geographical range of species, with a very few outstanding exceptions. The crux of the matter is that the characteristics of a species at isolated points in its range cannot give an adequate indication of the species' total variability or its ultimate genetic potential. It is a principle objective of plant exploration systematically to uncover the potential genetic variation of species, whether this is to be realized by access to previously undiscovered germplasm within the species itself or from related species by the use of suitable breeding techniques. The continued improvement of adaptive characteristics, yield characteristics, protein quality and amino-acid balance, maturity characteristics, morphology, responses to temperature and photoperiod, and resistance to diseases, pests, cold and drought in crop varieties depends in the last analysis on successful plant exploration.

Systematic exploration of the genetic variability of cultivated plant species barely pre-dates the present generation. In this context the chapters in this section—for all that they do no more than outline the barest problems of exploration—may be regarded as breaking new ground. One interesting outcome is that in every case taxonomy emerges as of major importance at every stage of exploration work. This is an encouraging boost to a scientific discipline that has long suffered a dusty and academic image but which now must be regarded as a vital practical tool in applied plant science, for the past neglect of which we may yet have to pay a heavy price.

The extent to which active cooperation between workers in many disciplines, and specialists in many crops, leads in the immediate future to effective measures extending our knowledge of variability in crop species and to its rapid incorporation into plant breeding programmes, will determine the success of a new generation of crop varietics similar to but on an even wider scale than those which have already been produced with such effect by the Rockefeller Foundation in Mexico. Effective plant exploration and the conservation of the materials collected all over the world will provide the added guarantee that such progress can be maintained by ensuring a ready supply of genetic variability upon which plant breeding may continue to draw for many generations to come. Such measures will also determine the extent to which the chapters in this section may require to be re-written in the coming decade.

WILD WHEATS

DANIEL ZOHARY

Department of Botany, The Hebrew University,
Jerusalem, Israel

INTRODUCTION

Wheats have a unique place among cultivated plants because a large amount of basic biological information on their wild relatives is readily available. We frequently consider the wheats as classic examples of evolution through polyploidy. Indeed the identification of the three diploid donors that contributed their genomes to the hexaploid bread wheats is regarded as a milestone in plant evolution. But from the point of view of crop exploration and the utilization of wild relatives as sources for plant breeding, wheat is exceptional for another reason. It is one of the very few crops in which the wild relatives are botanically and genetically satisfactorily known. This is in sharp contrast with most of our cultivated crops. In fact the wheat group (i.e. the species conventionally grouped in *Triticum* and *Aegilops*) is one of the very few plant genera of which we already have sound biological information on *all* species—both wild and cultivated.

The wheat group contains twenty-two wild species (see Table 19.1), and on all of them we have comprehensive information on morphological divergence, ecological specialization and geographical distribution (for review see Zohary, 1965). Furthermore, the wheat group is exceptional among plants as to the extent to which it has been studied genetically. Almost all the species of *Aegilops* and *Triticum* have been subjected to cytogenetic analysis (for reviews see Kihara, 1954; Sears, 1959; and Riley, 1965). Genetic affinities between species are worked out and genomic relationships between diploid and polyploids are soundly established. Finally we have in this group critical information about species interconnections in nature, and the role of introgression in the build up of variation in polyploid species has been studied (Zohary, 1965).

The wheat group thus presents us with a rather exceptional example. The basic elements of information necessary for planning a comprehensive utilization of wild gene pools are already available here. This is an ideal situation which is at present only a desired goal in most other crops and particularly in crops complicated by polyploidy. In the

TABLE 19.1.

Species and species groups in *Aegilops* and *Triticum*
Genomic formulation after Kihara (1954) and Kihara et al. (1959)

Natural units	Species	Genome type
DIPLOID GENOMIC GROUPS		
Genome B(= S)	*Ae.bicornis* (Forsk.) Jaub. et Sp.	S^b
	Ae.sharonensis Eig.	S^1
	Ae.longissima Schweinf. et Musch.	S^1
	Ae.speltoides Tausch	B(= S)
Genome D	*Ae.squarrosa* L.	D
Genome C	*Ae.caudata* L.	C
Genome M	*Ae.comosa* Sibth. et Sm.	M
	Ae.uniaristata Vis.	M^u
Genome C^u	*Ae.umbellulata* Zhuk.	C^u
Genome A	*T.boeoticum* Boiss.	A
	* *T.monococcum* L.	A
POLYPLOID COMPLEXES		
Genome D species cluster	*Ae.crassa* Boiss. 4x	DM^{er}
	Ae.crassa Boiss. 6x	DD^2M^{er}
	Ae. juvenalis (Thell). Eig.	DC^uM^j
	Ae.ventricosa Tausch	DM^v
	Ae.cylindrica Host	DC
Genome C^u species cluster	*Ae.triuncialis* L.	C^uC
	Ae.columnaris Zhuk.	C^uM^c
	Ae.biuncialis Vis.	C^uM^b
	Ae.triaristata Willd. 4x	C^uM^t
	Ae.triaristata Willd. 6x	$C^uM^tM^{t2}$
	Ae.ovata L.	C^uM^o
	Ae.variabilis Eig.	C^uS^v
	Ae.kotschyi Boiss.	C^uS^v
Genome A species cluster	*T.dicoccoides* Koern.	AB
	* *T.durum* Desf.	AB
	* *T.dicoccum* Schubl.	AB
	T.araraticum Jakubz.	AG
	* *T.timopheevi* Zhuk.	AG
	* *T.aestivum* L.	ABD

*Cultivated wheats

following sections an attempt will be made to survey the various *wild* sources available in wheat, and to evaluate what has actually been achieved.

World wheat agriculture is presently based on two main wheats:
- (*a*) *hexaploid wheat* or bread wheat (*T.aestivum*) which combines three different genomes (genomic constitution ABD).
- (*b*) *tetraploid wheat* or durum wheat (*T.durum*) with AB genomic constitution.

Genome analysis has elucidated the origin of both cultivated wheats. This can be summarized in the following sketch:

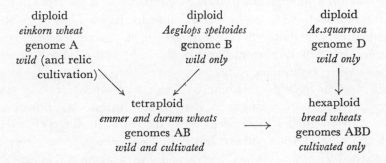

Thus we have in the wheats four independent wild gene pools, each carried on a chromosome set fully homologous to the ones found in the cultivated species. For the purpose of breeding tetraploid durum wheats one can easily draw from the wild gene pool present in the tetraploid progenitor *T.dicoccoides*. Here the procedure is simple since both wild and tame have the same chromosome constitution (both A and B). With some cytogenetic manipulation, breeding of *durum* wheats can also draw upon its two diploid donors, namely wild einkorn (genome A) and *Ae.speltoides* (genome B). For breeding work in hexaploid bread wheats, these three wild gene pools are supplemented by a fourth: by the source present in diploid *Ae.squarrosa*, the bearer of D genome.

The distribution and ecology of the wild progenitors of wheat can be summed up as follows:

A. *Wild einkorn* (genome A) : This diploid wheat (conventionally named *Triticum boeoticum* or *T.aegilopoides*) is widely spread over Western Asia and penetrates also to the southern Balkans (Greece, Turkey, Syria, N. Iraq, Transcaucasia). Its distribution centre lies in the 'fertile crescent' belt of S. Turkey and N. Iraq and adjacent territories in Iran and Syria. Here wild einkorn is massively spread as a component of open herbaceous park forest and steppe-like formations. It also occurs in masses at the edges of cultivation. West and north of this region wild einkorn is less common and more sporadic in its distribution and is mainly restricted to segetal or secondary habitats.

Relative to other diploids in the wheat group wild einkorn shows a considerable amount of genetic variation, which is apparent from the amount of morphological variation encountered in it. It is also indicated by the relatively wide ecological amplitude that wild einkorn shows. This plant is distributed over a wide area of soils and climates from the summer-dry, hot Euphrates basin to the cold and elevated Anatolian plateau with its summer rains.

B. *Aegilops speltoides* (genome B) : This wild wheat grass is again a common annual component in herbaceous formations and edges of cultivation in the 'fertile crescent' belt. Its distribution largely overlaps with the area of wild einkorn but it has a somewhat more restricted range (it does not occur in N. Iran and Transcaucasia). It also shows stronger affinities to typical Mediterranean habitats along the Eastern shore of the Mediterranean Sea. Its distribution and variation centre lies in a longitudinal belt just opposite the northeast corner of the Mediterranean Sea, i.e. in South Turkey, North Syria and North Iraq. In this centre it occurs in masses, both in primary habitats and at edges of cultivation in the alluvial plains. More sporadically, it is spread over the Anatolian plateau and penetrates westward as far as Thrace. To the south it is spread along the eastern shore of the Mediterranean Sea as far as Central Israel.

Compared to wild einkorn, *Ae.speltoides* possesses a somewhat more restricted amount of morphological and ecological variation. Yet it occurs on a wide amplitude of soils and climates which encompass the majority of types occupied by wild einkorn. (These two diploid progenitors often occur together). The relative wealth of variation here becomes obvious when *Ae.speltoides* is compared to other diploids in the wheat group. Upon such comparison it emerges as a relatively variable species.

C. *Aegilops squarrosa* (genome D) : This is the eastern-most diploid species in the wheat group. Its centre of distribution is in the South Caspian area. It is widespread and very common in Iran, and adjacent Transcaucasia and Transcaspia. Further away from this center *Ae. squarrosa* spreads westwards as far as East Turkey and Western Iraq, and eastward toward Pakistan and Kashmir. In Soviet Central Asia it is recorded as far east as Kirghizia and adjacent parts of Kazakhstan. *Ae.squarrosa* is also recorded as a rare plant from the Caucasus and Crimea. Both morphologically and ecologically *Ae.squarrosa* exhibits an extraordinarily wide amplitude. Its variation centre lies in the South Caspian belt. Here it is represented by a multitude of forms. Its exact ecological range still requires detailed study, but it is clear that this diploid occurs over a strikingly wide range of climatic conditions from dry sage brush (*Artemesia*) steppes and margins of deserts, to the rain-soaked temperate hyrcanic forest belt at the southern coast of the Caspian Sea.

Ae.squarrosa occupies both primary and segetal habitats. In its centre of distribution, i.e. North Iran, and adjacent Transcaspia, this plant is a frequent component in several types of genuine steppe and 'forest-steppe' formations. At the same time it is a noxious follower of man and is a common weed in cultivated wheat fields. Towards the periphery of its distribution it is apparently mostly a weed. In South Iran, South Afghanistan, and the Quetta area of Pakistan, it penetrates deeply into the warm arid plains as a weed companion of irrigated wheat.

In summation, the range of ecological and morphological variation exhibited by *Ae.squarrosa* is very wide. It apparently exceeds any other diploid in the wheat group. Furthermore, in comparison to the more Mediterranean progenitors previously described, this plant occurs in the more continental territories of Western and Central Asia.

D. *Wild emmer* (genomes AB) : There are two main types of wild tetraploid wheat : one which is usually referred to as *Triticum dicoccoides* is spread over Palestine and Syria. A second type often regarded as *T.araraticum* is distributed over Soviet Armenia and Georgia and adjacent parts of East Turkey, Iran and Iraq. These wild tetraploids wheats are morphologically very similar (and thus often intermixed) but genetically they are very distinct : the Syro-Palestinian wild tetraploid shows close genetic affinities to our common cultivated tetraploid wheats of the durum-emmer series. Wild and cultivated plants here are completely interfertile and show full genome homology. (Both

*J

have AB genomic constitution, see Table 1). The Armenian *T.araraticum* shows strong sterility barriers when crossed with either cultivated or wild AB tetraploids. Genetically it is an independent type. Its only close cultivated relative is *T.timopheevi* (genome AG, see Table 1), a restricted (relic) cereal in Georgia, USSR.

In the present discussion we will treat only the wild emmer proper (genome AB), since only these wild wheats are genetically close to our common cultivated wheats.

The distribution area of wild emmer (*T.dicoccoides*, genome AB) is over Israel, South Syria, and Transjordan (Harlan and Zohary, 1966). Wild emmer is also found in South Turkey, but the situation there needs further clarification. *T.dicoccoides* occurs in masses in the steppe-like formations and the park-forest belt from the Eastern Galilee to Mount Hermon, the Jebel Druz and the Gilead Mountains. It is particularly common on basaltic soils and hard limestone slopes.

In contrast to wild einkorn and *Ae.squarrosa*, *T.dicoccoides* is restricted mainly to primary habitats. It seldom occurs as a weed. It has an eco-geographic range somewhat more restricted than its diploid counterparts. It is centred in warmer, more southerly areas as compared to wild einkorn. In its geographic centre, *T.dicoccoides* shows a multitude of easily distinguishable forms and often builds conspicuously polytypic populations. Ecologically it again shows a rather wide altitudinal range, from early types growing in the basin of the Sea of Galilee (altitude, minus 100 metres) to later types which occur on the much cooler Hermon slopes at an altitude of 1200–1400 meters.

UTILIZATION OF WILD PROGENITORS

It is obvious from the previous section that all the four wild progenitors present us with rich pools of genetic variation. Furthermore, in the last few years we have acquired in each of them a relatively sound picture of ranges of variation and distribution patterns. Securing wild material here is a relatively simple task. But from the practical point of view, the wild progenitors have not yet been utilized as much as possible today. In fact, it is surprising how little representation one finds of these four wild species in world collections, and how small is their present weight in wheat breeding work.

Ae.squarrosa (genome D) presents us with perhaps the best case of a systematic attempt at utilization. This species was extensively explored by a Japanese expedition to Iran and Afghanistan headed by H. Kihara. Numerous types have been collected and a substantial effort has been made in the last decade (particularly by the Japanese group) to evaluate disease resistance and other economic traits.

There are at present several attempts to transfer disease-resistant genes and other economically important characters from diploid *Ae. squarrosa* to the hexaploid bread wheat. Various cytogenic manipulations are being employed such as the production of *durum* × *squarrosa* artificial hexaploids.

In comparison to *Ae.squarrosa* the two other diploids, namely wild einkorn (genome A), and *Ae.speltoides* (genome B) have been much less studied. This is in spite of the fact that only they can be used as diploid sources for both the durum wheats and the bread wheats. Perhaps the most comprehensive study of these two diploids has been carried out by Wahl and his group in Israel. They have examined some 60 collections representing the various eco-geographic types of these two diploids and found among them a considerable amount of resistance to the major stem-rust races affecting wheats in the East Mediterranean area. However, there has been no wide scale attempt to transfer disease-resistance from these two diploids to the cultivated wheats.

Cytogenetically such transfers can be achieved by artificial synthesis of AB tetraploids. In addition, another method can be recommended, namely, the utilization of triploids as bridges. Tetraploid *durum* × diploid einkorn and tetraploid *durum* × diploid *speltoides* hybrids are not completely sterile. When back-crossed they do produce occasional seeds. Introgression of genetic material from diploid progenitors to the tetraploid cultivated types can be thus effectively achieved here by back-crossing of triploid hybrids. In fact, successful transfer of stem rust resistance from wild einkorn to cultivated *durum* via a triploid bridge has been achieved in our laboratory.

Finally tetraploid *T.dicoccoides* (genome AB) has to be considered. Again, Wahl and his group have explored disease resistance in numerous collections of wild emmer from Israel and South Turkey. Several collections have turned out to be resistant to various stem-rust and yellow-rust races. But even in this wild tetraploid which shows no chromosomal level barrier for incorporation, up-to-date practical application is disappointingly meager. One exception is the transfer of yellow-rust resistance encountered by Wahl. This has been successfully accomplished by Dutch wheat breeders in Holland.

In summation, we have in the wild progenitors of wheat ready and available sources for immediate screening and exploitation. In contrast with the primitive cultivated varieties of wheat which are quickly disappearing the wild progenitors maintain their richness. Some of them apparently even continue to evolve and spread today. It is therefore tempting to predict that wheat breeding in the near future will see a drastic change towards the wild progenitors with more and more extensive exploitation of these sources in practical breeding work.

CONTRIBUTIONS OF ALIEN SPECIES

In addition to the four progenitors of cultivated wheats, all the other species of the wheat group can be regarded as potential donors of valuable genes to the cultivated polyploid wheats. That transfer of alien genetic material to polyploid wheats can easily be achieved is demonstrated by numerous hybridization experiments and the loose connections between polyploid entities in the field. In fact, inter-specific introgression at the polyploid level in *Triticum* and *Aegilops* is very common. It actually characterizes the variable weedy *Aegilops* forms. Thus the genetic variation present in the whole wheat group (Table 1) can be regarded as potential sources.

With utilization of alien genetic material, however, we face the difficulties of non-homology. While transfers of specific genes are easily accomplished, they are usually brought about by introduction of a whole alien chromosomal segment which cannot be easily broken down by crossing over. A good demonstration of this difficulty is given by E.R. Sears in his attempt to transfer rust-resistance from *Ae.umbellulata* to bread wheats. Incorporation of the resistance factor was relatively easily achieved. But it was accompanied by linked genes with deleterious effects on commercial qualities. The progenitors proper should therefore be considered as our most promising sources for the near future, but we should be aware of the fact that other *Aegilops* and *Triticum* species are potential sources as well and that with refined cytogenetic manipulations the problem of chromosome blocks could be solved as well.

REFERENCES

HARLAN R.J. & ZOHARY D. (1966) Distribution of wild wheats and barley. *Science* **153,** 1074–1080.

KIHARA H. (1954) Considerations on the evolution and distribution of *Aegilops* species based on the analyzer-method. *Cytologia* **19,** 336–357.

KIHARA H., YAMASHITA H. & TANAKA M. (1959) Genomes of 6 species of *Aegilops*. *Wheat Inform. Serv.* **8,** 3–5.

RILEY R. (1965) Cytogenetics and the evolution of wheat. In *Essays on Crop Plant Evolution* (Ed. Hutchinson J. B.). Cambridge University Press, Cambridge.

SEARS E.R. (1959) Weizen I: The systematics, cytology and genetics of wheats. In *Handbuch der Pflanzenzüchtung* (Eds. Kappert H. and Rudorf W.) Vol. II, pp. 164–187. Parey, Berlin.

ZOHARY D. (1965) Colonizer species in the wheat group. In *The Genetics of Colonizing Species* (Eds. Baker H.G. and Stebbins G.L.). Academic Press, New York.

20

PRIMITIVE WHEATS

H. KUCKUCK

Institut für Angewandte Genetik,
Hannover, Federal German Republic

INTRODUCTION

CHARACTERISTICS OF PRIMITIVE WHEATS

In the chapter on wild wheats, Zohary describes three diploid wild species and an allotetraploid wild species, progenitors of the cultivated wheats, from the point of view of their genetic variation, ecological specificity and geographical distribution. Although the genetic processes of evolution in cultivated wheats cannot always be individually traced, it can be said with some certainty that in the development from wild species to cultivated forms and the further differentiation of these, different genetic mechanisms have played a part, among them polyploidy, chromosome structural changes resulting in deficiencies, duplications, translocations, gene mutations, and recombination through hybridization.

The evolution of the wheats has occurred step by step over a long period of time. As an end result of this development, partly influenced by man, high-yielding cultivars have arisen in almost all the countries of the earth. Between the recently bred varieties on the one hand and the wild species on the other so-called primitive forms of wheat are still to be found in some countries, particularly those with a still undeveloped agriculture, as intermediate evolutionary products. In these forms the individual stages of evolution may be traced. Further, on account of their enormously great genetic variation, these primitive forms are an important source of raw material for the further improvement of varieties by plant breeders.

By what characters can primitive forms now be recognised? At an early stage of evolution stand the so-called spelt-forms. The grains are firmly enclosed by the glumes and cannot be freed by threshing, as is the case also with wild species. The rachis breaks more or less easily into individual spikelets, upon the application of pressure or in threshing, although not spontaneously when ripe as is the case with wild species.

The next stage in development of the wheats is marked by the occurrence of free-threshing forms (naked grain) with a tough rachis. These can also be described as primitive forms since they are cultivated as *populations* and are more the product of natural selection and adaptation than conscious breeding by man. Compared with modern, genetically homogeneous cultivars the yield potential of these populations is low and their response to improved cultivation, particularly increased fertilizer, is small and may even be negative as, for example, through lodging. Populations of primitive forms are, however, characterised by good adaptation to local ecological conditions and, consequently, by a certain security of yield.

SYSTEMATICS, ORIGIN, DISTRIBUTION AND CHARACTERISTICS OF PRIMITIVE WHEATS

(a) *Diploid Wheats* (Table 20.1a). From the diploid wild species, *Triticum aegilopoides*, only *T.monococcum* has evolved as a cultivated speltoid form. The presence of intermediate forms in Asia Minor (Schiemann 1948) makes it likely that the evolution to cultivated forms took place through numerous gene mutations. *T.monococcum* was already widely distributed, as one of the oldest of cultivated plants, also in Europe from Spain to Scandinavia in the early neolithic period (about 4,300 B.C.), according to radio-carbon dating of material found in the Cote d'Or in the province of Alicante in Spain (Hopf and Schubert 1965). *T.monococcum* is found only sporadically today as an agricultural crop. Borojevic (1956), for example, reports on the cultivation of about 4,000 hectares in Yugoslavia, where peasants in mountainous regions with severe climate and poor soil sown to wheat and barley cultivate small areas of *monococcum* on account of its great resistance to cold and rust. The grain, however, is seldom used for the preparation of bread but rather as fodder for horses and pigs. A few areas in Turkey, particularly in the neighbourhood of Ankara and between Bursa and Balikesir, are also sown to einkorn. A special food (pilaff) is prepared from this in which the grain is first moistened, then dried and milled and the product is finally prepared with salt and butter.

In India a population of einkorn (an accession from Japan) is reported by Rao (1963) to be resistant against all the races of *Puccinia graminis* and *P.glumarum* (10 and 13 respectively) which occur there.

TABLE 20.1a. Diploid wheats.

	Genome	Distribution	Origin	Important characteristics	Remarks
I. WILD FORM *T. boeoticum* Boiss.	A	Western Asia, Asia Minor, Balkans.			See Zohary (chapter 19)
II. SPELTOID CULTIVATED FORM *T. monococcum* L.	A	Formerly widely distributed in Europe. Present in early Neolithic 4300 B.C. (Hopf and Schubert, 1965). Today limited to mountain places in Yugoslavia and Turkey.	Apparently free mutation from *T. boeoticum.* Transition forms present in Asia Minor.	Genotypes occur with resistance against *Puccinia graminis* and *P. glumarum.*	Fodder for horses and pigs; seldom used in bread production but used for pilaff.

TABLE 20.1b. Tetraploid wheats.

		Genome	Distribution	Origin	Important characteristics	Remarks
I.	WILD FORMS					
	T.dioccoides Koern.	AABB	Transcaucasia, East Turkey, Iran, Iraq, Palestine, Syria.	Amphidiploid from *T.aegilopoides* × *Aegilops speltoides*		See Zohary (chapter 19)
	T.araraticum Jakubz.	AAB'B'				
II.	SPELTOID CULTIVATED FORMS					
	T.dicoccum Schübl.	AABB	Asia, Africa, Europe.	from *T.dicoccoides* by mutation.	resistant to rust.	The oldest cultivated wheat. C.4000 B.C.
	T.timopheevi Zhuk.	AAB'B' (AAGG)	Georgia (Transcaucasia).	D- and G-genomes differing structurally from B-genome occur also in *T.dicoccoides*.	resistant to rust and mildew.	Interaction between *T.aestivum* nucleus and *T.timopheevi* cytoplasm results in male-sterility.
	T.georgicum Dek.	AABB		Dense-eared variety or sub-species of dicoccum.		Cultivated in mixtures with *T.macha* which it resembles phenotypically.

TABLE 20.1b. (cont.)

	Genome	Distribution	Origin	Important characteristics	Remarks
III. FREE-THRESHING CULTIVATED FORMS					
T.carthlicum Nevski	AABB	Transcaucasia, East Turkey.	Cross between T. dicoccum and T. aestivum (??)	Resistant to brown and yellow rust; smut, and mildew; summer wheats but frost hardy; short vegetative period.	In mixtures with T. aestivum ssp. vulgare; in areas with long, snow-rich winters.
T.durum desf.	AABB	Asia Minor Ethiopia.			
ssp expansum Vav.					
ssp abyssinicum Vav.					
T.turgidum L.	AABB	Transcaucasia.	Related to T.durum.		
T.polonicum L.	AABB	Transcaucasia.	Complex-mutant from T.durum?		
T.turanicum Jakubz. = T.orientale Perc.	AABB	Iran, Iraq (limited distribution)	T.durum × T.polonicum		
T.ispahanicum Heslot.	AABB	Province of Ispahan (Iran) (limited distribution)	unknown		

Evolutionarily einkorn has remained at the stage of the spelting cultivated forms. The A-genome has shown itself in mutation experiments to be very stable; only a very few mutations can be induced. Yamashita obtained a 14-chromosome ring by reciprocal translocations. Einkorn is of interest today in the re-synthesis of tetraploid wheats in the production of rust resistant genotypes.

(b) *Tetraploid Wheats, AB-genome* (Table 20.1b). Corresponding to the great variation of the tetraploid wild wheats, which Zohary has placed in *T.dicoccoides* and *T.araraticum*, there is also a large diversity of form to be found in spelting cultivated forms. The *araraticum* genome is structurally different from the B-genome in *dicoccoides* and therefore generally designated as the G-genome. It is found in the spelting cultivated forms of *T.timopheevi*. Genetically, however, both genomes may be homologous and stem originally from the same donor species (see also Sachs, 1953). Both the amphidiploid from *T.dicoccoides* × *Aegilops squarrosa* and the amphidiploid from *T.timopheevi* × *Ae.squarrosa* yield *T.spelta*.

T.dicoccum (emmer) is the oldest cultivated wheat. It was already widely distributed between 3,000 and 4,000 B.C. in Africa (the Nile delta), in the Near East (Mesopotamia and other areas) and Europe (from Spain to Scandinavia). Today emmer has been widely replaced by tetraploid and hexaploid free-threshing wheats. It is still to be found only in a limited area in Ethiopia, Iran, Eastern Turkey, Transcaucasia, and sporadically in the Balkans (Yugoslavia) where it is mixed with oats and barley (see Borojevic 1956). Its contemporary importance for breeding lies in the production of rust-resistant genotypes (see the following section 'Maintenance and Utilization of Genetic Variation in Primitive Wheats').

T.timopheevi has only a limited distribution in Transcaucasia. *T.georgicum* may be considered as a variety of *dicoccum* rather than a species and is distinguished particularly by its dense ears. It occurs in mixed stands with hexaploid spelt wheats such as *T.spelta*, ssp. *macha*, which it resembles phenotypically.

While the evolution of a spelting cultivated form from the tetraploid wild species *T.dicoccoides* may be explained in terms of numerous small mutation steps, particularly with regard to quantitatively important characters, the origin of free-threshing cultivated forms possessing a tough rachis has still not been fully explained genetically.

From the morphological, physiological and ecological viewpoint speltoid and free-threshing forms are clearly distinguished from each other and transitional forms have not yet, to the author's knowledge, been encountered. Even artificial mutants derived from emmer show no forms that can be regarded as traditional to *T.durum* or other tetraploid species with naked grains (Kuckuck, 1964).

It is, therefore, possible that the tetraploid naked wheats have arisen from crossing of *T.dicoccum* with hexaploid naked wheat. This may also apply in the case of *T.carthlicum*, which is difficult to distinguish morphologically from the hexaploid *T.aestivum*. From the physiological point of view and from its ecological specificity *T.carthlicum* is markedly different from the other tetraploid species; it occurs above all in high mountain localities with snow-rich winters in East Turkey and in Transcaucasia and in mixtures with *T.aestivum* populations. It is an early ripening summer form in which many genotypes resistant to rust and *Erysiphe graminis* are to be found. It has, therefore, found considerable and successful use in plant breeding.

Among the tetraploid species that of the greatest importance as a cultivated wheat is *T.durum*. It has been safely established as having been present in Egypt and other countries in Graeco-Roman times (Schiemann, 1948). *T.durum* prefers areas with mild warm climates and a long vegetative period. The greatest diversity of *T.durum* today is found in Ethiopia, while the genetic variation in the south-west Asian gene centre (Turkey, Iran) now appears to be less, as a result of the replacement of primitive land races by improved varieties. Thus the hexaploid cultivars are becoming more widely distributed at the expense of the tetraploid. The *durum* wheats in south and west Persia have almost completely disappeared from cultivation. This is a consequence of the greater range of genetic variation and adaptability of the hexaploids compared with the tetraploids, and the consequently greater successes in the breeding of hexaploid varieties.

Other tetraploid species, such as *turgidum, polonicum, turanicum* and *ispahanicum* do not have major significance from the breeding point of view. Details of their origin and distribution may be seen in Table 1b.

(c) *Hexaploid Wheats, Genome ABD* (Table 20.1c). The greater range of variation and adaptability of the hexaploid wheats compared with the tetraploid wheats which has been referred to above can be attributed to the incorporation of the D-genome.

Among early cultivated forms are to be found primitive speltoid forms with a fragile rachis. As a result of materials discovered in the last 20 years in Iran and Transcaucasia (Kuckuck and Schiemann, 1958; Dorofeev 1966), and their description and genetic analysis (Gökgöl,

TABLE 20.1C. Hexaploid wheats.

		Genome	Distribution	Origin	Important characteristics	Remarks
I.	WILD FORMS					
	T.spelta ssp *macha* var. *megrilicum.*	AABBDD	Georgia (Transcaucasia).		Shattering spontaneously, small grained.	
II.	SPELTOID CULTIVATED FORMS.					
	T.spelta ssp. *macha* Dek. et Men.	AABBDD	Transcaucasia.	Amphidiploid from *T.dicoccum* or *T.dicoccoides* × *Ae. squarrosa.*		
	T.spelta ssp. *kuckuckianum* Gökg.	AABBDD	Iran, (Transcaucasia).			
	T.spelta ssp. *vavilovi* Zhuk.	AABBDD	Transcaucasia, Eastern Turkey (Lake Van).	Mutation in chromosome 5A and elongation of rachilla.	Drought resistant.	
	T.spelta ssp. *europaeum* Dorof.	AABBDD	Switzerland S.W. Germany (Transcaucasia).			
	T. spelta ssp. *europaeum* convar. *transcaucasicum* Dorof.	AABBDD	Transcaucasia.		Variable resistance against rust, mildew and lodging.	Cultivated alone and in mixtures with *T. aestivum.*

TABLE 20.1C. (cont.)

	Genome	Distribution	Origin	Important characteristics	Remarks
T.zhukovskyi Men. *et* Er.	AAAABB	Transcaucasia.	Amphidiploid from *T.timopheevi* × *T. monococcum*	Resembles *T.timopheevi* in ear form, resistance to fungal parasites and desynaptic system.	
III. FREE-THRESIHNG CULTIVATED FORMS					
T.aestivum ssp *vulgare* (Vill. Host.) MacKey.	AABBDD	Transcaucasia (greatest variation) Asia Minor, S.W. Asia (Hindu Kush, Pamirs, Himalayas).	Macromutation Q (Duplication) in Chromosome 5A. Complex inheritance. Breakage of complex nature (Kuckuck, 1964).		Introduction from Russia. Important basis of U.S.A. cultivars.
T.aestivum ssp *compactum* (Host) MacKey.	AABBDD	Transcaucasia Asia Minor.	Dominant macro-mutation C in chromosome 2D, complex inheritance.		The oldest cultivated wheat in Europe?
T.aestivum ssp. *sphaerococccum* (Perc) MacKey.	AABBDD	Punjab (India).	Macromutation (Duplication?) in chromosome 3-D; complex inheritance, breaking by X-rays (Swaminathan and Rao, 1961).		

1961 ; Kuckuck, 1964), a wide ecological tolerance with a correspondingly wide morphological diversity and geographical distribution has
been revealed in this group. All these forms posse₁s in common the
genetic characteristics of the spelt complex—invested grains and a
rachis which is fragile under pressure or on threshing—so that all the
speltoid species so far described, with one exception, may be classified
in the single species-complex *Triticum spelta* (Table 20.1c). The single
exception is *T.zhukovskyi*, which has been established on the basis of
morphology, rust and mildew resistance and from cytogenetic evidence
(genome formula AAAABB) as an amphidiploid of *T.timopheevi* ×
T.monococcum, a fact which has been confirmed by resynthesis (Upadhya
and Swaminathan, 1963). The origin, distribution and identification
of the speltoid species is to be seen in Table 20.1c.

The description of a variety of *T.macha*, the variety *megrelicum*
Dek. *et* Men. in West Georgia (Transcaucasia), is of particular importance (Dekaprelovich, 1961). This variety is distinguished by spontaneously shattering ears, as in *T.dicoccoides*. This discovery has established that the view previously held that no wild forms exist in the
hexaploid wheat series is no longer tenable. The occurrence in Transcaucasia of wild spelting forms which show such a great diversity of
form, as well as cultivated forms, leads one to conclude that Transcaucasia is the centre of origin of the hexaploid wheats.

Hexaploid spelt wheat is cultivated in areas of climatic extremes and
particularly in mountain places with much snow cover. It is often
characterised by considerable resistance against fungal diseases and
particularly rust. The invested grains are naturally protected against
bird damage, so that spelt is frequently found in small areas in the
immediate vicinity of villages. Spelt is also characterised by a high
flour quality and used for the preparation of the so-called Grünkern,
a sort of soup made from dried unripe grain. Not only in Europe but also
in Asia spelt is cultivated less and less. The large acreage on the high
plateau of Shahr Kord (2,000 metres) in the neighbourhood of Isfahan
in Iran in which spelt has for a long time been cultivated is today almost
completely extinct.

The free threshing cultivated forms are characterised by the so-
called Q-factor (MacKey, 1954) which suppresses the spelt complex.
Apparently this is associated with a duplication of variable effect in
chromosome 5A which is at times dominant, at times recessive, which
has been identified as Q (Kuckuck, 1964). In the area of distribution
of *T.spelta* in Iran, as also in Transcaucasia, transitional forms with a

fragile rachis but with naked grain have been found, so also have the so-called speltiform types, the ears of which resemble spelt only externally but are, however, free threshing and have a tough rachis (Kuckuck, 1964). Associated with the chromosomal Q-factor there are also small gene mutations which lead to the development of the naked cultivated form. The free threshing primitive forms are brought together in the nomenclature of MacKey* in the species *T.aestivum* in which *vulgare*, *compactum* and *sphaerococcum* are regarded as sub-species.

The classification of the *vulgare* wheats presents great difficulties on account of the extremely wide morphological and physiological variation and range of ecological adaptation (and with it the extensive geographical distribution) of this group. Koernicke was the first to attempt to bring order to its genetic diversity by describing varieties on the basis of combinations of a number of morphological characters. His method, however, did not reflect the taxonomic-phylogenetic relationships of the varieties he described, nor did it take account of ecological adaptation and geographical distribution. The school of Vavilov, on the other hand, established ecological-morphological groups, the so-called proles, which in turn were divided into a number of groups to which the term 'grex' was applied; these represent geographical groups with special morphological characteristics, and in turn were divided into varieties according to the scheme of Koernicke. The greatest genetic variation of the *vulgare* wheats is found in Transcaucasia, Turkey, Iran, the Hindu Kush and the Pamirs.

Triticum aestivum ssp. *compactum*—recognised by the dominant C-gene for extremely dense ears—was apparently already cultivated in Europe during the neolithic period; it is, therefore, an extremely old cultivated species. Today compactum is still found as an impurity in the Alpine land races of Europe and in the land races of the Near East (Transcaucasia, Iran and Turkey). In their requirements *compactum* and *vulgare* appear to be complementary and almost symbiotic; otherwise it would be difficult to understand why *compactum* forms, with their low growth and complete overshadowing by *vulgare*, are not eliminated from the population. *Compactum* forms do not have any particular importance in breeding apart from the short straw which is correlated with the dense ear.

The same is the case with *T.aestivum* ssp. *sphaerococcum*, which has only a very limited distribution in India. The characteristic growth

* MacKey (1954) has also treated *macha, spelta, vavilovi* as sub-species of T. *aestivum*.

and ear type with spheroid grain is inherited as a complex, genetically controlled by a duplication in chromosome 3D.

USE AND MAINTENANCE OF GENETIC VARIATION

The first successful expeditions for the investigation of the genetic variation of primitive wheats and their geographical distribution were conducted by Vavilov and his colleagues in a very systematic way. The material which was collected was analysed from different points of view, above all by the use of the differential phytogeographic method, and a large part of the genetic variation was conserved in living collections (Vavilov, 1950). These collections today still represent an important source of material for breeding programs, not only in the Soviet Union but also in other countries. As a result of the outstanding work of Vavilov and his school, collecting expeditions were conducted by other countries also, but the techniques and results of only a few of these have been described as accurately as has been the case for the Soviet expeditions.

How can the genetic variation of the primitive wheats be used? What results should be aimed at? First of all, it is in the developing countries that long-adapted primitive land race populations of high diversity, capable of being used as basic selection material in long-term breeding programs, are to be found. They represent a most important starting point for the successful development of improved varieties (cultivars) by exploiting genetic complexes governing adaptation or adaptability to the often very extreme environmental conditions of these countries. The experience and results of plant breeding at Svalöf in Sweden may serve as an illustration of this. Here, about 60 or 70 years ago, improved cultivars such as Sammet, Pudel and Kotte were selected from primitive land races on the basis of their extreme winter hardiness. These cultivars were then used in a crossing program with introductions of the high-yielding but not winter hardy squarehead-wheats, and later with quality wheats from Hungary, such as Bankuti 178. Today many widely distributed wheats such as Stark and Eroika contain germplasm of the old Swedish land races (Fajersson, 1963). Unfortunately, apart from a few exceptions, the possibilities of increasing yields offered by the use of the genetic variation of adapted land races in breeding, have been little exploited. In fact, breeding is often limited and restricted by the spread of new introductions. Frivolity and ignorance of the possibilities result not in increased yields, but merely in the loss of valuable genetic material.

The work of Gökgöl in Turkey may be referred to as an exception. Gökgöl, formerly Director of the Agricultural Research Institute at Yesilköy near Istanbul, analysed 18,000 wheat populations from almost every part of Turkey in the 1920s and the 1930s from the point of view of their genetic and taxonomic diversity, and the geographical distribution of species and varieties. This led to the development of three *durum* varieties by direct pedigree selection, and four *aestivum* cultivars by crossing selections from Turkish populations with introduced varieties. These varieties are still cultivated in Turkey. All this genetic material was selected and maintained by Gökgöl in living collections and in a herbarium but was lost when he retired in 1960.

Wheat breeding by Mudra in Iran is similarly based upon the collection of native races, in this case by Garibagli and Kuckuck, the last consisting of 11,000 lines selected from 536 populations (Kuckuck, 1955). Using the pedigree method, four varieties were developed from these which out-yielded unimproved local varieties by from 30% to 50%. On the Iranian plateau they also out-yielded all introductions (some hundreds) which have been tested to date.

From the collections in Iran 2,500 lines have been maintained. A second part of the Kuckuck collections of approximately 11,000 lines has been tested under the auspices of the F.A.O. Near East Wheat and Barley Improvement Program at Yesilköy. In addition, approximately 1,899 samples were distributed to 21 institutes in different countries. The maintenance and distribution of the Iranian material has been all the more important because in the last ten years very serious genetic erosion has taken place. The widespread replacement of *T.spelta* and *T.durum* cultivation by *aestivum* cultivars, already referred to, is an example of this.

Further results of Mudra (personal communication) have a special significance in the utilization of primitive races; the varieties Ommid, Roshan and Shahi which are derived from native populations and are susceptible in Iran to yellow rust (*Puccinia glumarum*) have been found at Braunschweig in Germany, to be highly resistant or immune to six important rust biotypes. The breeder of *aestivum* wheats, therefore, is not limited to the tetraploid sources of rust resistance only, such as *T. dicoccum*, *T.timopheevi* and *T.carthlicum* in which resistance to rust and mildew is relatively widely distributed, but can also use *aestivum* material as a source of resistance genes. The same results indicate that it is also essential to evaluate genetic material under different environmental conditions (see Krull and Borlaug: chapter 37 of the present volume).

The introduction of primitive winter wheats from Russia between 1873 and 1900 played an outstanding role in the development of wheat breeding in North America, so much so that a monument in Newton, Kansas, commemorates the introduction of 'Turkey' wheat (Reitz and Ward, in Allard, 1960). The varieties Hope C.J. 8178 and H.44 have also played an important part in North American wheat breeding; *durum* and *dicoccum* contributed to the origin of these varieties. The *aestivum* varieties, Gabo and Timstein, carry resistance to stem- and leaf-rust which has been introduced from *T.timopheevi* (or *T.durum*).

Wienhus (1959) tried to transfer the mildew resistance of *T. carthlicum* (=*persicum*) and *T.timopheevi* to *aestivum* varieties which were lodging-resistant and high-yielding. The derivatives of his first crosses have been used in many further breeding programs in Germany; they are also used (Pugsley, 1963) as test hosts against physiological races of mildew (*Erysiphe graminis tritici*). The early ripening and short straw of the primitive races of Asia and Ethiopia have been used with much success by Wienhus (1959) in recombination breeding. Primitive forms from Asia have also played a part in the development of Italian cultivars.

In recent years there has been mounting interest in the use of primitive wheats in the production of hybrid varieties. It is now possible to confer male sterility by combining specific *aestivum* or *durum* genotypes with certain cytoplasms, such as for example of *T. timopheevi* and *T.boeoticum*, along with fertility restorer genotypes. For further information the papers of Wilson and Ross (1962), Kihara (1963), and Maan and Lucken (1966) should be referred to.

CONCLUSIONS

In order better to consider what regions should receive the attention of future collecting expeditions we may first review briefly a few important expeditions of recent years. These are:

(1) Expedition undertaken by Kyoto University in 1955, under the leadership of Kihara, to Karakorum, the Hindu Kush and neighbouring Afghanistan and Iran. (For report see Kihara, 1959).

(2) Kyoto University sent a second expedition under the leadership of Yamashita to the Mediterranean countries in 1959. (Yamashita, 1959).

(3) The Institute of Plant Industry in Leningrad undertook a very extensive collecting expedition through Transcaucasia in

1961–64, under the leadership of Dorofeev. A first report, containing many important conclusions, has already been published (Dorofeev, 1966).

(4) A British expedition sponsored by the University of Reading Exploration Society collected 1500 samples in Afghanistan; this material is at present being examined at Cambridge in England and Wagga Wagga in New South Wales (Halloran, 1965).

The results of earlier expeditions, particularly those cited above, make it clear that a great number of wild and cultivated *Triticum* species with a particularly extensive diversity are endemic in Transcaucasia. Transcaucasia may not only very rightly be described as a centre of great genetic variation (Dorofeev, 1966), but also may be regarded as a centre of origin of cultivated wheat. The genetic variation of the primitive forms of Transcaucasia and the neighbouring areas of Turkey and Iran therefore requires to be collected and preserved. In this connection co-operation with Soviet research workers, who have initiated a long-term plant exploration program in order to fill the gaps in existing Soviet collections, should be established.

After Transcaucasia, Ethiopia with its tremendously wide variation of tetraploid wheats requires to be explored. My own observations in 1965 (unpublished FAO report) indicate the evolution of new variation in *T.aestivum*, especially through the crossing of indigenous *durum* wheats with *aestivum* cultivars introduced by the Italians during the years 1935 and 1936.

It is also important that the diversity of the primitive wheats be utilized in those countries in which they naturally occur, if necessary by establishing breeding stations and breeding programs. In the developing countries with indigenous land races, the use of these in plant breeding should receive high priority. Plant breeding institutes in the countries of origin and diversity can assist maintain native populations, where these are in danger of replacement by introduced varieties.

Genetic variation of the primitive wheats should not only be maintained as single pure lines selected more or less at random from a population, as has been the case with most collections to date, but should also be maintained in the form of populations. In the USDA world collections of wheat, populations are maintained (Rcitz and Ward, in Allard, 1960). It is then a matter for the breeder to select pure lines from this material when he requires to use them in crossing or any other way.

When local races have been replaced by bred varieties in their countries of origin the question arises whether certain representative populations might not be maintained in special rotations in limited areas of half to one hectare. Local varieties may thus be conserved dynamically. The proportions of particular genotypes in a land race can change under environmental pressures such as, for example, the use of fertilizers, irrigation, drainage and so on. Further, new genotypes can arise as a result of mutation and chance crossing, and under altered environmental conditions may find a chance of survival. The effect of such associated genera as *Secale* and *Aegilops* on genome and karyotype constitution through introgressive hybridization, chromosome-segment substitution and chromosome addition lines, may also be considerable (see Zohary: chapter 3 of the present volume). Crossing-over between gene loci can release latent genetic variability. The longer populations are maintained in this way the greater are the chances of crossing-over between closely linked genes and with this the origin of new genetic variants.

If it is possible to employ such an evolutionary method of maintaining representative populations of primitive wheats in their countries of origin gene pools adapted to new environmental conditions will continue to be available as valuable material for the use of future breeding programmes.

REFERENCES

ALLARD R.W. (1960) *Principles of Plant Breeding.* John Wiley, London.

BOROJEVIC S. (1956) A note about the 'New dates for recent cultivation of *Triticum monococcum* and *Triticum dicoccum* in Yugoslavia'. *Wheat Inf. Service* **4,** 1.

DEKAPRELEVICH L. (1961) Die Art *Triticum macha* Dek. et Men. im Lichte neuester Untersuchungen über die Herkunft der hexaploiden Weizen. *Zeitschr. Pfl. züchtung* **45,** 17–30.

DOROFEEV V.F. (1966) Die geographische Lokalisierung und die Genzentren hexaploider Weizen in Transkaukasien. *Genetica* (Moscow) **3,** 16–33 (in Russian) German translation available.

DOROFEEV V.F. (1966) *Triticum spelta* L. in Transkaukasien. *Biologica* **1,** 133–138 (in Russian) German translation available.

FAJERSSON F. (1963) Methods and achievements in Swedish wheat breeding. *Proc. II Wheat Genet. Symp. Hereditas Suppl.* **2,** 11–26.

GÖKGÖL M. (1941) Über die Genzentrentheorie und Ursprung des Weizens. *Zeitschr. Pfl. züchtung* **23,** 562–578.

GÖKGÖL M. (1961) Die iranischen Weizen. *Zeitschr. Pfl. züchtung* **45,** 315–333.

HALLORAN G.H. (1966) Wheat collecting expedition to Afghanistan. *Wheat Inf. Service* **22,** 12–13.

HESLOT H. (1959) *Triticum ispahanicum*: a new species of cultivated wheat from Iran. *Wheat Inf. Service* **9–10,** 15.

HOPF M. & SCHUBERT H. (1965) Getreidefunde aus der Coveta de l'or (Provinz Alicant). *Madrider Mitteilungen* **6,** 20–38. Kerle Verlag, Heidelberg.

KIHARA H. (1959) Japanese Expedition to the Hindukush. *Proc. I. Int. Wheat Genet. Symp.* 243–248.

KIHARA H. (1963) Nucleus and chromosome substitution in wheat and *Aegilops* I. Nucleus substitution. *Proc. II. Int. Wheat Genet. Symp. Heriditas Suppl.* **2,** 313–327.

KIHARA H., YAMASHITA K. & TANAKA M. (1965) Morphological, physiological, genetical and cytological studies in *Aegilops* and *Triticum* collected from Pakistan, Afghanistan and Iran. *Wheat Inf. Service* **19–20,** 5–8.

KUCKUCK H. (1956) Report to the Government of Iran on distribution and variation of cereals in Iran. FAO Report 517.

KUCKUCK H. (1959) Neuere Arbeiten zur Entstehung der hexaploiden Kulturweizen. *Zeitschr. Pfl. züchtung* **41,** 205–226.

KUCKUCK H. (1964) Experimentelle Untersuchungen zur Entstehung der Kulturweizen. I. Die Variation des iranischen Spelzweizens und seine genetischen Beziehungen zu *Triticum aestivum* ssp. *vulgare* (Vill. Host) MacKey, ssp. *spelta* (L.) Thell. und ssp. *macha* (Dek. et Men.) MacKey mit einem Beitrag zur Genetik des Spelta-Komplexes. *Zeitschr. Pfl. züchtung* **51,** 97–140.

KUCKUCK H. & SCHIEMANN E. (1957) Über das Vorkommen von Spelz und Emmer in Iran. *Zeitschr. Pfl. züchtung* **38,** 383–386.

MAAN S.S. & LUCKEN K. (1967) Additional cytoplasmic male sterility—fertility restoration systems in *Triticum*. *Wheat Inf. Service* **23–24,** 6–9.

MACKEY I. (1954) The taxonomy of hexaploid wheat. *Svensk. Bot. Tidskr.* **48,** 579–590.

MATSUMURA S., NEZU M. & KOSHIBA Y. (1958) Genome analysis of *Triticum georgicum*. *Wheat Inf. Service* **7,** 7–8.

OEHLER S. & INGOLD M. (1966) New cases of male sterility and a new restorer source in *Triticum aestivum*. *Wheat Inf. Service* **22,** 1–3.

RAO M.V. (1963) Genetics of field resistance of wheat varieties to the races of stem, leaf and stripe rust prevalent in India. *Wheat Inf. Service* **15–16,** 17–20.

SACHS L. (1953) Chromosome behaviour in species hybrid with *Triticum timopheevi*. *Heredity* **7,** 49–58.

SWAMINATHAN M.S. & RAO M.V.P. (1961) Macromutations and sub-specific differentiation in *Triticum*. *Wheat Inf. Service* **13,** 9.

SCHIEMANN E. (1948) *Weizen, Roggen, Gerste: Systematik, Geschichte und Verwendung.* Fischer, Jena.

UPADHYA M.D. (1967) Genome constitution of *Triticum ispahanicum* Heslot. *Wheat Inf. Service* **23–24,** 1–2.

UPADHYA M.D. & SWAMINATHAN M.S. (1963) Genome analysis in *Triticum zhukovskyi* Jacubz., a new tetraploid wheat. *Chromosoma* **14,** 589–600.

VAVILOV N.I. (1951) The origin, variation, immunity and breeding of cultivated plants. *Chron. Bot.* **13,** 1–364.

WIENHUS F. (1959) *Weizenzüchtung in Europa.* In *Handbuch der Pflanzenzüchtung* **2,** 216–267.

WILSON I.A. & ROSS W.M. (1962) Male sterility interaction of the *Triticum aestivum* nucleus and *Triticum timopheevi* cytoplasm. *Wheat Inf. Service* **14,** 29–30.

YAMASHITA K. (1959) II Preliminary report of the Botanical Mission of the University of Kyoto to the Eastern Mediterranean countries, April–May 1959. *Wheat Inf. Service* **9–10,** 43–48.

YAMASHITA K. & TANAKA M. (1960) II Exploration Results of the Botanical Mission of the University of Kyoto 1959. *Wheat Inf. Service* **11,** 24–31.

ZEVEN A.C. (1967) On the ancestry of *Triticum vulgare* varieties *Gabo* and *Timstein.* *Wheat Inf. Service* **23–24,** 2–5.

ZHUKOVSKY P.M. (1950) *Cultivated Plants and their wild relatives.* (Abr. transl. by P.S. Hudson, 1962) Commonwealth Agricultural Bureaux, Farnham Royal, Bucks.

21

RICE

T. T. CHANG

International Rice Research Institute
Los Baños, Laguna, Philippines.

INTRODUCTION

The genus *Oryza* is comprised of about twenty valid species, of which only two species are cultivated : *O.sativa* L. and *O.glaberrima* Steud. The wild and primitive forms are distributed over four continents : six in Africa, twelve in Asia, two in Australia and four in South America (Table 21.1). A few taxa such as *O.eichingeri*, *O.nivara* and *O.rufipogon* are distributed in two or more continents. Both diploid (2n = 24) and tetraploid forms exist in the African, Asian and American taxa. The taxonomy and nomenclature of certain taxa in the genus remain in dispute. Groups of such controversial entities are often conveniently referred to as species-complexes, e.g., the '*O.sativa* complex', '*O.latifolia* complex', '*O.officinalis* complex' and *O.meyeriana* complex'. Intra- and interspecific sterility exists in a number of species which include both cultivated and wild forms. Six basic genomes have been postulated for about sixteen taxa in the genus, but the relationship among the A, B and C genomes has not been fully elucidated.

In spite of the great genetic diversity in the genus, past cytogenetic and biosystematic investigations were often based on a small and narrow sample of the existing germplasm. For instance, all of the interspecific crosses involving *O.australiensis* made in several countries can be traced back to one single strain. The advent of modern agriculture has wiped out many of the truly primitive forms in endemic centres. As a result of hybridization with cultivars in adjacent fields, many of the Asian strains identified as *O.rufipogon* or *O.nivara* and *O.breviligulata* collected in tropical Africa are highly introgressed hybrids intermediate between the primitive and the cultivated forms. Living plants of a few exotic taxa such as *O.angustifolia* and *O.schlechteri* are disappearing rapidly and are unavailable to investigators.

267

K

TABLE 21.1. Species of *Oryza*

Code	Species (and synonyms)	Chromosome No. (2n)	Distribution
a	*O.alta* Swallen	48	Central and S. America
	O.angustifolia C.E. Hubbard (= *Leersia angustifolia*)[1]	—	Africa
	O.australiensis Domin	24	Australia
b	*O.barthii* A.Chev. (= '*O.perennis* subsp. barthii')[2]	24	Africa
c	*O.brachyantha* A.Chev. *et* Roehr.	24	West and Central Africa
d	*O.breviligulata* A.Chev. *et* Roehr. (= *O. stapfii*)	24	West Africa
e	*O.coarctata* Roxb. (= *Sclerophyllum coarctatum* (Roxb.) Griff.)[1]	48	Burma, India and Pakistan
	O.collina Trimen (= *O.eichingeri*)	24	Ceylon
f	*O.eichingeri* A. Peter	24, 48	East and Central Africa
g	*O.glaberrima* Steud.	24	West Africa
h	*O.grandiglumis* (Doell) Prod.	48	South America
	O.granulata Nees *et* Arn. *ex* Hook f.	24	South and Southeast Asia
i	*O.latifolia* Desv.	48	Central and S. America
j	*O.longiglumis* Jansen[3]	48	New Guinea
	O.malampuzhaensis Krish. *et* Chand[3]	48	India
l	*O.meyeriana* (Zoll. *et* Mor. *ex* Steud.) Baill	24	Southeast Asia
m	*O.minuta* J.S. Presl *ex* C.B. Presl	48	Southeast Asia
n	*O.nivara* Sharma *et* Shastry (= *O.fatua*, *O.sativa* f. *spontanea*, *O.rufipogon*)	24	South and Southeast Asia, N. Australia
o	*O.officinalis* Wall. *ex* Watt	24	South and Southeast Asia, New Guinea.
p	*O.perrieri* A. Camus (= *Leersia perrieri*)[1]	24	Malagasy
q	*O.punctata* Kotschy *ex* Steud	24, 48	Africa
r	*O.ridleyi* Hook f.	48	Southeast Asia
s	*O.rufipogon* Griff. (= *O.perennis*, *O. fatua*, *O.sativa* f. *spontanea*, '*O.perennis* subsp. balunga'[2], '*O.perennis* subsp. cubensis', *O.cubensis*)	24	South and Southeast Asia, South America
t	*O.sativa* L.	24	Asia
	O.schlechteri Pilger[3]	—	New Guinea
	O.subulata (= *Rynchoryza subulata*)[1]	24	South America
u	*O.tisseranti* A. Chev. (= *Leersia tisseranti*)[1]	24	Central Africa

[1]Recently removed from the genus *Oryza* by agrostologists.
[2]Temporary designation given at the 1963 Symposium on Rice Genetics and Cytogenetics (IRRI, 1964).
[3]Taxon of questionable status.

In areas where varietal improvement and national seed multiplication programs are being advanced, primitive and unselected cultivars of *O.sativa* are rapidly disappearing from highly localised habitats. The areas where rich genetic diversity is rapidly diminishing are Upper Burma, Cambodia, Laos, Vietnam, Indonesia, Oceania, Borneo Island, and East Pakistan.

EXPLORATION

Past efforts in exploration and collection have been few in number and limited in scope. During 1957–63 several Japanese workers and one Japanese-Chinese team made twelve collection trips and obtained about six hundred strains of various entities (Table 21.2). The Central Rice Research Institute of India collected twenty-six weed forms of *O.sativa* in the Jeypore tract of Orissa. The Indian Agricultural Research Institute also has collected wild forms inside India. The U.S. Department of Agriculture is supporting Indian workers in collecting primitive material and cultivars in Assam. Since the International Rice Research

TABLE 21.2. Collection trips for *Oryza* taxa.

Year	Locality	Workers	Material collected No. taxa and Code	Total No. Strains
Oct. 57–Jan. 58	India, Ceylon	H.I. Oka T. Tateoka T. Narise	7(e,l,n,o,r,s,t)	464
Oct. 58–Jan. 59	Thailand	H.I. Oka	4(l,o,s,t)	125
Jan.–Mar. 59	Malaya and Java	I. Hirayoshi	4(o,r,s,t)	266
Oct.–Dec. 59	Sikkim and Assam	H. Kihara S. Nakao	4(n,o,s,t)	386
Oct.–Dec. 59	Burma	K. Katsuya	4(l,o,s,t)	72
Oct. 59–Jan. 60	Africa	K. Furusato	6(b,c,d,g,q,t)	245
Oct. 60–Feb. 61	S. America	H.I. Oka	5(a,h,i,s,t)	70
Jan.–Mar. 61	Philippines, New Guinea	T.C. Katayama	6(f,l,m,o,s,t)	142
Jan.–Feb. 63	Philippines	T. Tateoka	4(l,m,o,s)	43
Mar.–May 63	Borneo and Java	T.C. Katayama	5(l,o,r,s,t)	126
Oct. 63–Jan. 64	West Africa	H.I. Oka W.T. Chang	7(b,c,d,g,q,t,u)	159
May–Aug. 64	East Africa, Malagasy	T. Tateoka	5(b,f,p,q,s)	39

Institute began its operations in 1962, it has supported some of the recent activities and is serving as a central depository for herbarium and seed material. The Institute's collection of wild forms numbers about nine hundred strains and covers thirty-eight entities. Other collections totalling several hundreds or more are being maintained at the Taiwan Provincial Chung-Hsing University (China), Central Rice Research Institute (India), Indian Agricultural Research Institute, All-India Co-ordinated Rice Improvement Project, and National Institute of Genetics (Japan). The Food and Agriculture Organization of the United Nations and its designated agencies in India and Japan, the U.S. Department of Agriculture, and the International Rice Research Institute maintain varietal collections of *O.sativa*, each collection numbering over several thousands.

The preservation of primitive germplasm is complicated by a high frequency of outcrossing, low percentage of seed fertility, and extreme shattering of ripening spikelets. A number of transported wild forms often succumb to some of the prevalent diseases which are endemic at the new sites of culture. Another problem involves the maintenance of the original population structure in bulked seedlots of a heterogeneous nature. One difficulty revolves around the need for correct morphologic and cytologic re-identification while the taxonomy of the genus is still in a state of flux. The problem of long-term seed storage in tropical areas is compounded by prevailing high humidity and high temperatures. As a result, the number of viable accessions in most of the existing collections is decreasing annually at an appreciable rate.

Further collection in several geographic areas is urgently needed to enrich the germplasm at hand for a number of specific objectives and to preserve valuable gene pools before the effects of progressive agriculture reach those areas which are still rich in primitive forms. Intensive explorations in the following areas are suggested:

1. West, North, Central and East Africa—Additional samples of exotic taxa (*O.angustifolia*, *O.tisseranti*) and diploid and tetraploid strains of *O.eichingeri* and *O.punctata* are desired to assist further studies on the taxonomy and biosystematics of primitive African species. Forms which are intermediate between *O.barthii* and *O.breviligulata* would provide an additional link in the evolution of the cultivated form, *O.glaberrima*.

2. Northern India, East Pakistan, Vietnam, Laos, Cambodia, Borneo Island, the sparsely inhabited islands of Oceania, and northern Australia—a wider spectrum of wild strains belonging to the complex

of O.rufipogon, O.nivara and *O.sativa* f. *spontanea* is needed to elucidate the evolution of *O.sativa* and to enrich germplasm of potentially useful genes.

3. Ceylon—diploid relatives of *O.officinalis* classified either as *O. eichingeri* or *O.collina* need to be augmented in number to aid in the biosystematic clarification of the '*O.officinalis* complex'.

4. Indonesia, Malaysia, Brunei and New Guinea Island—additional samples of *O.longiglumis*, *O.meyeriana*, *O.ridleyi* and *O.schlechteri* are desired in order to clarify these taxa of uncertain taxonomic status.

5. Tropical America, especially the Amazon basin—a wider array of diploid wild relatives of *O.sativa*, known either as *O.rufipogon* or '*O.perennis* subsp. *cubensis*', would be useful in relating these forms to the evolution of *O.sativa* and in enriching the pools of potentially useful genes.

6. Burma, Cambodia, Laos, Vietnam, East Pakistan, Indonesia, Borneo Island, Philippines and Thailand—primitive or unimproved forms of *O.sativa* need to be collected to provide a broader genetic basis for rice breeding.

While the need for international and inter-agency co-operation in exploration and collection efforts is widely recognized by scientists, the awareness and conscientious efforts of national and local governments in preserving the primitive germplasm and in assisting collection teams hold the key to fruitful ventures. Moreover, the composition of field teams should be broadened beyond the taxonomic discipline to insure a wider scope in collecting plant material of economic significance and pertinent information on agronomic traits and plant-environment interactions. Collection records should also be expanded in content to include information on the biophysical environmental conditions in which the rice plants grow, reproduce, and compete with other plants.

When some of the proposed collections materialize, the evaluation, cataloguing, preservation and utilization of useful genes and gene complexes in the primitive forms will constitute a formidable challenge to the rice scientists who will be involved in this work.

REFERENCES
for further reading

BARDENAS E.A. & CHANG T.T. (1966) Morpho-taxonomic studies of *Oryza glaberrima* Steud. and its related wild taxa, *O. breviligulata* A. Chev. *et* Roehr. and *O. stapfii* Roschev. *Bot. Mag. Tokyo* **27,** 791–798.

CENTRAL RICE RESEARCH INSTITUTE (1964) *Technical Report of the Central Rice Research Institute of the Year* 1963. Cuttack, India.

CHANG T.T. (1964) Present knowledge of rice genetics and cytogenetics. *Int. Rice Res. Inst. Tech. Bull.* **1**, 1–96.

CHANG T.T. & BARDENAS E.A. (1965) The morphology and varietal characteristics of the rice plant. *Int. Rice Res. Inst. Tech. Bull.* **4**, 1–40.

INTERNATIONAL RICE RESEARCH INSTITUTE. (1964) *Rice Genetics and Cytogenetics.* Elsevier, Amsterdam.

NATIONAL INSTITUTE OF GENETICS. (1959, 1960, 1962, 1963) *Annual Report, Nos.* 9, 10, 12, 13. Misima, Japan.

OKA H.I. & CHANG W.T. (1964) *Observations of Wild and Cultivated Rice Species in Africa.* 73: 1. National Institute of Genetics, Japan (mimeo).

SHARMA S.D. & SHASTRY S.V.S. (1965) Taxonomic studies in genus *Oryza.* I. Asiatic types of *O. sativa* complex. *Indian J. Genet. Pl. Breed.* **25**, 245–259.

TATEOKA T. (1963) Taxonomic studies of *Oryza* III. Key to the species and their enumeration. *Bot. Mag. Tokyo* **76**, 165–173.

TATEOKA T. (1965) Taxonomy and chromosome numbers of African representatives of the *Oryza officinalis* complex. *Bot. Mag. Tokyo* **78**, 198–201.

22

MAIZE

AURELIANO BRANDOLINI

Istituto di Ricerche Orticole, Minoprio, Como.

INTRODUCTION: ORIGIN AND EVOLUTION OF MAIZE

The increasingly rapid and wide diffusion of improved varieties of maize and especially of Corn Belt hybrids has led to the disappearance of most of the pre-existing ecotypes in many regions by substitution or uncontrolled hybridization. Modern local varieties are a result of hundreds or thousands of years of evolution in balance with the environment. Through generations these varieties have accumulated a number of gene combinations conferring productive potential as well as better adaptability to the particular conditions of their environment, climate and cultivation.

In view of the prevalence of allogamy, maize ecotypes appear to consist of groups of biotypes that, by crossing, selfing and recombination, present morpho-biological characteristics which vary greatly from individual to individual. A certain number of more or less evident characteristics, derived from the original ancestors, remain constant in every population. Some have yielded improved combinations as a result of either natural or anthropic selection pressure. Local cultivars are still largely unexplored, and possess great potential. Their disappearance deprives plant breeding of genetic material not easily replaced.

MODERN VIEWS ON ORIGIN AND PHYLOGENY

The species *Zea mays* L. belongs to the family *Gramineae*, tribe *Maydeae* or *Tripsaceae*. *Zea mays* L. has clear relations with some species of *Andropogoneae* of American origin. The tribe *Maydeae* is divided in two geographically well isolated groups: American *Maydeae* (*Zea mays* L., *Tripsacum* L., *Euchlaena* Schrad.) and Oriental *Maydeae* (*Coix* L., *Polytoca* R. Br., *Sclerachne* R. Br., *Chionachne* R. Br., *Trilobachne* Schench.). Maize cannot survive and reproduce itself without the aid of man: for this reason many hypotheses have been proposed concerning the original maize characteristics as well as the place and time of its origin and domestication. The principal hypotheses have considered :

1   Derivation of *Zea* by mutation from *Euchlaena* (Ascherson, 1880 ; Langham, 1940 ; Longley, 1941).

2   Hybrid origin from *Euchlaena* and an unidentified member of the *Andropogoneae* (Collins, 1912 ; Harshberger, 1893).

3   Amphidiploid origin from Asiatic species of *Maydeae* and *Andropogoneae* (Anderson, 1945).

4   Separate origin of *Zea*, *Euchlaena* and *Tripsacum* from a common ancestor (Montgomery, 1906 ; Weatherwax, 1918, 1955).

5   A tripartite hypothesis (Mangelsdorf and Reeves, 1939)

(*a*) the separate origin of *Zea* and *Tripsacum* from a common ancestral form ;

(*b*) the hybrid interspecific origin (*Zea* × *Tripsacum*) of *Euchlaena* ;

(*c*) the derivation of many evolved forms of *Zea* by introgressive hybridization from *Tripsacum* or *Euchlaena*.

6   Derivation of *Tripsacum* from an amphidiploid hybrid between primitive *Zea* and *Manisuris cylindrica* (Galinat *et al.* 1964).

The results of research in archaeology and genetics in the last 30 years permit some certainty on a number of basic points of maize evolution. Fossil pollen described by Barghoorn *et al.* (1954) proved that a type of *Zea* able to survive before domestication co-existed in the Mexican highlands with one or more *Tripsacum* species in the period between 100,000 and 80,000 years B.C. The presence of *Euchlaena* is identifiable there only at a much later time, between 7,000 and 6,000 years B.C. More recent archaeological discoveries of maize ears and tassels by Mangelsdorf and McNeish (1964) have permitted determination of the first phases of maize domestication in Mexico. In the Tehuacan Valley the sequence of wild and primitive maize of tripsacoid form helps further to clarify the course of evolution of maize. A comparison between the forms studied in Tehuacan and those found in Bat Cave (3,650 B.C.), La Perra Cave (2,500 B.C.) and Sierra de Tamaulipas suggested the possibility of a polycentric domestication of the species. On the basis of ethnological evidence a similar proposition has been made by Grobman *et al.* (1961), as also by McClintock (1960) on the basis of comparative studies of the chromosome morphology of similar forms from different regions.

Present knowledge concerning the origin and phylogeny of maize may be summarised as follows :

1   Wild forms of maize were widespread over the Mexican highlands (and possibly over central and south America) before man's first immigration to America.

2   Between 5,200–3,400 B.C. wild forms of *Zea mays* were utilized by 'gathering-stage' man in Tehuacan Valley. The main characteristics of wild maize were similar to the modern ones, apart from the greater size of the latter.

3   At the end of the above period more productive forms appeared, better fitted to cultivation.

4   Before 2,300 B.C., some tripsacoid forms of maize had been introduced from outside the region.

5   Domestication possibly took place simultaneously elsewhere in a similar way: consequently slightly different forms of primitive maize arose.

6   Present maize germ plasm appears to be composed of a number of racial forms, strictly related to wild *Zea*, differing as to the degree of direct evolution or of *Tripsacum* introgression.

7   *Tripsacum* introgression occurred at different times and places, directly by *Tripsacum australe* in Austral America, through *Euchlaena* in Meso America.

The *Tripsacum* contribution to maize can be summarized as follows:

(*a*) an increase in maize mutability (Mangelsdorf, 1958).

(*b*) higher chromosome knob frequencies (Mangelsdorf and Cameron, 1942 ; Wellhausen *et al.* 1957).

(*c*) additional heterotic complexes (Grobman *et al.* 1961).

(*d*) tissue hardening, mainly in ear structures (Mangelsdorf, 1961 ; Wellhausen *et al.*, 1957).

(*e*) diffusely tillering habit of the plant (Mangelsdorf and Reeves, 1939).

(*f*) higher insect and disease resistance (Horovitz and Marchioni, 1940 ; Rodriguez and Avila, 1964).

(*g*) higher fitness to growing conditions in tropical climates (Wellhausen *et al.* 1957).

Maize differentiation into ecologic-qualitative races appears to have followed two main paths:

1   A slow and constant selection in isolated populations of mutant genes and favourable modifier gene-combinations.

2   A similar process, in segregating generations, following hybridization with *Tripsacum* and *Euchlaena* as well as with occasionally and deliberately introduced germ plasm.

K*

CENTRES OF ORIGIN, DOMESTICATION
AND DIFFERENTIATION

The discovery of fossil pollen in Mexico definitely excludes the hypothesis of an Asiatic origin of maize, advanced by Bonafous (1836) and
more recently proposed by Anderson (1945). According to the phytogeographical criteria defined by Vavilov (1926) that the centre of origin of a
cultivated species coincides with the area where the greatest variability
of its wild forms persists, several authors are in favour of a Mexican or
central-American origin of maize (Harshberger, 1893; Vavilov, 1926;
Kempton and Popenhoe, 1937; Randolph, 1955). Darwin (1875) indicated Peru to be a possible centre of origin of maize and de Candolle
(1885) identified a centre of evolution of maize in the Colombian region.
On the other hand, Saint Hilaire (1829), Körnicke and Werner (1885),
and later Mangelsdorf and Reeves (1939), concluded that a domestication centre of maize must be assumed to be situated in the Paraguay
lowlands because of the presence there of primitive characters in local
strains. However, Mangelsdorf *et al.* (1964), Grobman *et al.* (1961) and
Brieger *et al.* (1958) stressed that the absence of maize wild forms does
not permit the application of Vavilov's criteria, which is therefore insufficient for the identification of a centre of origin. This also leaves
much uncertainty as to centres of differentiation; quite high variability is likely to be recorded in any centre where different races
converge.

There is a general agreement on some conclusions concerning the
origin of maize based on evidence from phytogeography, botany,
cytology, and also from the history, archeology and ethnology of the
regions concerned:

1   It looks highly probable that the origin of cultivated maize has been
polycentric (McClintock, 1960; Grobman *et al.*, 1961; Mangelsdorf and
McNeish, 1964). Although no ancient occurrence had been ascertained
outside Mexico, it is widely assumed that wild maize was present
generally in various habitats of the middle altitude regions of sub-
tropical America. The domestication process can have started in any
place where stability of settlements created the possibility and at the
same time the necessity of cultivating a cereal crop.

2   In both Meso America and Austral America it is possible to collect
scattered populations with primitive characters, which appear to be
remnants of 'evolutionary branches' with a wider diffusion during some
primitive stage of the domestication process. Most of the forms of the

Everta group and many of the 8-rowed *Indurata* and *Amylacea* groups have to be considered as such.

3 Due to lack of wild forms in maize, definitions of primary and secondary centres of differentiation do not appear to be entirely suitable. A 'primary centre' should be regarded as a 'domestication centre' and 'secondary centres' more properly as 'differentiation centres' distinct from the zones of domestication.

PRIMARY CENTRES

Climatic-orographic considerations and phylogenetic evidence permit a number of differentiation centres to be identified in both Meso America and Austral America.

The region where the primary stages of evolution under domestication probably occurred appears to have been paralleled after different periods by differentiation in smaller zones of ecological specialization. As a consequence, each primary centre of differentiation appears to be composed of a central nucleus of lower ecological specialization and by several peripheral zones of more specific climatic character where new races and ecotypes have become differentiated and specifically adapted to local climatic conditions and quality preferences.

A number of considerations lead us to define two great 'differentiation areas' (Table 22.1):

1 The region north of the equator (Meso America) including the southern United States, Mexico, Guatemala, Central America, Colombia, Venezuela and the West Indies, where germ plasm from the Mexico-Guatemala primary centre appears to prevail.

2 The region south of the equator (Austral America), under the influence of the Peru-Bolivian primary centre, which includes Ecuador, Peru, Chile, Bolivia, Paraguay, Argentina and Brazil.

MAIN SECONDARY CENTRES OF DIFFERENTIATION

Introduced into other ecological regions by migrations and along different exchange routes, maize continued to differentiate further, either along original evolutionary trends or along new paths imposed by new environmental conditions and by changes in selection criteria imposed by new human populations.

TABLE 22.1. Evolutionary trends in primary differentiation centres

Region	Habitat	Main associated civilisations	Maize races*	Evolutionary trends in the region
MESO AMERICA				
N.W. Mexico	New Mexico–Arizona drylands with irrigation; Pacific coast lowlands: 100–200 meters asl.	Bat Cave, Hopi-Papago Swallow Cave Culture Sonora Indians	(Sonora Cylindrica) CHAPALOTE Harinoso de Ocho	Hopi Southeastern Cylindrical Floury complex. Big-grain Cylindrical, Floury, Flints, 8-rowed Tabloncillo. Multirowed Cylindrical Popcorns, Floury, Flints, 'Sonora' maize
Central Mexico	Highlands: 2,000 to 2,800 meters asl.	Tehuacan Culture Aztec Empire	PALOMERO TOLUQUENO ARROCILLO AMARILLO Cacahuacintle	Conical Dents, deep grain complex Deep grain complex, cylindro-conical Dents
South Mexico, Guatemala, etc.	Tropical highlands and lowlands 0 to 2,500 meters asl.	Olmec Culture Maya Empires	NALTEL Oloton Quincheño, etc. Salpor	Cylindrical tropical Dents 8-rowed tropical Dents and Flints Highland early small-eared orange
Caribbean Middle Colombia	Coasts and islands Central Cordillera: 100 to 200 meters asl.	Taino-Arawak Culture Caribbean tribes	NEGRO/CAPIO Fira Andaqui	Lowland and highland Negro Floury complex. Coastal tropical Orange Flints and derived forms
ANDEAN AUSTRAL AMERICA				
(Colombia, Ecuador) Eastern Cordillera	Colombian highlands and Cordilleras: 2,000 to 3,600 meters axl.	Proto-Chibcha Chibcha	POLLO PIRA IMBRICADO Cacao	Highland small conical Flint complex Highland cylindrical 8-rowed Flints and Floury Derived forms

Region	Elevation	Culture	Native / introduced forms	Complex / derived forms
Peru and the Pacific Coast	Coast to 1,000 meters asl.	Chavin Culture Tiahuanaco influence (Inca Empire)	CONFITE CHAVINENSE PROTO CULLI PROTO ALAZAN MOCHERO	Mochero-Chaparreño early Floury complex, Alazan-Huayleño conical complex, Pardo cylindrical Floury complex
Valles	Central valleys of the Andean Cordilleras, 2,000 to 2,800 meters asl.	Pre-Inca cultures (Quechua, Aymará) Inca Empire	CULLI KAJBIA HUALEÑO CHUSPILLU	Hualtaco-Cuzco Big-grain Floury/Flint complex Huillcaparu complex
Valle Alto Altiplano	High valleys and highlands: 2,800 to 3,600 meters asl.	Tiahuanaco Aymará (Inca Empire)	CHECCHI HUACA SONGO JAMPE TONGO	Valle Alto short-plant, deep-grain. Very early, cold resistant
Central and South Bolivia	Medium and high valleys: 1,500 to 2,600 meters asl.	Yamparaez Culture (Inca Empire)	KARAPAMPA PISANGALLO MOROCHILLO Suave 8-hileras	Kellu-Morecho Indurata complex
Valles Orientales	Mid-altitude Andean valleys and south-facing slopes (Yunga); 100 to 600 meters asl.	Pre-Inca culture Inca Empire	CHUSPILLO PATILLO Hualtaco	Perla-del-Valle White Flint complex
Llano Oriental	Eastern lowlands: 100 to 600 meters asl.	Lowland tribes (Guaraní influence)	PURITO PORORO Perla del Valle Amazonica	Perla de Llano White Flint complex (Calchaqui White Flint) Guarani cylindrical Floury and Flints
Oriente (Amazonas)	Eastern Amazonian slopes and adjacent lowlands: 200 to 1,500 meters asl.	Mojos-Tupis Chiquitanos Arawaka Quechua influence	ENANO PURA COROICO Tusilla Perlas	Amazonian slopes and lowlands hybrids and Floury and Flint derived forms

* Native forms in capital letters, introduced forms in lower case.

United States and Canada

Secondary racial differentiation began in America in the present Northern Lakes Region and in New England, where nomad tribes met favourable conditions for establishing stable agricultural settlements. About the same time, Indian populations living in the southern Atlantic regions (Georgia, Florida, etc.) brought into cultivation maize races introduced from the Mexican lowlands and the West Indies. The westward migrations of European settlers, during the nineteenth century, caused a further phase of evolution of maize in the Middle West of the United States. Contemporary introductions to the same environment of northern and north eastern 8-rowed flints and of southern prolific dents (Anderson and Brown, 1952a) gave rise to the Corn Belt dent, on which the agricultural economy of the middle West was built.

Eastern Austral America

In the same century European immigrants to southern Brazil, Uruguay and Argentina permitted new contact between, and progressive blending of, races from the Amazonian and Paraguay lowlands with 'coastal tropical flints' from the West Indies, as well as with different flint races from the southern slopes of Bolivia. From this were derived a number of ecotypes, mainly orange, white and yellow flints which still predominate in southern Brazil and in the Argentine corn belt (Table 22.2).

Europe

Discovered by Columbus in the Bahamas (16 October, 1492) and first introduced into cultivation in Seville fields during 1494, West Indies flint maize was scattered in southern Europe without wide adoption into agriculture until the middle of the sixteenth century, when a further introduction of maize germ plasm from the Andean slopes and Mexican highlands permitted an increased variability, and better adaptability. Not widely adopted in Spain, a number of acclimatized forms spread from southern Italy through Mediterranean regions as far as south-eastern Europe, the Black Sea coast and the Near East and northern Africa. From Veneto a number of very early types were introduced (1590) into the Austrian and Hungarian plains, after crossing the Alps. Later, other varieties better adapted to warmer conditions were diffused by Venetian traders as far as the Balkan plains through Dalmatian ports.

TABLE 22.2. Secondary centres of differentiation of *Zea Mays*: Americas

Region	Habitat	Culture	Introduced races	Provenance	Derived race complexes
North and North-eastern U.S.A., southern Canada	Temperate Atlantic coast and Great Lakes: level and hilly: cool short season	Winnebago-Dakota Minnesota Indians	Cylindrical Floury and Flints Early Dent	Arizona via Ozark (Missouri)	8-rowed Northern Flint × Dent, 8-rowed north-eastern Flint × Floury, Canadian extra-early 8-rowed Flints
Southeastern U.S.A.	Southern Atlantic Coast: Warm temperate	Florida—Georgia Indians	Conical Deep Grain Dents Cylindrical Dent Tuxpeño Tropical Flints	Mexican Coast and Highlands Caribbean Islands	Prolific Southern Dents Gourd seed (Shoepeg) Dents, Big-grain 8-rowed white Dent (Hickory King) Cylindro-conical smooth Dents
Corn Belt	Continental Plains: Temperate: Medium Season	European settlers	8-rowed Northern Flint 8-rowed Northeastern Flint Southeastern Dents	North Central States N. Atlantic States S. Atlantic States	Modern multi-rowed Cylindrical yellow and white Dents
South Brazil and Argentine	Southeastern Hills and Plains: Subtropical	Portuguese settlers	Early small-eared Flints	Andes/Europe	Cateto Prolific Flints
		Spanish and Italian immigrants	Coastal Tropical Flint Guarani Cylindrical Flint Amazonian Flints 8-rowed Morochos Multi-rowed Morochos	W. Indies/Europe Paraguay Amazonian lowlands S. Bolivian slopes	Piamontés long-eared orange Flint, Quarentén early orange Flint, Colo-rado 8 hileras, Inter-mediate forms
		Calchaqui Indians	Perola/Calchaqui white Flints	E. Tropical slopes and Lowlands	Perola complex White Semiflints
		Guaranies Caingang Indians	Guarani white soft Caingangdent Floury US white Dents	E. Tropical lowlands E. Tropical U.S.A. Corn Belt	White Semiflints White Dents Flint-Dent complex

In the middle of the seventeenth century, maize was already widely grown in the whole of southern Europe, to become the main food crop of the peasants, contributing thereby to reduce and even to eliminate the earlier risks of recurrent famine. During the eighteenth century, from the French and English settlements of Canada and New England a number of very early forms were imported to Northern France, England, Holland and southern Germany. In the following century early 8-rowed varieties were introduced to southern Poland, Czechoslovakia, Hungary, Russian Galicia, and from there into the border regions of northern Italy, Croatia, Slovenia and Romania. During the nineteenth century a new flood of germ plasm from the newly settled regions of the American Mid-West helped to improve yield levels of the maize crop in the Balkans as a consequence of the introduction of Cornbelt Dent into the Danubian plains.

Quite a large number of strains from different American locations, mainly from the Caribbean coast and subtropical-temperate highlands, have given rise to a new complex of races and ecotypes in the Mediterranean and Balkan regions, fitted to diversified types of climate and to new cultivation and utilization needs (Table 22.3).

The main bulk of derived European germplasm at the end of the nineteenth century was of Indurata type, which responded better to transportation by sea and at the same time was able to ripen safely in the rainy autumns of southern Europe. Endosperm type caused no difficulties, because all European regions were already well equipped with mills for the processing of wheat flour.

Asia

Maize reached Asia from three directions soon after the discovery of America. Through the Mediterranean trade route it was taken into cultivation in Syria about 1565, from where it possibly spread to the Euphrates basin (Rauwolf 1574) and the southern Black Sea coast. Maize was introduced, mainly by Portuguese navigators and traders by way of the Atlantic and Indian Ocean sea routes, to southern India and Japan where its introduction was reported in 1565 in Kyushu. From the mid-sixteenth century, after Magellan's long voyage of circumnavigation of the earth, the Spanish fleet carried corn into the Pacific and especially to the Philippines and eastern Indonesia. About 1573 maize is described by the writer Li Shih-Chên as being grown in southern China, introduced recently from the South, possibly by land through Burma or Indochina (Laufer, 1907) (Table 22.4).

TABLE 22.3. Secondary Centres of differentiation of *Zea Mays*: Europe

Region	Habitat	Introduced races	Provenance	Derived race complexes
EUROPE				
1. Southern Europe and Mediterranean				
Southern-central Spain, Southern France, Southern-central Italy, Yugoslavia (Dalmatia and Macedonia), Albania Greece, Bulgaria, Turkey	Mediterranean summer-dry climate	Pollo-Naltel, Sabanero, Alazan, Tusilla, 8-rowed Morocho, Perola complex, Cylindrical red soft Early Caribbean Canguil Popcorn	Meso America Austral America / Central America Caribbean Andes	Early conical Mediterranean Flint, Medium late conical Mediterranean semiflint / Early northern Flints 8-rowed Mediterranean Flints
2. European Corn Belt				
Northern Italy, Yugoslavia (Sava, Danube basin) Romanian plain, S. Hungary, Bulgaria (Danube valley)	Intermediate climates	Pollo-Naltel, Sabanero, Tusilla, Imbricado 8-rowed Morocho Multi-rowed Morocho Cateto Flint Pisankalla/Pororo Perola complex, White Dent S. eastern conical Dent 8-rowed N. eastern Flint Pepitilla, Conico-Norteño USA Corn Belt Dent Hickory King 8-row Dent	Meso America Austral America / Atlantic coast / Mexico / USA Corn Belt Southern USA	Early conical Mediterranean Flint 8-rowed Mediterranean Flints Long eared orange Flints Pignoletto complex / White Dents Modern Dents Perola white Flints
3. Atlantic and Continental Corn Growing Regions				
Portugal, Northern Spain, Southern Netherlands, Southern Germany, Austria, Czechoslovakia, Southern Poland, Southern Hungary, Russia	Cool humid Atlantic or Continental climate with short growing season	Pollo-Naltel 8-rowed N. eastern Flint N. eastern 8-rowed Flint 8-rowed Tabloncillo Conical early Sabanero	Meso America Atlantic coast N. eastern USA Mexico Colombian Andes	Early 8-rowed Flints Early cylindrical Flints Early conical Flints

TABLE 22.4. Secondary centres of differentiation of *Zea Mays*: Asia and Africa

Region	Habitat	Introduced races	Provenance	Derived race complexes
ASIA				
Near East Transcaucasia, Turkey, Iran, Afghanistan	Dry Subtropical climate with very short dry growing season	Sabanero Chococeño	Meso America	Prolific small-eared orange Flints
Southern Himalayas	Highland tropical climate with rainy season and or irrigation	Sabanero Early orange Flint Pira Naranja Chococeño Coastal tropical Flint	Meso America	Multiple-rowed orange Flints. Prolific small-eared orange Flints. Long-eared orange Flints
Eastern and Southeast Asia China	Continental and Intermediate climate. Temperate oceanic climate. Tropical Oceanic climate	Sabanero Early orange Flint Coastal Tropical Flint 8-rowed Flint	Meso America	Long-eared orange Flints

AFRICA

Egypt: Nile basin	Dry subtropical climate with irrigation	Pearl Popcorn, Caribbean orange Flint, Pearl white Flint, USA white Dent	Caribbean, via the Nile	White Flint/Dent complex
West Africa	Tropical climate	Caribbean yellow and white Flint	Bahia, via Ghana	White and yellow Flint complex
		Brazilian yellow and white Floury		Yellow and white Floury complex
South Africa	Dry subtropical climate	Caribbean coastal orange Flint, Brazilian Floury, Hickory King		Botman-Cango white Flint
				Bushman Kaffir Meelie
East Africa (Somalia)	Dry tropical climate, hilly	Corn Belt Flint/Dent complex, White Flint	Southern USA	Flour, Hickory King, Potchfstroem Dent
East Africa (Kenya, Ethiopia)	Rainy tropical climate		U.S.A.	

Compared with the Mediterranean region, flint germ plasm from southern America and the West Indies spread rapidly in Asia, developing into a number of land races characterized by orange endosperm, deep flint grain and a broad and differentiated adaptation to tropical, subtropical and highland climates in most of the important regions of southern and eastern Asia. Although maize growing developed rapidly in inland China, on the southern slopes of the Indian Himalayas, in Burma, Indochina and on the Java hills, it remained relatively unimportant in all other regions of the continent.

Africa

From Italy and Spain maize reached northern Africa by the mid-sixteenth century: since 1560 it has been grown in Egypt and the Tripoli oasis, well fitted to local conditions where irrigation was available. Along the Atlantic navigation routes, Spaniards and Portuguese rapidly distributed the new cereal crop to African coastal countries: in 1560 maize was already grown in West Africa in Guinea and the Congo. A complementary route of introduction of yellow flint germ plasm from the Mediterranean basin to West Africa has been detected by way of the Nile valley and lake Chad region (Stanton, 1963). Apart from the imports of early Caribbean germ plasm by Arab traders as a consequence of the prevalent influence of Portuguese navigators, for about three centuries the bulk of maize introduced to the African coast originated from South American tropical regions, mainly from Brazil (Bahia), the Guyanas and the Paranà basin.

Dutch settlers introduced flint and floury types into South African agriculture at the time of their early settlements in the seventeenth century. Floury or Soft dent forms were adopted by native populations on account of the ease of processing by substituting cornmeal for sorghum flour. In general, a high frequency of white corn types grown by the native populations can be recognised, with a minority of orange-grained forms of Cateto origin, all with a special adaptation to the long season of tropical and subtropical regions.

During the late nineteenth and early twentieth centuries new introductions have been made from the southern part of the U.S.A. and from northern Mexico, especially to South and East Africa, synchronous with the development of European settlements.

PLANT EXPLORATION

The modern collection and description of maize germ plasm has illustrious antecedents in the Great Herbals of the sixteenth and seventeenth centuries as well as in the basic botanic studies of Bonafous (1836), Körnicke and Werner (1885) and Sturtevant (1899). A fresh impulse to exploration was given by Kuleshov (1933), Cutler (1948) and Anderson and his collaborators (1945, 1946, 1947, 1948, 1952b). Their studies covered a wide range of genetic material collected in all the places of possible origin of the species, and had as their main goal the phylogenetic relationships of *Zea mays* and its racial variability in relation to ecology and utilization. Further interest has been stimulated by the researches on the origin of maize by Mangelsdorf and Reeves (1939), as well as by the development of maize breeding techniques based mainly upon the dominance of complementary gene combinations, followed by hydridization between different strains.

An extensive programme for the conservation of maize germ plasm was begun in Mexico (1945–1952) by the Rockefeller Foundation, which made collections of cultivars and preserved and classified the resulting material. Modern methods of maize classification and preservation have been developed on the basis of this work.

The Race Concept in Maize

After the classification of maize by Bonafous (1836), the first subspecific classification was by Sturtevant (1899). Maize varieties gathered in North America were classified according to grain type into six groups, and further subdivided according to grain pattern and colour. The basic taxonomic criterion was the persistence of grain type through generations. The Sturtevant classification was criticized by Anderson (1945) as corresponding only slightly or not at all with phylogenetic evidence. Be this as it may, it is only reliable at the higher levels of intraspecific classification.

In order to resolve possible difficulties at lower taxonomic levels, Anderson and Cutler (1942) advanced as a practical solution the definition of the *race unit* later defined by Brieger *et al.* (1958) as a 'group of populations having a sufficient number of distinctive characters in common, maintaining itself through panmictic reproduction within populations, and occupying definite areas'. Thus a race complex is 'a group of races having a number of distinctive morphological characters in common being phylogenetically related'.

Methodology of collection and preservation

The methodology of collection and preservation has been little studied to date. Procedures may be summarized in general terms, on the basis of what is known of genetics and physiology, as follows :

(*a*)   direct collection of samples of local strains (5–30 ears each) in many locations,

(*b*)   preliminary preservation of local strains by sibbing and storage in controlled environments (relative humidity 40–50%, temperature 0–4°C),

(*c*)   taxonomic studies, in order to determine phylogenetic relations at a racial and subracial level,

(*d*)   multiplication of related strains in *subracial bulks*, having a high number of phenological and physiological characters in common, by open pollination in isolated plots, in order to obtain seed of the minimum subracial unit able to maintain most of the variability for each race (distinguished by special adaptation characters, growing period, photo-periodic response, specific distribution in relation to altitude, thermal requirements, etc.),

(*e*)   permanent storage in controlled environments and, if possible, controlled atmosphere (inert, or with low $O_2 < 2\%$, and $CO_2 < 3\%$) in special containers, in at least 2 locations (a national and a regional centre).

Methodology of classification

The taxonomic study of maize is made difficult by the existence of many small systematic units at the level of agro-ecotypes (Gregor, 1933) within varieties, differing in adaptive characters, with a narrow genetic basis but having, on the other hand, certain genetic traits in common with other varieties. Due to the prevalence of allogamy and to multiple introductions of germ plasm from different sources, a systematic survey of the different forms can be done only by determining phylogenetic relationships at the *racial* level. Many local varieties—populations in balance with the ecological and biotic environment in which they have evolved—are included within each race.

Relationships and the resulting taxonomic scheme are based on :

(*a*)   historical and ethnological records. These can help to identify introduction sources, migration routes, and indicate likely introgressions and genetic exchange between races.

(*b*)   morphological analysis of every sample collected, including :

3 phenological records	7 tassel morphology records
5 plant morphology records	3 resistance records

5 ear morphology records   6 morphological indices
6 grain morphology records

(c)   karyotype analysis, including the number, size and localization of chromosome knobs.

(d)   genetic records, derived from observations on segregating generations from single strains, or on inter-racial crosses or topcrosses to identify the specific contributions of each strain or race.

Recently, in 1967 at Montpellier, special emphasis has been given to the need to extend taxonomic studies of regional germ-plasm to cover several locations chosen on the basis of different climatic conditions, so that comparison of data can contribute to an understanding of the ecogenetic mechanisms involved in racial differences.

Half a century of classification work on a world scale following the Bukasov–Kuleshov expedition (1928) leads to the conclusion that taxonomic studies can be conducted efficiently only internationally by the examination of germ plasm from major geographical regions, defined by orographic patterns and the routes of contact between civilizations.

Meso and Austral America

The first systematic study on maize races in the western hemisphere was carried out by Wellhausen and his collaborators in the period 1945–1952. On the basis of more than 2,000 samples collected all over Mexico, these authors propose a race classification on the basis of morphological, genetic and archaeological evidence. At the same time they initiated a conservation programme by the reproduction of single races in the field and the long-term low-temperature storage of seed. Following this work several national programmes for the collection and classification of maize ecotypes were started in Latin American countries. As a result, a series of publications was issued by the National Academy of Sciences and National Research Council, among others, for Mexico (Wellhausen *et al.* 1952), Central America (Wellhausen *et al.* 1957), Cuba (Hatheway, 1957), Colombia (Roberts *et al.* 1957), Brazil and other eastern countries of South America (Brieger *et al.* 1958), West Indies (Brown, 1960), Bolivia (Ramirez *et al.* 1960), Peru (Grobman *et al.* 1961), Chile (Timothy *et al.* 1961), and Ecuador (Timothy *et al.* 1963) ; a new study of Bolivian maize (Rodriguez *et al.* 1968) has just been published by F A O.

Table 22.5 reports data on maize collections and the classification of individual races on the basis of their origins and endosperm characteristics is given.

TABLE 22.5. Maize exploration in the Americas
(Number of Races of Maize Collected and Classified 1942–64)

Country	Number of Samples	Ancient		Derived		Indurata Flint	Amylacea Floury	Indentata Dent	Everta Pop
		Native	Exotic	Prehistory	Modern				
Mexico	2000	4	4	13	4	2	1	16	5
Guatemala	1054	2	7	2	2	5	3	4	1
Central America	173	—	1	1	5	4	2	1	—
West Indies	212	—	3	2	2	4	—	2	1
Colombia	906/1999	2	9	8	4	10	—	3	3
Ecuador	675	4	5	9	10	8	12	7	1
Peru	1600	5	6	19	22	7	33	9	3
Bolivia	844	10	4	14	4	6	15	8	3
Chile	134	1	9	7	3	4	7	1	7
Brazil, etc.		0	5	7	4	10	4	1	1
Paraguay		1	1	2	1	2	2	—	1

Source: *Nat. Acad. Sci. Nat. Res. Counc. Publs.* 453, 510, 511, 593, 747, 792, 847, 915, 975.

Europe, Asia and Africa

In the Old World, the collection and classification of maize cultivars was started in a number of countries about 40 years ago. Descriptions of national collections gathered before 1930 were submitted to the 1st International Maize Meeting in France in 1931. Country monographs have been published in Italy (Succi, 1931) and Romania (Enescu, 1922). Less detailed descriptions have been issued in other countries since (Scossiroli 1953; Leng *et al.* 1962; Brandolini and Covor 1967; Brandolini *et al.* 1967).

At the FAO Eighth European Hybrid Maize Meeting, a cooperative plan of collection of European cultivars was outlined on the pattern of the Rockefeller Foundation Programme for Latin America. Although this programme was actively developed in some countries such as Spain, France, Italy, Yugoslavia, Romania, Bulgaria and Hungary, it was not developed on an international scale. Until now, only the Spanish collection has been described in a publication by Sanchez-Monge (1962). Studies of Italian, Yugoslav and Romanian collections are shortly to be published. In other countries classification work continues and we are, therefore, able to give only preliminary data. At the Fourth Maize Section Meeting of *Eucarpia* (Montpellier, 1967) its Southern Committee decided on a new programme of collection, classification, conservation and exchange of maize ecotypes, coordinated by a working group including representatives of the major maize growing countries, with a restricted working team on methodology composed of the Southern Committee President, and of single specialists from Italy, Spain, Yugoslavia and Romania.

In Asia a study of Everta and Indurata local varieties from Turkey has been made by Anderson and Brown (1953). On the basis of this work the authors discussed a classification of the material into two main groups, Asiatic and Aegean, according to their possible routes of introduction. Other collections from Nepal, Japan and India, and taxonomic studies on the collected material, have been made by Murakami (1963), Sprague (not published), and others (Table 22.6).

WORLD VARIABILITY OF *Zea Mays* L.

Kuleshov (1929) first outlined the phenotypic diversity of world maize. This work is still important not only because it was the first attempt to

TABLE 22.6. Maize Exploration in the Old World
(Number of Races of Maize Collected and Classified 1954–1967)

Country	Number of Samples		Racial groups							
			Indurata					*Amylacea*	*Indentata*	*Everta*
	Collected	Studied	Early Flint	8-rowed Flint	Coastal Flint	White Flint	Deep grain Flint	Conical Floury	Conic./cyl. Dent	Cylindrical Popcorn
EUROPE										
Spain	459	459	4	5	2	1	1	3	—	2
France	200	50	2	1	—	2	1	—	—	—
Italy	900	700	4	2	2	6	4	2	4	2
Yugoslavia	1500	900	2	1	1	—	2	—	5	—
Romania	2100	550	2	1	5	2	3	—	5	1
Bulgaria	800	(800)	1	1	1	1	2	—	+	—
Hungary	600	(600)	1	1	1	2	2	—	2	1
ASIA										
Japan	150	(150)	+	+			+			+
China*			+	+	+	+			+	+
India/Nepal	500	(500)	+	+	+		+			+
AFRICA										
Morocco*				+	+	+	+		+	
Egypt*					+	+			+	+
South Africa*					+	+		+	+	
West Africa (Nigeria, etc.)*						+		+	+	
East Africa (Somalia, etc.)	120	(120)			+			+	+	

* figures not available or incomplete   ( ) data still not complete   + present, but not further classified

TABLE 22.7. Variability of some Characteristics in *Zea Mays* L. (by Subspecific Group)
(Source: Original Data and References Cited)

Racial Group	Altitude of Collection (meters a.s.l.)	Growing Season (days)	Leaf Number	Plant Height (cm)	Ear		Grain		
					Length (cm)	Number of Rows	Length (mm)	Width (mm)	1000 Grain Weight (gm)
Amylacea	0–4000	68–480	10–44	110–400	9–25	8–18	6·0–21	5·4–18	100–1200
Indurata	0–3000	70–260	8–42	70–400	9–40	8–20	5·0–18	4·5–16	70–710
Indentata	0–2000	90–170	13–38	90–700	12–50	8–24	9·0–20	5·0–14	100–700
Everta	0–3500	90–140	14–27	40–300	4–20	8–20	2·8–13	2·9–7	50–220
Saccharata	0–2000	80–150	9–22	90–350	8–25	8–16	5·5–18	6·6–13	70–300
Amyleosaccharata	0–3500	120–172	28–33	90–210	10–18	8–20	11·0–18	8·0–9	300–550

evaluate maize variability in world terms, but also because it was the only attempt to do so in the temperate zone before hybrid dent maize began to spread and replace the native germ plasm of entire countries (USA, France, Romania, Hungary) in the most important areas of maize production. This process has had the effect of confining the old land varieties to marginal regions in many countries.

Modern maize is the result of a multiple evolutionary process conducted in diverse environments from the equator as far as latitude 52°. The goal has been to increase production, and has affected grain type, the size of the plant or its parts, its nutritive quality and its growth cycle, within the context of many regional environments (Table 22.7). As a result a very broad range of variability is now available on a world scale, which can provide a basis for further major evolutionary advance if carefully utilized and not wasted or destroyed.

Zea mays is grown from sea level up to 4000 meters, with a development period of 68–70 days for the Russian cultivar Viatka, and up to 16 months for a Colombian variety; from 8 leaves for a very early form grown in dry conditions, up to 42 leaves for a late variety grown in southern Colombia. Plant height may vary from 40 cm in dry areas up to 700 cm for Mexico Jala maize. Ear and grain characters also exhibit astonishing differences. Ear length may vary from 4 cm to 40 cm, ear rows from 8 to 26, grain length from 2·8 mm to 18·0 mm, and the 1000-grain weight may range from 50 grams for a Peruvian Everta cultivar to 1,200 grams for a form of Cuzco soft maize, also from Peru.

Distribution of endosperm types

Amylaceous types predominate, along with a small amount of Indurata, in the Andean Region. In the Old World and in eastern South America Indurata is dominant, while Indentata shows an increasing frequency from Mexico towards the American Corn Belt. Eight-rowed Indurata, and Amylacea, of great importance before the middle of the nineteenth century, appear only as traces in northern marginal area.

Endosperm type distribution is given in Table 22.8, after the data of Kuleshov (1929). This describes the distribution of the different types before the spread of hybrid maize, as the percentage of types found in collections from the most important maize-producing countries In the Old World frequencies appear to shift in favour of the Indurata group, due to the nature of the native germ plasm and to the better climatic adaptation of this type.

TABLE 22.8 Frequencies of *Zea Mays* Endosperm types in world collection
(Kuleshov, 1929)

New world

Region	Number of Samples	Percentage frequency		
		Indentata	Indurata	Amylacea
Canada	47	27·5	54·4	15·0
Northern USA	360	54·5	35·9	7·6
Central USA	217	89·9	8·3	1·8
Southern USA	77	81·8	5·2	12·0
Northern Mexico	67	80·6	17·9	1·5
Central Mexico	438	68·7	6·4	24·9
Southern Mexico	221	78·3	21·3	0·4
Central America	105	28·6	69·5	1·9
Northern Colombia	88	5·0	88·6	5·7
Southern Colombia	184	0·0	48·9	51·1
Ecuador	450	0·5	27·0	72·5
Peru	539	0·6	13·2	86·2
Bolivia	92	—	21·8	73·9
Argentina	—	5·0	90·0	5·0
Brazil	—	5·0	90·0	5·0

Old world

	Number of Samples	Percentage frequency					
		Indentata	Indurata	Everta	Amylacea	Saccharata	Ceratina
South western Europe	191	14	67	1	7	11	—
Continental Europe	77	10	75	1	1	13	—
Ukraine and Crimea	292	13	83	2	1	1	—
Northern Caucasus	648	15	77	4	2	2	—
Transcaucasia	281	38	56	5	1	—	—
Central Asian Repubs.	117	4	92	1	3	—	—
Iran	111	—	100	—	—	—	—
Afghanistan	24	—	100	—	—	—	—
India	39	3	95	2	—	—	—
Near East	70	11	83	6	—	—	—
Syria and Palestine	3	33	33	33	—	—	—
Siberia and Far East	98	—	92	2	2	1	3
China	106	—	84	2	—	7	4
Japan	26	—	77	4	—	—	19
Africa	23	13	87	—	—	—	—

Biological and vegetative characters

Maize originated in the different environments of the American continent. The movement of forms between American regions and from the
Americas to the Old World continued in an irregular way and at
different rates over four centuries. Primitive forms have had a variable
impact on the composition of modern maize gene pools according to the
frequency of different introductions.

Environment has necessarily conditioned the survival and the later
success of each different introduction by its effect on the relative survival
of different provenances during the process of development of new local
populations, the first and main requirement of which in each case has
been a photo- and thermo-period permitting optimal balance with the
specific conditions of its own environment. Among other environmental
factors, latitude and water availability have exercised a dominant
influence on maize adaptation and evolution. These factors have determined the present high variability of the species, evidenced, for
example, in the length of the growing season (figures 22.1 and 22.2),
or in leaf number (figure 22.3).

When the first attempts were made to introduce maize from the
equatorial and tropical belt to the temperate areas of Europe and Asia,
difficulties were encountered. However, adaptation occurred easily
when latitudinal differences between the original and the receiving
regions, e.g. between temperate regions of America and Europe or
between tropical regions, are minimal.

The success of acclimatation has been linked with the character of
the photoperiodic response of the strains involved. The extensive
adoption of Everta and Indurata germ plasm is explained by recent
studies (Brandolini and Pons 1964, Rodriguez *et al.* 1968) which have
shown that a number of strains (Everta from the Andean slopes and
Zapalote Chico from Mexico) are insensitive to photoperiod, while other
varieties from Indurata group are still segregating for photoperiodic
response.

In southern Europe and the Near East it seems that rainfall or
irrigation has been the main factor determining adaptation of maize
races to the ecological conditions of the Mediterranean. In Italy the
influence of germ plasm from the Caribbean islands, Central America,
Mexico and southern USA is encountered in the irrigated northern
regions, while in the non-irrigated areas of the South early strains
introduced from high latitudes or highlands of the Andean Cordilleras
are to be found.

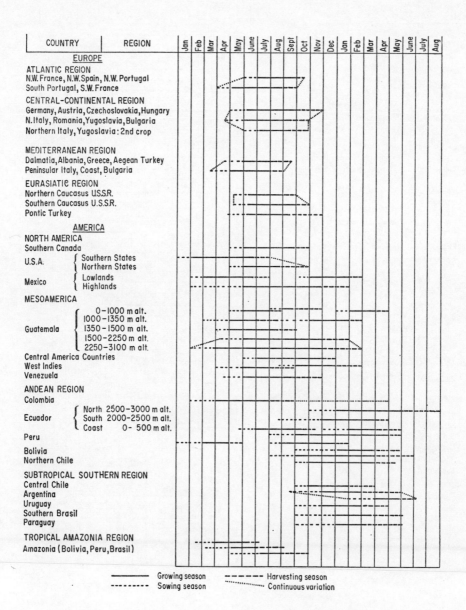

FIGURE 22.1. Growing seasons in *Zea mays* L.—Europe and America.

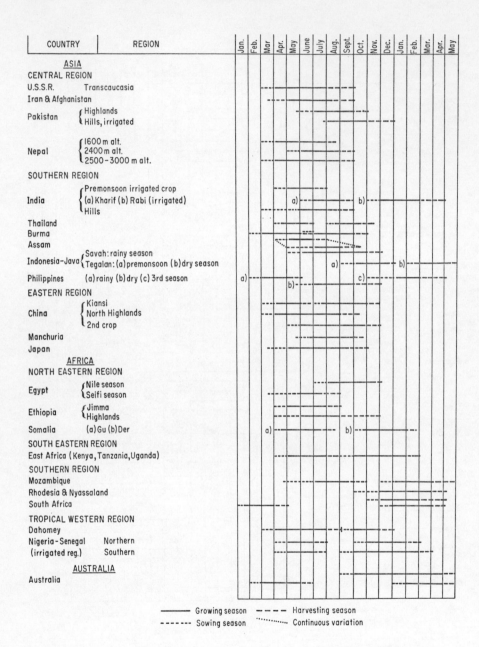

FIGURE 22.2. Growing seasons in *Zea mays* L.—Asia, Africa and Australia.

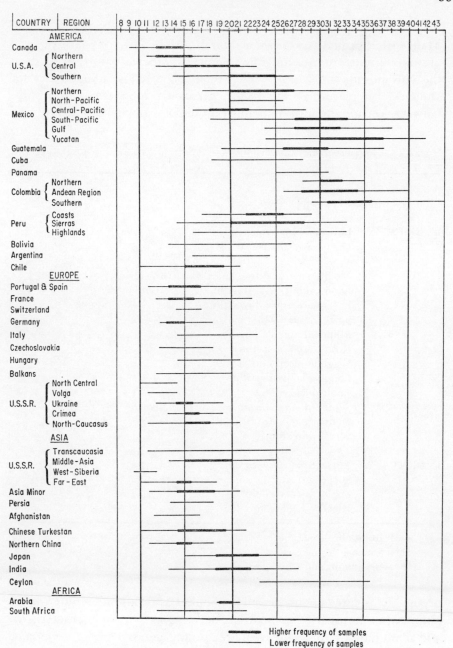

FIGURE 22.3. Leaf number in *Zea mays* L.—range of variations (from Kuleshov, 1929).

Genetic and chromosomal characteristics

Mangelsdorf (1961) has shown a relationship between the latitude and altitude of maize strains and the average number of knobs present on the chromosomes. Bianchi *et al.* (1963) reported similar results for Italian germ plasm. The work of Lorenzoni (1965) on relationships between certain quantitative morpho-biological characters and the

TABLE 22.9 Frequency of Chromosome Knobs in European Maize Races

Racial group		Italy (*)	Spain (**)	Romania (***)
EVERTA	Late rice popcorn	4	—	—
	Prolific pearl popcorn	4	3–4	—
INDURATA	Mediterranean 8-row flint	3–4	3	2–3
	Long cylindrical 8-row flint	6	5	3–5
	Big square grain 8-row flint	—	1–2–3	—
	Small-eared prolific flint	4–5–6	2–3	—
	Elliptical pignole flint	8	—	—
	Rostrato pointed flint	6	—	—
	Scagliolo deep flint	4	2–3	—
	Long-eared orange flint	4–6	2	2–3–4
	Conical-eared flint	0–2–3	1–2	3
	Southern cinquantino	1–3–4	0–2	—
	Southern cylindro-conical	3–5	4–6–7	—
	White pearl flint	4	—	—
INDENTATA	Ancient floury types	5	—	3
	Shoepeg dent	5	—	—
	U.S.A. modern dent	5–6	—	2
	Hickory King white dent	—	4	4

(*) Brandolini *et al.* 1967
(**) Sanchez Monge, 1962
(***) Brandolini and Covor, 1967

presence of isolated knobs, as well as peculiar associations of some knobs, establishes a number of correlations between karyotype characteristics and plant habit, stem length, leaf area, and vegetative cycle, conferring adaptation to the conditions of the Po valley. In American races of maize similar studies have been used to investigate phylogenetic relationships between races. The number of knobs appears to be highly

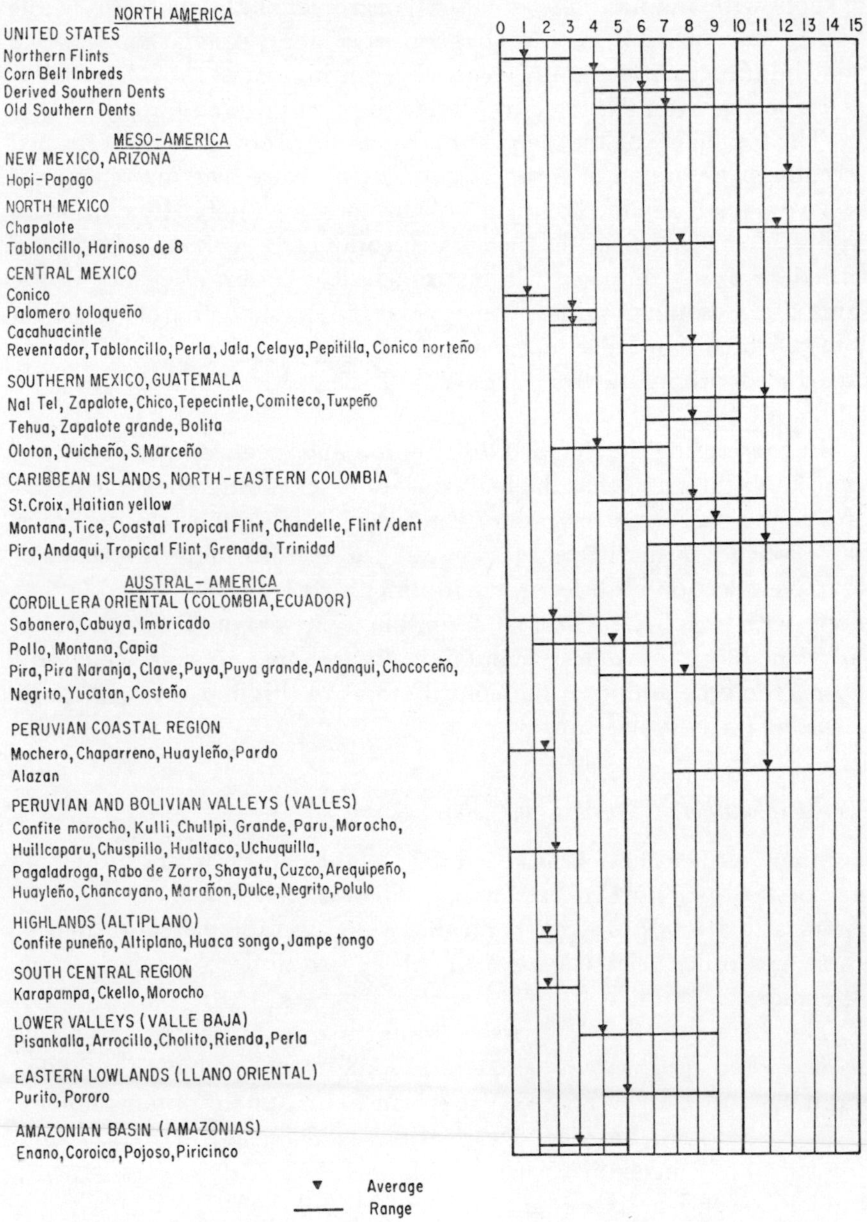

FIGURE 22.4. Frequency of knobs in American races of maize—racial averages and variation.

variable within races (figure 22.4), but an association of higher numbers of knobs with adaptation to equatorial or tropical habitats, possibly due to *Tripsacum* or *Euchlaena* introgression, is evident. Amylaceous, Everta and Indurata maizes from Andean slopes or highlands show few knobs, as has been previously stated by Mangelsdorf and Reeves (1939).

The frequency of knobs in European racial groups has been studied recently by a number of authors (Table 22.9). European maize appears to have a relatively low frequency of chromosome knobs. In a few local strains of early conical flints they are completely lacking. Most local varieties appear endowed with extremely few knobs, often not in the same chromosome positions. Some racial groups show frequencies from 4 to 7, which is usually linked with a long growing period in strains introduced originally from the West Indies, Meso America or the southern USA.

In considering the detailed distribution and localization of chromosome knobs, it seems that the high variability encountered is due to the broad range of germ plasm which converged into Southern Europe over four centuries from different regions, and to the distinctive processes of adaptive selection in different environments. It is highly probable that along with the heterochromatic combinations (knobs) a number of polygenic blocks have been maintained by selective pressure which still permit the recognition of the contributions of original races, through persisting phenotypic features.

Plant Exploration of Maydeae and related genera

Until now little attention has been paid to the collection and preservation of the genera *Euchlaena* and *Tripsacum*, beyond the supply of botanical materials to workers on the origin and phylogeny of maize. These and other related genera (Tables 22.10 and 22.11) have been little studied.

The systematics and phytogeographical distribution of species of *Euchlaena* and *Tripsacum* have received some study, including a monograph by Cutler and Anderson (1941) and a treatment of morphology by Reeves (1953). Phylogenetic relations of *Euchlaena*, *Tripsacum* and *Zea mays* have been discussed by Mangelsdorf and Reeves (1939), Randolph (1955) and Galinat *et al*. (1964).

Several authors (Mangelsdorf and Reeves, 1939; Reeves, 1953; Mangelsdorf and McNeish, 1964; Rodriguez and Avila, 1964;) have emphasized the important contribution of *Tripsacum* and *Euchlaena* germ

TABLE 22.10 Chromosome Numbers in *Zea* and Related Genera

	2n	*Author*
American *Maydeae*		
Zea mays L.	20	Kuwada (1919)
Euchlaena mexicana Schrad.	20	Kuwada (1915)
Euchlaena perennis Hitchc.	40	Longley (1937)
Tripsacum australe Cutler and Ander	36	Graner and Addison (1944)
Tripsacum dactyloides L.	36	Reeves and Mangelsdorf (1935)
Tripsacum dactyloides L.	72	Reeves and Mangelsdorf (1935)
Tripsacum floridanus Porter ex Vasey	36	Longley (1937)
Tripsacum latifolium Nash	72	Reeves and Mangelsdorf (1935)
Tripsacum laxum Nash	72	Reeves and Mangelsdorf (1935)
Tripsacum maizar Hern. and Rand.	36	Hernandez and Randolph (1950)
Tripsacum pilosum Scribn. and Mer.	72	Reeves and Mangelsdorf (1935)
Tripsacum zopilotense Hern. and Rand.	36	Hernandez and Randolph (1950)
Oriental *Maydeae*		
Coix aquatica Roxb.	10	Mangelsdorf and Reeves (1939)
Coix lachryma-jobi L.	20	Longley (1924)
Polytoca barbata Stapf.	20	Reeves and Mangelsdorf (1935)
Sclerachne punctata Brown	20	Reeves and Mangelsdorf (1935)
Andropogoneae		
Manisuris cylindrica (Michx.) Kuntze	18	Reeves and Mangelsdorf (1935)
Sorghum dimidiatum Stapf.	10	Janaki-Ammal (1939)
Sorghum halepense Pers.	40	Longley (1932)
Sorghum intrans F. Meull.	10	Garber (1947)
Sorghum purpureo-sericeum Schw. and Arch.	40	Longley (1932)
Sorghum randolphianum Paredi	40	Randolph (unpublished)
Sorghum versicolor Anders.	10	Longley (1932)
Sorghum vulgare Pers.	20	Kuwada (1915)

plasm to the genetic improvement and breeding of maize, as a source of mutability and of genetic traits controlling morphology, adaptation and resistance. A detailed study on *Euchlaena* races has been more recently published by Wilkes (1967) (Tables 22.12 and 22.13).

TABLE 22.11 Native Habitat of American *Maydeae*

	Chromosome Number 2n	
		DIPLOIDS
Euchlaena		*MESO AMERICA*
Eu. mexicana Schrad	20	Mexico to Honduras
Tripsacum		
T. dactyloides	36	Kansas, U.S.A.
T. floridianum	36	Florida, U.S.A.
T. zopilotense	36	New Mexico, U.S.A.
T. maizar	36	Guerrero, Mexico
		AUSTRAL AMERICA
T. australe	36	British Guyana-Venezuela — Savannah and slopes up to 800 m/asl
		Ecuador — Slopes up to 1200 m/asl.
		Bolivia — Lowlands up to 1500 m/asl.
		Brazil — Lowlands
		Paraguay — Latitude 26° S.
		TETRAPLOIDS
Euchlaena		
Eu. perennis Hitch.	40	
Tripsacum		
T. dactyloides	72	Indiana, Illinois to Texas, Georgia, Florida.
T. pilosum	72	South West Mexico to Guatemala.
T. lanceolatum	72	Arizona to Guatemala.
T. lemmoni	72	Mexico to Guatemala.
T. laxum	72	South Mexico to Central America.

Recently, interest in *Tripsacum australe* has increased and a collecting expedition to the Bolivian lowlands was made by Cardenas and Timothy in 1966. More careful collection and an intensified study of different strains from the various habitats of each species should lead us to a better knowledge of the phylogenetic relations within the tribe as well as to a richer source of genetic materials for use in maize breeding programmes, with the attainment of improved yielding ability and the further expansion of maize cultivation into tropical regions.

TABLE 22.12. Races and Habitats of Teosinte, *Euchlaena Mexicana* Schrad.
(after H. Garrison Wilkes, 1967)

Race	Habitat	North Latitude	Altitude (meters a.s.l.)	Days to Anthesis	Knob number Range	Average
Nobogame	West Sierra Madre	26° 15′	1750–1920	70	5·0	
Central Plateau	Guanajuate-Michoacan	21°	1750–2100	79	6–11	8·5
Chalco	Mexico Valley	19°	2180–2500	82	8–13	10·0
Balsas	South Michoacan-Guerrero	18° 30′ – 17° 15′	800–1950	86–91	4–13	8·5
Huehuetenango	North Guatemala	16°	1000–1650	104–108	9–12	
Guatemala	SE Guatemala	14° 30′	1000–1300	99		11
	Honduras	—	600–700	—	—	—

TABLE 22.13. Average Morphological Characters of Races of Teosinte, *Euchlaena Mexicana* Schrad. (After H. Garrison Wilkes, 1967)

Race	Height (cm)	Node Number	Tiller Number	Fruiting Nodes	Length (cm)	Width (cm)	Leaf Area (cm^2)	Rachis Segment Weight (gr/100)	Seed Weight (g/10)	Seed Number per Spike	Pollen Size (microns)
Nobogame	116·1	10·4	8·7	7·4	41·6	4·2	132·0	0·62	0·30	9·7	66·4
Central Plateau	158·0	12·9	5·6	9·5	42·6	5·4	173·1	0·86	0·62	10·6	76·5
Chalco	190·0	14·2	3·9	8·4	50·9	6·6	250·1	1·16	0·50	11·3	79·2
Balsas	129·3	12·0	9·6	9·2	47·0	4·9	173·4	0·51	0·24	8·8	56·0
Huehuetenange	178·1	14·8	12·3	10·6	64·2	5·4	256·9	0·61	0·25	8·6	78·4
Guatemala	116·2	12·0	10·5	10·3	49·0	4·6	167·0	0·74	0·33	6·4	83·0

REFERENCES

ANDERSON E. (1945) What is *Zea mays?* a report of progress. *Chron. Bot.* **9,** 88–92.

ANDERSON E. (1946) Maize in Mexico: A preliminary survey. *Ann. Missouri Bot. Gard.* **33,** 147–247.

ANDERSON E. (1947) Field studies of Guatemalan Maize. *Ann. Missouri Bot. Gard.* **34,** 433–467.

ANDERSON E. and BROWN W.L. (1948) The southern dent corns. *Ann. Missouri Bot. Gard.* **35,** 255–268.

ANDERSON E. and BROWN W.L. (1952a) The history of the common maize varieties of the United States Corn Belt. *Agric. Hist.* **26,** 2–8.

ANDERSON E. and BROWN W.L. (1952b) Origin of Corn Belt Maize and its genetic significance. In *Heterosis* (Ed. Gowan J.W.), 124–148. Iowa State College, Ames.

ANDERSON E. and BROWN W.L. (1953) The popcorns of Turkey. *Ann. Missouri Bot. Gard.* **40,** 33–48.

ANDERSON E. and CUTLER H.C. (1942) Races of *Zea mays:* I. Their recognition and classification. *Ann. Missouri Bot. Gard.* **29,** 69–88.

ASCHERSON P. (1880) Bemerkungen über ästigen Maiskolben. *Bot. Ver. Prov. Brandenburg* **21,** 133–138.

BARGHOORN E.S., WOLFE M.K. and CLISBY K.H. (1954) Fossil maize from the Valley of Mexico. *Bot. Mus. Leafl. Harvard Univ.* **16,** 229–240.

BIANCHI A., GHATNEKAR M.V. and GHIDONI A. (1963) Knobs in Italian maize. *Chromosoma* **14,** 601–617.

BONAFOUS M. (1836) *Histoire Naturelle Agricole et Economique du Mais.* Paris.

BRANDOLINI A. and COVOR A. (1967) *Razze di mais in Romania.* Milano (in press).

BRANDOLINI A., LORENZONI C. and VANDONI G.C. (1967) I Mais Italiani. In *Enciclopedia Agraria*, REDA, Rome.

BRANDOLINI A. and PONS A. (1964) *Elementos desarrollo agricola del Ecuador: Maïz.* O.E.A., Washington.

BRIEGER F.G., GURGEL J.T.A., PATERNIANI E., BLUMENSCHEIN A. and ALLEONI M.R. (1958) Races of maize in Brazil and other eastern South American countries. *Nat. Acad. Sci. Nat. Res. Counc. Publ.* 593.

BROWN W.L. (1960) Races of *Zea mays* in the West Indies. *Nat. Acad. Sci. Nat. Res. Counc. Publ.* 792.

CANDOLLE A. de (1885) *Origin of Cultivated Plants.* London.

COLLINS G.N. (1912) Origin of Maize. *J. Washington Acad. Sci.* **2,** 520–530.

CUTLER H.C. (1948) Races of maize in South America. *Bot. Mus. Leafl. Harvard Univ.* **12,** 257–291.

CUTLER H.C. and ANDERSON E. (1941) A preliminary survey of the genus *Tripsacum. Ann. Missouri Bot. Gard.* **28,** 249–269.

DARWIN C. (1875) *The Variation of Animals and Plants under Domestication.* John Murray, London.

ENESCU J. (1922) *Porumburile Rominesti.* Atelierele Grafice Socec., Bucuresti.

GALINAT W.C., CHAGANTI R.S.K. and HAGER F.D. (1964) *Tripsacum* as a possible amphidiploid of wild maize and *Manisuris. Bot. Mus. Leafl. Harvard Univ.* **20,** 289–316.

L*

GREGOR J.W. (1933) The ecotype concept in relation to the registration of crop plants. *Ann. Appl. Biol.* **20,** 205–219.

GROBMAN A., SALHUANA W. and SEVILLA R. in collaboration with MANGELSDORF P.C. (1961) Races of maize in Peru. *Nat. Acad. Sci. Nat. Res. Counc. Publ.* 915.

HARSHBERGER J.W. (1893) Maize, a botanical and economic study. *Contrib. Bot. Lab. Univ. Pennsylvania* **1,** 75–202.

HARSHBERGER, J.W. (1895) Fertile crosses of teosinte and maize. *Garden and Forest* **9,** 522–523.

HATHEWAY W.H. (1957) Races of maize in Cuba. *Nat. Acad. Sci. Nat. Res. Counc. Publ.* 453.

HOROVITZ S. and MARCHIONI A.H. (1940) Herencia de la resistencia a la langosta en el maíz 'Amargo'. *Ann. Inst. Fitotéc. Santa Catalina* **2,** 27–52.

KEMPTON J.H. and POPENOE W. (1937) Teosinte in Guatemala. *Carnegie Inst. Washington Publ.* 483, 199–218.

KÖRNICKE F. and WERNER H. (1885) *Handbuch des Getreidebaues I. Die Arten und Varietäten,* 355–360, Berlin.

KULESHOV M.N. (1929) The geographical distribution of the varietal diversity of maize in the world. *Bull. Appl. Bot. Gen. Pl. Breed.* **20,** 506–510.

KULESHOV M.N. (1933) World's diversity of phenotypes of maize. *J. Amer. Soc. Agron.* **25,** 688–700.

LANGHAM D.G. (1940) The inheritance of intergeneric differences in *Zea-Euchlaena* hybrids. *Genetics* **25,** 88–107.

LAUFER B. (1907) The introduction of maize into Eastern Asia. *Proc. XV Int. Congr. Americanists* **1,** 223–257.

LENG E.R., TAVČAR A. and TRIFUNOVIC W. (1962) Maize of Southeast Europe and its potential value in breeding programmes. *Euphytica* **11,** 263–272.

LONGLEY A.E. (1938) Chromosomes of maize from North American Indians. *Jour. Agr. Res.* **56,** 177–195.

LONGLEY A.E. (1941) Knob positions on teosinte chromosomes. *Jour. Agr. Res.* **62,** 401–413.

LONGLEY A.E. and KATO T. (1965) Chromosome morphology of certain races of maize in Latin America. *CIMMYT Res. Bull.* **1.**

LORENZONI C. (1965) Knob e caratteri quantitativi nei mais italiani. *Ann. Fac. Agrar. Piacenza* **5,** 343–366.

McCLINTOCK B. (1960) Chromosome constitutions of Mexican and Guatemalan races of maize. *Carnegie Inst. Washington Yearbook* **59,** 461–472.

MANGELSDORF P.C. (1958) The mutagenic effect of hybridizing maize and teosinte. *Cold Spring Harbor Symp. Quant. Biol.* **23,** 409–421.

MANGELSDORF P.C. (1961) Introgression in maize. *Euphytica* **10,** 157–168.

MANGELSDORF P.C. and CAMERON J.W. (1942) Western Guatemala, a secondary center of origin of cultivated maize varieties. *Bot. Mus. Leafl. Harvard Univ.* **10,** 217–252.

MANGELSDORF P.C. and McNEISH R.S. (1964) Domestication of Corn. *Science* **143,** 538–545.

MANGELSDORF P.C., McNEISH R.S. and GALINAT W.C. (1956) Archeological evidence on the diffusion and evolution of maize in Northeastern Mexico. *Bot. Mus. Leafl. Harvard Univ.* **17,** 125–150.

MANGELSDORF P.C. and REEVES R.G. (1939) The origin of Indian corn and its relatives. *Texas. Agr. Exp. Sta. Bull.* 574.

MONTGOMERY E.G. (1906) What is an ear of corn? *Pop. Scien. Monthly* **68**, 55–62.

MURAKAMI K. (1963) List of native corn varieties in Japan. *Nat. Inst. Agric. Sci.* (*mimeographed report*).

RAMIREZ R.E., TIMOTHY D.H., DIAZ B.E., GRANT U.J. in collaboration with NICHOLSON G.E., ANDERSON E. and BROWN W.L. (1960) Races of maize in Bolivia. *Nat. Acad. Sci. Nat. Res. Counc. Publ.* 747.

RANDOLPH L.F. (1955) History and origin of corn II. Cytogenetic aspects of the origin and evolutionary history of corn. In *Corn and Corn Improvement* (Ed. Sprague G.F.), 18–57. Academic Press, New York.

REEVES R.G. (1953) Comparative morphology of the American *Maydeae*. *Texas Agr. Med. Coll. Bull.* 761.

ROBERTS L.M., GRANT U.J., RAMIREZ E.R., HATHEWAY W.H. and SMITH D.H. in collaboration with MANGELSDORF P.C. (1957) Races of maize in Colombia. *Nat. Acad. Sci. Nat. Res. Counc. Publ.* 510.

RODRIGUEZ A. and AVILA G. (1964) *Tripsacum* factor de variabilidad genetica. *Univ. Cochabamba Bol. Tec.* **1.**

RODRIGUEZ A., ROMERO M., QUIROGA J., AVILA G. in collaboration with BRANDO-LINI A. (1968) *Maices Bolivianos.* FAO, Rome.

SAINT HILAIRE, A. de (1829) Lettre sur une variété remarquable de mais du Brésil. *Ann. Sci. Nat.* **16**, 143–145.

SANCHEZ-MONGE E. (1962) *Razas de Maiz en España.* Madrid.

STANTON W. (1963) Archeological evidence for changes in maize types in West Africa. *Man* **150**, 117.

STONOR C.R. and ANDERSON E. (1949) Maize among the hill peoples of Assam. *Ann. Missouri Bot. Gard.* **36**, 355–404.

STURTEVANT E.L. (1899) Varieties of corn. *U.S.D.A. Off. Expt. Sta. Bull.* 57.

SUCCI A. (1931) Il granoturco. In *Nuova Enciclopedia Agraria.* Torino.

TIMOTHY D.H. *et al.* (1961) Races of maize in Mexico. *Nat. Acad. Sci. Nat. Res. Counc. Publ.* 847.

TIMOTHY D.H. *et al.* (1963) Races of maize in Ecuador. *Nat. Acad. Sci. Nat. Res. Counc. Publ.* 975.

VAVILOV N.I. (1926) Studies on the origin of cultivated plants. *Bull. Appl. Bot. Gen. Pl. Breed.* **16**, 139–246.

WEATHERWAX P. (1918) The evolution of Maize. *Bull. Torrey Bot. Club* 45, 309–342.

WEATHERWAX P. (1955) Early history of corn and theories as to its origin. In *Corn and Corn Improvement* (Ed. Sprague G.F.), 1–16. Academic Press, New York.

WELLHAUSEN E.J., FUENTES O., ALEJANDRO H. and CORRO A. in collaboration with MANGELSDORF P.C. (1957) Races of Maize in Central America. *Nat. Acad. Sci. Nat. Res. Counc. Publ.* 511.

WELLHAUSEN E.J., ROBERTS L.M. and HERNANDES X.E. in collaboration with MANGELSDORF P.C. (1952) *Races of Maize in Mexico.* Bussey Inst. Harvard University, Cambridge, Mass.

WILKES H.G. (1967) *Teosinte: the closest relative of maize.* Bussey Inst. Harvard University, Cambridge, Mass.

23

POTATOES

J. G. HAWKES
University of Birmingham,
Birmingham, U.K.

INTRODUCTION

Although the potato is a world crop of the greatest importance, it is extremely sensitive to diseases and pests, and is adapted to a rather narrow range of environmental conditions. Breeding work is, therefore, mainly concerned with problems of disease resistance and adaptation to a wider climatic range. Other problems, such as increase in dry weight, protein and vitamin C content, as well as flavour and market acceptability, are also being investigated.

Until comparatively recently commercial varieties were rather narrowly based genetically, having been derived from a limited number of primary introductions in the late sixteenth century and a few more in the nineteenth and early twentieth centuries. Hence, to widen the genetic basis of this crop, breeders in this century from the 1920s onwards have endeavoured to introduce material from South America, where the plant is indigenous and where the range of variability is high.

TAXONOMY AND ADAPTATION

The cultivars of South America, where the potato has been grown for a very long period and where it first originated as a crop plant, represent only a small proportion, in their turn, of the total genetic variability available to breeders. Thus, there are only seven cultivated species, whilst at least about 150 wild species can be recognised. Against this, however, one must place the fact that each cultivated species comprises a very wide range of cultivars, so that the total variability in this group is high. Detailed studies of the wild species indicate even so, that the more widespread of these are also highly variable. It is therefore extremely important to realise that just one or two samples of a species from one point in its range do not by any means give a fair indication of the total variability of the species. Mass sampling and large-scale evaluation are essential if the potentialities of this vast and incredibly useful gene pool are to be fully exploited.

We have mentioned that the cultivated species are indigenously confined to South America, though it would seem that they were conveyed to Central America and Mexico not long after the Spanish conquest. They are typically grown in the high cool-temperate regions of the Andes at altitudes of 2,500 m and over. Two frost-resistant species, *S.juzepczukii* and *S.curtilobum*, are cultivated from 3,500 m to even higher altitudes. One species is grown on the east-facing slopes of the Andes from 2,000 m upwards in frost-free areas (*S.phureja*), where its lack of tuber dormancy enables it to be grown all the year round. The most widespread species, *S.tuberosum*, extends throughout the Andes from Venezuela southwards to North Argentina (subspecies *andigena*) and also in the coastal lowlands of southern Chile (subspecies *tuberosum*). The climate in this latter region is rather similar to that of the high Andes, though the summer day-length is very much longer. On the whole, then, the range of tolerance of the cultivated species is not very great.

The wild species, on the other hand, are found in a wide range, geographically, extending from the States of Colorado and Nebraska in the U.S.A., southwards through Mexico and Central America, and thence into South America along the length of the Andes from Venezuela to southern Argentina and Chile. They also spread out over the plains of the La Plata basin into Paraguay, Uruguay and southern Brazil. The range of adaptation is great, from drought and heat-resistant species growing at or near sea-level in the tropics to frost resistant ones in the high Andes at over 4,000 m, and in the high mountains of Mexico and Guatemala at some 3,500 m. Others grow in the mountain rain forests, whilst others again seem quite well adapted to the deserts of Mexico and Argentina, and the dry intermontane basins and valleys in the Andes and elsewhere. Details of resistance to disease, adaptation to special environmental conditions, and the development of improved biochemical qualities are discussed more fully by Ross (1958), Rothacker (1961), Ross and Rowe (1965) and Hawkes and Hjerting (1969).

EXPLORATION

Even before the disastrous *Phytophthora* epidemics of the 1840s in Ireland and elsewhere which caused potato crop failures and famines, attempts were being made to introduce 'fresh blood' from the original home of the potato, South America, so as to improve its general yielding ability, resistance to disease, and quality. Thus, a number of botanists and horticulturists in England, France, Germany, and the U.S.A. obtained a few samples from time to time though with little practical success. Mention must be made here of the variety Rough Purple Chile, obtained by Goodrich in the U.S.A. and used by him and others subsequently with great success in breeding first early varieties. The introduction of the wild species *S.demissum* from Mexico by the German botanist Klotzsch may also have contributed to the *Phytophthora* resistance of the later German varieties. Salaman, in England, probably was the first investigator to demonstrate, in 1909 and 1910, resistance to *Phytophthora* in a hybrid of *S.demissum* by *S. tuberosum*.

It was left to the Russian investigators from 1929 onwards, under the leadership of N.I. Vavilov, to begin a really systematic study of the genetic resources of wild and cultivated potatoes. The expeditions of Bukasov and Juzepczuk, as well as that of Vavilov himself, set the pattern for the modern era of study and exploitation of potato germplasm (see Table 23.1). When the results of these expeditions and the subsequent work of evaluation began to be published from 1929 onwards, other countries were quick to realise the value of such work, and collections were made by scientists from Germany, Sweden, U.S.A. and the British Commonwealth from 1930 to 1939. After the second world war more detailed collections in specific areas began to be made, some collectors concentrating on wild species, whilst others confined themselves entirely or almost entirely to a study of cultivars. As can be seen from Table 23.1, the expeditions and collecting trips are still continuing, sponsored generally by countries in Europe or by the United States, though the funding has not of course always come from Government sources. Some collectors, such as Correll, Hjerting, Hawkes, and others were primarily interested in taxonomic problems of wild species, though most kept firmly in view the actual or potential breeding value of the material gathered. Considerable interest was also shown by certain South American governments, as well as by individuals, as can be seen in Table 23.2. Thus, the present writer has been invited by two South American governments (Colombia and Uruguay) to set up schemes for the scientific evaluation and utilization of the genetic resources of potatoes in their own areas; and excellent pioneering work has been done in other countries by far-sighted individuals, such as Vargas and Ochoa in Peru and Cárdenas in Bolivia. The work of

TABLE 23.1. Potato Collecting Expeditions from 1925 onwards

Date	Collector(s)	Areas Visited	Material collected	Sponsoring country[1]
1925–6	S.M. Bukasov	Mexico, Guatemala, Colombia	Mainly cultivated species	U.S.S.R.
1927	S.W. Juzepczuk	Peru, Bolivia, Chile, Argentina	Mainly cultivated species (some wild)	U.S.S.R.
1930	D. Reddick	Mexico (Central regions)	Wild species	U.S.A.
1930	Bauer and Schick	Peru, Bolivia, Argentina	Cultivated species	Germany
1932	N.I. Vavilov (and Kesselbrenner)	Mexico, S. America	Mainly cultivated species	U.S.S.R.
1932	Macmillan and Erlanson	Peru, Bolivia, Chile	Cultivated species	U.S.A.
1933–4	C. Hammarlund	Peru, Bolivia	Cultivated species	Sweden
1938	E.K. Balls and W.B. Gourlay	Mexico (Central regions)	Wild species	British Common-wealth
1939	E.K. Balls, W.B. Gourlay and J.G. Hawkes	Colombia, Ecuador, Peru, Bolivia, Argentina	Wild and cultivated species	British Common-wealth
1947–8	D.S. Correll	Mexico	Wild species	U.S.A.
1949	J.G. Hawkes	Mexico	Wild species	U.K.
1955	H.J. Toxopeus	Peru	Cultivated species	Nether-lands
1956	J.P. Hjerting, E. Petersen and K. Rahn	Argentina, Chile	Wild species	Denmark
1957–60	D.S. Correll et al.	Colombia, Ecuador, Peru, Bolivia, Chile, Argentina	Wild species (? and cultivars)	U.S.A.
1958	J.G. Hawkes, J.P. Hjerting and R.N. Lester.	U.S.A., Mexico, Central America	Wild species mainly	U.K., Denmark
1958	P.M. Zhukovsky	Latin America	Wild and cultivated species	U.S.S.R.
1959	H. Ross et al.	Peru, Bolivia, Argentina	Wild and cultivated species	Germany

TABLE 23.1 *(contd.)*   POTATOES   315

1960	K.S. Dodds and G.J. Paxman	Andes of S. America	Cultivated diploid species U.K.
1960	J.P. Hjerting	Peru, Chile	Wild species	Denmark
1962	K.S. Dodds and N.W. Simmonds	Andes of S. America	Cultivated species U.K.
1964	J.G. Hawkes, C. Ochoa and C. Vargas	North and South Peru	Wild species	U.K.
1965	J.G. Hawkes *et al.*	Mexico	Wild species	Rockefeller Foundation
1965	H. Ross	Coastal lomas of Peru	Wild species	Germany
1966	J.G. Hawkes, J.P. Hjerting and K. Rahn	Argentina	Wild species	U.K., Denmark

[1]Some expeditions were 'unofficial' and were funded from non-government sources

TABLE 23.2. Collections made on behalf of (or with funds from) Latin American Governments or Universities by their own nationals or by others on contract to these bodies

Date	Collectors	Areas Visited	Material	Country
1936–	C. Vargas	South Peru	Cultivated and wild species	Peru
1939–	M. Cárdenas	Bolivia, Peru	Cultivated and wild species	Bolivia
1948–53	E. Petersen and J.P. Hjerting	Argentina, Bolivia, Peru	Cultivated and wild species	Argentina
1948–51	J.G. Hawkes, N. Estrada *et al.*	Colombia, Venezuela, Ecuador	Cultivated and wild species	Colombia
1951–	N. Estrada	Colombia	Cultivated and wild species	Colombia
1948–63	H. Brücher	Argentina, Chile	Cultivated and wild species	Argentina
1950–	C. Ochoa	Peru, Ecuador, Bolivia	Cultivated and wild species	Peru
1958	J.G. Hawkes	Argentina (B. Aires), Uruguay, S. Brazil	Wild species	Uruguay
1960–	R. Flores Crespo	Mexico	Wild species	Mexico
1967	K. Okada	Argentina	Wild species	Argentina

Petersen and Hjerting in Argentina, as well as Brücher in the same country, also deserves mention.

If all the material collected by these expeditions and individuals was still being grown in experimental stations in Europe and elsewhere, or was stored as seed in gene banks, breeders would be in a very fortunate position indeed. This is far from the case, however. Until comparatively recently there were few institutes or experimental stations of the size and with the facilities to make possible a really exhaustive program of screening, with subsequent storage of useful genetic material for the benefit of breeders in all parts of the world. The potato is highly susceptible to disease and most of the material from the Americas will not form tubers well except under short days, which must be provided artificially if the plants are grown in northern Europe or the U.S.A. Nevertheless, the material already collected has provided the basis for breeding programs of the greatest value ; and we now know a great deal about the taxonomy, breeding behaviour, cytogenetics and disease resistance of a large proportion of the species, all of which is essential for the successful pursuit of modern scientific breeding programs.

Amongst the wild species we know that there are two important gene centres : (1) Mexico and (2) the Andes of South America from Peru southwards, through Bolivia to north-west Argentina. In these two centres the majority of species are to be found, though specific resistance to certain diseases has been encountered outside them, also. In the Mexican centre, genes providing different types of resistance to *Phytophthora* are to be found, as well as genes for resistance to several viruses (the Y group) and to insect damage. In the Andean area some resistance to *Phytophthora* is also found, as well as resistance to *Heterodera rostochiensis*. Virus and insect resistance is known from *S.chacoense* in the plains of Argentina and elsewhere, and several species in both centres show useful resistance to bacterial diseases. Unfortunately, it is not possible in a paper of this length to go into more detail, but suffice it to say that we know enough of the wild and primitive cultivated species to make us quite certain of their importance for breeding, now and in the foreseeable future. In practically every case where resistance to disease or adaptation to specific environmental conditions has been looked for in the indigenous potatoes of the Americas, this has been found when enough material has been examined.

It is not possible, however, at this stage to be over-optimistic, to the extent of asserting that all problems in potato breeding are solved, or are even within sight of solution. We know a great deal about

FIGURE 23.1. Indian guide holding a wild potato plant (*Solanum agrimonifolium*) collected in the high mountain rain forest of Chiapas State, southern Mexico.

FIGURE 23.2. Digging wild potatoes on the borders of a maize field at Saltillo, Coahuila State, northern Mexico.

the genetic variation of the wild species and primitive cultivated forms ; yet there are many problems of gene transference that have not yet been solved and good resistance to all diseases has not yet been found. Although many expeditions have collected material from the overall range of distribution of these species there are still notable gaps. Many collectors have obtained material from regions where others have looked already, though this was necessary in some cases, where the original collections had been lost or discarded. Areas which would repay exploration still exist, therefore, as can be seen in Table 23.3. Much work

TABLE 23.3. Areas where potato collections have not been made or where little material has so far been collected

Country	States, provinces, etc.
U.S.A.	Arizona, Texas
Mexico	Sonora, Sinaloa, Baja California, Nayarit, San Luis Potosí, Vera Cruz, Guerrero, Oaxaca
Honduras	Central mountain area
Panama	Western area near Costa Rican border
Venezuela	Western highlands of Táchira, Mérida and Trujillo
Ecuador	Southern provinces
Peru	More remote valleys in north and centre. Southern coastal lomas
Bolivia	Eastern slopes and valleys of more difficult access
Argentina	Eastern areas of provinces Jujuy and Salta
Paraguay	No expedition has ever sampled potatoes in this country
Brazil	Paraná, Santa Catarina, Minas Gerais
Chile	Central provinces, south of Santiago. Highlands of Antofagasta and Tarapacá. Southern lake district.

still remains to be done in Mexico, Peru and Bolivia, whilst Paraguay has not yet been collected, so far as potatoes are concerned. Further collections from Chile would be rewarding, also.

The work of collecting is only the first stage in the utilization of potato germplasm. Of equal importance is the evaluation and storage of material in gene banks. At present, large and valuable collections of material exist in the following countries outside the gene centres themselves :

(1) The N.I. Vavilov Institute of Plant Industry, Leningrad, U.S.S.R.

(2) The Commonwealth Potato Collection, Edinburgh, U.K.

(3) Erwin–Bauer–Sortiment, Cologne, Germany.

(4) American Potato Introduction Station, Sturgeon Bay, Wisconsin, U.S.A.

Plans are also under way for the establishment, under the auspices of the European Association for Research in Plant Breeding (EUCARPIA) and O.E.C.D., of an international European Potato Gene Bank.

Inside the gene centres the following gene banks have been established or are being projected:

(1) Toluca, Mexico (Government of Mexico and Rockefeller Foundation).

(2) Tibaitatá, Bogotá, Colombia (Government of Colombia and Rockefeller Foundation).

(3) La Molina, Lima, Peru.

(4) Balcarce, prov. Buenos Aires, Argentina (I.N.T.A., Argentina).

These gene banks are steps in the right direction, since with the spread of improved cultivars the variability within the indigenous cultivated species is being depleted and there is now a very great danger that genes of potential value may be lost for ever. Similarly, the spread of improved methods of agriculture and the pressure of population is destroying or changing the natural vegetation to such an extent in some areas that many of the wild species are threatened also. Much collecting work is thus urgently needed, if possible on an international scale, to preserve material for posterity.

It may at first sight be supposed that the rather large number of gene banks, both inside and outside the gene centres, to some extent duplicate efforts. Of the gene banks listed above, the American Potato Introduction Station at Sturgeon Bay is by far the most important, and it might be thought that this would be sufficient for world needs. It is hoped to be able to rationalise the use and preservation of material by establishing a similar bank in Europe. It is felt very strongly, however, that two or three large collections outside the gene centres, in regions where potato breeding work is very active, would complement rather than duplicate the gene-centre stations. These latter would serve also as exploration centres and laboratories where field work on the wild and cultivated species as well as on their specialised diseases and parasites could be carried out in their natural environments.

On the other hand, the gene banks in Europe and the U.S.A. would serve as important centres of basic research on wild and primitive cultivated species and could also provide training for research workers from gene-centre countries. Indeed, this program of research and training has already been under way in the American Station for a number of years.

Much work remains to be done on the potato. With international co-operation and understanding, as well as with adequate financial support, it should be possible to accomplish a very great deal indeed in the next twenty years or so on this valuable crop and to evaluate, utilize and preserve vital genetic variation before it disappears completely.

REFERENCES

HAWKES J.G. & HJERTING J.P. (1969) *The Potatoes of Argentina, Brazil, Paraguay and Uruguay—a biosystematic study.* Chapter 5. Oxford University Press.

ROSS H. (1958) Ausgangmaterial für die Züchtung. *Handbuch der Pflanzenzüchtung*, Vol 3, 2nd edition (Eds. Kappert H. and Rudorf W.). Paul Parey, Berlin.

ROSS R.W. & ROWE P.R. (1965) Inventory of tuber-bearing *Solanum* species. Bulletin 533, Agricultural Experiment Station, University of Wisconsin, Madison, Wisconsin, U.S.A.

ROTHACKER D. (1961) *Die wilden und kultivierten mittel- und südamerikanischen Kartoffel-species. Die Kartoffel*, Vol. 1 (Eds. Schick R. and Klinkowski M.). Deutscher Landwirtschaftsverlag.

PISUM

STIG BLIXT

Weibullsholm Plant Breeding Institute,
Landskrona, Sweden

INTRODUCTION

The high protein content of the seeds and green matter of leguminous plants makes the family to which they belong one of very considerable agricultural interest. In the tropics particularly, where there is a critical need for protein sources for human consumption, *Leguminosae* are especially important.

Pisum is a genus of the temperate zones. Its principal centre of genetic diversity is the Mediterranean gene centre, and there are secondary centres in the Near East and in Ethiopia. But in spite of this the pea is of great interest in semi-tropical areas such as India. The extension of the range and the conservation of the genetic variability at the disposal of plant breeders is therefore desirable.

From the genetic point of view, *Pisum* is already the best-known among the genera of the *Leguminosae*. Since Mendel's classical work researchers have devoted considerable time to this species, e.g., Pellew, Fedotov, Wellensiek, Nilsson, Lamprecht, only to mention some, and of the many genera within the family which are of agricultural value it is perhaps the most extensively studied. This has led to the development of co-operation between *Pisum* geneticists and plant breeders on an international scale of a sort which might serve as a model to be advantageously applied to programs of conservation and systematic utilization in other cultivated plant taxa also. The present chapter, therefore, will confine itself to outlining briefly the nature of the organization which has arisen as a result of this co-operation. Purely genetic matters will be discussed only briefly.

GENETIC VARIABILITY IN THE GENUS PISUM

Divers activities are involved in the present work with *Pisum*. There are, first, the exploration and collection of genetic variability in the genus, followed by its classification and conservation. A great deal of material already is held in collections, so that the emphasis of the present phase of the work is placed upon the tasks of its classification. A start has been made towards solving certain problems of maintenance, to deal with the large amount of material already held and with the expected increase of this material from future collections.

As is the case with any other group of plants, the sources of genetic variation in *Pisum* are to be found in primitive cultivars and wild species, in existing cultivars, in special genetic lines and in mutant stocks.

Primitive and wild material still exists in many regions, such as Ethiopia, the Near East and Israel, and the exploration, collection and preservation of this material should be carried out before there is further loss in the face of the advance of modern agriculture and a wide distribution of advanced cultivars. The urgency of the need to collect and preserve this material cannot be sufficiently stressed. As in the case of other crop plants, these primitive forms are a major source of genetic variability which may be used to extend the genetic possibilities of the cultivated forms of the species. In Turkey alone there exist (Zagaja, personal communication) for example, some 20 primitive varieties and many local forms, adapted to very widely varying conditions, which represent a potential of great value.

The primitive forms, which have evolved in South America during 400 years of evolution in isolation, in an environment favouring outbreeding through the presence of insects capable of effecting cross pollination (Harland 1948), may be cited as illustrating material whose genetic potentialities should not be overlooked in exploration or conservation programs. Such forms, of which there may yet be many unknown examples, must be collected and investigated.

At present, however, the greatest source of useful genetic variability and genes are the existing cultivars of *Pisum sativum*. The preservation of this material is a major problem. Although the preservation of certain types of cultivars is well organised, the information which could be made available relating to this material is not systematised, is often insufficiently specific, and sometimes difficult of access.

Genetic lines which have been used by different groups of workers on the genetics of the pea provide another and well-documented source of gene material. Information on this material is frequently available in very great detail, though it is somewhat scattered, and may be referred to in numerous works by Lamprecht, Wellensiek, Gottschalk, Blixt, Yarnell and others (see for example, Lamprecht 1961, 1964;

Blixt 1959, 1964). The review of Yarnell (1962) is perhaps most useful as an introduction.

Finally, one must refer to the extremely powerful sources of genetic variation created by the action of mutagenic agents. The literature of such variation may be referred to in the papers of Blixt (1961, 1962, 1965a, 1965b, 1966a, 1966b, 1966c, 1966d) and Gottschalk (1964).

At present we are involved in the early planning stages of the classification of existing collections, and the preservation of these and of material which is expected to be collected in the future. To enable this work to be done more effectively, the Pisum Genetics Association has been formed.

THE PISUM GENETICS ASSOCIATION

The P.G.A. is an international organization devoted to the study of *Pisum*. It was initiated because of the recognition of the increasing danger of extinction of irreplaceable genetic material. This danger comes at the moment mainly from two directions. Most important and alarming is the threat to the wild and primitive forms ('land races') which arises from the accelerating introduction of advanced cultivars in many important areas of genetic diversity. A second danger stems from the fact that, for economic reasons, the cultivation of peas in many advanced agricultural countries is at the moment becoming more and more restricted to a narrow range of forms, which can lead to serious losses of very important material if appropriate measures to prevent this are not taken in time.

The P.G.A. was modelled on the Tomato Genetics Co-operative, but from the first aimed at the broadest possible international basis. In the present initial stages, the group numbers among its members Snoad at the John Innes Institute in England, Marx at Geneva, New York, Monti at Casaccia, Rome, Sharma at New Delhi, and Blixt at Weibullsholm. Gottschalk at Bonn is expected soon to become active. It is hoped that soon the P.G.A. will increase its membership considerably, and that individual scientists and institutes will be invited to participate.

The program of the P.G.A. seeks to secure the collection and systematization of all genetic traits in *Pisum*, the collection, maintenance, evaluation and systematization of commercial varieties, primitive and wild material, and mutation stocks, the mapping of existing and new mutations, and the supply of suitable plant material to geneticists, plant breeders and other scientists throughout the world, upon request.

The first, immediate task of the Pisum Genetics Association is the compilation of lists of all *Pisum* stocks at present held in different collections, in order to provide basic information for future work. In this, as in all stages of the program, co-operation with all interested organizations and institutes is especially important. In the same connection, the value of the recent F.A.O. international survey of genetic stocks held in research institutes is acknowledged. Such projects, however, themselves depend upon co-operation. It is foreseen that the P.G.A. will play a role in ensuring the spirit of collaboration among the many groups whose interests are interdependent, and by its example to encourage similar initiative in other fields of activity in genetic exploration and conservation.

The recommendations of the recent Conference on the Exploration, Utilization and Conservation of Genetic Resources represented by primitive cultivars and wild species-relatives, as well as existing and obsolete cultivars, (Bennett, 1968) are a welcome indication of a growing international awareness of the urgent need to rescue the cultivated and wild genetic resources of plants before they become extinct. There is no time to be lost if invaluable genetic material is to be saved.

The P.G.A., for its part, is willing—and planning—to undertake all the necessary investigations, and the preservation, of *Pisum* collections, whatever their origin. It undertakes thoroughly to evaluate and classify material through its member institutes, which will work in co-operation with each other and with plant introduction centres and similar institutions if desired. Allowance will of course be made for the environmental conditions of the localities from which collections have been made. Figure 24.1 indicates how the work with *Pisum* collections will be organized. All existing and future collections will be distributed to the different co-operating members of P.G.A., who will carry out the necessary investigations, and maintain all the information relating to them. It is intended to publish the work of the P.G.A. in Pisum Newsletters.

It is envisaged that the Pisum Genetics Association will provide for the long-term storage of genetic stocks in co-operation with its own and other institutes. Developing countries which lack suitable facilities for evaluation and storage will thus also benefit greatly from the project.

In the immediate future it is hoped that the improved continuity of investigations, better efficiency and the elimination of duplication of

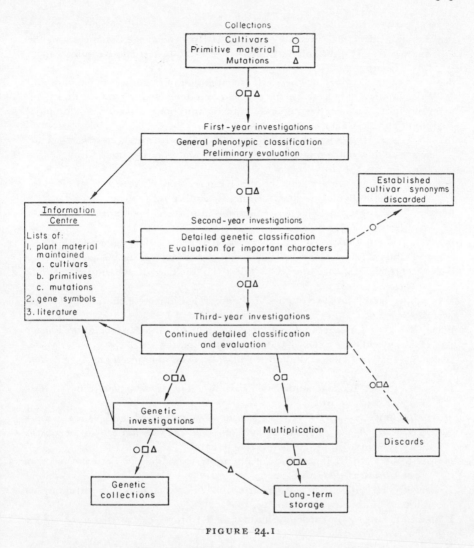

FIGURE 24.1

effort which result from the work of the P.G.A. will be major benefits to all. Above all, assurance of the safe maintenance of genetic stocks is a matter of primary concern in the present planning stages.

On a somewhat longer term, the P.G.A. aims to undertake other work such as the standardization of the rules of nomenclature and gene symbolization, the centralization of all information services relating to collections, and the preparation, storage and distribution of relevant data relating to *Pisum* on a world scale.

REFERENCES

BENNETT E. (Ed.) (1968) Record of the FAO/IBP Technical Conference on the Exploration, Utilization and Conservation of Plant Genetic Resources, 1967. FAO, Rome.

BLIXT S. (1959) Cytology of *Pisum* III. Investigation of five interchange lines and co-ordination of linkage groups with chromosome. *Agri. Hort. Gen.* **17,** 47–75.

BLIXT S. (1961) Quantitative studies of induced mutations in peas. V. Chlorophyll mutations. *Agri. Hort. Gen.* **19,** 402–447.

BLIXT S. (1962) Studies in induced mutations in peas. VI. Mutations in seed-colour, flower-colour, maculum-colour, pod-colour, and grey spotting of leaves. *Agri. Hort. Gen.* **20,** 95–110.

BLIXT S. (1964) A presentation of the Lamprechtian *Pisum*-material. Report, Weibullsholm Plant Breeding Institute, November 1964. 76 pp.

BLIXT S. (1965a) Studies of induced mutations in peas. X. Spontaneous mutations. *Agri. Hort. Gen.* **23,** 43–47.

BLIXT S. (1965b) Linkage studied in *Pisum*. I. Linkages of the genes Chi2, Chi3, and Chi4, causing chlorophyll deficiency. *Agri. Hort. Gen.* **23,** 26–42.

BLIXT S. (1966a) Linkage studies in *Pisum*. II. Linkage of the mutant *aurea*R3. *Agri. Hort. Gen.* **24,** 7–156.

BLIXT, S. (1966b) Linkage studies in *Pisum*. III. Linkage of the mutant *aurea*R5 *Agri. Hort. Gen.* **24,** 157–163.

BLIXT S. (1966c) Linkage studies in *Pisum*. IV. The mutant *chlorina* and the linkage of the determining gene, Ch3. *Agri. Hort. Gen.* **24,** 164–167.

BLIXT S. (1966d) Linkage studies in *Pisum*. V. The mutant *albina*R2. *Agri. Hort. Gen.* **24,** 168–172.

BLIXT S. (1966e) Linkage studies in *Pisum*. VI. The *luteo-maculata* mutant. *Agri. Hort. Gen.* **24,** 173–194.

GOTTSCHALK W. (1964) *Die Wirkung mutierter Gene auf die Morphologie und Funktion pflanzlicher Organe, dargestellt an strahleninduzierten Mutanten von Pisum sativum.* Botanische Studien 14, Fischer Verlag, Jena.

HARLAND S.C. (1948) Inheritance of immunity to mildew in Peruvian forms of *Pisum sativum. Heredity* **2,** 263–269.

LAMPRECHT H. (1961) Die Genenkarte von *Pisum* bei normaler Struktur der Chromosomen. *Agri. Hort. Gen.* **19,** 360–401.

LAMPRECHT H. (1964) Partielle Sterilität und Chromosomenstruktur bei *Pisum. Agri. Hort. Gen.* **22,** 56–148.

YARNELL S.H. (1962) Cytogenetics of the vegetable crops. III. Legumes. A. Garden peas, *Pisum sativum* L. *Bot. Review* **28,** 465–537.

25

TEMPERATE ZONE TREE FRUITS

S. W. ZAGAJA

Research Institute of Pomology,
Skierniewice, Poland

INTRODUCTION

Temperate zone tree fruits are a very heterogeneous group of plants with respect to their origin, taxonomy, ecological requirements and breeding system.

From the pomological point of view temperate fruits are classified into four major groups :

pome fruits (apple, pear, etc.)

stone fruits (peach, apricot, cherry, etc.)

berry fruits (gooseberry, raspberry, etc.)

nuts (walnut, hazelnut, etc.)

Different as they are, fruit trees have in common a long life cycle, large size, and the fact that under cultivation they are propagated as clones. They are therefore highly heterozygous. In these respects fruit trees differ considerably from the majority of other economic plants.

Most temperate zone fruits have originated in the northern hemisphere of the Old World while only a few are native to either North or South America and none to Australia (Vavilov, 1926; Zielinski, 1955).

Many of the temperate zone tree fruits have been cultivated since very early times. Archaeological excavations indicate that the apple was known to man in the Stone Age. Apples, pears, plums, grapes and cherries were very well known to the ancient Greeks and Romans who described several varieties of these fruits and also described methods of propagation by both grafting and budding (Sekowski, 1956; Zielinski, 1955). Peaches and apricots were domesticated first in China where their cultivation was known from at least 2,000 B.C. (Sekowski, 1956).

Already during his very early migrations man carried fruits along with him and was establishing their cultivation in newly occupied areas. In this way the temperate zone fruits spread over large areas of the Old World very early in human history. Once introduced and established in the new areas, fruits were exposed to evolutionary forces as a result of which secondary centres of genetic diversity developed. The main

centres of genetic diversity in the temperate zone fruits are described by
Vavilov (1926, 1930) and Zielinski (1955). This chapter describes
experiences in one area of genetic diversity in fruits only, namely
Turkey.

TAXONOMY AND ADAPTATION

The following temperate zone tree fruits or their wild relatives are
indigenous to Turkey: Apple (*Malus* spp.), Pear (*Pirus* spp.), Sweet
cherry (*Prunus avium*, L.), Sour cherry (*Prunus cerasus*, L.), Mahaleb
cherry (*Prunus mahaleb*, L.), Plum (*Prunus* spp.), Grape (*Vitis vinifera*,
L.), Walnut (*Juglans regia*, L.) and Hazelnut (*Corylus* spp.). Some other
temperate zone fruits such as Apricot (*Prunus armeniaca* L.), Almond
(*Prunus amygdalus* L.), and Peach (*Prunus persica*, L.), were introduced
for the first time into Turkey about 2000–4000 years ago (Sekowski,
1956). An account of the distribution of these fruits and their wild
relatives in Turkey was published by Zhukovsky (1933).

One of the most striking characteristics of these fruits is their
adaptation to a very wide range of ecological conditions. Almonds, for
example, are grown from the almost frost-free zone of the Muğla region
and up to 1600 m elevation in the Torus Mountains. In Central
Anatolia, almonds are found at elevations ranging from 700 m to
1000 m in the Corum, Malatya and Kayseri areas. Sweet cherry is
reported by Zhukovsky to occur from the Black Sea coast to an
elevation of 2000 m in the Pontic Mountains.

Other temperate zone fruits such as apple, pear, plum and sour
cherry are also grown in Anatolia over a wide range of climatic conditions. The data presented by Zhukovsky strongly suggest that in
some fruits in Turkey and particularly in almond, apricot and cherry,
the range of adaptation for winter chilling requirements, as well as for
winter-hardiness, is much wider than that in the improved cultivars
grown commercially elsewhere.

EXPLORATION

Tree fruits indigenous to Turkey, with the exception of walnut and
hazelnut, can be found there in the following four forms:
    wild form,
        locally developed cultivars representing various degrees of improve-
            ment,

old varieties developed elsewhere and introduced to Turkey in the
distant past,

highly improved varieties developed elsewhere and introduced
into Turkey within the last 50 years or so.

Many of the introduced varieties of fruits, particularly the older
ones, are grown under Turkish names and are considered locally as being
indigenous.

As far as is known no introductions of walnuts, hazelnuts or almonds
have been made into Turkey in the last several hundred years, so that in
those fruits only indigenous populations or cultivars are grown.

In apricot and in peach, where there are no wild progenitors, three
forms of cultivars can be found, corresponding to the forms listed in
paragraph 1 above. From the germplasm point of view only truly
indigenous Turkish cultivar populations are of interest since even
relatively early introductions of foreign varieties grown today in
Turkey are preserved elsewhere.

Explorers from Europe and from the United States have visited
Turkey and made fruit collections. However, they collected germplasm
material mainly for limited and specific purposes (Hatton, 1917). Until
very recently, no attempt has been made systematically to survey the
genetic resources of wild and cultivated fruits in Turkey, with the
purpose of collecting representative samples, making them available
for the present fruit improvement programs and preserving them for
future use. In 1963 the United Nations Development Program and the
Government of Turkey signed an agreement jointly to establish a
Crop Research and Introduction Centre (CRIC) in Turkey 'for the
survey, collection, introduction, maintenance, selection, breeding and
cultural study of valuable genetic material from Turkey and other
countries of the Near Eastern region, with a view to developing
improved varieties of field, horticultural and industrial crops'. The
Crop Research and Introduction Centre commenced operations in
1964. Despite the need more fully to explore the genetic potential of the
whole Anatolian region, facilities and funds available to CRIC are
limited. A completely satisfactory exploration program has been
impossible for this reason.

Surveys conducted in 1965–1967 by the Crop Research and
Introduction Centre supplement the data of Zhukovsky (1933),
particularly on the distribution of genetic resources in tree fruits in the
case of apple, apricot and sweet cherry. Zhukovsky does not report these
species as occurring in the Aegean region. In fact, well-adapted native

cultivars of all three are grown in Western Turkey. For example, selected cultivars of *Malus pumila* are grown successfully at sea level, near Çeşme, in Izmir province. Primitive cultivars of sweet cherry are grown near Ephesus. In the same area apricots, plums and peaches have been grown since very early times, not only at the higher elevations but also almost at sea level. This indicates that the range of adaptation of these fruits to climatic conditions is even wider than can be concluded from Zhukovsky's work. It is worth noting that in the early fifties some introductions of apricots from Malatya (East-Central Anatolia) to the Izmir area were made. Those introductions produced large trees but did not yield a commercial crop because of insufficient winter chilling. This nicely demonstrates the genetical differences which exist between the apricots of Central Anatolia and those of Western Turkey.

The population of sweet cherries growing in the Ephesus area appears to be interesting, not only in view of its adaptation to low-chilling requirements but also because closer examination of these trees showed them to be free from the symptoms of virus and bacterial diseases. It is, of course, possible that diseases are absent in this isolated area. This is unlikely, however, since in other areas of the Izmir region the symptoms of virus and bacterial diseases are very common in cherry trees.

There is extreme variation in the fruit characteristics of almonds of Western Turkey, as is also reported by Zhukovsky (1933). Studies conducted in 1966 and 1967 fully confirm Zhukovsky's findings. But at the same time the recent studies show that there is no less variation in the time of flowering of almond populations in the same area. During the winter of 1965/66 the season of flowering in almond lasted for over six weeks, from the middle of January until the beginning of March, in climatically comparable areas.

In 1966 and in 1967 mazzard and pear trees producing rooted suckers were found in the Pontic Mountains and in Eastern Turkey. This material will be of great value in developing vegetatively propagated rootstocks for cherries and pears. Rooting pear (*Pyrus communis*) found in 1966 was successfully propagated under mist in 1967 at the Crop Research and Introduction Centre.

During the 1967 expedition to Eastern Turkey, a dwarf *Prunus divericata* was found in Artvin. It may probably offer a solution for developing dwarf rootstocks for plums, prunes and possibly also for other stone fruits such as peach and apricot. Selected types of *Malus pumila* grown at higher elevations in Eastern Turkey and particularly in the regions of Ardahan, Kağizman and the Lake Van area must possess considerable winter hardiness, since winter temperatures there fall to − 30°C. This material, therefore, offers great promise in developing winter-hardy vegetatively-propagated rootstocks for apple ; the vegetative apple rootstocks selected in East Malling (Hatton, 1917) which are used at present lack winter-hardiness and because of this their value is limited (Zagaja and Czynczyk, 1966). In the same area, particularly in Artvin and Kağizman, very high-quality local apricots were found.

There are at least two other important types of adaptation in temperate zone fruits in Turkey which should be mentioned here. It has been observed in some regions that populations of native fruit varieties, adapted to highly calcareous soils, are grown successfully on soils of very high pH, at 8 or above. Under such conditions, trees of introduced varieties suffer greatly from iron-, zinc- and other microelement deficiencies. Adaptation to calcareous soils has been observed, particularly in apple and apricots in Western Turkey, in the Marmara Region and in some parts of Central Anatolia.

In some fruits another type of adaptation which has been observed in native varieties of apple and pear is the ability of the fruit to withstand storage for a very long time under relatively high air temperature and low relative humidity. The native apples, Amasya and Demir, and also a variety of pear called Ankara, are good examples of such adaptation. It might be noted that similar adaptations are also found in Turkish muskmelons.

DANGER OF EXTINCTION

As in many other gene centres germplasm resources of the temperate zone tree fruits in Turkey are threatened with extinction. The danger varies according to species and with the degree of its improvement. The most serious threat comes from the modernization of fruit production.

About thirty years ago large commercial tree fruit Government-owned nurseries were first established in Turkey, which today contribute about 80 per cent of tree-fruit stocks in the country. At the same time lists of varieties of different fruits recommended for growing were prepared. Although fully justified from the commercial point of view, these undertakings prevented further propagation of an extremely large number of local varieties by the commercial nurseries. This has been particularly so in the case of the peach, pear, sweet cherry and apricot.

M

Commercial nurseries use improved methods of fruit propagation. Until quite recently apricot was propagated to a very large extent from seed. Today it is propagated almost exclusively by grafting, using only a limited number of varieties.

Highly improved fruit varieties were later introduced from abroad in order further to improve fruit production in Turkey. Peach introductions have been so successful that they have almost entirely replaced local types. Introductions of apples, pears, and cherries have also been successful and have eliminated many local varieties. This trend continues, eliminating increasing numbers of native fruits from commercial and home garden production. Many local cultivars of genetic value have almost completely disappeared. Many others will disappear as old orchards are replaced by new ones.

Rapidly improving transportation conditions in Turkey are another threat to the native fruits. There is no longer any need for even remote regions to be self-sufficient in fruit. High-quality fruits grown in favourable areas are now being distributed over most of the country, quickly ousting native cultivars in the less favourable regions.

The fruits least seriously threatened with genetic erosion are hazelnut, almond and walnut; only the native varieties of these fruits are grown at present.

The wild relatives of temperate zone tree fruits are also disappearing rapidly in Turkey. This is due in part to the developments already described but is due also to the fact that in many parts of the country fruit trees are being cut down for fuel and timber, and are not replaced.

METHODOLOGY

Because of the presence of large numbers of old introductions from Europe and elsewhere, field collecting teams should consist of pomologists familiar with the old varieties of fruits, particularly of apple, pear and sweet cherry of foreign origin. Otherwise it will be difficult to avoid collecting cultivars which are already preserved elsewhere.

Collections of wild fruits, and also of seed-propagated fruits (walnut, almond, and the older plantations of apricot) should be done on the basis of random sampling. This, however, should not exclude a bias towards the collection of individuals the value of which can be readily recognised, which may often result in a shortening of the time required for the assessment of the genetic potential of the population of which the selected individual is a member. In the case of vegetatively propagated fruits, the collection and preservation of all indigenous cultivars should be attempted.

Again in the case of seed propagated fruit populations either vegetative material or seed may be collected, according to convenience. Each method has its advantages and its disadvantages, which depend upon the limited life expectancy of material of either type without certain technical facilities. Thus, the efficient collection of vegetative material would seem to indicate the provision of some kind of mobile refrigeration equipment in the exploration vehicles, and good receiving arrangements to store, or graft and bud, material received from the field are indispensable. This implies the need for refrigeration facilities at a stable centre within reach of the exploration areas and for at least two specialists, one in the field and one at the receiving centre.

For the vegetatively propagated native fruits, however, the collecting of vegetative material should be preferred.

Before large scale samplings of the temperate zone fruit germplasm resources in Turkey are started, arrangements should be made for establishing and preserving the collected material. A thorough exploration of the fruit germplasm resources in Turkey might result in some thousands of collections. To establish and to maintain such a large collection of fruits will require a considerable and continuous expense which no single country can be expected to bear.

REFERENCES

HATTON R.G. (1917) Paradise apple stocks. *J. R. hort. Soc.* **42,** 361–399.

SEKOWSKI B. (1956) *Pomologia.* Poznan.

VAVILOV N.I. (1926) *Studies on the Origin of Cultivated Plants.* Leningrad.

VAVILOV N.I. (1930) Wild progenitors of the fruit trees of Turkestan and the Caucasus and the problem of origin of fruit trees. *Proc. 9th Int. hort. Congr. London,* 271–278.

ZAGAJA S.W. & CZYNCZYK A. (1966) Winter injuries of the dwarfing apple rootstocks during the winter of 1962 and 1963. *Pr. Inst. Sadow. Skierniew.* **10,** 93–95.

ZHUKOVSKY P.M. (1933) *Agricultural Turkey.* Acad. Sci. U.S.S.R. Moscow-Leningrad.

ZIELINSKI Q.B. (1955) *Modern Systematic Pomology.* Iowa.

26

GENE POOLS IN THE NEW WORLD
TETRAPLOID COTTONS

S. C. HARLAND

Casilla 5, Chaclacayo,
Peru

INTRODUCTION

It is a truism that a plant breeder should have free access to the whole germplasm material, first, of the species with which he is working, and secondly of all species in the genus which are crossable with it, and which have genes of value for transference to it. It is probably correct to say that no cotton breeder is in such a position at the present time. There are, however, in various parts of the world comprehensive collections of both cultivated and wild species. For the most part these have been insufficiently studied morphologically, and have not been adequately screened for resistance to insects or pathogens. They have certainly not been properly evaluated for their physiological attributes.

Although, as will appear in this chapter, there are a number of important areas which have either not contributed to collections at all, or have been insufficiently surveyed, it is unlikely that any breeder is at the present time held up for genetic material. If we look at the breeding work which is being carried out in various parts of the world, it is evident that the great wealth of germplasm immediately available is being insufficiently exploited.

One reason is that much apparently useless material is present in the collections, of a deadly monotonous morphological sameness. The sameness is, however, more apparent than real, since biotic and physiological screening may reveal characters which the breeder wants. For example, when the writer was looking for new sources of *Verticillium* resistance, a large number of samples of the Peruvian *barbadense* backyard cottons were examined. Careful examination of these revealed outstanding resistance in two types only.

Another reason is that many of the superior commercial cottons of today are the end products of many years of breeding. They are so highly specialized in their industrial characters that the introduction of even a few genes from extraneous sources results in some degree of inferiority. It must always be borne in mind that the incorporation of new genes into a specialized genotype means not only that the alleles of the new genes are substituted, but also that each new gene carries with it a chromosome segment upon which unwanted genes may be present.

Even a single gene substitution may confer inferiority. Evelyn, in St. Vincent, was able to introduce the gene for red plant body from a perennial *G. barbadense* into Sea Island. In spite of the large number of back crosses made, the effect of the gene substitution showed up in a spinning test. The new red Sea Island was significantly inferior in spinning properties to the original type.

If a desired character is polygenic in its genetical make-up, such as appears to be the case with resistance to *Verticillium*, it is probably not possible to introduce this into a highly selected cultivar. Gene pools should therefore be screened for what I have termed 'Dictator' genes, i.e., single powerful genes which confer resistance without the need of modifier complexes. Knight has met with these in the wild, diploid and genetically remote species which he has used in his work on angular spot resistance in Egyptian cotton.

I shall now treat of some areas as yet genetically unexploited, or insufficiently studied. Many of these contain a wealth of genetic material.

MARIE GALANTE HIRSUTUM—THE UPLAND GROUP

The current theory that the centre of origin of the Upland group lies in Central America is probably incorrect. Several years ago the writer visited the cotton growing areas of the state of Rio Grande do Norte in northern Brazil. Here he was given material of a wild type from the arid mountainous region of the interior. This was an exceedingly primitive perennial type of *G.hirsutum* (Marie Galante). It was found growing among xerophytic scrub in a region of very low and sporadic rainfall. From its characters, it was certainly a truly wild species which had never been under cultivation. This area is almost certainly the centre of origin of the whole Upland group. From here the lines of dispersion appear to be as follows: first, northwards to the Amazon where it splits into two streams. The first of these goes up the Amazon, thence across the Andes into Ecuador, western Colombia and possibly still further north. The second goes northward through the Guyanas to the

West Indies, leaving representatives in all the West Indian Islands, thence passing into eastern Colombia, and further north into central America via Yucatan. For all its wealth of material, the whole central American region must be regarded as a secondary centre of diversity. Another end point of this stream is in Florida where wild or semi-wild Marie Galantes could be found up to a few years ago. In this region they may now be extinct.

In addition to the northern lines of dispersion there is also a line of dispersion to the South. Marie Galantes are found in the eastern coastal region of Brazil almost as far south as Rio de Janeiro though nothing seems to be known about them.

In this very large geographical area a range of types occurs from the wild prototype of Rio Grande do Norte, with excessively short and coarse staple, to the long, fine linted types of Moco, eastern Colombia, Haiti and the Caribbean. At its best the Moco of Rio Grande do Norte and Pernambuco may be as good as a good Egyptian. Marie Galantes occurring in uninhabited islands such as Patos, near Trinidad, appear to be not far from the wild prototype.

Marie Galantes are used extensively for hammock making, which is practised not only by the South American jungle Indians, but also in elaborate forms by the inhabitants of North Brazil. The South American Indian is an assiduous distributor of plants. Wherever he goes he takes planting material with him of all his useful plants, so that every settlement has a range of 'backyard' cottons. Most houses have one or two perennial Marie Galantes in their gardens, or nearby. Hammock making and in some areas primitive weaving have contributed to the domestication, sometimes only partial, of the Marie Galantes. In recent years the area of cultivated Marie Galantes has diminished owing to replacement by other varieties. In the early 18th century they were extensively cultivated in the West Indies. At the present time North Brazil is the principal cultivated area, with small areas in the Grenadines (Windward Islands), Haiti and eastern Colombia.

An important point is that the backyard cottons, at any rate of the smaller West Indian islands, breed true when taken into cultivation, thus constituting a valuable series of pure lines. This is mainly due to isolation, or to inbreeding in small populations. Absence of pollinating agents is also a factor.

In 1914 the writer observed that cotton in the island of St. Croix was not cross-pollinated by bees, which worked only the extra-floral nectaries without entering the flowers. But some time in that year they suddenly learned to enter the flowers for the sake of the pollen, and thereafter cross-pollination was extensive.

It may be mentioned that an important centre of variability exists in western India (and also Goa), where numerous Marie Galantes, some with lint of high quality, are found as backyard cottons. These were probably introduced from South America by the Portuguese as early as the 17th century.

A final point worth noting is that the use of cotton as a medicinal plant has contributed to the backyard conservation of both Marie Galante and *G.barbadense*.

THE PUNCTATUMS

The *Punctatums* constitute an important sub-section of the Marie Galante group. They are small-bolled perennial types, now found in Polynesia, the Marquesas, Fiji and in northern Australia. The Cape York peninsula of Queensland is said to contain numerous specimens of these. The writer has grown one from Port Essington in the northern territory of Australia. The valuable Hopi cotton grown by the Hopi Indians of Arizona appears to be a sympodial type of *punctatum*. *Punctatums* also occur in West Africa (Gambia).

THE BARBADENSE GROUP

To this group belong the most valuable of all cottons, the Sea Island and Egyptian types. The centre of origin of *barbadense* is almost certainly in northern Peru, in the arid mountainous interior of the province of Tumbes. The species, or sub-species, *darwinii*, is closely related and occurs as an endemic in the Galapagos Islands, where it has become strongly contaminated by hybridization with exotic introductions. Both the Tumbes and Galapagos types are truly wild and follow the general rule that the wild species of *Gossypium* are xerophytes, occurring in arid and usually mountainous regions where scanty rainfall does not permit of cultivation. Peru is also the centre of domestication of the Tumbes *barbadense* and the pre-Inca inhabitants evolved an advanced textile culture based on improved forms of it. The commercial cotton which is grown most extensively in Peru—the Tanguis variety—is basically Tumbes modified by selection. As backyard types, *barbadense* perennials occur sporadically over the whole of Peru. Southwards they extend into Chile, the last remnants being found only a few miles north of

Santiago. The backyard *barbadense* forms of Chile are physiologically of great interest, as they occur at the extreme southern limit of the area of distribution. They are used for home spinning and weaving, and their presence in this area is due to the fact that the pre-Inca peoples took cotton with them from Peru when they spread South. The *barbadense* of Peru and Chile constitute what I have termed the Pacific assemblage, which as a whole is characterised by broad leaves and intense hairiness of the underside of the leaf, a character which confers resistance to jassids. Some of the backyard forms are highly resistant to *Verticillium* wilt. Tanguis used to be resistant, but resistance has broken down in recent years, doubtless through strains of *Verticillium* of increased virulence.

In 1964 the writer found an entirely new type of *barbadense* in Ecuador, occurring sporadically in an intensely arid region a few miles to the south-west of Guayaquil. The *barbadense* group in general, with the exception of Sea Island and Egyptian, is characterised by coarse lint which may rarely attain a length of $1\frac{3}{8}$ inches in selected Tanguis. The new Ecuador type is long—up to $1\frac{1}{2}$ inches, and is fine and silky. It is in fact very similar to a modern Egyptian cotton, and may be the progenitor of the whole of the Sea Island-Egyptian complex, the origin of which has always presented a mystery. At any rate it is a valuable addition to the *barbadense* germ plasm pool.

Somewhat sharply contrasted with the Pacific assemblage are the *barbadense* cottons of the eastern side of the Andes, which include the kidney cottons. These we may term the Atlantic assemblage. They are, in general, glabrous and narrow leaved, and are adapted to regions with a well marked rainy season. In some cases adaptation occurs to high and almost continuous rainfall. They are found over the whole of the Amazon region, extending also as xerophytes into northern coastal Brazil. In Brazil they occur as far south as the state of Santa Catarina. From Brazil they extend northwards through the Guayanas into Venezuela and the Caribbean, thence to Cuba, Haiti, Puerto Rico and Jamaica. They have been taken from South America to Africa, where in Nigeria a cultivated form known as Ishan is grown, as well as to most tropical regions of Asia—India, Ceylon, Indonesia, etc. The *barbadense* kidney form appears to be morphologically uniform wherever it occurs. The Pacific assemblage extends northwards into Ecuador and Colombia, where in the Cauca valley genetical variability is so great that the writer was at one time led to believe that this region may have been the centre of origin of *brasiliense*.

M*

In some regions where the old cottons have not been replaced by modern selected types, it is not unusual to find Marie Galante and *barbadense* grown as a mixture, though with the Marie Galante component more abundant. This is the case in north Brazil, and at one time in some of the smaller islands in the Windward group (Union Island, Carriacou). In the West Indies this mixture appears no longer to be grown.

In Egypt the prevalent *barbadense* cultivations carry a small component of naked-seeded Upland. In central Asia, Afghanistan and India, the Uplands often carry small numbers of diploid *herbaceum* or *arboreum*. These 'weeds' should be collected and preserved, as they may have a quite considerable genetic potential. Continued association of the two components has probably led to some slight introgression and to morphological convergence, so that in an annual crop both components are sympodial although originally one may have been perennial and monopodial. The value of a minor component is illustrated by the case of Peruvian Tanguis, which originated as a selection from a field of Upland.

Where there are two components, both are subjected to the same agricultural and ecological conditions, and the consequent adaptation to these becomes of importance. In some parts of the world new irrigated areas are being created. Existing Uplands are usually grown under moderate rainfall and are not well adapted to irrigation. The Naked-seeded Upland weed of Egypt could provide a genetic pool adapted to irrigation, although at present it is just regarded as a nuisance.

Any germ plasm collection should naturally contain representative material from all the sources I have mentioned, as well as the wild tetraploid *tomentosum* (the Hawaiian endemic), and all the wild diploids. The latter have been fairly adequately collected and are available for breeding purposes. But it should be mentioned that the valuable Peruvian diploid, *raimondii*, is now extinct in the area in which it was first found, so that existing collections of it should be carefully preserved by those who still have them.

27

SWEET POTATO

D. E. YEN

B. P. Bishop Museum, Honolulu,
Hawaii.

INTRODUCTION

The sweet potato, *Ipomoea batatas* (L.) Lam., is one of two species of the Convolvulaceae widely cultivated for human food in tropical and sub-tropical environments. The other is *I.aquatica* Forsk., utilised as a leafy vegetable in Southeast Asia. As a root crop cultivar, the sweet potato is of pantropic distribution, which, in its historical aspect, has raised ethnological questions concerning its provenances in almost every area—America, Asia, Africa and the Pacific Islands. The plant, whose normal mode of reproduction is vegetative, is inevitably associated with indigenous agricultures. The implications of difficulty of natural distribution of the species have called forth hypotheses of the agency of man in transfers, associated with complex migration patterns of man and plant in pre-historic and historic times. In the vegetal complexes of modern agriculture, the sweet potato takes varying roles; as a root vegetable in the United States where it is rated as third in importance among vegetable crops (Martin, *in press*) and in New Zealand; as a vegetable, stock feed and important source of industrial starch and alcohol in Japan; and as a supplementary stock feed in tropical Australia. Nevertheless its future development, as many papers to the 1967 First International Symposium on Root Crops held in Trinidad would indicate, lies in its potential as a major contributor to the calorific intake of emergent native populations throughout the world.

The centre of origin for sweet potato is not well established, but the concensus of opinion from the time of de Candolle (1886) through to Vavilov (1951) has been toward an American origin. Sauer (1950) has indicated that the area of greatest diversity is in Peru rather than Mexico. More recently, the evidence of Japanese workers has been summarised by Nishiyama (1963) in relating *I.batatas* with the wild species, *I.trifida* (H.B.K.) Don., an American species with a distribution extending from Mexico to Bolivia. The direct ancestral derivation of the *batatas* form from *trifida* by cultivation has not met with agreement, since the criteria of common chromosome number ($2n=90$), ability to hybridize, similarity in the self-incompatibility systems, and morphological parallels, may merely convey close relationship of similar, or indeed identical ancestral species, with subsequent segregation.

The ethnobotanical issues, rather than the genetic, were the spur to the Pacific sweet potato project which was sponsored by the Rockefeller Foundation, New York. As an example of plant exploration, the relevant portions of the work are summarised here from its two phases; firstly, field observations during the collecting of clonal varieties in South America, the Pacific Islands and eastern Asia, and, secondly, the comparative cultivation of the collection in experimental-field tests at the Otara Vegetable Research Station, D.S.I.R., New Zealand.

THE FIELD PHASE OF EXPLORATION

The wide adaptability of the sweet potato plant is reflected in the range of edaphic and climatic conditions over which it has been collected: the littoral coral and sand soils of the Pacific Islands and coastal Peru, the alluvia of river beds of South America and New Guinea from the coasts to 7,000 feet a.s.l., mountain soils in excess of 8,000 feet in those areas, with some examples of cultivation in drained swamps in New Guinea at varying altitudes, and in irrigated mountain terraces of the Philippines.

Within these environmental contexts, there is considerable variation in agricultural treatment of the plant. Planting methods vary from the extremely simple soil preparations associated with slash-and-burn clearing operation and planting slips with a dibble stick, to quite elaborate preparations which involve breaking up of soil, mounding or drainage and green manuring. The correlation of methods with environmental factors has been treated by Brookfield (1962) for New Guinea. In considering the total agricultural systems, it is found that often there is more than one method of cultivation applied to the plant within a given group of agriculturists. Some systems include two phases of cultivation (i) permanent areas of occupation such as artificial terraces, or of long occupation such as on river flats and (ii) areas of shifting cultivation, generally situated on adjacent hilly or mountainous slopes. The first is characterised by more elaboration of agricultural technique, with the permanent areas exhibiting crop rotation (e.g. among the Bontoc of the Philippine Mountain Province where sweet potato

TABLE 27.1. Sweet Potato varieties collected for study in New Zealand, 1957–1964

Collection Area		No. specimens collected	No. studied in N.Z.
AMERICA			
U.S.A.—Louisiana		6	6
MEXICO		2	2
CARIBBEAN IS.		15	5
PERU, North Coastal	—Piura, Libertad	67	48
South Coastal	—Lima, Tacna	27	9
Mountains	—Ancash, Arequipa, Cuzco	24	12
Jungle Lowland	—Loreto, Huanuco	44	8
BOLIVIA, Mountains	—La Paz, San Simon	5	2
ECUADOR, Coastal	—Daule	4	2
Mountains	—Equatorial region	8	4
COLOMBIA, Coastal	—Valle del Cauca, Cordoba	39	14
Mountains	—Cundinamarca, Antiquoia	14	4
	Total American Varieties Studied		116
POLYNESIA			
EASTER ISLAND		17	11
MARQUESAS IS.—Nukuhiva, Ua pau, Uahuka,			
	Hiva Oa, Fatuhiva	26	16
SOCIETY IS.	—Borabora, Raiatea, Moorea,		
	Tahiti, Fakarava (Tuamotus)	30	11
NEW ZEALAND	—Maori varieties, Auckland Province	4	4
	European-introduced, Auckland		
	Province	9	9
COOK IS.	—Aitutaki, Rarotonga, Mangaia	27	27
SAMOA	—Upolu	2	2
TONGA	—Tongatapu	22	20
	Total Polynesian Varieties Studied		100
MELANESIA			
FIJI	Viti Levu	10	10
NEW CALEDONIA	Noumea area, Balade	25	17
NEW HEBRIDES	Espiritu Santo, Efate	28	21
SOLOMON IS.	Malaita, Guadalcanal	11	6
NEW BRITAIN	Northern area	21	8
AUSTRALIAN NEW GUINEA,	Coastal—Moresby, Lae	22	18
AUSTRALIAN NEW GUINEA,	Eastern Highlands—		
	Watabung, Asaro,		
	Aiyura, Namura,		
	Gitunu	41	19

TABLE 27.1 *(contd.)*

AUSTRALIAN NEW GUINEA,	Western Highlands—Kaugel, Simbai, Kaironk	93	57
WEST IRIAN, Coastal	—Merauke, Hollandia, Biak	32	16
WEST IRIAN, Mountains	—Wissellakes, Baliem	32	17
	Total Melanesian Varieties Studied		189

ASIA

TIMOR (Portuguese) Baucau, Dili		24	17
PHILIPPINE IS.			
Luzon, Mountain Province		188	107
Luzon W., Coastal—Ilocos N. & S., Batangas		46	8
Mindoro		21	0
Basilan and Zamboanga		13	2
JAPAN, Southern		4	4
RYUKYU IS.—Ishigaki, Kobama		19	12
HONG KONG, CHINA		14	14
THAILAND Central Plateau		14	11
Total Asian Varieties Studied			175

follows rice in the artificial terraces in a regular annual cycle), and the long occupation areas a rotational procedure which appears to maintain fertility and soil condition by some form of manuring, and broadly cyclic fallow between crops within the restricted areas. The second (ii) may be seen as more extensive, for it is practised as a ground rotation with long intervals of fallow between cropping, which are however quite irregular, and dependent on the judgement of the cultivators. It is in this phase that the sweet potato figures in most areas as the main component. In Peru, the terraced cultivations are usually used for grain crops, while the peripheral areas may contain, among other root crops, the sweet potato. The same situation obtains in Southeast Asia, for, with the exception of the Bontoc, either two crops of rice are grown in permanent terraces, or there is an intervening fallow between annual crops. In many such areas, the contribution of the sweet potato from the shifting phases of the agricultural systems may exceed that of rice. The South Pacific provides some contrast within such systems, for from eastern Melanesia to eastern Polynesia, the plant which most commonly occupies the 'permanent' phase is taro (*Colocasia esculenta*) (L.) Schott., a root crop.

The exclusively shifting systems are widespread from southeast Asia to the eastern Amazonian jungle areas of Peru and Ecuador. The sweet potato is not a major focus of agriculture except in New Guinea, where in the steep mountains of median altitudes of 3–5,000 feet, it is the present-day staple. Elsewhere, such cultivations are typified by mixed species plantings ; in Asia tree and root crops may be intermingled with grain plants, while in America, the dominants are likely to be maize and manioc.

There has been little in the way of technological development associated with the utilization of the sweet potato in America. In Polynesia, it was used for food by adapting the preparation methods for the earlier traditional plants like taro. Techniques for storage, however, may be looked on as responses to environment, for outside the tropic zones, the New Zealand Maori was able successfully to convert the tropical perennial to an annual plant with the overwintering of the plant for food and planting material by storage techniques. In China, this is also practised, together with the storage of processed material in the shape of dried or powdered starch for consumption. It is notable that in New Guinea, where many live at high altitudes with severe incidences of frost, no organised storage is evident. Thus famines as the result of frost call forth the social adjustment of migration of human populations, as instanced by Meggitt (1958).

Most indigenous peoples recognize the value of the plant as feed for domestic animals, and both tops and roots are used. The former may be harvested purposely from growing crops, and with roots in excess of human requirements, fed to pigs. The animals are also turned onto exhausted cultivations to forage, and there are not many societies which do not fear the depredation of domesticated or feral pigs in sweet potato cultivations unharvested or at an early stage of growth. The plant is used also as a green vegetable for humans through most of its distribution, but this has been least recorded in America, as has the use of the plant in animal husbandry.

In its cultivation in native agricultures, the sweet potato is universally found as a mixture of varieties in the same garden. There are no differential treatments of varieties, but, usually, each one is recognised by name. The names adopted may indicate the areas from which the varieties were introduced, the names of persons who made the introductions, or distinguishing features of the plants such as colour of root skin or flesh, the shape of leaves or roots, applied in direct or metaphorical terms. The criteria for discrimination among varieties are essentially similar to our own, for with additional plant variations such as colour of leaves and stems and the hairiness of the above-ground parts, quite positive identifications are made. Flowering occurs throughout the tropics, but its significance as far as the production of seed is concerned seems to escape most cultivators, who nevertheless claim that all varieties flower. Seed formation has been observed in every area, and it is posited that the number of varieties and the comparatively rare duplication of varieties between areas without constant communication are due to the occasional accidental finding of seedling varieties. Their selection provides for a situation of changing varieties in time in a given area. This process of genetic recombination, together with the added effect of introduction, is considered a more frequent source of variability than somatic mutation.

The bases for human influence in selection of sweet potato in native agricultures are established with the general recognition of morphological variability and the sources of variability itself. In contrast to some modern selection points dictated by consumer partiality, there are no examples of choice of such characters as colour of roots or shape of leaves. Standards are utilitarian, and the differences in flavour or sweetness are recognized as diet variations, rather than as preferences. Morphological characters are functional in the ethno-taxonomy at the level of varietal separation. That some adaptive functions are recognised, however, may be seen in the typification of some varieties as being more suited to higher altitudes or wetter soils. The selection of accidentally discovered seedlings, then, may be viewed as a part of the empirical process of adaptation, complementary to the fitting of environments to the requirements of the plants by the development of agricultural techniques.

THE EXPERIMENTAL PHASE

A cytological survey of the collected material showed a common chromosome number throughout its distribution. Bivalent associations in meiosis, as recorded by Ting, Kehr and Miller (1957) for North American sweet potato were also found throughout, indicating a similar stage of evolution.

Continuous ranges of variation were found in 41 observable characters. These included the measurement of size, colour, hairiness of relevant parts of the plant—stems, leaves, flowers, roots, and some physiological reactions, ability to set flowers and edible roots under

FIGURE 27.1. Contrast between growth forms of two South American sweet potato varieties. The two plots planted on the same day, photographed after 90 days at Crop Research Division, Otara, New Zealand. Scale 12″/division. Note also the difference in leaf shape.

(photographed by A. Underhill)

New Zealand conditions, reaction to cold, and to three fungous organisms. Apart from two characters, the ranges of the American material in most cases exceeded or equalled those exhibited by material from other areas. The lowest specific gravity reading for edible roots was made from a variety from the Marquesas Islands, while the only example of a glabrous ovary was recorded from Thailand. These transgressions may be explicable on the basis of random genetic drift.

Geographic distribution does not reveal differentiation at a sub-specific level, and the propositions are that the plant, as an extremely variable but single species, is of American origin, and that immigration of the plant, even where pre-historic contacts are suggested, occurred in comparatively recent times. The conservative effect in evolution of the mode of reproduction of the sweet potato, however, must be considered in this.

Native selection appears to have influenced the plant phenotypes as expressed in two characters. In varietal populations of mountain cultivators, e.g. in New Guinea and the Philippines, there is a higher frequency of sprawling longer stem types than in those of flat-land dwellers. In Tonga, the varieties are of the compact bush types in the main. At the same time, none of the Pacific varieties has the length of stems exhibited by some mountain varieties from Peru and Colombia. While it is possible that the genotypes conferring extreme length were not introduced originally, it may be that selection is toward the middle of the range of variability. For the longest stemmed forms are not as branched as the median, are slower in growth, and are thus not as valuable for either soil holding on slopes, nor to provide green material as vegetables for human consumption or as bulk feed for pigs. This, then, may provide an example of modal selection in indigenous contexts, tending to preserve genetic variability. For despite the fact that selection and vegetative propagation of desirable clones could eliminate unadapted types, a small proportion of these are present in most mountain varietal populations. While such a lack of selection pressure may be attributed to neglect, it is suggested that the different natures of the environments used within agricultural systems, in this case the use of flat *as well as* sloping topographies, militates against intensive selection in the plant habit character.

The varieties of highland New Guinea appear to have been selected for tolerance to cold, for the types which succumb to early frost in New Zealand are absent from there. Perhaps there is no real resistance to cold in the species, but the variability within the New Guinea populations in the degree of tolerance indicates again a lack of selective intensity which may be due to the fact that a social adjustment like migration following frost attack and the new importation of varieties from lower altitudes on resettlement is a more effective measure. The New Zealand example of agricultural adjustment is of interest, for the Maori varieties extant are among the least cold-tolerant in the collection.

THE SIGNIFICANCE OF EXPLORATION IN
SWEET POTATO IMPROVEMENT

The variability of the species in its distribution among indigenous peoples may be compared with that of modern commercial varieties. For example, the morphological variability available to American breeders early this century (Groth, 1911) is not now generally obtainable. It is not known how much useful variability has been lost by selection to established consumer standards, but some indication is gained in the present material from assessments of disease reaction to three fungi. Tests with the pathogens responsible for scruf, *Monilochaetes infuscans* Ell. and Halst., black rot, *Ceratocystis fimbriata* Ell. and Halst. reported by Nielson and Yen (1966), and, for soil rot *Streptomyces ipomoea* (Person and Martin) Waks. and Henrici, as indicated by histological techniques by Martin (pers. comm.), indicate resistance above what might be expected in modern varieties. Most of the clones showing resistance were derived from South America.

One of the smallest plant growth forms was found in the Caribbean. On cultivation in New Zealand, it consistently produced high root yields, and was to be incorporated in the breeding program there, for the form would be useful in mechanical harvesting procedures.

If the agricultural patterns of the underdeveloped countries are to undergo rapid change, then the application of modern breeding methods to improve the sweet potato will follow. The weaknesses at present, however, with this lie in the lack of definitions of production problems for the direction of breeding aims. The disease and pest problems are not those of temperate agriculture, e.g. the leaf disease caused by *Elsinoe* spp., regarded as unimportant, may reach epidemic proportion in the tropics; the dependence for nutrition on the plant, hardly an issue in modern horticulture, is of considerable import in native contexts. While nobody in the United States or New Zealand would calculate on the sweet potato to supply significant amounts of protein in the diet, this is not the case in areas like New Guinea. Following the demonstration of Oomen *et al.* (1961) of significant variability in this character in sweet potato clonal varieties, Ruinard (1961) proposed a program of upgrading the nutritive value of the crop in the Highlands of West Irian by the introduction of the higher value clones. The pursuance of such programs, with appropriate extension methods to encourage the cultivation of such clones may have further effects, genetic in nature, for the common growing of high-protein clones may repeatedly contribute beneficial genes into what is an essentially inter-breeding population. In other words, local selection may in itself develop varieties which combine the adaptiveness of the indigenous varieties with the higher quality of the adventive.

The present collection has not yet been assessed for its potential in food quality, but if the results of such investigation follow the trends shown by other characters, it may well be that the South American populations might make significant contributions in this phase.

THE PRESERVATION OF GERM PLASM

The difficulties of preservation of gene sources of vegetatively reproduced plants is shared somewhat by the sweet potato. However, since the species is far from sterile in its sexual mode of reproduction, the possibility of preservation in seed form is present. The natural longevity of the seed, combined with the application of modern methods of seed preservation should make practicable the long-term storage of a gene pool. Controlled growing of seed in temperate New Zealand, where the collection is being held now, is difficult owing to the non-flowering of many clones. However, the possible transfer of the collection to tropical environments should overcome this. Such a device has been used by the United States plant breeders to obtain surer supplies of seed for experimental purposes (e.g. see Jones, 1966), by sending clones to Puerto Rico for natural cross-pollination.

The varietal population of South America has been shown to possess the widest ranges of variability in most of the characters assessed in this exploration of sweet potato species. At least this portion of the collection should be conserved; for the inroads of modern society in which the demands on vegetable food production are for uniformity may have the effect of diminishing the genetic variability that we know exists in the species now.

REFERENCES

BROOKFIELD H.C. (1962) Local study and comparative method: An example from Central New Guinea. *Annals. Assoc. American Geographers* **52,** 242–254.

CANDOLLE A. DE (1866) *Origin of Cultivated Plants.* New York, Hafner 1959 (reprint of 1866 edition).

GROTH B.H.A. (1911) The sweet potato. *Contributions from Botanical Laboratory of University of Pennsylvania,* IV, 1.

JONES A. (1966) Morphological variability in early generations of a randomly intermating population of sweet potatoes. *University of Georgia College of Agriculture Experiment Station Technical Bulletin,* N.S. 56.

MARTIN F.W. The sterility-incompatibility complex of the sweet potato. *Proc. 1st International Root Crops Symposium,* Trinidad, 1967 (in press).

MARTIN W.J. (1965) Results of tests for soil rot reaction of clones from Pacific sweet potato collection, Louisiana State University. Personal communication.

MEGGITT M.J. (1958) The Enga of the New Guinea Highlands: some preliminary observations. *Oceania* **28,** 253–330.

NIELSEN L.W. & YEN D.E. (1966) Resistance in sweet potato to scurf and black rot pathogens. *N.Z. J. Agric. Research* **9,** 1032–1041.

NISHIYAMA I. (1963) The origin of the sweet potato plant. In *Plants and the Migrations of Pacific Peoples* (Ed. Barrau J.), 119–128. Honolulu, B.P. Bishop Museum Press.

OOMEN H.A.P.C., SPOON W., HESTERMAN J.E., RUINARD J., LUYKEN R. & SLUMP P. (1961) The sweet potato as the staff of life of the Highland Papuan. *Tropical and Geographic Medicine* **13,** 55–56.

RUINARD J. (1961) Agricultural research in Netherlands New Guinea. *South Pacific Commission Bulletin* **11,** 22–24.

SAUER C.O. (1950) Cultivated plants of South and Central America. In *Handbook of the South American Indians* (Ed. Steward J.H.), Vol. 6: 487–543. Washington, D.C., Smithsonian Institution Bureau of American Ethnology, Bulletin 43.

TING Y.C., KEHR A.E. & MILLER J.C. (1957) A cytological study of the sweet potato plant, *Ipomoea batatas* (L.) Lam. and its related species. *American Naturalist* **91,** 197–203.

VAVILOV N.I. (1951) The origin, variation, immunity and breeding of cultivated plants. *Chron. Bot.* **13,** 1–364.

B·EXPLORATION IN FORESTRY

28

GENE POOLS IN FORESTRY

S. D. RICHARDSON

Department of Forestry, University College of North Wales,
Bangor, United Kingdom

INTRODUCTION

That the long life cycle and large size of forest trees create substantial problems which have effectively discouraged the application of genetics to silviculture, forms an *apologia* that prefaces many a review paper on forest tree improvement; but the advantages that these distinctive features give the forest geneticist over his agricultural and horticultural colleagues are often ignored. In any consideration of the conservation and utilization of gene pools, however, they become apparent. For example, the size, stand structure and regenerative powers of forest tree species render them less liable to catastrophic elimination than most herbaceous species; while the wide genetic diversity existing in both natural and man-made forests (Gustafsson and Mergen, 1964; Bannister, 1965) offers a wide scope for selection. Furthermore, the long life cycle ensures that by the time forest trees have reached maturity they have experienced (and survived) a greater range of environmental vicissitudes than other crop species and the choice of material for propagation and conservation can be made with a correspondingly greater degree of confidence. Finally, as with all perennial species, it is usually possible to evaluate the progeny of artificial selections and crosses within the lifetime of the parents and the propagator can, if necessary, return to the progenitors for more material.

The concept of gene pools in forestry is a wide one and can include natural forests, artificial plantations of both indigenous and exotic species, seed stands, arboreta, provenance collections and clone archives. The present chapter reviews briefly past and current attitudes to each of these sources of germ plasm and outlines progress in seed collection, certification and exchange. It concludes with a short evaluation of requirements for a more objective approach to the utilization of gene pools in production forestry.

NATURAL FORESTS

Despite evolutionary pressures (Stern, 1964), so-called dysgenic selection in the commercial exploitation of forests (Minckler, 1953; Lindquist, 1954), and environmental change involving widespread forest destruction, the natural forest offers a rich source of germ plasm. And because the objectives of tree improvement programs are, in general, ill-defined and—under the influence of rapid technological change in wood utilization—subject to constant modification, it is important that the genetic variability of natural forest populations be preserved. The exceptional magnitude of this variability (e.g., Muller, 1952; Langlet, 1962; Callaham, 1964), even in species with only a limited geographic distribution (Bannister, 1965; Forde, 1962; Wright, 1962), however, necessitates the protection and exclusion from commercial exploitation of significant areas. Toda (1965), for example, suggests a minimum of 10,000 individuals for each of the restricted coniferous species of Japan, while the retention of genotypic diversity in widely distributed species such as *Pinus sylvestris* would demand conservation on a gargantuan scale.

Because of the difficulties involved in the reservation of stands solely for use in forest genetics, it is necessary to combine these objectives with resource conservation for other scientific and economic purposes (Bialobok, 1965; Toda, 1965), for instance, wildlife management, recreation and amenity, water conservation and catchment protection. Particularly in densely populated and developed countries, public awareness of the value of forest conservation in national parks, nature and game reserves, etc., is being fostered and exploited by the forest geneticist.

Considerations of genetic diversity in forest tree species (Vidakovic and Zufa, 1965) and the lack of definition in the objectives of tree improvement programs also emphasize the importance of population genetics and studies of breeding systems. Although foresters preceded other scientists in recognising intra-specific variability (Langlet, 1962), it is only within the last decade that they have begun to use the theory of population genetics; yet it is clear that tree populations provide better material in this field than the domestic animals and crop plants (far removed from their wild ancestors) from which the theory has been developed. Stern (1964) illustrated the value of population genetics as a basis for tree selection by describing a mathematical model for some indigenous populations. He concludes that, within any particular region, a tree population does not have a random-mating structure but comprises sub-populations 'each of which may be considered as being derived from a random-mating population'. Using this model, genetic parameters (heritability, genetic correlation and the coefficient of inbreeding) can be estimated. Obviously, the model is inappropriate for populations which propagate mainly by vegetative means (e.g., some populations of *Populus*), species which are prevailingly self-fertilizing (as is probably the case with many tropical rain forest species (Baker, 1959)), or where the natural population structure has been destroyed. There are also difficulties in the delineation of 'regions' (Callaham, 1964) and a dearth of information relating to the extent of population sub-division. Studies specifically designed to measure variability of tree populations in the sense used by Stern have been described, *inter alia* by Langlet (1959), Zobel and McElwee (1960), Wright (1962), Stern (1962) and Bannister (1963). It is significant that they are all recent; they indicate the belated recognition by foresters of the value of the methodology of quantitative genetics as a basis for tree improvement.

Another feature of natural forests as gene pools relates to areas subjected to commercial exploitation. Particularly in sub-tropical and tropical areas, logging is highly selective. The tree flora is rich and the demands of wood-users extremely conservative, with the result that over vast areas, harvesting involves the removal of only one or two individual trees per hectare. Moreover, the low level of technology in the logging industry has hitherto imposed size restrictions on trees harvested, and over-size individuals (which from the utilization viewpoint may well represent superior genotypes) have often escaped the axe. Undoubtedly, current developments in wood-use (e.g., increasing demands for pulpwood, fibreboard and chipboard; technological improvements in traditional processing industries; and changing market requirements) will increase the range of utilizable species and size-classes. Other factors, however, (the need for political stability as a prerequisite for high-capital investment in forest industries, economic considerations of accessibility, etc.,) militate against a rapid increase in the *tempo* of exploitation and suggest that the threat of forest destruction comes less from timber harvesting operations than from such factors as population pressures on cultivable land and modern methods of warfare.

At present, therefore, in regions of low-population density, even cut-over forest can be regarded as a potential source of germ plasm. Given adequate international cooperation, a suitable organizational

framework, and greater open-mindedness among foresters with respect
to tree improvement objectives, the outlook for the conservation of the
germ plasm of natural forests is by no means dismal.

ARTIFICIAL PLANTATIONS AND SEED STANDS

There are now few countries of the world which do not have plantations
of indigenous and exotic tree species. The vast majority of such
plantations are established for the commercial production of timber and
ancillary products to supplement existing forest resources and, provided
questions of reservation do not arise, there is usually no opposition to
their temporary use as gene pools. But in general, plantations established
more than two decades ago derive from limited seed lots, unrecorded and
unselected except for accessibility. (In many countries of the world,
perhaps most, the majority of artificial plantations are, in fact, still
established on the same basis). In species with a severely restricted
natural distribution (e.g., *P.radiata*), the genetic variability of the
plantations may equal, or even exceed, that of the natural population
but generally it represents only a fraction of the species diversity; and
with silvicultural treatment this variation is further reduced. Plantations
established from selected seed, and seed stands themselves, are likely
to be even more homozygous, in view of the *ad hoc* selection criteria
employed.

The use of commercial plantations as gene pools could be justified
if it could be assumed that the criteria of the superior phenotype would
not change with time, and if more precise knowledge were available
concerning the heritability of 'desirable' characters (Lerner, 1958;
Wright, 1962; Toda, 1963; Hattemer, 1963). To some extent, prognoses
can be made. Thus, rapid rate and evenness of growth, straight stem
form, and disease and pest resistance are always likely to be economically
desirable. Unfortunately, few of these characters show a high degree of
heritability, while any attempt to forecast future requirements in wood
properties, physiological or silvicultural characteristics (e.g., resistance
to wind or frost, site adaptability, etc.) can only be speculative.
Furthermore, changes in forest policies brought about by increasing
population pressures are forcing plantation development more and more
on to infertile, high-altitude, and other intractable sites; while the
application of scientific management (e.g., the use of fertilizers) offers
means of tree improvement that may be more immediate and spectacular than the hopes of the geneticist.

The Final Report of the World Consultation on Forest Genetics and Tree Improvement included summary papers (Björkman, 1964; Segaard, 1964; Zobel, 1964) on the progress in selection and breeding for specific properties that illustrate the subjective character of allegedly 'desirable' features and the inadequacy of our knowledge of heritability. Certainly, the last decade has seen the publication of many papers purporting to estimate heritability for a wide range of characters; unfortunately, though the mathematical treatment may be impeccable, the statistical bases of the data often leave much to be desired. Also, it is seldom possible to extrapolate results from individual population studies beyond their confines.

Changing concepts of desirable wood properties could be extensively documented. The centuries-old searches of British naval surveyors for oak-trees with low, spreading crowns (from which to cut ships 'knees') stand in sharp contrast to modern requirements for oak veneer bolts; while even in the most technologically complex of wood-based industries—pulp and paper manufacture—doubts about the continuing desirability of long-fibred softwoods are prompting companies to establish seed-orchards of short- as well as long-fibred trees. Similarly, the widespread acceptance of new pulpwood species (e.g., *P.radiata*, *Eucalyptus* spp. and other hardwoods) in recent decades, illustrates the rapidity and magnitude of change in the forester's notion of what is 'desirable'. The extent to which traditional timber markets are being invaded by non-wood substitutes provides further evidence.

The probability exists, then, not only that phenotype selection criteria will change in the future but that, by selecting for a limited number of characters of economic importance, certain desirable recessive genes have been eliminated from commercial plantations and seed stands. Since the primary purpose of gene pools should be to preserve intraspecific variability, most artificial plantations have a limited usefulness. Current attitudes (e.g., Toda, 1965) advocate plantation establishment from scattered open-pollinated mother trees in sufficient numbers to reproduce the population diversity and to reduce the risk of inbreeding in subsequent generations (Stern, 1959). In cases where a high degree of inbreeding has occurred, however, genetic variability can be increased by mixing populations in a single plantation.

Despite this change in approach, gene pool plantations, since they are destined for exploitation, present special problems: they must be large enough to attract the support of commercial interests; in general, they have to be limited to currently desirable species—though, in Japan, it is hoped to plant the slow-growing less sought-after species in protective belts around the commercial plantations (Toda, 1965); and the analysis of genetic variation (by means of single-tree progeny trials established in parallel with each population at the onset of sexual maturity) is a *sine qua non*.

ARBORETA, PROVENANCE COLLECTIONS AND CLONE ARCHIVES

The most important limitation of artificial plantations as gene pools applies equally to most existing tree populations in these categories; they have been created with severely restricted objectives. Thus, arboreta have generally been established as collections of individual trees for limited scientific purposes, or for educational and recreational use; provenance collections, although preserving a degree of genetic variation, usually purport to determine the most suitable seed source for the afforestation of specific areas (Edwards, 1956; Bouvarel, 1958; Langlet, 1963; Pryor, 1963; Callaham, 1964); and clone archives (or 'tree-shows') are normally designed to test the productive capacity of a restricted number of genotypes (selected from currently desirable phenotypes) over an economic rotation. Nevertheless, because they are created specifically as gene pools (albeit with limited objectives) and because of changing attitudes of foresters and arboriculturists to genetic sciences, they provide the most convenient media currently available for the preservation and utilization of gene pools in forestry. It is, indeed, on the evidence provided by arboretum-type plantings that most of the man-made forests of the world—amounting to more than 50 million hectares (FAO, 1966)—have been created.

Traditional arboreta have particular relevance for the conservation of species in which the gene pool is small and under pressure of destruction; and for individuals having distinctive characteristics which are at present of no apparent economic significance. They also serve as field laboratories for cytological and genecological studies—essential concomitants of the effective utilization of gene pools. The recognition by foresters of the need for cytogenetic investigations of trees is a major development of the past decade (Gustafsson, 1960; Mehra, 1960; Righter, 1960; Duffield, 1962; Wright, 1962; Khoshoo, 1963), while studies of inter- and intra-specific hybridisation—often carried out in arboreta—are giving the practical tree-improver a valuable appreciation of the limitations and possibilities of his raw material (Wright, 1962;

1964). Particular attention has been focussed on the genera *Pinus*, *Populus* and *Quercus*.

In modern arboreta, scientific purpose takes precedence over ornamentation, and the need to illustrate genetic variation within species is increasingly recognized. International cooperation to this end is improving and it seems probable that the future use of arboreta as gene pools will be limited more by inadequate finance than by deliberately limited objectives. Particularly in the developing world, there is still a need to establish arboreta—if only as a stop-gap measure until larger scale gene pools can be created.

Turning now to provenance collections, a reappraisal of the objectives and methodology of such tests is underway in many countries. Again, the restricted aims of earlier trials (e.g., the international provenance trials of *P.sylvestris* begun in 1907 and 1922, *Picea abies* in 1938, *Larix decidua* in 1944, and numerous national collections) have become apparent. Designed to evaluate stand productivity on particular sites, they were often unreplicated, unrepresentative of a species range or of individual populations, and unreproducible because seed was often collected during felling operations or from vaguely specified locations. At the same time, areas devoted to provenance trials in many countries are so large that adequate maintenance and assessment have become impractical; and too frequently the genecological studies which should precede their establishment are lacking. Critical reviews of many of these aspects have appeared in recent years (Edwards, 1956; Callaham, 1961, 1962, 1964; Jackson, 1962; Langlet, 1962; Shiue and Pauley, 1961; Wright and Freeland, 1960; Vyskot, 1963; Giertych, 1965; Schober, 1963; Wright, 1962, 1963). Argument has concerned the criteria for species and seed-tree selection, seed certification, experimental design and plot size, assessment techniques and silvicultural treatments. The need to maintain intra-specific genetic diversity and the importance of genecological investigation are now generally acknowledged, as is indicated by a recent report (Lines, 1967) of a Working Group (established in 1962 with more than 60 members) of the International Union of Forestry Research Organizations (IUFRO).

A problem that is of particular concern in provenance research (and relevant to a discussion of gene pools) concerns choice of species (Champion and Brasnett, 1960). Extensive data are available, from empirical trials, on the performance of exotic species (usually of unknown provenance) in several countries of the world, and some of the factors governing successful introductions can be recognized (Wright, 1962). Plasticity and similarity of habitat are important features, while monotypic genera have a particular value, since they are remarkably free from serious pests. On the other hand, neither the extent of a species' natural range nor its economic significance are strongly correlated with its potential usefulness as an exotic and, in general, it has been the ability of species to satisfy particular economic demands in the country of introduction that has determined their widespread use (e.g., *Eucalyptus* spp. in the dry, warm/temperate timber-deficient areas of the world; fast-growing *Pinus* spp. in countries with a slow-growing native flora, such as East Africa and New Zealand; Pacific-Northwest conifers in species-poor Great Britain). It seems probable that economic considerations will always figure prominently in the selection of exotics and, hence, in the provenance research programs of forest services. With the abandonment of 'serendipity research', however, adequate gene pools of the more commonly used species are likely to be maintained. It is the currently uneconomic and little-known species (especially those of tropical and sub-tropical zones and the highland regions of Mexico and Western China) that will remain under-represented; their incorporation into provenance trials is an urgent need.

Clone archives are comparative plantings of rooted cuttings, layered or grafted material, set out in such a way as to test the productive capacity of individual trees and to serve as reference collections. Their use as gene pools is restricted by limited and subjective phenotypic selection and, in addition, by topophysis, difficulties of propagation in many species, and delayed graft incompatibility in others. They may be useful, however, in determining total genetic variance within a small population, in facilitating controlled pollination, and in seed production.

Current discussion of clonal plantings is more concerned with seed orchards (design, treatment, assessment and estimation of genetic gain, etc.) and clonal tests to demonstrate genetic variability, than with clone archives *per se* (Wright, 1963; Matthews, 1964). The need to represent geographic regions in seed orchards (so-called 'provenance seed orchards') has been recognized (Anderson, 1960), and the value of archives in screening clones for phenological response, self-compatibility etc. as a prelude to orchard establishment has been stressed (Matthews, 1964). The establishment of a IUFRO Working Group on the international testing of clones underlines the importance of cooperation between national forest services and may extend the scope of clone archives.

THE UTILIZATION OF GENE POOLS

The belated recognition by professional foresters of the importance of genotypic selection has meant that forest management (as distinct from research) has so far derived little practical benefit from the concepts discussed above. On a world basis, most countries involved in plantation establishment still obtain the bulk of their tree seed from unimproved sources and management practices in natural forests are determined almost entirely by *ad hoc* economic and technological expedients rather than biological criteria. Unfortunately, the time-scale of genotypic improvement in forest trees (Schreiner, 1966) and the logistics of the translation of genetics research into production forestry militate against the kind of development that has occurred in agriculture.

An essential element of the efficient utilization of gene pools is a facility for the collection, storage, and movement of germ plasm; and increasing awareness among foresters of the opportunities for tree improvement has given impetus to the development of such facilities in many countries (Matthews, 1964). Forest services concerned with artificial plantations normally maintain seed-source registers and collecting agencies (usually in the research branch) and some 12 countries have comprehensive seed certification schemes. Individual countries have mounted collecting expeditions to more remote geographical areas (e.g., Hinds and Larson, 1961; Zobel, 1961), while for provenances of species that are much desired but difficult of access (e.g., *Eucalyptus* spp. and Mexican pines) national collection and distribution centres have recently been established. Pollen banks are maintained in at least 30 countries. At the international level, various groups operating under the aegis of FAO (e.g., the International Poplar Commission, the Teak Sub-Commission), IUFRO (various Working Groups), the International Seed Testing Association (Forest Seeds Committee), the International Crop Improvement Association, the Organization for Economic Cooperation and Development (Working Group on Forest Tree Seed Certification), and other organizations take a lively interest in the certification and movement of tree seed and plant material. Recently, the Forestry and Forest Products Division of FAO has developed plans for the strengthening of regional centres in order to facilitate seed exchange between member nations.

With few exceptions, however, the activities mentioned above are restricted to developed countries in the North Temperate Zone and are concentrated on a few commercial species. Sub-tropical and tropical resources are scarcely being tapped.

CONCLUSION

During the past two decades, foresters have come to appreciate the potential of gene pools as practical implements of silviculture and, although they lag behind agriculturists and horticulturists in the application of genetic science to crop improvement, their increasing reliance upon the artificial regeneration of forests has provided a stimulus that could do much to mitigate past neglect. In this chapter their efforts have been criticised on the grounds of overly restricted objectives, neglect of all but a few species commercially important in developed economies, and excessive concentration on *ad hoc* selection criteria—deficiencies which are, perhaps, understandable in the light of the rapid technological changes occurring in the utilization of forest products and consequent inability to forecast requirements. It is suggested that in the establishment of gene pools these difficulties can be exploited, since they provide a political justification for the preservation of a much wider range of germ plasm than is of immediate use. They also give urgency to the need for increased basic research in population genetics, cytology and genecology in relation to forest trees.

Priorities have to be established in the conservation and utilization of gene pools in forestry. *A priori*, populations with a severely restricted distribution and monotypes should receive immediate attention, together with biotypes known to have, or suspected of having, a high combining ability. As to species choice, it is impractical to avoid economic speculation or to ignore existing artificial gene pools, despite their limitations. It is suggested that high priority should be given to the extension of existing provenance collections and clone archives by supplementary sampling designed to achieve better representation of species diversity; and that, in the selection of other species, attention should be paid to properties which are most likely to remain 'desirable' (e.g., adaptability to intractable sites, high growth rate in softwoods, and wood working properties in decorative hardwoods).

Along with the conservation and extension of germ plasm resources, forest scientists must also accelerate the evaluation of currently non-commercial species and widen the bases of such evaluation. In all these endeavours, enhanced international cooperation with scientists in other disciplines will be of crucial importance.

REFERENCES

ANDERSON E. (1960) Fröplantager i Skogsbrukets *tjänst K. Skogs-o. Lantbr. Akad. Tidskr. Stockholm,* **99,** (1–2), 65–87.

BAKER H.G. (1959) Reproductive methods as factors in speciation in flowering plants. *Cold Spring Harbor Symp.* **24,** 177–191.

BANNISTER M.H. (1963) Planning a genetical survey of *Pinus radiata* populations. In *Proceedings of the World Consultation on Forest Genetics and Tree Improvement, Stockholm*—**1,** 4/1, 1–10. FAO, Rome.

BANNISTER M.H. (1965) Variation in the breeding system of *Pinus radiata*. In *The Genetics of Colonizing Species* (Eds. Baker H.G. and Stebbins G.L.), 353–372. Academic Press, New York.

BIALOBOK S. (1965) Conservation of natural forest populations in Poland. *International Union of Forestry Research Organizations Special Meeting Zagreb. Section* **22.**

BJÖRKMAN E. (1964) Breeding for resistance to disease in forest trees. *Unasylva* **18** (2–3), 71–81.

BOUVAREL P. (1958) Les peuplements artificiels—conséquences d'ordre génétique. *J. Forêts Sci.*, **8/9,** 524–535.

CALLAHAM R.Z. (1961) Experimental taxonomy: more than seed source studies. In *Recent Advances in Botany* (Ed. Bailey D.L.), **2,** 1695–1699. Univ. Toronto Press, Canada.

CALLAHAM R.Z. (1962) Geographic variability in growth of forest trees. In *Tree Growth* (Ed. Kozlowski T.T.), 311–325. Ronald Press, New York.

CALLAHAM R.Z. (1964) Provenance research: investigation of genetic diversity associated with geography. *Unasylva* **18,** (2–3), 40–50.

CHAMPION H.G. & BRASNETT N.V. (1960) Choice of forest species for planting. *FAO Forest Dev. Pap.* 13.

DUFFIELD J.W. (1962) Forest tree improvement: old techniques and the new science of genetics. H.R. MacMillan Lect. *Pub. Univ. British Columbia* **12,** 1–16.

EDWARDS M.V. (1956) The design, layout and control of provenance experiments. *Z. Forstgenet.* **5,** 169–180.

FOOD and AGRICULTURE ORGANIZATION (1966) Wood: world trends and prospects. *Unasylva* **20** (1–2), 1–135.

FORDE M.B. (1962) Variation in the natural populations of Monterey pine (*Pinus radiata* Don.) in California. Doctoral thesis, Univ. Calif. Davis.

GIERTYCH M.M. (1965) Adapting provenance trials towards most efficient selection and preservation of desirable forest populations. *International Union of Forestry Research Organizations Special Meeting Zagreb. Section* **22.**

GUSTAFSSON Å. (1960) Polyploidy and mutagenesis in forest tree breeding. *Proc. 5th World For. Cong., Seattle, U.S.A.,* 793–805.

GUSTAFSSON Å. & MERGEN F. (1964) Some principles of tree cytology and genetics. *Unasylva* **18** (2–3), 7–20.

HATTEMER H.H. (1963) Estimates of heritability published in forest tree breeding research. *Proceedings of the World Consultation on Forest Genetics and Tree Improvement, Stockholm* **1**, 2a/3, 1–14. FAO, Rome.

HINDS H.V. & LARSEN E. (1961) Collecting tree seed in Mexico. *Emp. For. Rev.* **40** (1), 43–53.

JACKSON D.S. (1962) Parameters of site for certain growth components of slash pine (*Pinus elliottii* Engelm.). *Duke Univ. Sch. For. Bull.* **16**, 1–118.

KHOSHOO T.N. (1963) Cytogenetical evolution in conifers. *Proceedings of the World Consultation on Forest Genetics and Tree Improvement, Stockholm* **1**, 1/2, 1–5. FAO, Rome.

LANGLET O. (1959) Skogsforskningens nya granproveniensflörsök. *Skogen* **18**, 370–371.

LANGLET O. (1962) Ecological variability and taxonomy of forest trees. In *Tree Growth* (Ed. Kozlowski T.T.), 357–369. Ronald Press, New York.

LANGLET O. (1963) Practical results and current problems in provenance research in Sweden. *Proceedings of the World Consultation on Forest Genetics and Tree Improvement, Stockholm* **1**, 3/1, 1–10. FAO, Rome.

LERNER I.M. (1958) *The Genetic Basis of Selection.* Wiley Inc., N.Y.

LINDQUIST B. (1954) *Forstgenetik in der Schwedischen Waldbaupraxis* Newmann Verlag, Berlin.

LINES R. (1967) Standardization of methods for provenance research and testing. (International Union of Forestry Research Organizations. Working Group, compiled by Lines, R.) *Proc. 14th IUFRO Cong., Munich* **3**, 672–718.

MATTHEWS J.D. (1964) Seed production and seed certification. *Unasylva* **18** (2–3), 104–108.

MEHRA P.N. (1960) Cytology and breeding of conifers. *Proc. 5th World For. Cong., Seattle, U.S.A.* 728–733.

MINCKLER L.S. (1953) Recent advances in the field of forest genetics. *Trans. Illinois Acad. Sci.* **46**, 56–62.

MULLER C.H. (1952) Ecological control of hybridization of *Quercus:* a factor in the mechanism of evolution. *Evolution* **6**, 147–161.

PRYOR, L.D. (1963) Provenance in tree improvement with particular reference to *Eucalyptus. Proceedings of the World Consultation on Forest Genetics and Tree Improvement, Stockholm* **1**, 3/2, 1–6. FAO, Rome.

RIGHTER F.I. (1960) Forest tree improvement through inbreeding and interspecific hybridization. *Proc. 5th World For. Cong., Seattle, U.S.A.* 783–787.

SCHOBER R. (1963) Experience with the Douglas fir in Europe. *Proceedings of the World Consultation on Forest Genetics and Tree Improvement, Stockholm* **1**, 4/5, 1–18. FAO, Rome.

SCHREINER E.J. (1966) Future needs for maximum progress in genetic improvement of disease resistance in forest trees. In *Breeding Pest-Resistant Trees* (Eds. Gerhold H.D., Schreiner E.J., McDermott R.E. and Wineski J.A.), 455–466. Pergamon Press, New York.

SHIUE C. & PAULEY S.S. (1961) Some considerations on the statistical design for provenance and progeny tests in tree improvement programmes. *For. Sci.* **7**, 116–122.

SØEGAARD B. (1964) Breeding for resistance to insect attack in forest trees. *Unasylva* **18** (2–3), 82–88.

STERN K. (1959) Der Inzuchtgrad in Nachkommenschaften von Samenplantagen. *Silvae Genet.* **8,** 37–42.

STERN K. (1962) Preliminary estimates of the genetic structure of two sympatric populations of birches as determined by random effects and natural selection. *Northeast Forest Tree Improv. Conf. Proc.* **9** (1961), 25–34.

STERN K. (1964) Population genetics as a basis for selection. *Unasylva* **18** (2–3), 21–29.

TODA R. (1963) Mass selection and heritability in forest tree breeding. *Proceedings of the World Consultation on Forest Genetics and Tree Improvement, Stockholm* **1,** 2a/2, 1–7. *Section* **22.**

TODA R. (1965) Preservation of gene pool in forest tree populations. *International Union of Forestry Research Organizations Special Meeting Zagreb. Section* **22.**

VIDAKOVIC M. & ZUFA L. (1965) The preservation of the gene pool in natural stands for genetical research. *International Union of Forestry Research Organizations Special Meeting Zagreb.* FAO, Rome,

VYSKOT M. (1963) Standardization of methods for provenance research and testing. *Proceedings of the World Consultation on Forest Genetics and Tree Improvement, Stockholm* **1,** 3/5, 1–7. FAO, Rome.

WRIGHT J.W. (1962) Geographic variation patterns in forest trees. *Proc. Second Cent. States For. Tree. Imp. Conf.* (1960) 15–20.

WRIGHT J.W. (1962) Genetics of forest tree improvement. *FAO For. and For. Prod. Studies,* No. 16.

WRIGHT J.W. (1963) The design of field tests. *Proceedings of the World Consultation on Forest Genetics and Tree Improvement, Stockholm* **1,** 3/4, 1–6. FAO, Rome.

WRIGHT J.W. (1964) Hybridization between species and races. *Unasylva* **18** (2–3), 30–39.

WRIGHT J.W. & Freeland F.D. (1960) Plot size and experimental efficiency in forest genetic research. *Mich. State Univ. Tech. Bull.* **280,** 1–28.

ZOBEL B.J. (1961) Pines in the tropics and sub-tropics. *Proc. 13th International Union of Forestry Research Organizations Cong., Sec.* 22/10, 1–8. Vienna.

ZOBEL B.J. (1964) Breeding for wood properties in forest trees. *Unasylva* **18** (2–3), 89–103.

ZOBEL B.J. & McELWEE R. (1960) Plans for progeny testing seed orchards. North Carolina State Coll. For. (Mimeogr.).

29

MEXICAN PINES

BRUCE ZOBEL

North Carolina State University,
Raleigh, N.C., U.S.A.

INTRODUCTION

As for many plants in Mexico, pines show great variability. Large morphological and adaptive differences are to be expected because of the extremely varied environments under which pines grow. In addition, there is a blending of species through hybridization and introgression. Several 'species complexes' have evolved which consist of a number of closely related species with no clear-cut barriers and with all kinds of intergrading forms.

There is, therefore, ample scope for the exploration of Mexican pines for use in afforestation throughout the world. The pines grow from sea level to timberline, from tropical to cold temperate climates, from desert to rain forest. They grow on good soils and poor, in pure stands and in mixtures with other species. Some are found on soils so poor that practically no other vegetation is found. Botanically, the species range from strictly western types into more eastern types (as in the Group *Australes*). Although man has not yet successfully crossed the eastern and western *Australes*, 'intermediate' *Australes* are found in Mexico. There is recurring argument whether Mexico is the meeting ground for the eastern and western forms or whether it is the center of origin from which these forms arose.

PLANNING THE COLLECTION TRIP

The first collection trip made by Zobel to Mexico in 1954 was made without knowledge of proper equipment and supplies and with practically no preplanning, on the invitation of several Mexican organizations, to study and collect pines in the state of Nuevo Leon. In 1954 there was a cone crop failure but many yearling cones were observed, indicating a good crop would be produced in 1955. Therefore, in late 1955 a further trip was made to Nuevo Leon which was well prepared and successful.

Seed collecting requires considerable preplanning and definition of objectives. Difficulties are likely to occur in obtaining proper clearances, guides and contacts, the environmental conditions are widely varied, and long travel distances are involved. A careful choice of objectives is essential if one is to cover the required area in the limited time and with limited resources.

The flora of Mexico is so rich that if one does not plan correctly, resources are soon exhausted and frustration results. The necessary scientific equipment, chemicals and supplies must be brought in adequate quantity by the collection crew, because they are not always readily available in the collection areas.

Based upon their experiences in 1962, Saylor and McElwee outlined some basic needs for collection of pine seed in Mexico:

Permits to collect seed. Obtainable from the Office of the Secretary of Agriculture and Livestock, the National Institute of Forestry Investigations, and the Forestry Commission of the State of Michoacan.

Permit to export seed. Obtainable from the Office of Agricultural Economics.

Permit to import seed. Such a permit must be obtained from the plant quarantine division of the country into which seed will be brought.

Guides and interpreters. A knowledgeable guide in Mexico is essential. He needs to know where the desired species are growing that can be easily and legally collected. He needs to know the people, the local governments and the large landholders because each has to be contacted before collection can proceed. The number of obstacles a good guide can overcome is amazing.

Climbers to collect cones. Even in the most isolated areas there are strong reasons why cones cannot be obtained by shooting off limbs or by other methods that cause damage to the trees. Climbing equipment such as spurs or Swedish Bicycles need to be brought into Mexico.

A sturdy, four-wheel-drive vehicle. Essential for traversing unimproved back roads. Such equipment is difficult to hire in Mexico.

Prior information of potential cone crops. A good estimate of future crops can be obtained from estimates of yearling (one-year-old) cones in the late spring prior to fall cone collection. This job must be done by a reliable observer, preferably the person who will later act as guide. A yearling estimate will save fruitless, frustrating trips, since frequent cone crop failures occur in the pines in Mexico.

Extraction, treatment, packing and shipment of seed. This can be the most time-consuming and frustrating part of the whole operation and complete preparations, prior to the trip, must be made.

FIELD SAMPLING

The intensity and kind of field sampling depends on the objective of the trip. Very often it is desired to collect races, species or ecotypes which will be tested as exotics under specific environmental conditions. This is a difficult kind of field sampling which requires the following :

A decision as to the species complex or species to be studied. Environmental conditions under which a species in Mexico grows often are quite varied, which emphasizes the need for notes on the environmental conditions of individual collecting sites. This is not easy, since much necessary information, such as rainfall, maximum and minimum and average temperatures are not available in many of the areas where natural pine stands occur. One of the most serious complications involves species determination since a wide range of intergrading forms occurs. Publications dealing with the taxonomy and characteristics of the Mexican pines are helpful but sometimes misleading, especially in the areas where hybridization is evident.

Collection of an adequate sample representative of a given population or taxon. For practical purposes, sometimes a sample of as few as five trees per population are used, but samples of up to 25 trees are preferable. Mixing seeds from different trees within a population is not satisfactory because sometimes, after seedlings are grown, it is found that an individual tree is a hybrid or even a different species.

Ensuring that the cones are ripe and seeds are sound. Cone maturity varies greatly according to species and environment. Cone ripening in the hard pines occurs from November to late January, while it is earlier in the white pines. Some cones from each plot should be cut to determine the number of sound seed, as seed may be unfilled or may be infested with seed and cone insects. Many apparently good collections have yielded nothing because the seed obtained would not germinate.

Correct and permanent labelling. Under field conditions of mass collection and imperfect extraction facilities it is essential to have material double-labelled to prevent a chance of confusion or loss. Such an obvious precaution is often not taken, which results in severe impairment of the value of the collection.

COLLECTION TRIPS

Our experience is based on three separate trips to Mexico. The first, without prior preparation, was made by the writer in 1954 to the wild, high lands of the state of Nuevo Leon. Since there was a cone crop failure that year, and as the writer did not have suitable equipment and supplies, the main activities were to scout collection areas, make proper contacts, and learn the requirements for a properly organized collecting trip.

In 1955, Cech and Zobel went into the same area, renewed their local contacts, and had a very successful collection trip. Working on tree improvement in the Texas Forest Service, the principal objective was to obtain pines growing in areas of very low rainfall, that might be suitable to plant in the very droughty 'Post Oak Region' of east Texas. Collections were obtained mostly from the drier areas of the northern state of Nuevo Leon, although some specimens were obtained from moister environments at higher elevations, up to 12,000 feet. Twenty-eight separate collections were made, three of which turned out to be new species or hybrids that could not be identified (Zobel and Cech, 1957).

Seed and botanical specimens were taken to Texas, where the seed was extracted and planted in the nursery. Growth and survival were very disappointing. The numerous collections from hot, dry areas (rainfall as little as nine inches per year) froze in Texas in the very severe, late season cold 'northers' that occur in this area. The trees withstood colder temperatures in their native habitat, but cold weather occurred only after they had hardened off. In Texas they started growth in the spring with the first several weeks of warm weather and were killed by the sudden cold and very low humidity during the northers. The trees from high elevations survived the cold but died from the drought and heat during the summer. Most of the few trees that did survive grew so much more slowly than the native drought-resistant loblolly pine that there is no hope for their use in commercial plantings.

Seed and plants were sent to a number of arboreta throughout the southern United States. Most of them froze a year or two after planting out. It was most disappointing that several grew ten feet or more tall and then were killed by an unusually early or late freeze. Very few still survive at this time. There is one exception, a collection from a single tree growing on top of a peak in the middle of the desert north of Monterey, Mexico. This tree did not fit any species description and was labelled 'Mex. 28'. Its progeny grow well and seem to be resistant to unseasonal cold periods. They are planted at several places in the south-eastern United States. Although some of the plants are more than 20 feet tall, they have as yet produced no pollen or female conelets.

The third collection trip was a major enterprise, well planned and organized, and financed by six members of The Cooperative Tree Improvement Program at North Carolina State University. Two three-man teams went to Mexico in 1962. One started near Mexico City and worked westward in the Sierra Madre Oriental and the Great Cross Range, and the other started in the north-central part of Mexico and worked south in the Sierra Madre Occidental mountain range. They eventually met in the state of Michoacan. As for the earlier trips, cooperation from Mexico was excellent after preliminary difficulties were overcome.

The trip had both practical and scientific objectives. One major problem of the member companies of the North Carolina State-Industry Cooperative Tree Improvement Program is to determine what to grow on marginal lands. Such marginal areas range from extremely dry, low elevation sites to high elevation sites in the northern part of the southern pine region. Collections were made to see if any species could be found that would grow well in these problem areas.

From a scientific standpoint, information was desired on evolution, speciation and hybridization taking place in natural populations of pines in Mexico. A secondary objective was to determine the range of variability in wood qualities from various species of the Mexican pines and to determine how they varied, within and between species, for trees growing under different environmental conditions.

A total of approximately 42,000 cones were collected from 128 trees representing the following 18 species:

P.arizonica	lawsoni	patula
chihuahuana	leiophylla	pseudostrobus
lutea	lumholtzii	rudis
durangensis	michoacana	tenuifolia
engelmanni	michoacana var. cornuta	teocote
hartweggii	montezumae	
herrerai	oocarpa	

Two 10-mm wood samples were taken from each tree in addition to necessary herbarium specimens and fixed needle samples. Black and white and color photography were used to record features of individual trees, stands, and herbarium collections. More than 7,000 miles were travelled in eight states in making these collections.

N*

The scientific and wood studies were successful and some results have been published (Zobel, 1965). Even though the collections required the efforts of six persons and support from the industries and North Carolina State University and the help of numerous people and organizations in Mexico, collections are still not sufficiently complete to draw sound conclusions about variation patterns or species relationships.

Seedlings have been grown on nearly 15 outplanting sites from Tennessee to south Florida, Hawaii and two places in Brazil. All of the plantings north of Florida have frozen, except the high elevation sources, which have a very slow growth rate. Growth in Hawaii has been poor; survival in Brazil has been excellent, as has been growth of some collections. The plantings have been a near failure in the south-eastern United States, which can be directly traced to lack of adaptability to temperature and moisture fluctuations in the plantation areas. This occurred partly because, in spite of the extensive preparations, cone failures were found in several key areas which prevented collections from populations deemed most likely to succeed.

DISCUSSION

Despite the apparent potentialities for use, the Mexican pines as a group have been a disappointment, if not a failure, when tested in other parts of the world. A few species have been successful, and are used because of their good growth and wide adaptability, e.g., *P. patula*, but most attempts to grow Mexican pines as exotics have met with little success.

Part of the problem is caused by the 'shotgun' approach in which species and races have been tried, irrespective of their potential for success. Ecotypic and clinal effects have been ignored, as have geographic sources. The general idea has been, 'get some Mexican pine seed and let's try it', with no attempt to match growth and adaptability of the seed source to the area where it is to be grown. Such efforts would be expected to produce unsatisfactory results or failures, and they have. Some *Eucalyptus* species and Monterey pine, coming from rather limited habitats but well adapted to grow in a wide variety of conditions, have been used by foresters in justification of the contention that the seed source and planting area is not needed for success of introduction.

It can be expected that a careful matching of seed source with potential planting site will be fruitful in the Mexican pines. Very little of this has been tried, but even in those few instances where a reasonable correlation has been established some failures have been encountered. Poor data about environments at the seed source, misjudgment due to using climatic averages instead of sequences and extremes, lack of proper mycorrhizal infection in the exotic environment have all contributed to failures. Specific adaptations of certain species to unusual environments have also produced difficulties. For example, the well-known 'grass stage' or 'semi-grass stage' may give the tree a unique ability to survive and compete under natural conditions, but it renders the species unfit for intensive forestry conditions.

The Mexican pines appear to have produced species or races particularly suited to nearly every condition under which commercial forests could conceivably be planted in their natural range, but few efforts have been as unrewarding as the movement of Mexican pines to exotic planting sites. Thus far we have not been able to exploit the variation present in Mexican pines. The reason for failure appears to be simple : insufficient knowledge of the biology and ecology of this group of species. If the Mexican pines are to play a significant role in plant introduction in the future, intensive, detailed studies are needed. This requires cooperation of agencies both inside and outside Mexico. It also requires speed since some of the best genotypes are nearing extinction because of logging and fires. Our tree improvement programs sometimes go into intensive breeding programs to produce something that nature has already produced but which has been neglected—all too frequently because of ignorance.

REFERENCES

SAYLOR L.C. & McELWEE R.L. (1962) Collecting pine material in Mexico for provenance trials and wood studies. *Tech. Rept. No.* 18, 1–23. School of Forestry, North Carolina State University, Raleigh.

ZOBEL B.J. (1965) Variation in specific gravity and tracheid length for several species of Mexican pine. *Silvae Gen.* **14,** 1–12.

ZOBEL B.J. & CECH F.C. (1957) Pines from Nuevo Leon, Mexico. *Madroño* **14,** 133–144.

LOW ALTITUDE TROPICAL PINES AND FAST GROWING HARDWOODS

A. F. A. LAMB AND E. N. G. COOLING

U.K. Overseas Aid Scheme, Commonwealth Forestry Institute,

Oxford, England

INTRODUCTION

The British Government's Tropical Pines Overseas Aid Programme based on the Commonwealth Forestry Institute, Oxford, started in September 1963 with a survey of the species *Pinus caribaea* in the literature and in the field where it had been planted in tropical countries. Tours of East, Central and South Africa, and the Caribbean by Lamb in 1964 showed that there were many other pines on trial which could prove equally important and that a broader basis for the scheme was desirable. These tours showed also that practical help was urgently needed to assist countries in obtaining the seed they required for species and provenance trials, and in comparing the wood quality produced by tropical pines when grown in exotic plantations.

At the end of the first two year grant for the scheme, a revised programme was approved covering a three year period from April 1966, and extending the scope to embrace all lowland tropical pines and fast growing hardwoods likely to prove successful in commercial plantations. A sum of £30,000 to be spread over three years was made available and approval given to employ a second Senior Research Officer and a technician. At the same time the staff at the Tropical Products Institute, London, was expanded to deal with pulping trials and a capital grant for equipment was used by the Commonwealth Forestry Institute to obtain instruments for rapid measurement of timber strength properties, wood fibres, spiral grain, etc. This pilot series of tests of wood properties was co-ordinated with the programme of major timber tests of tropical species in progress at the Forest Products Research Laboratory at Princes Risborough, which is financed from the same source but from a separate grant.

THE INFORMATION SERVICE

As first-hand data accumulated from visits to tropical plantations, a series of reports in the form of 'Impressions' was issued in cyclostyled form to all interested British Commonwealth Forest Departments and to FAO, Rome. These did not pretend to be comprehensive monographs on individual species but were up-to-date comments on techniques and on the performance of species in a number of tropical countries under very varied conditions. They were supplemented by first-hand data from the countries of origin. These reports were designed to supply information needed by forest officers in the field and therefore included bibliographies and summaries of useful papers on species.

The initial collection of data on the numerous fast growing tropical hardwoods was done by means of a questionnaire; the results were summarised and issued in May 1966 as a cyclostyled Part I of data on fast growing hardwoods. This is being followed by Part II—a series of compilations on individual species taken from the short list of 'Probables' in Part I which are likely to be, or are already, widely planted. Such compilations have been prepared for *Gmelina arborea* and *Cedrela odorata*, and are in preparation for the genera *Terminalia* and *Cordia*. Similar reports have been published on *Pinus merkusii* and the genus *Araucaria*.

SEED SERVICE

One of the practical services offered under the scheme is a seed supply service. Owing to the recent improvement in techniques, the seed store installed at the U.K. Forestry Commission's Research Station, Farnham, had spare space which was made available for the storage of tropical seed. This made it possible to bring batches of seed from all over the tropics to England and store them under the best conditions until countries not yet having controlled storage conditions were ready to sow the seed. It is now possible to build up sets of seed of all the major provenances of a species and organize comparable, replicated provenance trials in several countries. So far stocks of seed have been made available for the three major provenances of *P.caribaea* and for several provenances of *P.merkusii*.

In addition, help has been given in obtaining bulk supplies of seed of tropical pines where for one reason or another a country has been unable to deal direct with the supplier of the seed. Two visits have been made to the Bahamas and two to South East Asia and Australasia to obtain as much seed as possible of indigenous tropical pines. On occasion, some of this seed has been exchanged for seed of a provenance which could not easily be obtained by purchase.

In spite of this, inadequate seed supplies for both research and commercial plantations remain a bottleneck in the development of tropical plantation silviculture. Several countries put restrictions on the export of seed which raise the price and reduce the supply. Fortunately, over the past twenty years large stocks of exotic tropical pines have been built up in a few countries where tree improvement programmes are under way. These countries should be encouraged to plan to export surplus seed of selected strains over and above their own requirements as soon as possible.

SELECTION OF SUPERIOR PHENOTYPES

The selection of superior phenotypes for individual seed-tree collections in the country of origin has been attempted only in British Honduras and the Bahamas, and only for *P.caribaea*. It could be done wherever the local forest service agrees, and can ensure the safety of the selected trees. However, reasonable accessibility and adequate mapping of the open-pollinated parents are a *sine qua non* in such work.

TIMBER TESTING

The work on timber testing, so far, has been concentrated on the major tropical pines and *Gmelina arborea*. A sampling procedure for testing within-tree, between-tree and between-site differences was used. Lamb sampled the indigenous pine populations of both *P.caribaea* and *P.oocarpa* in British Honduras. Discs cut at every ten per cent of height were brought to Oxford for detailed study of anatomy, physical properties, and pulping properties. A similar set of discs of the Bahamas provenance of *P.caribaea* was obtained through the co-operation of the Forest Supervisor and an American pulpwood exporter. For comparison with these indigenous samples, discs were cut from *P.caribaea* plantations in Trinidad, Jamaica, Fiji, Sabah, and Malaya. Most of these were obtained from young plantations showing much more rapid growth. In consequence, very great differences in wood density and pulping qualities have been revealed.

Small wood samples of *P.khasya* and *P.merkusii* (two small sample logs) from the Philippines, *P.occidentalis* from the Dominican Republic, and numerous increment borings have been assembled for examination.

PROVENANCE RESEARCH

In view of the pioneer work of Luckhoff (1964) and Nikles (1966) on *P.caribaea*, it was considered unnecessary to re-examine the differences between the anatomical characteristics of the major provenances of this species. Such work had not been done for *P.merkusii*, until undertaken by Cooling under this scheme. During a recent visit to the natural forests over much of the distribution of *P.merkusii*, a series of botanical, wood, bark, and resin samples of this heterogeneous species complex was obtained. These will help greatly to expand the evidence of provenance variations already provided by provenance trials in Zambia, and the evidence obtainable in trials of this species in South Africa, Malaya, Tanzania, Queensland (Australia) and Indonesia. To complete the survey of this species, visits will be necessary to Assam and Burma, and wood sampling will have to be done in exotic plantations as soon as they are old enough for wood testing.

Similar studies of *P.khasya* and *P.oocarpa* will follow. Much is already known about the former from Zambian experience. The slower growing, low altitude tropical pines (*P.tropicalis*, *P.cubensis* and *P.occidentalis*) have lower priority but are being included in species trials. The medium level species, *P.strobus* var *chiapensis* and *P.tenuifolia*, are border-line cases which will be given further study when the opportunity arises; they are already represented in several species trials.

TROPICAL HARDWOODS

Practical work on fast growing tropical hardwoods is at an earlier stage. Very few provenance trials have yet been planted, and very little has been done to test the wood properties of plantation-grown hardwoods. Work in this Institute on *G.arborea* has revealed its exceptional wood properties when grown fast in plantations. Approval is now awaited to commence a major test of Nigerian-grown *C.odorata* from a plantation at Sapoba now thirty-eight years old.

In order to reduce overlap of activities, close contact has been maintained with FAO, Rome, with tropical research stations in France, Australia, the Philippines, Malaya, India, Indonesia, East and Central and South Africa, Costa Rica, Puerto Rico, and with the Danish Co-ordinating Centre on Procurement of seed for Provenance Research at Humlebaek which is run by Mr. Barner, under the auspices of I.U.F.R.O. Our object is to offer a series of services to tropical countries which will assist them in developing productive timber plantations of the most suitable species and sub-species for their conditions, to promote regional tree improvement programmes, and to help to ensure that the wood produced is suitable for the industries using it.

REFERENCES

Luckhoff H.A. (1964) The natural distribution, growth and botanical variation of *Pinus caribaea* and its cultivation in South Africa. *Ann. Univ. Stellenbosch* **39** (1), 1–160.

Nikles D.G. (1966) Comparative variability and relationship of Caribbean pine (*Pinus caribaea* Mor.) and slash pine (*Pinus elliottii* Engelm). Thesis, (unpublished). North Carolina State University, Raleigh.

EXPLORATION, EVALUATION, UTILIZATION AND CONSERVATION OF EUCALYPT GENE RESOURCES

E. LARSEN* AND D. A. N. CROMER

Forest Research Institute,
Canberra, Australia.

THE GENUS EUCALYPTUS

The genus *Eucalyptus* is one of the largest and most complex genera of woody plants in the world. Blakely (1955) listed more than 1000 published species and varieties of which 675 were considered to be valid. Some 225 of these are now thought to be either hybrids or forms for which specific or varietal ranks are not justified (Johnston and Marryatt, 1965). About half a dozen new species are awaiting formal description, and more will undoubtedly be discovered. A division of the genus into two new genera: *Eucalyptus* and *Symphyomyrtus* has been suggested (Carr and Carr, 1962), but this has not been generally accepted by taxonomists.

EXPLORATION

The number of described species and varieties of Eucalypts is evidence of the genetical diversity of the genus. It is not possible here to give an account of the very large volume of work leading up to the present taxonomical classification of the genus. For the present purpose it may be accepted that some 450 nomenclative entities constitute the basic framework for further genetical investigation. The question to consider, then, is the nature and extent of genetical diversity within each species.

Studies of intra-specific variation fall into two groups:

1. Studies of variation in a population or a small section of the natural range: *E.pauciflora/niphophila/de beuzevillei* (Pryor, 1956), *E.regnans* (Eldridge, 1964), *E.gunnii* (Anon, 1961; Hillis and Koichiro, 1965; Marris, 1966), *E.urnigera* (Barber and Jackson, 1957; Hall *et al.*, 1965), *E.citriodora*, *E.dives*, *E.radiata* (Penfold

*The death of Egon Larsen during an expedition, on 29th April 1969, is announced with regret.

and *Morrison*, 1927; Willis, McKern and Hellyer, 1963), and *E.sideroxylon* (Hillis and Koichiro, 1965). Generally, these studies deal with the variation of one characteristic only, e.g., leaf dimensions, glaucousness (leaf waxes), essential oils or polyphenols:

2. Studies of variation of a species in its entire natural range of occurrence: *E.maculata* (Larsen, 1965), *E.camaldulensis* (Karschon, 1967; Larsen, 1967), and *E.pauciflora*. Studies in this category are dealt with in more detail under 'Utilization and Evaluation'.

The elucidation of the hybrid nature of many Eucalypts and the heritability of their distinguishing characteristics is largely due to Pryor. Hybrids are common in natural stands in Australia and possibly even more common in plantations in other countries where species that are geographically isolated in their natural habitat are brought together. Hybrid progeny generally exhibits a range of characteristics intermediate between the parent species, tending to break down the distinctions between species. This tendency towards genetic instability is only partially compensated for by breeding barriers between certain species groups (Pryor, 1959), and by species coherence (Hartley, 1965).

The natural Eucalypt forests rarely consist of only one species, but form complex patterns of several species with changes reflecting often minute differences in edaphic, topographical or climatic conditions. The balance is easily upset by changes brought about by fires, land clearing, or other causes. Elevational and/or latitudinal clines are common and are likely to exist in most species. Very few species, however, have a continuous distribution over a large area, and patterns of discontinuous variation are usually superimposed on the clinal pattern. Discontinuities which cannot be attributed to breaks in the natural occurrence of a species appear to be due largely to introgression. As far as is known, there is no case where gene mutation has been the suspected cause of variation.

Some of the widespread Eucalypts can be divided into major geographical 'races', e.g., *E.camaldulensis* (Karschon, 1967; Larsen, 1967), but these 'races' are too variable to be considered as units of sampling.

UTILIZATION AND EVALUATION

The utilization of the Eucalypts in world forestry has been largely at the species level, and until recent years little attention has been given to within-species variability. Early introductions in many countries consisted of small amounts of seed, originating no doubt in many cases from single parent trees in Australia. Some of these genetically 'narrow' plantations subsequently provided seed for extensive planting over whole regions, e.g., *E.microtheca* and *E.camaldulensis* in the Mediterranean. Some 100 Eucalypt species are now commonly planted in more than 50 countries. The most important species are '*E.alba*' in Brazil (not true *E.alba* but an undescribed species, probably originating in Timor) ; *E.camaldulensis* in arid zones in the Mediterranean, Pakistan, etc. ; *E.citriodora* ; *E.globulus* ; *E.grandis/saligna* in Africa ; *E.robusta* and *E.tereticornis* in India. In addition, the following species are important in more restricted regions, for planting under special conditions : *E.deglupta, gomphocephala, maidenii, microtheca, occidentalis, regnans* and *viminalis*.

The origin of the seed used to establish these Eucalypt plantations is generally not known, and it is difficult to estimate the extent to which the gene resource of a species has been utilized. It is, however, possible to make some general comments. In Australia, Eucalypt seed is collected from felled trees and if a species is not being logged commercially, seed would normally be collected from a tree cut for the purpose, or from trees with low branches. Heavy-crowned trees of poor form frequently carry the heaviest seed crop, and it is probable that this method involves a negative selection with respect to genes controlling stem form and branching habit. Seed of the main commercial species would in most cases have been collected from logging areas, and as only the best trees are cut for logs, some degree of positive selection for stem form, vigour, branching habit, and timber quality is likely to have been the result. Eucalypt seeds are very small, and a single tree may easily yield 5 lb of seed which, for a species such as *E.grandis*, would equal about 3 million viable seeds, or sufficient seed to plant about 2,000 acres of forest. The implication is that many of the early introductions are bound to have originated from a single parent tree, and for some of the rare species it is quite conceivable that all stands planted outside Australia could be single tree progenies. The further spread of original introductions can be very rapid as most Eucalypts produce seed at a very early age.

Some Eucalypts are thought to have developed into local 'strains' under cultivation. Examples of this are *E.'saligna'* or '*saligna/grandis*' in Africa (possibly *E.grandis* of Queensland origin) ; *E.'C'* in Zanzibar which is probably *E.tereticornis* from northern New South Wales ; the

'Mysore Hybrid' in India, another form of *tereticornis* (Boden, 1964);
E.trabuti in Italy, known to be hybrid forms of *E.botryoides* and *E.
camaldulensis*. It has been suggested that *E.camaldulensis* in Israel is of
South Australian origin (Karschon, 1967), and this appears quite
likely, but recent work has shown that its leaves contain three polyphenols which have not been found in the species anywhere in Australia.
This lends support to the suggestion that *E.camaldulensis* in Israel has
developed into a distinct form not found in the natural habitat.

The systematic testing of different seed sources (provenances) of
Eucalypts did not commence until 1964. In that year the New South
Wales Forestry Commission established trials of *E.cloeziana*, *maculata* and
pilularis in several localities throughout the State. Trial plantations of
these and many other species have since been established in some 25
countries in all parts of the world. The species and number of provenances which have been collected by the Forest Research Institute
in Canberra for distribution to other countries are as follows:

E. *alba*	15	*kingsmillii*	3
amplifolia	2	*maculata*	6
blakelyi	3	*nitens*	4
botryoides	3	*pilularis*	18
brevifolia	3	*pruinosa*	2
camaldulensis	50	*radiata* var. *australiana*	4
citriodora	6	*rudis*	3
cloeziana	2	*saligna*	8
dalrympleana	1	*seeana*	2
deanei	3	*tereticornis*	12
dives var. 'C'	2	*viminalis*	3
grandis	7	Undescribed Exsertae	5

The oldest trials are still too young to provide reliable evidence of
differences in growth rate and other aspects of importance to forestry.
Morphological differences between seedlings, however, are of considerable magnitude and indicate that plantations of different seed
origin of the same species may have significantly different potential for
utilization in practical forestry. Significant differences in tolerance to
frost and soil salinity have been demonstrated in *E.camaldulensis*
(Larsen, 1967).

CONSERVATION

The conservation of *Eucalyptus* gene resources may be dealt with in
two ways: (1) Preservation of representative natural stands, or (2)

establishment of trees or populations in regional centres in Australia and elsewhere.

In dedicated forest areas the gene pool is largely intact. Eucalypt forests in Australia are as a rule replaced by natural regeneration, and planting is very limited. Outside State Forests, or National Parks, the conservation of Eucalypts is a matter of urgency for some species threatened by extensive land clearing for agriculture. However, up to the present time fairly wide strips of the natural vegetation have been preserved along the roads for the droving of sheep and cattle. With increasing motorized transportation, and the extent of wheat growing in whole regions, such reserves may not be retained in future land development schemes. For the vast majority of Eucalypts, however, there is not much danger of any serious depletion of the natural gene resource during the next few decades.

The conservation of Eucalypt gene resources *in situ* is essential, but for most purposes of study and utilization, it is of course necessary to bring the material together in central collections. The Technical Commission on Tree Improvement and Afforestation, 6th World Forestry Congress, 1966, recommended that 'Regional centres for the preservation of genetic stocks should be developed under F.A.O. organization and within the framework of the germ plasm conservation program being envisaged by F.A.O.'

The systematic collection of Eucalypt seed for seed origin research started in 1963 and the Forest Research Institute now maintains a collection team for this purpose. The work has so far been concentrated mainly on species of commercial importance either in Australia or in other countries. The main object is to provide seed of a range of provenances of each species so as to enable the growers to determine the most suitable seed sources for use in subsequent plantation establishment. The work may be summarized as follows:

Study of the species and described varieties, survey of the natural range of occurrence, and determination of sampling intensity.

Collection of seed, botanical specimens and wood samples from 10 trees in each locality.

Permanent marking of parent trees, or preservation of these by grafting.

Establishment of seedlings of each parent.

Study of variation of parent material and seedlings.

Distribution of seed to other countries.

This work is carried out in accordance with the recommendations made by the 'Working Group on Provenance Research and Testing' of Section 22 of I.U.F.R.O. (Vyskot, 1964). The main problems are the determination of sampling intensity, and the preservation of the seed parents. 'Gene pool' or 'gene resource' are terms which are difficult to define and consequently the exact determination of sampling intensity is not possible. In the present program of work, the aim is to sample a number of trees which may reasonably be considered to represent the range of variation in characteristics relevant to forestry practice. Regionally, collection points are decided on the basis of known morphological variation of the species, geographical and climatical features of its natural range, and zones of overlap with closely related species. In addition, attempts are made to sample optimum areas as well as areas where the species is under environmental stress of one kind or another. Each collection is made from 10 trees in an area of from 5 to several hundred acres. Material is collected from the best available trees selected for straightness of stem, vigour and branching habit. Thus, the sampling is in no sense random and probably results in only a partial representation of the total gene pool.

The permanent marking of seed parents is possible only when collection can be made from standing trees, and the preservation of such trees in Australia presents many problems. For these reasons it is considered desirable to reproduce the seed trees vegetatively and plant them in special clone orchards. It is at present not possible to root cuttings from mature Eucalypts, and grafting has been only moderately successful. The main difficulty is to get the scion material from the point of collection to the grafting site in a satisfactory condition. Pieces of semi-woody branchlets wrapped in plastic and air-mailed generally arrive in usable condition during cool weather, but often deteriorate during the hot summer months. Tip-cleft grafting onto young, vigorously growing root-stock is used, and temperature and humidity control in the glass house is necessary for a good take. Mortality after planting-out is heavy, possibly due to root-stock-scion incompatibility.

This collection work is being supported financially by F.A.O., and the seeds are distributed gratis. The establishment of replicated trials is now proceeding on a large scale in many countries. The level of testing of the different seed origins of a species varies from the establishment of plots of single-tree progenies to plots of regionally grouped provenances representing some 100 parent trees each. Thus, the extent to which these provenance trial plantations can be utilized as gene resource archives will vary from country to country. It would, however, be a fairly simple matter to set up a formal system for registering and classifying these plantations in a central Eucalypt register.

FUTURE WORK

The genus *Eucalyptus* represents a vast natural gene resource which the world has barely begun to exploit. Natural stands occur from latitude 43°S in Tasmania to 7°N in the Philippines, from the humid tropics to the arid desert in Central Australia, and in the alpine environemnt of the Snowy Mountains. Tree form ranges from the small many-stemmed mallees to some of the tallest trees in the world, and the genus yields timbers suitable for practically any use to which wood can be put. The natural range of occurrence varies from a few square miles for some species to some 2 million square miles for others (*E.camaldulensis*).

The exploration, utilization and conservation of the gene resources of some 450 Eucalypt species is obviously an enormous task. The first essential step is to study in detail the intra-specific variation of each species. Studies of this nature are known to be in progress for *E.obliqua*, *E.propinqua-punctata*, *E.regnans*, *E.tereticornis*, *E.viminalis*, and with the electronic data processing techniques developed in recent years, major progress can be expected in this field of research during the next decade. The collection of material for this kind of research can easily be combined with the collection of seed, which opens the way for the testing and utilization of the gene resource in plantation forestry. Seed collection is already progressing fairly rapidly and will continue at a somewhat increased pace in future years. Regional arboreta are not contemplated at present in Australia, except for the dozen or so species of major commercial importance, and these are likely to be mainly in the form of provenance test plantations. Numerous such provenance trials are being established in many countries at the present time, and some thought should be given to ways of developing them into permanent gene archives. The establishment of special regional gene pool collections divorced from practical forestry does not appear feasible at present.

In view of the very limited manpower, funds and facilities that are available for work of this nature, it is important that botanical collection, seed collection, study of variation, testing of seed sources, and conservation should not be dealt with independently by different workers and organizations. To avoid duplication, it is desirable that these related aspects of the work be coordinated as far as possible.

REFERENCES

ANON. (1961) Bibliography on Eucalypts. *IInd Wld. Eucalyptus Conf.*, Brazil.

BARBER H.N. & JACKSON W.D. (1957) Natural selection in action in *Eucalyptus*. *Nature, Lond.* **179**, 1267–1279.

BLAKELY W.F. (1955) *A Key to the Eucalyptus*. Forestry and Timber Bureau, Canberra, 1st. Ed.

BODEN R.W. (1964) Hybridisation in *Eucalyptus. Indian Forester* **90**, 581–586.

CARR S.G.M. & CARR D.J. (1962) Convergence and progression in *Eucalyptus* and *Symphyomyrtus. Nature, Lond.* **196**, 969-972.

ELDRIDGE K.G. (1964) Breeding *Eucalyptus regnans*—Five year progress report. *Forestry* **28**, 34–50.

HALL D.M., MATUS A.I., LAMBERTON J.A. & BARBER H.N. (1965) Infra-specific variation in wax on leaf surfaces. *Aust. J. biol. Sci.* **18**, 323–332.

HARTLEY J. (1965) Coherence in *Eucalyptus. Aust. J. biol. Sci.* **18**, 190–192.

HILLIS W.E. & KOICHIRO I. (1965) Variation in the chemical composition of *Eucalyptus sideroxylon. Phytochemistry* **4**, 541–550.

JOHNSTON R.D. & MARRYATT R. (1965) Taxonomy and nomenclature of Eucalypts. Forestry and Timber Bureau Canberra, Leaflet 92.

KARSCHON R. (1967) Ecotypic variation in *Eucalyptus camaldulensis*. In *Contributions on Eucalypts in Israel III*. Nat. Univ. Inst. Agr. Ilanoth.

LARSEN E. (1965) A study of the variability of *E. maculata* and *E. citriodara*. Forestry and Timber Bureau, Canberra, Leaflet 95.

LARSEN E. (1967) Geographic variation in *E. camaldulensis*. ANZAAS Conference, Melbourne, (Unpublished).

MARRIS B. (1966) A bibliography of Australian references to Eucalypts 1965–1966. Forestry and Timber Bureau, (mimeo).

PENFOLD A.F. & MORRISON F.R. (1927) The occurrence of a number of varieties of *Eucalyptus dives* as determined by chemical analysis of the essential oils. *J. Proc. R. Soc. N.S.W.* **61**, 54–67.

PRYOR L.D. (1956) Variation in Snow Gum (*E. pauciflora*). *Proc. Linn. Soc. N.S.W.* **81**, 299–305.

PRYOR L.D. (1959) Evolution in *Eucalyptus. Aust. J. Sci.* **22**, 45–48.

VYSKOT M. (1964) Standardization of methods for provenance research and testing. In *Proc. World Consultation on Forest Genetics, Stockholm, FAO FORGEN*-63, **1**, 3/5, 1–7.

WILLIS J.I.., McKERN H.H.G. & HELLYER R.O. (1963) The volatile oils of the genus *Eucalyptus* (Fam. *Myrtaceae*). *J. Proc. R. Soc. N.S.W.* **96**, 59–64.

32

GENETIC RESOURCES FOR SILVICULTURAL USE IN RELATION TO POPLAR AND SOME TROPICAL SPECIES

L. D. PRYOR

Department of Botany,
Australian National University, Canberra, Australia

Compared with agriculture, forestry is singularly deficient in the array of plant material available for silvicultural use and this critically limits what is available for plantation establishment. It is evident that there is a need for considerable innovation in silviculture, and some of the possibilities are foreshadowed by the extraordinary development or work with poplar in the last few decades. With this group of trees and with willows, there is indeed a need for the collection, conservation and exploitation of gene resources in much the same way as for a number of cereal crops. This need in poplar is better known, and can be more adequately set out, by those dealing intensively with the genus in Europe; but a few comments upon the problem as it is seen from outside Europe may be warranted, to indicate the silvicultural potential which almost certainly resides in certain groups of tropical species.

POPLAR

Poplar is of particular importance in forestry because of the innovation it introduces into silvicultural practice. The special features associated with poplar culture are likely to be of great import in the future development of plant material for forest use. In broad terms, the value of poplar lies in the fact that it can be propagated clonally; that there are continentally separated species, hybrids between which have distinct advantages; that it is possible to use intensive cultural techniques on land of agricultural quality; and that the wood produced has intrinsic qualities which meet a wide range of current and possible future technological needs.

Because of its particular importance, some considerable effort has already been made to bring basic material together in collections to

conserve it for future exploitation and use. The Populetum Mediter-
raneum near Rome is a very good example of such a collection. Nevertheless, in spite of the effort that has been put into this, it still merits
considerable amplification and it is certainly desirable that there
should be more than one such collection on a world basis. For example,
as evidence of a need for further collection, one may note that it is only
relatively recently that material of different genetic background from
within the wide-ranging and important species, *Populus deltoides*, of the
United States, has been added to this collection and even such additions
are far from complete.

It is evident that poplar has been cultivated for very long periods in
Asia and scattered about amongst relatively isolated communities from
the Mediterranean to India, and probably through other parts of Asia
into China; there are clones which have been selected in the past and
which are still cultivated for local use. A systematic exploration and
collection of these would be of inestimable value and would complement
the rather meagre collections so far made by the sporadic efforts of collectors who have often worked under considerable difficulty, and by
taking advantage of travel opportunities have made such collections
almost by chance.

In addition to clones which are in cultivation, or have survived from
ancient cultivation, such as the Maktar White Poplar in Tunisia, there
are certain relatively isolated species which should be preserved in collections. For example, a species, presumably a part of *Populus euphratica*,
occurs naturally in Kenya at high elevations near the equator. In view
of the importance of day length response in poplars, the opportunity to
obtain propagating and breeding material of this species is of very considerable importance, but so far this has remained inaccessible. Likewise, *Populus ciliata* growing in the Himalaya has been obtained only
with considerable difficulty, and it has a somewhat similar importance.
In such cases, at the most, an isolated collection has been made and no
opportunity has so far existed to sample populations over the range of
the species.

A special place is occupied by *Populus yunnanensis*. This appears in
cultivation in most places apparently only as a single male clone. It has
importance because, like the southern extension of *P.deltoides* in Texas,
it is found in low latitudes. It hybridizes readily with the black poplar
group, and therefore it would be of considerable value to assemble
material this species collected from a range of provenances (which

are probably fragmentary) in south-west China. The same is no doubt true of other Chinese species.

TROPICAL SPECIES

The almost unique situation with poplar leads to a consideration of an important way in which plant material might be developed for future silvicultural use. Special features in poplar are that the trees produce timber which is low in density, light in colour, without marked structural features, and which peels readily into rotary veneer. In addition, they grow quickly, respond to intensive cultural treatment, can be propagated from cuttings and thrive in full sunlight. There is virtually no other presently grown forest crop which is managed silviculturally in the way that poplar is handled. Yet in the large array of tropical species, in the main so far scarcely exploited at all, it is probable that there are several with some or all of these features. In many cases, though timber quality is known in a general way, the capacity for vegetative propagation is a complete unknown, so that a first step is to obtain seed from a number of species throughout their range, test them for capacity to propagate vegetatively, and then proceed with cultural and technological tests.

In searching for species which combine the capacity to endure full sunlight and which at the same time have rapid growth, (two essentials in the choice of material for use as contemplated) it is likely that those species which are characteristic of second growth forest in the tropics are the ones to provide the answer. Amongst such there are several which have light coloured wood of even texture and low density and peel satisfactorily. Often these are regarded as weed species and while some of them are indeed useless, others have timber qualities which modern needs demand, though they find little or no place in the traditional wood-using industries. In Australia and South East Asia the following preliminary list has been prepared of species that in the main meet these requirements :

> *Anthocephalus cadamba*
> *Endospermum moluccanum*
> *Elaeocarpus sphericus*
> *Trema* spp.
> *Hibiscus papuodendron*
> *Albizzia moluccanum*
> *Alstonia actinophylla*

Canaga spp.
Piptadenia novaguiniaensis
Canarium australe
Cordia dichotoma

Without special effort it is usually particularly difficult to obtain seed and propagating material of tropical species of this type, even as single collections ; and unless it were part of a deliberate programme, it would be virtually impossible to obtain a range of samples throughout their natural distribution range, or indeed, in many cases, to obtain any seed at all. Nothing is known about the capacity of any of them to strike from cuttings for silvicultural use, and since vegetative propagation is vital to such a programme, this must be tested concurrently with any screening which is contemplated. The above list has been prepared in a quite preliminary way. A well developed programme seeking the silvicultural innovation that would result from selecting species which produce wood of desired characteristics from trees which have the necessary silvicultural characteristics, including vegetative propagation, could be done effectively on a world basis only if a carefully prepared programme is organized. This could take the following course :

> Screening records of species characteristic of tropical second growth to select those which have the desired wood and growth features.
>
> Collection of seed and other propagating material for testing capacity for vegetative reproduction, at appropriate centres.
>
> Building up reserve collections for subsequent evaluation and utilization.
>
> Carrying out more detailed surveys, collections and tests to provide more precisely selected material from within the group of species subsequently designated as meeting the necessary requirements.

SECTION 4
EVALUATION AND UTILIZATION

EVALUATION AND UTILIZATION— INTRODUCTORY REMARKS

O. H. FRANKEL

Division of Plant Industry, CSIRO, Canberra,
Australia

This section deals with the characterization, evaluation and utilization of plant material which results from exploring and collecting activities. It does not attempt to present a detailed treatment of this large and diverse subject; an adequate treatment of evaluation alone would require a multi-disciplinary textbook. This introduction and the chapters which follow attempt to present an outline of general principles, problems and approaches, illustrated where possible by practical experiences. As in other sections, the discussion is confined to wild species and to primitive cultigens, (i.e. cultivated material which has not resulted from selection by plant breeders).

When plant material is introduced from elsewhere, there are risks of introducing diseases, pests or weeds, hence plant quarantine procedures must be applied (chapter 34 by Kahn). If not done previously, the introductions are classified and recorded, prior to being examined, tested and evaluated (chapter 35 by Hyland). In some countries a national body accepts responsibility for plant introduction (chapter 36 by Hartley), though not necessarily for all phases of evaluation. Introductions are either for direct use, or for recombination with adapted types (chapter 37 by Krull and Borlaug). Perhaps the most extensive use of primitive and especially of wild material has been in the breeding for resistance to diseases and pests, and the search for various kinds of resistance is likely to be intensified in the future (chapter 38 by Watson). The ease of transfer of genetic elements from wild to domesticated material depends on cytogenic and genetic relationships between the respective species. Such relationships have been discussed in several chapters of section 1, where also references to relevant literature can be found.

At some stage there will arise the need for multiplication to provide material for tests and for distribution to others. This, and some of the other steps outlined in this section, require careful planning and a workable organization. The remarks which follow are to serve as a general introduction to the subject.

EVALUATION AND UTILIZATION—INTERACTIONS

Introductions are used either directly, i.e. in their original form, sometimes after selection ; or as parental material, often in combination with locally adapted types. Needless to say, these different purposes necessitate different processes of evaluation.

Direct use of introduced *wild material* is confined to types of plants which themselves have not been thoroughly 'domesticated'—forest trees, pasture, medicinal and many ornamental plants. Fitness, or general adaptation, in the new environment is clearly an essential requirement ; productivity may be improved by selection and recombination.

In most countries and situations, the direct use of introduced *primitive cultivars* is now probably confined to horticultural species, where the borderline between 'primitive' and 'advanced' types is not as sharp as in agricultural crops.* But this was not the case until the second half of last century, when the first cultivars were being developed from local or introduced land races, and when towards the end of the century cross-breeding began in England, France, Sweden, Australia, Germany, the United States and Canada, which started a new era of crop improvement.

In all agriculturally advanced countries, and in most agricultural and many horticultural crops, a plateau of productivity was reached which, until recently, has not been substantially raised, except by the incorporation of 'resistance genes' conferring resistance to pests, diseases or agronomic hazards. The general structure of 'production characters' (Frankel, 1947), i.e. plant characteristics relating to yield, such as the number of heads or of grains, or the weight of a grain, have as a rule not been drastically or at any rate deliberately, changed.† This, it would appear, may have been the result of the narrowing of the effective parental gene pools.

*Where cultivation expands into areas beyond the normal ecological range of a species, as may well happen under pressure of increasing population, primitive cultivars from comparable stress environments may provide at least the raw materials for development of adapted cultivars.

†The one major exception, heterosis breeding, is not relevant to this discussion.

The history of wheat breeding in Australia and New Zealand presents illustrations of both closing and extending parental gene pools. In Australia, out of the large number of varieties that had been introduced in the first 60 years of wheat breeding, in 1948–49 all the then prominent varieties had descended from a mere handful of primary introductions, and very nearly all the new introductions which had been used in the preceding twenty years had contributed mainly disease resistance genes transferred by back crossing. By contrast, New Zealand had been able to use varieties introduced from Mediterranen and Western European countries. Yields were high, and, with no major disease problems, cross-breeding was not started till the late twenties. A deliberate attempt was then made to raise yields directly, i.e. through improvement of 'production characters', using a number of widely different stocks in multiple crosses with adapted varieties. The attempt was successful, with yield levels raised by over 20 per cent, whereas in Australia the 'closing of the ring' appeared to have inhibited further progress. Clearly, tremendous progress had been made in the earlier years in the quest for adaptation to the harsh Australian environment ; and in later years the understandable preoccupation with rapidly evolving rust fungi seemed to overshadow other avenues for raising productivity. Indeed, when a high level of adaptation is reached the plant breeder is all the more reluctant to run the risk of breaking it up. Such conservatism leads ultimately to an evolutionary cul-de-sac (Frankel, 1954).

In this situation the obvious alternative would be 'infiltration' with genotypes likely to improve the production characters. But there is an even bolder possibility. It could scarcely be suggested that the few primary parents which constituted the Australian gene pool were the only or even the best possible sources for the successful adaptation of wheat in Australia. Indeed, there is a possibility that other material might have facilitated even further progress.

This situation is by no means unique ; and in many countries modern cultivars have a relatively narrow genetic base. The question might be asked whether it 'might . . . not be worth while starting again, with the greater gene resources of the world's wheat now available to draw upon,' to go back to 'primitive' sources for new pathways of adaptation (Frankel, l.c.).

Some encouragement comes from one of the most striking instances of a yield increase *per se* in contemporary plant breeding other than heterosis breeding—the high-yielding semi-dwarf and dwarf wheats developed in the United States and in Mexico (Vogel, Allan and Peterson, 1963; Borlaug, 1958). These new varieties derive from the Japanese wheat Norin 10 their short straw (the reason for the choice of this wheat as a parent), but, in addition, 'an exceptionally high tillering capacity and a consistently higher number of fertile florets per spikelet' were incorporated as 'fringe benefits' (Krull and Borlaug, chapter 37). These benefits, as the authors remark, are proving of great value even where lodging does not occur. An analogous improvement in yielding capacity was achieved in the production of the new short-strawed Philippine rice variety, IR8 (International Rice Research Institute, 1967). Just as the valuable yield characteristics were incorporated as a fortunate by-product, so it is possible that the vast, as yet unexploited gene pools of primitive cultigens contain potential but as yet unexplored contributions to 'production breeding'. Production characters are the resultant of many physiological processes which are only beginning to be understood. It is possible that the long duration and diversity of conditions under which the primitive agricultural flora has evolved, have resulted in various pathways which in the context of present-day genotypes may be of great value.

There are then three ways in which primitive and wild material can be utilized, and although they overlap and interact, they call for different attitudes and methods of evaluation.

(1) Introductions for direct use—forest trees, pasture species etc. These are examined for adaptation and economic fitness (i.e. productivity, quality characteristics, growth type, growth rhythm, quality of various kinds, susceptibility to diseases and pests, etc.; see chapter 35 by Hyland).

(2) Introductions which are to confer particular characteristics to adapted cultivars to improve their agronomic or economic fitness. In this case general adaptation is less relevant than the genetic background —there may be 'fringe benefits' or detrimental linkages (chapter 37 by Krull and Borlaug). This type of utilization is now, and is likely to remain, the most prominent way in which primitive material of domesticated species is used, and the only way for the use of wild relatives of such species. Evaluation may include a great variety of tests ranging from morphological and observational examination to phytopathological, physiological and biochemical tests (see chapter 35 by Hyland).

(3) Introductions to increase productivity *per se*, irrespective of resistance to physical or biotic components of the environment. The role of introductions may range from 'infiltration' into adapted genotypes to

complete reconstruction of adaptation *de novo*. Evaluation for 'production potential' is difficult to specify at the present state of our knowledge. A pragmatic test might be derived from tests for combining ability (Finlay, 1964). However, an analytical approach is emerging from the growing understanding of some physiological processes relevant to productivity (cf. Frankel, 1969). Notwithstanding the great difficulties of evaluation, an empirical approach is open by means of composite cross populations (Harlan, 1956). Populations derived from multiple crosses among selected groups of primitive parents could not only provide useful material, but may shed light on the potential of such an approach, especially if complemented by tests for combining ability.

Reference to the examination and testing for specific characteristics is made in several chapters of this book, especially by Creech (chapter 17), Hyland (chapter 35) and Brezhnev (Appendix). The diversity of the subjects and in many instances the highly technical nature of the tests emphasize the need for a multidisciplinary approach, and, to keep abreast of advancing science, the participation of a variety of research institutes. Moreover, as stressed by Krull and Borlaug in chapter 37, some tests require to be conducted in different environments. This is most important for the unravelling of the true potential of a genotype—be it disease resistance, as emphasized by Krull and Borlaug, or adaptability over a range of environments, or adaptation to specific environments such as high or low moisture, temperature or nutrient status. Few countries have the size and the resources to satisfy these requirements. In consequence, *international collaboration* in evaluation is not only desirable, but essential.

This co-operation, as is also stressed in several chapters, but especially in chapter 39 by Finlay and Konzak, must be complemented by an international records and retrieval system which alone can make all the results emerging from evaluation anywhere in the world available for all. There is no nation which does not stand to gain from such an approach.

MULTIPLICATION

The need for multiplication may arise any time after a collection is made. It is nearly always attended by trouble, risk or loss—trouble in growing and harvesting, risk of contamination, of infection, or loss through natural selection—the nature and extent of these difficulties depending on a number of factors:

(i) size of original sample. The larger the original sample, the easier and safer it is to test, conserve and multiply. Collections of wild material are often so small that they must be multiplied even for conservation*, let alone evaluation. There should be less difficulty with cultigens; but being populations, they may contain rare components.

(ii) reproductive system. Prevention of unwanted hybridization during multiplication is as essential as it is difficult.

(iii) environmental conditions should favour survival and reproduction of all components. This necessitates careful site selection, and sometimes duplication of sites to reduce the bias of natural selection at any one site. Some wild plants are exceedingly hard to grow outside their natural range. It may be necessary to arrange for multiplication sites that are climatically suited as well as convenient.

(iv) protection against fungous, bacterial or virus diseases for all multi-plications is necessary and in some instances essential.

A number of procedural principles apply generally.

(1) Splitting versus pooling. A decision has to be made in each case whether, and to what extent, a collected sample should be separated into component parts if there are recognizable variants, whether it should be treated as a unit, or whether it should be pooled with other samples related to it ecologically or genetically. This decision should not be made solely or mainly on grounds of convenience, for it cannot be undone at a later stage unless reserves have been stored. In some circumstances, it may be sounder to reduce the number of strains to be multiplied rather than to combine them. In this decision the reproductive system will be a major factor. In general it is advisable to delay pooling of strains till after their evaluation and characterisation is completed (cf. Allard p. 493). Evaluation can be extended over a number of years by the retention of individual strains in storage.

(2) Conservation *versus* evaluation and distribution. It is advisable to make provision for *conservation* at the earliest stage, i.e. from the original material wherever possible. If multiplication of material for conserva-tion is inevitable, every precaution should be taken to preserve its integrity as far as this is possible (cf. chapter 40 on conservation). Larger quantities are needed when multiplication is made for *evaluation* and for *distribution* to other institutions. Size in itself reduces some of the

---

*Reproduction of original samples may also become necessary when seed has been collected in a state which renders it unfit for long-term storage, as may be unavoidable during collecting expeditions (cf. chapter 43, p. 506).

intrinsic hazards of multiplication ; nor is there quite the same need for extreme care. Thus one may envisage two separate streams, one for conservation, to be drawn upon if and when required, the other for evaluation and general distribution. It is advisable to retain adequate stocks of the latter in first-rate storage, so as to reduce as far as possible the trouble, expense and risk attendant upon multiplication.

(3) Methods and facilities. Methods and facilities for multiplication of introductions are not different from those commonly used in the breeding of the respective plants. Similarly, facilities required correspond to those of well-equipped plant breeding stations. These may include greenhouses, isolation houses, and ample facilities for the control of fertilization. There must be an adequate and experienced professional and technical staff; the requirements outlined by Hawkes (p. 496ff.) apply generally.

REFERENCES

BORLAUG N.E. (1958) The impact of agricultural research on Mexican wheat production. *Trans. N.Y. Ac. Sci.* **20**, 278–295.

FINLAY K.W. (1964) Adaptation—its measurement and significance in barley breeding. *Proc. First Int. Barley Gen. Symp.* 351–359.

FRANKEL O.H. (1947) The theory of plant breeding for yield. *Heredity* **1**, 109–120.

FRANKEL O.H. (1954) Invasion and evolution of plants in Australia and New Zealand. *Caryologia*, **6**, *Suppl.* 600–619.

FRANKEL O.H. (1969) The dynamics of plant breeding. *Proceedings of XII International Congress of Genetics*, Vol. 3 (in press).

HARLAN J.R. (1956) Distribution and utilization of natural variability in cultivated plants. *Brookhaven Symp. Biol.* **9**, 191–206.

INTERNATIONAL RICE RESEARCH INSTITUTE (1967) Annual Report, 1966. Los Banos.

VOGEL O.A., ALLAN, R.E. & PETERSON C.J. (1963) Plant and performance characteristics of semidwarf winter wheats producing most efficiently in Eastern Washington. *Agron. Jour.* **55**, 397–398.

INTERNATIONAL PLANT QUARANTINE

ROBERT P. KAHN

U.S. Plant Introduction Station,
Glenn Dale, Maryland.

INTRODUCTION

The objectives of international plant quarantine in connection with any plant gene collection and conservation program are to provide safeguards against inadvertently upsetting the balance of nature in a given country or region. Man's previous experience in disrupting this system of checks and balances has resulted in devastating losses to human, plant, and animal life such as : the introduction of rabbits into Australia ; Klamath weed into Canada, the United States and Australia ; measles into Africa ; Japanese beetles into the United States, and both giant snails and foot-and-mouth virus into many countries.

In characterizing destructive pests and pathogens that reach such epidemic proportions when introduced into new regions, we often use the terms 'risks' and 'hazards'. 'Risks' are defined as pests or pathogens of quarantine significance, i.e., those that are not known to occur in a country or if they do occur, they are not yet widely distributed. Some noteworthy risks include :

> The coffee rust fungus, *Hemileia vastatrix* Berk. and Br.—not known in Central and South America.
>
> The cacao witches' broom fungus, *Marasmius perniciosus* Stahel.—not reported in Africa.
>
> The tobacco veinal necrosis strain of potato virus Y—not known to be in the U.S. or Canada.

'Hazards' may be defined as risks which have gained entrance and become established, resulting in extensive damage to crops. Some organisms in this group are :

> Grape phylloxera aphid, *Viteus vitifoliae* Fitch. (United States to Europe).
>
> European corn borer, *Catrinia nubilalis* (Rubn.) (Europe to North America).
>
> Downy mildew fungus, *Plasmopara viticola* Berk. and Curt. Berl. and Det. (United States to France).

Chestnut blight fungus, *Endothia parasitica* (Murr.) P.J. & H.W. Anderson. (Asia to United States and Europe).

Sigatoka disease of banana caused by *Cerespora musae* Zimm., first noted in Java and introduced into many banana-growing areas.

Blue mold of tobacco fungus, *Peronospora tabacina* Adam. (Australia into Europe).

A given pest or pathogen may be classified as either a risk or hazard depending on geographic location. In Madagascar the occurrence of the Fiji disease of sugarcane may be considered a hazard since it has already been introduced from the Fiji Islands. However, the occurrence is considered a risk for the rest of Africa since it is not known to occur on the continent.

LEGAL BASIS FOR PLANT INTRODUCTION QUARANTINE

The legal basis for quarantine in connection with plant introduction may be found in the International Plant Protection Convention, inter-governmental agreements that set up plant protection bodies, or in regulations issued by departments or ministries of agriculture.

The International Plant Protection Convention (Ling, 1953) was approved at the 6th FAO Conference in Rome, Nov.—Dec. 1951. Fortyfour countries are parties to this convention.

Inter-governmental plant protection bodies organized within the framework of FAO and in conformity with the FAO Constitution include: (a) Plant Protection Committee for South East Asia and the Pacific Region (FAO, 1965a; O'Connor, 1961; South Pacific Commission, 1964); and (b) Near East Plant Protection Commission (FAO, 1965b). In addition the organization of a Caribbean Plant Protection Organization (Anon, 1965) has been proposed for establishment within the framework of FAO.

International governmental plant protection bodies with agreements approved by the various governments but not within the framework of FAO include: (a) Organismo Internacional Regional de Sanidad Agropecuaria (Organismo Internacional Regional de Sanidad Agropecuaria, 1961); (b) Comite Interamericano de Proteccion Agropecuaria; (c) Organizacion Bolivariana de Sanidad Agropecuaria; (d) European and Mediterranean Plant Protection Organization (European and Mediterranean Plant Protection Organization, Annual Report 1965) and (e) Inter-African Phytosanitary Commission (Inter-African Phytosanitary Commission, 1962; Inter-African Phytosanitary Commission, 1965). FAO co-operates with all these organizations.

QUARANTINE STATUS OF PLANT INTRODUCTION

When plants are received at an inspection station or port of entry, we recommend that they be placed in one of four categories with respect to their quarantine status : (a) absolute prohibition : (b) quarantine : (c) post-entry quarantine : (d) restricted entry. Since these terms may have different meanings in different countries, we define them as follows :

(a) *Absolute prohibition.* Genera imported from foreign countries are placed in absolute prohibition category when the risk of introducing pests and pathogens is so great that importation should be denied even to government services. Absolute quarantine is invoked by the importing country when there are no adequate safeguards and when isolation from commercial crop production is not feasible. For example, the Southwest Pacific Commission recommends an absolute prohibition against coconuts from 8 specified geographic areas because of diseases of obscure origin such as Cadang-oadang in the Philippines (South Pacific Commission, 1964).

(b) *Quarantine.* Genera imported from a given country are placed in the quarantine category when pests or pathogens have been reported on these genera in that country. Where such quarantines are authorized, safeguards consist of trained personnel, adequate methods of detection, phytosanitation, and quarantine facilities. Admission of plants under quarantine is usually reserved for government services and is not available to the general public. In the United States, the term 'prohibited genera' is used for the term 'quarantine' since the entry of these genera is prohibited to all but the Department of Agriculture.

(c) *Post-entry quarantine.* Genera are placed under post-entry quarantine when pests and pathogens have been reported in some but not all foreign countries but the importation originates from a country where such risks have not been reported. Safeguards consist of inspection upon arrival and during the post-entry quarantine which may be maintained on the premises of the importer. Post-entry quarantine is available to government services as well as public and private institutions or qualified individuals whose facilities meet post-entry quarantine requirements but may not be to the general public.

(d) *Restricted entry.* All genera that are admissible, i.e., those not excluded by absolute prohibition or detained at quarantine stations should be considered 'restricted'. 'Restricted' is defined as subject to inspection and treatment upon arrival at a port of entry or inspection station. Restricted plants may be received by the general public. Safeguards consist of inspection and treatment, if necessary, upon arrival.

MAINTAINING THE QUARANTINE

Having defined the four categories, we will be concerned in the remainder of this discussion with only the quarantine category which pertains to genera that originate in countries where pests and pathogens of quarantine significance are known to occur. It should be emphasized here that the importation of quarantined genera should be confined to plants for scientific or research purposes and not permitted for commercial importations.

A. *Quarantine regulations*. The details of these regulations need not be discussed here since they have been abstracted and summarized for all countries (Inter-African Phytosanitary Commission, 1962; Ling, 1952; Ling, 1954; Sheffield, Dickinson and Boundford, 1964; South Pacific Commission, 1964; USDA, 1955). Procedures for handling introductions have also been described in detail (Inter-African Phytosanitary Commission, 1962; O'Connor, 1961; Sheffield, 1955; Sheffield, 1958; South Pacific Commission, 1964; USDA; Kahn, 1967). However, in general, the regulations of various countries have several features in common. They usually :

specify prohibitions

require import permits

require phytosanitary certificates which stipulate inspection during the growing season and may require additional declarations about freedom from certain pests

require certificates of origin

stipulate inspection on arrival

prescribe treatment upon arrival to eliminate a risk

prescribe quarantine or post-entry quarantine if a risk is involved.

These regulations have been instituted by governments as phytosanitary actions for the most part directed against large or commercial shipments. It should be feasible to set up regulations and procedures to expedite the introduction of research plant materials into countries or regions.

B. *Quarantine facilities*. The type of quarantine facilities depends on the climate at the introduction station, the crop and its temperature requirements, pest and pathogen risks, and duration of the quarantine period as it affects plant size. Obviously, potato (cool temperature, dormant period, quarantine for 2 growing seasons) requires different facilities than does citrus (warmer temperatures, no comparable dormant period, and a 3 to 8-year quarantine).

Features that can be incorporated into a greenhouse to improve phytosanitation and thus facilitate quarantine include : compartments (or series of small greenhouses), positive air pressure, filtered air, air conditioning, concrete floors with drains, raised benches, humidity control, container-grown plants, double door air lock arrangements, screened vents (30/30 mesh copper or saran), soil sterilization, incinerators, steam sterilization facilities, fumigation chambers, service and laboratory facilities in the same building. Other features are pathogen-free water supply, sealing of structural joints, heat therapy, meristem tip culture, and hot water treatment facilities, black-light insect traps, shoe disinfectants, and fungicide and insecticide spray programs.

The extent to which these features are incorporated usually depends on availability of funds. An example of a facility incorporating some of these features is the greenhouse as designed for the Nuclear Stock Association (Ornamentals) Ltd., at the Glasshouse Crops Research Institute, Littlehampton, England. Other quarantine-type facilities that have been described, include those for the Republic of South Africa (Nel, 1964) and East Africa (Sheffield, 1955; Sheffield, 1958; Sheffield, Dickinson and Boundford, 1964). Quarantine facilities are currently under construction or expansion including India (FAO, 1965a; Lal, 1959; Renjehn, 1962), Australia and Southwest Pacific territories (Renjehn, 1962), Japan (Renjehn, 1962), Canada, and Turkey.

In addition to the greenhouses, quarantine screenhouses are widely employed in plant introduction because of the lower construction costs and usefulness in maintaining larger plants for longer periods. These screenhouses should be constructed with at least 30/30 mesh screen, high roofs, and double-door entrances. Plants should be pruned to keep foliage from touching screen or else a double screen wall should be installed. Plants should be container grown where feasible to prevent root grafting and sprayed frequently with insecticides and fungicides.

C. *Location of quarantine facilities*. Genera that enter a country under quarantine may be maintained in either centralized or localized facilities. An example of centralization is the United States Plant Introduction Station, Glenn Dale, Maryland, which is the quarantine center for the quarantine of all plant genera. An example of localization is in

Great Britain where regulations stipulate that the maintenance of quarantine is the responsibility of a plant pathologist or entomologist at each of the requesting institutes which differ in crop specialization.

D. *Quarantine principles.* Although regulations of countries spell out specific requirements pertaining to the entrance of each of many quarantine genera, certain general concepts are appropriate regardless of the crop and its pest and pathogen relationships. For example:

> Seed rather than vegetative material should be introduced unless clonal propagation is necessary.
>
> For clonal propagations, non-rooted propagative material such as scions or cuttings should take precedence over rooted plants.
>
> Woody plant introductions should not be more than 2 years old.
>
> Shipments of vegetatively-propagated material should be small; i.e., each variety or species should be represented by a few tubers, scions, or cuttings.
>
> A stock plant should not be re-used for propagation if a foreign bud or scion failed to survive on that stock. Bud or graft failures may be caused by pathogens such as viruses transmitted from the introduction to the stock.
>
> One should never assume that all vegetative propagations of a given species or variety were derived from the same mother plant.
>
> Each scion, cutting or tuber of a clonal introduction should be considered as a sub-clone.
>
> When pest or pathogen detection tests indicate that a particular sub-clone is eligible for release from quarantine, propagations for release should come only from the sub-clone that was tested and not from other sub-clones that were not tested even though these sub-clones constitute part of the original accession.
>
> If introductions are received as roots, such as sweet potato, cuttings derived from the roots should be released rather than the original root itself. It should be destroyed.
>
> Visual observation is not satisfactory for diagnosing virus diseases because neither the presence nor absence of virus-like symptoms is necessarily indicative of the presence or absence of virus.

Of all the types of pests and pathogens that affect plants, perhaps the most difficult to detect are the viruses. Most fungi, bacteria, nematodes, insects, mites, snails, etc., can be detected by observation. However, viruses are difficult to detect because (a) viruses cannot be seen even under high magnification of a light microscope and (b) neither the presence nor absence of virus-like symptoms indicates the presence or absence of virus. Some virus-like symptoms such as chlorosis can be induced by viruses, nutritional imbalance, or genetic factors. Symptomless plants could be carriers of latent viruses, particularly in vegetatively propagated plants.

Since observation is unsatisfactory as a method of virus detection, a plant introduction center should be able to conduct virus indexing tests. Indexing is a procedure whereby grafting, sap transfer or insect vectors are used to transmit the virus from the foreign plant, in which it may be latent, to susceptible domestic indicator plants known to show diagnostic symptoms.

In the United States, virus indexing tests have been conducted since 1957 for vegetatively-propagated plant introductions of *Citrus, Vitis, Solanum, Ipomoea,* and *Prunus* (Kahn, *et al.,* 1963 ; Kahn, *et al.,* 1967). Sixty-two percent of 1300 plant introductions including crop and wild species, were virus infected yet less than 20 percent showed virus-like symptoms. We concluded that there was at least a 50 percent chance of introducing virus-infected plants in vegetative propagations of old-line varieties or new varieties or breeding lines grown in the field in non-isolated sites.

Although emphasis has been placed on vegetative propagations and viruses, it is not intended to suggest that the introduction of seeds is without risk. Many fungi and viruses are borne internally and therefore escape chemical treatment. In addition, viruses are commonly seed-borne in many families such as Leguminosae, Solanaceae, Chenopodiaceae and Rosaceae.

INTERNATIONAL CO-OPERATION

Although no cost estimates have been prepared in connection with the U.S. Plant Introduction program during the past 10 years, such projects are definitely expensive as far as trained personnel and facilities are concerned. The process of importing and establishing introductions ; maintaining a quarantine for long periods, especially for rapidly growing woody plants ; and of producing and maintaining indicators, particularly woody ones, over long incubation periods also contributes to these high costs.

In view of these costs and the high incidence of latent virus infection, international co-operation in the exchange of plant materials presents the most logical solution to the cost of indexing vs. high incidence of virus infection problems. If plant introduction specialists could obtain materials from institutions where 'virus-free' plants have been obtained as a result of indexing and selection, or by heat treatment followed by meristem or stem tip propagation, the chances of introducing a virus-free clone would be increased. The need for indexing by the recipient would not be eliminated but the number of introductions that index negatively would be increased. Consequently, the chances of introducing virus infected plants would be decreased.

International co-operation is needed to publicize the availability and location of 'virus-free' or improved clones and to co-ordinate their exchange countries. Plant introduction specialists who are able to import improved clones rather than run-of-the-mill clones would be able to justify the high cost of indexing and quarantine by a greater yield of plants indexing negatively.

REFERENCES

ANON. (1965) Caribbean Plant Quarantine Conference. News and Notes. *F.A.O. Pl. Prot. Bull.* **13,** 96.

EUROPEAN AND MEDITERRANEAN PLANT PROTECTION ORGANIZATION (1965) *Annual Report,* 1964–65.

FOOD AND AGRICULTURE ORGANIZATION (1965a) *Report of the 5th Session of the Plant Protection Commission for S.E. Asia and Pacific Region.* Canberra, Australia, 1964.

FOOD AND AGRICULTURE ORGANIZATION (1965b) *Report of the First Session of the Near East Plant Protection Commission,* June 7–14, 1965.

INTER-AFRICAN PHYTOSANITARY COMMISSION (1962) A memorandum for phytosanitary procedure in Africa. *Publ. No.* 82.

INTER-AFRICAN PHYTOSANITARY COMMISSION (1965) The protection of Africa south of the Sahara against the introduction and spread of plant pests. Informational note (mimeographed).

KAHN R.P. (1967) Plant quarantine aspects of plant introduction. In *Proceedings of the International Symposium on Plant Introduction.* Escuela Agricola Panamericana. Tegucigalpa, Honduras, November 30–December 2, 1966. pp. 55–60.

KAHN R.P., HEWITT W.B., GOHEEN A.C., WALLACE J.M., ROISTACHER C.N., NEUER E.M., BRIERLEY P., COCHRAN L.C., MONROE R.L., ACKERMAN W.L., CREECH J.L., SEATON G.A. & SCHOEN J. (1963) Detection of viruses in foreign plant introductions under quarantine in the United States. *Plant Dis. Reptr.* **47,** 261–265.

KAHN R.P., MONROE R.L., HEWITT W.B., GOHEEN A.C., WALLACE J.M., ROISTACHER C.N., NEUER E.M., ACKERMAN W.L., WINTERS H.F., SEATON G.A. & PIFER W.A. (1967) Incidence of virus detection in vegetatively-propagated plant introductions under quarantine in the United States, 1957–1967. *Plant Dis. Reptr.* **51,** 715–719.

LAL K.B. (1959) *Directorate of Plant Protection, Quarantine and Storage: Functions and Organizations.* Ministry of Food and Agriculture, Government of India.

LING LEE (1952) Digest of plant quarantine regulations. *FAO Development Paper No.* 23. Revision of 1949 edition. F.A.O., Rome.

LING LEE (1953) International Plant Protection Convention, its history, objectives, present status. *F.A.O. Pl. Prot. Bull.* **1,** 65–72.

LING LEE (1954) Digest of Plant Quarantine Regulations Supplement 1 (mimeographed). F.A.O., Rome.

NEL A.C. (1964) Plant quarantine in the Republic of South Africa. *Leaflet No.* 13, *Department of Agricultural Technical Service, Republic of South Africa.*

O'CONNOR B.A. (1961) Plant quarantine in the South Pacific Commission's Area. South Pacific Commission, August 1961. 24 pages. Mimeo.

ORGANISMO INTERNACIONAL REGIONAL DE SANIDAD AGROPECUARIA (1961) *Cinco años de labores del OIRSA.*

RENJEHN S. (1962) Plant quarantine in India. *Sci. Cult.* **28,** 215–218.

SHEFFIELD F.M.L. (1955) Plant quarantine in East Africa. *E. Afr. agric. J.* **21,** 10–17.

SHEFFIELD F.M.L. (1958) Requirements of a Post-Entry Quarantine Station. *F.A.O. Pl. Prot. Bull.* **6,** 149–152.

SHEFFIELD F.M.L., DICKINSON P.J. & BOUNDFORD L. (1964) Extension to the East African Quarantine Station. *Commonw. phytopath. News* **10,** 25–26.

SOUTH PACIFIC COMMISSION (1964) *Report, Regional Plant Quarantine Conference,* 10–19 *March.*

UNITED STATES DEPARTMENT OF AGRICULTURE (1955) Rules and Regulations of the Plant Pest Control Branch and Plant Quarantine Branch. Title 7, Chap. III of the *Code of Federal Regulations.*

UNITED STATES DEPARTMENT OF AGRICULTURE *Export Certification Manual, Vols. I and II.*

DESCRIPTION AND EVALUATION OF WILD AND PRIMITIVE INTRODUCED PLANTS

H. L. HYLAND

New Crops Research Branch, Agricultural
Research Service, USDA, Beltsville, Maryland

INTRODUCTION

To most crop specialists the term 'plant introduction' means, in its broad sense, the transfer of a living genetic entity from a location where the plant usually has survived through several generations, to a new location. It may range from the wild and primitive forms to the more highly developed economic varieties, or to cultivars which are the result of man's manipulation of desirable characteristics. The purpose of this chapter is to outline here the general methodology related to the description and evaluation of wild and primitive material. A well-planned approach will provide plant specialists with readily accessible data that can easily be obtained during the initial stages of screening under a new environment.

In outlining such methodology, it is convenient, in the main, to draw upon procedures and experience gained in the United States, where plant introduction activities have been handled on an organized basis for 70 years. Most other countries which have organized such work appear to be following similar patterns.

The controlled use of 'wild' plant germ plasm is largely dependent upon accurate description and taxonomic identification, followed by comprehensive evaluations by competent authorities. The thoroughness of such evaluation depends upon the number of accessions under observation at a given time, the diversity of genera or species, and the availability of specialists. Transferring a plant from its original habitat to a different location and environment often results in phenotypic differences and in many cases unconscious selection results in genetic change. Thus descriptive records, from the time of original discovery and throughout the evaluation period become highly important. They should be prepared for long-term reference, and assembled methodically for computer adaptation.

The basic descriptive process starts with the field collector's first observation at the site of the original collection. Obviously, the details will vary, depending upon the interests of the collector. However, in general, he should record the following:

1. Tentative taxonomic identification
2. Morphologic characteristics
3. Stage of growth; general health
4. Surrounding plant climax
5. Density of population
6. Environmental factors: altitude, soil, rainfall, etc.

Highly important among the above points is taxonomic identification, and voucher specimens are a requirement for later verification.

The format for recording these descriptive notes is likely to prove as variable as the training and experience of the collector who records the data. Field collectors for the United States Department of Agriculture are using standardized forms, size 4 × 8 inches, for ready filing. The cards include the following information:

1. Collector's name and date
2. Latin name
3. Local name
4. Locality data
5. Plant description
6. Special notes
7. Whether wild or cultivated form
8. Herbarium specimen taken

There are few additional descriptive data of value to be recorded at the time of collecting, unless other facts are required for verification of the taxonomic names. Further description will follow during, and in combination with, the evaluation processes when first generation progeny are examined in the new environment.

EVALUATION

Where the purpose of introduction is clearly known evaluation is relatively simple. This applies with introduced cultivars, ornamentals, medicinal and some forage plants. In these cases there is generally sufficient information available from the country of origin to permit either direct utilization as cultivars or to provide genetic variability in breeding programs.

However, with most wild or primitive plant collections, evaluation aims to reveal potentially useful variability. This necessitates an initial evaluation, generally in nurseries, followed by a more detailed field study to characterize growth habit and general potential. A variety of specialized observations is also required to locate specific characters such as disease or pest resistance.

For initial tests a favorable environment comparable to the original habitat of the species is usually provided. However, abnormal conditions may reveal useful characteristics, therefore planting should not always receive optimal environmental treatment. Locations should be chosen where competent specialists (agronomists, geneticists, pathologists, etc.) can collect specialized information. It is preferable to use more than one planting site when sufficient material permits.

Most countries have specific locations or facilities to conduct evaluations covering only one or relatively few crops in which they have immediate interest. For example, a potato station in Germany will be quite competent to make preliminary evaluations of Solanums, but may not be concerned with other vegetables. A station in Japan may be able to screen a wide assortment of carrots, onions, eggplants, and other vegetables. This situation is common, and it usually results in specialized collecting of primitive materials by the interested agency. It also assures an efficient organ for evaluating them locally. Therefore, the selection of an agency for screening or preliminary evaluation will depend upon facilities already existing within the country.

In the United States, two main types of evaluation agencies exist. Where well-coordinated national programs exist for research testing, they also include evaluation of introductions. Wild collections of cotton, sugarcane, small grain cereals and soybeans are evaluated by those research units responsible for the improvement of such crops. This is comparable to the potato station in Germany referred to previously. In addition, four regional plant introduction stations accept the responsibility for evaluating other introduced stocks. These regional stations take a team approach. During the evaluation process, their staff members (an agronomist, a horticulturist, a pathologist, and an entomologist) work closely with local university or State Experiment Stations.

When collections arrive at the evaluation center, they are catalogued. Then field plantings are made—in most cases, by transplants from greenhouses, or direct field seeding if there is sufficient initial stock. If alfalfa is used as an example of a common forage plant, some idea of the scope of the evaluation needed can be gained from the following listing of proposed characteristics recommended by alfalfa breeders.

A. *Plant characteristics:*
　　1. Vigor of growth
　　2. Habit of growth
　　3. Crown width
　　4. Fall growth (habit, height)
　　5. Foliage color
　　6. Recovery after cutting
　　7. Seed production
　　8. Stand survival (present stand as percent of original)
　　9. Winter injury
　10. Plant height
　11. Uniformity of plant type
　12. Latitude where collected
　13. Leaves:
　　　　Number
　　　　Size
　14. Stems:
　　　　Number
　　　　Size
　15. Yield
　16. Flower color
　17. Desirability

B. *Diseases:*
　　1. Bacterial wilt: (*Corynebacterium insidiosum* (McCull.) H.L. Jens.)
　　2. Common leaf spot: (*Pseudopeziza medicaginis* (Lib.) Sacc.)
　　3. Black stem: (*Ascochyta imperfecta* Pk.)
　　4. Alfalfa mosaic: (*Marmor medicaginis* Holmes var. *typicum* Black & Price.)
　　5. Cercospora leaf spot: (*Cercospora zebrina* Pass.)
　　6. Root rots and wilt: (*Fusarium* spp., *Cylindrocarpon* spp.)
　　7. Yellow leaf blotch: (*Pseudopeziza jonesii* Nannf.)
　　8. Downy mildew: (*Peronospora trifoliorum* DeBary)
　　9. Alfalfa dwarf: (*Morsus suffodiens* Holmes)
　10. Witches' broom: (*Chlorogenus medicaginis* Holmes)
　11. Bacterial stem blight: (*Pseudomonas medicaginis* Sackett)
　12. Crown rot: (*Sclerotinia* spp.)
　13. Aster yellows: (*Chlorogenus callistephi* Holmes)

14. Root rots : (*Leptodiscus terrestris* Gerdemann
    Phytophthora cryptogea Pethyb. & Laff.
    Rhizoctonia violacea Tul.)
15. Leptosphaeria leaf spot : (*Leptosphaeria pratensis* Sacc. &
    Briard)
16. Verticillium wilt : (*Verticillium albo-atrum* Reinke & Berth)
17. Southern anthracnose : (*Colletotrichum trifolii* Bain & Essary)
18. Pepper spot : (*Pseudoplea trifolii* (Rostr.) Petr.)
19. Rust : (*Uromyces striatus* Schoet. var. *medicaginis* (Pass.) Arth.)
20. Zonate leaf spot : (*Pleospora herbarium* (Fr.) Rab. and
    Stemphylium botryosum Wallr.)
21. Nematodes :
    Stem : (*Ditylenchus dipsaci* (Kuehn) Filip.)
    Dagger : (*Xiphinema* spp.)
    Northern root knot : (*Meloidogyne hapla* Chitwood, 1949)
    Cotton root knot : (*M.incognito acrita* Chitwood, 1949)
    Southern root knot : (*M.incognito incognito* (Kofoid & White,
    1919) Chitwood, 1949)
    Javanese root knot : (*M.javanica javanica* (Treub, 1885)
    Chitwood, 1949)

C. *Insects :*

1. Potato leafhopper (*Empoasca fabae* (Harris))
2. Pea aphid ((*Acyrthosiphon pisum* (Harris))
3. Spotted alfalfa aphid (*Therioaphis maculata* (Buckton))
4. Alfalfa weevil (*Hypera postica* (Gyllenhal))
5. Southwest alfalfa weevil (*Hypera brunneipennis* (Boh.) =
   Egyptian alfalfa weevil)
6. Meadow spittlebug (*Philaenus spumarium* (Linnaeus))
7. Clover seed chalcid (*Bruchophagus platyptera* (Walker))
8. Lygus bug (*Lygus* spp.)
9. Alfalfa looper (*Autographa californica* (Speyer))
10. Alfalfa webworm (*Loxostege commixtalis* (Walker))
11. Two-spotted spider mite (*Tetranychus urticae* (Koch))
12. Green peach aphid (*Myzus persicae* (Sulzer))
13. Grasshoppers (*Acrididae*)
14. Pale western cutworm (*Agrotis orthogonia* (Morrison))
15. Red-backed cutworm (*Euxoa ochrogaster* (Guenee))

For evaluating certain vegetable crops, these data recorded for peas give some idea of the scope:

1. Uniformity
2. Habit
3. Vigor
4. Tall or dwarf
5. Plant height in inches
6. Nodes to first flower
7. Number of branches at base of individual plants
8. Stem size
9. Color of axils
10. Leafiness
11. Leaf size
12. Leaf color
13. Tendrils present or absent
14. Days from seed sown in field
15. Days from seed sown to pods
16. Flower color
17. Set
18. Pod doubling (frequent, intermediate, rare)
19. Pod characteristics:
    Length in centimeters
    Width in centimeters
    Color
    Surface—smooth or neoplastic
20. Pod edible or not
21. Number of days from sowing in field to harvest of ripe seed
22. Seed characteristics:
    Size
    Surface
    Color
23. Category of causal agent
24. Fungus species (includes variety, form or race)
25. Bacterial genus
26. Bacterial species
27. Virus
28. Insect genus
29. Insect species
30. Nematode genus

31. Nematode species
32. Physiological or genetic abnormality
33. Disease rating
34. Degree of resistance

These formats have been designed to attain a degree of uniformity in evaluation records. They could also be used later for documenting world gene pool collections. Revisions and consolidations may of course occur, depending upon plant category (cereal, oilseed, ornamental), priority, problem areas and so on. In some instances, depending upon the ultimate purpose of the wild or primitive accession, certain categories would be reduced, or others, such as characters of taxonomic or evolutionary significance, may be added.

The evaluation of primitive plant material requires competent personnel and sufficient time to do the task thoroughly. It becomes more difficult when large numbers of accessions are to be screened, particularly if the accessions involve several genera or species. One of the most controversial and difficult tasks in the evaluation phase is the maintenance of the genetic composition of cross-pollinated plants during testing (cf. Chapter 33 page 401).

REFERENCES
(for further reading)

ALEXANDER L.J. & HOOVER M.M. (1955) Disease resistance in wild species of tomato. *North Central Regional Publication* 51. *Ohio Agr. Exp. Station Research Bull.* 752.

CORLEY W.L. (1966) Some preliminary evaluations of *Vigna* plant introductions. *Georgia Agr. Exp. Station Bull.* N.S. 165.

HODGE W.H. & ERLANSON C.O. (1955) Plant introduction as a federal service to agriculture. *Adv. Agron.* **7**, 189–211.

LANGFORD W.K. & KILLINGER G.B. (1961) New plants for the South. *Southern Cooperative Series Bull.* 79.

McCRORY S.A. (1958) Preliminary evaluation and descriptions of domestic and introduced fruit plants. *North Central Regional Publication* 90. *South Dakota State College Bull.* 471.

RADCLIFFE E.B. & LAUER F.I. (1966) A survey of aphid resistance in the tuber-bearing *Solanum* (Tourn.) L. species. *Univ. of Minnesota Tech. Bull.* 253.

ROSS R.W. & ROWE P.R. (1965) Inventory of tuber-bearing *Solanum* species. *Univ. of Wisconsin Agr. Exp. Station Bull.* 533.

36

PLANT INTRODUCTION SERVICES: AN APPRAISAL

WILLIAM HARTLEY

Commonwealth Scientific and Industrial Research Organization,
Australia

This chapter reviews the place and functions of national and regional plant introduction services in relation to the collection, evaluation and exchange of primitive and advanced cultivars, and their role as focal points for international collaboration.

No-one familiar with the history of plant exploration and introduction throughout the world can fail to be impressed by the great part which has been played, and continues to be played, by individual botanists, both professional and amateur, who have been inspired by the fascination of the subject, and who, often at great personal hardship and danger, have contributed enormously to the crops of our fields and the beauty of our gardens. Frequently such individuals, especially in the early days, were people whose main responsibilities lay elsewhere but whose natural love of plants was stimulated by the opportunity to visit distant countries. Often, also, botanic gardens, societies and associations promoted plant exploration and plant exchange. An outstanding example is the work of the Royal Horticultural Society of Great Britain which, through the sponsoring of collecting expeditions to the Himalayan region and many other parts of the world, has been instrumental in bringing into cultivation some of our most beautiful garden plants. Especially in more recent years, university groups have taken a great interest both in the exploration of gene centres and in the introduction and study of special groups of plants of importance for plant breeding or genetic study.

Unfortunately, the activities of such isolated and uncoordinated groups and individuals often involve unnecessary risks and lost opportunities. The risks are mainly that diseases and pests may be introduced, and that undesirable weeds may become established. Examples of serious diseases and pests introduced as by-products of plant collecting are given by Granhall (1963), and some of the procedures designed to minimize the dangers have been described by Kahn (1967, and Chapter 34).

Australia offers many examples of plants introduced as ornamentals which have become serious weeds, notably lantana and St. John's wort, while the establishment of the blackberry as a serious pest in many parts of south-eastern Australia was largely due to deliberate, but ill-advised distribution by enthusiastic botanists.

The lost opportunities resulting from uncoordinated plant introduction, though less obvious than the quarantine risks, are no less serious. The specialist collector, concentrating on a defined objective, may fail to collect many other plants which could have value for other purposes. He may even be blind to the true potentialities of the plants which he himself collects. In their paper in the present volume, Krull and Borlaug (Chapter 37) have stressed that collection teams should include scientists with broad agronomic backgrounds as well as taxonomists and cytogeneticists. Only such multi-disciplinary teams, usually drawn from several institutions or from a central national plant introduction agency, can ensure that potentially valuable plants are not overlooked.

The 'individualist' plant collector suffers from further handicaps when faced with the problems of evaluating in their new home the plants which he has collected. Assuming that he is fully aware of the quarantine risks, he will rarely have at his disposal adequate facilities to ensure that the plants can be grown, multiplied and tested under proper phytosanitary control. He will usually be able to test his plants only under a limited range of climatic conditions. Many potentially valuable introductions fail to gain recognition simply because they are tested in the wrong environment. And even if he is able to make use of some of his introductions, the time must come when his work ceases. At this stage, collections of great intrinsic value, which may be irreplaceable, are lost through neglect, with attendant risks that dangerous weeds will have an ideal opportunity to escape and become established. The records, too, are frequently lost, leading to unnecessary duplication of work and further lost opportunities.

It is largely with the purpose of obviating the risks and lost opportunities so frequently associated with uncoordinated plant introduction that many countries have decided to establish national plant exploration and introduction services. Some of these, most notably those of the United States and the Soviet Union, have a very long and distinguished history and have contributed greatly not only to the agriculture of the countries themselves, but also to the knowledge of the origin, distribution and evolution of economic plants. In more recent years these countries have been joined by many others, including several countries in eastern Europe, Australia, India and Argentina.

Information about the organization and operation of these national plant introduction services is given in a number of publications. A general account of the United States service is given by Hodge and Erlanson (1955), and has been supplemented by more recent descriptions by Hyland (1963, see also Chapter 35), Ryerson (1967) and Winters (1967). The earlier papers of Vavilov described Russian plant exploration activities, but there is no readily available publication in English which gives a comprehensive review of the Soviet service as it exists today. Useful information is, however, contained in an unpublished report by Erlanson (1964.)* The organization of plant introduction in Australia is described by Hartley and Neal-Smith (1963), and in India by Joshi and Singh (1963). Shorter references to work in other countries appear in the reports of the Technical Meeting held in Rome in 1961 (Whyte and Julen, 1963), and in the Proceedings of the International Symposium on Plant Introduction held in Honduras in 1966, while Whyte (1958) gives a review of the whole subject.

The services operating in different countries vary considerably, especially in the degree of centralisation. However, all national introduction services have some features in common which facilitate their efficient operation. The following deserve special mention.

The plant introduction service usually forms part of the Department of Agriculture or a major research organization, and hence is able to draw upon extensive resources in carrying out its work.

The service either has direct responsibility for plant quarantine or works in close collaboration with the quarantine authority.

The service has at its disposal good testing facilities in all the major climatic zones of the country concerned.

The service maintains records of introduced plants, usually including plants introduced by other agencies, and is thus able to ensure that national requirements are met without unecessary duplication.

By maintaining extensive collections, and by establishing close collaboration with its counterparts abroad, the service is able to provide plant material needed by specialists.

The service conducts foreign plant exploration, both on its own

* cf. also Appendix by Brezhnev.

behalf and in collaboration with crop and forage plant specialists, and is an invaluable source of 'know-how' for all collecting
expeditions.

The service provides a contact point for international collaboration through F.A.O. and other agencies.

In view of these advantages it is perhaps surprising that national
plant introduction services have not been more generally established.
The reasons for this are fear of duplicating existing activities, and perhaps
a belief that national services may tend to maintain large collections
without regard to the effective use of the material by plant breeders
and others.

The surveys of plant exploration and introduction conducted by
Delhove (1966/67) for F.A.O. furnish information about the attitude in
many countries to the establishment of national plant introduction
services. The replies indicate that most countries in Europe and the
Mediterranean region—other than north-western Europe—would
favour the establishment of such services, the main restriction being
finance. On the other hand, there is opposition in countries with highly
developed agricultural research centres, which regard a national plant
introduction service as harmful rather than helpful. There is, however,
support in Western European countries for *regional* specialised introduction centres dealing with a single crop or group of related crops. Opinion
is divided in most of the African countries, with a tendency to favour
national services in principle, but with a recognition that resources
would only permit the establishment of multi-national services. It is
perhaps significant that the surveys do not indicate any substantial
opposition to national services where these are already in existence.

One may conclude that national plant introduction services have
played an important role in the exchange of useful plant material, in
the exploration of gene centres, and in the collection and preservation
of primitive cultivars and their wild relatives. Reference need only be
made to the work of Vavilov and his successors at the All-Union Institute of Plant Industry in Leningrad, and to the establishment of the
National Seed Storage Laboratory by the New Crops Research Branch
of the U.S. Department of Agriculture.

There is indeed need for international collaboration, especially to
ensure the preservation and utilisation of threatened gene resources.
But it is all too evident that such collaboration is not easily established
or maintained. The European Potato Introduction Station is not yet a
reality in spite of the almost unanimous support given to it by potato

specialists and international conferences ever since it was proposed in 1960. And the efforts of F.A.O. to promote international collaboration so far have not met with the success which they deserved. International action can best be assured if it is firmly based on strong national plant introduction services, which can complement the work of more specialist institutions and individuals by providing centralised quarantine control and records, and by ensuring the safe-guarding of collections. There is in existence a valuable framework of such services scattered throughout the world, often working in comparative isolation. They merit more support to enable them to exercise more fully their national and international responsibilities.

REFERENCES

DELHOVE G.E. (1966/67) *F.A.O. Plant Introduction Newsletter*, Nos. 16, 17, 18, 20 and 21. F.A.O. Rome.

ERLANSON C.O. (1964) Trip report of C.O. Erlanson to the Soviet Union, Poland and Czechoslovakia. 22 pp., (Unpublished mimeo.)

GRANHALL I. (1963) Plant introduction and plant quarantine. *Genet. agr.* **17**, 537–542.

HARTLEY W. & NEAL-SMITH C.A. (1963) Plant introduction and exploration in Australia. *Genet. agr.* **17**, 483–500.

HODGE W.H. & ERLANSON C.O. (1955) Plant introduction as a Federal service to agriculture. *Adv. Agron.* **7**, 189–211.

HYLAND H.L. (1963) Plant introduction objectives and procedures in the United States. *Genet. Agr.* **17**, 470–482.

JOSHI A.B. & SINGH H.B. (1963) Plant introduction and exploration in India. *Genet. agr.* **17**, 526–536.

KAHN R.P. (1967) Plant quarantine aspects of plant introduction. *Proceedings of the International Symposium on Plant Introduction*, 55–60. Escuela Agricola Panamericana, Tegucigalpa, Honduras.

RYERSON K. A. (1967) The history of plant exploration and an introduction in the United States Department of Agriculture. *Proc. Intern. Symposium on Plant Introduction*, 1–19.

WHYTE R.O. (1958) Plant exploration, collection and introduction. *F.A.O. Agricultural Study No.* 41.

WHYTE R.O. & JULEN G. (Eds.) (1963) Proceedings of a Technical Meeting on Plant Exploration and Introduction. *Genet. agr.* **17**, 573 pp.

WINTERS H.F. (1967) Mechanics of plant introduction. *Proc. Intern. Symposium on Plant Introduction*, 49–53.

THE UTILIZATION OF COLLECTIONS IN PLANT BREEDING AND PRODUCTION

CHARLES F. KRULL AND NORMAN E. BORLAUG

Wheat Program of the International Maize and Wheat
Improvement Center (CIMMYT), Mexico 6, D.F., Mexico

INTRODUCTION

Although plant collecting is extremely useful in elucidating the taxonomic and evolutionary relationships between different species and varieties, its principal justification is to obtain natural variability that can be useful in broadening germ plasm pools for plant improvement. Others have presented suggestions for improving the thoroughness, efficiency and utility of collections as well as proposals for their multiplication, storage and subsequent distribution to interested parties. If these commendable efforts are to have an impact on crop yields, the genetic variability must also be effectively incorporated into improved types.

NECESSITY OF A CLEARLY DEFINED GOAL

The key to successful utilization of variability from broad gene pools requires that the crop breeder have a clear concept of what he is trying to introduce, and why. Knowing this, he can search for the trait and in turn incorporate it genetically into a usable variety, (i.e., cultivar), hybrid or synthetic.

After crossing, the breeder must rigorously select among the progeny for the desired trait combined with good agronomic type, and accept only a minimum of undesirable characteristics that are introduced from the wild type. Some workers seem to have an almost mystic respect for any type of variability coming to them from a wild source. There are many desirable genes in the world collections, but most of the variability is detrimental. Most wild types have very low yield potential. The task and art is to incorporate the desirable characteristics into a cultivar without becoming drowned in undesirable material. This can only be done by having a clear concept concerning the characteristic being introduced and its potential value. Moreover, the breeder must

P

have a sound grasp of the relative effectiveness of different breeding methods for incorporating valuable genes into cultivars.

To define the goal and the methods is fairly straightforward in the case of a search for genetic resistance to a new pest or disease, such as a new virulent race of a cereal rust. The scientist develops an effective test to identify resistance to the pathogen or insect. He then screens all available material until he encounters adequate resistance. This resistance must then be incorporated into a suitable background. While the principle of finding and utilizing resistance genes is quite simple and has been widely used in plant breeding for the past 50 years, the actual breeding procedure can be both long and difficult. The pathogen must often be separated into races and the screening done on an individual race basis. The pest or pathogen generally must be cultivated artificially under laboratory conditions. Efficient screening must often be done with seedlings or only portions of a plant and this must be related to field attack on the whole plant. Host-pathogen relationships, the effect of environment, the stability of the reaction under different ecological conditions and many other aspects must be established; nevertheless in such specific cases the breeder usually has a clear idea of the type of character being introduced.

The search for truly revolutionary traits for use in the overall improvement of crops plant is more complicated. It involves recognizing the potential of a given characteristic and visualizing its value when incorporated into a commercial variety or hybrid. Unfortunately, there does not seem to be any substitute for the ingenuity and vision of the individual scientist in recognizing a valuable new trait in a wild background and appreciating its potential usefulness for crop production. As with the more specific cases of resistance to insects or disease, there still remains the more difficult task of actually incorporating the desirable trait into an appropriate background while minimizing the effects of related problems including undesirable linkages, the unsuitable performance of the trait in a new background, negative relationship with other desirable agronomic and disease factors, etc.

THE NORIN WHEAT EXAMPLE

An example of such a trait and its impact will illustrate several principles. Following the second world war, Dr. S.C. Salmon of the USDA, visited Japan in order to study the agricultural research that had been done in that country. Among the materials that attracted his attention was a group of short statured, high tillering wheats. Dr. Salmon envisaged the value of this dwarf trait in areas where weak straw is a limiting factor in increasing fertilizer use in wheat, and he sent samples to some scientists including Dr. O.E. Vogel, USDA wheat breeder at Washington State. Dr. Vogel crossed some of these with the variety Brevor and subsequently sent some F_2 and F_3 seeds to many interested workers.

In addition to excellent straw strength and high tillering the Japanese Norin dwarf wheats were found to have a large number of seeds per head (largely due to more fertile florets per spikelet). However, they were very poorly adapted to Washington and extremely susceptible to disease. An even greater problem was the fact that the dwarf complex was soon found to be tightly linked to a shrunken, poor quality grain type. Many workers tried to break this linkage and failed. Dr. Vogel, however, had the vision and perseverance to break this linkage and produce dwarf selections with acceptable grain type. The resultant variety, Gaines, is the most significant winter wheat variety in several decades and has shattered yield records throughout its area of adaptation. Yields of 10 tons per hectare (i.e., 150 bu./acre) are not uncommon among the better farmers, and verified yields of more than 14 tons have been obtained.

The Norin × Brevor crosses were also the basis of a revolution in the yields of Mexican spring wheats. The same problem of a close association between short stature and shrivelled grain was encountered and also finally broken by means of a vigorous program of hybridization and selection. The results have been very rewarding. Within three years of the introduction in 1962 of the two first semi-dwarf commercial varieties, the Mexican national yield rose one ton per hectare (i.e., 15 bu./acre), and yields have continued to increase. The national average yield now stands at three tons per hectare (45 bushels per acre). Many farmers harvest five ton yields on large acreages and a few of the best achieve yields of seven to eight tons per hectare.

Of even greater world wide importance is the fact that the Mexican wheats have shown high yield in almost all spring wheat regions of the world. They have had the highest overall yield in the Inter-American Spring Wheat Yield Nursery, the Near East American Spring Wheat Yield Nursery and the subsequent International Spring Wheat Yield Nursery every year in which they have been entered. This includes ten sets of international yield trials (Borlaug, Ortega, and Garcia, 1964; Borlaug, Ortega and Rodriguez, 1964a, b, c, d; Krull et al., 1966).

Additionally, these wheats are providing the basis for a sharp change in the production patterns and yields of wheat in several Near Eastern countries. Pakistan and India have both moved vigorously in buying, multiplying and distributing these high yielding, fertilizer responsive varieties. During 1967 alone, more than 60,000 tons of seed of these varieties were purchased from Mexico for planting in other countries, the largest amounts going to Pakistan and Turkey. There will be between 10 to 13 million acres of Mexican semi-dwarfs grown in Pakistan, India, Turkey and Afghanistan in 1967–68 crop season. The results of collecting a few grains of Japanese wheat are indeed impressive.

There are several lessons that can be drawn from this example that are rather generally applicable to the identification and utilization of variability from collections:

Principle 1. The person who made the collection had the vision to see its possible application. A collecting team should consist of people with a wide range of competence and training. This should include fields ranging from basic cytogenetics and genetics to a broad agronomic background in soil fertility, water management and commercial crop production practices. A person with only a narrow interest in cytology and evolution would probably not have appreciated the production potential of these dwarf wheats and might have thought of them at most as an interesting genetic marker. By the same token a person only concerned with soil fertility would be unlikely to appreciate the significance of a taxonomically important 'missing link'.

For this reason we maintain that collection teams should include a scientist with broad agronomic background as well as a taxonomist, a cytogeneticist and a pathologist. Thus, the likelihood of recognizing and collecting new types of both academic and practical importance would be enhanced. The inefficiency in utilizing genetic variability of the present collections is often due to the fact that the person making the collection did not appreciate the potential of the new type and never brought it to the attention of the appropriate scientists.

It might, of course, be argued that the collector has no such responsibilities and that collections should be evaluated by specialists and the information distributed to interested scientists. This kind of evaluation is also important. Nevertheless, the incorporation of an important new characteristic and the reorientation of a breeding program can usually be dated from a casual remark from one scientist to another, rather than from the massive exchange of data. It would be desirable if the collectors could appreciate some of the significance of a new type and try to interest the appropriate scientist at an early stage.

While most of the emphasis here is on new traits within the presently cultivated crops, the broadly oriented collector would also be more likely to visualize the agronomic value of a new race or species. This is particularly applicable to forage plants and other species that could possibly be used directly or with little genetic improvement.

Principle 2. Additional desirable characteristics other than the ones actually apparent and being incorporated will frequently appear. The primary reason for using the Norin wheats was to incorporate short, strong straw and thereby avoid lodging. However, an exceptionally high tillering capacity and a consistently higher number of fertile florets per spikelet were simultaneously obtained from these wheats. These additional features have played a significant role in markedly raising the yield potential of wheat in addition to the increase provided by superior lodging resistance. Indeed the Washington State winter wheats and the Mexican spring wheats are being widely used for crossing in order to increase the yield potential in areas of the world where lodging is not a problem.

The possibility of such fringe benefits is usually well appreciated. Indeed, this is often the reason given for indiscriminately saving progeny of crosses involving wild types. One must, as suggested earlier, have a definite concept of the primary goal but should always be cognizant of possible additional desirable traits that can be obtained.

One of the basic defects of long backcrossing usually used for the incorporation of new rust resistance genes is that genes with additional fringe benefits are eliminated and have no opportunity to express themselves. If doublecrosses or only one or two backcrosses are used, most of the parental type can be recovered but there is still some opportunity for other new desirable genes to be introduced assuming very large F_2 populations are grown. The often cited advantage of the strict backcross method of plant breeding is that the parental type is fully recovered with the exception of the one gene being added. This is also its chief disadvantage. The insistence of five or more backcrosses has limited many cereal breeding programs to only the incorporation of new resistance genes with almost no possibility of improving the yield base. Unfortunately, these short-sighted methods still prevail in many areas of the world, including the developed countries.

Principle 3. The desirable character(s) which are incorporated may be genetically associated with objectionable traits. Such linkages caused a great many difficulties both in Washington and Mexico in using the Norin wheats, and the tightness of the linkage completely discouraged many other workers. High grain yield in Norin derivatives was strongly linked to such undesirable characteristics as shrivelled grain (low test weight), weak gluten, partial pollen sterility, especially in late tillers, and extreme susceptibility to all three of the rusts. Persistence with the use of large populations at both Washington State and in Mexico, however, prevailed with the aforementioned results. A high negative correlation between two desirable traits does not mean it is impossible to get the desired combination but simply indicates that more work and larger segregating populations are necessary.

GENERAL CONSIDERATIONS

It is difficult to generalize about how to utilize gene resources or even where valuable new genes are likely to be found. Plant scientists must be constantly on the watch for indications of characteristics that might allow major breakthroughs in production. The manner of utilizing these characteristics often depends on the manner of inheritance (whether simply inherited or multigenic), relationship with other traits, ease with which the trait can be identified., etc.

However, some general considerations relating to choice of methods are worth mentioning. Plant collections should be evaluated under a wide range of environmental conditions. Some characteristics are easily identified under certain environments but indistinguishable under others. Indeed almost any trait will vary its expression with differing environments, the exceptions being traits such as awned vs. awnless. Both maturity and plant height vary considerably with soil fertility, water availability, temperature and day length. Not only do the actual values differ but the relationship between varieties may vary. In wheat, for example, Penjamo 62 and C-271 are similar in height under low fertility and/or drought conditions, but C-271 grows very tall under more optimum conditions while Penjamo 62, possessing a Norin gene, stays relatively short and therefore is more lodging resistant. Thatcher and Sonora 64 will head within one day of one another at 50° N latitude at Winnipeg, Manitoba, but Thatcher may head 80 days later than Sonora 64 at the 28° latitude of Ciudad Obregon, Sonora, in Mexico. The effect of date of planting—as it influences whether days are increasing or decreasing in length—also strongly influences Thatcher's behaviour in both maturity and grain yield, while it has little effect on Sonora 64. This day length response has great significance. Sonora 64 is well adapted and high yielding over a wide range of latitudes whereas Thatcher cannot be grown successfully with good yields at latitudes of less than 38° to 40°.

Disease reaction may vary widely between locations due to differences in race complexes as well as the effect of climatic factors. Testing with purified races of a pathogen under controlled conditions is helpful in establishing the relative effects of these factors. However, such tests are not always completely applicable to field conditions and are more costly than testing with a severe field epiphytotic.

Collections of wild relatives of crop plants are often tested under a wide range of environments. It is important that data from such plantings be conveyed to other interested scientists. There is considerable interest today in developing a system by which data can be stored and distributed to interested parties. Unfortunately, the data available on even the best collections have usually been taken rather haphazardly. There is often little appreciation of the effect of environment in the expression of nearly all characters of interest to plant breeders, in establishing the relative effects of these factors (see Chapter 39 by Finlay and Konzak).

A rather systematic scheme of testing under environments that are known to reveal easily distinguishable differences would be very helpful in gathering more useful data from the plant breeding viewpoint. For example, wheat stripe rust data from Damascus, Syria, where the disease is seldom damaging, are not as useful in choosing parental material as are data from Quito, Ecuador, or Njoro, Kenya, where the disease is severe and where very virulent races prevail. Race changes make it necessary to periodically re-evaluate lines in critical zones. Unfortunately, there is no known way to evaluate the resistance to races that have not yet appeared.

The same principle of re-evaluation applies to a whole range of agronomic traits as production practices are constantly being up-graded around the world. For example, lodging resistance is much more important today than it was in the days before inexpensive nitrogen fertilizers became available. Today, Mexican farmers are clamouring for double dwarf and triple dwarf wheat varieties to replace the semi-dwarf varieties which now lodge under their intensive programs of fertilization.

Even with the limitations they possess, the present available world collections of the major crop plants contain a tremendous range of variability. The major hurdle to unlocking their secrets and utilizing the valuable characters has been our inability to satisfactorily classify this variability. Classification studies have been frowned upon as routine, while at the same time mutation research to induce variability has been glamorized. The natural variability in collections has been ignored. Mutation research has clearly shown that genetic variability can be produced by various mutagenic agents. However, up to now this induced variability has made little impact in agricultural production.

Progress in varietal improvement in the past has seldom, if ever, been restricted because of the lack of available variability in wild and primitive populations, as well as in the world's cultivars. Progress has been slow rather because of the lack of imagination, vision and efficiency in identifying and incorporating the existing variability into improved varieties.

Induced mutations simply contribute some additional variability to that already available, and there is little evidence that this additional variability is radically different in type or amount from that already available in even fairly rudimentary crop collections. It should be clearly understood that mutation research is seldom a substitute for plant breeding but simply a means of extending genetic diversity when limited. Developing countries frequently divert their limited funds and trained personnel from the urgent task of feeding people to the more academic work in mutations. The trend is confounded further by the glamor generally associated with this type of work.

This is not to say that useful mutants cannot be created. When talented mutation geneticists work side by side with outstanding plant breeders their programs are likely to be better oriented and more likely to produce significant results. A case in point is the recent development of Sharbati Sonora, a white grain mutant from red grained Sonora 64 by Drs. Swaminathan and Varughese. Because white grain is preferred in India for chappatis, Sharbati Sonora will likely replace Sonora 64 as a commercial variety.

There is a need to emphasize the urgency of increasing the completeness of the collections of the major crop plants. After untold centuries of traditional agriculture, many of the countries that contain the primary and secondary centers of origin of these genera are rapidily changing their production pattern by introducing varieties or hybrids of high yield potential with the fertilizer and other management factors to realize this yield potential. The native types and older varieties can not compete under these new conditions and are being rapidly replaced. This applies particularly to wheat in the Near East as well as to sorghum, rice, millet, and maize in Africa, Asia and the Americas. During the past two years, Afghanistan, one of the richest countries in diversity of native wheats, has begun to move aggressively in changing its traditional patterns of wheat production. The same is happening in Turkey.

NEW TYPES OF VARIABILITY NEEDED

Finally, it might be worthwhile to consider some of the types of agronomically important variability that are particularly worth searching for and could make a strong impact on production.

1. *New disease resistance sources*. Probably the most valuable contribution of the present collections of wheat, oats and barley has been to provide resistance to new diseases and new races of diseases. The incorporation of this resistance has allowed high stable yields while minimizing the hazards of disease attack. The best manner of continuing this sucess is to have large, diverse collections of these important cereals available so that resistant types can be found to any new race or disease.

It is also important that different and broader types of resistance be found. There are indications that certain wheat varieties have an adult broad-spectrum of field resistance to many races and that this resistance is much more stable to race changes than seedling, hyper-sensitive resistance genes. Increased stability and breadth of resistance would allow the breeder to spend a higher percentage of his efforts on yield and agronomic factors rather than disease resistance.

2. *Resistance to pests*. Almost all important economic plants from forage grasses to forest trees are occasionally menaced by a new pest or plague. Large collections of diverse germ plasm are the only means of confronting such threats. Once the problem becomes apparent, the collection can be screened and the resistant types introduced into commercial production either directly or in crosses.

A recent example of this is the increasing importance of the cereal leaf beetle in the northern United States. The collections are being intensively tested to find resistance to this insect. A considerable number of the pubescent leaf types of wheat from India, Afghanistan and Pakistan show resistance.

3. *Dwarfness*. Dwarf varieties were responsible for the success of grain sorghum in the southwestern United States. These dwarf varieties and subsequent hybrids contain at least two dwarfing genes and allow intensive management and high yields without lodging. Short statured types have been very successful in rice, wheat and millet, and considerable effort is being devoted to developing them in maize, oats, barley

*P

and many other crops. Dwarf fruit trees are becoming popular because of the ease in harvesting from shorter trees.

There is a great need for new types of dwarfing in all of the major crop plants. For example, with the discovery of the cytoplasmic sterility restorer mechanism for hybrid wheat, it has become quite important to find dominant dwarf genes. The Norin dwarf genes behave as recessives, and the F_1 of a cross between a normal and semi-dwarf variety is almost as tall as the taller plant. Such an F_1 hybrid could not be grown in Mexico at the present time since the presently grown varieties are all dwarf and strong strawed. A dominant dwarf gene would, however, allow the use of a tall parent in the cross. It appears that the variety Tom Thumb, originating from a collection made in the 1930's in Tibet may carry such a dominant dwarf factor, but additional sources would be of interest (CIMMYT, 1967).

4. *Cytoplasmic sterility—fertility restorer mechanisms for hybrids.* Systems involving cytoplasmic male sterility and the corresponding fertility restorers have allowed scientists to develop hybrid onions, sorghums, millets, maizes, etc. which commercially utilize the yield advantage of heterosis. A similar mechanism for wheat is being intensively studied in several countries. There is also a need for such a mechanism in most of our agricultural and horticultural plants. Collections, particularly those involving wild species, have generally been the source of these mechanisms.

Even for the crops presently using hybrids, there is a need for improved sterility–fertility mechanisms. In wheat, for example, pollen fertility restoration depends on at least two major genes plus a number of important modifying factors. Large populations must be handled to get the required recombinations and it is, therefore, very difficult to produce lines that will fully restore fertility in the F_1 hybrid. A one-gene restorer mechanism would save endless hours of work and millions of dollars of research money (CIMMYT, 1967 ; Rodriguez *et al*, 1967).

5. *Earliness.* Improved varieties and hybrids of crop plants are almost always earlier in maturity than native types, and there is a need for new earliness genes in almost all crop plants. As fertilizer use increases, a given variety tends to have a longer life cycle. The plant breeder must produce still earlier varieties since fertilizer use is increasing rapidly in all countries. Earlier commercial varieties also allow double cropping in many areas of the world.

6. *Quality factors.* The Opaque-2 factor in maize has also been shown to be associated with high lysine content and consequently with

increased nutritional value. The protein in these lines is, in fact, nearly as nutritious as that in milk. Several institutions including the Rockefeller Foundation are beginning large programs to identify and utilize genes controlling the amino acid content of several of the basic food crops. Recently, certain ryes and Triticales have been found to be as high in lysine content as the Opaque-2 maize (Mertz, Bates and Nelson, 1964; Villegas, unpublished thesis).

Currently genes are being sought that will increase the quantity as well as the quality of protein. Until recently there was very little evidence in wheat of important genetic differences in protein percentage at the same yield level. However, within the past few years, the variety Frondozo and its derivative Atlas 66 have been shown to carry a factor that contributes a 2–3 per cent higher protein content at the same yield level. These types of genes undoubtedly occur in many species and could represent a significant improvement in nutrition for many countries (Johnson, Schmidt, Mattern and Haunold 1963).

New genes are also needed to improve the industrial quality of several crops. This would include higher test weight and weight per seed as well as milling and baking characteristics, malting and brewing quality, and cooking quality. Not only are the genes needed to improve the industrial quality but types are needed that are simpler in inheritance. There are indications, for example, that the excellent milling and baking quality of Argentine wheats is more simply inherited (and therefore easier to incorporate) than the quality of the hard red spring wheats such as Thatcher and its derivatives in Canada and the United States. The gluten quality of Thatcher depends upon multiple recessive genes for gluten strength.

7. *Drought and cold tolerance*. Increased drought resistance would be desirable in almost any economically important plant. The range of adaptation could be increased allowing at least some production where there is none now. Of even greater importance would be the ability to resist the periods of drought that occur at least occasionally in all non-irrigated regions.

Cold tolerance is a valuable trait in the cereals and many forage crops. It is interesting to note that spring as well as winter varieties of cereals often contain valuable genes for cold tolerance. If adequate cold or frost resistance could be found to shift the winter wheat belt northward 300 miles across the prairies and steppes of northern U.S.A., Canada and U.S.S.R. it would be of enormous benefit. Since winter wheats generally utilize moisture much better than spring sown varieties this would be reflected in higher yields and a vast jump in production throughout these regions.

8. *Other specific factors.* All crops have some particular problem for which genes from collections might be important. A gene for longer coleoptile length in dwarf wheat would be valuable for many areas in the Near East where the seed is planted quite deep. Most sorghums do not set seed well in cool temperatures and genes allowing them to do so would be valuable in extending the range of adaptation of the crop to more extreme latitudes and to higher elevations in the tropics and subtropics. Certain Ethiopian collections apparently have this ability and are now being used in breeding programs with this objective in mind.

REFERENCES

BORLAUG N.E., ORTEGA J. & GARCIA A. (1964) Preliminary report of the results of the first cooperative inter-American spring wheat yield nursery grown during 1960–61. *International Center for Maize and Wheat Improvement Miscellaneous Report No.* 1. Mexico, D.F.

BORLAUG N.E., ORTEGA J. & RODRIGUEZ R. (1964a) Preliminary report of the second inter-American spring wheat yield nursery grown during 1961–62. *International Center for Maize and Wheat Improvement Miscellaneous Report No.* 2. Mexico, D.F.

BORLAUG N.E., ORTEGA J. & RODRIGUEZ R. (1964b) Preliminary report of the third inter-American spring wheat yield nursery grown during 1962–63. *International Center for Maize and Wheat Improvement Miscellaneous Report No.* 3. Mexico, D.F.

BORLAUG N.E., ORTEGA J. & RODRIGUEZ R. (1964c) Preliminary report of the results of the first cooperative Near East–American spring wheat yield nursery. *International Center for Maize and Wheat Improvement Miscellaneous Report No.* 4. Mexico, D.F.

BORLAUG N.E., ORTEGA J. & RODRIGUEZ R. (1964d) Preliminary report of the second cooperative Near East–American wheat yield nursery grown during 1962–63. *International Center for Maize and Wheat Improvement Miscellaneous Report No.* 5. Mexico, D.F.

CIMMYT (1966-67) *Report, International Maize and Wheat Improvement Center (CIMMYT)*, pp. 76–9. Mexico, D.F.

JOHNSON V.A., SCHMIDT J.W., MATTERN P.J. & HAUNOLD A. (1963) Agronomic and quality characteristics of high protein F_2 derived families from a soft red winter-hard red winter wheat cross. *Crop Science* 3, 7–10.

KRULL C.F., NARVAEZ I., BORLAUG N.E., ORTEGA J., VAZQUEZ G., RODRIGUEZ R. & MEZA C. (1966) Results of the third Near East–American spring wheat yield nursery, 1963–65. *International Maize and Wheat Improvement Center Research Bulletin No.* 5. Mexico, D.F.

MERTZ E.T., BATES L.S. & NELSON O.E. (1964) Mutant gene that changes protein composition and increases lysine content of maize endosperm. *Science* **145,** 279–280.

RODRIGUEZ R., QUINONES M.A., BORLAUG N.E. & NARVAEZ I. (1967) Hybrid wheats: their development and food potential. *International Maize and Wheat Improvement Center Research Bulletin No.* 3. Mexico, D.F.

VILLEGAS E. Variability in the lysine content of wheat, rye and Triticale proteins. Unpublished Ph.D. thesis. North Dakota State University, Fargo, N.D.

THE UTILIZATION OF WILD SPECIES IN THE BREEDING OF CULTIVATED CROPS RESISTANT TO PLANT PATHOGENS

I. A. WATSON

Department of Agricultural Botany,
The University of Sydney, Australia

INTRODUCTION

The breeding of crops resistant to plant pathogens has met with spectacular success in many countries of the world, but, since pests and diseases continue to cause considerable losses in the world's food production, every conceivable method to reduce their attack must be exploited by plant breeders, plant pathologists and others.

Prospects for the control of pests and diseases by breeding always remain bright while an adequate source of resistance is available. The genes controlling such resistance may reside in the wild progenitors of the cultivated species found growing in remote areas. Since crosses between cultivated and wild types are often difficult, these latter have mostly been left as a last resort and it can be expected that a reservoir of valuable resistant material still remains among them. Before they are lost there is an urgency to assess and catalogue the host genes for resistance, and to assemble and identify the genes for virulence in the pathogen by planned international cooperation.

THE BIOLOGICAL BALANCE BETWEEN HOST AND PATHOGEN

Long periods of association between plants of primitive species and their pathogens have often led to a situation where the host is able to propagate itself in spite of the organism existing as a multiplicity of strains. A balance has been reached where, in the particular environment concerned, the two populations coexist in a compatible relationship. Should the host, the pathogen or the environment change, this relationship may pass from one of stability to one of disruption and this could lead to the eventual elimination of one or both partners in the association.

Man's efforts in introduction, in breeding, and nature's role in dissemination of spore material are all calculated to disturb this balance.

Many examples of the disturbance of natural associations are available. *Hevea brasiliensis* is a native of the western hemisphere and abounds in the Amazon valley of South America. Great variability exists from plant to plant, especially for resistance to the leaf blight fungus *Dothidella ulei*, also a native of the area. When the rubber industry of South East Asia was established, seeds free of the fungus *D.ulei* were taken from the Amazon valley. High producing individuals were developed by the appropriate breeding and selection methods and it was possible to increase markedly yields of latex by moving from a jungle to a plantation type of husbandry. The improved clones were then taken to tropical America and a similar husbandry was tried. The uniformity of the clones and the susceptibility to *D.ulei* provided a medium for growth that was especially congenial. Devastation resulted because the balance had been disturbed (Stakman and Christensen, 1960).

Breeding disease resistant varieties has had the same disruptive effect. There are many examples but the only one cited will be that of breeding stem rust resistant wheats in Australia over a period of 50 years. Before the work began, the country was populated by six standard races of stem rust which presumably were wild types of unknown origin (Waterhouse 1929, 1936). These have been gradually replaced over the period (Fig. 38.1), first by an aggressive strain which probably originated from outside the country (Waterhouse, 1936) and subsequently by other strains which had combined genes for aggressiveness with specific genes for virulence (Watson and Luig, 1966). The result has been a complete change in the rust flora over 50 years to a point where the original strains are not now recognisable. Man's intervention has undoubtedly influenced this situation but it is impossible to predict what would have happened without the natural gene flow, first from strain 126–6,7 in 1925 and from 21–0 in 1954. The influence of the wheat breeder has necessitated a build up in the number of genes for virulence in the fungus, and the wild types of the fungus have been unable to survive following the creation of these artificial conditions.

GEOGRAPHICAL CENTRES OF DIVERSITY

Since the original observation of Vavilov (1951) concerning the major centres of origin of crop plants we have come to recognise that for any crop species, the diversity in its relatives may vary from place to place

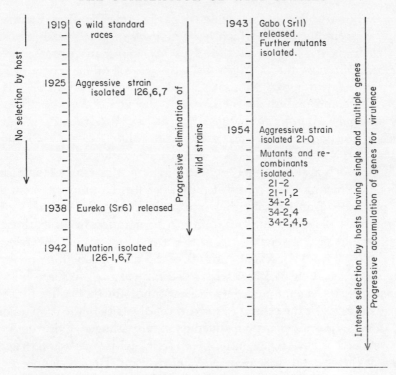

FIG. 38.1. Replacement of original races of *P. graminis tritici* by specialised strains during the period 1919 - 1968.

throughout the world. We can probably assume that the plant pathogens in their most diverse and primitive forms will be found where the ancestors of the cultivated crops still exist as wild species (Zhukovsky, 1964). If this is true it may be possible to trace the evolution of plant pathogens.

Holmes (1951) suggested that it may be possible to locate the point of origin of several viral diseases by studying areas where virus resistant plants are most in evidence. Any attempt to do this for plant pathogens in general, however, is fraught with complications because not only has man transported these organisms from place to place, but they have also been blown considerable distances as spore material. In the case of Tobacco Mosaic Virus (TMV), Holmes compared the geographical areas characterised by relatively resistant species and varieties with areas showing closely allied but highly susceptible species. He concluded that TMV probably originated in Peru, Bolivia or Brazil since the greatest resistance was found in the species such as

Nicotiana rustica and *N.glutinosa* which occur in these countries. Examples of fully susceptible species which have evolved in places well removed from the centre of origin of the virus are found in Australia, e.g., *N.debneyi*, *N.suaveolens* and *N.maritima*. Species of other genera which have evolved within and without the alleged area of origin of TMV, follow the same pattern as members of the genus *Nicotiana*. Hence *Solanum nigrum* (Europe probably), *Petunia hybrida* (Argentina), *Atropa belladona* (Europe and Asia) are susceptible, while *Solanum capsicastrum* (Brazil) and *S.tuberosum* (Bolivia–Peru) are resistant.

A lack of parallelism between the genetic diversity of host and pathogen sometimes occurs and it may arise from a number of causes. The presence of an alternate host species necessary for sexual reproduction may allow extreme variability to be manifest in the pathogen, but if such a species is lacking from the area of maximum diversity of the primary host only asexual variants of the pathogen will be present. This is the situation in Israel where *Thalictrum*, the alternate host of *Puccinia recondita*, is not found. Hence we cannot always be sure that the centres of origin or the centres of maximum diversity of the crop species will provide the greatest genetic diversity in the pathogen. Evidence from the work of Knight (1954) and Innes (1965) with *Xanthomonas malvacearum* of cotton, and from that of Wilkinson and Hooker (1968) with *Puccinia sorghi* of maize, suggest that a host species which has been moved from place to place by man, may have acquired additional variability by independent hybridisation and/or mutation. Work by Nelson (1961) on gene pools for pathogenicity, makes it clear that the accumulation of genes for virulence will be influenced by the total complex of the host species present in any area. Reassembling of host genes collected in many areas of the world may reveal the extent of the diversity in the sources of resistance.

WILD SPECIES AS SOURCES OF RESISTANCE

There have been extensive searches for disease resistance in the wild relatives of cultivated crops. We know that there are valuable genes in the wild potatoes, tomatoes, beets, sugar cane and the progenitors of cultivated wheat, oats and barley. It is believed, but not yet fully understood, that these wild species have in addition to the easily recognised genes for resistance, a genetic system which enables the plants to survive and reproduce in spite of pathogenic changes in the organism. A simplified classification of the types of disease resistance that may be in the wild species and of potential value in breeding is as follows :

1. Specific Resistance.
   A. Operating throughout the life of the plant :
      (i) controlled by a single major gene ;
      (ii) controlled by several major genes.
   B. Operating in adult plants only.
   C. Operating throughout the life of the plant due to a combination of A and B.
2. Non-specific Resistance controlled by a complex genetic system.
3. A combination of Specific and Non-specific Resistance.

In most agricultural crops by far the greatest effort has gone into the breeding of improved cultivars with resistance controlled by one or two genes whose presence is easily recognisable. This is true of the early work in potatoes where resistance to specific strains of *Phytophthora infestans* was obtained utilising the genes of *Solanum demissum* (Black, 1952). It is also true of the cereal rusts where resistance has been obtained from intergeneric crosses (Sears, 1956 ; Riley, Chapman and Johnson, 1968 ; Knott, 1964) and of the potatoes where resistance to the nematode *Heterodera rostochiensis* has been obtained from *Solanum andigenum* and *S.multidissectum* (Cole and Howard, 1966).

The hypersensitivity to *P.infestans* and to the cereal rust fungi is probably differentiated from susceptibility by some relatively simple biochemical process, as variants that have the capacity to overcome this type of resistance commonly arise by mutation. Usually, only one host gene at a time is affected (Flor, 1958). Since the genes for virulence in the organism show a complementary relationship with the genes for resistance in the host, the resistance displayed is referred to as specific.

Many of these genes for specific resistance operate throughout the life of the plant so that, to the same strain and in the same environment, seedlings and adult plants react alike. But each specific resistance is not necessarily of this type. For example, when Hope wheat was developed having its resistance from Yaroslav Emmer, it was believed that the so-called 'field resistance' was valuable in that it operated only in the adult plants and to that extent would be unaffected by variation in the fungus. We now know that in this case adult plant resistance to some strains does not mean resistance to all strains (McIntosh, Luig and Baker, 1967). It is true that there may be differences in the relative ease with which seedling and adult plant resistance become ineffective but this probably indicates differences in the stability of the complementary gene for gene relationship.

Breeders of blight resistant potatoes and of certain other crops now recognise a type of resistance that they consider to be controlled by the combined action of a number of minor genes. Results so far obtained suggest that this type of resistance may operate regardless of the microbial strain. For the purpose of this discussion such resistance will be referred to as non-specific. Driver (1962) believes that it is more permanent than the specific resistance characterised by hypersensitivity, because it tends to select mutations that allow the fungus to live with the host, growing on it but not killing it. Moreover, Graham and Hodgson (1965) have shown that the appearance of race 1,3,4 of *P.infestans* was more frequent on potato selections having the genes R_1, R_3, R_4 combined with little or no minor gene resistance, than on the selections having the same major genes plus minor gene resistance.

While the major work with cereals has been devoted to the transfer of easily recognisable genes from wild species it is very likely that a genetic system remains in them which could be exploited as a source of non-specific resistance. There are several observations that suggest the likelihood of this being the case and two will be given. The first relates to the fact that *Solanum demissum* has contributed altogether 9 different R genes for hypersensitivity to the appropriate strain of *P.infestans*. Six of these nine have been isolated from the same clone of the wild species (Malcolmson and Black, 1966). This species is, however, also a source of the field resistance which is associated with minor genes (Dodds, 1966). By using this multigenic resistance the possibility of mutants or recombinants in the pathogen overcoming it should be reduced although Niederhauser (1964) in Mexico has even found evidence of the 'erosion' of field resistance.

The second example comes from the work of Murphy *et al.* (1967) in which *Avena sterilis* was studied in association with *Rhamnus palaestina*, the alternate host of the crown rust fungus, *P.coronata* f. sp. *avenae*, in Israel. Commercial fields of oats are often destroyed by crown rust when conditions are favourable. *Avena sterilis*, although infected under the same conditions, produces seed of good quality. There is a relatively high level of outcrossing in *Avena sterilis* and a wide range of resistance to crown rust develops. On the basis of work with other crops we can now assume that this wild species has a type of resistance which is effective against all strains of crown rust in Israel.

WILD SPECIES IN RELATION TO CROP HYGIENE
AND PATHOGEN VARIABILITY

The control of plant pathogens is achieved most effectively by an integrated approach involving the breeding of resistant cultivars, the elimination of sexual reproduction in the organism where possible, and the removal of overseasoning inoculum. Wild species may provide genes for resistance but they also have an important role in the generation of new variability in the pathogens concerned.

Since many wild species exist in precarious circumstances in remote areas of the world, it is essential to maintain them under more favourable conditions. If assurance could be given that such living collections were available, there would be many arguments in favour of eradicating susceptible wild species and their relatives from areas where crops related to them are cultivated commercially. Many wild species do not discriminate against strains of the pathogen and consequently the variability among strains collected on them is greater than among those collected on cultivars with resistance to specific strains (Watson and Luig, unpublished). Moreover, on such wild species occurs somatic hybridisation, for example, *Puccinia graminis* on *Agropyron* species, or sexual hybridisation, e.g., *Melampsora lini* on *Linum marginale*. In other words crop sanitation can be improved by the elimination of the continuous infection chain provided by wild susceptible hosts.

TRANSFER OF RESISTANCE FROM WILD SPECIES

A. *Specific resistance*
When the effects of the genes controlling disease resistance in wild species can be readily identified, a number of methods have been proposed and used to transfer those genes to cultivated crop species.

(i) *Conventional crossing and backcrossing with homologous chromosomes*
There has been little difficulty in transferring disease resistance from wild to cultivated species where there is sufficient homology between the chromosomes of the parents. This has been shown by Rick and Butler (1956) within the genus *Lycopersicon* where chromosome numbers may be the same and by Pridham who produced Timvera ($2n = 42$) from a cross between Steinwedel and *Triticum timopheevi* (Watson and Luig, 1958b). Vardi and Zohary (1967) suggested the use of the triploid bridge to make the cross between *Triticum durum* and *T.boeoticum*,

and Gerechter-Amitai (1967) has indicated that these triploids can be used in the transfer of stem rust resistance from the diploid to the tetraploid species.

Amphidiploidy may also be used in the incorporation of genes from wild species and this has been successfully demonstrated by Kimber (1967b) in experiments where he transferred the resistance to eyespot (*Cercosporella herpotrichoides*) from *Aegilops ventricosa* to *T.aestivum*. The fact that the gene(s) were on a chromosome of the D genome of the wild species allows for a reduction in the size of the segment concerned by normal recombination.

(ii) *Chromosome transfer with non-homologous chromosomes*

Where chromosome homology is non-existent and meiotic isolation is complete, it may be possible to locate resistance factors on particular chromosomes by creating either addition or substitution lines. Provided there are no epistatic effects, the resistance to disease residing in the alien chromosome would be recognised in the appropriate derived line.

Resistance to a strain of *Puccinia recondita* has been shown in an addition line of *T.aestivum* by Kimber (1967a) and resistance to TMV in material derived by Holmes has been shown by Gerstel (1946) to be due to the substitution of a pair of chromosomes from *Nicotiana glutinosa* into *N.tabacum*.

It cannot be expected that such addition and substitution lines will have immediate acceptance as commercial cultivars, but they can serve as a step in the ultimate transfer of only small segments of chromosomes on which the gene for resistance is located.

(iii) *Chromosome breakage*

Highly productive cultivars are mostly unique genotypes which will tolerate, at best, only small portions of chromosomes from wild, alien and unadapted forms. Two methods have been used to reduce the length of the chromosome segment which involves the gene(s) required. In the first method Sears (1956) transferred the leaf rust resistance of *Aegilops umbellulata* to *T.aestivum*. The chromosomes were broken by irradiation and the translocation which resulted between the chromosome of wheat and the alien species carried the gene for resistance.

The second method which has been used by Riley, Chapman and Johnson (1968) involved the use of *Aegilops speltoides* to interfere with the pairing mechanism of *T.aestivum* so that chromosome 2M from *Aegilops comosa*, which carried the gene Yr8 for yellow rust resistance, could pair and recombine with the homoeologous chromosome 2D.

The hexaploid line Compair has been developed by this procedure and carries Yr8 for resistance from *A.comosa*.

B. *Non-specific resistance*

All the above transfers have involved genes whose effects are clearly seen. The methods have not been attempted to the same extent with multigenic resistance and the experimental procedures, particularly in the selection of the strains of the pathogen, would need to be different.

Assuming that a wild species has both specific and non-specific resistance, the essential steps in transferring the latter would be as follows :

(i) Separate the non-specific resistance using the appropriate strains of the pathogen.

(ii) Determine the mode of inheritance and the chromosomes involved using aneuploid techniques where possible.

(iii) Intercross among lines having non-specific resistance to determine the possibility of raising the level of resistance.

(iv) Transfer the resistance to agronomically desirable genotypes using selection methods appropriate for multigenic characters and pathogens capable of eliminating the effects of genes for specific resistance.

(v) Test the derived lines with the widest possible range of fungal genotypes.

Once derived and established, the genes for specific resistance can be added to these proven types by routine procedures.

HOW GENES FOR RESISTANCE BECOME INEFFECTIVE

In those organisms which have been studied in detail, it has been found that provided we are dealing with specific resistance, the variability of the organism, and hence the stability of the resistance, will be dependent to a large extent on the mode of reproduction of the organism. For this reason it is appropriate to examine some of the ways in which these organisms may vary.

Briefly these are :

1. By sexual reproduction.
2. By asexual reproduction involving :
   (a) Mutation.
   (b) Nuclear exchange and heterokaryosis.
   (c) Parasexualism.

(d) Progressive changes in virulence.

(e) Physiological adaptation.

(f) Cytoplasmic changes.

It is a generally accepted principle that sexual reproduction results in the maximum expression of genetic variability. There are many examples to substantiate this when we consider the segregation of genes for virulence which enable plant pathogens to overcome the resistance of their hosts. Collections of wheat rust taken in and around barberries are much more dissimilar pathogenically than those collected in areas well removed from the alternate host. Stakman and co-workers in 1949 (Stakman and Harrar, 1957) identified 43 races and biotypes of *P.graminis tritici* in the immediate vicinity of barberries in Pennsylvania, U.S.A. and only 5 from areas well removed from them. In other cases they isolated races in association with barberry which had not been found elsewhere. On the average the ratio between races and collections of uredospores was about 1 : 50 or 1 : 80. From aecidiospores however, the corresponding ratio was about 1 : 5 or less. A similar result was obtained by Dinoor, Khair and Fleischmann (1968) and the ratios could be even more dissimilar since Roane *et al.* (1950) and Fleischmann (1967) have discussed reasons for the failure of sexual recombinants to survive.

Flor (1946) also demonstrated the diversity resulting from sexual repoduction. In the F_2 of a cross between race 22 from South America and race 24 from the United States he isolated 64 races and of these 62 had not been previously described.

Wild species of crop plants and species sufficiently related to harbour pathogens attacking the cultivated crops, probably have a more intimate role with the alternate host than the crops themselves. The reasons for this are clear. The alternate host does not normally occur in the crop itself but mostly along fences and in hedges adjacent to it. The closer the association the more likely will be the infection of both species. Under Australian conditions it would be almost impossible to find *Berberis vulgaris* infected by sporidia originating in a cereal crop. However, in Tasmania, where the alternate host is regularly infected by *P.graminis secalis*, the sporidia originate from teleutospores on *Agropyron repens*, a species closely associated with barberry as a weed in parks, gardens and roadsides (Watson and Luig, 1958a).

Species of *Thalictrum* are not found naturally infected by *P.recondita* in Australia and it would be unusual to find them infected in countries where grasses susceptible to this species are absent. By contrast in

Portugal, Freitas (1966) found *Thalictrum speciosissimum* naturally infected by race 58 of *P.recondita*. Since this rust species occurs in that country on species of *Aegilops* it seems certain that wild grasses provide much of the teleutospore material for the infection of the naturally occurring alternate host.

The role of *Agropyron scabrum* in the hybridisation of varieties of *P.graminis* has already been mentioned. Similar results were obtained many years ago by Levine and Cotter (cited by Stakman and Harrar, 1957) working at the haploid level, and they obtained hybrids that combined in the one strain the genes for virulence on both wheat and rye. Strains derived in this way could overcome the resistance of rye transferred to wheat, since Watson and Luig (unpublished) and Sanghi (1968) have shown that the genetic systems governing the resistance to the wheat and rye stem rust organisms are independent. Other varieties of *P.graminis* may show similar results when hybridised (Cotter and Roberts, 1963).

In many countries and with many organisms sexual reproduction cannot be invoked to explain the variability in virulence that has been observed. The alternate hosts for the rust fungi may be absent or the environment unfavourable for the germination of the teleutospores. This situation obtains with *Puccinia graminis* and *P.recondita* on the Australian mainland. It applies to *P.striiformis* in both North America and Europe and it applies to *Phytophthora infestans* in Europe where only one mating type occurs (Romero and Erwin, 1967). Under these circumstances a search has been made for other mechanisms to explain the origin of the variants. Mutation has been demonstrated repeatedly and this must be regarded as a process that commonly occurs, the variants being readily detected when the appropriate screening procedures are used (Flor, 1958). Watson and Luig (1968) have recently presented evidence that the change from avirulence to virulence for a specific host gene may not proceed in a single step in the case of *P.graminis tritici*. Heterokaryosis has been suggested as a cause of variation in cereal rusts but Caten and Jinks (1966) question the importance of this mechanism with other fungi under natural conditions.

Until more studies are conducted we must conclude that where sexual reproduction is not possible the plant pathogens are still able to show tremendous variation. The control of this variation will depend for its success on the manipulation in the host of the genetic mechanisms that are concerned in resistance.

STABILITY OF DISEASE RESISTANCE

Breeders of disease resistant cultivars always hope that the materials they have developed will maintain their characteristics. The results of many experiments, however, show that specific resistance, especially when controlled by a simple genetic system, is of limited value. This has been especially true for those genes controlling hypersensitive reactions which operate throughout the life of the plant. There are some suggestions that resistance controlled by a single gene which operates only in the adult plant may be more lasting in its effects. The resistance of Chinese Spring wheat to *Puccinia recondita* and Hope wheat to *P.graminis tritici* could be given as examples but more evidence is needed to confirm this proposal. Experiments with resistance to *Phytophthora infestans* on potato (Niederhauser, 1964) and to *Puccinia sorghi* on maize (Hooker, 1967) suggest that the multigenic non-specific resistance is more permanent.

The theoretical considerations of the usefulness of the classified types of resistance can best be discussed in relation to the gene for gene theory of Flor (1956) which has been found to have acceptance in a number of different host-pathogen relationships (Person, 1967) and possibly in similar relationships with nematodes (Jones and Parrott, 1965). Any given interaction can be changed by gene mutation at the appropriate locus in either the host or the pathogen. Since the population of pathogens far exceeds in size that of the host, we can assume that for any complementary situation, detectable variability will mostly come from changes in the pathogen.

From the work of Flor (1958), it is clear that the stability of rust resistance is different from one host gene to another. In his experiments with mutant strains of flax rust, the cultivars Dakota, Cass and Polk were less stable in their resistance than Kota, Leona and Abyssinian, and these relationships held regardless of whether the variants were obtained spontaneously or by using artificial mutagens. Work with wheat suggests that the gene in Thew for resistance to *P.recondita* is concerned in a relatively unstable system with the corresponding gene for avirulence in the fungus, since from strains avirulent on seedlings of Thew, their virulent counterparts readily appear spontaneously.

Genes for specific resistance, especially those transferred from wild species, are often effective against all strains of the organism in the area where the work has been done. Since much time and manipulative skill has been involved in transferring these genes it seems unwise to expose them singly to natural populations of the organism. A better approach would be to incorporate them into a genotype already protected by one or more genes. Pelham (1966) makes this comment on using wild species in breeding tomatoes resistant to TMV :—'breeders should not release varieties which carry only one gene for resistance', such a policy will result in 'a gradual frittering away of the few forms of resistance available' and this is an 'unforgivable waste of the world's natural resources'.

So far there is no good evidence that the genes for resistance from the wild species are superior to those already present in cultivated types, although Clayton (1953) claims there is a difference. There is nothing to show that the relationship between pathogen gene and host gene is any more stable, as indicated by lower mutation rates, when alien chromatin material is transferred from one group to the other. The work of Samborski (1963) and of Luig (unpublished) shows clearly that the specific resistance to *P.recondita* in *Aegilops umbellulata* can be easily overcome when in a background of hexaploid wheat. Stubbs reports (personal communication) that the resistance of *Aegilops comosa* is ineffective against certain strains of *P.striiformis*.

Single genes for resistance do not provide the stability required of breeders' material; however, evidence is accumulating that combinations of genes are superior in this regard. The more genes for resistance in a particular host, the less likely it is to be made susceptible by a mutation in the pathogen. In wheat, the low average coefficient of infection against *P.graminis tritici* has been found associated with multiple resistances. Rajaram (1968) took 5 lines of wheat which, on the basis of world tests, were highly resistant and he analysed the genetic nature of their resistance. He obtained no evidence of simple genetic systems giving widespread protection. The most comprehensive resistance was in all cases attributed to gene combinations.

While combinations of genes for specific resistance afford useful protection against disease, the availability of a non-specific type of resistance should be exploited. There may be environments where multigenic (non-specific) resistance is ineffective (Walker, 1963) or undesirable (Van der Plank, 1966) but many advantages are to be gained from combining the specific and non-specific types. Simple methods for doing this with field resistance and seedling resistance to rusts are available. Apart from the more permanent resistance provided by these combinations of genes we can anticipate a retardation of the rate of spread of disease in a single season which has been shown graphically by Van der Plank (1966). In the breeding programme the main difficulty will be in determining with certainty that the non-specific resistance is present. Careful selection of strains which eliminate all other resistances can be used in the field and the exact genotypes for the specific resistance can be determined by laboratory tests.

CATALOGUING OF GENES FOR VIRULENCE

From what has been written in the preceding sections it is clear that variation in virulence may occur from one geographical area to another. The most comprehensive resistance, combining both specific and non-specific types, can only be achieved with confidence by exposing the material to those organisms having the greatest number of genes for virulence. The most effective way to determine the potential resistance of a line is to test it at one centre to a collection of those strains of an organism having the greatest number of genes for virulence. For reasons connected with quarantine this procedure would be extremely unwise. However, if the breeders had information to show them where the strains having certain combinations of genes for virulence are located, host material could be assembled and assessed at these places. It should be possible to analyse the complete genotype of any resistant culture by knowing its performance against the total array of genes for virulence. To derive such information and to catalogue it for breeders, is an important project that should immediately be undertaken for all organisms where detailed knowledge is available.

REFERENCES

BLACK W. (1952). Inheritance of resistance to blight (*Phytophthora infestans*) in potatoes. Interrelationship of genes and strains. *Proc. Roy. Soc. Edinburgh.* **64**(B), 312–352.

CATEN C.E. & JINKS J.L. (1966). Heterokaryosis: its significance in wild homothallic Ascomycetes and Fungi Imperfecti. *Trans. Br. mycol. Soc.* **49**, 81–93.

CLAYTON E.E. (1953) The genes that mean better tobacco. In *Plant Diseases. United States Dept. Agric. Year Book* 1953, 548–553.

COLE C.S. & HOWARD H.W. (1966). The effects on a population of potato-root eelworm (*Heterodera rostochiensis*) of growing potatoes resistant to pathotype B. *Ann. appl.. Biol.* **58**, 487–495.

COTTER R.U. & ROBERTS B.J. (1963). A synthetic hybrid of two varieties of *Puccinia graminis. Phytopathology* **53**, 344–346.

DINOOR A., KHAIR J. & FLEISCHMANN G. (1968). Pathogenic variability and the unit representing a single fertilisation in *Puccinia coronata* var. *avenae. Can. J. Bot.* **46**, 501–508.

DODDS K.S. (1966). The evolution of the cultivated potato. *Endeavour* **25**, 83–88.

DRIVER C.M. (1962). Breeding for disease resistance. *Scot. Plant Breeding Sta. Rec.* 28–38.

FLEISCHMANN G. (1967). Virulence of uredial and aecidial isolates of *Puccinia coronata* Corda f. sp. *avenae* identified in Canada from 1952 to 1966. *Can. J. Bot.* **45**, 1693–1701.

FLOR H.H. (1946). Genetics of pathogenicity in *Melampsora lini*. *J. agr. Res.* **73**, 335–357.

FLOR H.H. (1956). The complementary genic systems of flax and flax rust. *Adv. Genet.* **8**, 29–54.

FLOR, H.H. (1958). Mutation to wider virulence in *Melampsora lini*. *Phytopathology* **48**, 297–301.

FREITAS A.P. de C. (1966). *Puccinia recondita* Rob. IV–Novas Raças fisiológicas em Trigo para o Continente Portugues e Prospecçao Nos Anos de 1962 e 1963. *Agron. lusit.* **28**, 47–64.

GERECHTER-AMITAI Z. (1967). Wild grasses as sources of resistance to the wheat rusts. *The First Israel Congress of Plant Pathology*, p. 43.

GERSTEL D.U. (1946). Inheritance in *Nicotiana tabacum* XXI. The mechanism of chromosome substitution. *Genetics* **31**, 421–427.

GRAHAM K.M. & HODGSON W.A. (1965). Effect of major and minor gene interaction on adaptive parasitism in *Phytophthora infestans*. *Phytopathology* **55**, 73–75.

HOLMES F.O. (1951). Indications of a New-World-origin of tobacco mosaic virus. *Phytopathology* **41**, 341–349.

HOOKER A.L. (1967). The genetics and expression of resistance in plants to rusts of the genus *Puccinia*. *Ann. Rev. Phytopathology* **5**, 163–182.

INNES N.L. (1965). Inheritance of resistance to bacterial blight of cotton. 1. Allen (*Gossypium hirsutum*) derivatives. *J. Agric. Sci. Camb.* **64**, 257–271.

JONES F.G.W. & PARROTT D.M. (1965). The genetic relationship of pathotypes of *Heterodera rostochiensis* Woll. which reproduce on hybrid potatoes with genes for resistance. *Ann. Appl. Biol.* **56**, 27–36.

KIMBER G. (1967a). The addition of the chromosomes of *Aegilops umbellulata* to *Triticum aestivum* (var. Chinese Spring) *Genet. Res.* **9**, 111–114.

KIMBER G. (1967b). The incorporation of the resistance of *Aegilops ventricosa* to *Cercosporella herpotrichoides* into *Triticum aestivum*. *J. Agric. Sci. Camb.* **68**, 373–376.

KNIGHT R.L. (1954). Cotton breeding in the Sudan. 1. Egyptian cotton. *Emp. J. exp. Agric.* **22**, 68–80.

KNOTT D.R. (1964). The effect on wheat of an *Agropyron* chromosome carrying rust resistance. *Can. J. Genet. Cytol.* **6**, 500–507.

McINTOSH R.A., LUIG N.H. & BAKER E.P. (1967). Genetic and cytogenetic studies of stem rust, leaf rust and powdery mildew resistances in Hope and related wheat cultivars. *Aust. J. biol. Sci.* **20**, 1181–92.

MALCOLMSON J.F. & BLACK W. (1966). New R genes in *Solanum demissum* Lindl. and their complementary races of *Phytophthora infestans* (Mont) de Bary. *Euphytica* **15**, 199–203.

MURPHY H.C., WAHL I., DINOOR A., MILLER J.D., MOREY D.D., LUKE H.H., SECHLER D. & REYES L. (1967). Resistance to crown rust and soil borne mosaic virus in *Avena sterilis*. *Pl. Dis. Reptr.* **51,** 120–124.

NELSON R.R. (1961). Evidence of gene pools for pathogenicity in a species of *Helminthosporium. Phytopathology* **51,** 736–737.

NIEDERHAUSER J.S. (1964). Genetic studies on *Phytophthora infestans* and *Solanum* species. *Abs. Xth Int. bot. Congr. Edinburgh,* 87.

PELHAM J. (1966). Resistance in tomato to tobacco mosaic virus. *Euphytica* **15,** 258–267.

PERSON C. (1967). Genetic aspects of parasitism. *Can. J. bot.* **45,** 1193–1204.

RAJARAM. (1968). The genetic basis for low coefficient of infection to rust in common wheat. Ph.D. Thesis, University of Sydney.

RICK C.M. & BUTLER L. (1956). Cytogenetics of the tomato. *Adv. Genet.* **8,** 267–382.

RILEY R., CHAPMAN V. & JOHNSON R. (1968). Introduction of yellow rust resistance of *Aegilops comosa* into wheat by genetically induced homoeologous recombination. *Nature, Lond.* **216,** 383–384.

ROANE C.W., STAKMAN E.C., LOEGERING W.Q., STEWART D.M. & WATSON W.M. (1950). Survival of physiological races of *Puccinia graminis* var. *tritici* on wheat near barberry bushes. *Phytopathology* **50,** 40–44.

ROMERO S. & ERWIN D.C. (1967). Genetic recombination in germinated oospores of *Phytophthora infestans. Nature, Lond.* **215,** 1393–1394.

SAMBORSKI D.J. (1963). A mutation in *Puccinia recondita* to virulence on Transfer, Chinese Spring x *Aegilops umbellulata. Can. J. Bot.* **41,** 475–479.

SANGHI A.K. (1968). Studies on the genetic nature of resistance in common wheat to strains of stem rust possessing unusual genes for avirulence. Ph.D. Thesis, University of Sydney, 1968.

SEARS E.R. (1956). The transfer of leaf-rust resistance from *Aegilops umbellulata* to wheat. *Brookhaven Symp. Biol.* **9,** 1–21.

STAKMAN E.C. & CHRISTENSEN J.J. (1960). The problem of breeding resistant varieties. In *Plant Pathology—an advanced Treatise,* **3,** (Eds. Horsfall J.G. & Dimond A.E.) 567–624. Academic Press, New York.

STAKMAN E.C. & HARRAR J.G. (1957). *Principles of Plant Pathology.* Ronald Press, New York.

VAN DER PLANK J.E. (1966). Horizontal (polygenic) and vertical (oligogenic) resistance against blight. *Am. Potato J.* **43,** 43–52.

VARDI A. & ZOHARY D. (1967). Introgression in wheat via triploid hybrids. *Heredity* **22,** 541–560.

VAVILOV N.I. (1951). The origin, variation, immunity and breeding of cultivated plants. In 'Selected Writings of N.I. Vavilov'. Trans. by K. Starr Chester, *Chronica bot.* **13,** 1–364.

WATERHOUSE W.L. (1929). Australian Rust Studies, I. *Proc. Linn. Soc. N.S.W.* **54,** 615–680.

WATERHOUSE W.L. (1936). Some observations on cereal rust problems in Australia. *Proc. Linn. Soc. N.S.W.* **61,** 5–38.

WALKER J.C. (1963). The physiology of disease resistance. In 'The physiology of fungi and fungus diseases'. *West. Va. Univ. Agr. Exp. Sta. Bul.* 488T.

WATSON I.A. & LUIG N.H. (1958a). Widespread natural infection of barberry by *Puccinia graminis* in Tasmania. *Proc. Linn. Soc. N.S.W.* **83**, 181–186.

WATSON I.A. & LUIG N.H. (1958b). Timvera—A Steinwedel x *Triticum timopheevi* derivative. *Agron. J.* **50**, 644.

WATSON I.A. & LUIG N.H. (1966). Sr15—a new gene in the classification of *Puccinia graminis* var. *tritici. Euphytica.* **15**, 239–247.

WATSON I.A. & LUIG N.H. (1968). Progressive increase in Virulence in *Puccinia graminis* f. sp. *tritici. Phytopathology* **58**, 70–73.

WILKINSON D.R. & HOOKER A.L. (1968). Genetics of reaction to *Puccinia sorghi* in ten corn inbred lines from Africa and Europe. *Phytopathology* **58**, 605–608.

ZHUKOVSKY P.M. (1964). Main achievements in the U.S.S.R. since Vavilov's time on problems of origins of cultivated plants and gene centres in relation to plant breeding. *Abs. Xth Int. bot. Congr. Edinburgh*, 124.

SECTION 5
DOCUMENTATION, RECORDS AND RETRIEVAL

INFORMATION STORAGE AND RETRIEVAL

K. W. FINLAY[1] AND C. F. KONZAK[2]

[1]Waite Agricultural Research Institute, Glen Osmond, South Australia.
[2]Washington State University, Pullman, Washington, U.S.A.

INTRODUCTION

The amount of information accumulating about the world distribution of cultivated plants, their evolution, sub-division into species and sub-groups, breeding systems, ecology, and agronomic performance, is increasing rapidly year by year. Some of this information is systematically assembled in great detail, e.g., the taxonomic classification of most of our plant species. On the other hand, documentation of the collection, maintenance, description and evaluation of genotypes of a wide range of domesticated species is generally poor, and although large amounts of data have been accumulated over the years, few have ever been published.

Electronic computers are extensively used for information storage and retrieval in various fields of commerce, industry and science. Computers are already used for this purpose by plant breeders (Carmer *et al.*, 1963 ; Carmer, 1965 ; La Bastide, 1967 ; Smith *et al.*, 1963) and taxonomists (Sokal and Sneath, 1963 ; Sokal, 1965 ; Williams, 1967), though not with international links. It is now proposed that this system be adopted on an international scale for the storage and utilization of data concerning plant gene resources.

AN INTERNATIONAL STORAGE AND RETRIEVAL SYSTEM

At the initiative of FAO and IAEA, a group of experts was assembled in Vienna to consider 'International Standardization, Integration and Mechanization of Crop Data Recording and Processing' (Konzak and Sigurbjörnsson, 1966). This group proposed an international network of information centres, linking individual scientists and institutions, through national centres, to an international centre which is to be established at FAO in Rome. The network is to be organized to allow information on plant genetic stocks to be assembled and, as need arises, to be relayed to participants.

To accomplish this aim it has been necessary to devise a record system which is sufficiently adaptable to permit, but not require, computer storage and retrieval of the information, and to allow for the inevitable variations required to describe biological material. To encourage widespread adoption, it must be adequately described and widely publicized.

The *objectives* of the system are:

> To store and disseminate classified information on genetic stocks of cultivated plants and their wild relatives, which are contained in germ plasm collections or experimental material of experiment stations, research institutes, etc., in reserves, and possibly even in natural habitats; such stocks to include currently used, obsolete and primitive cultivars, wild relatives, breeding material and genetic stocks of special interest, induced mutations, and any other material of potential value or interest.
> To assist in the standardization of terminology and methodology of data recording relating to the history, characterization and performance of genetic stocks.
> To encourage international, regional and national coordination in the following areas:
>
>> Collaboration in the assembly, evaluation and utilization of collections of new germ plasm, of hybrid material, and of induced mutations.
>> Collaboration in maintenance and distribution of stocks, reducing duplication and loss of potentially valuable stocks.
>> Evaluation of stocks for characteristics of general interest such as physiological and biochemical characters, disease resistance, adaptability, quality, etc., and integration and analysis of performance records.
>
> To provide an information service for workers in plant taxonomy, breeding and introduction, plant pathology, pest control and other fields concerned with the characterisation of plants, and also to FAO and other international agencies and to governments.

THE RECORD FORMAT

The record format will be divided into sections to facilitate use of the information in data processing and in research.

The basic record

The first section is designed for use as a master for data processing and other applications. Each accession will be identified by name, number, genus, species, subspecies, lifespan, reproductive system, nature of population, and use. The country and maintaining station, the year of accession and the date of recording will be included to facilitate international interchange and the integration and addition of new information.

Other sections will carry information on the origin of the accession, its scientific name, synonyms and vernacular names. The complete pedigree of an accession will be retrievable. In the early developmental stages of the system, notable features and special information will be included in an open-ended remarks section.

Crop specific records

Information to be entered on a separate form will describe the various attributes of each accession. Such information will be coded to conserve storage space, reduce retrieval time and to simplify collation. The information will be decoded after retrieval. Initially this section will provide sufficient information to describe the more important features of an accession. Eventually complete and uniform descriptions should be achieved. While the aim is ultimately to accumulate in an open central file a complete record of information on all of the many recognized traits of accessions, it is obvious that such a goal is not immediately practicable.

Guides for standardization of procedures

Handbooks will be compiled containing instructions and guides for the description and recording of plant characteristics and recommendations for standardization of performance ratings from experimental tests. The first of these handbooks will deal with wheat, the second with rice. Others will be developed in order of the importance of the crop and the ease of compilation.

THE CENTRAL FILE

The central file at FAO will fulfil two main roles. First, by accepting records from all holders of collections willing to exchange seed and, by adding information on new material, it will become a current record of stocks available throughout the world. Second, by also accumulating

information about material which has a severely restricted seed supply
or for which seed is not available, the central file will become an archive
for records of genetic variation.

Retrieval

The purpose of the use of computers for storage of information is to
eliminate, or greatly reduce, the need for publication of detailed results.
At regular intervals a brief summary of the central records will be published, for example a table showing the number of accessions for each
crop, and the number which have been scored for each individual
characteristic. The summary publications will be used as a guide for
obtaining specific information.

Records of plant exploration

The record system has been designed to accommodate detailed
descriptions of collecting sites, of the collections themselves, their
characteristics and their evaluation. Collections will be classified by an
accession coding to facilitate their retrieval. Open ended formats will
allow additional information to be added as it is accumulated and
periodic revision of the files will allow alteration of information if more
specific or more accurate data become available.

Should some of the entries be utilized for agronomic studies or commercial exploitation, or should they be subdivided into subgroupings,
a cross reference will enable the data to be readily obtained in a normal
survey of the records.

Analysis of accumulated information

Broad scale studies of world gene pools present great difficulties.
Many of the data collected by uncoordinated expeditions have been
poorly documented, or not recorded at all. Vavilov was able to formulate
generalizations about world gene pools, because of his personal involvement not only in most of the expeditions conducted by his Institute, but
in the extensive classification and evaluation of the vast collections
which were their result.

The gradual accumulation within the central records of information
from all over the world about wild and primitive plant stocks and modern cultivars will facilitate a broader type of study than is now possible.
Not only will such data become generally available, but the computer
will be able readily to assemble them in any selected form. This should
not only speed up breeding, and hence increase world food production,

but also could open the doors to a new appreciation of world gene pools. It should also strengthen international cooperation in research, improve coordination in plant exploration and introduction, and preserve for posterity the accumulated knowledge of scientists around the world.

REFERENCES

CARMER S.G. (1965) Computer programs for the construction of experimental layouts. *Agron. J.* **57,** 312–313.

CARMER S.G., SEIF R.D. & JACOB W.C. (1963) The use of computers for the analysis of data from variety trials. *Agron. J.* **55,** 585–587.

KONZAK C.F. & SIGURBJÖRNSSON B. (1966) International cooperation in standardization of procedures in crop research data recording. Fifth Yugoslav Symposium on Research in Wheat. *Contemporary Agriculture* **11–12,** 691–696.

LA BASTIDE J.G.A. (1967) A computer program for the layouts of seed orchards. *Euphytica* **16,** 321–323.

SMITH Y.C., WILLIAMS B. & BEATTY E.R. (1963) Computer programming of yield data. *Agron. J.* **55,** 208.

SOKAL R.R. (1965) Statistical methods in systematics. *Biol. Rev.* **40,** 337.

SOKAL R.R. & SNEATH P.H. (1963) *Principles of Numerical Taxonomy.* W.H. Freeman & Co.

WILLIAMS W.T. (1967) Numbers, taxonomy and judgement. *Bot. Rev.* **33,** 379–386.

SECTION 6
CONSERVATION

GENETIC CONSERVATION
IN PERSPECTIVE

O. H. FRANKEL

Division of Plant Industry, CSIRO,
Canberra, Australia

THE STRATEGY OF CONSERVATION

The need for conservation of genetic resources is widely recognized. But there has been little discussion on what one might call the strategy of conservation, i.e. its objectives and perspectives. This chapter is intended as a contribution to this discussion. The subject is not only important but most urgent, since without well-planned measures of conservation even the most comprehensive collections have ephemeral value.

The strategy of conservation depends on the nature of the material and on the objective and scope of conservation. The nature of the material is defined by the length of the life cycle, the mode of reproduction, the size of individuals, and the ecological status—whether wild, weed or domesticated. The objective—research, introduction, breeding, etc.— may determine the degree of integrity which it is essential or desirable to maintain. The scope is the time scale over which preservation is projected, and the area, or space, to which it relates—a locality, a region, the world. The strategy will determine methodology, including the size of a population or sample which it is appropriate to preserve ; in particular, whether to seek the preservation of a population as such, or of its genetic potential.

The discussions in this chapter and those that follow refer to a broad range of conditions and objectives, from the working collection of an introduction or breeding station maintained as part of its current operations, to a world gene pool to be preserved in perpetuity. The emphasis that is placed on the long-term preservation of broadly based gene pools is due to the previous lack of a comprehensive treatment for this subject, possibly because the need for preserving our genetic heritage had not been widely recognised. Material which is deemed to be potentially useful today may be even more so in the future when the growing depth of biological knowledge will doubtless enhance the precision and scope for identification and transfer of genetic elements. Yet by then this material may have vanished unless urgent steps are taken now to safeguard its preservation. It is, of course, possible that biologists may discover more direct means for manipulating genetic controls, which would render the ancient gene assemblies redundant, as could scientific or technological developments in entirely different fields, such as food or textile technology. Yet until the time that their redundancy is recognized beyond a doubt, evolutionary responsibility predicates that what we regard as our genetic heritage must be preserved for future generations.*

There is another aspect of conservation, and that is the conservation of information. It is not only important to conserve areas, communities, populations or individuals, it is also important that information relating to them is adequately recorded, safeguarded, and made available. This applies to communities observed or studied in reserves, or to material in collections. The site, nature and status of the material should be recorded, as should be observations, assays or experiments (*cf.* chapter 39 by Finlay and Konzak). The value of the material grows with the information relating to it. This should be borne in mind when material has ceased to be of interest to its owners. The accumulated information enhances the value of the material, in comparison with similar material which might be obtainable from the same locality. This is a strong argument for the long-term preservation of material which has been studied extensively.

Strategy must take note of innate limitations. There are practical limits to the scale and scope of conservation as there are to the scope of collection and evaluation. But there are further limitations which are intrinsic in the process of conservation. There is in fact no practicable way in which plant material can be maintained with complete genetic integrity. Hybridization, mutation and natural selection, changes in the environment and human error, all contribute towards erosion of integrity ; even seed is not immune from genetic change, not to mention the inevitable process of rejuvenation of seed kept in storage (see p. 483). Hence, where the aim is a high degree of integrity, in practice no more than an approximation can be expected. On the other hand, what

*Perhaps the earliest warning 'that the world will have lost something irreplaceable' should 'the world's priceless reservoir of germ plasm' be destroyed, comes from H. V. Harlan & Martini (1936).

happens when controls on the environment and on genetic recombination are relaxed in a process of 'adaptive panmixis'? Existing information is limited indeed—too limited to permit categorical conclusions. Commonsense indicates compromise.

Compromise between technical, administrative and economic factors may be called for in choosing the appropriate method of conservation. But there is one area where compromise seems wholly inappropriate, because it is, or should be, avoidable, and that is the technical competence of storage facilities for seed.

The technology of seed storage is well understood (*cf.* chapter 43 by Harrington), and the facilities needed are neither complex nor unduly expensive. Considering the great cost of establishing and evaluating a collection, and indeed the incalculable value of its genetic potential, it seems indefensible to provide anything but optimal storage conditions for the seeds (see pp. 482 f.).

This chapter is intended as a perspective, but not as a comprehensive treatment, less still as a review of the subject. It raises as many questions as it answers; and some of the positive statements it makes are likely to be challenged. This gives point to the observation that the method of conservation of gene pools itself requires study and evaluation. The present treatment is viewed merely as a forerunner to a much needed intensive and detailed study which, one may hope, it may help to stimulate and encourage.

NATURAL MASS RESERVOIRS

A. *Wild Communities*

There can be little doubt that valuable gene pools of the wild plants we use in forests, pastures and elsewhere, and those which are related to our domesticated plants, not only should be preserved in perpetuity, but as far as is possible with the genetic integrity of their natural state. A community in balance with a stable environment—the stability being subject to the general vagaries of natural environments—is the ideal model of long-term conservation.

It is still easy to cite examples of important communities which have retained their integrity, although in each case it is possible to visualize dangers in the near or distant future.

The hills of Eastern Galilee in Israel abound with a great diversity of wild wheat, barley, oats and Aegilops, among rocks and ancient trees, where the rough terrain creates a natural sanctuary. The 'wild orchards' of Anatolia, consisting of wild pears, apples, plums, pistachio, on rocky slopes at the edges of cultivation, were similarly preserved for hundreds, or more probably thousands of years, being used as stock for grafting of cultivated forms (M. Zohary, personal communication). Eucalypts in Australia, now domesticated in many parts of the world, were protected, until a century and a half ago, by the absence of economic man.

Each of these, like countless other communities, is vulnerable in the face of modern pressures and technologies. Aerial application of fertilizer and seed could presumably transform the Galilean hills into more productive pastures, with certain destruction for gene pools bridging the millenia. The bulldozer is reputed to be dealing with the wild orchards. And even in vast Australia there is very real danger of some invaluable gene pools being completely replaced by pastures and crops before the end of the century.

As has become evident from some of the preceding chapters, gene pools of many wild species which are directly used in forestry or as range and forage plants are more immediately threatened. Foresters are acutely concerned at the loss of valuable genetic resources in various parts of the world, but especially in the tropics, through the cutting out of indigenous forests, deforestation for agricultural development, replacement by exotics, or destruction by fire or introduced parasites (*cf.* chapter 29 by Zobel). The expansion of agricultural crops, made necessary by rapid population growth, causes overgrazing of the contracting pastures in the Middle East and elsewhere, threatening the continued existence of important gene centres of forage species. The threat to the wild and weed relatives of domesticated plants as yet is not as acute, although one must bear in mind, as Baker (in Bennett, 1968, p. 62) has pointed out, that 'the wild relatives of *Zea mays*, *Armoracea rusticana*, *Gingko biloba*, and many other relatives of tropical economic plants [had] become extinct in the days before modern pressures began to be felt'.

Today neither physical nor social environments are as stable as they used to be, hence a 'community in balance with a stable environment' is likely to be an exception. There is rapidly growing a threat to an increasing range of species and areas. This is a world problem as much as a local one, and often more so. A centre of diversity for a genus may be outside its area of cultivation, as in the case in *Arachis* : South America is the home of the wild species of the genus, but does not cultivate groundnuts in the areas where the crop originated.

In principle we are here on common ground with nature conservation in general; but there is one important difference. Nature conservation aims to protect areas representing habitats and communities which can be identified. Gene pool conservation goes further. It is concerned with *genetic* differences which often can only be surmised, but not identified. It is therefore concerned with population samples, possibly along latitudinal or altitudinal transects, often over extensive areas; hence a 'genetic reserve' should include a spectrum of ecological variability so as to provide a spectrum of genetic variability. It may therefore have to be either extensive, or scattered—the latter, as conservationists know, being difficult to manage.

The hills of Galilee are now protected against any form of land use except light grazing. Partly through altitudinal, partly through climatic gradients—sandwiched as they are between the Mediterranean and the desert—they provide a great range of ecological, hence genetic, variation. They are the home of a large number of Mediterranean species which have enriched the economic flora of many parts of the globe, as food, forage, fibre, ornamental, medicinal plants, and as weeds. This rich and unspoiled flora has stimulated important research in the evolution, cytogenetics, systematics and ecology of many species of economic significance, and recently has become a fertile source of wild material for plant breeders.

Similar needs and opportunities for protection exist in many parts of the world. But as yet the need is not widely recognized. Nor has the large body of information which exists been brought together to serve as a basis for national and international conservation programmes.

The first requirement then is to provide an inventory of wild and weed communities which urgently need and deserve protection. Needless to say, such an inventory cannot help being somewhat inaccurate and incomplete, but it is bound to include many of the most important and most threatened sites and species. A great deal of information can be obtained from taxonomists, ecologists, evolutionists, plant geographers, plant explorers, foresters, agronomists, which would assist national and international organizations to designate and pin-point species, communities and sites in need of urgent protection.

The second requirement is to find ways to effect protection. Most countries possess the legal and administrative structure for the conservation of sites for economic, scenic or recreational purposes, including forest or watershed reserves, national parks, nature and historical reserves, etc. The International Biological Programme is gathering information which is to prepare the ground for 'ecological reserves' which would extend protection to any important habitat or community which is not protected at present. 'Gene pool reserves' could be designated along similar lines, either within or as an extension of an existing system. Considering how important the protection of such resources is for the world as a whole, national efforts may need to be reinforced by international support, linked with long-term agreements on maintenance, access and availability.

A third requirement is to provide permanent protection for wild plants that have been taken from their habitats to make them available for research and plant breeding. While exposed to the vicissitudes that this involves (*cf.* the next section), they are readily accessible, and observation and study relating to them will render such individuals or strains worthy of continuing preservation.

B. *Primitive cultivars, or land races*

The position of the primitive cultivars differs widely from that of wild material. Here there simply is no possibility of a 'steady state' : the communities are a vanished or vanishing asset, and the environments in many of the areas concerned are in a state of rapid and drastic change. Where in Vavilov's time, and even twenty years ago (*cf.* e.g. Harlan, 1950, 1951), ancient land races of wheat and barley were abundant, now only traces of the former diversity can be found in Turkey, Iran, Ethiopia and neighbouring countries (Kuckuck, personal communication). This process of erosion was initiated by introductions from abroad—not always with good results (Kuckuck, in Bennett, 1968, pp. 32 and 61)—and by selections from indigenous land races. But in recent years it has received enormous momentum through the rapid spread of nitrogenous fertilizer and of highly productive and adaptable varieties which are capable of utilizing the fertilizer ; of mechanization and irrigation, and of disease and pest control. The short-strawed Mexican wheats and Philippine rices and their derivatives adapted to the local conditions of many parts of Asia, are now spreading as fast as seed becomes available. They are having the most beneficent effect upon the food supply of hundreds of millions, but the most destructive effect upon what remains of our genetic heritage built up since the beginnings of agriculture. Another example of a species which is rapidly disappearing is the African rice, *Oryza glaberrima*, which was domesticated in West Africa independently of the Asian rice. A survey conducted in 1936 on the plain of Banfora, Upper Volta, showed African rice to be the dominant rice grown. Another survey in 1967 showed it to represent less than 10% of the rice, with a reasonable prediction that there will be none there in ten years. It is going out all over West Africa and the complete gene pool faces extinction (J.R. Harlan, personal communication).

The application of hybrid vigour mediated by male sterility is spreading rapidly to ever more agricultural and horticultural crops, superseding the genetic diversity of primary and secondary centres. The production of tobacco resistant to blue mould (*Peronospora tabacina*) or of a seedless water melon would wipe out important secondary gene centres in Turkey, just as the introduction of hybrid maize to Europe wiped out the secondary centres of that crop in Italy and the Balkan Peninsula.

This process is not one that could or should be arrested or impeded. Our concern must be to extend protection to the valuable gene pools which remain. In this, as in the preceding section, the discussion is confined to the possibilities of *conservation in the original habitats*. Other ways of conservation are discussed in the following sections.

What can be done about this? Farms cannot simply be preserved, like forests or national parks. They involve people with a way of life which is bound to change. Based on years of experience in Iran and Turkey, Kuckuck (in Bennett, 1968, pp. 32 & 61) proposed the establishment of what might be called 'crop reservations'—areas of 1 to 2 acres in size where a local crop variety would be maintained under the supervision of a local agricultural officer. The areas would be subject to changes in the environment brought about by agricultural development—fertilizers, cultivation, etc.—and to genetic change mediated by hybridization, mutation and natural selection. They would thus form 'mass reservoirs' with opportunities for gradual adaptation to changing environments and with genetic self-renewal through mutation and introgression.

One may feel doubtful about the practicability of small areas retaining anything like their integrity under the supervision of officers hard pressed by more immediate responsibilities, with predatory man, beast and other parasites to contend with, in addition to contamination, both biological and mechanical, which is likely to overwhelm a small isolate. Some of the difficulties would be met by inclusion of the crop areas suggested by Kuckuck within a 'plant exploration centre' of the kind proposed by Rudorf (1963), where at least expert supervision would be forthcoming.

But, one may well ask, what is the purpose of maintaining primitive cultigens in a 'dynamic state' in their original site, if the site itself is changing beyond recogition? The virtue of these populations rests in their internal diversity, as a store of variability which can be released by environmental change (*cf.* Bennett, 1965) and recombination, replenished by mutation and by introgression from wild or weed species (Harlan, 1961). They can give rise to evolutionary bursts in 'microcentres' (Harlan, 1951), one may suppose when a combination of circumstances is just right, such as retention of farmers' own seed, availability of interspecific diversity with surmountable barriers, possibly occasional seasonal conditions favouring outcrossing, introgression with mutator effect, as from teosinte to maize (Mangelsdorf, 1958), or destabilization of a genetic system as a consequence of the breakdown of a supergene, as observed in wheat (Frankel *et al.*, 1969). Both stability and instability in these adaptive populations appear to be the result of highly complex interactions of environmental and genetic factors. Could such a system be maintained in a drastically changed environment? Modern agriculture is a great leveller. Heavy applications of fertilizers, mechanisation, pest and disease control, let alone irrigation see to this. We know little enough of the dynamics of 'primitive' populations in their traditional environments, less still when exposed to such challenges; but it is certain that their composition and character could not escape the powerful influence of the new environment, nor of the new neighbours in the shape of high-yielding, largely alien varieties which together with improved cultivation are likely to supplant the former wild and weed introgressors. The difficulty is to find the border line between 'adaptive change' and 'genetic erosion'. Bennett (1968 p. 63) sees 'no advantage in the "steady state" [since] the purpose of conservation is not to capture the present moment of evolutionary time, in which there is no special virtue, but to conserve material so that it will continue to evolve'. Such changes are desirable as long as 'genetic erosion does not take place'. But how is one to know? The outcome will depend on the dynamics of complex and uncontrollable components, resulting in changes which may well lead to massive erosion. There can be no objection to the idea proposed by Kuckuck; at the least the resulting populations could serve as mass reservoirs for local plant breeders. But if there is any virtue in preserving the ancient genetic reservoirs for the good of mankind as a whole, then I should prefer to find a safe niche to protect them from the hurricane of change which as likely as not may destroy the genetic system for which we value them. Change is inevitable, whatever approach one chooses. The question is whether one should attempt to control and minimize it, or whether to encourage it—with unforeseeable consequences.

From the adaptive mass reservoirs in the native habitat there is only one step, though a major one, to mass reservoirs in altogether different environments, which will be discussed in the next section. Harlan (1956) has shown how mass reservoirs resulting from polyallel crosses can produce 'evolutionary bursts' resembling in principle those he observed in 'microcentres'. But all this is a far cry from what conservation is normally understood to be.

We conclude that the prospects of long-term conservation of 'primitive' populations in their native habitat, with anything like their current population dynamics, is generally much more tenuous than that of wild plants. Long-term conservation may depend mainly or wholly on protection in areas under scientific control, i.e. in experimental stations or areas, suitably dispersed to cover a range of communities and environments. This would seem the most effective, and perhaps the only way in which primitive communities of short-lived sexually reproduced plants can be maintained with a reasonable degree of integrity. A further compromise suggests itself along Allard's example of limited bulking (p. 493). Individual population samples from related sources (i.e. similar material and environment) could be bulked to form 'race reservoirs'. This would result not only in a saving of labour, but in facilitating a substantial population size—always an essential for effective conservation. Such a procedure would anyway be almost inevitable in cross-fertilized plants. The cost of maintenance would be considerable ; but this could be reduced by seed storage (see p. 482). The conservation of short-lived asexually reproduced plants presents a special problem and is the subject of chapter 42.

In the maintenace of vegetable, fruit and plantation crops, which always receive a good deal of care, hence are less subject to natural selection, few difficulties are likely to arise—apart from expense. Indeed in fruits, as in all vegetatively propagated plants, preservation in the home country has obvious advantages.

CONSERVATION IN COLLECTIONS

To form a collection of genotypes or populations representative of a region, or of the world, it is necessary to bring genotypes from an environment in which they are adapted into one in which they are not, an altogether more drastic situation than that contemplated in the preceding section. By comparison, the scope for natural selection will be greatly increased as will be the opportunities for natural hybridization with alien material, and even increased mutability has been reported to follow. In general, the effect on the population structure is likely to be determined on the one hand by the differences between climatic, edaphic and biotic components of the original and the new environments, on the other hand by the length of the life cycle, the reproductive system, the intensity of competition, and the degree of care which is extended in the cultivation of a crop. Asexually reproduced plants in general are more buffered than are plants which are reproduced from seed, as are widely spaced tree crops by comparison with crowded field crops ; and ornamentals or greenhouse crops may, with reasonable sanitary protection and suitable daylength and temperature, remain altogether unscathed.

This spectrum of factors will determine the method by which any particular collection can best be maintained, as will the purposes and objectives which it is to serve. If its purpose is to provide material for research in evolution, systematics, cytogenetics, physiology, pathology, etc., every effort must be made to retain, as far as is possible, the integrity of its components. The other extreme is presented by the requirement of plant breeders for a pool of broadly based variability, maintained in 'panmitic mass reservoirs' which are to 'supply the mass of locally adapted variability which is needed for sustained crop improvement' (Simmonds, 1962). Such mass reservoirs may be intended to serve both short and long term needs. But their purpose is local by definition, and can only be broadened to the extent to which the 'adaptive gene pool' is replicated in other environments.

Which of these approaches, or what compromise or combination is adopted in any specific case, will depend not only on the purpose of the collection, but on the length of the life cycle of the species and its mode of reproduction. Three main groups can be recognised : A. long-lived plants, including forest trees (*cf.* chapter 44), fruit trees and shrubs* ; B. sexually reproduced, short-lived plants (*cf.* chapter 41) ; and C. asexually reproduced short-lived plants which are dealt with by Hawkes

*Owing to illness of the invited author at a time when the completion of this book could be no longer delayed, it was not possible to include a chapter on the conservation of fruit trees.

in chapter 42. Between them lie the various groups of long-lived herbaceous (and some woody) plants with different, though mainly short-
cycle modes of reproduction, including many forage, vegetable, berry
and ornamental plants combining features of two or even three of the
main groups.

A. *Long-lived plants*

The techniques and problems of conserving forest tree species in
arboreta, provenance collections, etc., are discussed by Bouvarel (chapter
44) and also by Richardson (p. 358) ; and the maintenance of diverse,
including exotic, genotypes in experimental plantings is familiar to
fruit geneticists and breeders. But since forest and fruit trees have
features in common which are directly relevant to methods of conservation, a brief discussion of the principles of tree conservation seems
appropriate.

In most respects the maintenance of trees is easier than that of
smaller plants. Wide spacing removes or reduces competition, cultivation and pest control are common practice, and a long life reduces
the changes of biological erosion resulting from rapid turnover of generations. Against this there is the greatly increased space and expense per
plant, which tend to restrict population size. In fruit trees most of which
are asexually propagated, this is of less consequence than in forest tree
species most of which are normally reproduced from seed.

With the kind of care which is usually given to collections, including
adequate nutrition and pest and disease control, the main limiting
factors are climatic ; and if irrigation is provided, these are restricted to
temperature and day length. Fruit varieties are generally widely adaptable within the main distribution range of the species. It is therefore
both possible and efficient to establish fruit collections on a regional
basis, as recommended by Zagaja (in Bennett, 1968, p. 67). Organized
on a co-operative basis with reciprocity of access, such collections could
provide widely representative gene pools of all important fruit species at
small expense to the individual institution or nation.

Some species of forest trees are much less adaptable (*cf.* Zobel, pp.
371-373). For such species conservation *in situ* may be a necessity (*cf.* pp.
523-525).

Storage of both pollen and seed are discussed in chapter 43. Conservation of pollen is an attractive prospect especially in fruit trees,
where wild or primitive material is unlikely to be used except in crosses.
Long-term storage of pollen is as yet not fully solved.

Conservation of long-lived, large organisms is expensive, hence a prospect of preservation in tissue culture may be of interest in some circumstances. So far the technical problems have not been solved, but clearly this technique would, theoretically at least, facilitate the maintenance of large numbers of individuals in a small space. From all we know about tissue culture, this is unlikely to be trouble free or inexpensive.

B. *Short-lived plants*

This section is concerned with annual or biennial plants which are solely or mainly reproduced from seed. Short-lived asexually propagated plants are the subject of chapter 42.

In his chapter on Problems of Maintenance (p. 491 ff.) Allard provides a succinct assessment of the merits and limitations of the two contrasting approaches, individuality *versus* panmixis, and shows how a judicious synthesis can provide a workable compromise solution. His treatment has the advantage not only of being founded on personal experience, but in fact on very nearly the only available precise experimental evidence. While Allard's statement speaks for itself, it seems desirable to discuss further the general implications.

Let us consider the merits of collections which perpetuate the individuality of original entries, and which Simmonds (1962) has called 'museum* collections'; and in doing so let us assume that their integrity can be preserved within acceptable limits. Only such collections make it possible to study individual gene pools and their components and to relate their characteristics to the original environments and to integrate environment-heredity relationships of different gene pools in an ecogenetic and evolutionary synthesis of the species as a whole. Such studies may include morphological, physiological, genetic, cytogenetic, agronomic, pathological characterizations of direct value to the plant breeder, and of great interest to biologists in general.† They are facili-

---

*The choice of word is apt, though not in the sense apparently intended by its author. Museums nowadays are places of active research and community involvement, in which the accumulated beauty and experience of past ages not only are preserved for the future, but brought into close relationship with the present. The art treasures of great museums are taken to remote places to be admired and studied; but they are not refurbished to make them compatible with changing conditions.

†A recent example is the meticulous study of a world collection of barley conducted by Ward (1962).

tated by being conducted in a standardized environment (as against the wide variation of natural habitats). Naturally, such observations greatly gain in value when conducted in several environments, or when complemented by studies in controlled environments (McWilliam, 1966).

But even at a more empirical level, broadly based collections of this kind are valuable to the plant breeder. In no other way can he inform himself of the breadth of variation within a species; and this information gains as much as it loses from the fact that the observations are made in the environment in which he works, rather than the environments to which the material is adapted. Such a collection not only informs and instructs, it stimulates the imagination and generates new ideas. The group of semi-dwarf and dwarf wheats found in a Japanese collection which gave rise to record-breaking new varieties in the United States and in Mexico is a good example; and some of the high-yielding New Zealand wheats are in part derived from a group of entries in a world collection which had been noted for their exceptionally large grain. It is more than doubtful that either of these ideas—dwarf stature of extra-large grain—would have been taken up if such types had occured as odd plants in a 'composite cross'. It is, of course, natural and justified for breeders often (though not exclusively) to be concerned with 'characters', although more often than not they are not based on one or a few genes as Simmonds (*l.c.*) and Bennett (1965) insist, with the exception of specific genes for disease resistance. The 'characters' with which a plant breeder is mostly concerned can be as broad as resistance to lodging or shattering in the cereals, protein content and composition, flowering or ripening time—involving major anatomical, physiological or biochemical processes with no doubt complex genetic controls. And changes involving such characters must be integrated into the adaptive system of the plant, which cannot be done, and probably is never attempted, by back crossing (as asserted by the same authors) since as a rule far too many genes are involved.

To the plant breeders of the last eighty years such collections have not only been sources of information and inspiration, but of raw materials for the breeding of varieties without which the world would now be starving. Even today it is, of course, quite incorrect to say, as Simmonds (*l.c.*) does, that 'they supply a steady trickle of useful genes', and nothing more. The great collections of the Vavilov Institute of Plant Industry in the USSR have been used in the breeding of hundreds of varieties of various crop plants (Brezhnev, Appendix); and this is equally true of many institutions elsewhere. It should also be noted that the Russian collections have been maintained with little loss throughout the years, with regular rejuvenation (Ter Avanesyan, personal communication), and that the extensive collections of the Institut für Kulturpflanzenforschung at Gatersleben are similarly maintained (Lehmann and Mansfeld, 1957).

If what has been said in defence of 'museum collections' justifies their maintenace for the present, then their preservation for the future would seem at least as justified (*cf.* p. 469). The difficulties in maintaining collections are changes in population structure through natural selection and genetic drift, and outcrossing (Allard, pp. 491 f.), loss of ill-adapted types and expense (Simmonds, 1962). All of these are mitigated by long-term *seed storage* under optimal conditions; for it is obvious that the less a collection is exposed to the risks of life, the safer and cheaper is its maintenance.

It almost goes without saying that the preservation of a collection is entirely compatible with its utilization. A collection can be observed, studied, and used in plant introduction and breeding, while at the same time being safely stored away for preservation. Institutions conducting long-term seed storages (e.g. the Welsh Plant Breeding Station, Aberystwyth) make arrangements for accessibility of stored seeds, and this can be done in a variety of ways. Storage of seed is only a device for effecting the preservation of populations as near as possible to the state in which long-term, and for the greater part slow evolutionary processes, have bequeathed them to this revolutionary age. There is nothing to prevent the same material being used in any way or for any purpose (see chapter 33 by Frankel).

The question is, first, how safe is maintenance in storage, second, what are the consequences of the inevitable rejuvenation. The first is the subject of chapter 43 by Harrington. It appears that under optimal conditions extended storage periods do not drastically impair viability or genetic constitution. We have a good deal more information on the consequences of storage under poor (Harrison, 1966) or indifferent conditions than under optimal ones; and, as already emphasized, *none but optimal storage conditions should be considered acceptable*. It will take a long time before we can be quite sure that we have adequate information on the nature and extent of genetic change under optimal storage conditions. This is important since selection among components of a population in storage has no relevance to the normal conditions of cultivation. But at the present state of our knowledge I for one regard it as more than likely that collections in this kind of storage will be much less of a 'wasting asset', as Bennett (1968, p. 63) suggests, than collections maintained in any other condition. Comparisons with panmictic conditions are discussed below.

Rejuvenation, as Allard (p. 492) points out, inevitably presents an opportunity for natural selection (and hybridization) to occur. The aim must be, by judicious selection of climatic conditions and cultural measures, to prevent losses rather than to maintain genotypic frequencies—which is probably impossible to achieve.

As repeatedly emphasized, various practical considerations, and, especially, the mode of reproduction, necessitate compromise. When the size of a collection becomes unmanageable, entries related in origin and ostensible characteristics can either be culled or, as Allard (p. 493) suggests, pooled, preferably after individual study. This is inevitable in mainly cross-fertilized species. Ecogenetic 'micropools' of this kind are a plausible compromise; but they are a far cry from 'mass reservoirs'.

Finally, organization and expense. The organization of preservation —as distinct from study, evaluation and utilization* which emerges from this discussion consists of four steps : seed storage, rejuvenation, records, and distribution. It is an advantage, though not a necessity, that these be under the direction, though not necessarily under the physical care, of one authority for any one crop or group of crops, especially in the case of central collections which are to serve a region or the world. This indicates the participation of an international organization.

Long-term storage of seed requires an expert staff, though not necessarily a large one, and a number of rooms in which temperature and humidity can be controlled. At the levels required, these conditions are neither difficult nor expensive to achieve and maintain; but it is a fact that even institutions and countries which maintain some of the largest collections do not as yet possess adequate storage facilities—although the need is well recognized. Yet it is clear that a small number of first-rate storage laboratories could efficiently and inexpensively preserve all gene pools for the whole world. This would require agreements on access and on quarantine.

Rejuvenation should take place wherever the environment is most suitable and where there is an institution competent and willing to conduct it. A species with a wide ecological range may require a number of centres for rejuvenation. Experience will indicate the optimal storage

*cf. p. 480 above, also chapter 33 by Frankel.

period ; in the meantime a proportion of a collection could be rejuve-
ated annually thus reducing the burden to manageable proportions.
A collection of 10,000 entries and an expected storage life of 20 years
would require an annual planting of 500 entries—in a self–fertilized
crop an insubstantial burden for a large institution ; but pooling on a
commonsense basis, as previously suggested, would, in practice, reduce
the size of the collections to much smaller numbers.

Records of stored seed and its distribution should form part of a record
and retrieval system embodying all information on exploration and collection. *Distribution* of seed from long-term storages should be subject to
the principles discussed in chapter 39 by Finlay and Konzak.

The main *expenses* would derive from the provision of storage facilities. As already said, these are not heavy if spread over many crops
and used by a number of countries. The costs would be offset by savings
in the maintenance of collections which are now kept for the contin-
gency of need without being actively used.

MASS RESERVOIRS

In earlier parts of this chapter it has been shown that pooling of lines
or populations with ecological and genetical affinities may be necessary
or inevitable .This is widely different from panmictic populations which
have been called 'mass reservoirs' by Simmonds (1962). The idea came
from composite crosses started by H.V. Harlan in 1929 and reported
upon by Suneson and Stevens (1953), Suneson (1956) and J.R. Harlan
(1956). The composite cross which was first described and exploited
consisted of the progeny of 28 polyallel crosses ; but, as has been pointed
out, the composition of such populations need not be fixed, since promising new material can be added from time to time. It seems essential,
however, that the material should contain types of considerable
diversity to attain the level of variability which will provide the scope
for natural—and later deliberate—selection which is desired.

Such populations are 'an adjunct to breeding' (Simmonds, 1962) and
as such have been found highly productive by several breeders. But it
has also been suggested, e.g. by Simmonds (l.c.), that they can be regarded as 'reserves of locally adapted variability against unforeseen future
demands for new adaptation,' or, in other words, as a method for
long-term conservation of variation, currently adapting to changing
environments, and available as a pre-adapted gene pool for future
needs.

The question is whether genetic elements, viz., genes and gene combinations are retained which do not confer an advantage upon the individual. This clearly is an essential requirement of long-term conservation. For genes it is not so much a matter of frequencies, since, provided their effects are 'observable' (Frankel, 1947) an efficient screen will bring to light genes with very low frequencies; and it appears that such genes tend to be retained in populations though at low frequencies; (*cf.* Allard, p. 493). However, 'characters', which depend on the interaction of many genes tend to be less observable, hence frequencies are more relevant.

So what about the fate of the gene combinations and complexes which condition the 'characters' that are of such concern to plant breeders? And what about the gene associations which must be responsible for the genetic balance which conditions the as yet elusive quality of 'adaptation' which has provided the foundation of the modern crop varieties of the last eighty years? What if a plant breeder decides to start afresh from these mostly forgotten sources (*cf.* chapter 33 by Frankel)? If one is prepared to tolerate the loss of potentially valuable genes, will one be content with the break-up or loss of ancient gene assemblies which is likely to occur under the impact of competition or recombination or both?

There are many examples on record of the elimination of agronomically valuable types under conditions of competition, hence may it suffice to refer to the earliest and to one of the most recent studies. In their classical study of competition among 11 varieties of barley observed in 10 stations over from 4 to 12 years, H.V. Harlan and Martini (1938) found that at all stations there was a rapid elimination of the less adapted varieties; few varieties survived at all stations. As J.R. Harlan (personal communication) remarks, 'the results of this study are among the strongest reasons for *not* using bulk methods for preserving germ plasm'.

The recent example is a study of competition between traditional tall (and low-yielding), and the new short (and high-yielding) types of tropical rice (Jennings and de Jesus, 1968; Jennings and Herrera, 1968). The production of these short and erect types which respond to high nitrogen fertilization is revolutionizing tropical rice production. Yet in a mixture of varieties in which types of this kind contributed as much as 40 per cent of the original composition, they were wiped out after three cycles (each consisting of one wet and dry season crop). This confirms the experience in mass reservoirs: 'Bulk breeding, especially with progenies of crosses involving contrasting plant types, results in a progressive loss from generation to generation of desired intermediate recombinants and types resembling the introduced parental plant types'. In this case these are the types possessing the desirable agronomic characters of short stature and stiff straw.

The effect of recombination may be as drastic, though not quite as lethal. It will bring about the incorporation of chromosomes or chromosome segments in an 'adapted genotype', which is the purpose of the exercise; it may thus achieve a short-term advantage at the expense of the unredeemable loss of the original assembly. For it is hard to conceive how any of the subtly balanced genotypes, unadapted to the physical environment and to modern agronomy, can escape unscathed. Yet they might prove of immense value as building stones in the future. For it is a misconception to assume that evolution at the will of man need be a straight-line process, progressing from one step to the next. Indeed, new ideas or objectives may render irrelevant the adaptations to current environments.

Replication in different environments would reduce the risk of loss, and increase the breadth of variability. But it would not succeed in retaining for future generations the great reservoir of genetic variation which man built up over the millenia, without tearing it apart in a biological mincing machine.*

CONCLUSIONS

1. If the wild and primitive material which is the subject of previous chapters is deemed to be of value today, it is our responsibility to preserve it for future generations. This involves conservation of plant material in a form which retains as far as possible the genetic structure it has acquired, and also the preservation of information relating to the material.

2. All conservation involves compromise: at the least the limitations of sampling of sites, populations, individuals; at the worst the conse-

---

*It is worthy of note that H.V. Harlan, according to a personal communication from his son, Dr. J.R. Harlan, 'was very meticulous about maintenance of his world collection. He grew it out every five years partly because seed storage in Washington, D.C. was very poor in those days and partly to refresh his memory and gain perspective on what he was doing. He grew the collection in both Arizona and Idaho and would never dream of bulking it or converting it to a composite cross as a means of preserving germ plasm.'

quences of natural selection, hybridization, and outright loss. The objective must be to choose methods of conservation which minimize the losses and maximise the gains in terms of usefulness, knowledge, and integrity.

3. Conservation of *wild plants* is most effective in their natural environment. If this is threatened, selected sites may require protection, as is already the case with regard to important gene pools in forestry. Where necessary, protection in reserves should be sought, either in connection with, or as an extension of existing systems of conservation.

4. A world-wide inventory of areas requiring and deserving permanent protection would assist national and international endeavours.

5. Inclusion of representatives of wild species in collections makes them accessible for research and for utilization. Such stocks should be properly documented and preserved.

6. *Primitive cultigens* or land races, when threatened with displacement, can be preserved within their original environment, but only when grown on large areas and under scientific supervision, i.e. in experiment stations and their sub-stations. Drastic changes in the environment and/or extensive introgression from alien cultivars may disrupt the genetic system which they have acquired. One may be doubtful whether such attempts are likely to be successful or, in view of their cost, even worth while ; in the long run, the safest place is, almost inevitably, in collections. Maintenance in collections within the country of origin has few if any advantages over maintenance in homoclimes elsewhere. Notable exceptions are asexually reproduced plants, and especially fruit trees.

7. *Plant collections* consist of individual lines, clones or populations with a common ecological or genetical origin. They are generally maintained in plantations or in field plots, alternating with periods of storage, commonly of seed, but in the future possibly of pollen or of tissue culture. Depending on the length of life, mode of reproduction, degree of competition, and interactions with the physical environment, plant collections are subject to changes in population structure arising from natural selection and hybridization. These effects are smallest in trees and in asexually reproduced plants, largest in short-lived, cross-fertilized plants. In spite of these limitations, collections alone present opportunities for continuing studies of the material, and for preservation with a reasonable degree of integrity.

8. Preservation is safest in storage, which does not prevent simultaneous study and utilization ; but storage must be conducted under

optimal conditions. This is not only the most effective, but the cheapest method of preservation.

9. '*Mass reservoirs*' or panmictic populations derived from crosses of a wide array of material, including locally adapted types in combination with introduced primitive and, if so desired, wild types, have shown distinct promise as an adjunct to plant breeding. Even if replicated in different environments to multiply opportunities for adaptation and reduce the risk of losses, they cannot be considered a form of conservation, since the very existence of the genetic elements to be preserved is broken up and submerged in a process of adaptation which may have no meaning in the conditions of the future.

10. We derive the general conclusion that for all plant gene pools which need and deserve conserving and which cannot be conserved in their natural habitat, the most effective, and in many instances the only effective manner is in collections wherever and whenever possible maintained in storage.

11. The conservation of the world's genetic resources requires the *co-operation of many nations*. No single nation can hope to marshal and preserve all species it uses. Maintenance even of a single species may have to be spread over a number of environments. Observation and research which is correlated between environments is of great mutual benefit. Storage facilities can be more efficient and economic if centralized. An internationally co-ordinated storage and retrieval system for information on plant genetic resources would provide wide coverage and perpetual availability of information to all nations. Above all, *safety and permanence* for irreplaceable collections can be secured only by mutual agreement under international supervision : too many valuable collections have been jettisoned by their owners.

12. The conservation of gene pools should therefore be a joint responsibility of all nations, and co-ordination should be vested in a United Nations agency.
This would involve—

    (i) the planning and establishment of central collections in collaborating countries and institutions which would be responsible for assembly and rejuvenation,

    (ii) arrangements for suitable storage facilities,

    (iii) agreements for availability and distribution of material, and

    (iv) a comprehensive record system (*cf.* chapter 39).

REFERENCES

BENNETT E. (1965) Plant introduction and genetic conservation: genecological aspects of an urgent world problem. *Scottish Pl. Breed. St. Rc.*, 27–113.

BENNETT E., (ed.) (1968) *Record of the FAO/IBP technical conference on the Exploration, Utilization and Conservation of Plant Genetic Resources*, 1967. FAO, Rome.

FRANKEL O.H. (1947) The theory of plant breeding for yield. *Heredity* 1, 109–120.

FRANKEL O.H., SHINEBERG B. & MUNDAY ANNE (1969) The genetic basis of an invariant character in wheat. *Heredity* (in press).

HARLAN H.V. & MARTINI M.L. (1936) Problems and results in barley breeding. USDA Yearbook of agriculture 1936: 303–346.

HARLAN H.V. & MARTINI M.L. (1938) The effect of natural selection in a mixture of barley varieties. *J. Agric. Res.* 57, 189–199.

HARLAN J.R. (1950) Collection of crop plants in Turkey, 1948. *Agron. Jour.* 42, 258–259.

HARLAN J.R. (1951) Anatomy of gene centers. *Am. Naturalist*, 85, 97–103.

HARLAN J.R. (1956) Distribution and utilization of natural variability in cultivated plants. *Brookhaven Symposia in Biology* 9, 191–206.

HARLAN J.R. (1961) Geographic origin of plants useful to agriculture. In *Germ Plasm Resources* (Ed. Hodgson R.E.), Pub. No. 66, AAAS, Washington.

HARRISON B.J. (1966) Seed deterioration in relation to storage conditions and its influence upon germination, chromosomal damage and plant performance. *J. Nat. Inst. Agric. Bot.* 10, 644–663.

JENNINGS P.R. & DE JESUS J. (1968) Studies on competition in rice. I. Competition in mixtures of varieties. *Evolution* 22, 119–124.

JENNINGS P.R. & HERRERA R.M. (1968) Studies on competition in rice. II. Competition in segregating populations. *Evolution* 22, 332–336.

LEHMANN CHR. O. und MANSFIELD R. (1967) Zur Technik der Sortimentserhaltung. *Ber. Mitt. Inst. Kulturpflanzenforschung* 5, 108–138.

McWILLIAM J.R. (1966) The role of controlled environments in plant improvement. *Aust. J. Sci.*, 28, 403–407.

MANGELSDORF P.C. (1958) The mutagenic effects of hybridizing maize and teosinte. *Cold Spring Harbor Symp. Quant. Biol.* 23, 409–421.

RUDORF W. (1963) Exploration centres within the areas of gene centres and introduction centres in remote countries with large areas of cultivated plants. FAO Tech. Meeting on Plant Exploration and Introduction, 1961. *Genetica Agraria* 17, 436–463.

SIMMONDS N.W. (1962) Variability in crop plants, its use and conservation. *Biol. Rev.* 37, 442–465.

SUNESON C.A. (1956) An evolutionary plant breeding method. *Agron. Jour.* 48, 188–191.

SUNESON C.A. & STEVENS H. (1953) Studies with bulked hybrid populations of barley. *U.S. Dept. Agric. Tech. Bul. No.* 1067.

WARD D.J. (1962) Some evolutionary aspects of certain morphologic characters in a world collection of barleys. *U.S. Dept. Agric Tech. Bul. No.* 1276.

PROBLEMS OF MAINTENANCE

R. W. ALLARD

University of California,
Davis, California, U.S.A.

The problems of evaluation and maintenance of a collection have been alluded to in Chapter 8. It is clear that these problems cannot be considered independently of sampling. Thus, for example, the million seeds in an hypothetical collection of wild oats might at one extreme be maintained as one million separate entries, or perhaps as 500 entries based on individual collection sites, and at the other extreme they could be combined into a single large bulk. Whether one or the other procedure, or some intermediate course, were to be followed in maintaining the collection would, of course, have important implications on activities in the field during the collection and also on the effectiveness with which the materials collected can be evaluated and preserved. Fortunately, since detailed studies have been made in a few species the pros and cons of lumping versus splitting can be discussed in something more than general terms.

First, let us suppose that the collection is to be maintained as 500 separate entries corresponding to the individual collection sites. Further suppose that the materials are to be maintained in cold storage with rejuvenation only when this is necessary to maintain viability. Although it is commonly assumed that this procedure of 'static' preservation will capture and preserve the variability as it exists at the time the collection is made, both population genetic theory and practical experience indicate that this is in general not the case.

The main factors involved in the changes which occur are as follows :

(1) *Differential survival in storage*. Practical experience shows that there are substantial differences in the ability of different genotypes within the same species to survive in storage. Some entries fail to survive periods of storage that hardly reduce the germination of other entries. Frequently when the germination of an entry has been reduced to say 50 percent of the original germination, the genetic composition of the entry is drastically changed due to differential survival of the various genotypes within the entry. In some cases such changes occur even when germination

percentage does not change in storage, apparently because a different set of genotypes germinates before and after storage.

(2) *Selection during rejuvenation.* When a collection is grown to rejuvenate the seed, the plants are of course subject to selection. Even though each entry may be grown under the best possible conditions that can be provided in order to maximize survival and minimize selection, selection still takes place and it is frequently sufficiently powerful to bring about substantial changes in the genetic composition of the entry. Compounded over two or three cycles of rejuvenation, the effect of selection is often great enough so that the entry bears little resemblance to the original parent(s) collected in nature.

(3) *Outcrossing with other entries.* It is often difficult to provide adequate isolation to prevent outcrosses from occurring between different entries. This is more of a problem with outcrossing than with inbreeding species but it is a serious problem even with the latter when there are many entries to maintain.

(4) *Genetic drift.* If a large number of entries are to be maintained, practicalities require that each must be propagated as a population of restricted size and each such small population inevitably drifts toward fixation of particular alleles. It is easy to show theoretically that this drift toward fixation, with the accompanying 'genetic erosion', occurs at much the same rate in small populations whether the mating system is one of outcrossing or predominant selfing (Allard and Hansche, 1964). Studies of actual populations show that this drift is more powerful than all except the most stringent of selection favouring heterozygotes and the result, after a few generations, is near homozygosity within any single entry for a largely random sample of the original genes of the entry.

Since fixation in small populations is largely independent of the selective value, many entries become fixed for deleterious genes. Their vitality becomes low and they become increasingly difficult to maintain. The fact that fixation is largely independent of selective value is at the same time one of the strengths of this system of maintenance. If the original collection includes a large number of different entries, nearly all of the non-lethal genes of the original population will become fixed in one entry or another. Hence this system can be highly effective in the preservation of genetic variability, even though the variability will not be preserved in its original form.

The labor requirement of this system of storage is largely a function of the amount of time the seeds can be preserved without significant change in viability or genetic composition. If the period of survival is 20 years or more, or can be increased to such a span of years through provision of ideal storage conditions, the method will clearly preserve variability effectively with a relatively small labor requirement. However, when good storage facilities are not available, as is often the case, or when viability decreases rapidly even under the best of storage conditions, the labor requirement of the method is high.

Maintaining a collection by combining all items into a large bulk, i.e., as a so-called living collection, also has advantages and disadvantages. The outstanding advantage of the mass-reservoir system is the small amount of labor and expense required to grow and harvest many thousands or even hundreds of thousands of plants. Another advantage is the prospect for evolutionary progress as shown by various studies with bulk populations (see, for example, Suneson, 1956 and Allard, 1967). In theory this is at the same time one of the advantages of maintenance in large populations, because in providing opportunity for selection to operate the growing of large populations also provides maximum opportunity for the elimination of genes which are at a selective disadvantage in the environment where the population is maintained. In practice, however, we have found that large bulk populations retain enormous stores of variability (Allard and Hansche, 1964). The evidence suggests in fact that although some alleles are reduced to low frequency few if any are completely lost from the population. The basis of this result often appears to be frequency dependent selection having the effect that rarity in itself leads to an increase in selective value, promoting retention of variability in the population (Harding, Allard and Smeltzer, 1966). If a mass reservoir is maintained in several different environments, or is switched from one environment to another, the chances of losing any given allele are much smaller than if the mass-reservoir is grown continuously at one place. The chances of loss are, of course, also reduced if part of the harvest of early generations is placed in cold storage and the number of cycles of rejuvenation kept to a minimum.

Perhaps the main disadvanage of bulking is that in amalgamating all the materials into a single amorphous mass, opportunity to discover and study interesting properties of individual items is lost (see p. 480).

The nature of the deficiencies of the two extreme procedures suggests that a combination of procedures may be called for in many if not most instances. In settling on the most appropriate combination two facts have to be considered. First, collections once combined cannot be studied individually and valuable information may be lost if lumping is done prematurely. Second, materials can be combined on an increasingly rational basis as more and more is learned about them. In general it would, therefore, appear that collecting in the field should be on the finest net that can be managed and that lumping should be held off as long as possible. This was the procedure followed with the lima bean collection mentioned in Chapter 8. In some cases the situation in the field indicated that lumping was in order and many of the collections were made as composites of single plants, or as composites of closely related populations. Nevertheless the total collection ultimately consisted of more than 2000 items, a number that it was not possible to maintain indefinitely. After the first round of evaluation only about 200 items were judged sufficiently interesting to be maintained separately and the remainder were combined to form about 30 populations. These 30 populations have been maintained by growing them in several different environments to promote the maintenance of maximum variability. Subsequently, further consolidations have taken place and at present fewer than 100 items are maintained separately and the number of populations has been reduced to about 15. It is felt that this opportunistic manipulation of this collection has provided for effective preservation, evaluation and utilization of the original variability contained in the collection with a minimum of labor and expense.

REFERENCES

ALLARD R.W. (1967) Population structure and performance in crop plants. *Cienc. e Cult. S. Paulo* **19,** 145–150.

ALLARD R.W. & HANSCHE P.E. (1964) Some parameters of population variability and their implications in plant breeding. *Adv. Agron.* **16,** 281–325.

HARDING J., ALLARD R.W. & SMELTZER D.G. (1966) Population studies in predominantly self-pollinated species. IX. Frequency dependent selection in *Phaseolus lunatus. Proc. Natn. Acad. Sci. U.S.A.* **56,** 99–104.

SUNESON C.A. (1956) An evolutionary plant breeding method. *Agron. J.* **48,** 188–191.

THE CONSERVATION OF SHORT-LIVED
ASEXUALLY PROPAGATED PLANTS

J. G. HAWKES
University of Birmingham,
Birmingham, United Kingdom

Many of the problems of conservation of the sexually propagated plants are encountered also with the short-lived asexually propagated ones. There are also other difficulties, concerned with the preservation of clones from year to year without loss, admixture or infection by disease.

Asexually propagated crops have originated in many parts of the world, but were perhaps especially common in the New World tropics. Well-known plants of this type are potatoes (*Solanum tuberosum* and relatives) from South America, manioc (*Manihot esculenta*) from South America and the Caribbean, sweet potatoes (*Ipomoea batatas*) from South America and Central America, pineapples (*Ananas comosus*) from South America, Jerusalem artichoke (*Helianthus tuberosus*) from North America, various species of tropical yams (*Dioscorea* spp.) from the Old and New World tropics, taro (*Colocasia esculenta*) from South East Asia and the Pacific, and sugar cane (*Saccharum officinarum*) from South East Asia and New Guinea. There are also, of course, many ornamental plants belonging to the genera *Hyacinthus*, *Narcissus*, *Crocus*, *Iris*, *etc.*, which are propagated by corms, bulbs and rhizomes, which should be mentioned, but which perhaps come outside the scope of the present discussion.

Often the asexually propagated plants can also reproduce readily from seed, but because commercial varieties are highly heterozygous it is clearly in the interests of the growers to propagate a well-adapted genotype asexually. Examples of this type are potatoes and sugar cane. Generally, however, in crops of this sort certain varieties are sterile or produce flowers rarely, whilst others produce seed more freely. In some plants, however, infertility due to chromosomal or genetic causes is much more widespread (pineapple, for instance), so that a sexual reproduction is practically obligatory.

I shall outline some of the problems connected with the long-term preservation of short-lived asexually propagated crops, and the ways in which these problems can be solved. In the main I shall illustrate my points by reference to potatoes, which is the crop I know best.

1. *Preservation of material.* In potatoes, and possibly in some other crops, preservation in 'mass reservoirs' can be effected by mass hybridization between types of the same group or from the same original areas, thus preserving the genetic variability in the form of true seed. This would then only require sowing every five years or perhaps even longer, depending on the length of seed viability of the crop in question. This method cannot be used with highly sterile crops, or where particular genotypes need to be preserved. With such plants it may be necessary to propagate them every year asexually.

With modern advances in the development of plant environment chambers, phytotrons, plant hormones and the like, it ought to be possible, however, to preserve tubers, rhizomes, cuttings, etc. for at least one year or even longer. Potatoes can be kept at 4°C without sprouting from October to the following April or May (6–7 months), and without too much difficulty for a further year (18–19 months). Planting in alternate years would be no problem, therefore, and research designed to determine the optimum moisture content and temperature for storage of potatoes and other crops should help us to store material for two, or even perhaps for three years. This would enable a large collection of, say, 3000 samples to be sown out in batches of 1000 per year— an immense saving in time and effort.

2. *Growth procedures.* These will vary according to the plant in question, but a well-equipped station or institute is essential to maintain whatever gene bank is being considered. Some crops would require field plots only, whilst others would need glasshouses, screen houses or the like, to effect greater environmental control. Glasshouses are absolutely necessary where there is risk of infection by insect-transmitted viruses, so that fine mesh wire or nylon screens can be fitted.

Those plants which develop tubers on long underground stolons some distance from the mother plant must be grown in pots, so as to prevent admixture of clones (potatoes, sweet potatoes, etc.). In plants where a cluster of tubers or rhizomes is produced near the base of the mother plant or which are propagated by above-ground stem cuttings (pineapple, sugar cane), pot culture is not so necessary, even though it is often quite convenient.

3. *Photoperiodism.* Many plants, such as primitive forms of potatoes and the other Andean tuber crops, which are indigenous to the tropics, will form tubers only under short 9–12-hour days and therefore present problems when cultivated in high latitudes with 18-hour summer day length. Blinds or curtains, or darkening boxes and screens are then necessary to reduce the photoperiod to the required length. However, many tropical plants can be grown in temperate climates under glass during autumn or winter when the day length is short. Under these conditions, and with artificial heating, as well as mercury vapour lamps to increase light intensity, the plants will give satisfactory yields.

4. *Quarantine measures and disease control.* Perhaps the greatest difficulty in the conservation of asexually propagated plants is to keep them free from viruses, whether transmitted by insects or by other means. Insect-proofed glasshouses with wire or nylon mesh over windows, and insect traps at the entrances are essential in keeping virus-sensitive crops such as potatoes in a healthy condition.

General control of fungal diseases and insect pests is a matter of correct horticultural practice, and need not concern us here. However, the problem of infection of vegetatively propagated crops by viruses is a most serious one. Until recently, the only known way of curing most plants of virus infection was to grow them from true seed. This is not always possible or desirable : one may need to preserve a particular genotype, or the plant concerned may be sterile, or at any rate self-incompatible, as with diploid potato species. Recent work on potato and other viruses has shown that a cure may be effected in clones of vegetatively propagated material, either by heating the tissues above the thermal death point of the virus, or by tissue culture of stem tips in rapidly growing material, where the virus seems to lag behind the growing point of the host plant. It is still easier to prevent than to cure such virus diseases, however.

This brings us to the question of quarantine methods (cf. chapter 34). In any gene bank it is clearly essential to keep a very careful check on virus and other infection in newly introduced material and to isolate it from already quarantined specimens. Even these should be checked over now and again and infected lines destroyed or, if possible, renewed from seed. The control of virus diseases in vegetatively propagated crops is thus the biggest problem in maintaining a gene bank for such crops.

5.   *Technical personnel*. In all gene banks where material has to be
     grown from year to year it needs to undergo various handling
     operations such as planting, harvesting, checking, sorting, etc. In
     each of these operations errors may occur. Even during the growth
     phase it is only too easy for labels to 'disappear' or to be mysteri-
     ously exchanged from one pot or garden plot to another. It is
     absolutely essential, therefore, to cut down handling to a mini-
     mum number of operations and to entrust it only to technical
     personnel who are well-trained, careful and meticulous, who
     carry out instructions carefully and who, if they do make a
     mistake, record it and do not try to hide it.

6.   *Scientific personnel*. The scientific personnel involved in the conser-
     vation of gene bank material must possess a detailed knowledge
     of the taxonomy of the group in question, to the extent of being
     able to identify errors of labelling or arrangement. They should,
     ideally, make detailed descriptions of each accession to ensure that
     the actual material being grown is the same as it was when it
     first came into the collection. Vegetative mutations may occur in
     vegetatively propagated material and should be looked out for.

     The scientific personnel should carry out an active research
     programme where possible, running parallel to their routine
     duties. It is essential that there should be a continuity of person-
     nel, and a research programme, besides contributing information
     of value, would help to retain a continuity of interest and of effort.

7.   *Records* (cf. chapter 39). It is essential to keep records, not only of
     the morphology of the clones grown but of the results of screening
     for resistance to disease and adaptation to environmental condi-
     tions. A herbarium of voucher specimens should also be built up.

8.   *Location of collections*. There are here two opposing concepts : (i) A
     gene bank should be located in the centre of variability of the
     crop concerned. This has the advantage that a more intimate
     knowledge of the crop, its specialized parasites, its over-all vari-
     ability and its resistance to disease can be built up. New collections
     can be made from time to time and the environmental conditions
     of the gene bank should be correct for the material grown. The
     disadvantages are that centres of variability of many crop plants
     are often backward regions with poor communications, and offer-
     ing little inducement to the scientific personnel or their wives and
     families to settle in them permanently, or even longer than a year
     or two. (ii) The alternative solution is to situate the gene bank in

an area where active research and breeding is in progress. This generally solves the problem of conditions for the personnel but does not provide so much interest as regards contact with centres of variability of the crop concerned.

Sometimes the two concepts can be resolved or a compromise can be reached. Another way is to provide gene banks both in the areas of variability and in the area where active research and breeding is in progress. With the potato, gene banks are in existence or projected in Mexico, Colombia, Peru and Argentina, and it has been possible to site them in or near the centres of variability and to carry out fundamental research as well; in addition a bank has been in existence for some time at Sturgeon Bay, U.S.A., and another is projected for Europe. This, it seems to me, is the ideal solution; groups of well-trained people are working or will work at all these centres and by exchange of material, ideas and personnel, active research is maintained and the materials are preserved in the best possible way.

Some such means of preservation of the other asexually propagated crops is urgently needed, since if gene banks for these are not established quickly we shall be in danger of losing for ever much of the variation that may be essential in solving future problems of yield and disease resistance in our major crop plants.

R*

43

SEED AND POLLEN STORAGE FOR CONSERVATION OF PLANT GENE RESOURCES

JAMES F. HARRINGTON

University of California,
Davis, California, U.S.A.

INTRODUCTION

Probably the easiest and least expensive way of preserving plant gene resources is seed storage. Under proper conditions the seed of many species remain viable for up to hundreds of years, but proper conditions include both optimum techniques of seed preparation and optimum storage environment. Even so, unfortunately, the seed of a few species will not survive for long periods under any storage regimes known, although proper preparation and environment can prolong their life. Even under ideal storage conditions, however, genetic changes may occur—both by gene changes in individual seeds and by population changes created by irregular losses of viability in a seed lot.

Pollen, too, can be stored under proper conditions. The practical maximum, however, appears to be a few years, far less than the storage life of seeds.

This chapter discusses the techniques for preparing seed and pollen for storage, the storage environment necessary for retention of high viability of seeds and pollen, the problems involved, and some of the exceptions among species.

IDEAL STORAGE CONDITIONS

Optimal storage environments, expectedly, differ with different species, but common factors of importance are the relative humidity and temperature of the ambient atmosphere.

The relative humidity of the air usually determines the moisture content of seeds. Exceptions are seeds possessing a seed coat impermeable to moisture, usually called 'hard' seeds.

Immature seeds developing on a plant have a very high moisture content. As the seed matures, an abscission zone develops, reducing the flow of water into the seed. Finally the seed is completely cut off from the mother plant and dries until it is in equilibrium with the relative humidity of the air around it. If, however, the seed is harvested before it has reached such an equilibrium, or if the air is very humid, the moisture content may be dangerously high. Seeds of a moisture content of around 40 percent or higher will germinate unless they are subject to the inhibiting influences of a fruit. Once the seeds have germinated they cannot be stored or redried without death of the seedling. In a range of seed moisture between approximately 20 and 40 per cent, respiration of both the seeds and associated microorganisms results in heating. This respiration can be anaerobic, and the temperature can rise rapidly to levels lethal to the seed. If the seed moisture is in the range between approximately 14 and 20 per cent, the seed will deteriorate rapidly from destruction of the embryo by invasion of microorganisms. Christensen (1957) has done extensive work on the microorganisms involved. Even if the seeds are sterilized there is still rapid respiration, and, through factors not yet understood, the seed of many species will lose viability quickly whereas seeds of other species will survive for long times. Examples of these latter types of seeds are found in various buried-seed experiments. In these species, other factors (such as high CO_2 in the soil air) may reduce respiration or inhibit processes that otherwise lead to a rapid decline in viability.

Below 14 per cent seed moisture, several investigations (for example, Harrington, 1963) indicate that, for many seeds, a 1 per cent loss in seed moisture doubles the life of the seed. This rule of thumb applies down to about 4 per cent seed moisture. Thus, a seed of 4 per cent moisture will maintain viability approximately 1,000 times as long as a seed of 14 per cent moisture. This may seem incredible, but onion (*Allium cepa*) seed containing 14 per cent moisture stored at 35°C will be dead in one week whereas some seed will still be viable after 20 years if it contains only 4 per cent moisture. If, however, seeds of some species are dried below about 4 per cent moisture, deterioration, although still slow, is more rapid than in seed of a moisture content in the range of 4–7 per cent. Harrington (1965) theorizes, by analogy from research on the deterioration of dehydrated foods (Lea, 1962), that the more rapid loss in viability at these extremely low moisture contents is due to autoxidation of lipids in the cells of the embryo, especially in its meristematic areas, leading to destruction of the lipoprotein membranes and, by free-radical formation, destructive reactions of these lipids both with proteins (causing enzyme inactivation) and with nucleic acids (causing destruction of RNA and DNA molecules). However, this autoxidation may be minimized at a seed moisture content of near zero and seed life may be prolonged even longer if such seed is sealed in an oxygen-free, ultra-violet-proof container. An example would be vacuum packing of seeds at zero moisture content in a tin can. A further theory that at higher moisture contents there is a monomolecular layer of water around all macromolecules, retarding entrance of oxygen and preventing physical contact of the lipids with other cell macromolecules is now being critically examined.

Seeds of different species vary widely in chemical composition. The compounds most critical in relation to seed moisture content are the lipids, since they are hydrophobic. Seed of a species having only 4 per cent lipid content (Gramineae) can be contrasted with seed of a species having 36 per cent lipid content (Cruciferae). Compared on the basis of relative moisture content of the non-lipid fraction of the seed a water content of 6 per cent in the Gramineae seed would be equal to a water content of 4 per cent in the Cruciferae seed. At a higher seed moisture range, 16 per cent moisture in the Gramineae would be equivalent to 10.7 per cent in the Cruciferae. Hence if we compare seeds of the same moisture content (calculated on the basis of total fresh weight) the seeds with a high oil content are effectively 'wetter' than the seeds with a low oil content. Thus, seed of a species containing a high oil content will continue to be invaded by microorganisms to a lower seed moisture content, and also can be dried to a lower moisture content before autoxidation becomes serious.

Because of variations in chemical composition, each species has a different moisture equilibrium with a given relative humidity. Even within a single species the chemical composition varies among harvests and with climatic conditions and soil fertility. Further, because of the hysteresis effect (see 'Drying') and because moisture equilibrium increases slightly as temperatures are lowered, each individual seed lot may differ in equilibrium moisture according to its previous history and temperature of storage. Table 43.1 compares the moisture equilibria of several species at five relative humidities. These figures and the oil content of the seed make it possible to anticipate fairly accurately the moisture content that will be reached at a given relative humidity. Table 43.1 also illustrates that if 4–6 per cent seed moisture is ideal for maximum seed life, it will require storage near 15 per cent relative humidity.

TABLE 43.1. Approximate adsorbed moisture of seed in equilibrium with air of various humidities at approximately 25°C, showing a range from low-oil seeds to high-oil seeds (moisture content wet basis, in per cent).

Species	Oil content per cent	Relative humidity, per cent				
		15	30	45	60	75
Triticum vulgare	2	6·5	8·5	10·4	12·1	14·7
Zea mays	5	6·6	8·4	10·2	12·7	14·4
Phaseolus vulgaris	2	5·0	6·5	8·5	11·0	14·0
Soja max	19	—	6·5	7·4	9·3	13·1
Linum usitatissimum	39	4·4	5·6	6·3	7·9	10·0
Brassica campestris	35	4·0	4·5	6·0	7·0	9·0
Brassica oleracea	35	3·5	5·0	6·0	7·0	9·0

Temperature is equally important in influencing seed viability. The lower the storage temperature the longer the life of the seed. Another of Harrington's (1963) rules of thumb applies reasonably well here : between 50°C and 0°C, every 5° lowering of storage temperature doubles the life of the seed. Thus, seed stored at 0°C should have a life expectancy 1,000 times that of seed stored at 50°C. This spectacular increase in longevity is substantiated by the research of several workers. Since relative humidity and temperature appear to be independent in effects, seed with 4 per cent moisture stored at 0°C would be assumed to maintain viability 1,000,000 times as long as seed with 14 per cent moisture stored at 50°C (1,000 × 1,000). This point has not been verified by experiment, but Rocha (1959) found that onion seed of 13 per cent moisture stored at 50°C showed a significant decline in germination and vigor in only two hours. In contrast, Brison (1952) found no appreciable loss in viability in 10 years in onion seed of over 6 per cent moisture stored at 5°C. The life span difference here is more than 44,000 times, with the end point not yet reached and the storage conditions not even the ideal.

At temperatures around 50°C and higher, seed is injured quickly if it is air-dry or moister. The reason may be denaturation of the proteins, inactivating the enzymes and thus killing the seed. Very dry seed of many species, however, can stand 80 to 100°C for at least a few hours.

At the other end of the temperature spectrum, temperatures below 0°C have not been well explored. Temperatures below freezing kill seeds when moisture content is high, but do not harm seeds that are air-dry or drier. Where the break in seed moisture content occurs between injury and no injury is not precisely known. It would vary with the kind of seed, and probably with the rapidity of freezing.

If seeds are dry enough and stored at temperatures below 0°C, how long will they maintain viability? Will the storage life be lengthened as the temperature is lowered further below 0°C? The data available are not completely satisfactory, but there is some indication that reducing temperatures below freezing does prolong viability. Becquerel (1925) stored several species of seeds (dried to about 5% moisture and sealed in a vacuum) in liquid helium ($-269°C$) for four months without loss in germination. He stated that under these conditions there was complete suspension of life and the seed should remain viable forever.

Other environmental factors influencing longevity include the oxygen and carbon dioxide content of the ambient atmosphere and the effects of light and high energy radiation. Under long-term storage, seed viability is harmed by a high-oxygen atmosphere and benefited by a high-carbon-dioxide atmosphere. These phenomena reflect their effect on respiration. When seed is sealed in a container, respiration reduces oxygen and increases carbon dioxide (Harrington, 1963), automatically adjusting the atmosphere for prolongation of seed life. Light, particularly ultraviolet light, is harmful to seed. The cause is most probably autoxidation of lipids, but may be due to the formation of other deleterious compounds. High energy radiation has been found to be harmful, but the lower the seed moisture the less harmful is a given dose.

The causes of aging of seeds are not known for certain, but several factors are probably involved. Starvation of the entire seed is not a cause, for dead seeds contain abundant stored food. It is possible, however, that the meristematic cells of the radicle and plumule could starve even though food is abundant a few cells away, since food transport is impossible at moisture contents below 12 per cent. Some respiration does occur at these low moisture contents. Proteins may also denature slowly, leading to inactivation of enzymes. The possibility is very strong that lipid autoxidation, a nonenzymatic reaction, occurs in dry seeds. The free radicals resulting could react with enzymes, DNA, and RNA, causing their inactivation or destruction. Further, some high energy radiation damage always occurs when storage is for a very long time. Such damage seems to affect some species more than others. The free radicals from lipids and radiation damage could both affect the DNA, creating genetic changes and chromosomal abnormalities leading to death of the cells and, ultimately, to death of the seed.

COLLECTION OF SEED

Maximum viability depends first on collecting only seed that has the best potential for long-time survival. The seed should be obtained at the moment it has reached physiological maturity. Seed harvested when immature will usually not survive as long as mature seed, and seed that is mature soon begins to deteriorate. Deterioration can be slowed by proper techniques, but climatic conditions in the field are not often ideal for minimizing the aging process.

Many theories have been offered as to why immature seed may decline in viability more rapidly than mature seed. The reason may be that development is not complete. One aspect could be that certain compounds may be produced only as the seed reaches maturity. These might include dormancy-inducing compounds, lipid antioxidants such as the tocopherols, and a sufficient supply of energy compounds in the meristematic regions of the radicle and plumule. It is also possible that some proteins may not have reached a structural shape in immature seed that will allow for dehydration without denaturation ; thus, when immature seed is dried, the activity of enzymes may be lost or membranal structure may be injured.

Once a seed has passed physiological maturity, degradation begins that leads to death of the seed. Included are high respiration and deleterious end products as a result of high seed moisture and high temperature. Additionally, weathering may occur from wetting by rain, or a breakdown of compounds in the seed from sunlight.

It is useless to collect seed which has been killed by insects or disease. One should of course take immediate steps to establish conditions that shield the seed from insects or disease and ensure that any insect eggs or fungal spores will be killed or kept dormant. Since fumigation, insecticides, fungicides, and antibiotics may injure seed, these treatments, although beneficial to short-term storage, may reduce the maximum possible life of the seed. Therefore, it is desirable to dry seed to low moisture contents—below 12 per cent for control of diseases and below 9 per cent for insect control. Storage at low temperatures and in a modified atmosphere such as carbon dioxide is best for insect control.

Many seeds are in fleshy fruits at the time they are physiologically mature. While the seed is in the sound ripe fruit, germination inhibitors prevent deterioration. If, however, the seed is injured during extraction, rapid deterioration may follow. Hand methods of macerating the fruit are preferable to mechanical macerating devices. After removal from the fruit, the seed must be dried to a safe moisture level (see the following section).

A less easily controlled and less well understood factor influencing the longevity of seed is the environment in which the plant is grown and the seed matured. Seed viability is reduced by environmental stresses during seed maturation. Environmental stresses include insect and disease attacks on the plant, extremely high or low temperatures, water stress caused by drought or a desiccating wind, or a severe mineral deficiency (Harrington, 1960). Thus, seed should be harvested from the most vigorous and healthy plants.

DRYING

After the seed has been harvested, the moisture content must be reduced to a safe level, preferably to around 12–14 per cent, until the seed is cleaned. After cleaning, the seed can then be dried further to the moisture content most desirable for long-term storage. Seed is not dried to final moisture content before cleaning because it can reabsorb moisture rapidly during cleaning and may have to be redried. Further, seed that is extremely dry cracks easily during cleaning, with a loss of viability. Trash, light seed, and many unwanted species included with seed will not affect viability, but seed is usually cleaned for reasons of neatness and for conservation of space.

Cleaning is accomplished mostly by an air-screen separation. This can be done by hand screens (winnowing) or by machines in various sizes.

Moisture testing is best done in a drying oven—by weighing a thin layer of seed in a weighing dish, drying for two hours at 135°C or 24 hours at 105°C, cooling in a desiccator, and reweighing. The loss in weight is assumed to be only water, and it is further assumed that all the moisture is removed. Neither assumption is entirely true, but the results are close enough for determining whether the seed is dry enough. An accuracy of ±0.2 per cent seed moisture is sufficient.

The various electric moisture-measuring machines available require charts for each kind of seed, which are available for only the most common commercial seeds. Besides, these machines are less accurate in the range of 4–6 per cent seed moisture desired for maximum longevity. The most accurate method is to use the Karl Fisher reagent, which combines stoichiometrically with water, and the loss of reagent can be accurately measured. However, preparation of the sample is laborious, a skilled technician is needed to run the tests, and the reagent is expensive.

As explained above, it appears that, for many species, seed with a moisture content in equilibrium with 15 per cent relative humidity is at an ideal moisture content for longevity. Freshly harvested seeds are seldom so dry and under many climatic conditions it is impossible to keep them so dry in open storage. Obviously, the sooner the seeds reach this moisture content the longer they will survive, having had less time at the more injurious high moisture contents. Thus a proper drying technique is necessary, and, after the seeds are dried, a moisture-proof container is necessary to prevent reabsorption of moisture.

Drying can be accomplished by two techniques. One is to raise the temperature of the air, which reduces its relative humidity. The other is to remove moisture from the air without changing the temperature, which also reduces relative humidity.

If air at 5°C and 90 per cent relative humidity is heated to 35°C it will then have 15 per cent relative humidity, the level needed to bring the seeds to the most desirable moisture content. The air, heated to 35°C, is blown through the seed until moisture reaches equilibrium between the air and the seed. The time to equilibrium may be less than an hour with a seed layer only one seed thick, but can vary from a few days to over a week with a seed layer three or four feet thick. The time of drying is influenced by other variables such as speed of air flow, seed size, permeability of the seed coat, and cleanness of the seed lot.

Although 35°C is safe for drying seeds, 50°C can be very damaging to seeds of high moisture content. It is best never to exceed 35°C. A compromise may be made if speed of drying and the presence of warm moist air require higher temperatures: then, the temperature of the drying air can be raised as the seed dries, even to 45°C when the seeds have become quite dry.

There are climatic situations where raising the temperature even to 45°C will not produce a drying air of 15 per cent relative humidity. For example, in many tropical areas the air for weeks at a time may exceed 30°C and 90 per cent relative humidity. Raising the temperature of such air to 45°C will reduce the relative humidity only to 40 per cent. Under these conditions the water vapor must be removed from the air without raising the temperature—by : (a) refrigerating the air to below the dew point, condensing the water vapor on the cooling coils, and then reheating the air to 35°C ; or (b) using a desiccant. (The air is blown through the desiccant, which removes the water vapor, and then through the seed. Various desiccants can be used, but the most indestructible and easiest to reuse is silica gel.) There are advantages and disadvantages to both of these methods, and both are expensive for small lots of seed. For small lots of seed that have first been air-dried to a moisture content below 20 per cent, a third method is completely satisfactory. The air-dried seed is placed in a sealed container with an equal quantity of silica gel that has been freshly dried at 200°C and cooled. The silica gel, seed, and enclosed air will come to an equilibrium near 15 per cent relative humidity.

After drying, the seed must be stored in a moisture-proof container. Harrington (1963) described moisture-proof containers, including tin cans, glass mason jars, aluminium-foil polyester pouches, and 10-mil polyethylene bags. For large quantities, moisture-proof gasket-lidded drums and steel bins are available. Many commercial seedsmen and experiment stations have rooms dehumidified to 15 per cent relative humidity for the storage of seeds.

The relationship between seed moisture and the relative humidity of the surrounding air needs clarification. Surprisingly, the moisture content of the seed is a function not of the absolute water-vapor content of the air but of the relative humidity. For example, air at 50 per cent relative humidity contains 19 grams of water vapor per cubic foot at 5°C, and 124 grams per cubic foot at 35°C, yet the moisture content of the seed in equilibrium with these two atmospheres will be almost exactly the same. It will be slightly lower at the high temperature, because of the higher kinetic energy of the water in the seed. The relationship between relative humidity and seed moisture is sigmoid, as illustrated in Fig. 43.1. Note that at the same relative humidity the moisture content of the seed is higher if the moisture is being removed to reach equilibrium than if it is being added to reach equilibrium. This is known as the hystcresis effect. The hysteresis effect is explained by the fact that as the seed is dried structural changes occur in the macromolecules which are not completely reversed at low levels of resorption of moisture.

The flex point at about 4 per cent for wheat is assumed to be the point at which the monomolecular layer of water around the macromolecules begins to be removed. As can be seen from Figure 43.1, there is a very sharp rise in moisture content at about 95 per cent relative humid-

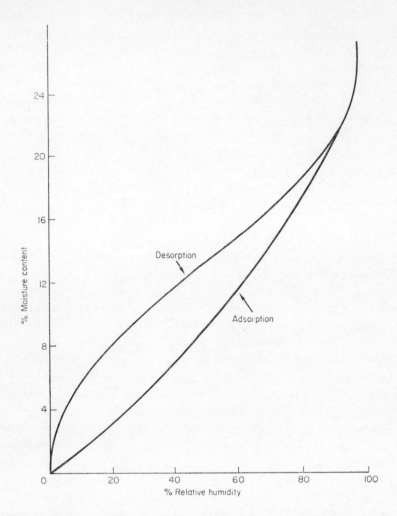

FIG. 43.1. The moisture content of wheat seed expressed on a fresh-weight basis as a function of the relative humidity of the air in equilibrium with it. From Babbitt (1949).

ity. It is extremely difficult to determine the equilibrium at 100 per cent because of the rapid growth of microorganisms. For most species the equilibrium moisture content of seed is between 20 and 30 per cent in the relative humidity range of 95–100 per cent. The International Seed Testing Association (1963) has an excellent monograph on seed drying.

It is essential to know the germination percentage of each lot of seed stored. The initial germination percentage is determined prior to storage and as soon after harvest as possible. If a lot of seed germinated 90 per cent before storage but germinated only 40 per cent after 20 years of storage, there might be grave suspicion that some genetic selection had occurred. If, however, even after the best cleaning techniques, a seed lot germinated only 40 per cent at the start of storage and still germinated 40 per cent after twenty years, then no genetic selection would have occurred during the storage period. If the initial germination is 40 per cent or less, the germination percentage might possibly be improved by refined cleaning techniques such as the gravity machine, electrostatic separation, flotation, or a more severe air separation to remove dead seed. A much more likely situation, however, particularly with seed of wild species, is that this lot of seed is partially dormant.

DORMANCY

Dormancy in seeds is important to preserving seed viability. Unfortunately, the term 'dormancy' has been used in different ways by various workers. The following definitions are used in the discussion below:

Dormant—a seed is dormant from the time it abscisses or is detached from the mother plant until germination begins.

External dormancy—a seed is dormant because environmental factors are unfavourable for germination. These include unfavourable temperature, insufficient or excess water, insufficient oxygen, or excess carbon dioxide.

Internal dormancy—a viable seed that does not germinate when placed in an environment favourable to germination. Internal dormancy may be caused by immaturity of the embryo, inhibitors present in the seed, impermeable seed coats (hard seeds), or lack of germination triggering compound. Internal dormancies usually disappear with time. In storage the embryo continues to develop until mature, the inhibitors break down, or the triggering chemical is accumulated.

Hard seeds usually remain hard until environmental conditions soften the seed coats. These conditions may be the action of micro organisms in soil breaking down the seed coat; changes in relative humidity affecting its permeability; cracking of the seed coat by expansion and contraction; or abrasion of the seed coat, as might occur when the seed is washed down a stream. Likewise, germination inhibitors can be leached from seeds by soaking. Further, immature seeds may mature only slowly or not at all at one temperature but much more rapidly at another. This can be said equally for destruction of inhibitors or accumulation of a triggering compound. For example, seeds of many species will not germinate until stratified—given a month to a few months of storage at around 5°C in an imbibed state. During stratification one or more of these processes occur, yet they will not occur if the imbibed seed is subject to higher temperatures. In fact, for some species dormancy is enhanced at temperatures of 25–35°C, suggesting an increase in the inhibitor or destruction of the triggering compound. Thus, internal dormancy can also be regulated by environmental factors.

Hence, maximum viability is obtained by maintaining dormancy. This includes controlling all the environmental factors in external dormancy and maintaining the maximum internal dormancy.

If a seed of a given species germinates best at 25°C, then a storage temperature well below 25°C is generally desirable. This usually means a colder temperature, but it is possible that seeds of *Lactuca*, for example, which have a high-temperature dormancy, may survive longer at 35°C than at 5°C.

If a seed has a hard seed coat, every effort should be made to preserve the hard seed coat. With these species, storage temperature and relative humidity may not be so important. Many Leguminosae species illustrate this possibility.

If high moisture in the seed allows a loss of internal dormancy, it is best to reduce the moisture to a low level, yet the seeds of certain water species appear to survive longer submerged in water than if allowed to dry out. In such seeds a low oxygen supply may maintain dormancy. If a seed cannot be dried without being killed, then a temperature below freezing will probably be injurious. However, in the great majority of the species, the colder the storage the better.

In the few species that have been studied intensively it is clear that the maximum life span of seed is achieved by creating a storage environment that maximizes the external and internal factors controlling dormancy.

It is necessary to know how to break these dormancies when germination is desired. This is complicated because many types of dormancies have evolved in different species.

Scarifying will usually break dormancy caused by hard seed. Stratifying in a moist environment at 5°C for 1 to 6 months, plus gibberellic acid treatment, will break some forms of dormancy. The reader is referred to Crocker and Barton (1953) for an extensive discussion of dormancy breaks.

LIFE SPAN OF SEEDS

There is some information about the life span of seeds of a few hundred species, but little is known for the rest of the species. In 1908, Ewart proposed three biological classes of seeds : (a) *microbiotic*, whose life span does not exceed 3 years ; (b) *mesobiotic*, whose life span ranges from 3 to 15 years ; and (c) *macrobiotic*, whose life span ranges from 15 to over 100 years. At that time he was pessimistic about the accuracy of many records and knowledge of the factors affecting seed longevity. Since his classical work much more reliable data have become available on the life span of many species of seeds, and much more is known about the environment and internal dormancy factors which influence the life span of seeds.

It is clear now, for example, that there are no discrete groups of seeds with similar life spans, but a continuum from the shortest-lived to the longest-lived. Even under ideal conditions the seed of most species of *Quercus* and *Citrus* will not survive past three years. In contrast, the seed of many species in Leguminosae will survive for over 100 years. Seeds of most species of *Allium* are dead in less than three years under open storage yet have been kept for 20 years without loss of germination if dried to 6 per cent moisture and stored at 5°C. By extrapolation, if this seed were kept at −190°C it should be viable for hundreds of years. Thus, depending on the environment available for storage, *Allium* species could be in any one of Ewart's three classes.

No comparative life-span studies have been made of a large number of species stored under ideal environmental conditions. Went and Munz (1949) tried to set up such an experiment, but the quality of the seeds at the start of the experiment was very poor. There is great need for a well-executed experiment of this type, and present knowledge makes it possible.

There are numerous references to the life span of seeds of different species. Ewart (1908), Crocker (1948), Owen (1957), and Mayer and Poljakoff-Mayber (1963) have extensively reviewed earlier data. It is difficult to combine data for different species into a common table because different experimental conditions have been used, the history of the seed before storage is not always known, and the environments used in most experiments were less than ideal. Even so, some generalizations can be made.

(1) The seeds of a group of species which cannot be dried without loss of viability have a very short life span, usually less than one year, even if stored near 0°C. These seeds cannot be frozen without injury. Modified atmospheres such as a high CO_2 atmosphere delay senescence in some species, but not enough to extend the life span much beyond a year. Seeds of several tropical species fall in this class, and more extensive studies would probably identify seeds of several other tropical species as unable to withstand drying.

Among the species in this group are:

Family	Genus and species	Common name
Gramineae	Zizania aquatica	wild rice
	Saccharum sp.	sugar canes
Palmaceae	Cocos nucifera	coconut
	Sabal sp.	palmetto palms
Salicaceae	Populus sp.	poplars
	Salix sp.	willows
Juglandaceae	Juglans sp.	walnuts, butternut
	Carya sp.	hickories, pecan
Fagaceae	Castanea sp.	chestnuts
	Fagus sp.	beeches
	Quercus sp.	oaks
Rutaceae	Citrus sp.	orange, grapefruit, lemon
Euphorbiaceae	Hevea brasiliensis	rubber tree
Aceraceae	Acer saccharinum	silver or river maple
Hippocastanaceae	Aesculus sp.	horse chestnuts
Theaceae	Thea sinensis	tea
Cucurbitaceae	Sechium edule	chayote

The elms (*Ulmus* sp.) are usually included in this group, but slow drying makes it possible to dry seeds to moisture contents in the 5 per cent range and increase their life span to many years. Possibly, with the proper techniques, seed of some of the species above could also be dried for long-term storage.

(2) Another group of species has seed that survive for long times in soil. The two most exhaustive experiments were established by Beal and Durel, comparing the life spans of seeds in soil. Published results cover 70 years of the Beal experiment (Darlington, 1951) and 39 years of the Durel experiment (Toole and Brown, 1946). Ødum (1965) has published a list of species of seed buried in sites dated by archeology which germinated when brought to the surface. The species in which seed germinated following burial in soil for twenty years or longer include:

Family	Genus and species	Common name	Life span
Gramineae	*Phalaris arundinacea*	reed canary grass	30
	Phleum pratense	timothy	21
	Poa pratensis	Kentucky bluegrass	39
	Setaria lutescens	yellow foxtail	30
	Setaria verticillata	foxtail	39
	Setaria viridis	green foxtail	39
	Sporobolus airoides	hairgrass dropseed	21
	Sporobolus cryptandrus	sand dropseed	39
Cyperaceae	*Cyperus esculentus*	yellow nutgrass	21
Urticaceae	*Boehmeria nivea*	ramie	39
	Urtica dioica	nettle	600
Polygonaceae	*Polygonum aviculare*	wire grass	400
	Polygonum hydropiper	—	50
	Polygonum pensylvanicum	smart weed	30
	Polygonum persicaria	ladysthumb	30
	Polygonum scandens	climbing false buckwheat	21
	Rumex crispus	curled dock	70
	Rumex obtusifolius	broad-leaved dock	39
	Rumex salicifolius	willow-leaved dock	39
Chenopodiaceae	*Beta vulgaris*	sugar beet	21
	Chenopodium album	Lambsquarter	1700
	Chenopodium hybridum	maple-leaved goosefoot	39
Caryophyllaceae	*Cerastium caespitosum*	chickweed	600
	Spergula arvensis	spurry	1700
	Stellaria media	common chickweed	600
Ranunculaceae	*Ranunculus repens*	creeping crowfoot	600
Amaranthaceae	*Amaranthus graecizans*	tumble-weed	40
	Amaranthus retroflexus	rough pigweed	40
Phytolaccaceae	*Phytolacca americana*	pokeweed	> 39
Portulacaceae	*Portulaca oleracea*	purslane	40
Nymphaeaceae	*Nelumbo nucifera*	East Indian lotus	1000
Fumariaceae	*Fumaria officinalis*	fumatory	600
Cruciferae	*Brassica campestris*	common mustard	600
	Brassica nigra	black mustard	50
	Lipidium virginicum	—	40
	Thlaspi arvense	field pennycress	30
	Capsella bursa-pastoris	shepherds purse	35
Rosaceae	*Potentilla norvegica*	rough cinquefoil	> 39
Leguminosae	*Cassia marilandica*	wild senna	30
	Lespedeza intermedia	lespedeza	> 39
	Lupinus arcticus	—	10000
	Robinia pseudoacacia	black locust	> 39
	Trifolium hybridum	alsike clover	30
	Trifolium pratense	red clover	> 41
	Trifolium repens	white clover	600

Family	Genus and species	Common name	Life span
Anacardiaceae	*Rhus glabra*	smooth sumac	39
Malvaceae	*Abutilon theophrasti*	velvet leaf	>39
	Hibiscus militaris	halberd-leaved rosemallow	39
Hypericaceae	*Ascryum hypericoides*	St. Andrew's cross	39
Violaceae	*Viola arvensis*	Field pansy	400
Onagraceae	*Oenothera biennis*	evening primrose	70
Umbelliferae	*Apium graveolens*	celery	39
Convolvulaceae	*Convolvulus sepium*	hedge bindweed	>39
	Cuscuta polygonorum	smartweed dodder	39
	Ipomoea lacunosa	small flowered white morning glory	39
Verbenaceae	*Verbena hastata*	blue vervain	39
	Verbena urticifolia	white vervain	39
Labiatae	*Glecoma hederacea*	grounding	400
	Lamium album	nettle	600
	Lamium purpureum	nettle	600
Solanaceae	*Datura stramonium*	jimson weed	>39
	Hyoscyamus niger	henbane	600
	Nicotiana tabacum	tobacco	>39
	Solanum nigrum	black nightshade	>39
Scrophulariaceae	*Verbascum thapsus*	common mullein	600
Plantaginaceae	*Plantago major*	common plantain	40
	Plantago rugellii	Rugel's plantain	21
Caprifoliaceae	*Sambucus nigra*	European elder	500
Compositae	*Ambrosia artemisiifolia*	ragweed	>39
	Ambrosia elatior	—	40
	Arctium lappa	burdock	39
	Carduus crispus	thistle	600
	Chrysanthemum leucanthemum	oxeye daisy	39
	Helianthus annuus	wild sunflower	30
	Onopordum acanthium	Scotch thistle	>39
	Rudbeckia hirta	black-eyed susan	>39
	Sonchus oleraceus	snow-thistle	600
	Anthemis cotula	mayweed	25
	Taraxacum vulgare	dandelion	600

The experiment of Durel included many cultivars. Very few seeds survived beyond one year in the soil. The maximum life span of seed of these cultivars, however, has not been determined with proper drying and storage in a sealed container. On the other hand, evidence indicates that the seeds of many weed species survive longer in the soil than in air storage. This is probably due to fluctuating storage temperature and relative humidity in air, as well as the possibility that soil storage may establish a low-oxygen high-carbon-dioxide atmosphere.

Nelumbo nucifera, which has survived a long time in soil (around 1,000 years), has a very thick hard seed coat and was found in cold peat soil at a depth where oxygen would be extremely limiting. All these conditions favour long seed life. Ødum (1965) found two species (*Chenopodium album* and *Spergula arvensis*) that were dated archeologically to be 1,700 years old and had no dormancy but germinated readily when brought to the surface. Porsild, Harington and Mulligan (1967) reported that seeds of *Lupinus arcticus* buried at least 10,000 years (radiocarbon-dated) in lemming burrows preserved in permanently frozen organic soil germinated when tested. In all three of these examples of extremely long-lived seeds, storage was under extreme cold and very low oxygen. Further, the lotus were hard seeds that needed scarification. Even so, all were high in moisture and nevertheless maintained viability.

(3) Group three contains many examples of seeds of species obtained from herbaria that still germinated after 50 years of storage. These seeds survived ambient relative humidities, usually quite low, and ambient temperatures. Many, if not all, have hard seeds. Becquerel (1934) and Ewart (1908) have the most inclusive lists:

Family	Genus and species	Life span
Iridaceae	*Watsonia* sp.	>50
Nymphaeaceae	*Nelumbo nucifera*	250
Leguminosae	*Albizzia julibrissin*	149
	Anthyllis vulneraria	90
	Astragalus massiliensis	86
	Astragalus utriger	82
	Cassia bicapsularis	115
	Cassia multijuga	158
	Cytisus biflorus	84
	Dioclea pauciflora	93
	Ervum lens	65
	Goodia lotifolia	105
	Hovea linearis	105
	Indigofera cytisoides	51
	Leucaena leucocephala	99
	Lotus uliginosus	81
	Medicago orbicularis	78
	Melilotus alba	81
	Melilotus gracilis	58
	Melilotus lutea	55
	Mimosa glomerata	81
	Trifolium arvense	68
	Trifolium pratense	81
	Trifolium striatum	90
	Species of at least 30 other genera	>50

Family	Genus and species	Life span
Tiliaceae	*Entelea arborescens*	51
Malvaceae	*Lavatera pseudo-olbia*	64
	Abutilon sp.	> 50
	Hibiscus sp.	> 50
	Modiola sp.	> 50
	Sida sp.	> 50
Sterculiaceae	*Hermannia* sp.	> 50
Euphorbiaceae	*Euphorbia* sp.	> 50
	Pseudanthus sp.	> 50
Labiatae	*Stachys nepetifolia*	> 50

(4) In addition to the species known to have short-lived seed and the two groups of species above known to have long-lived seed are the species whose life span is poorly understood. This includes most of the plant species of the world. However, it is probable that if viable seeds are stored under ideal conditions, most species will retain their viability for at least twenty years and probably much longer.

POLLEN STORAGE

Preserving the viability of pollen presents problems quite similar to those with seed, though the life span is generally shorter. There is a need for short-term storage of pollen in hybridization experiments where plants flower at different times or where populations are geographically separated. There is also a need to store pollen from season to season or for several years as a means of preserving plant gene resources.

For most species, pollen will maintain viability longer at low temperature than at high temperature. Visser (1955) stored pollen of *Pyrus malus* for two years in liquid air and found it as good as fresh pollen. He considered that pollen of *Pyrus malus* would keep indefinitely in liquid air. This is the same as the opinion held by some research workers that seed of many species will remain viable indefinitely at the temperatures of liquid air. On the other hand, the freezing of pollen of many Gramineae species is harmful.

Again, as with seeds, the viability of pollen of most species keeps longest at a low relative humidity. In most species the pollen stores best in a range of 10–30 per cent relative humidity, although there are some species (such as *Permistera typhoideum*) in which pollen remains viable longest at 0 per cent relative humidity. The lower relative humidities may cause lipid autoxidation in most species. The pollen of a few species including many of the species in Gramineae, cannot be dried without being killed. At 60 per cent relative humidity and above, however, bacterial and fungal growth are serious. Maize, wheat, rye, barley, and sugar cane pollen at 90–100 per cent relative humidity and 0–10°C can be kept viable for only a few days to three weeks at most.

Pollen viability is lost more rapidly when relative humidity fluctuates than when it is kept constant.

If pollen is dried to equilibrium with 10–30 per cent relative humidity, reconditioning is necessary by storing it at about 80 per cent relative humidity for a short while (a day with some species).

The gaseous atmosphere also influences the longevity of pollen. Increasing the oxygen concentration is less favourable, while increasing carbon dioxide is more favourable for longevity. The experimental evidence is conflicting on the advantage or disadvantage of a vacuum or nitrogen storage. Exposure to light, especially ultraviolet light, is detrimental.

King (1965) successfully freeze-dried (lyophylized) pollen and sealed it in a glass capsule either under vacuum or in nitrogen gas. The pollen remained viable for up to three years at uncontrolled room temperature. This technique should be extremely useful for shipping to any part of the world those pollens that can stand freezing and dehydration.

The viability of pollen can be measured by either the percentage of fruit set or by germination tests on artificial media. The two tests do not always give identical results. Some stored pollens that have an excellent pollen tube elongation in cultures will not set fruit. Stored pollen of other species may show no germination in cultures but set fruit. In the latter situation it is possible that the stigmas and styles were supplying materials which have become lacking in the pollen, since it has been found that stored pollen may have a higher sugar requirement or be more sensitive to boron than fresh pollen when germinated in cultures.

Stored pollen may show erratic germination. This may be due to improper rehydration or to the release of bound enzymes by freezing of pollen. Other tests of viability include tetrazolium, peroxidase, and acetocarmine tests. These are only indications at best.

Holman and Brubaker (1926) stored pollen of many species. Certain families contained species with long-lived pollen, others tended toward intermediate longevity, and still others were rather short lived.

Families with many species with long-lived pollen include : Primulaceae, Rosaceae, Leguminosae, Saxifragaceae, and Pinaceae.

Families with intermediate pollen viability include : Amaryllidaceae, Liliaceae, Ranunculaceae, Salicaceae, and Scrophulariaceae.

Families with short-lived pollen include: Alismataceae, Cyperaceae, Commelinaceae, Juncaceae, and, especially, Gramineae.

Additional data on individual species are provided in Table 154 of the Handbook of Biological Data (1956) and in tables of King (1965). None of these tables, however, are able to include the maximum storage life of pollen of a given species. The fact is that the ideal storage conditions are known only roughly, nor is even the approximate storage life of pollen of most species known, since fewer than 400–500 species have been examined.

Lindkens (1964) and Johri and Vasil (1961) list possible causes for aging of pollen. These are mostly the same causes proposed for the aging of seeds: (a) respiratory substrate exhaustion; (b) inactivation of enzymes, growth hormones, and particularly pantothenic acid, part of coenzyme A; (c) desiccation injury; (d) accumulation of secondary metabolic products, resulting in a blocking effect; and (e) changes in lipids of the exine of the pollen membrane (might also be lipid autoxidation?).

REFERENCES

BABBITT J.D. (1949) Observations on the adsorption of water vapour by wheat. *Can. J. Res.* **27,** 55–72.

BECQUEREL P. (1925) La suspension de la vie des graines dans la vide a la temperature de l'helium liquide. *Compt. Rend. Acad. Sci. Paris* **181,** 805–807.

BECQUEREL P. (1934) La longevité des graines macrobiotiques. *Compt. Rend. Acad. Sci. Paris* **199,** 1662–1664.

BRISON F.R. (1952) Influence of storage conditions on the germination of onion seed. *Prog. Rept. Texas Agr. Expt. Sta.* **1492,** 1–4.

CHRISTENSEN C.M. (1957) Deterioration of stored grains by fungi. *Bot. Rev.* **23,** 108–134.

CROCKER W. (1948) Life span of seeds. In *Growth of Plants*, 28–66. Reinhold, New York.

CROCKER W. & BARTON L.V. (1953) *Physiology of Seeds*. Chronica Botanica, Waltham, Mass.

DARLINGTON H.T. (1951) The seventy-year period for Dr. Beal's seed viability experiment. *Am. J. Bot.* **38,** 379–281.

EWART A.J. (1908) On the longevity of seeds. *Proc. R. Soc. Vict.* **21,** 1–210.

HARRINGTON J.F. (1960) Germination of seeds from carrot, lettuce, and pepper plants grown under severe nutrient deficiencies. *Hilgardia* **30,** 219–235.

HARRINGTON J.F. (1963) The value of moisture-resistant containers in vegetable seed packaging. *Calif. Agr. Expt. Sta. Bull.* **792,** 1–23.

HARRINGTON J.F. (1965) New theories on the biochemistry of seed aging. *Agron. Abstr.* p. 41. (1965 Annual Meeting of the American Society of Agronomy).

Holman R.M. & Brubaker Florence (1926) On the longevity of pollen. *Univ. Calif. Publs. Bot.* **13,** 179–204.

International Seed Testing Association (1963) Drying and storage. *Proc. int. Seed Test. Ass.* **28,** 689–1000.

Johri B.M. & Vasil I.K. (1961) Physiology of pollen. *Bot. Rev.* **27,** 326–381.

King J.R. (1965) The storage of pollen—particularly by the freeze-drying method. *Bull . Torrey bot. Club.* **92,** 270–287.

Lea C.H. (1962) The oxidative deterioration of food lipids. In *Lipids and their Oxidation* (Ed. Schultz H.W.). Avi Publishing Co., Westport, Connecticut.

Lindkens H.F. (1964) Pollen physiology. *Ann. Rev. Pl. Physiol.* **15,** 255–270.

Mayer A.M. & Poljakoff-Mayber A. (1963) *The Germination of Seeds.* Macmillan, N.Y.

Ødum S. (1965) Germination of ancient seeds. Floristical observations and experiments with archaeologically dated soil samples. *Dansk bot. Ark.* **24,** 1–70.

Owen B. (1957) The storage of seeds for maintenance of viability. *Bull. Commonw. Bur. Past. Fld. Crops* No. 43.

Porsild A.E., Harington C.R. & Mulligan G.A. (1967) *Lupinus arcticus* Wats. grown from seeds of Pleistocene Age. *Science* **158,** 113–114.

Rocha F.F. (1959) Interaction of moisture content and temperature on onion seed viability. *Am. Soc. Hort. Sci.* **73,** 385–389.

Spector W.S. (Ed.) (1956) *Handbook of Biological Data.* W.B. Saunders Co., Philadelphia.

Toole E.H. & Brown E. (1946) Final results of the Durel buried seed experiment. *J. agric. Res.* **72,** 201–210.

Visser T. (1955) Germination and storage of pollen. *Meded. van de LandbHoogesch. Wageningen* **55,** 1–68.

Went F. & Munz P.A. (1949) A long term test of seed longevity. *Aliso* **2,** 63–75.

THE CONSERVATION OF GENE RESOURCES OF FOREST TREES

P. BOUVAREL

Centre National de Recherches Forestieres (I.N.R.A.)

Nancy, France

INTRODUCTION

Until the 1940s, with few exceptions, forest tree collections were made by arboreta and botanical gardens. The major objective was to gather specimens of the principal taxonomic categories (species, sub-species, varieties, forms) for the use of taxonomic botanists. These arboretum collections have been very useful for determining the growth and development of exotic species for ornamental and afforestation purposes; their potential for tree breeding was hardly realized.

Experimental plantations had been established previously in certain countries to ascertain the performance of exotic species, but they had not been planned to conserve, with minimum modification, the gene resources of the species concerned. Since the last world war, the substantial development of tree breeding has changed the conception of tree collections, and has resulted in new collections more suitable for the conservation of the gene resources of interesting types, regardless of whether or not they are defined by classical taxonomy.

Forest trees possess three essential characteristics which govern the nature of the collections intended to conserve genetic resources:

Their size is large, therefore collections will cover large areas and it would be difficult for each type to be represented by a great number of individuals.

They are long-lived, ensuring permanence and stability in time.

They are wild species, predominantly allogamous, which grow over large natural regions, and possess *great genetic variability* at the individual level (pronounced heterozygosis) and at the infra-specific level (numerous ecotypes with pronounced differences).

CONSERVATION OF STANDS *in situ*

At first sight, it would seem that there is no serious risk of the loss of natural stands in countries where forestry tradition has long been estab-

S

lished and where good legislation against clear cutting has been enacted. There are risks however, as even these countries are not fully protected from extensive forest fires, insect and disease epidemics, and from the deleterious effects of air polution. Furthermore, modern silvicultural systems frequently lead to the substitution of natural stands at present considered to be of little economic value, by plantations of more productive species or provenances.

Conservation measures are fairly easy to apply in the case of such stands, autochthonous or allochthonous, *selected as seed stands*, either because of their good phenotypic characters or because of the value of their progeny. They should be protected :

Against the risk of premature exploitation of the trees. Seed stands in public forests may be excluded in the working plans ; in the case of private forests the loss of revenue incurred by maintaining the trees beyond their commercial maturity must be compensated by the sale of seed.

Against the risk of hybridization by pollen from stands of the same or other species. The width of a safe isolation distance will vary with the species, the method of pollination (by wind or insects), the direction of the prevailing winds, and the existence of a forested belt. The seed stands should be encircled by natural forested belts at least 100 meters wide and of the same genetic constitution as the seed stand itself.

These conditions are sometimes difficult to achieve for isolated and small artificial stands (Douglas fir in Western Europe, Schlitz larch in Germany) as well as for some autochthonous old stands surrounded by plantations (Scots pine of Saint-Die and Wangenbourg in the Vosges, Spruce in the Harz). It will often be necessary to establish special plantations or resort to vegetative propagation in order to conserve the gene resources of these highly valuable stands without adulteration.

But in other regions of the world, in particular in the developing countries where population pressure finds relief at the expense of the forest and where, from a social point of view, control by drastic legislation is not possible, millions of hectares of forest and thousands of valuable genotypes are on the point of rapidly disappearing through clearing, illegal exploitation, deliberate burning and grazing. The underlying forces are tremendously powerful and it is obvious that the conservation of gene resources cannot be the first and most important argument against such destruction. However, it is necessary to draw the

attention of governments and international organizations to the existence of such a problem in order that :

> Conservation measures to protect seed stands can be taken within
> the framework of integrated forest protection programs.
>
> Institutions concerned can be alerted in good time when a serious
> danger exists so that adequate measures can be taken or advised
> for the conservation *in situ* or in collections.

Obviously all possible efforts must be made to ensure the conservation *in situ* of the greatest possible number of stands considered valuable
because of their genetic resources. However, the countries in which
such stands are located, and which are therefore responsible for their
protection and conservation, are not always those most directly
interested.

It would be unwise to rely exclusively in the future on conservation
in situ. It is certain that increasingly the gene resources necessary for the
improvement of forest trees will be efficiently conserved in collection
plantations. The type of conservatory plantations will vary depending
upon :

> The normal reproduction method of the species ; sexual repro-
> duction or vegetative propagation.
>
> The objectives ; whether the aim is to conserve botanical types,
> selected populations, or selected individuals, and whether the
> collections are or are not to be used for seed production.

CONSERVATION OF SPECIES THAT CAN NORMALLY
BE PROPAGATED VEGETATIVELY

This mainly concerns poplars (with the exception of the section Leuce).
Collections are established from cuttings taken from a single individual,
the ortet ; each clone should be represented by about 10 ramets. It is
advisable to have, in another place, stools of these clones for the production of new cuttings. If mutant branches appear on trees of the
collection or on an ortet, the whole tree should be eliminated ; the
mutant if interesting should be conserved by cloning.

Vegetative reproduction is used mainly for the conservation of
selected clones. It is not practical for the conservation of natural poplar
stands which are essential to provide the tree breeder with as wide and
varied a genetic base as possible. In this case it is necessary also to use
seed, and therefore the problem is the same as the general problem of
the conservation of ecotypes.

THE DISADVANTAGES OF CONVENTIONAL ARBORETA—
MODERN CONCEPTION

Arboreta of an earlier type contained as large a number of species as possible, each represented by a few individuals, with no provision for statistical evaluation. They have had the great advantage of providing a start for the introduction of exotic species which enabled improvements in the productivity of afforestation. Nevertheless, they do have the following disadvantages :

Each species is usually represented by individuals from a single provenance, itself of uncertain or unknown origin. If that particular provenance was one of the best or one of the poorest, the potential of the species for afforestation has been over- or under-estimated.

Representatives of certain species are the offspring of seed collected in other arboreta, where the probability of hybridization would be increased by the arrangement of collections by genera. Sometimes this led to great confusion and has resulted in faulty nomenclature.

In other cases the seed used originated from self-pollination of isolated individuals of the same species. This may have resulted in lack of vigor of the offspring, in the underestimation of the value of the species in question, and in all the disadvantages of excessive consanguinity in cases where the seed from the later generations was also used.

Modern arboreta are given over chiefly to exotic species as yet little used or not used at all in the country where the arboreta are located. (Species currently used for afforestation are the subject of special types of collections which will be dealt with later). The purposes of these arboreta are :

To obtain preliminary estimates of the potential of these species for afforestation and/or ornamentation.

To enable the tree breeder to use these species for interspecific hybridization.

We believe that exotic species should be established on the following basis :

Each species should be represented by at least 2 provenances (area of optimum development ; marginal area) to ascertain its variability as accurately as possible.

At least 10 individuals per species per unit plot (if the layout calls for replications) is desirable in order to have at least five adult trees.

One arboretum should be established in each major ecological region to evaluate the performance of the species in relation to varying environmental conditions; it is better to have a network of small '*ecological arboreta*' rather than a few large arboreta.

The following two rules should be adhered to:

Seed obtained from arboreta must not be used for the establishment of other collections. If trees need to be multiplied and if is impossible to go back to the original seed stand, vegetative propagation must be utilized.

No selection program for a particular species should be based on the individuals growing in an arboretum because they are always too few for this purpose. This does not apply to the first stage of an interspecific hybridization program where the objective is to assess roughly the potential of an 'average hybrid' between two species.

CONSERVATION OF ECOTYPES

For each major afforestation species, hundreds if not thousands of batches of planting stock, derived from seed of well-defined origin, are needed for a selection program. These populations (provenances)—which can be regarded more or less as ecotypes if sampling has been adequate—are subjected to comparative trials (provenance test plantations) to identify the best provenances and to guide the collection and importation of seed for large-scale afforestation. When the experiment has been completed one is not always certain of again finding the same provenances (we have discussed the problems of conservation *in situ*). Therefore, provision must sometimes be made for their multiplication to provide seed-production plantations capable of supplying all the necessary seed. Such plantations are of three kinds:

Provenance test plantations. Although they are established primarily to identify the best provenances and are outplanted in an adequate experimental design, provenance test plantations can play a seed-production role. In fact they are the most common method used for the conservation of ecotypes. For this purpose they must fulfil certain conditions and suffer from some limitations in the further utilization of the material.

In order to have an ecotype adequately represented, the seed must be collected from at least 10 parent trees. These parent trees must be adequately scattered and the total number of trees of each provenance must be at least 100.

The multiplication of a provenance should be by vegetative propagation, not by seed, because of the considerable risk of hybridization between provenances. The trees thus established by vegetative propagation are generally intended for the creation of seed orchards.

Provenance conservation plantations. Where it is known that certain provenances available for provenance tests may not easily be found again, their conservation must be insured by the establishment of special plantations for each provenance, well identified and isolated from other trees of the same species.

Seed orchards for provenance conservation. These are established with grafted plants of a *single provenance* (ecotype). The number of clones used must be as large as possible to adequately represent the provenance if it is intended to maintain a faithful image of the gene frequencies. In no case must this number be less than 30 trees, covering the range of variation of the entire provenance. These seed orchards ensure the conservation of ecotypes too seriously threatened by hybridization with artificial stands to utilize their sexual progenies. They can be used also for the multiplication of the best provenances for seed production.

It should be noted that although these techniques, by proper sampling of the seed trees, may permit the conservation of ecotypes with gene frequencies reasonably similar to those in the natural stands, they do not guarantee reproduction of the gene arrangement. Consanguinity occurs in the stands subject to natural regeneration because of the limited effective dissemination distances of pollen and of seed. Such consanguinity is obviously eliminated in the stands established with seed collected in the plantations or in the seed orchards established for the conservation of provenances. In the latter case they exhibit lower homozygosis which generally makes for enhanced vigor, and to that extent does not reduce their practical value.

CONSERVATION OF INDIVIDUALS

This concerns either trees selected for improvement work (plus trees) or trees exhibiting some mutation that is worth exploiting for ornamental purposes. Vegetative propagation, most commonly by grafting, is obviously the only conservation technique. Ramets of these plus-trees clones

are grouped together in *clonal archives* which have a three-fold purpose :
Conservation of gene resources.
Production of scions for clonal propagation for the establishment of seed orchards to produce improved seed (synthetic varieties).
Production of flowers for controlled crossing.

These grafted plants may differ from seedling trees in habit and growth because of topophysis (varying from species to species).

The identity of clones must be very carefully preserved because clones of the same species are difficult to identify by their morphological characters. This also applies to the conservation of ecotypes.

CONSERVATION OF SEED OR POLLEN

This question is dealt with exhaustively for all plants by Harrington (cf. Chapter 43). The general principles, such as the storage of seed in airtight containers at low temperatures and at low moisture content, apply also to forest trees. Seed of the majority of conifers can be conserved for several years (up to 20 and perhaps longer) at low temperatures (-5 to $-20°C$) with a moisture content from 5 to 8 per cent. Seed of *Abies* and *Cedrus*, as well as some pines, is less long-lived. Broadleaved species pose more difficult problems, especially *Salix* and *Fagus* species. Pollen storage techniques are available to maintain pollen viability for several years. Although research has not yet developed methods for storage periods as long as for seed, it is possible to anticipate that pollen can be maintained viable for a very long time. Deep freezing or lyophilization give the best results for certain species ; the optimal moisture content varies in accordance with the species.

In cases of prolonged storage of seed or pollen, the risk of deterioration of chromosomes should not be overlooked.

CONCLUSION

The development of forest tree breeding programs has brought about important changes in the conception of forest tree collections : diversification of the genetic entities to be conserved (species, ecotypes, clones) ; diversification of the categories of collection plantations.

In view of the ever-increasing areas and costs of such specialized plantations it is often necessary, through certain accessory measures, to make use of experimental plantations (provenance test plantations, clonal archives) as collections of genotypes.

APPENDIX

MOBILIZATION, CONSERVATION AND UTILIZATION OF PLANT RESOURCES AT N.I.VAVILOV ALL-UNION INSTITUTE OF PLANT INDUSTRY, LENINGRAD

D. BREZHNEV

N.I. Vavilov Institute of Plant Industry, Leningrad, U.S.S.R.

The history of plant introduction in the U.S.S.R., as in other countries, goes back to ancient times. Major progress has, however, been made in this century in genetics and plant breeding, and in particular in the last decade during which a large variety of cereals, commercial, vegetable and fruit crops, have been developed using materials from a wide range of parental forms, both indigenous and introduced.

The use of breeding material with a maximum amount of diversity is essential for the development of varieties for the Soviet Union with its wide range of soil, climatic and agro-ecological conditions. The need for plant introduction was quickly realized in the U.S.S.R., and in 1920, shortly after the creation of the Union, a special Institute of Applied Botany and New Crops was established. This Institute later became the All-Union Institute of Plant Industry and now bears the name of its founder and first director, N.I. Vavilov. From 1920 to 1940, 140 expeditions in the U.S.S.R. and 40 expeditions to 64 foreign countries were organized. The expeditions were planned using Vavilov's theories of the origin of crops, their evolution and their variability in space and time which he had put forward in 'An Understanding of Wheat', 'The Centres of the Origin of Cultivated Crops', 'The Law of Homologous Series in Hereditary Variability', 'Paths of Soviet Plant Breeding', etc.

During its first 20 years the Institute collected a wide range of domestic varieties and forms of cultivated plants and discovered large resources of wild species of fruit, berry and fodder plants. The discovery of the centres of origin of the most important cultivated species such as wheat, barley, rye, flax and clover led to the collection of wild varieties of these plants from the southern regions of the U.S.S.R., which are in close proximity to the centres of origin.

A large amount of varietal plant resources was collected in Trans-Caucasian Republics—Azerbaijan, Georgia, Armenia, in the Soviet Republics of Central Asia ; the Uzbek, Turkmen, Tajik, Kirghiz and

Kazakh Republics; in the Ukrainian and Byelorussian Soviet Republics; and in many territories and regions of the Russian Federal Republic. As a result a considerable fund of domestic varieties of cultivated plants was formed and big resources of wild species of fruit, berry and fodder plants were revealed.

Many of the plants collected in these regions within the U.S.S.R. were found to have characterisitics of the greatest value in plant improvement. Winter wheats developed in our country are famous throughout the world for their drought resistance, frost resistance and grain quality. Large numbers of varieties of wheat, rye, berry plants and alfalfa were discovered on the territory of the Caucasus and Central Asia.

Valuable and mostly endemic species of apples, quince, myrobalan plum, medlar, apricot, sweet cherry, cherry, almond, pistachio, walnut, fig, pomegranate, grapes, actinidias grow wild in forests of the Caucasus, Central Asia, the Crimea, Primorsky territory, in the European part of the U.S.S.R. and partly in Siberia.

Bread grains and other crops, characterized by high productivity and large size of grain, are concentrated in the foothills of Azerbaijan and Daghestan. There are valuable winter durum wheats which grow only in these regions.

Simultaneously expeditions were sent to Africa, Asia and Europe, and very important collections were made in Central, South and North America. N.I. Vavilov participated in a large number of these expeditions. In addition to the expeditions an active exchange of seeds and vegetative materials was developed with many scientific institutions in other countries.

In 1940 the collection contained 200,000 varieties and samples and it was due to the great efforts of the Institute's scientists that the major part of the collection was removed from Leningrad at the approach of the invading armies and was transported to the eastern regions of the country.

The main task of the Institute is still the mobilization of plant resources, their study and their rational utilization. In order to carry out this work the Institute has a staff of more than 1,600 scientists and technicians grouped in 15 sections with 15 laboratories. There are 20 experimental stations and centres suitably located to represent all the agro-ecological zones of the country.

'Plant resources of the world are immense. In the field of studying plant resources throughout the world botanists will have much to do still in the centuries to come', wrote N.I. Vavilov, and it is for this reason that the Institute's scientists continue annual expeditions to different regions which have great resources of the various primitive forms of the cultivated plants and their relatives. From 5,000 to 6,000 samples of seeds and vegetative material are added annually to the Institute's collection as a result of these expeditions, the total for the period 1952 to 1967 being more than 100,000. Furthermore, contacts were established with 400 scientific institutions in more than 70 countries of the world and regular exchanges are made of plant material. About 5,000 to 6,000 samples are sent annually to foreign countries and approximately the same amount is received in exchange. The total number of samples in the collection at the Institute now amounts to 175,000. This material is carefully preserved in special seed depositories and is periodically sown to maintain viability. All new material is subject to a quarantine control in special nurseries before being included in the collection.

On the basis of the study of the collection the scientists of the Institute work on a number of theoretical questions pertaining to the problems of the origin, evolution, ecology, systematics and classification of cultivated plants, their interspecific differentiation, regularities of geographical variability and reaction to different factors of the environment, genetic potentials of species, methods of breeding (in particular, the development of heterotic hybrids), distribution of crops in the U.S.S.R. territory.

Special attention is being paid to the study of samples in relation to the main plant breeding problems, such as quality of grain or of other products, immunity, response to irrigation, response to high fertilizer applications, resistance to unfavourable conditions, etc. Laboratories have been created for the study of mutagenesis and polyploidy, heterosis, population genetics, frost and drought resistance, and photosynthesis. Research has been started in the field of genetic typing of all the specific and varietal variations in cereal and other crops using the genetic characteristics of species, varieties and ecological groups, by comparing the nature and strength with which a complex of definite properties are inherited, by comparing the values of various combinations, and by studying the reaction to mutagenetic agents and polyploidy.

Hybrid families of the soft wheat type, with high resistance to brown rust and powdery mildew, have been developed as a result of interspecific cross breeding ; forms with cytoplasmic male sterility have been found among interspecific hybrids and it has been established that the species *Triticum zhukovskyi* and *T. timopheevi* are sources of such sterility ; it has also been established that the immune species *T. zhukovskyi* originated from crossing *T. timopheevi* with *T. monococcum* and that its genomic composition is AAAABB. Work is being carried out to find new sources of cytoplasmic male sterility, through remote crossbreeding of wheat, and to make a comparative study of the different sources and of the nature of the genetic control.

The Institute has proved the ability of various wheat species and ecological groups of soft wheat to cross with rye and with Triticale with different chromosome numbers. The Institute has developed 3 amphidiploid wheats immune to fungous diseases, 3 Triticale forms, 2 samples of tetraploid rye, 2 samples of tetraploid barley, as well as polyploid forms of tomatoes, vetch, clover, cabbage, carrot and haploid potato. Since 1965 a study of the importance of self incompatability, male sterility, apomixis, as important factors in the genetic control of reproduction, has been carried out,.

In 1967 a laboratory of cyto-biochemistry was established to study the composition, fine structure and function of cell components. The study is mainly concerned with the chromatin in the nucleus. The nature of proteins and nucleic acids and their participation in molecular organization of chromatin and chromosomes are being studied. Regularities of changes in the composition and structure of chromatin in relation to developmental processes are being studied. This laboratory is also trying to discover the mechanism of inter-cell regulation of gene activity ; the morphogenetic function of the nucleus, which forms the basis for the productivity of the plant ; heterosis phenomena ; the effects of polyploidy ; and the development of new forms of cultivated plants.

The photosynthesis laboratory is carrying out studies on pure lines and hybrids of maize. Efforts are being made to develop methods which would make it possible to examine rates of photosynthesis of the Institute's world collections. The biochemistry section is making studies of seeds, fruits and the vegetative organs of the plants for variations in protein, oil, carbohydrates, vitamins, etc. The section of immunity has carried out research on the regularity with which immunity is distributed among species and eco-geographic groups of the Institute's collection, as well as the geography of immune forms, variations in resistance with place of origin, and the principles for selecting parents for hybridization. The laboratory for the technological evaluation of crops has completed a study of varieties in the soft wheat world collection, and 250 varieties of strong wheats have been identified. A study of the nature of wheat strength and its geographical variability is also being carried out. This laboratory is collaborating with the genetics laboratory in an examination of the combining ability of strong wheat varieties.

The collection of the Institute has become the main basis on which breeding institutions of our country have developed and are developing new varieties and hybrids of various cultivated plants. The Institute annually sends 50–60 thousand varietal samples to the experiment and breeding institutions of the country, for use as initial material. According to very incomplete information, various breeding institutions have developed from this material 725 varieties and hybrids, most of which are zoned in different parts of the country, including: cereal crops—128 varieties, groats and maize—80, pulses—33, industrial crops—85, vegetables and melon crops—143, potato—68, feed crops—51, fruit crops and grapes—137 varieties.

In addition, the scientists of the Institute and its experiment stations have developed over 400 varieties (excluding fruit and sub-tropical crops) most of which are also zoned in many territories, regions and republics, including: cereals—17 varieties, groat crops and maize—51, pulses—15, industrial crops—18, vegetables and melon crops—146, potato—36, and feed crops—13 varieties. A large number of varieties has been specified, developed and introduced into the culture of fruit and berry crops, subtropical plants and grapes.

All these varieties are grown on scores of millions of hectares. Wheat varieties alone developed on the basis of the use of the Institute's collection are cultivated on 30 million hectares, and barley varieties on 3 million hectares. Hybrids of maize, developed by the Kuban Experimental Station are sown on an area of about 8 million hectacres. Altogether the varieties developed by the scientists of the All-Union Research Institute of Plant Industry during 50 years of the existence of the Soviet State, as well as the varieties developed by other plant-breeders on the basis of the Institute's collections are grown on an area of about 60 million hectares.

Using the collection the scientists of our country have made big contributions to the development of new areas and the introduction of crop production in the North and North-East, to deserts and semi-deserts.

This brief report will give an indication of the studies and research being carried out in the Soviet Union in the field of mobilization, study and use of plant resources. The Institute is still, however, searching for new material and a number of expeditions to all the continents are planned for the coming years. In addition the Institute looks forward to the establishment of closer contacts with scientific institutes and workers throughout the world and for an increased exchange of seeds and vegetative material.

NAME INDEX

Bold figures indicate opening page of Contributor's article

SUBJECT INDEX

Bold figures indicate major references

547

533f; diffuse origins 22, 39, 276f; disease and host resistance 443f; polyploidy 39; primary centres 35f, 277; *see also* Centres of diversity, Evolution, Variability

Ornamental species 224

Outbreeding, and disease resistance 446

pH 133f

Pathogens evolution of 443; virulence 442

Phalaris 140

Phaseolus 226

Phenology 171f, 192, 195

Phenotype constancy of 125; plasticity of 123; uniformity of 125

Photoperiod 132, 497; photoperiod insensitivity 139

Photosynthesis 136, 536

Physiology *See* Environmental physiology

Phytogeographic technique 33, 158, 276

Phytophthora 122, 140, 312f, 316, 446, 451

Picea 359

Pinus 140, 354, 359–361, **367–379**; adaptation 367, 370–372; tropical pines 375–378

Piper 222

Pisum 118, **321–326**; exploration 321f; collections 323–325; conservation 322–325; maintenance 323–325; Pisum Genetics Association 323–325

Plant breeding 10–12, 236, 397, **427–439**; 535, backcrossing 431; changing objectives in 433; collections 221–224, 397, **427–439**, 481f; composite cross 484; disease resistance **441–457**; gene transfers in 447f; linkage 429, 431f; mutations 11f, 434, 448; production breeding 11, 397f; restricted gene pools, effect of 397; Vavilov Institute 537, *see also* Disease resistance

Plant formations classification of 192, 194

Plant introduction 139, 223, **395–401**, **413–425**, 533; cooperation 404–406, 424; diseases and pests 403, 421f; evaluation 370, 372, 396, **413–419**; national services 423–425; objectives 535; quarantine procedures 405–409, 497; wild and primitive material 396, 427, *see also* Provenance studies

Plant populations adaptation **119–121**; breeding systems 120; conservation of 475, 477; cultivated 102, **115**; differentiation of 100; forest trees 109f, 354f; gene frequency 164; genetic structure **97**, **109**, 112, 354f; maintenance of 264; natural 99, 115, 117–123; population parameters 112, 119f; population variance 118f, 164; primitive 10, 121f; sampling 97, **103–106**, **163–167**; selection pressure 115, 118f

Plant Protection Organizations 404, 406

Plant quarantine **403–411**, 497; facilities 406–408; general principles of 408f; and vegetative reproduction 497

Plant steroids 225f

Plantago 119

Plantations as gene sources **356–358**; provenance 527f

Platanus 59

Pollen fertility 436; forest trees 361, 529; storage 479, **518–520**

Pollination cotton 337f

Polycross 125

Polyploidy 28, 39, **63–65**, **87–96**, 110; and adaptation 92; and cultivated plants 63; diploidisation 88–90; and evolution 28, 39, 62, 76, 87, 90; forest trees 111; origin of 94; and origin of species **87–96**; pivotal genomes 90; taxonomy 63, 93; wheat 90f, 240

Population *See* Plant populations

Populus **389–392**

Potato 135, 139, 223, 227, **311–319**; adaptation 311f; collections 226, 317f; conservation **495–499**; disease resistance 75, 223, 313, 316f,